ON INSTAGRAM

IF YOU TAKE PHOTOGRAPHS,
DON'T SPEAK, DON'T WRITE, DON'T ANALYSE YOURSELF,
AND DON'T ANSWER ANY QUESTIONS.

/ *Robert Doisneau*

ON INSTAGRAM
DAVID HURN

RAP
REEL ART PRESS

INTRODUCTION / DAVID HURN

Early in 2016 – I must have had nothing better to do – I decided to flirt with Instagram, but I had also heard of blogging. I had little idea what either was, and certainly not how to 'do' them. I hoped I could find a way of passing on constructive photography advice: photo tips, things to read, exhibitions I had seen, books to buy, photographers I found interesting etc. I wished to be all embracing. It would be a sort of diary, clarifying my muddled thoughts. It would be as accurate as I could make it.

It took me time to work out how Instagram might work for me. I soon discovered that the essential attraction to each post was the picture. However, for me, the picture is simply there to promote the text.

The idea of photo tips, books, quotes, as the main mirror did not seem to work for viewers. I had shown four 'Book of the Month', four 'Photo Tips', six colour pictures (not the normal me). So all these categories were dropped from further posts. I needed a way of incorporating 'ideas' into the text.

Slowly, I hope, I found a way of making an instructive whole. I am not a writer, so the idea of confining myself to about 2,000 characters fitted into my skill from the past of constructing telegrams . . . a sort of postcard, a condensed letter, I suppose a sort of email to everyone.

Much later I realised that there was a sort of progression/clarification of thoughts and the possibility of doing a book seemed attractive. I had occasionally repeated pictures, often simply because my memory is lax, occasionally because the picture seemed appropriate and the first version had been shown over a year previously.

The posts shown are, as far as possible, in the original order, where changed it is for clarity. The texts are accurately reproduced, except where spelling was bad or grammar appalling. In a couple of cases I have expanded what is essentially an obituary. I never really understood hashtags so these have been adapted to what is more accurate.

All posts hinting at 'selling my wares' have been dropped.

THE CONVENTION IN CONVERSATION, AND I HOPE PHOTOGRAPHY,
IS TO TELL THE TRUTH, OTHERWISE NO COMMUNICATION HAS ANY MEANING.

IT SEEMS TO ME THAT IN WHATEVER FORM OF COMMUNICATION, BE IT PAINTING, SCULPTURE, MUSIC, DANCE, PHOTOGRAPHY, EVEN SPEECH, OUR JOB IS TO TRY TO COMMUNICATE TO OTHERS AS HONESTLY, ACCURATELY, AUTHENTICALLY, WHAT WE SAW, FELT, THOUGHT, AT A PARTICULAR TIME.

PHOTOGRAPHY SHOULD BE ABOUT TELLING US WHAT IT IS LIKE TO BE ALIVE.

/ *David Hurn*

2016

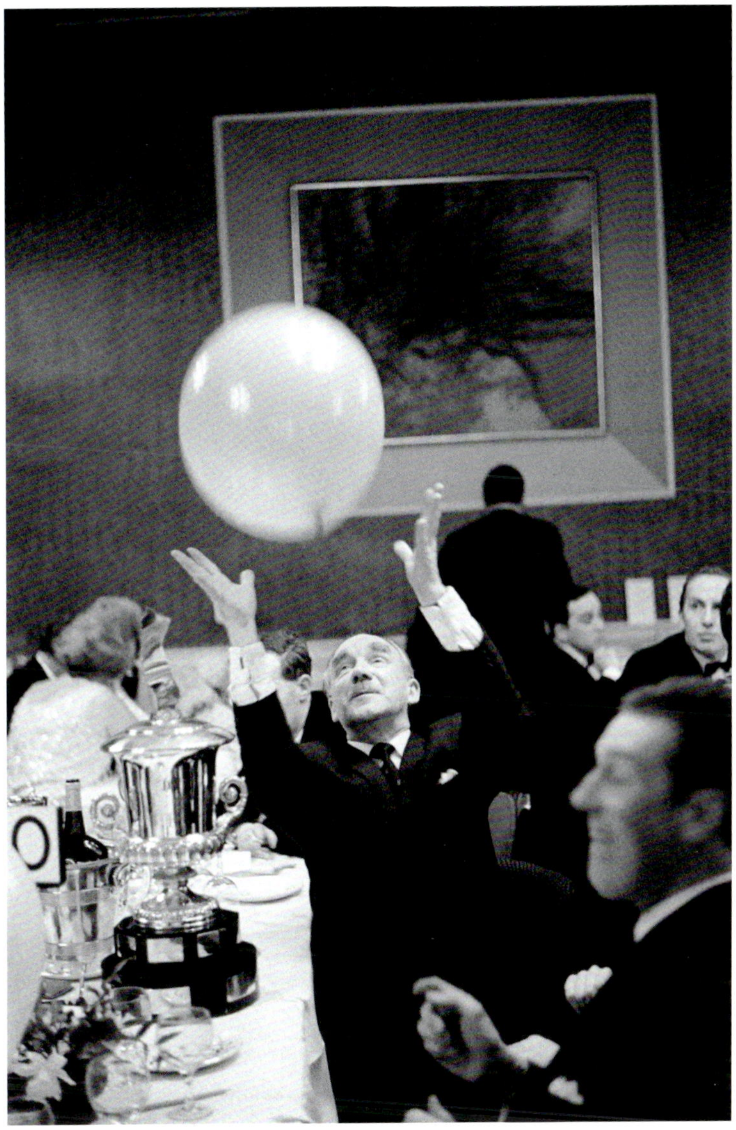

3 NOVEMBER 2016 / MG CAR OWNERS BALL. *EDINBURGH, SCOTLAND 1967*

Retired gentleman at the MG Car Owners Ball.

@davidhurnphoto @magnumphotos

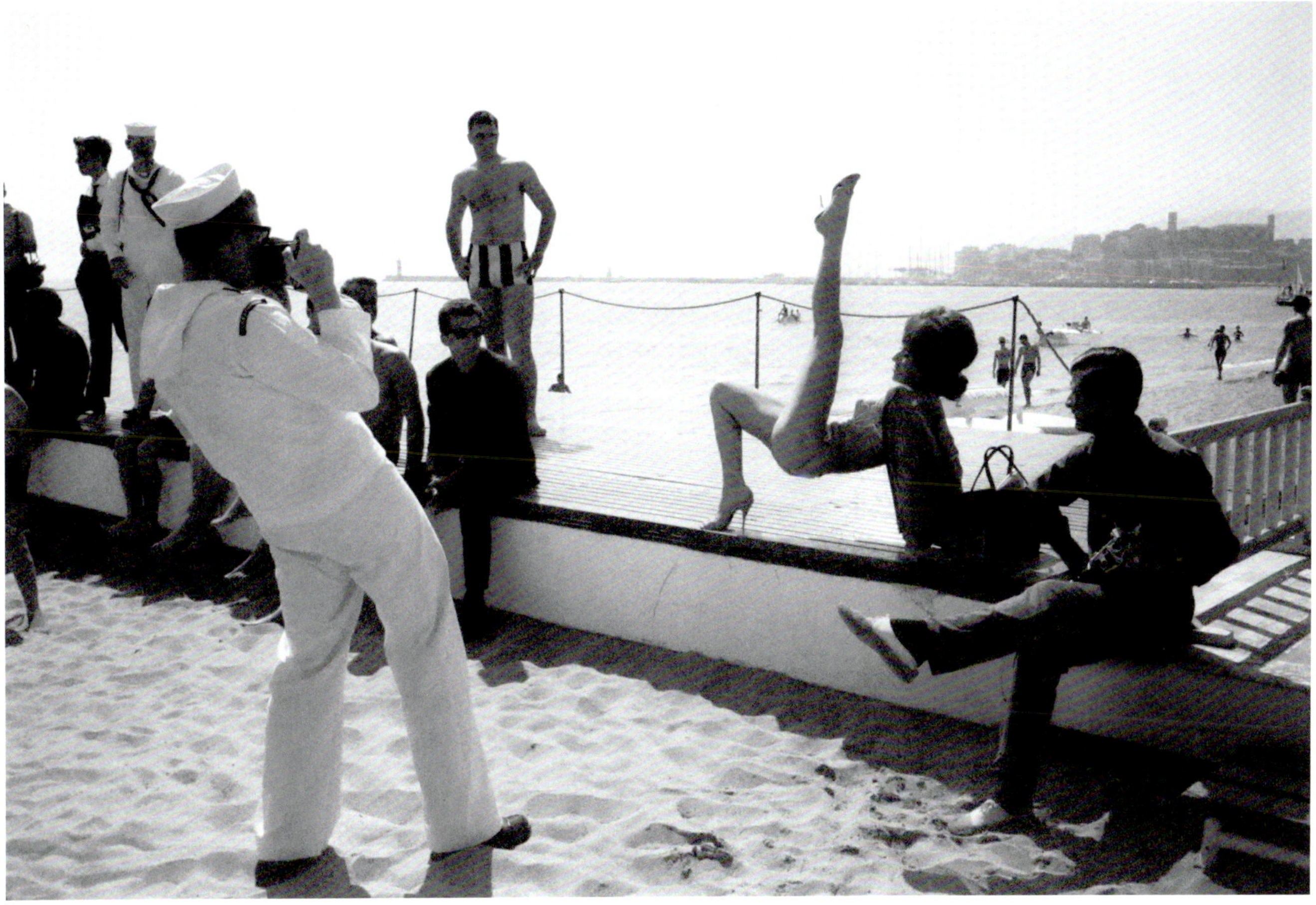

4 NOVEMBER 2016 / *CANNES, FRANCE 1963*

Amateur photographer photographs starlets at the Cannes Film Festival, 1963.

@davidhurnphoto @magnumphotos #cannesfilmfestival

PHOTO TIPS /

I have always enjoyed receiving and practicing practical tips that can be applied to photography. In my first months on Instagram I decided to share a few, with their heading text replacing my photographs in each post.

PHOTO TIP OF THE MONTH: NOVEMBER 2016

Photographers have to walk a lot

10 NOVEMBER 2016 / GOOD SHOES

The most important equipment for photographers is good shoes.

@davidhurnphoto @magnumphotos #phototip

PHOTO TIP OF THE MONTH: DECEMBER 2016

Play the piano a lot

14 DECEMBER 2016 / PLAY THE PIANO A LOT

In 1970 I shot pictures of Daniel Barenboim for *Look* magazine. I accompanied him when he gave a concert at the Wigmore Hall in London. I remember saying over dinner, 'I find it impossible to understand how a human being is capable of playing like that.' I went on to ask the question, 'How do you become a concert pianist?'

He replied, 'You play the piano a lot'.

If music, why not photography?

Take lots and lots and lots of pictures – it is likely you will get better.

@davidhurnphoto @magnumphotos #phototip

PHOTO TIP OF THE MONTH: JANUARY 2017

Sherlock Holmes

10 JANUARY 2017 / SHERLOCK HOLMES

Sherlock Holmes said, 'The trouble with you, my dear Watson, is that you see but you do not observe'.

It is easy to see. It takes deep concentration to observe but it's observation that gives one a chance of having a unique vision and saying,

'Do you find my observation interesting?'

@davidhurnphoto @magnumphotos #phototip #sherlockholmes #observe

PHOTO TIP OF THE MONTH: FEBRUARY 2017

Where and When

23 FEBRUARY 2017 / WHERE AND WHEN

We photographers really only have two controls when we take pictures. *Where* we stand and *when* we press the shutter. Stand in the right place and press the shutter at the right time and with luck you might produce an interesting picture. Of course, the right place often means much research and the right time requires concentrated observation.

Sharing the Magnum 70th anniversary hub which has just launched: www.magnumphotos.com/magnum-photos-70/

@davidhurnphoto @magnumphotos #phototip

PHOTO TIP OF THE MONTH: MARCH 2017

Lewis Hine

21 MARCH 2017 / LEWIS HINE

I sometimes feel quotes are useful, they can clarify one's own thoughts in a much clearer and more succinct way than one's own use of language.

When I was teaching, I had three quotes written in large letters on the wall. All by the photographer Lewis Hine: a photographer whose photographs, more than most, changed the world for the better.

1: 'If I could tell the story in words, I wouldn't need to lug around a camera.'

2: 'You and I know that this undoubted faith in the integrity of the photograph is often rudely shaken; for while photographs may not lie, liars may photograph. It becomes necessary, then, in our revelation of the truth, to see to it that the camera we depend on contracts no bad habits.'

3: 'I wanted to show the things that had to be corrected: I wanted to show the things that had to be appreciated.'

@davidhurnphoto @magnumphotos #phototip #lewishine #inspirationalquotes

BOOK OF THE MONTH /

Similarly, I have always enjoyed reading a wide variety of books in some way relating to photography. I decided to share a few, with their covers replacing my photographs in each post.

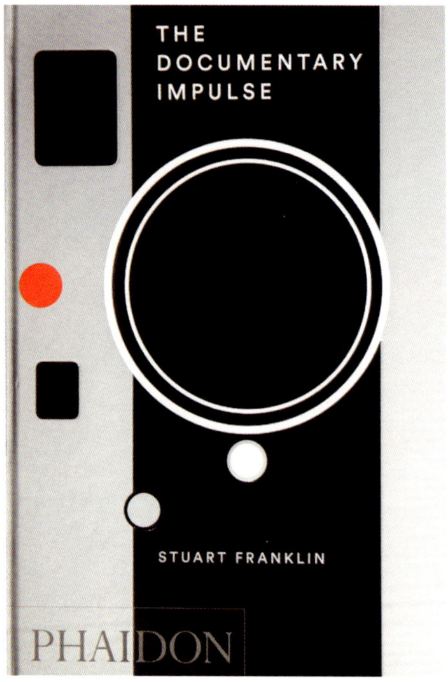

2 DECEMBER 2016 / STUART FRANKLIN

The Documentary Impulse by Stuart Franklin

I am interested in all genres of photography when realised to their limit. For me there are no hierarchies, but I want to see excellence in whatever is attempted. I am primarily involved in what is often called 'Documentary' although I think 'Reportage' is a better word, this genre of photography is my first love.

This book, by the very fine photographer Stuart Franklin, is beautifully written in understandable language. It is amazingly well researched, it makes me feel safe that the facts stated are actually facts and can be trusted.

Francis Bacon, the English philosopher, wrote:

'Read not to contradict and confute, nor to believe and take for granted . . . but to weigh and consider'.

Some books are to be tasted, others to be swallowed, and some few to be chewed and digested.

I think *The Documentary Impulse* fulfils these criteria splendidly.

@davidhurnphoto @magnumphotos #photobook #booktips

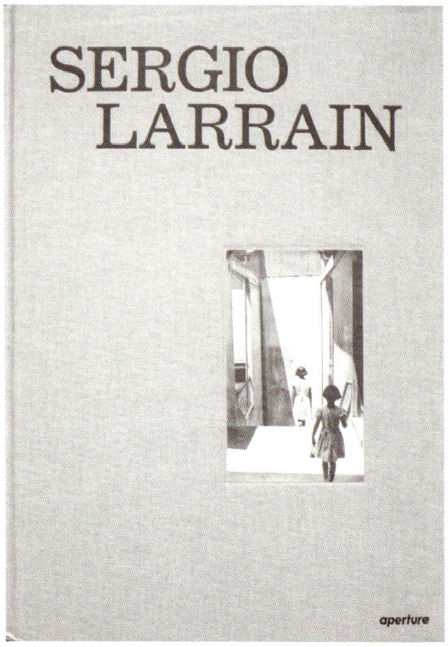

18 JANUARY 2017 / SERGIO LARRAIN

Sergio Larrain. Editorial concept Agnès Sire.

There are books one dips into but never really looks at everything. There are books one looks through at a single sitting but forgets days later. And books one looks at time and time again, they become part of one's life and alter it in productive ways. I met Sergio in London in 1958. We became close friends. If I were forced to suggest ten photographers that I found the most interesting from the history of photography he would be among the top of my list. He – perhaps also early Bruce Davidson – had a true feeling of poetry in his pictures. He constantly produced pictures that seemed to express the inexpressible. It's a reasonably expensive book. An inexpensive but also excellent alternative is *Sergio Larrain: London 1958-59*, published by Dewi Lewis.

@davidhurnphoto @magnumphotos @fondationhcb @dewi_lewis_publishing @aperturefnd #booktips #photobook

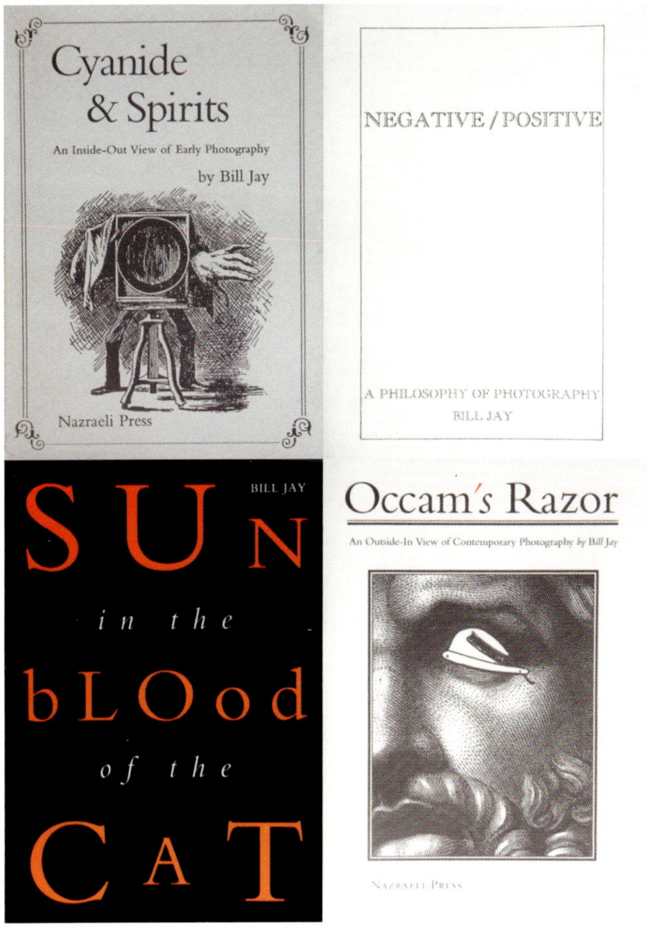

8 FEBRUARY 2017 / BILL JAY

Writings of Bill Jay

If you wish to get away from academic theoretical writing on photography I would recommend the writings of Bill Jay. In my opinion Bill was the major instigator of photographic changes in the UK in the late '60s and early '70s, primarily through his editorship of *Creative Camera* and *Album* magazines. Most of the time he either showed pictures or wrote an alternative history of photography telling, in an amusing way, what actually went on in photography from 1839.

I can, of course, be accused of biases. He was more a brother than a friend.

I would start by reading his essays:

www.billjay.com/articles

Then:

Cyanide & Spirits; *Negative / Positive*; *Sun in the Blood of the Cat*; and *Occam's Razor.*

The explanation of the title *Sun etc...* is worth the cost of the book alone.

@davidhurnphoto @magnumphotos #photobook #booktips #billjay

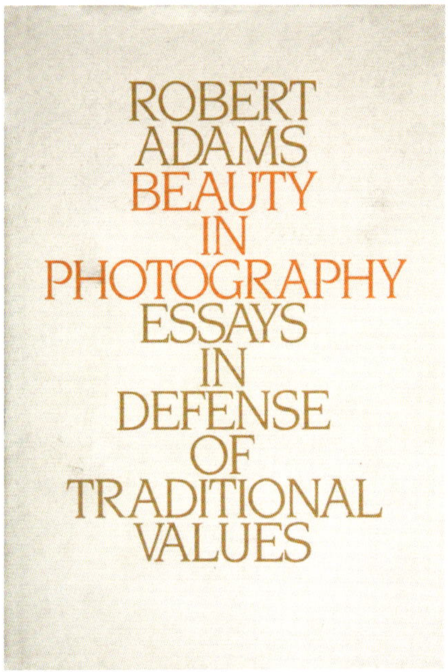

23 MARCH 2017 / ROBERT ADAMS

Beauty in Photography by Robert Adams

Part of the fun of looking at pictures is working them out for oneself.

For me the best textbooks about photography simply nudge and suggest, they do not tell you how to look.

The best books are written in simple language, not in that comparatively new writing that has become exceedingly odd; not talk about feelings or emotions or content but full of sentences of large words, opaque language, and fine distinctions that would make even an intelligent chimpanzee suspicious.

Robert Adams has a PhD in English. He taught English at Colorado College. He is an inspiring photographer who learned photographic technique from Myron Wood, a professional photographer who lived in Colorado.

All one needs to say about the publication is that it is a wonderfully uplifting book that makes me want to go out and shoot pictures.

@davidhurnphoto @magnumphotos @aperturefnd #booktips #photobook #robertadams

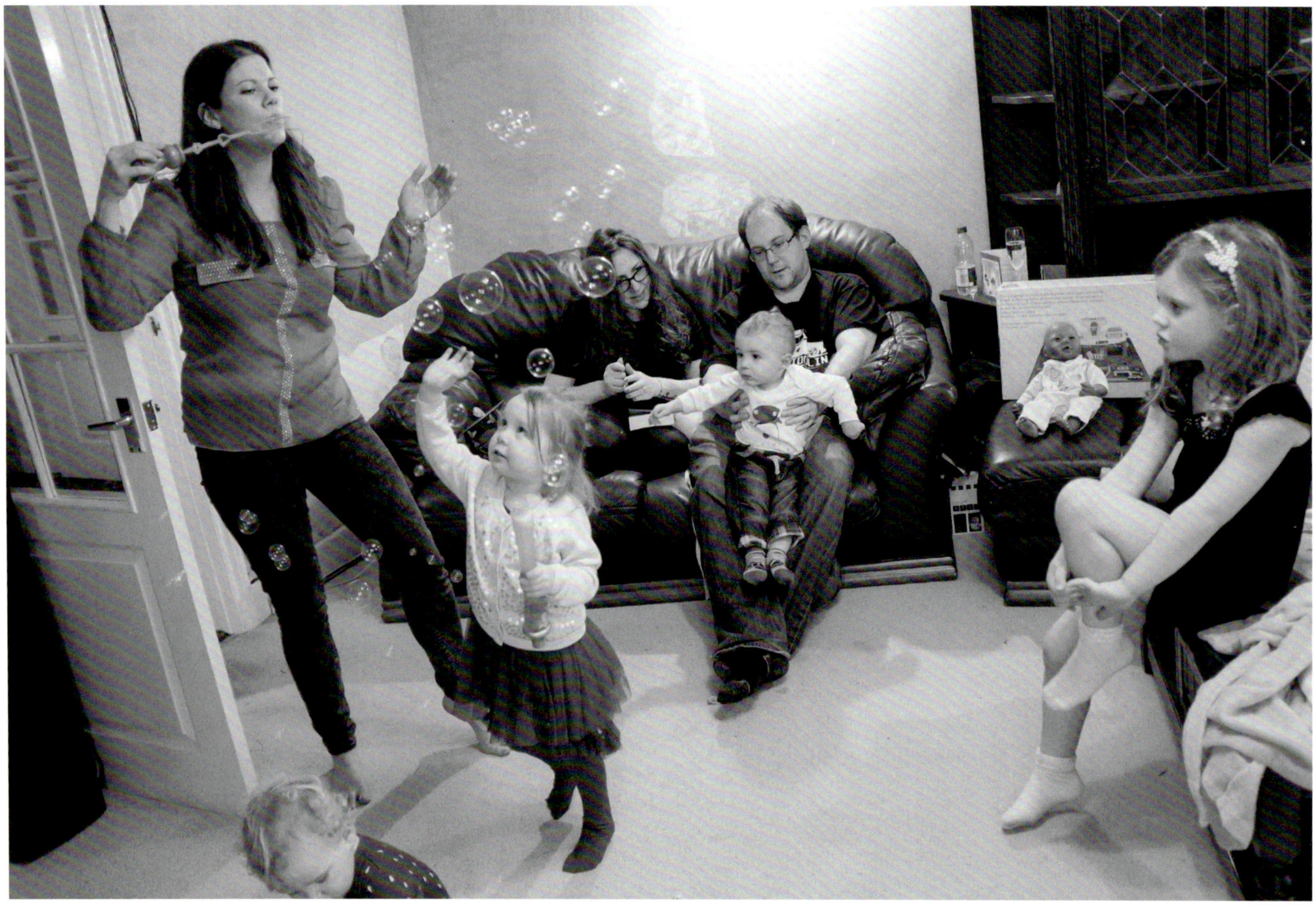

15 NOVEMBER 2016 / CHRISTMAS. *TINTERN, WALES 2015*

My local supermarkets inform me that Christmas is amongst us. Some time ago I was seduced by a quote from a favourite writer, John Updike, 'to give the mundane its beautiful due'. It started an ongoing project, photographing my exquisite village Tintern. The beauty in photographing the familiar is that, almost by definition, you have inborn trust, no problems with access, and it's never too far to walk.

I will show a few pictures from recent years, and then keep you up-to-date as I continue to photograph in my village in the future.

Tintern 1: I live by myself but I love to spend Christmas day with the Klinkerts – my dearest friends. I love the atmosphere of a large family and kids – at least occasionally.

@davidhurnphoto @magnumphotos #tintern #wyevalley #wales

www.tinternvillage.co.uk

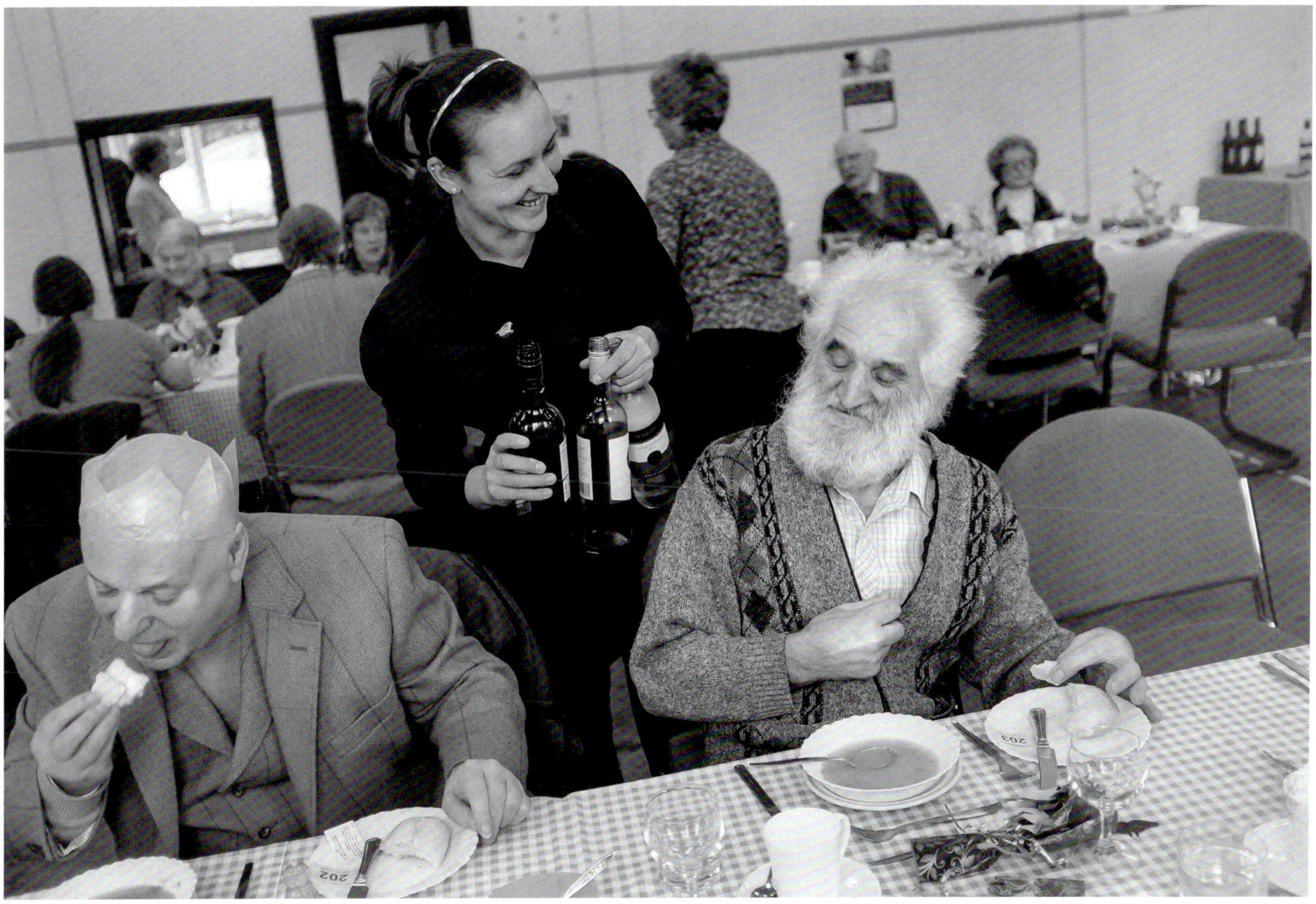

18 NOVEMBER 2016 / TINTERN SENIORS. *TINTERN, WALES 2013*

Tintern 2: The Seniors Lunch in the village hall is community at its best: hotel chefs, helpers, all generously muck in, and much joy is seen to be had by all. My waist gets bigger. Wonderful lunch, apple juice (I don't drink alcohol) and mince pies.

@davidhurnphoto @magnumphotos #tintern #wyevalley #wales

www.tinternvillage.co.uk

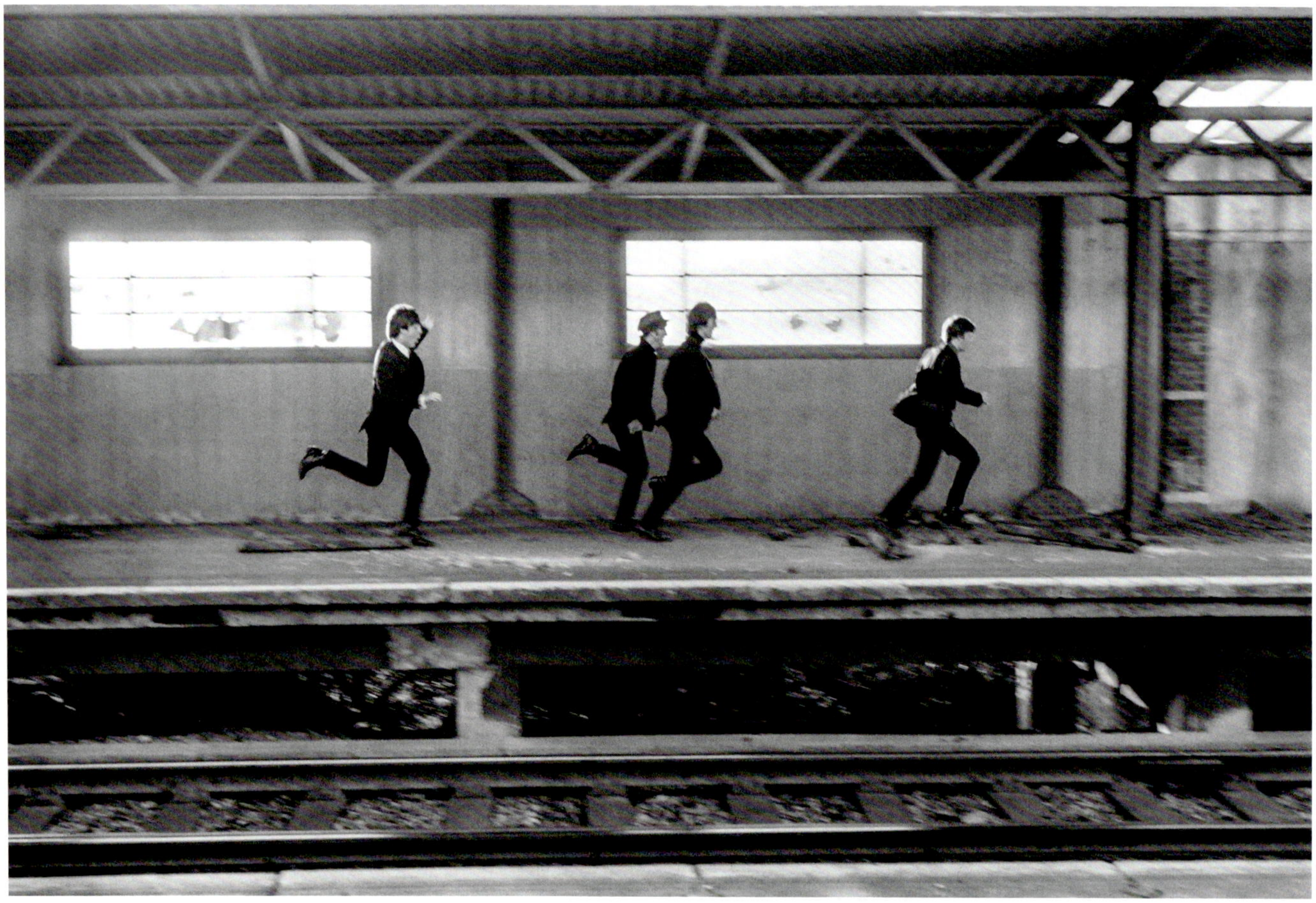

22 NOVEMBER 2016 / THE BEATLES. *LONDON, ENGLAND 1964*

From the cover of *The 1960s Photographed by David Hurn*
Published by @reelartpress

I had worked on the TV film *The Running, Jumping & Standing Still Film* (1959) featuring Spike Milligan and Peter Sellers, directed by Richard Lester. It was a favourite film of the Beatles. They asked Richard to direct their film, *A Hard Day's Night* (1965), and Richard, in his turn, asked me to act as a Special Photographer on the film. Bizarrely, most of it was shot on a hired train travelling each day between Marylebone and Minehead stations.

@davidhurnphoto @magnumphotos @reelartpress #photobook #the60s #thebeatles #aharddaysnight

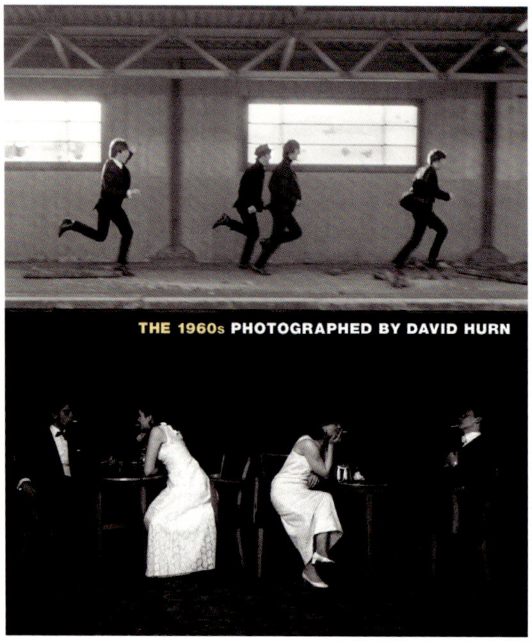

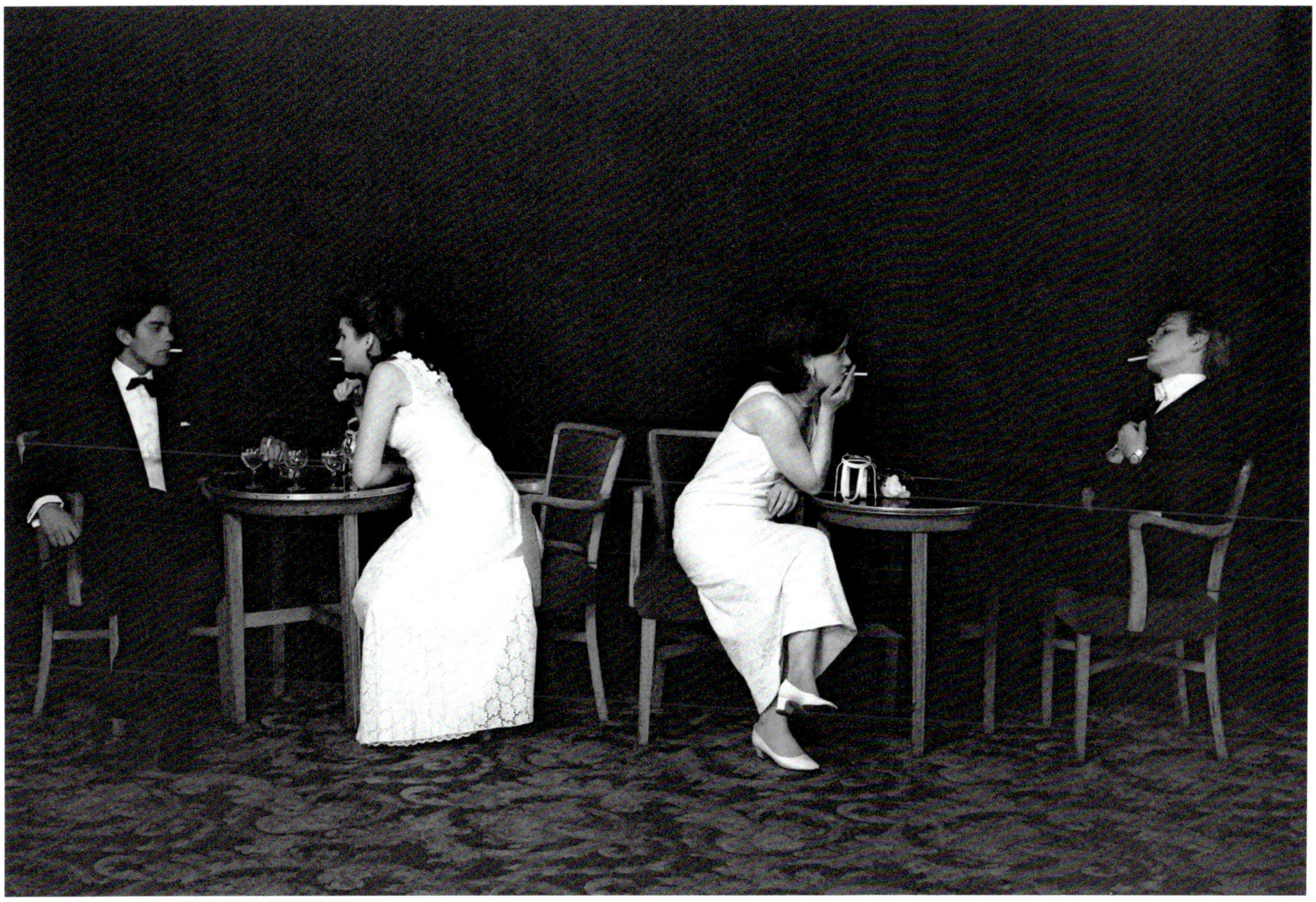

22 NOVEMBER 2016 / QUEEN CHARLOTTE'S BALL. *LONDON, ENGLAND 1967*

From the cover of *The 1960s Photographed by David Hurn*
Published by @reelartpress

Queen Charlotte's Ball was the highlight of what was called 'the debutante season' and 'coming out'. It had its roots in the 18th century when around 1780 the King, George III, held a ball for his wife's birthday. The ball was known as the Queen Charlotte's Ball and it was proposed that the 'well bred' and prettiest girls should attend to be presented at court to the Queen, in order that they could meet a suitable marriage partner, usually the brothers of the debs and known as the 'debs delights'. Only girls who had a relation who had herself been presented at court could come to the ball. When the Lord Chamberlain announced the end of the royal presentation ceremony in 1958, it provoked a record number of applications from distraught mothers. That year, 1,400 girls curtseyed in front of Queen Elizabeth II, over three days. The ball continued with the debs, bizarrely, curtseying to a giant cake in place of the Queen. The ball faded out in the '70s.

@davidhurnphoto @magnumphotos @reelartpress #photobook #the60s #thebeatles #aharddaysnight

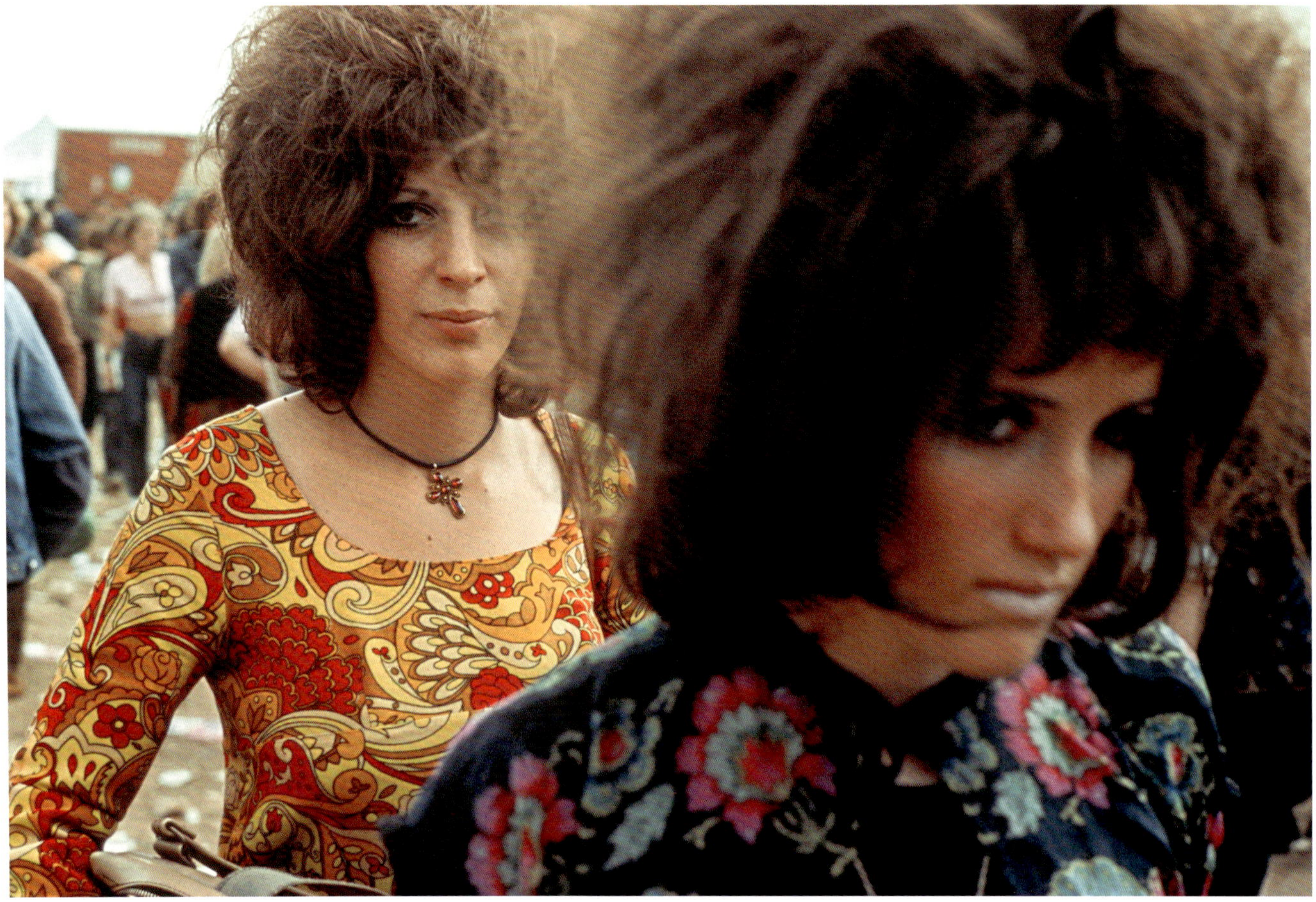

30 NOVEMBER 2016 / ISLE OF WIGHT FESTIVAL. *ENGLAND 1969*

The 1960s Photographed by David Hurn covers a wide range of happenings of the '60s, normally in the form of sets of pictures.

This picture is from 'Isle of Wight Festival'.

The festival was originally a counterculture event held from 1968 to 1970. An age of flamboyance in dress. Bob Dylan elected to come to the Isle of Wight rather than the Woodstock festival in USA. The 1970 Isle of Wight festival was said to be the largest human gathering in the world, with estimates of over 600,000 humans.

The full set is in the book, *The 1960s Photographed by David Hurn*.

@davidhurnphoto @magnumphotos @reelartpress #photobook #the60s #isleofwightfestival

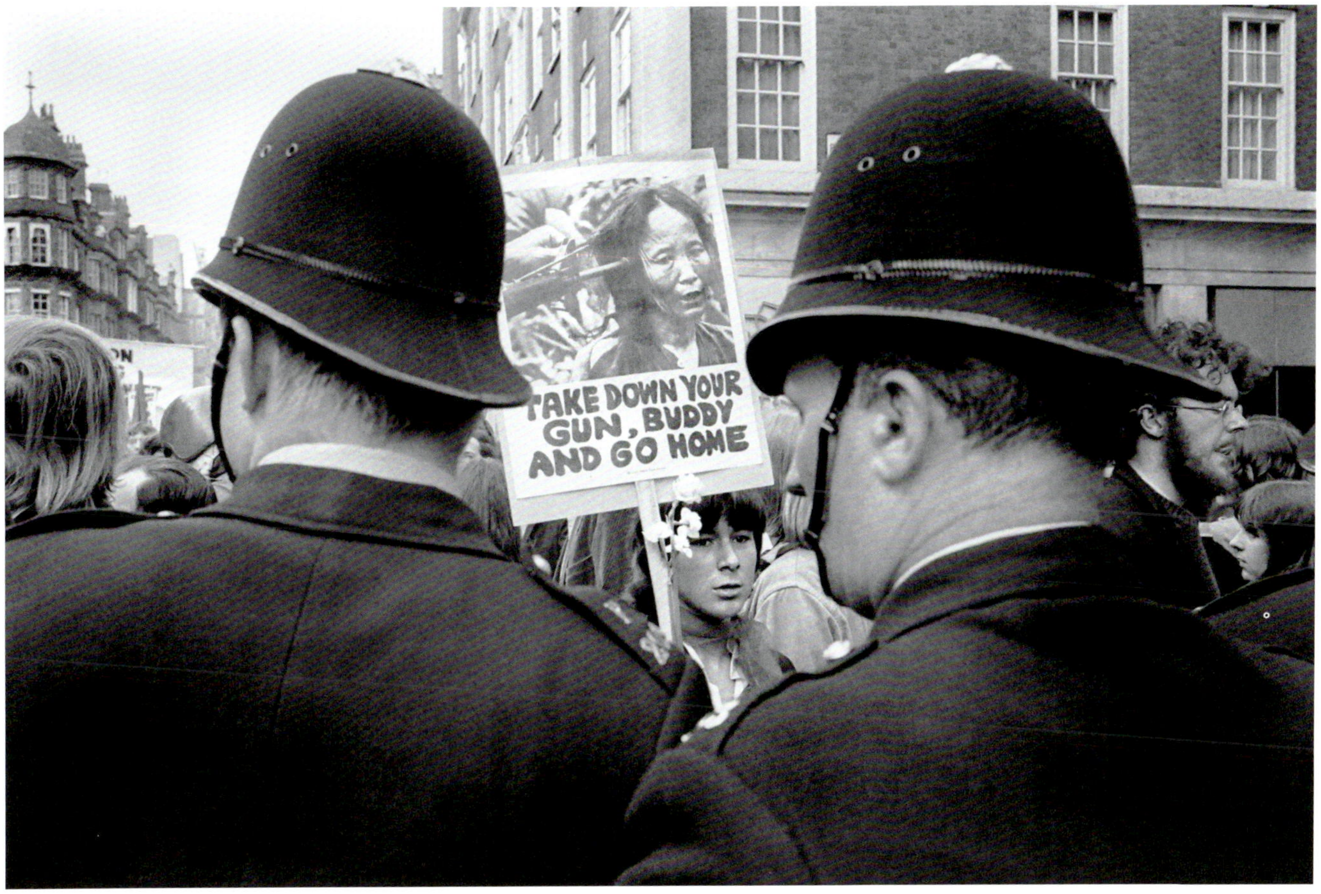

30 NOVEMBER 2016 / GROSVENOR SQUARE RIOTS. *LONDON, ENGLAND 1968*

The 1960s Photographed by David Hurn covers a wide range of happenings of the '60s, normally in the form of sets of pictures.

This picture is from 'Grosvenor Square Riots'.

Protest marches against the Vietnam war took place frequently. In London, the trouble in the late '60s centered on Grosvenor Square – home of the US ambassador to Britain. The demonstrations turned violent as activists in the march clashed with police.

The full set is in the book, *The 1960s Photographed by David Hurn*.

@davidhurnphoto @magnumphotos @reelartpress #photobook #the60s

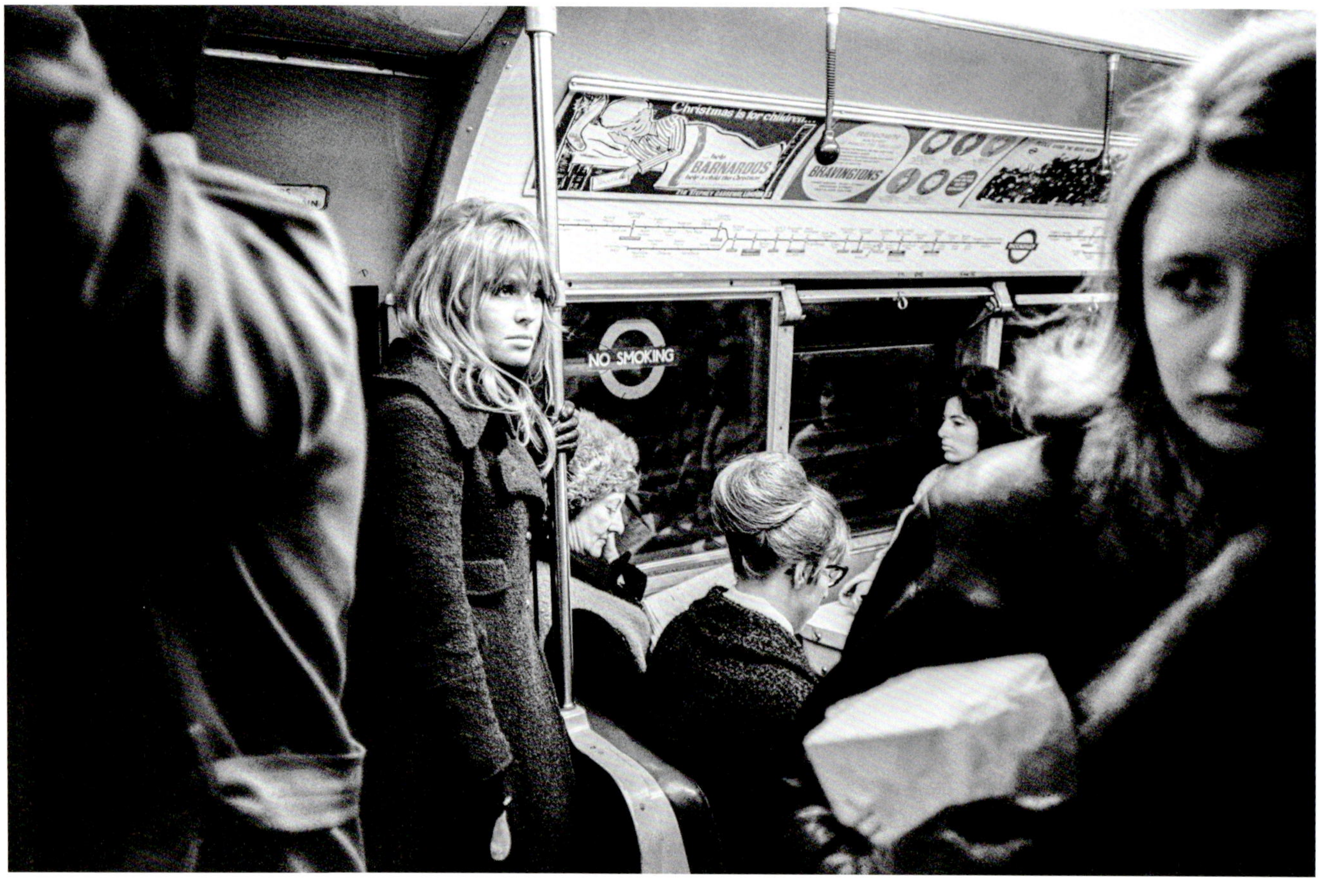

30 NOVEMBER 2016 / JULIE CHRISTIE. *LONDON, ENGLAND 1965*

The 1960s Photographed by David Hurn covers a wide range of happenings of the '60s, normally in the form of sets of pictures.

This picture is from 'Julie Christie'.

I did a photo essay about Julie Christie for *Look* magazine (USA). At this time she had just been in two films, *Darling* and *Dr. Zhivago*. For each film she received major actress awards. In life she was very unassuming and frequently could be seen travelling in London on the tube train.

The full set is in the book, *The 1960s Photographed by David Hurn*.

@davidhurnphoto @magnumphotos @reelartpress #photobook #the60s #juliechristie

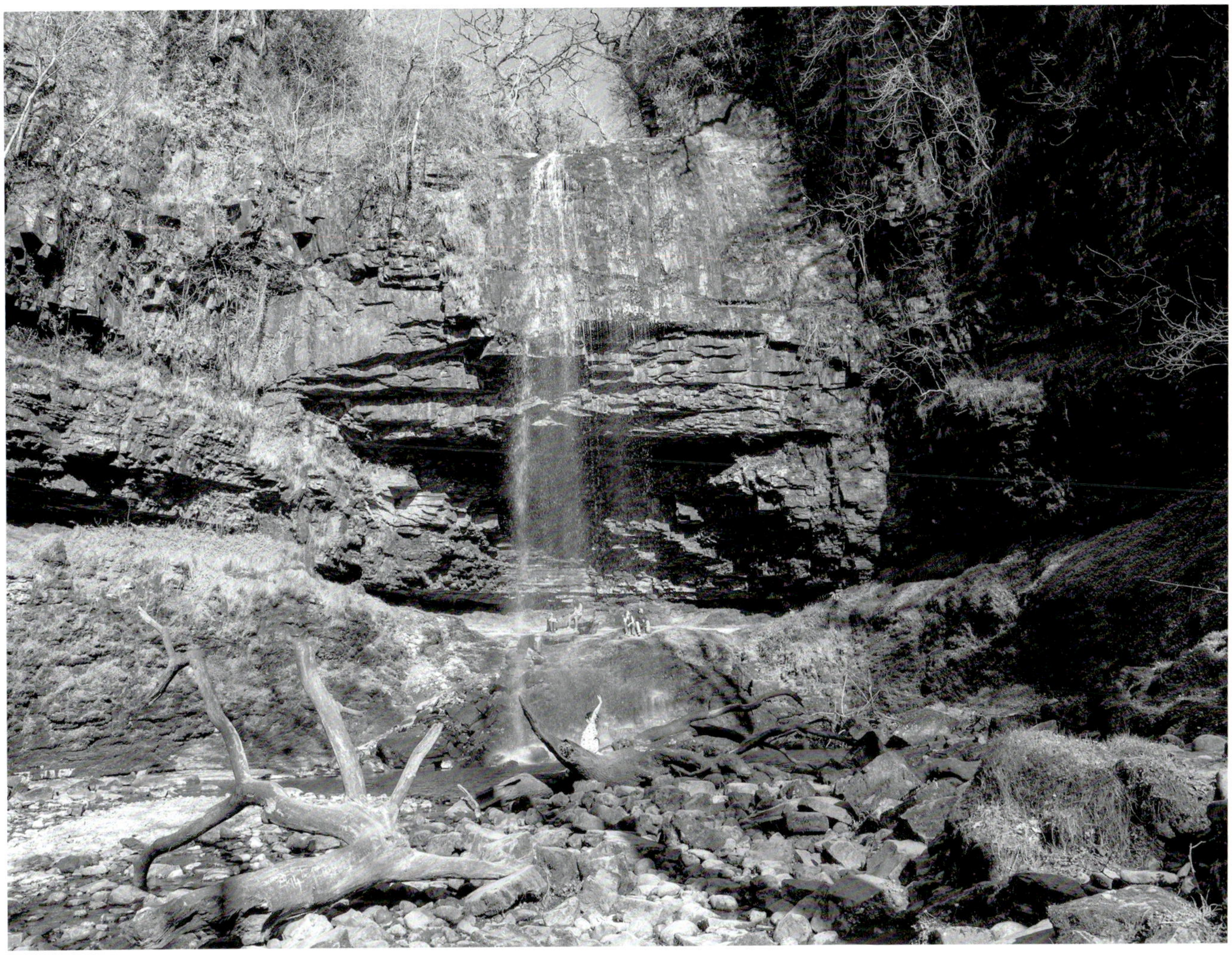

2 DECEMBER 2016 / BATMAN'S CAVE. *BRECON BEACONS, WALES 2015*

For the third in a series of three books trying to understand my culture, I am photographing landscape for the first time. I am trying to take my narcissism out of the equation but utilise my authorship on *others'* guidance.

I was surprised to find that the batcave in the blockbuster film *Batman: The Dark Knight Rises* (2012) was in fact filmed in Wales at Henrhyd Falls in the Brecon Beacons. It has now become a popular attraction for fans from all over the world. It is a beautiful location and is a Site of Special Scientific Interest.

@davidhurnphoto @magnumphotos #landscape #brecon #wales

21 DECEMBER 2016 / TRAVEL ESSAY 2016

A trip for a Magnum retreat, Chepstow to Paris, on to Trouville, back to Paris back to Chepstow.

Picture 1. Travel from Chepstow to London by coach.

@davidhurnphoto @magnumphotos

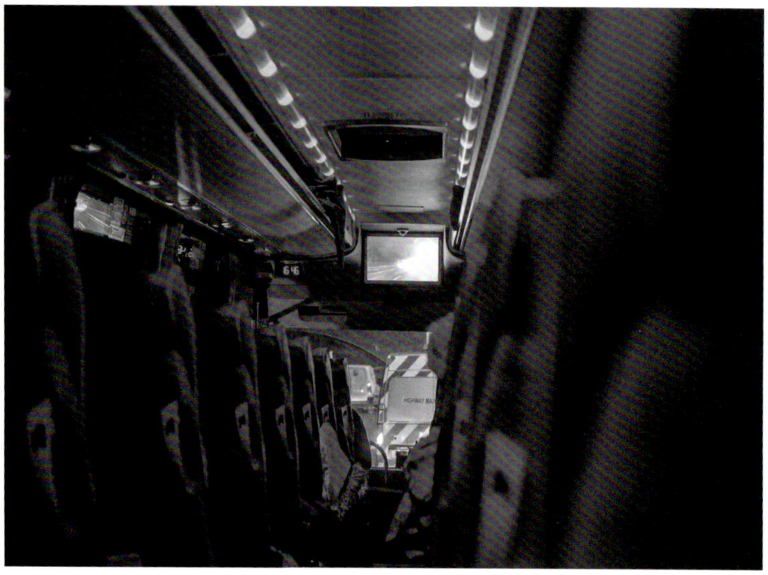

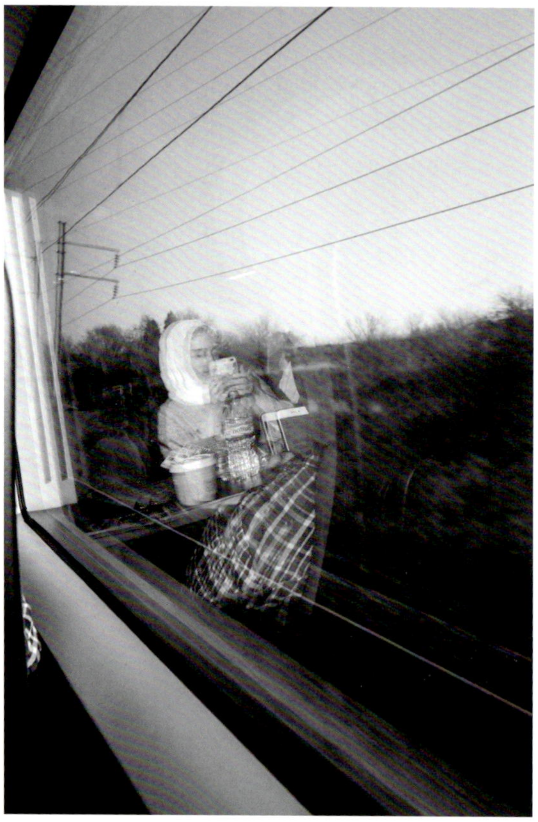

Picture 2. Eurostar London/Paris

Reflections in my seat window.

@davidhurnphoto @magnumphotos #eurostar

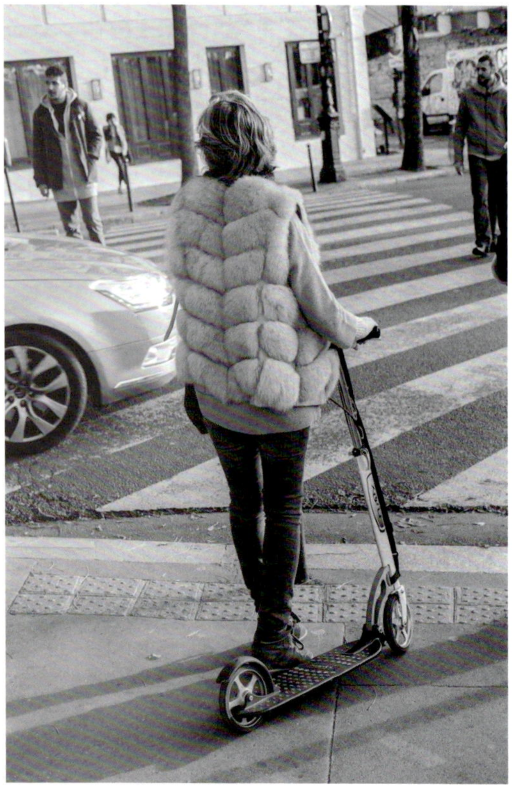

Picture 3. Place de Clichy, Paris.

@davidhurnphoto @magnumphotos #paris #placedeclichy

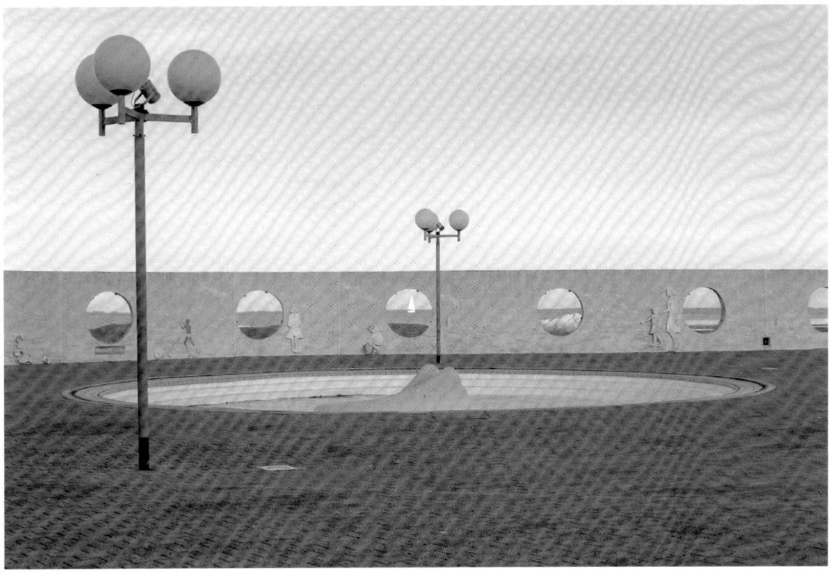

Picture 4. Trouville.
Favourite resort of Flaubert and Proust, Monet and Boudin.

@davidhurnphoto @magnumphotos #trouville

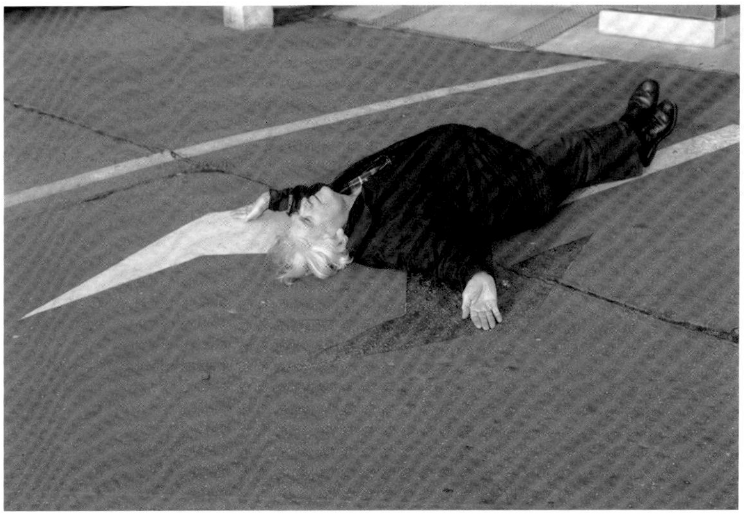

Picture 5. Wonderful photographer and humorist Richard Kalvar resting after a meeting.

@davidhurnphoto @magnumphotos @richardkalvar

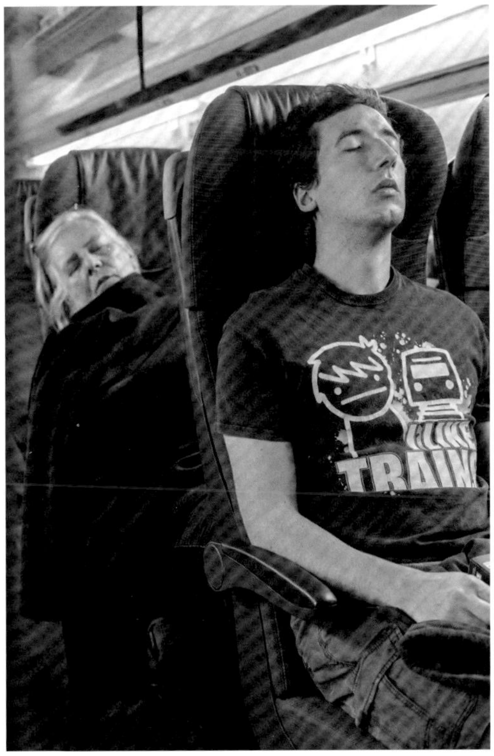

Picture 6. Eurostar Paris/London.

@davidhurnphoto @magnumphotos #eurostar

Sir DON

31 DECEMBER 2016 / SIR DON

Don McCullin, now Sir Don McCullin, has pursued an exemplary standard of photography for so many years. Plus, perhaps as important, he has represented photography in a dignified, thoughtful, and passionate way.

All photographers should thank him for he has enriched our lives.

@davidhurnphoto @magnumphotos @don.mccullin

THEY SAID, ‘YOU HAVE A BLUE GUITAR
YOU DO NOT PLAY THINGS AS THEY ARE’.
THE MAN REPLIED, ‘THINGS AS THEY ARE
ARE CHANGED UPON THE BLUE GUITAR’.

/ *Wallace Stevens*

2017

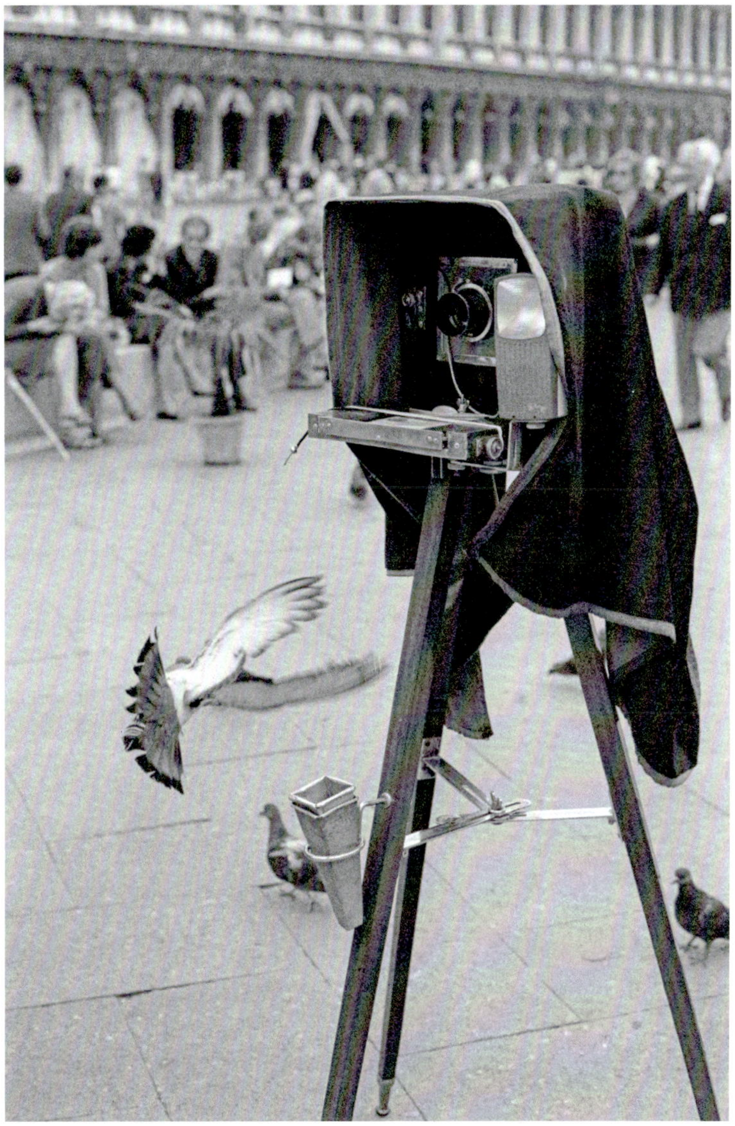

6 JANUARY 2017 / *VENICE, ITALY 1964*

It's the start of the New Year and I am already getting itchy feet. Fifty years ago I shot some pictures in Venice. I have an urge to go back, maybe just for a week, previous pictures plus new might make a gentle pleasing little essay.

@davidhurnphoto @magnumphotos #piazzasanmarco #venice #pigeon

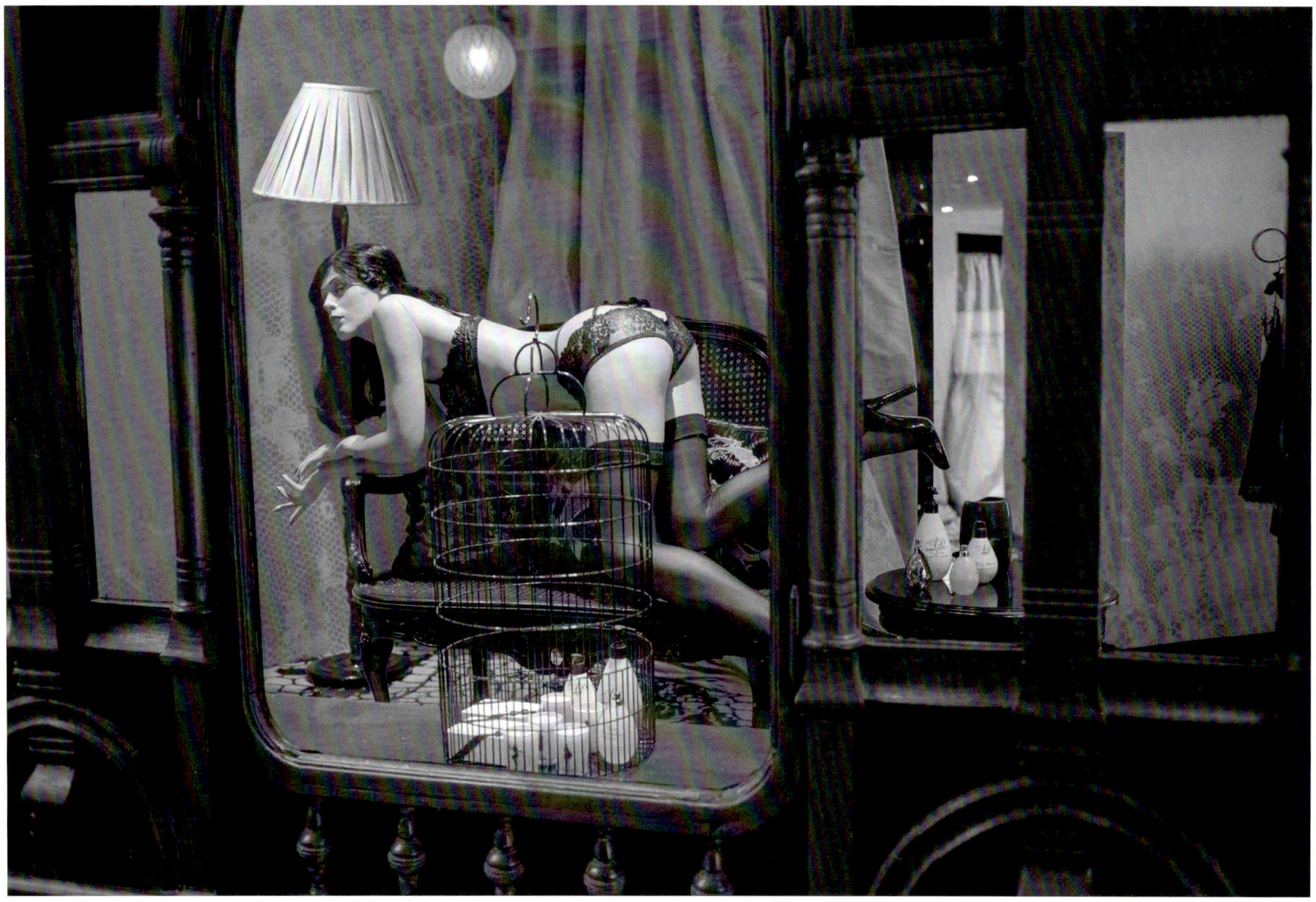

11 JANUARY 2017 / LINGERIE SHOP WINDOW. *STOCKHOLM, SWEDEN 2011*

Each year at this time I hope to go to Stockholm, a favourite city: I love cities where it is easy to walk. The city encompasses 14 islands and more than 50 bridges on an extensive Baltic Sea archipelago, it is fun to wander from island to island, or often even easier, go by boat. The Swedish speak better English than most of us so it is very easy to find one's way.

@davidhurnphoto @magnumphotos #stockholm

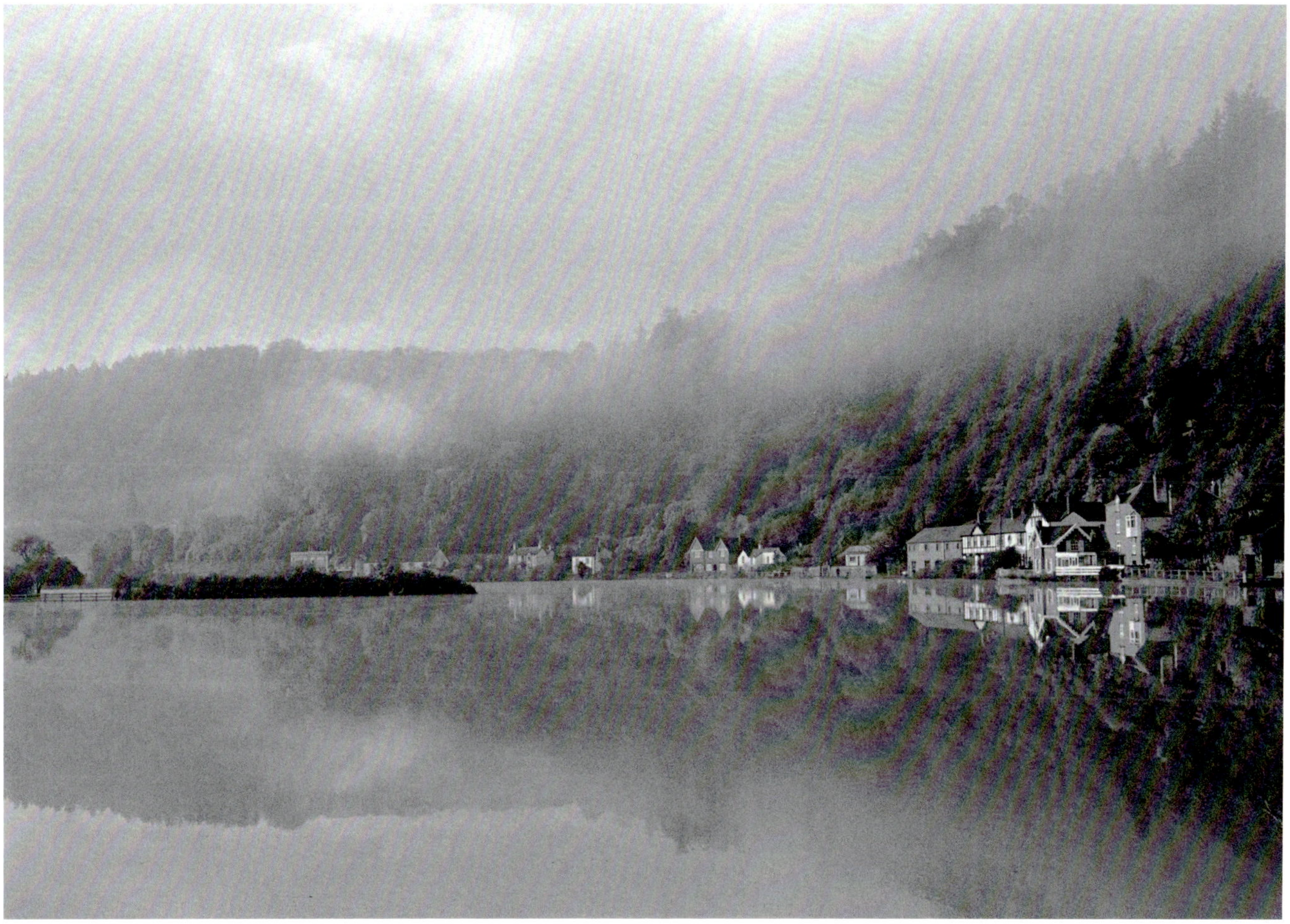

17 JANUARY 2017 / THE RIVER WYE HIGH TIDE. *TINTERN, WALES 1975*

I have woken this morning to the view from my bedroom window showing me the worse aspects of winter, dull and damp. The damp gets into my bones and I have a yen to go back to bed.

@davidhurnphoto @magnumphotos #tintern #wyevalley #wales #landscape

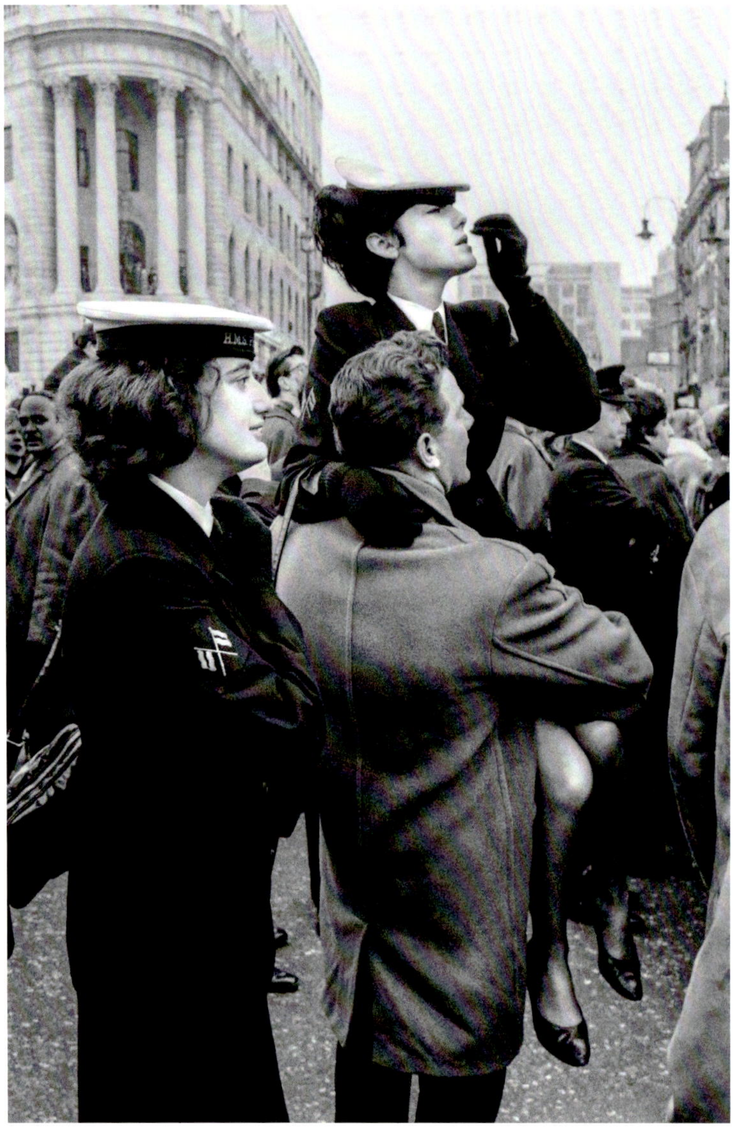

30 JANUARY 2017 / CHURCHILL FUNERAL. *LONDON, ENGLAND 1965*

I am working on archives and realise that 31 January is the anniversary of the funeral of Sir Winston Churchill who, in our years of greatest danger, became the personification of the will of the British nation. I was a comparatively young photographer of 31. I had elected to work totally on my own rather than take a pool position. I started at 4am as people arrived near the Houses of Parliament and wandered. I later spent time in Trafalgar Square as two Wrens attempted to have a better view of the cortège.

@davidhurnphoto @magnumphotos #churchill #wrens

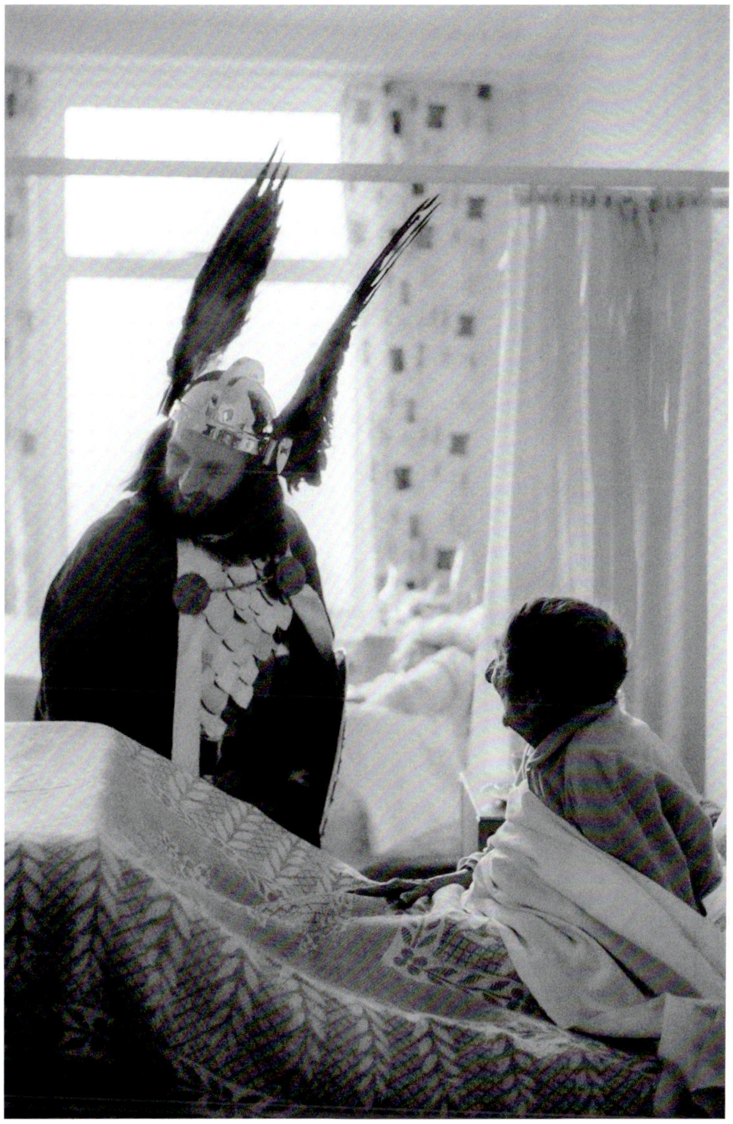

31 JANUARY 2017 / UP HELLY AA. *SHETLAND, SCOTLAND 1967*

On the last Tuesday of January, in Lerwick, Shetland, a festival procession takes place which culminates in flamed torches being thrown into a full-sized replica Viking longship. Afterwards the Guizer Jarl – main man – visits the local hospital.

@davidhurnphoto @magnumphotos #uphellyaa #scotland #viking

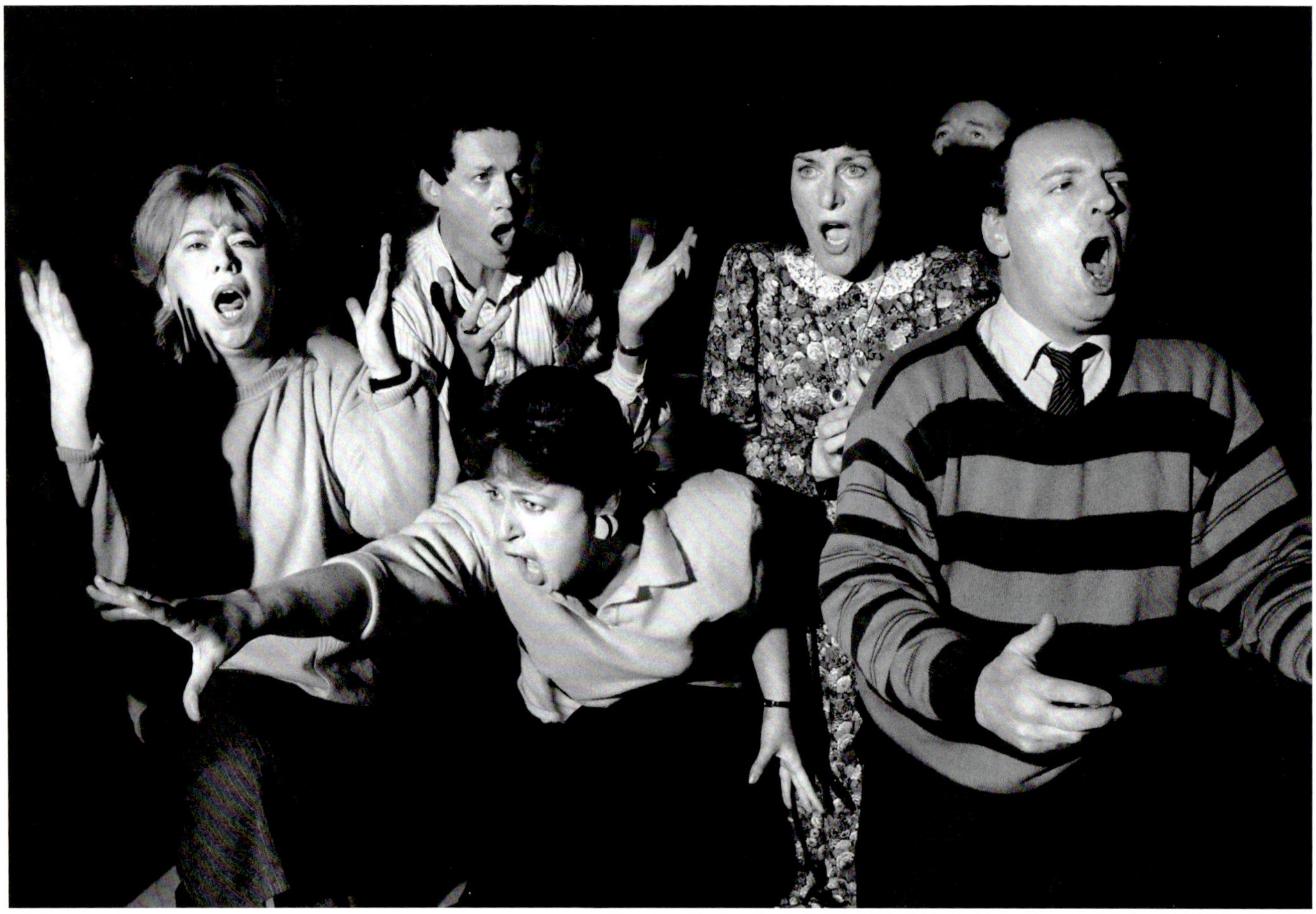

4 MARCH 2017 / WHAT'S HAPPENING? *CARDIFF, WALES 1986*

I enjoy the quality of strangeness within the familiar. We see a photograph – in my case one that is not stage directed but seen – yet we are puzzled, when logic suggests we should understand. Do you know what is happening in this picture?

@davidhurnphoto @magnumphotos #wales #violence #puzzle

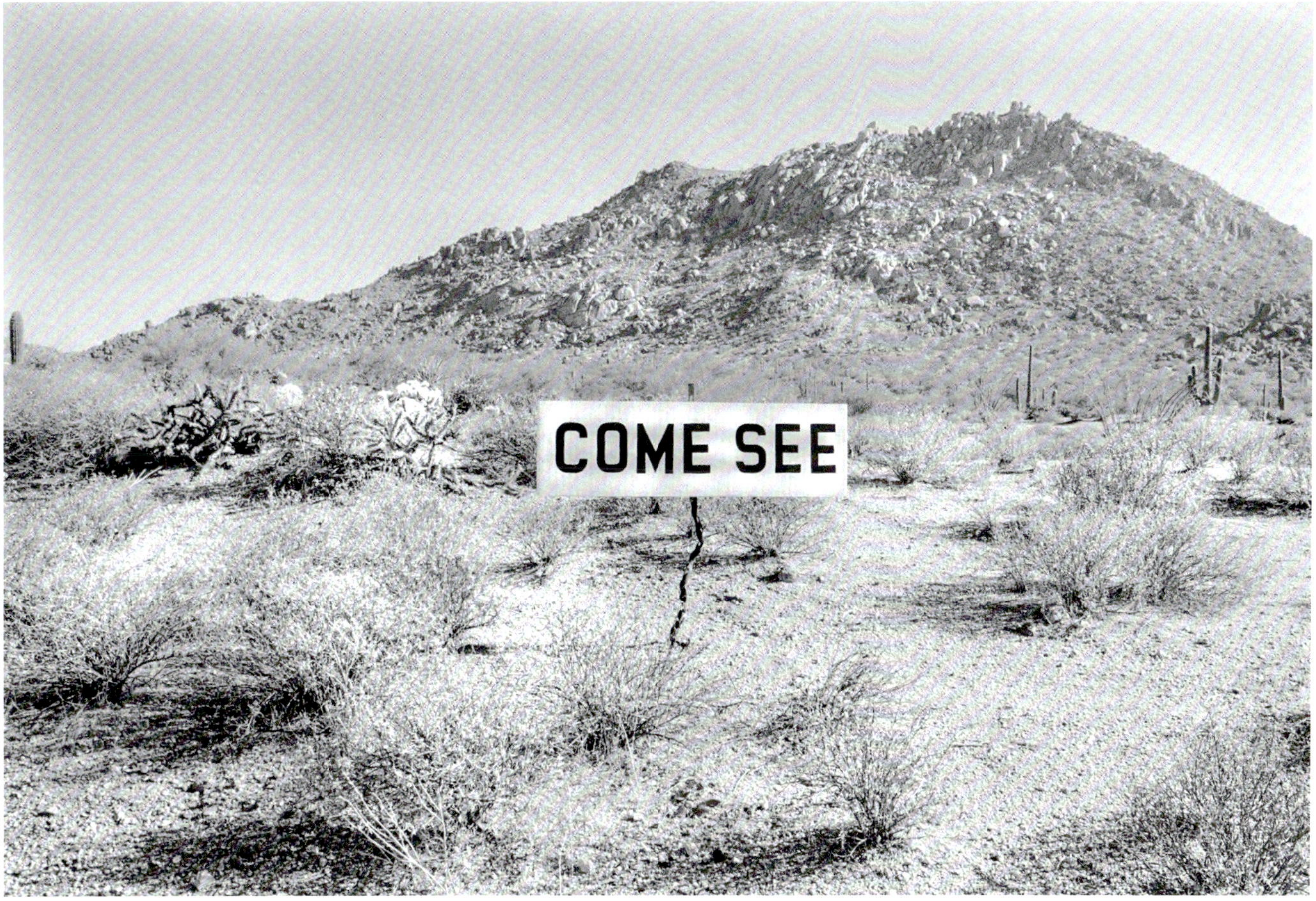

24 MAY 2017 / *ARIZONA. USA 1979*

Well, Photo London is over. Very taxing. Twenty interviews in eight days. The swaps show was an enormous success. As one eminent gallery said, 'It's good to see actual pictures again'.

R|A|P (Reel Art Press) are going to publish my Arizona pictures as my next book. We are working on the layout – easy as I tend to go with chronological order. Hopefully it will be published this year, we are going for the very best printing.

@davidhurnphoto @magnumphotos @reelartpress #arizona

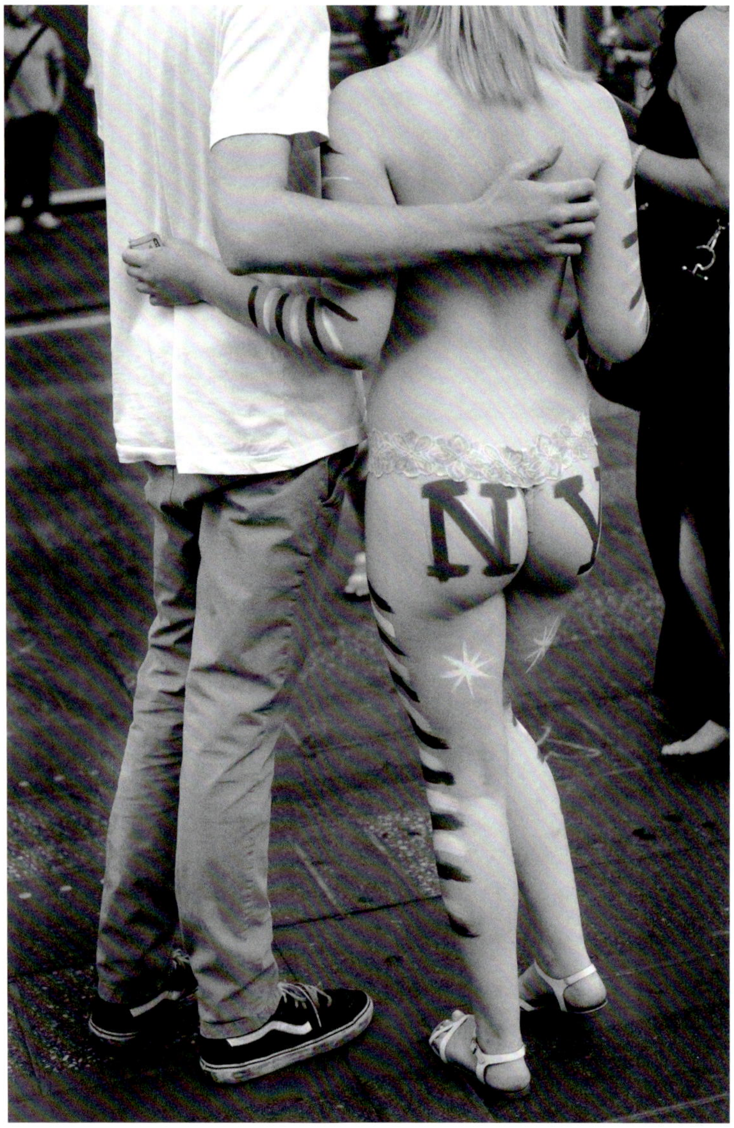

6 JULY 2017 / TIMES SQUARE. *NEW YORK, USA 2017*

Last post I apologised for not showing more pictures due to pressure of work.

I have now been even more lax. Have been in New York for Magnum meetings, saw Elliott Erwitt, Donna Ferrato and Sylvia Plachy, among others.

Shot a picture for *The New Yorker* magazine in Times Square, above.

@davidhurnphoto @magnumphotos @elliotterwitt @donnaferrato @newyorkermag #sylviaplachy #timessquare #newyork

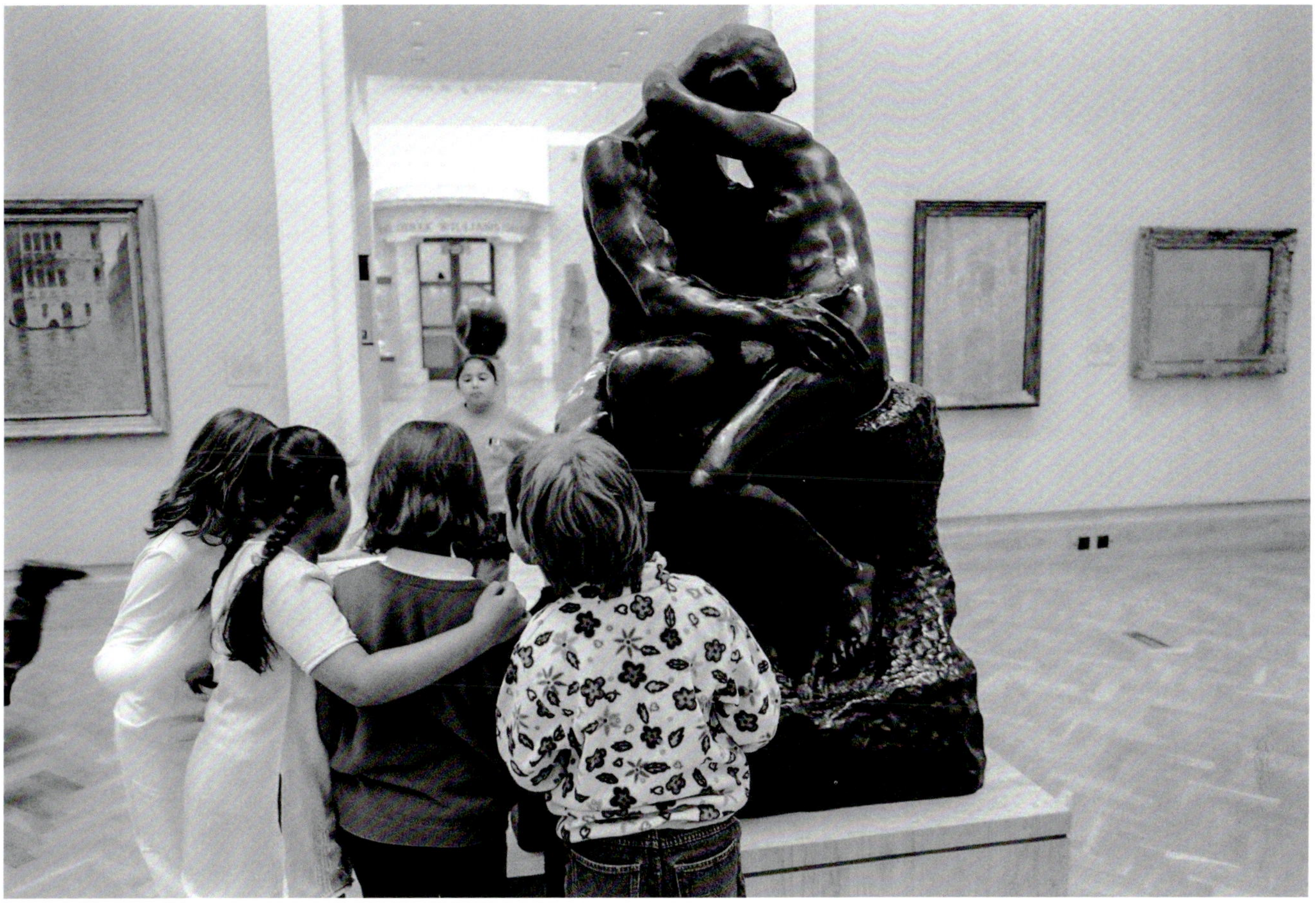

18 JULY 2017 / RODIN: 'THE KISS'. *CARDIFF, WALES 2004*

The BBC have commissioned a film on me to be shown probably in October.

One of the first sequences we have shot is revisiting my first visual memory, a statue, in the National Museum in Cardiff, Wales. My mother regularly took me into the museum when I was about six years of age – I remember a 'naughty statue', i.e. Rodin *The Kiss*.

@davidhurnphoto @magnumphotos @museumwales #nationalmuseumcardiff #rodin #bbc

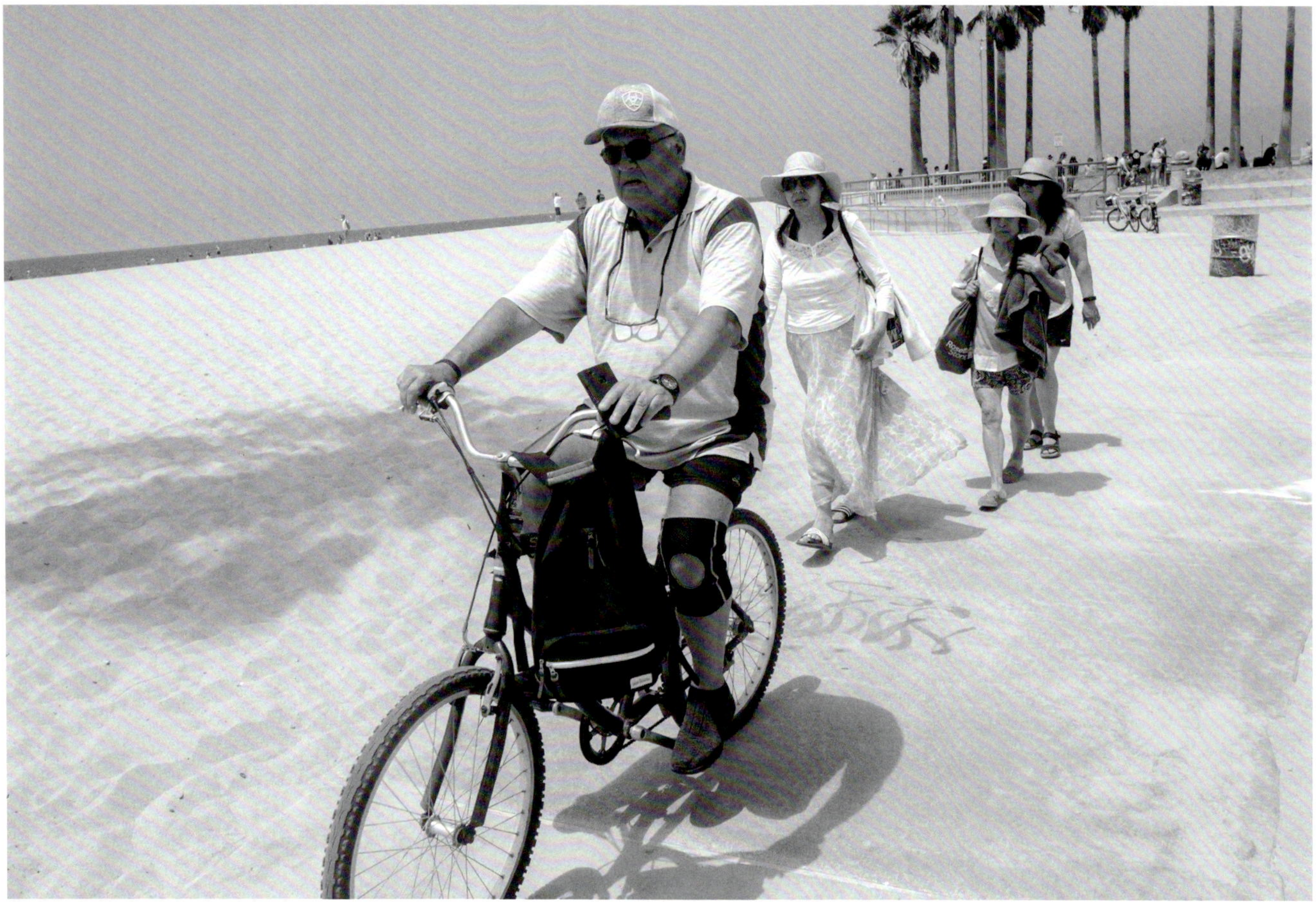

1 AUGUST 2017 / VENICE BEACH. *CALIFORNIA, USA 2017*

Continuing my filming with the BBC we revisited Venice Beach, a haunt of mine in the '70s and early '80s when I spent time with the very interesting photographer Garry Winogrand. This time, I visited Beverly Hills to see an old friend, actor Jane Fonda. She will be 80 in December, she looks and thinks amazing.

@davidhurnphoto @magnumphotos @janefonda #bbc #venicebeach #california

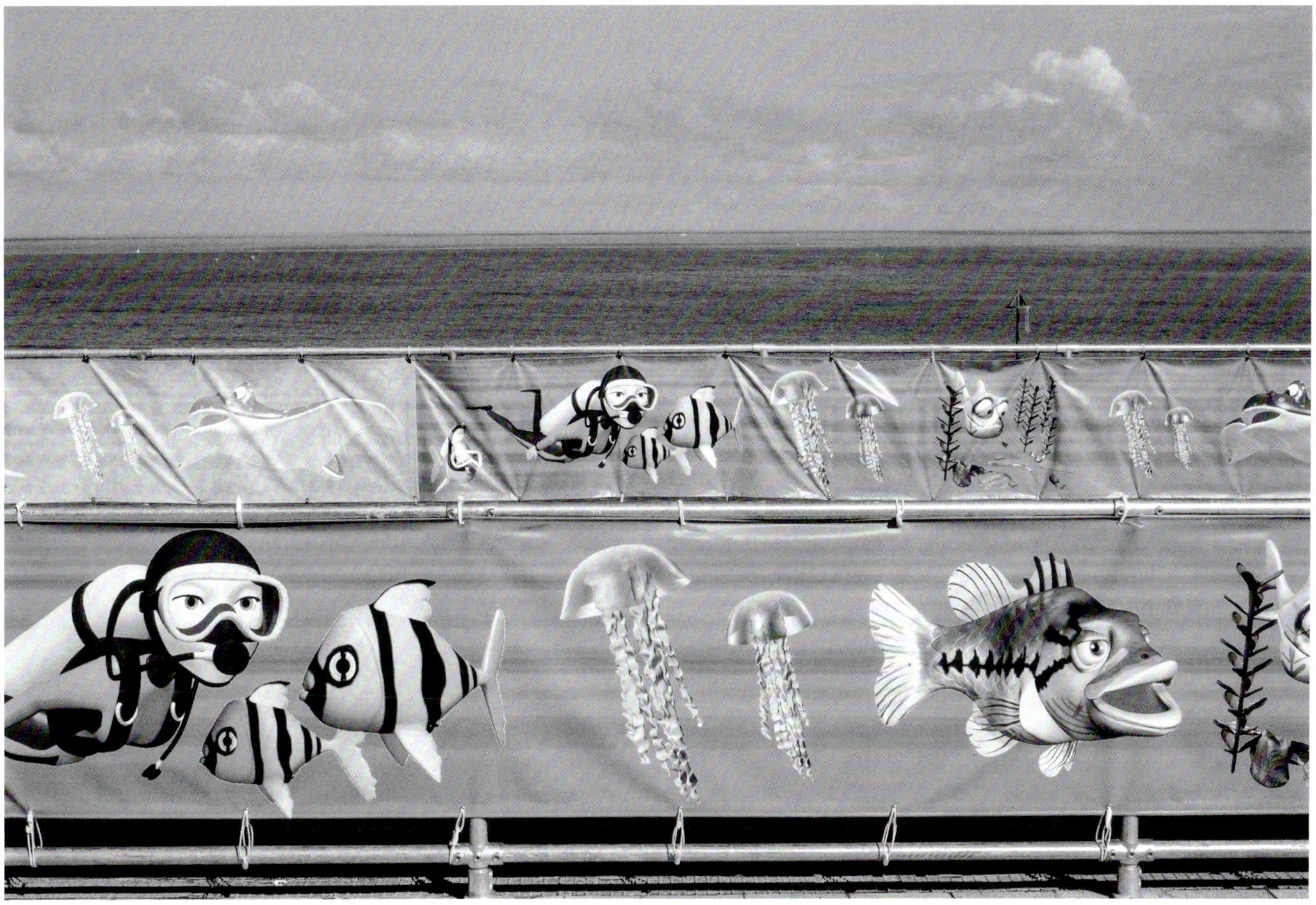

15 AUGUST 2017 / THE GREAT BRITISH SEASIDE. *ABERYSTWYTH, WALES 2014*

At last my shooting schedule is getting under control. I have an ongoing project on landscape but that is very flexible as landscape doesn't tend to go away. I am doing a talk at the Monmouth Photographic Club, rare as I have more or less given up doing lectures – but I like to keep on good terms with the locals. I am also shooting for a group exhibition, *The Great British Seaside*, at the National Maritime Museum next year. The other participants are Tony Ray-Jones, Martin Parr and Simon Roberts – a pretty distinguished group.

@davidhurnphoto @magnumphotos #monmouthphotographicclub #seaside #surreal

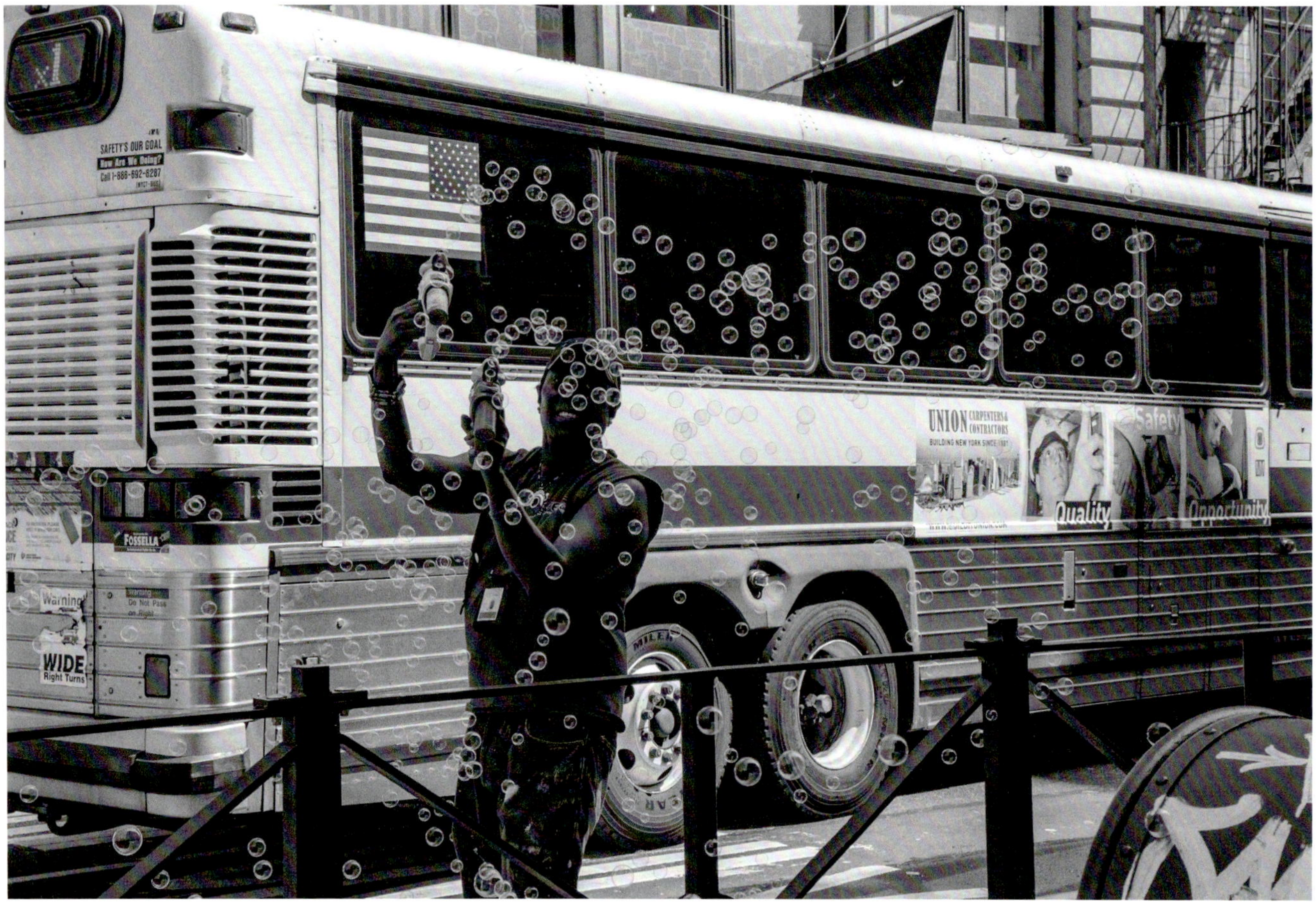

22 AUGUST 2017 / NEW YORK BUS & BUBBLES. *NEW YORK, USA 2007*

I did love being in New York – it revitalises me. Everything is moving fast, so many characters seemingly having fun. Sadly, I suspect it will have been the last time I go.

@davidhurnphoto @magnumphotos #surreal #newyork #bubbles

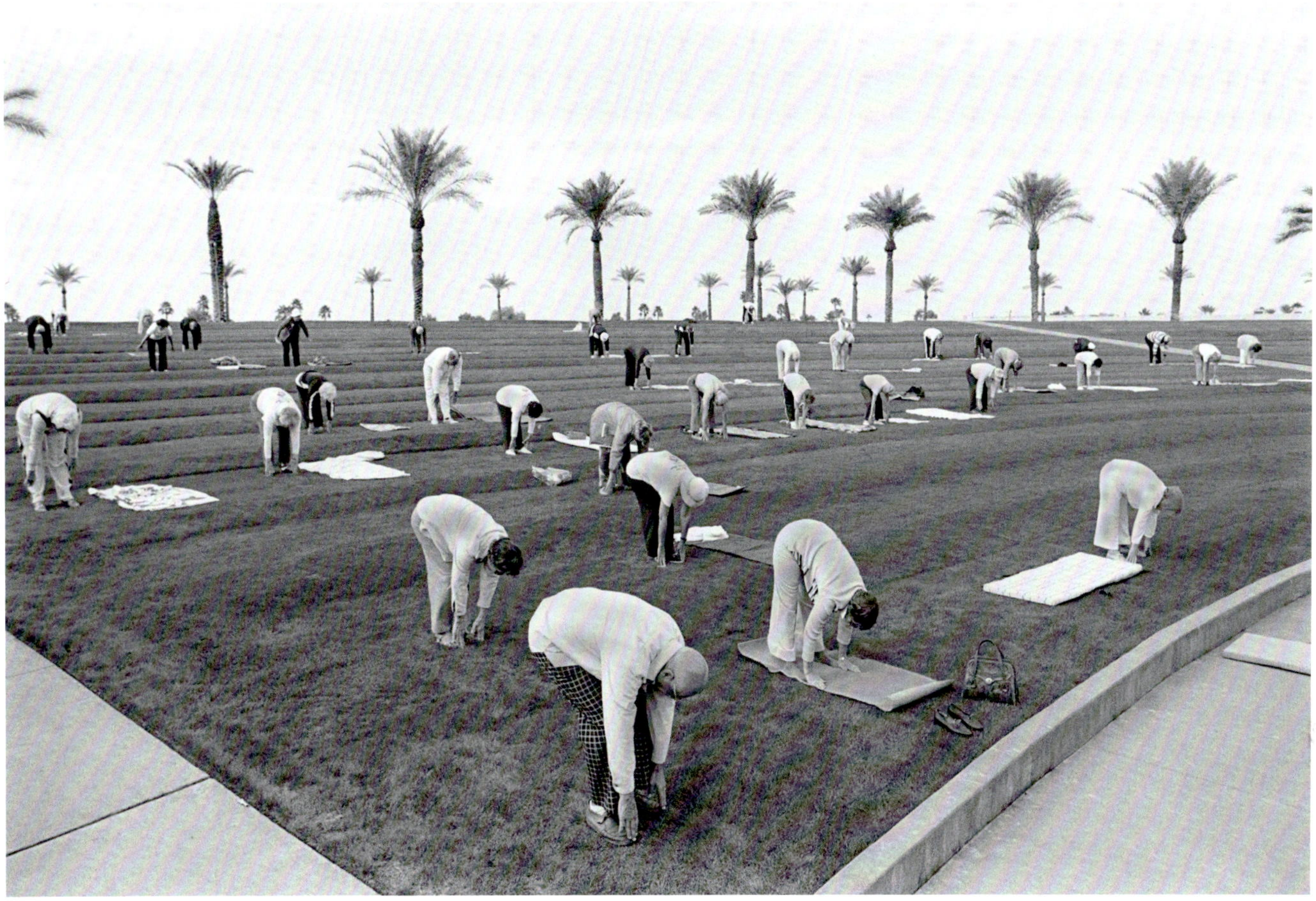

26 AUGUST 2017 / SUN CITY. *ARIZONA, USA 1980*

I have discovered that just walking and shooting does not really keep me fit. I am fine for stamina but my legs become weaker than I would like. Now I am home it's back to the gym, a month and I will be fine again.

@davidhurnphoto @magnumphotos #suncity #exercise #seniors #arizona

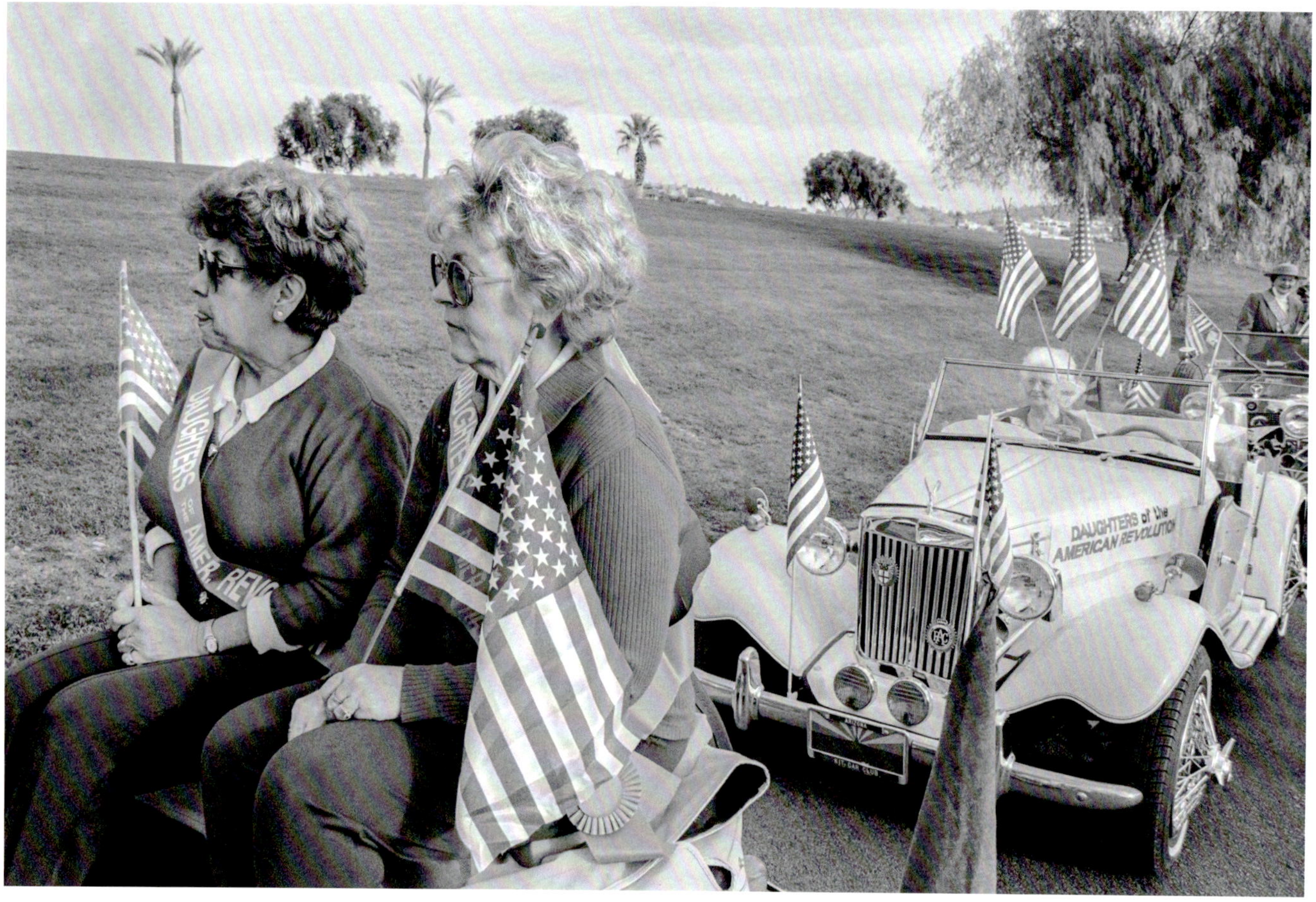

15 SEPTEMBER 2017 / DAUGHTERS OF THE AMERICAN REVOLUTION. ***ARIZONA, USA 1997***

Can't help wondering it there is a relationship between Brexit and The Daughters of the American Revolution? Nostalgia for mythical days.

@davidhurnphoto @magnumphotos #flags #daughtersoftheamericanrevolution #arizona

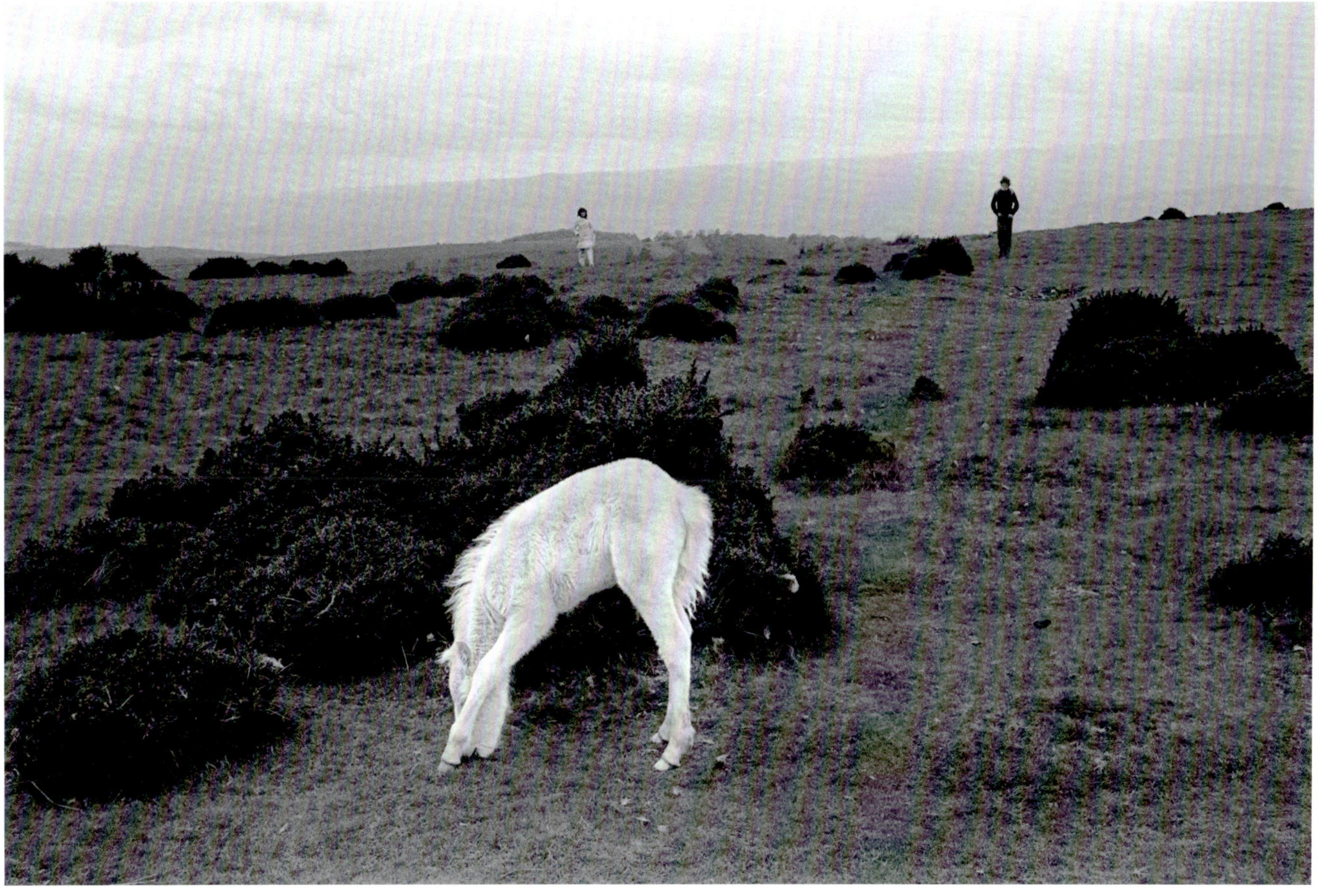

19 SEPTEMBER 2017 / BRECON BEACONS, *WALES 1974*

I seem to be coming to the end of a very hectic period. I have donated 700 prints that I have acquired from other photographers by 'Swapping', to the National Museum of Wales in Cardiff, they have opened a permanent gallery for photography. The first show will open 28/29 September and shows will last for six months then rotate, so there is always a reason to go to the museum.

I am off to the Beacons for a couple of days relaxing.

@davidhurnphoto @magnumphotos #wales #beacons #pony

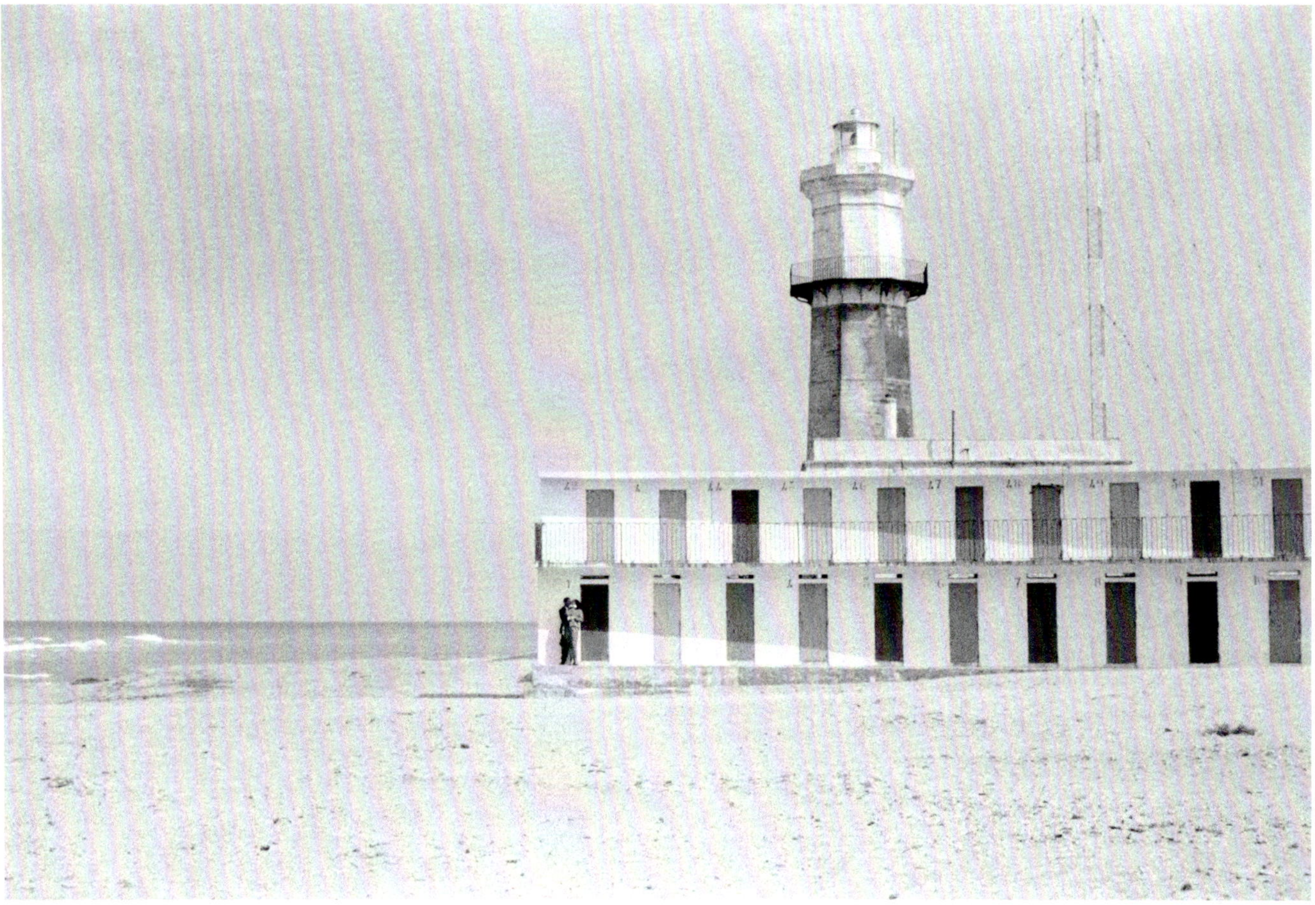

26 SEPTEMBER 2017 / *CATALDO, ITALY 1964*

I have a lot of themes stored in the back of my mind. It helps concentrate concentration. One of those is 'how small can the essential content be in a picture?'

@davidhurnphoto @magnumphotos #cataldo #detail #love #seascape

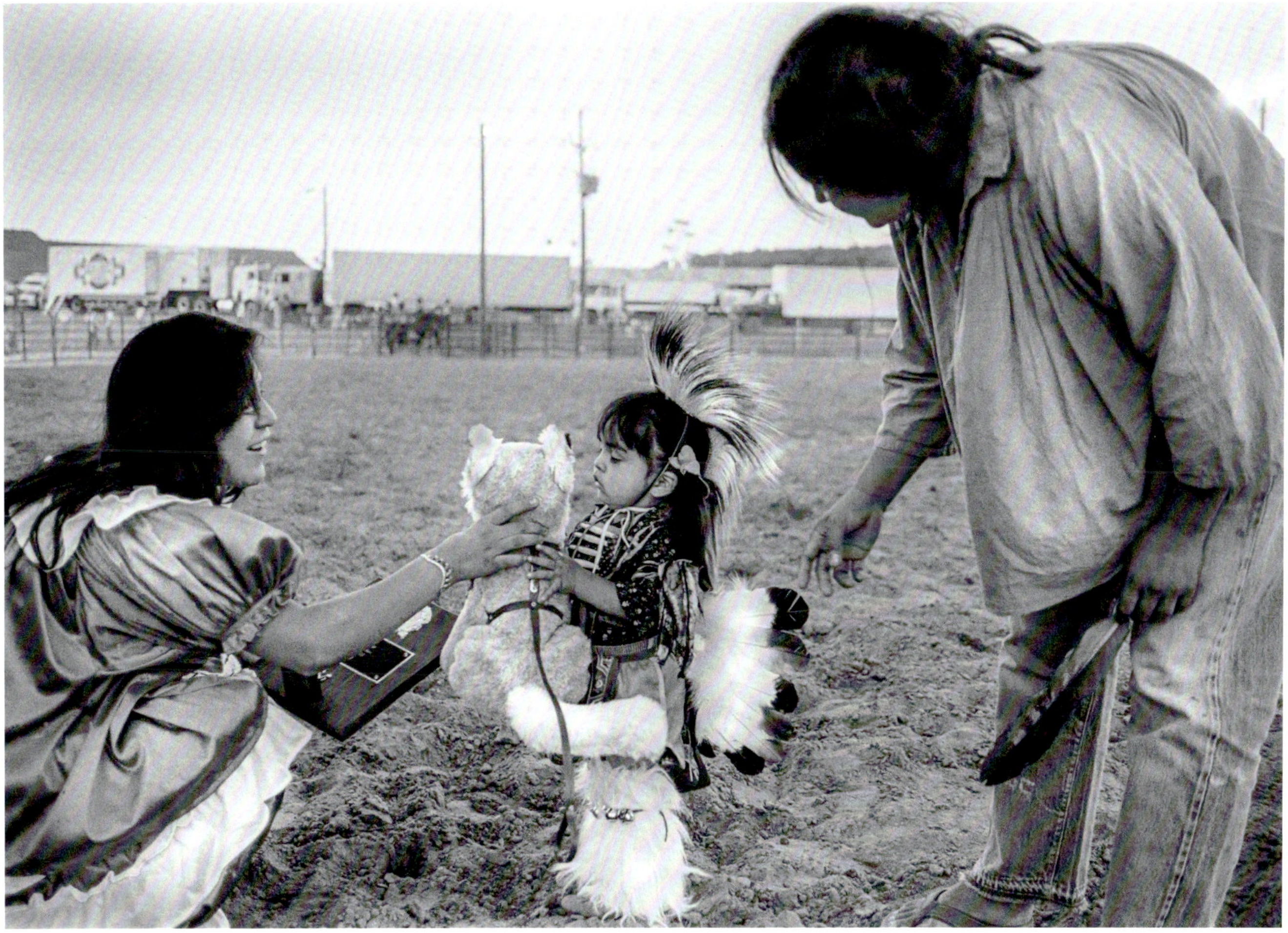

8 DECEMBER 2017 / WINNER OF 'APACHE BABY CONTEST'. *ARIZONA, USA 1980*

During my time in Arizona I spent a considerable time with various of the Native American Nations. I even had the honour of being invited to participate in a puberty ceremony. My contact to various tribes was facilitated by travelling to see them with doctors from St Josef's Hospital in Phoenix. I then built up mutual trust.

@davidhurnphoto @magnumphotos @reelartpress #arizona #apache

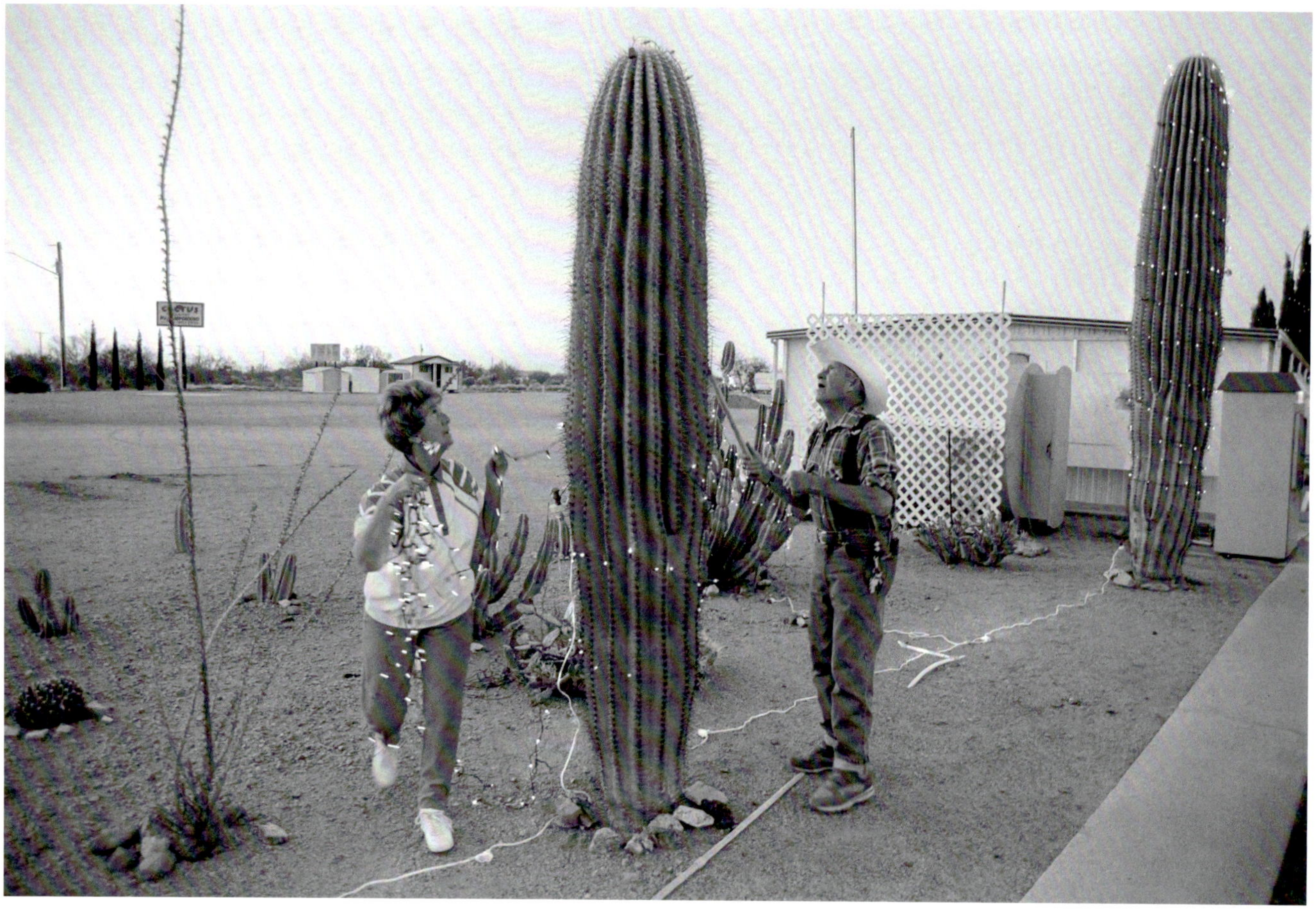

24 DECEMBER 2017 / ARIZONA CHRISTMAS TREE. *ARIZONA, USA 1997*

I wish you all a very positive holiday.

@davidhurnphoto @magnumphotos @reelartpress #arizona #cactus

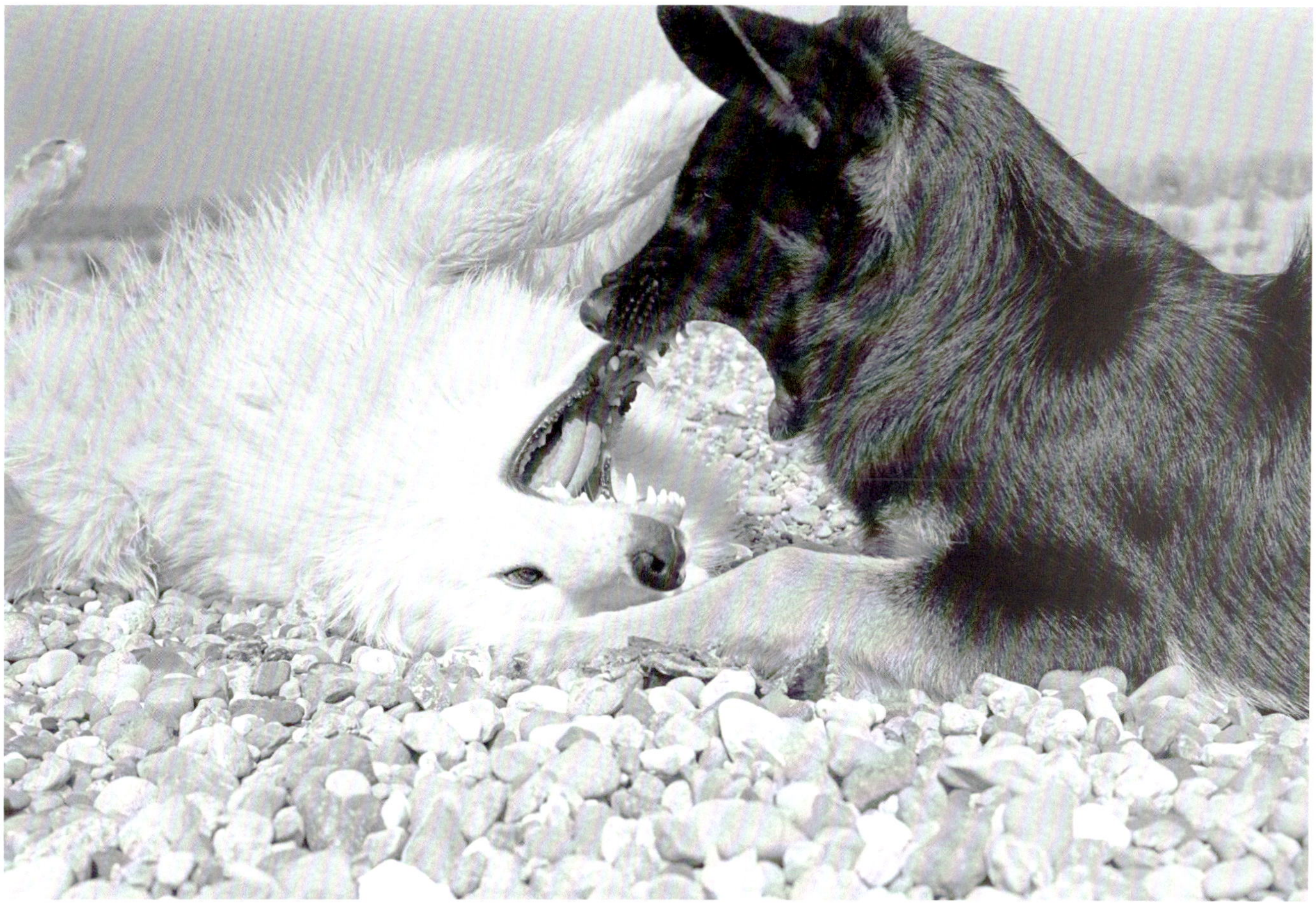

31 DECEMBER 2017 / MY DOGS. *RHYL, WALES 1976*

May you all be gifted a kind and productive year. Peace and goodwill to all.

I have bought myself three books to read in the next month.

Daemon Voices: On Stories and Storytelling by Philip Pullman: I heard one of the essays on the radio: although it was essentially about writing, it seemed to so easily, with a little lateral thinking, translate into photography. I find thinking about other disciplines as though they were photography very rewarding.

Art Can Help, essays by Robert Adams. For me anything he writes, and photographs, is worthwhile. How can one not like 'to keep an affection for life'.

Henri Cartier-Bresson: Interviews and Conversations, 1951-1998. I suspect I have read it all before, but maybe a gem was missed, and such clarity, as his, is worth re-reading.

@davidhurnphoto @magnumphotos #wales #dogs #booktips #newyear #philippullman #robertadams #henricartierbresson

I'M OBSESSED BY ONE THING, THE VISUAL PLEASURE.

/ *Henri Cartier-Bresson*

2018

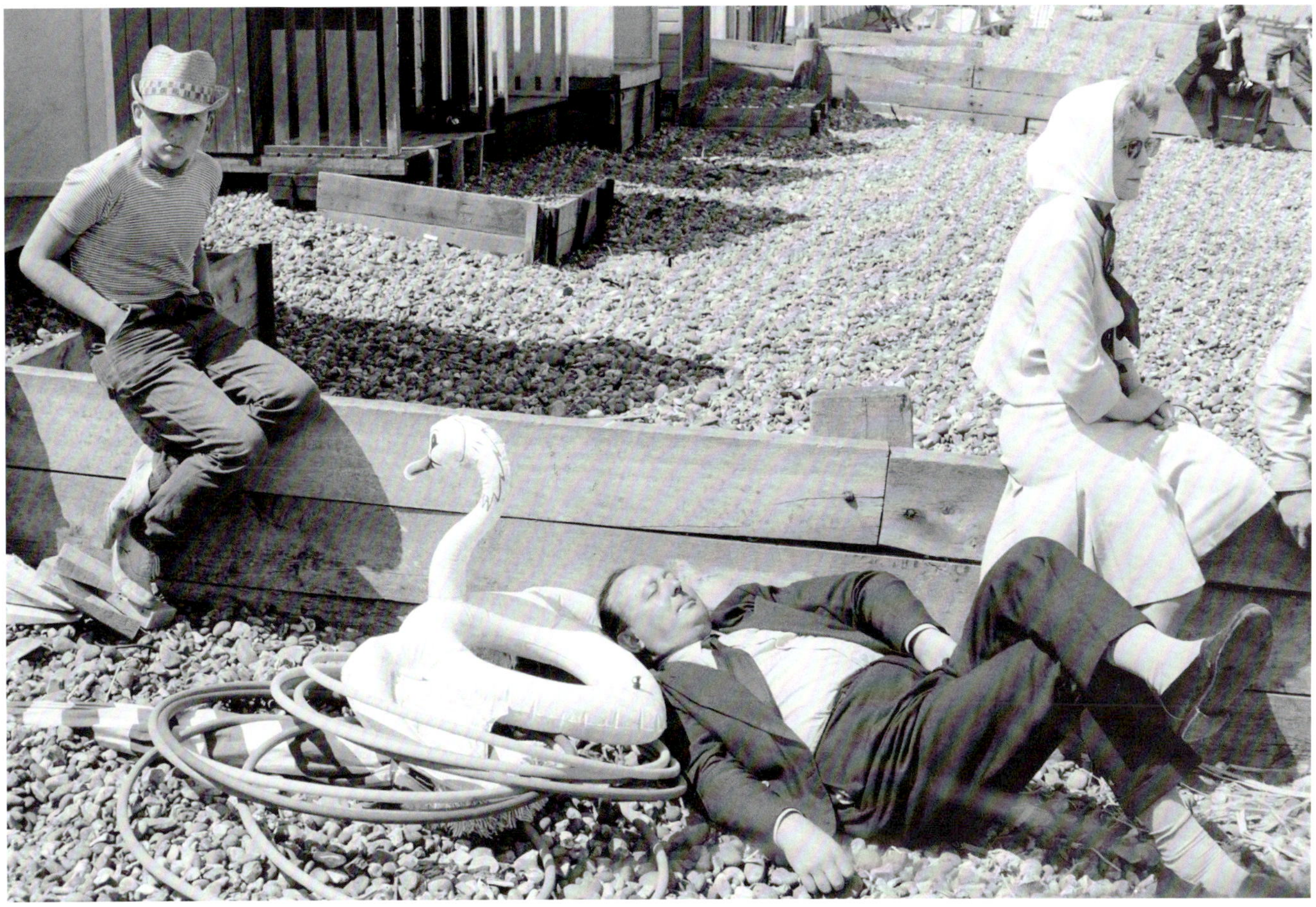

10 JANUARY 2018 / HERNE BAY, *ENGLAND 1963*

'On 23 March the National Maritime Museum (NMM) opens a major photography exhibition celebrating the nation's love affair with the seaside. Featuring over 100 works by four of Britain's most celebrated photographers – David Hurn, Tony Ray-Jones, Martin Parr and Simon Roberts – the exhibition explores our changing relationship with the seaside over the last six decades.' So reads the NMM's press release.

I think it will be a popular exhibition as it will show people having fun and dropping their inhibitions.

I started photographing in Herne Bay in early 1963 as it was an easy train ride from London and helped me have a relaxing weekend. I felt very much in the tradition of a lovely photographer, Paul Martin, who photographed in Yarmouth in 1892. In my opinion there are no better collection of holiday pictures than his.

@davidhurnphoto @magnumphotos @royalmuseumsgreenwich
#GBseaside #hernebay #seaside

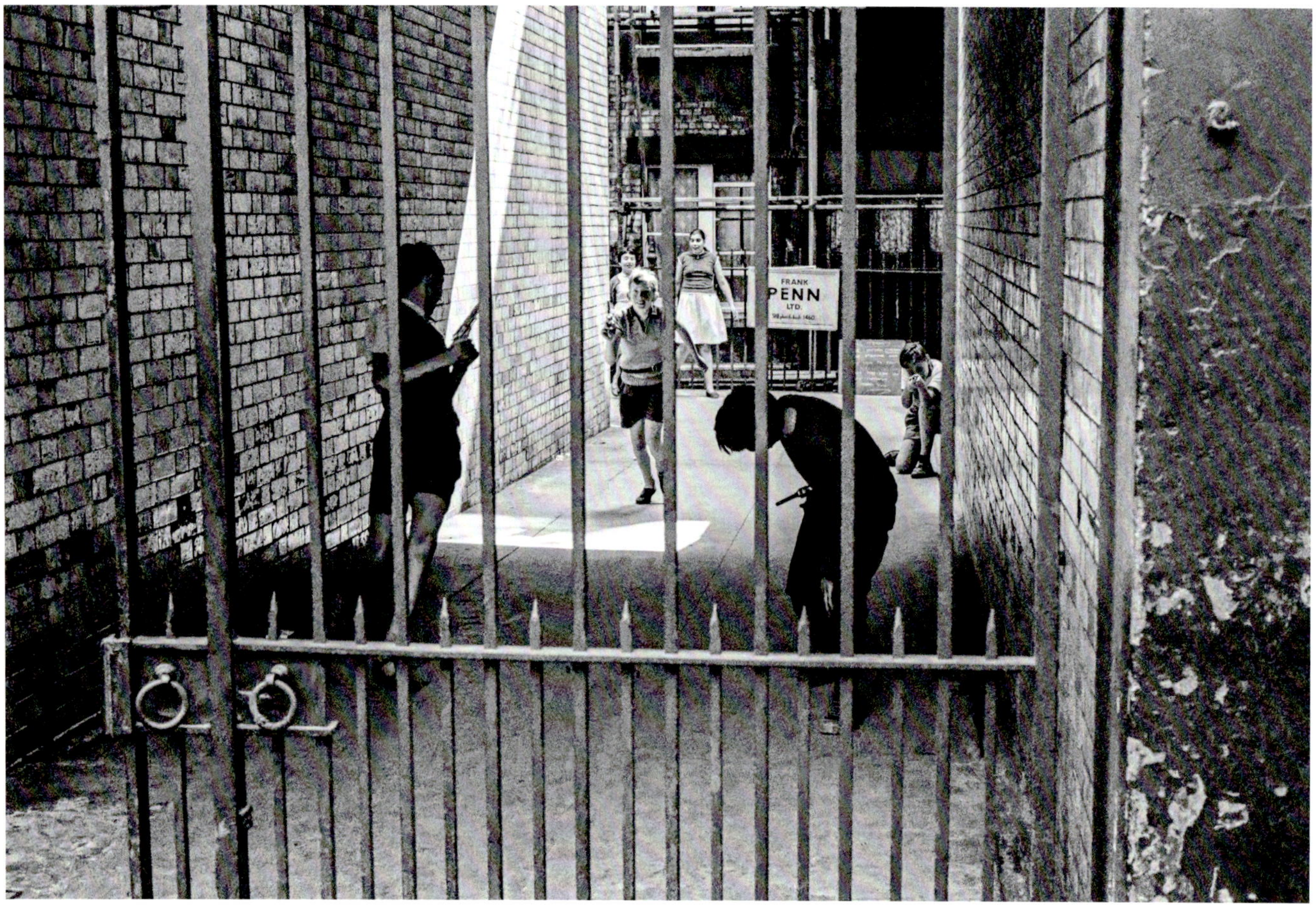

30 JANUARY 2018 / CHILDREN IN SOHO PLAYING WITH GUNS. *LONDON, ENGLAND 1955*

I seem to not be able to get out of the cycle of dealing with exhibitions and resulting organisation. It takes too much of my time.

So am having to put up another very early picture taken with my folding Kodak camera. Important to me as at that time I was resolving what subject matter I was most interested in. Until you manage this, it's difficult to progress.

I like a quote of William Hazlitt: 'You know more of a road by having travelled it than by all the conjectures and descriptions in the world.'

@davidhurnphoto @magnumphotos #soho

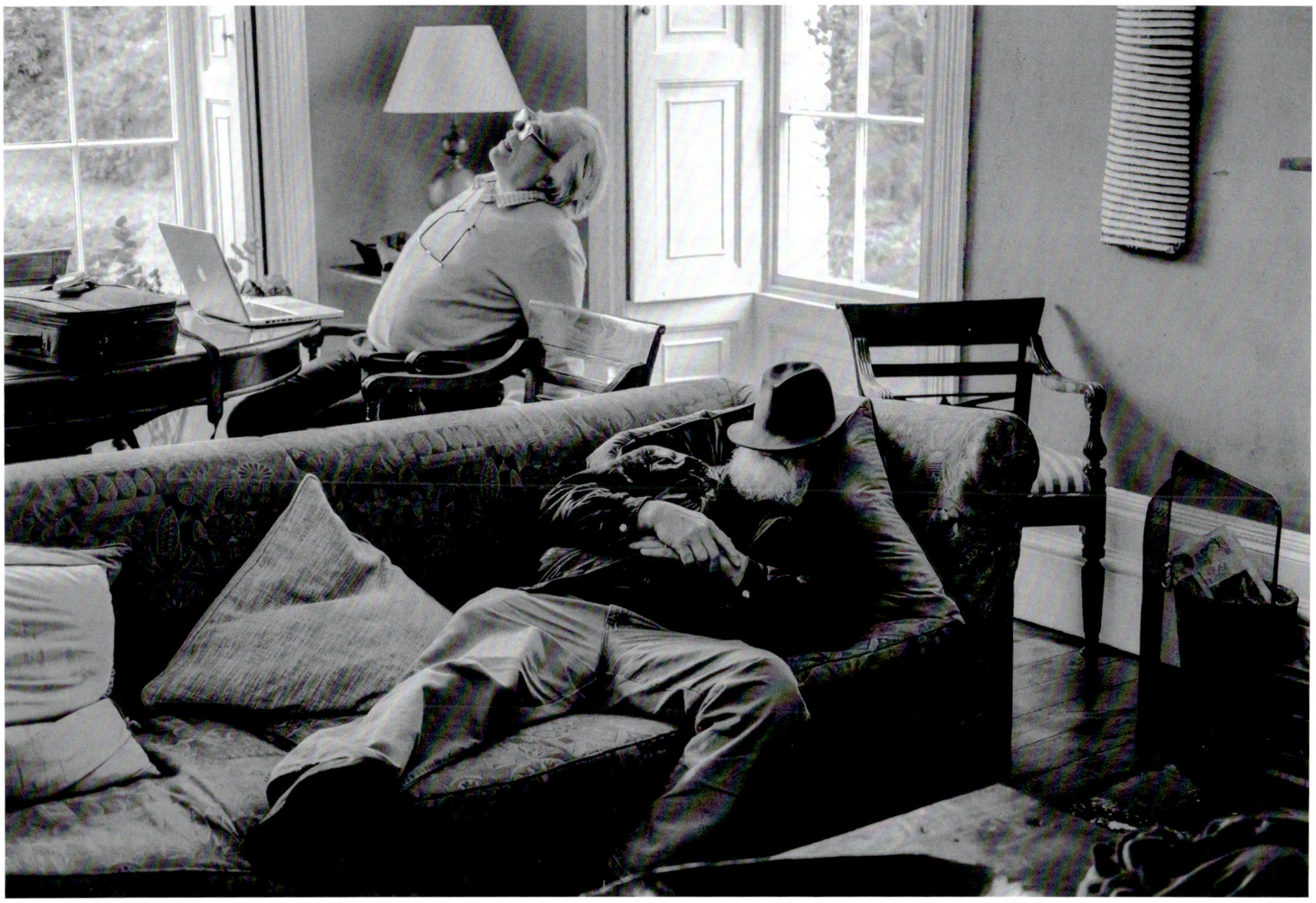

14 FEBRUARY 2018 / RETREAT IN THE BRECON BEACONS. *WALES 2018*

I have just returned from a delightful gathering in the Brecon Beacons. Thirty-four members of Magnum staff and photographers – 18 photographers – got together as family to make sure we still like each other. What a surprise any photographer in Wales would have had if they had wandered into the local pub at lunch time.

After exacting conversation, we see Richard Kalvar and Larry Towell sleeping it off.

@davidhurnphoto @magnumphotos @richardkalvar @larrysgeneralstore #nostalgia #sleep

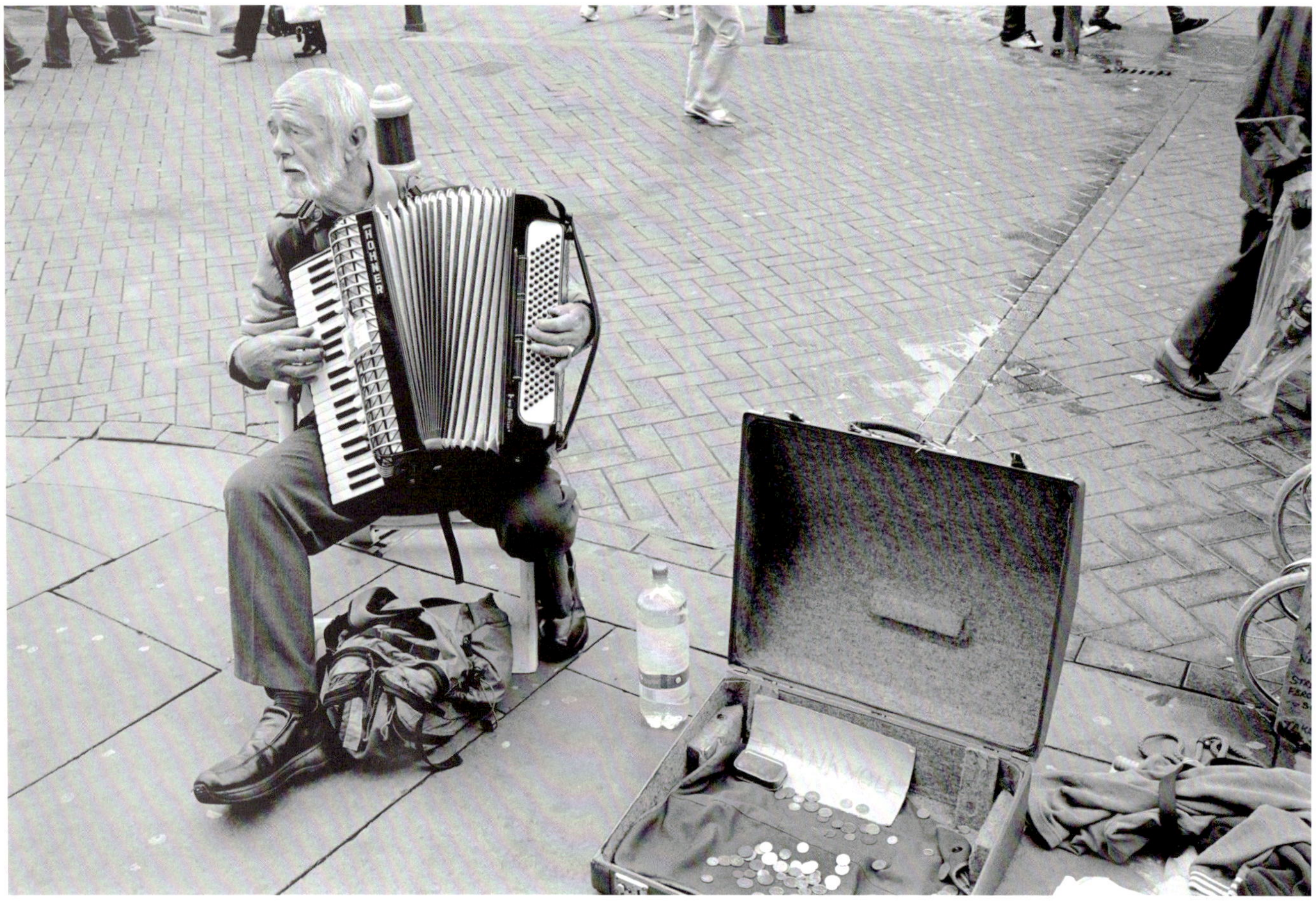

21 FEBRUARY 2018 / ACCORDION PLAYER. *NEWPORT, WALES 2008*

An excellent book is Geoff Dyer's *The Ongoing Moment*. He investigates the way photographers often investigate the same subject matter – as an aside he mentioned Walker Evans' advice to a learning Ben Shahn: 'Look Ben, there's nothing to it. F9 on the shady side of the street, F45 on the sunny side, twentieth of a second, hold the camera steady!' Returning to subject matter, Dyer refers to photographers recording accordion players. Ben Shahn, Walker Evans, Ed Clark and many André Kertész. I recently joined the queue.

@davidhurnphoto @magnumphotos #accordion

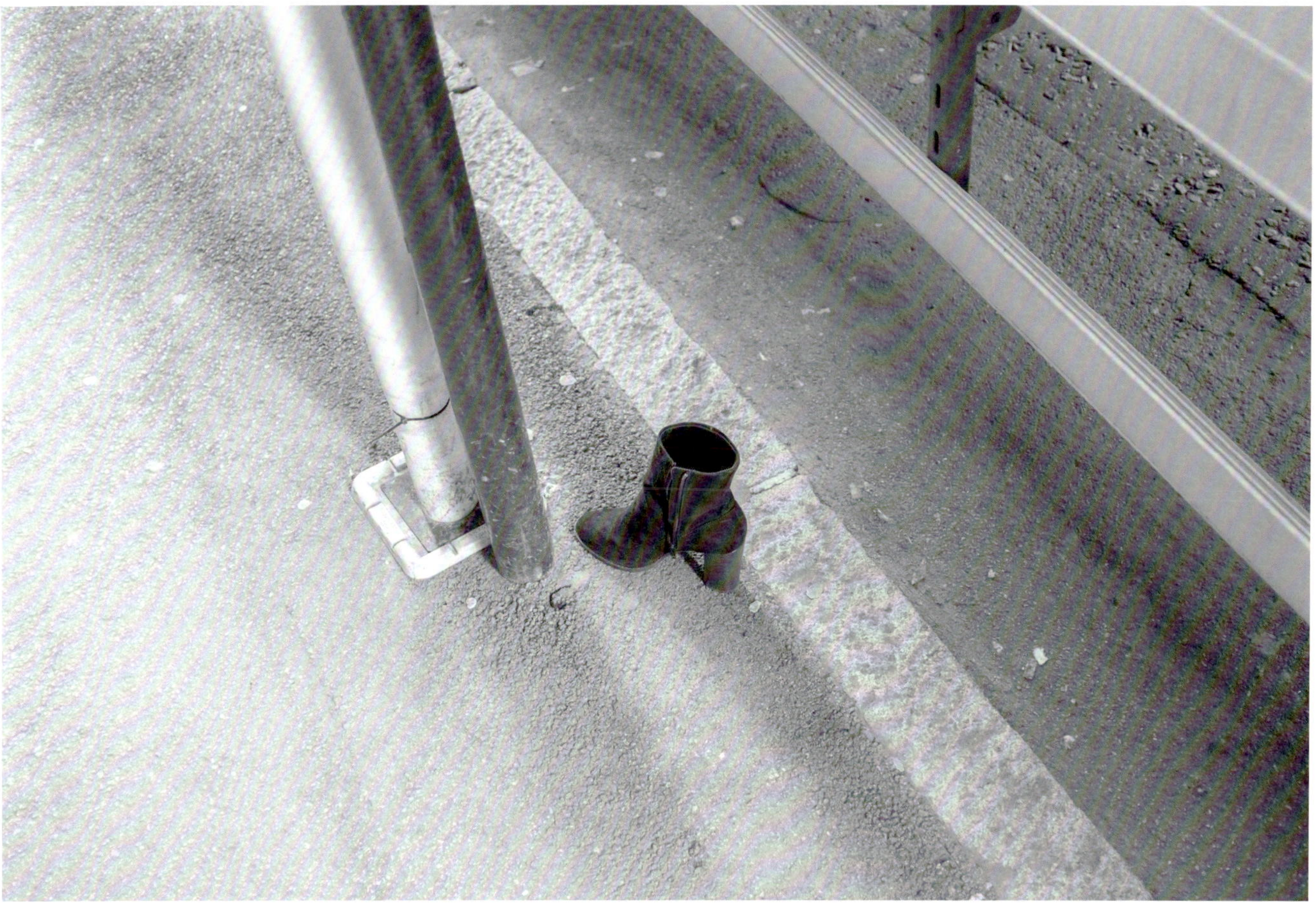

6 APRIL 2018 / THE MYSTERY OF 'THE LADY'S BOOT'. *LONDON, ENGLAND 2018*

I have just returned home, Tintern, from a successful conversation with Sir Christopher Frayling at the National Portrait Gallery.

When in London I nearly always stay in Gee Street, the street of the Magnum office. Every morning I go out to breakfast, my favourite meal.

For three mornings running I have noticed a single black lady's boot at the base of some scaffolding. The first day it was a passing puzzle, the second day mysterious – could it be art, perhaps conceptual? Anyway, I checked to see if it was glued down, it wasn't. The third morning it was still there, no-one had touched it, the mystery remains.

I enjoy the picture because I am sure it sets up a thousand explanations.

@davidhurnphoto @magnumphotos @christopherfrayling

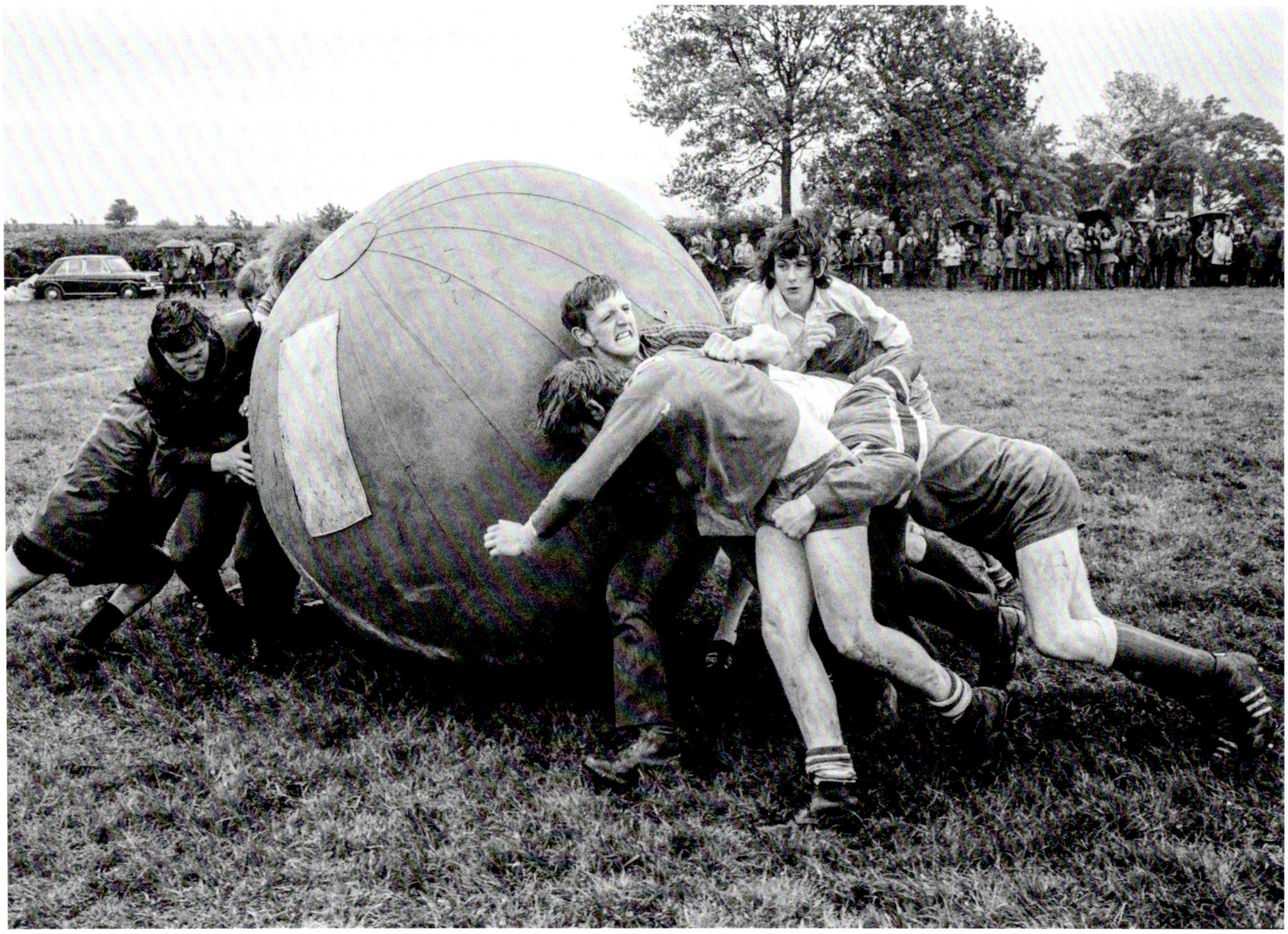

25 APRIL 2018 / YOUNG FARMERS DAY. *BRECON, WALES 1973*

A great photographer and friend, Abbas, died last night. He was an Iranian photographer who I suspect will be most remembered for his extensive essays on various religions. I often hear photographers claiming 'an in-depth study', Abbas actually fulfilled that claim. He seemed perpetually working, relentlessly attempting to get that last piece in his jigsaw vision of life. He was an inspiration for me and I am sure for many others.

The picture I have posted is a tenuous link with him. I was helping him with some connections to Muslims in Cardiff. He came with me on a day trip to a Young Farmers Club day in Brecon.

@davidhurnphoto @magnumphotos #abbasphoto #religion

29 MARCH 2021 / SOCIAL DISTANCING. *BRECON, WALES 1973*

I was browsing a 1978 edition (9) of the excellent *Camerawork* magazine – sadly ended 1985. I had written an article, 'The picture Story'.

A paragraph from it: 'The dental photographer X-rays your tooth to see if it is decayed. If he pulls out the right tooth, that is a good photograph. It might only interest another dentist, but it is still a successful photograph even if outside its context it is unlikely to be of interest except in some conceptual way.'

It reminded me that you don't have to 'do' something yourself to like and respect other work.

Many moons ago I bought some old Welsh chairs, ladles, and other Welsh crafts from Tim Bowen Antiques in Ferryside, ever since I have received their Stock Update catalogues. They are full of beautiful still-life pictures, virtually any one I would be happy to swap and own – I particularly loved one of a little dog coming out of a cupboard door. I don't know why they appeal so much, but they are very simple, and beautifully composed – I have no idea who takes the pictures.

I have once before talked of the garden catalogue of Sarah Raven, they continue to arrive by email, again I have no real idea why they seem so satisfactory, again it's something to do with excellent form, in one of the latest there is a picture of tomatoes and cosmos flowers called 'Companion Planting', the geometry is just perfect, again I would be happy with a print, again I have no idea who the photographer is.

Finally a new photographer who I am sure will be a future star in her genre – I am not sure what you would call that, fairies at the bottom of my garden – I have seen her start, struggle to find herself, self-teach herself to be technically superb, and now has her own voice – she just needs the right client to notice her. Veronika Lavey – please visit @veronikalavey

I guess I am saying photography is a broad church with many genres. What they all have in common is that the successful have beauty, attention to detail, clear purpose and, I suspect, hard work.

@davidhurnphoto @magnumphotos @veronikalavey @timbowenantiques @sarahraven #nonfictionphotography

25 APRIL 2022 / STRUGGLE. *BRECON, WALES 1973*

I was thinking back to the last visit I had to an exhibition. I was looking at over 300 pictures, all interesting, some memorable. But my memory retains about 12 of them.

I think that 12 of anything is the maximum my mind can cope with at a time. However, if I take those 12 out of the equation, I suspect I would have remembered 12 others.

I tested my thought on paintings in the National Museum Cardiff – by the way an extraordinary collection – the result was roughly the same, 12 pictures I clearly remembered from that visit. Of course, I have a residual memory of many others accumulating from previous visits but at least temporarily, they are shut out.

I am afraid that, nowadays, many exhibitions, for me, produce nothing, no thoughts to be passed on – in fact almost the opposite. I often play a game, 'how much would I pay *not* to be given any of the exhibits?' Particularly if a condition of gift was that I had to display them in my home, have to listen to them more than once a day, or eat them more than once a week.

Then a gem and the world lifts again.

@davidhurnphoto @magnumphotos @museumwales #nonfictionphotography #nationalmuseumcardiff

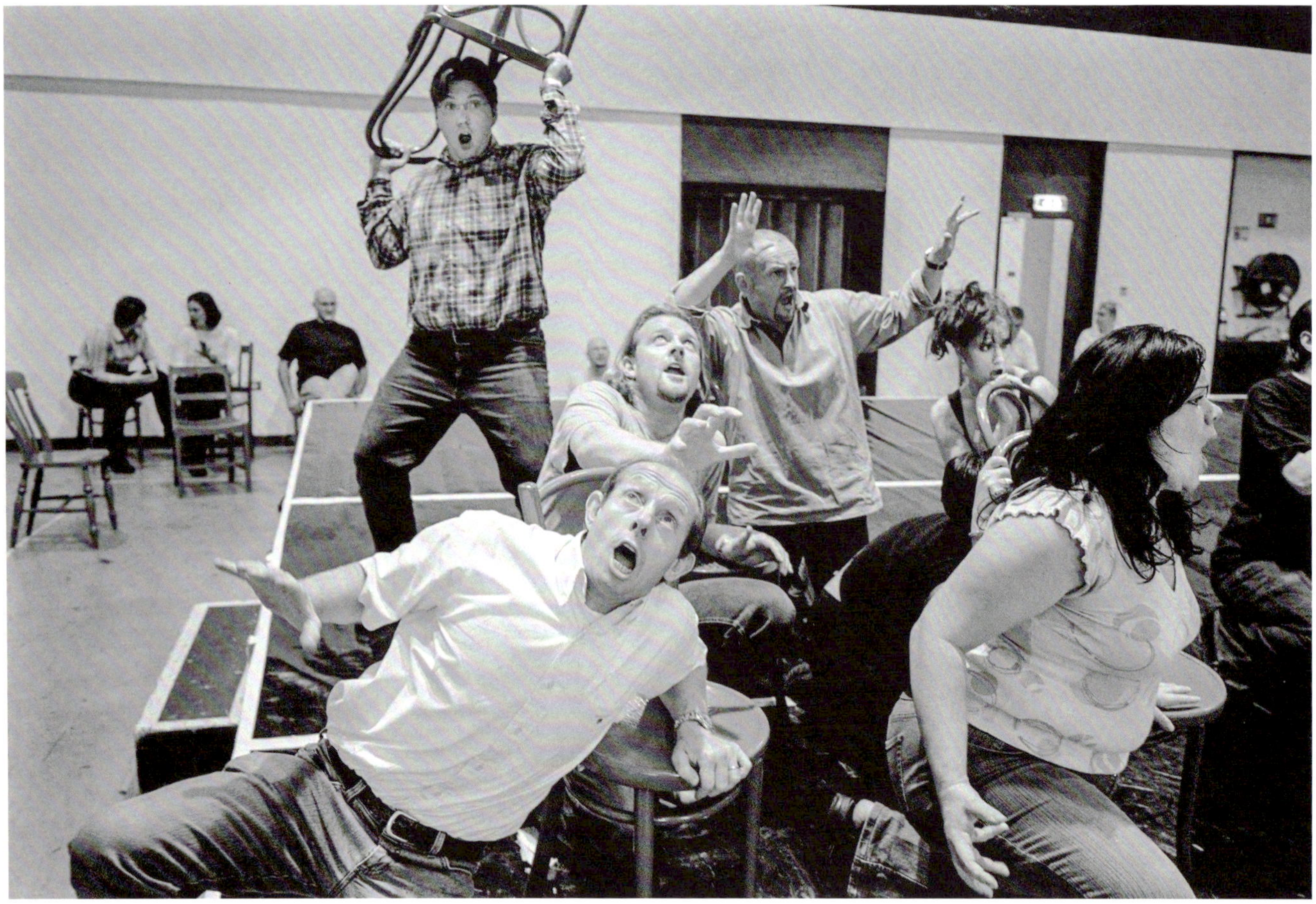

30 APRIL 2018 / *CARDIFF, WALES 2004*

I have just finished a remarkable book, *Sound*. It is about aspects of deafness. The author, Bella Bathurst, was at one time deaf herself, she has since recovered her hearing. In my opinion she is an arresting writer, elegant and simple in language, witty, authoritative, and with relentless research. What has this to do with photography? Well, the factual process of research is what should be ingrained into the minds of all photographers.

Reading the book, I was reminded of the sheer power and noise of singers in full flight. The Welsh National Opera chorus is one of the best in the world.

@davidhurnphoto @magnumphotos #bellabathurst #sound #wno

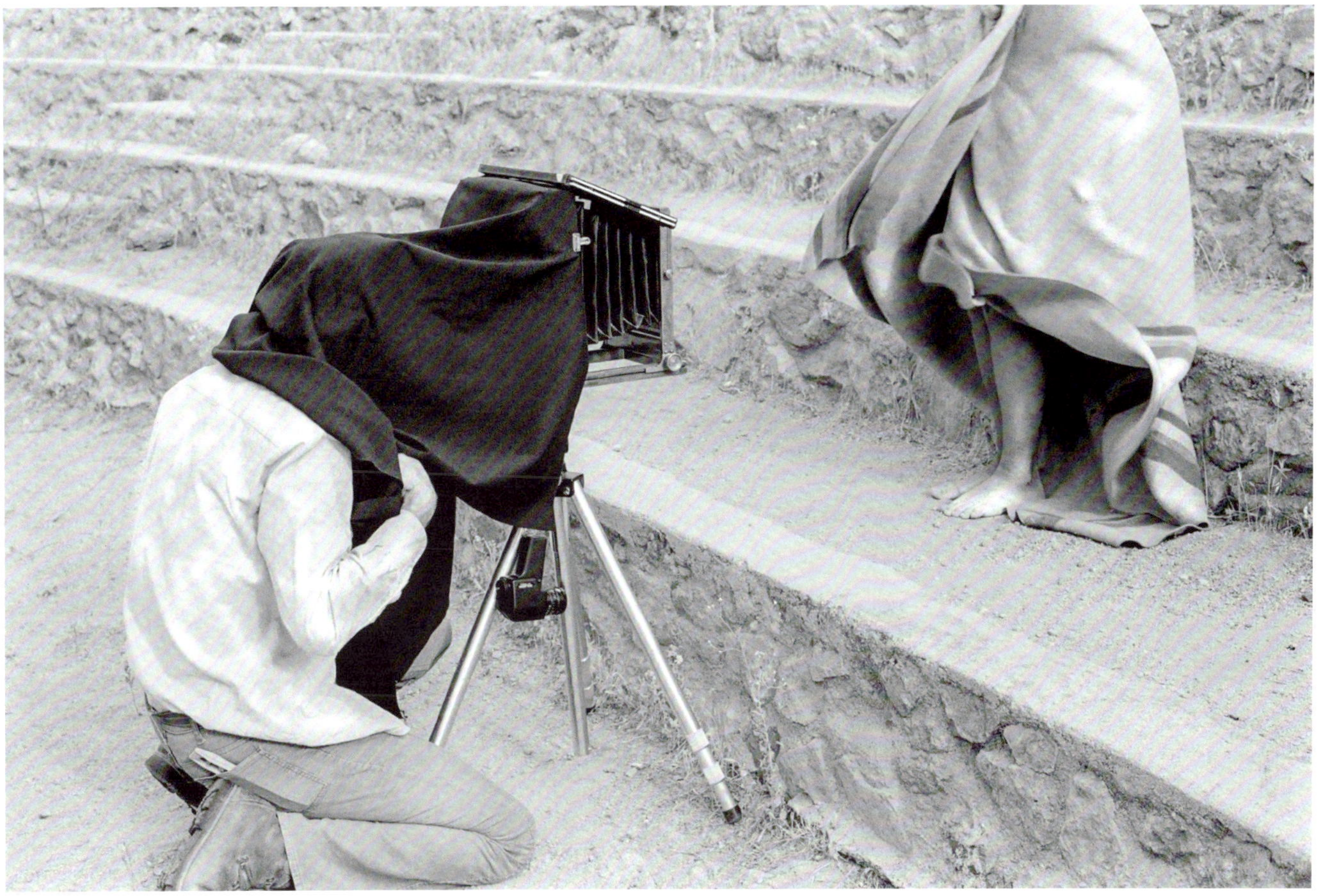

7 MAY 2018 / COLE WESTON PHOTO WORKSHOP. *ARIZONA, USA 1979*

I have been involved in many talks and meetings with fine photographers over the last few months. When the talks end with questions, I am frequently asked, what is 'the essential book' one should obtain to get an understanding about looking at pictures. There are many books, but most modern writers seem to fall into the narcissism of seemingly being as interested in showing off their knowledge of art history and philosophic quotations as in describing why they like a particular picture. So without reservation, I think the most important book is *Looking at Photographs*, 100 pictures from the collection of The Museum of Modern Art, described/discussed by John Szarkowski, a man so modest he doesn't even have his name on the cover.

Looking at a picture by Timothy H. O'Sullivan he writes:

'His landscapes are as precisely and as economically composed as a good masonry wall. It is as though every square inch of the precious glass plate, carried so far at so great effort, had to be justified completely.'

For me, it does not come better than that.

@davidhurnphoto @magnumphotos #johnszarkowski #booktips

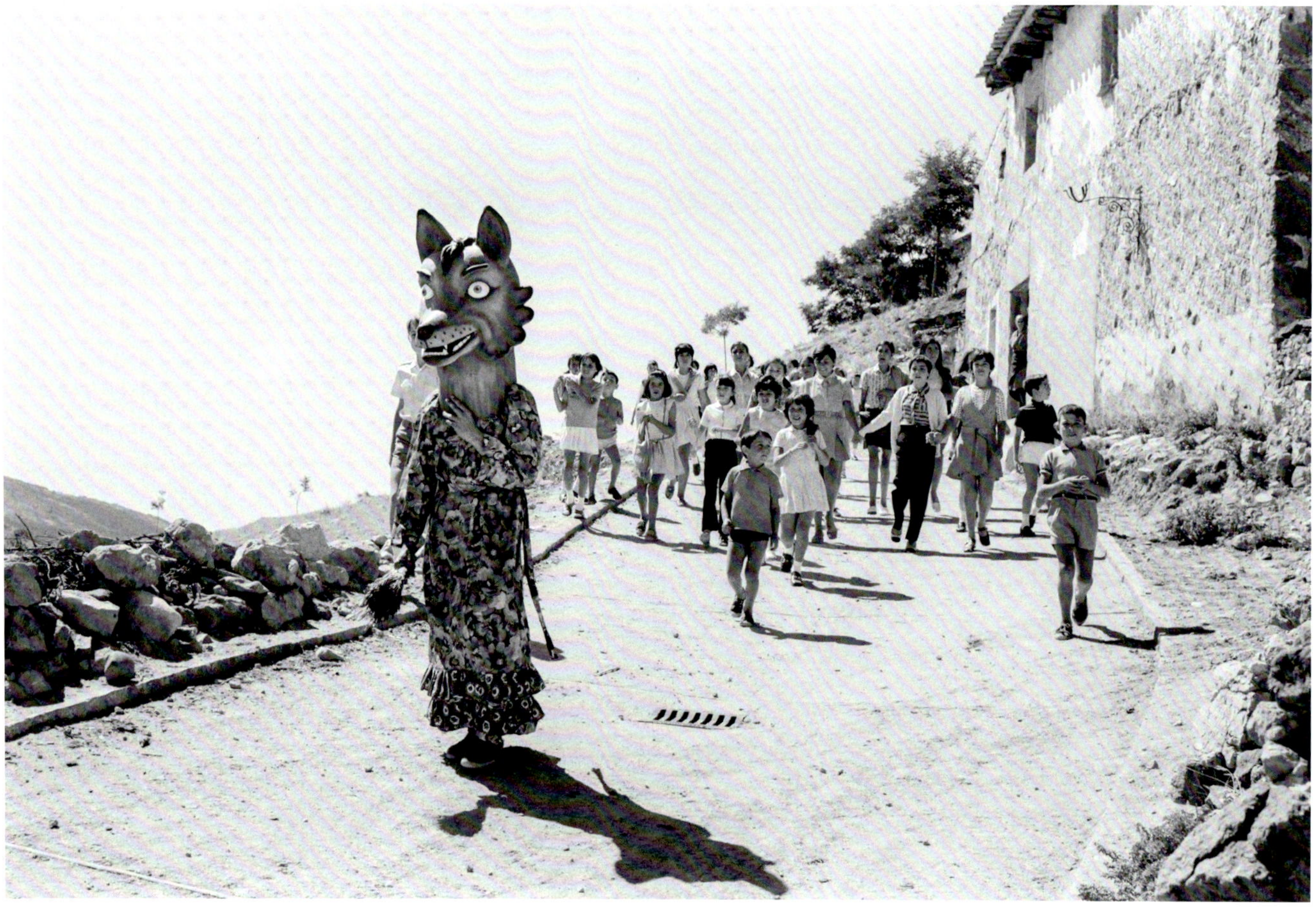

10 MAY 2018 / ATIENZA. *SPAIN 1970*

In 1970 I spent a couple of weeks in a small town, Atienza, in Northern Spain.

I was working on the making of the film *The Trojan Women* directed by Michael Cacoyannis and starring the wonderful Katharine Hepburn.

During off moments I would wander the streets of Atienza and shoot pictures purely for myself. I have an edit of 30 pictures I like – a few have been published but always as singles – 30 is a difficult number, not really enough for a book. I have decided to return to Atienza towards the end of this year and do a now and then. With luck, this I can get published.

@davidhurnphoto @magnumphotos #atienza

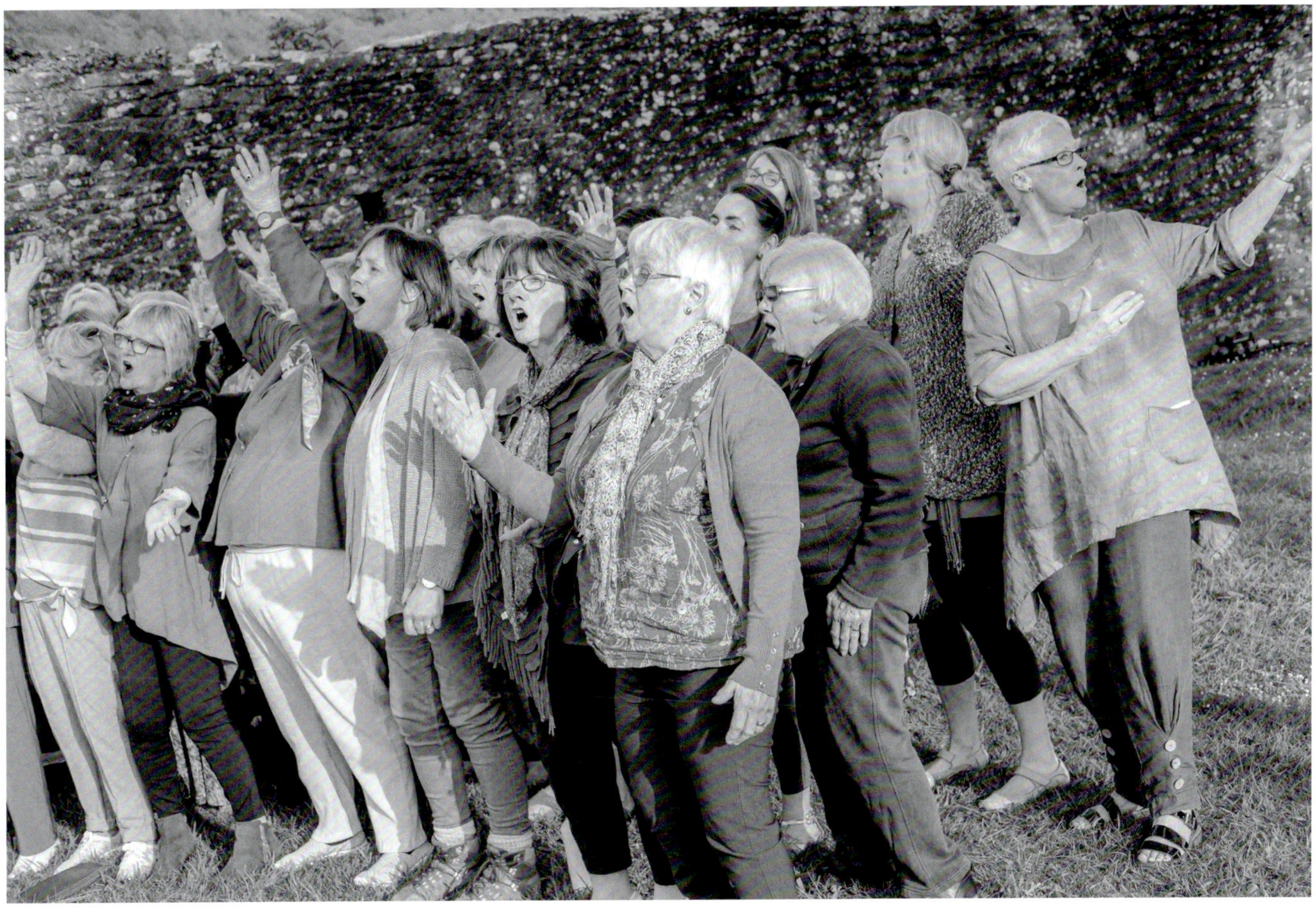

22 MAY 2018 / CHOIR IN TINTERN ABBEY. *TINTERN, WALES 2018*

I am slowly returning to shooting pictures.

A good starting point was 'The Museum of the Moon', a picnic held in Tintern Abbey as part of the Wye Valley River Festival. Apparently, Admiral John Byng – a Royal Navy officer who was notoriously court-martialled and shot dead by a firing squad – wrote in the 18th century:

'The way to enjoy Tintern Abbey properly ... is to bring wines, cold meat, with corn for the horses; bread, beer, cider and commonly salmon ... and spread your table in the ruins'.

Good advice. Fun was had by many picnicking in the grounds.

My mini photo essays are posted on the excellent Tintern website: *tinternvillage.co.uk*

I have been browsing though notes/letters from Bill Jay, he was very wise/funny. I have decided to pass on some of his thoughts.

'I have trouble imagining Attila the Hun as a landscape photographer.' – Bill Jay

@davidhurnphoto @magnumphotos #tintern #wales #billjay
www.tinternvillage.co.uk

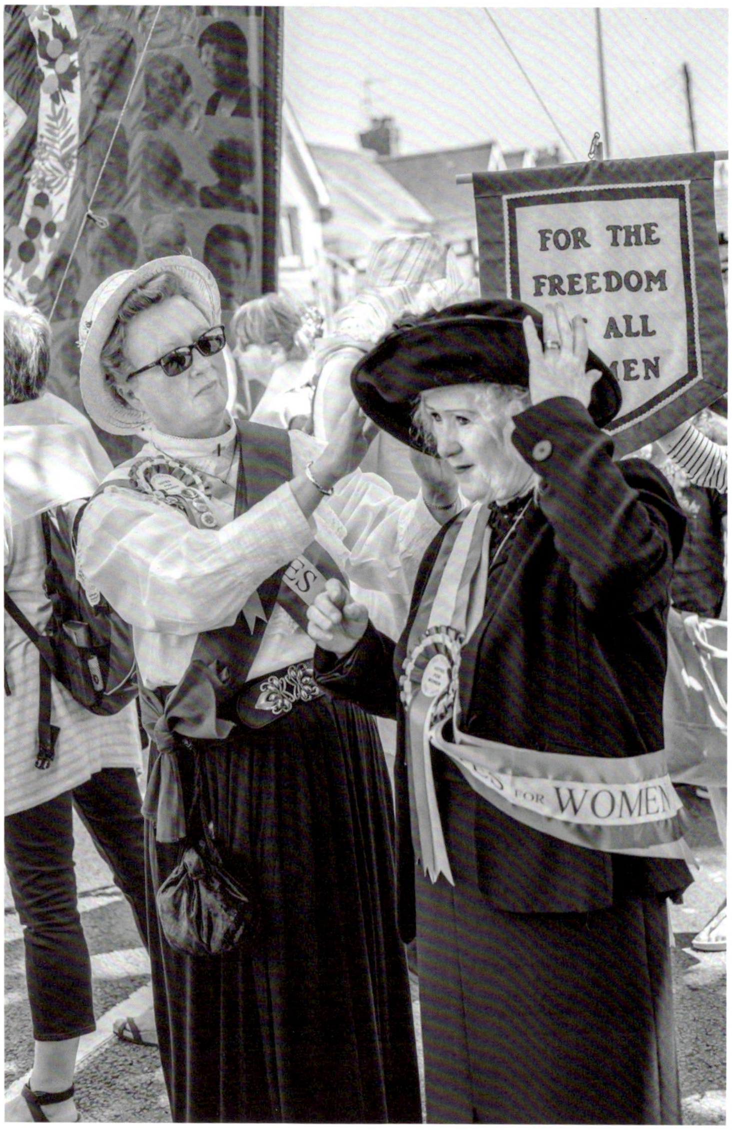

10 JUNE 2018 / WOMEN'S MARCH. *CARDIFF, WALES 2018*

I spent an uplifting afternoon, 10 June, observing/photographing the Women's March in Cardiff. Thousands of women of all ages marched together through Cardiff in celebration of women winning the right to vote. Mothers with babies were joined by older generations – some in mobility scooters. It marked 100 years since the Representation of the People Act was passed – which gave some women the right to vote.

For me, it is this sort of real occasion that made me want to have the privilege of being a photographer.

@davidhurnphoto @magnumphotos #womensmarchcardiff #womensmarch

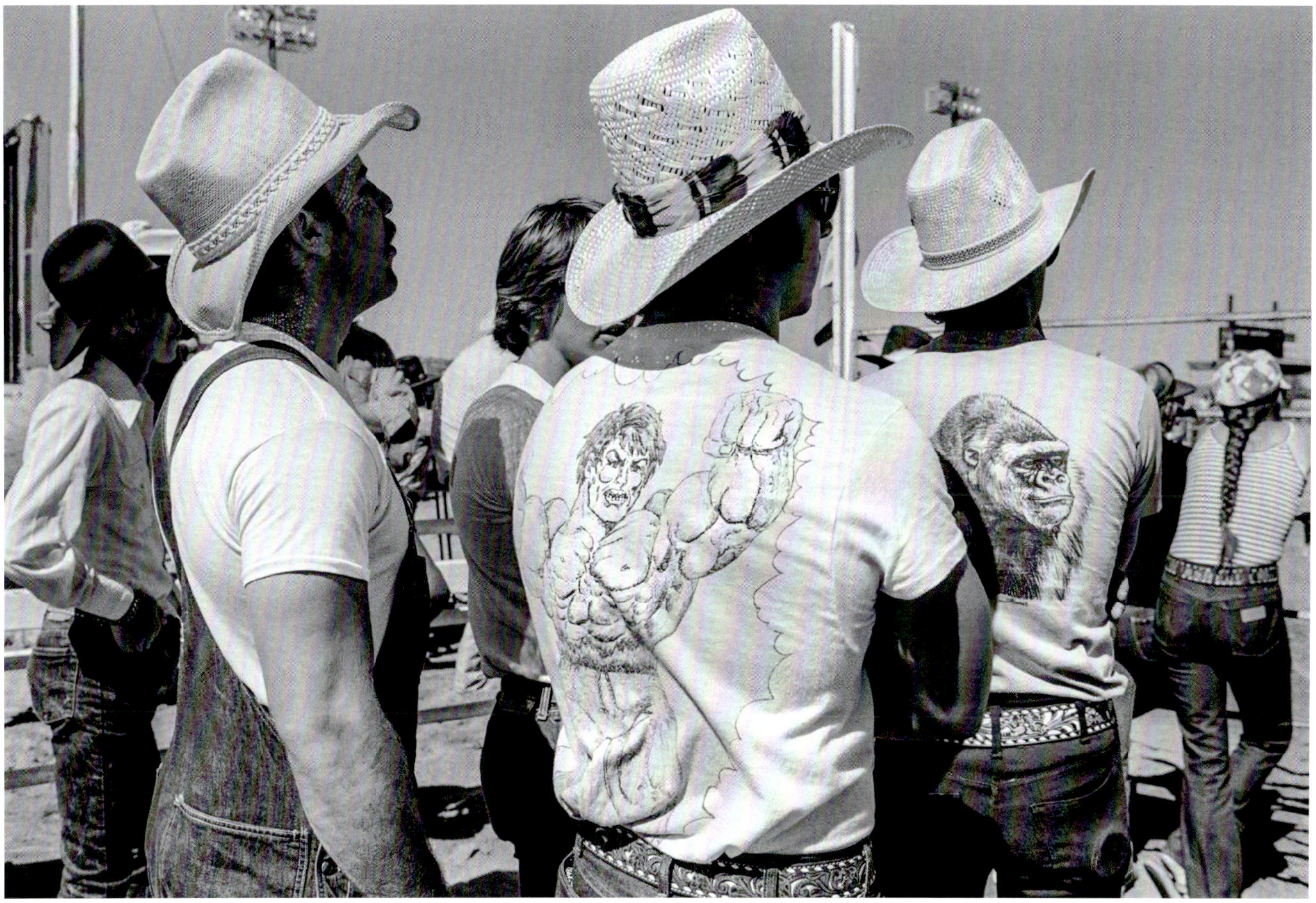

27 JUNE 2018 / BACK VIEWS. *ARIZONA, USA 1980*

I am beginning to think that my favourite watering hole is Martin Parr's Foundation in Bristol. I am just leaving to go to a talk by Geoff Dyer about Garry Winogrand. Geoff is a major writer of novels, essays, and other genre-defying titles. As far as I am concerned, his book about photographs, *The Ongoing Moment*, is as eye opening as one can find. An added bonus is that it is written in a language that most can understand.

At one point he writes about back views, hence my picture above.

Elsewhere he writes a provocative sentence – he talks of categories of pictures, one of which is 'photographs that look like photographs taken by someone else', that sets up enough thought in me to make the book worthwhile just for that.

Bill Jay quote: 'When they discover the centre of the universe, a lot of people will be disappointed they are not it'.

@davidhurnphoto @magnumphotos @martinparrfdn #geoffdyer #arizona #billjay

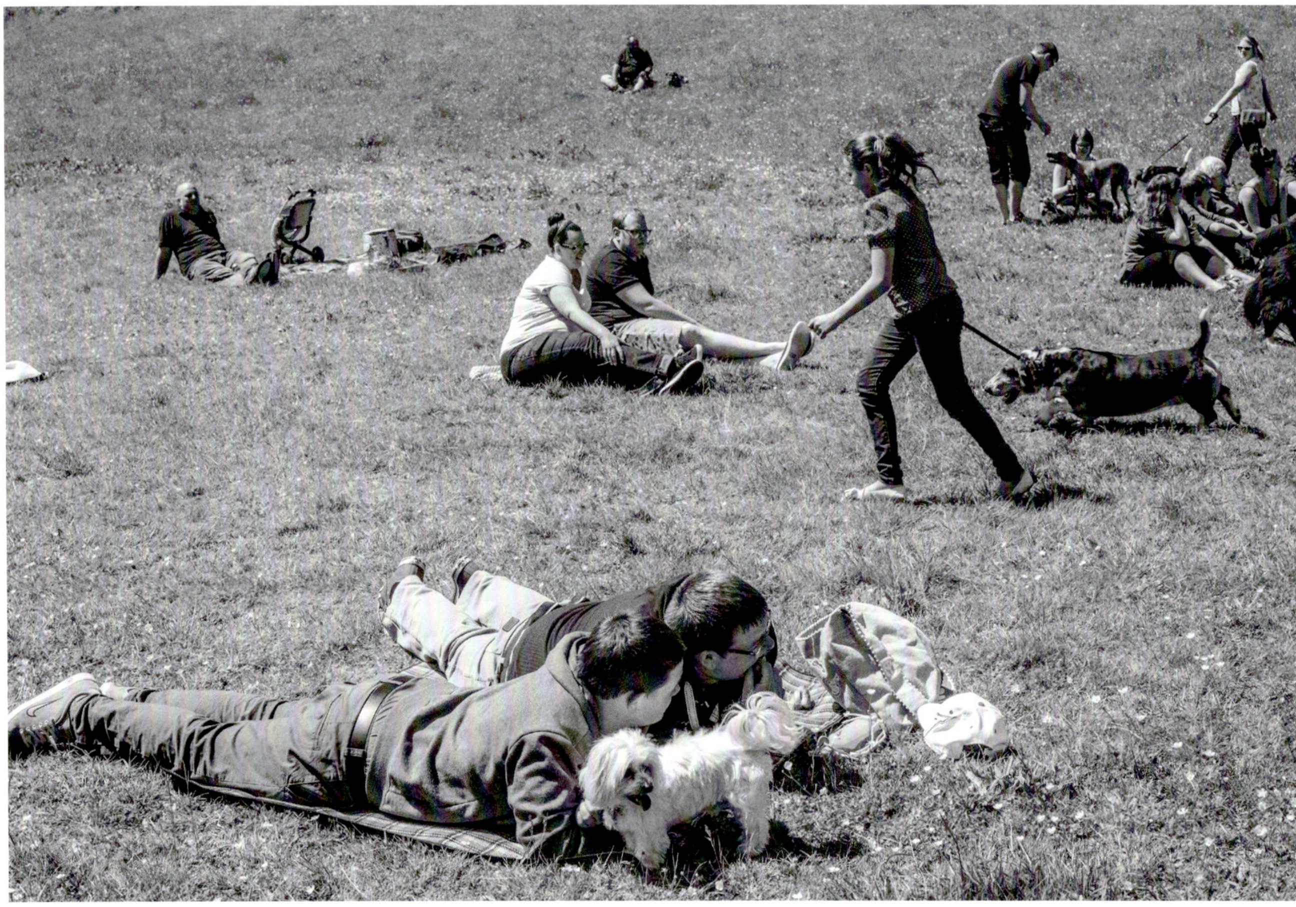

8 JULY 2018 / WALK IN THE MEADOW. *TINTERN, WALES 2013*

I am slightly frustrated. The longest stretch of summer I can remember and I am still hampered with a strained back. Still, I can do small walks in the village and my camera is very light.

I have just received my 'brother' Josef Koudelka's latest – maybe final – book, *Returning*. It is a résumé of his life's work designed particularly for his home country where his archives will end up in Prague. For me, he is in my group of the greatest photographers of all time.

Bill Jay quote:

'The Zen Master: a photograph of a tree is not a tree unless it is a tree, photographed.

The Catholic: It's OK to buy a new camera as long as you feel guilty.

The Hari Krishna: Photography while dancing is allowed but use the non-tambourine hand and a fast shutter speed.

The Existentialist: Photography is boring and your pictures bore others, good.'

@davidhurnphoto @magnumphotos @josef_koudelka

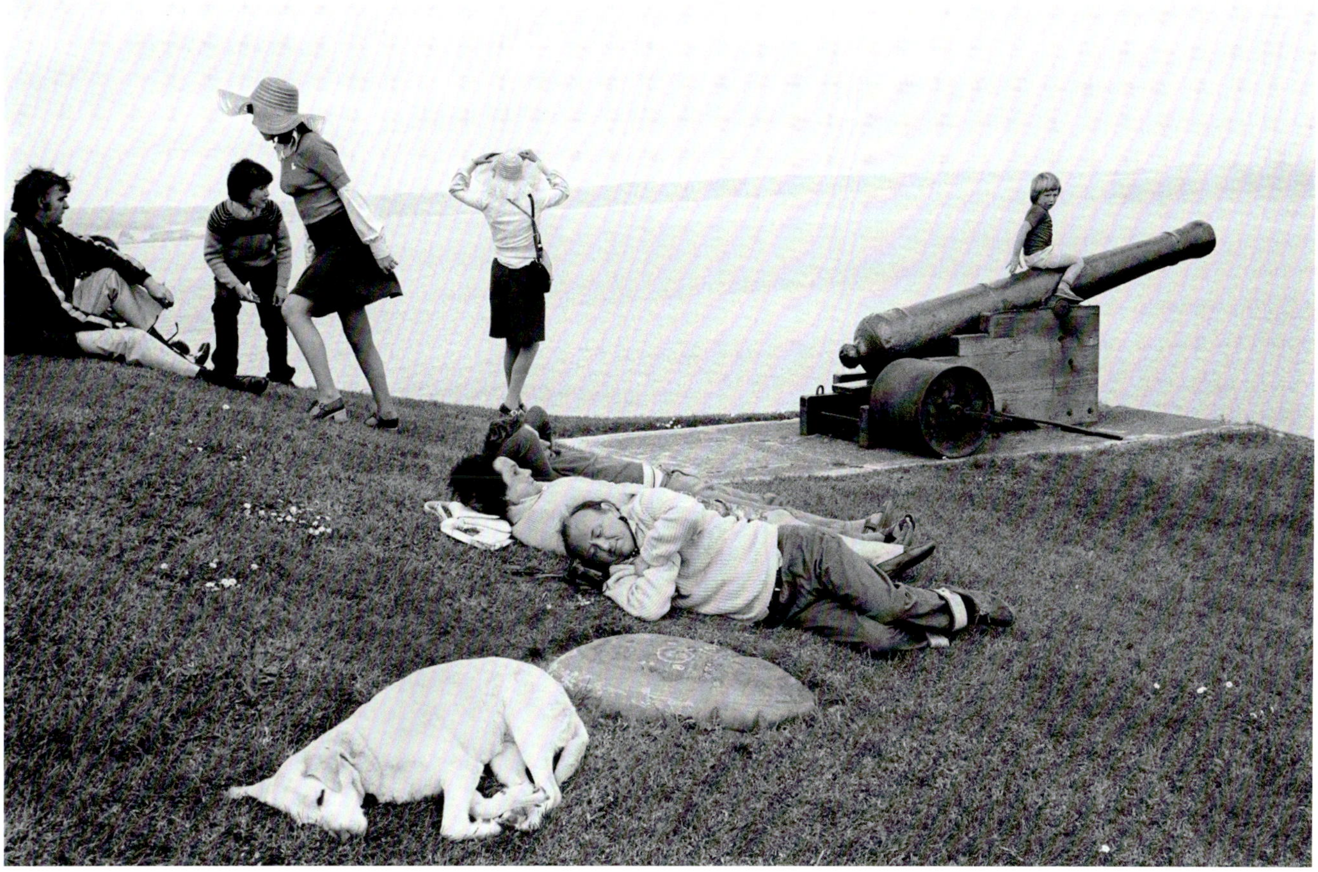

30 JULY 2018 / CASTLE HILL. *TENBY, WALES 1974*

I spent a relaxing couple of days in the rain with Martin and Susie Parr in Tenby. From their top floor apartment are amazing views. Martin and I wandered to where I had shot the holidaymakers and canon picture. Martin shot a portrait of me there. I later saw Susie's delightful book, *The Story of Swimming*, published by Dewi Lewis. What a wonderful gift for virtually anyone of any age. Well researched and written text and a great collection of pictures.

@davidhurnphoto @magnumphotos @dewi_lewis_publishing #martinparr #susieparr

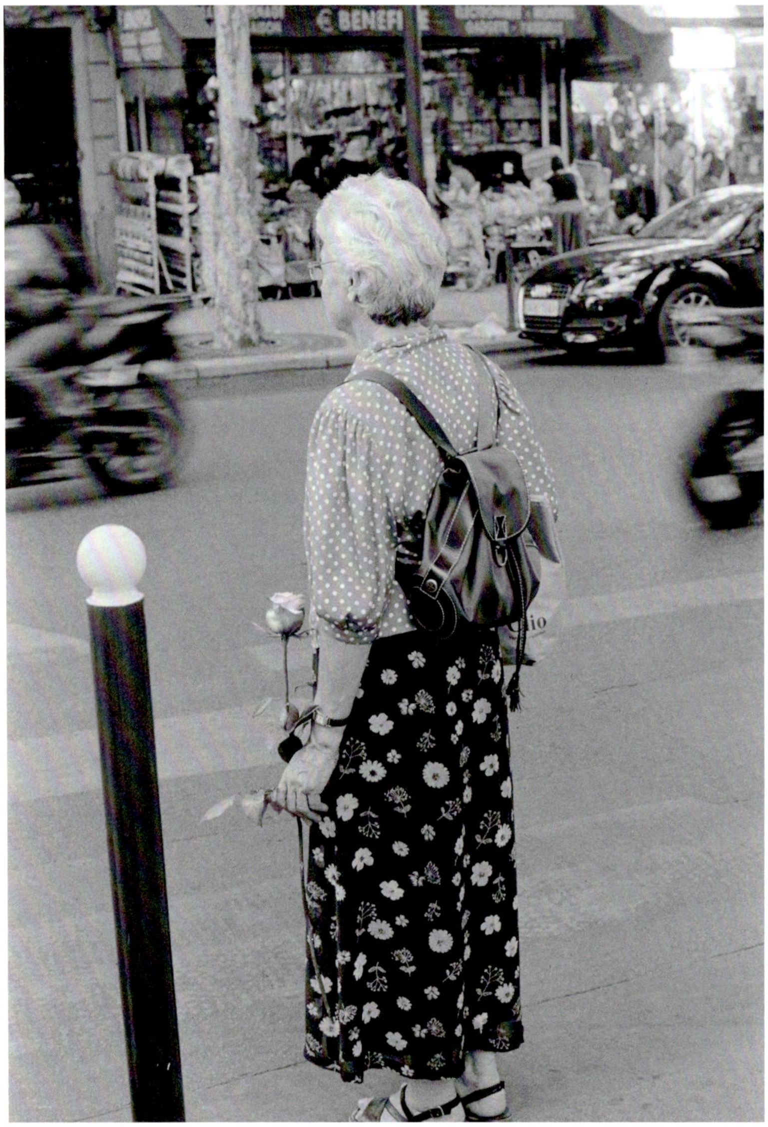

3 AUGUST 2018 / LADY WITH FLOWER CROSSING STREET. *CARDIFF, WALES 2008*

I remember seeing this lady mainly because her situation reminded me of a picture I like by a photographer I admire, Louis Faurer. His picture was of a man with a flower in New York. His, and I hope my, picture sets up questions: Where going to? Or where coming from? Is the flower a gift to him/her or will it be a gift for someone else? I love the quality of everyone having an opinion.

By the way, the book *Louis Faurer* published by Steidl, is well worth having.

@davidhurnphoto @magnumphotos @steidlverlag #louisfaurer

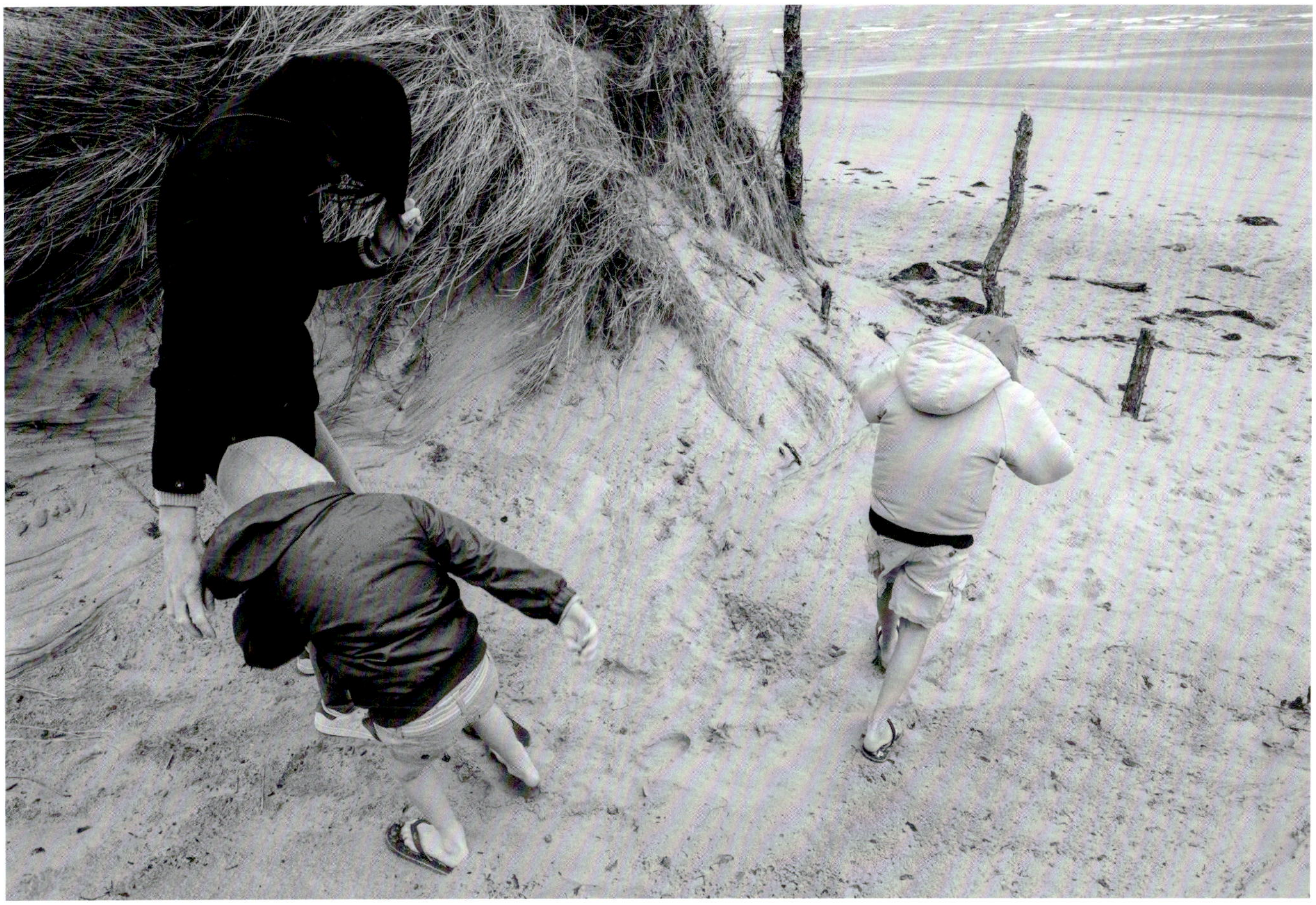

19 AUGUST 2018 / FAMILY HOLIDAY, WIND AND RAIN. *NEWBOROUGH WARREN, ANGLESEY, WALES 2018*

I have just returned from a rewarding road trip with my friends, Brian Carroll of Ffoton – who do really-worth-listening-to recordings of 'Conversations' among other positive things – and Gareth Phillips, in my opinion the best and most tenacious and thinking photographer in Wales. In theory, I was simply going to three places in Anglesey that I photographed some time ago – I now attach ten-figure OS map references to all my landscape pictures, and these three were done before I started this peculiarity so I needed to catch up. We then explored Dinorwig slate mines and later the lead mines at Cwmystwyth, incidentally the centre of Wales.

I was perpetually exhausted in the continual rain, Brian pushed me uphill and Gareth charged on ahead acting as chief scout. With frequent stops for tea we had a wonderful time.

My pictures all ended up in focus – I could not have done it without them.

@davidhurnphoto @magnumphotos @ffotonwales @garethphillips_ @jazzyfingers #landscape #wales

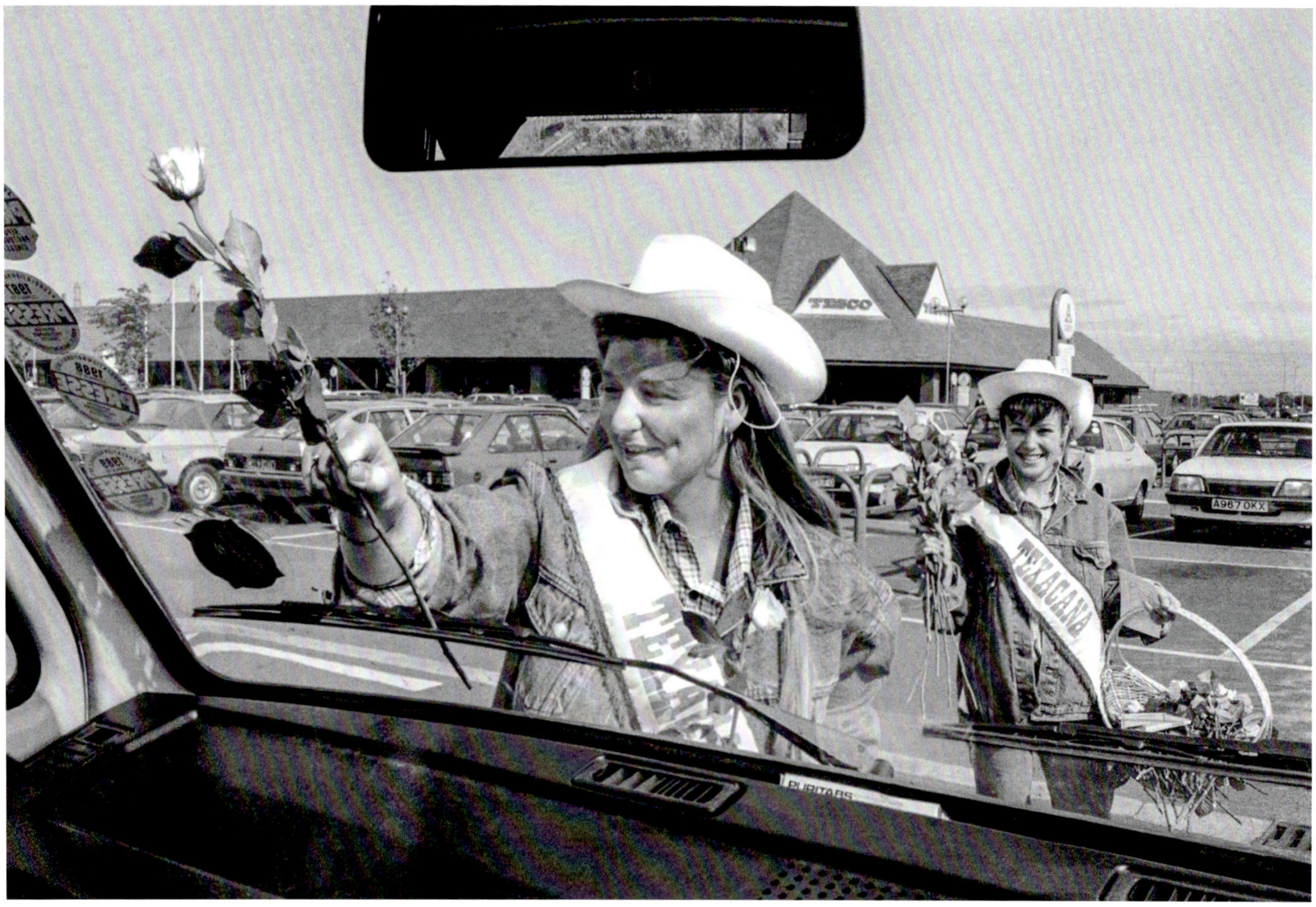

28 AUGUST 2018 / THROUGH A CAR WINDOW 2. *NEWPORT, WALES 1989*

Me only driving. To my delight I was given a rose at the opening of a new shopping centre.

@davidhurnphoto @magnumphotos #wales

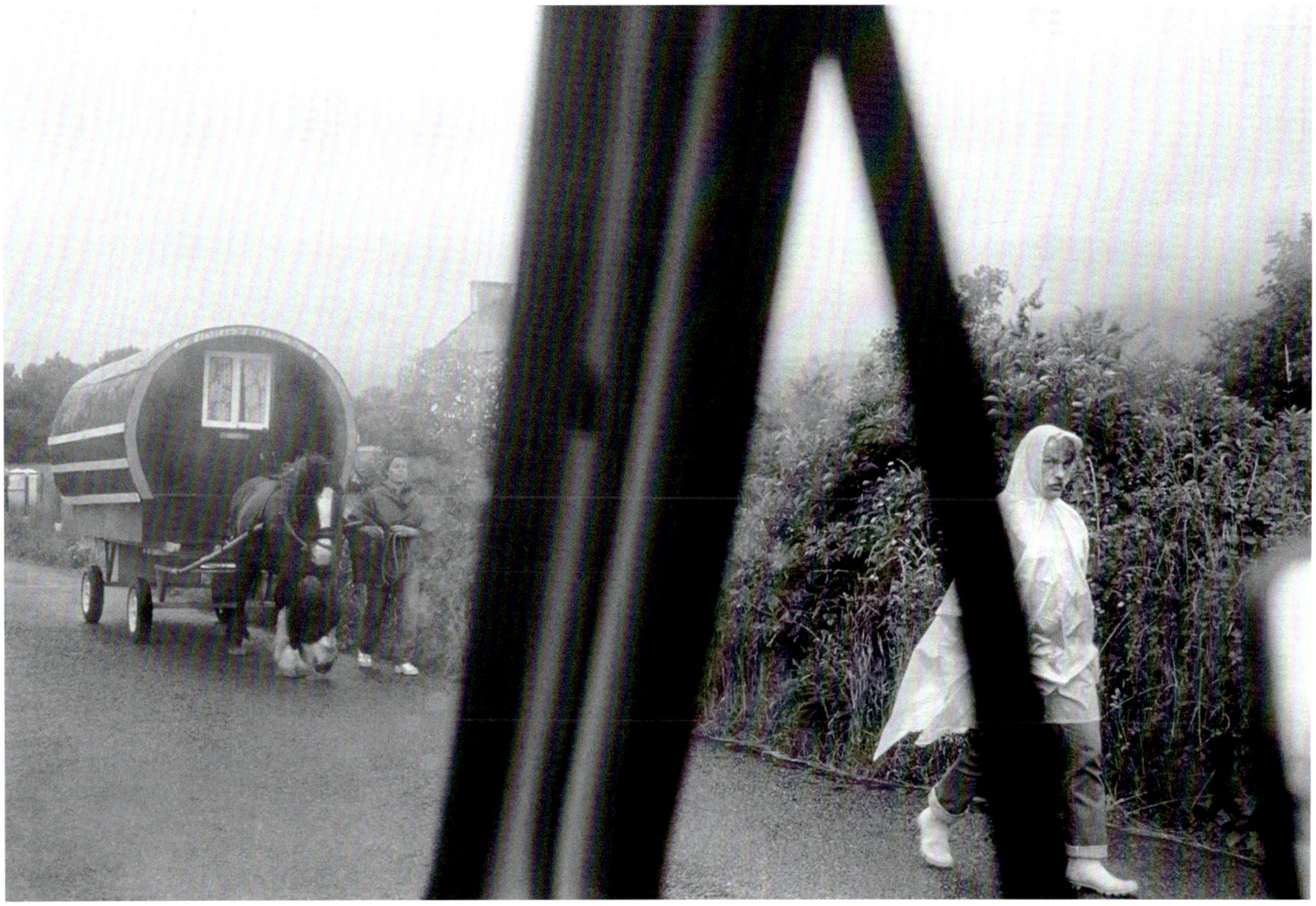

1 SEPTEMBER 2018 / THROUGH A CAR WINDOW 3. *COUNTY KERRY, IRELAND 1984*

I think my favourite area of Ireland.

@davidhurnphoto @magnumphotos #countykerry

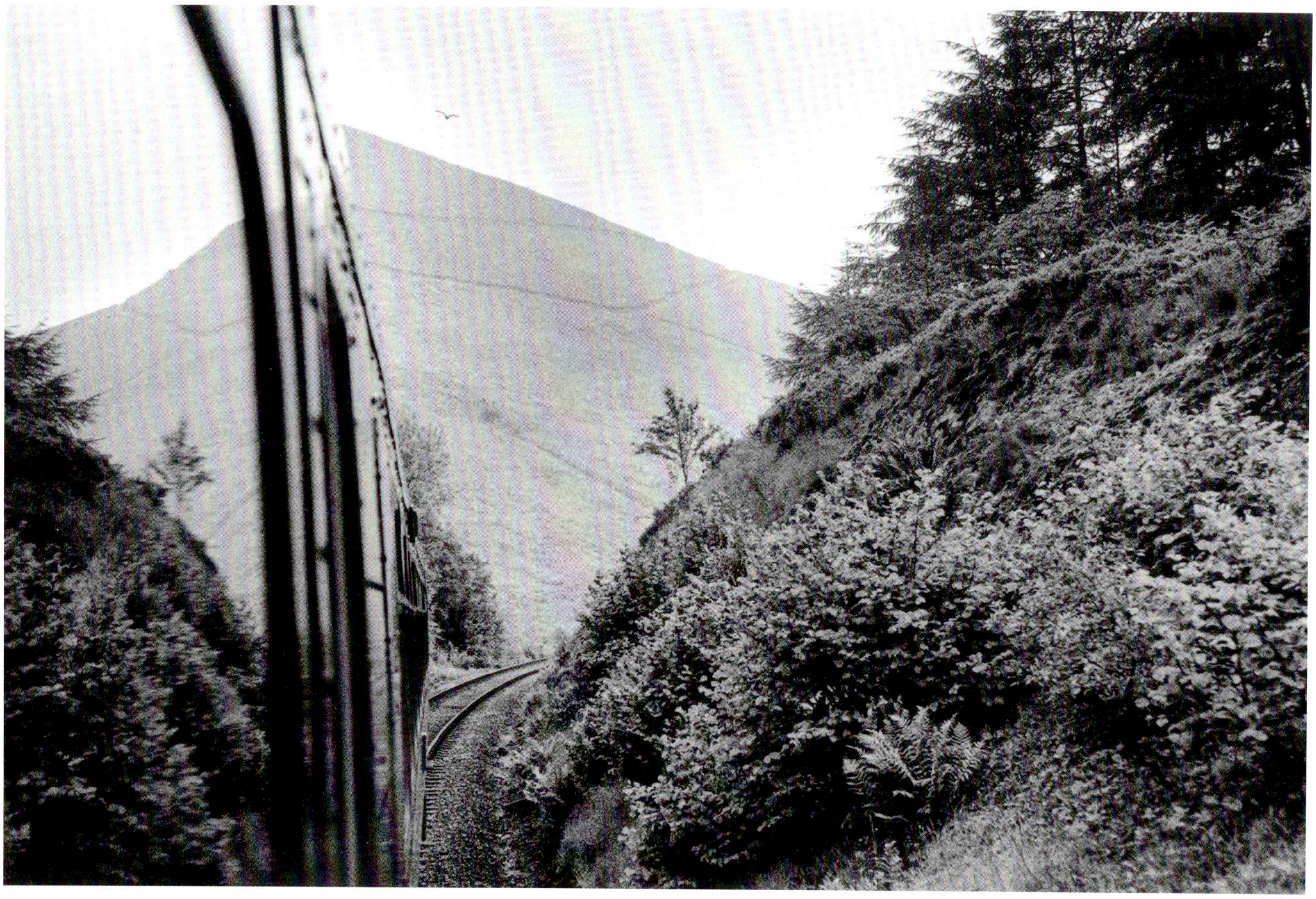

5 SEPTEMBER 2018 / THROUGH A TRAIN WINDOW. *CYNGHORDY, MID WALES, 1993*

I suspect interest in 'through car windows' is petering. I am switching to one through a train window. It is from a set of pictures I did on the 'Last Train Around Wales'.

Had a very enjoyable evening in conversation with Martin Parr at his foundation last night. A wonderful place to meet people – Denis Thorpe's son – what a lovely photographer Denis was, I think mainly for *The Guardian*, I hope he is still able to shoot. Sadly, he could not be there last night. Also a delight was re-meeting David Jones – he was on the very first intake on the Documentary course I started in Newport when it was still an art college – he is still shooting. We have now re-made contact to my delight.

By the way, Simon Roberts is talking at the foundation on Wednesday 19, an evening not to be missed. I will certainly try to be there.

@davidhurnphoto @magnumphotos @martinparrfdn @simoncroberts #train #denisthorpe #davidjones

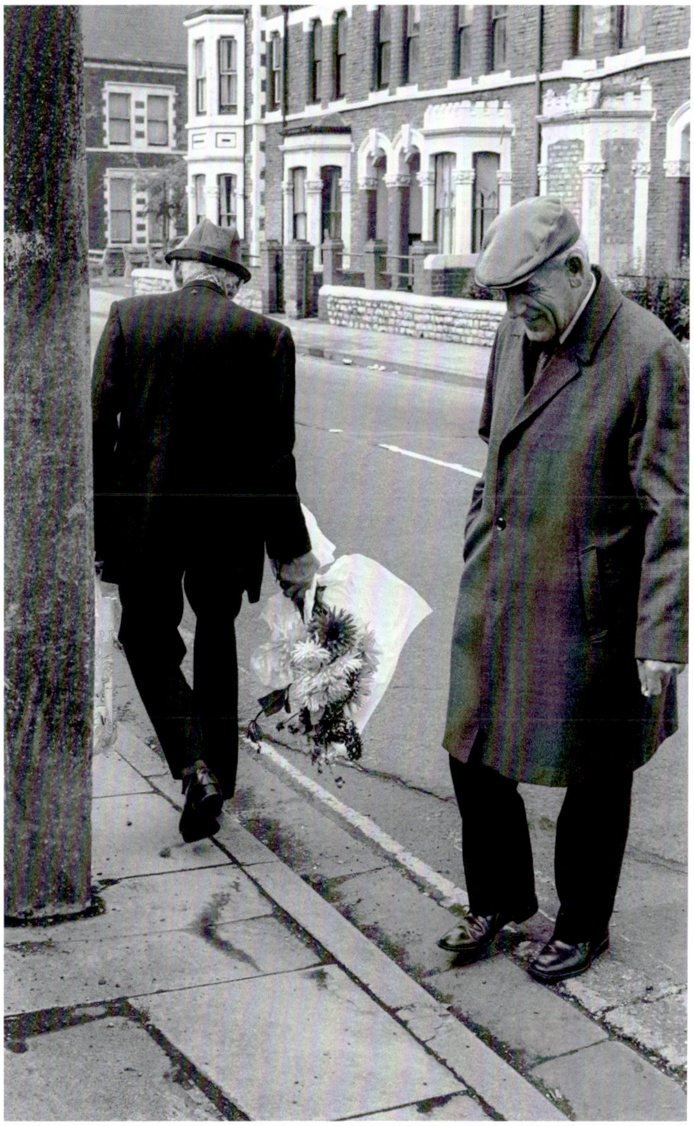

14 SEPTEMBER 2018 / FLOWERS FOR WHOM? *CARDIFF, WALES 1973*

A photograph is a very accurate trace of what is seen through a lens. But in my view, the photographer is someone who is showing viewers things by making photographs of them, and is simply asking the question. I found this interesting, even significant, do you? As a photographer I do not pretend to give meaning, in fact I enjoy most the innate ambiguity of photographs, the ability to construct different means for each viewer. It's the reason I love working with poets, they bring precision to their understanding – they tell another point of view.

By the way, at the moment I am reading *12 Rules for Life* by Jordan Peterson. Boy, there is a clear and thought-provoking thinker.

@davidhurnphoto @magnumphotos @jordan.b.peterson

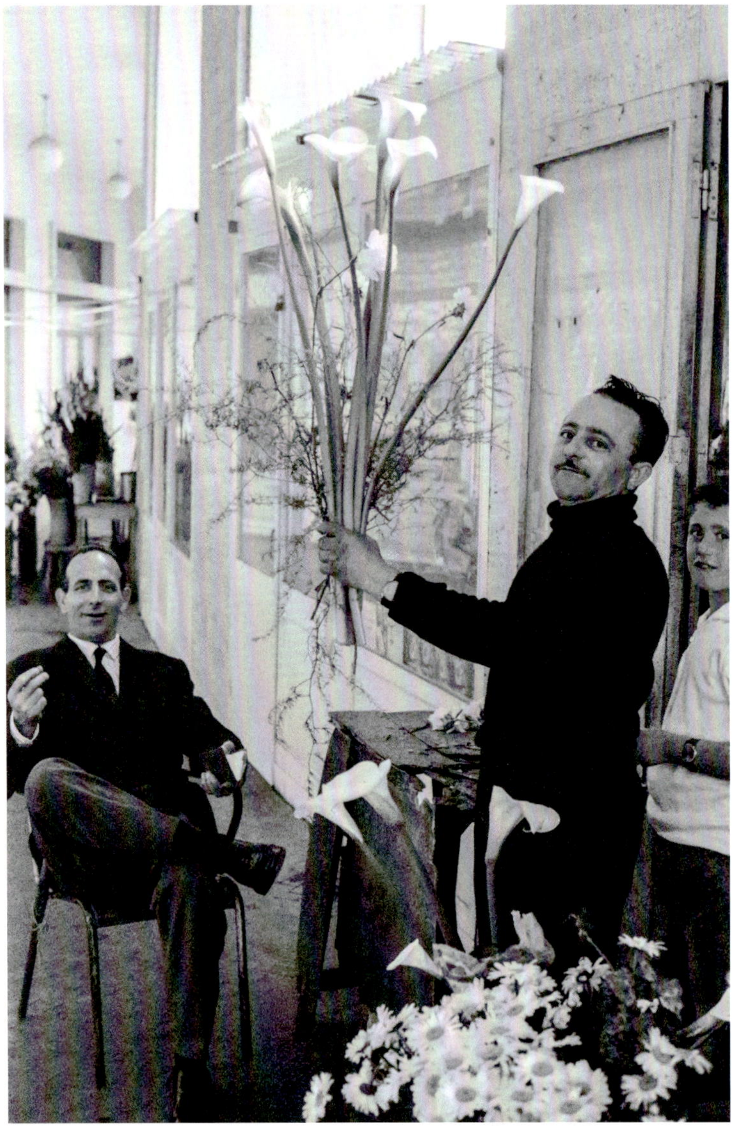

20 SEPTEMBER 2018 / FLOWER MARKET. *BRINDISI, ITALY 1964*

In 1964 I had my first really big assignment – it was for *Holiday* magazine – a wonderful American magazine where, if you can find past copies, you can see Henri Cartier-Bresson at his published best. I did a trip together with the author Irwin Shaw to 24 towns/cities around the coast of the Mediterranean.

I am toying with the idea of redoing the trip throughout next year – it has the advantage of no deadlines, so I could wander leisurely, a good thing at my age.

In my Instagram post picture I enjoy the obvious pride the participants have in their flowers, in their jobs. Photography can be so good at picking up nuance.

Last night I went to hear Simon Roberts speak at the MPF. He was superb. I will write more next post after I have gathered my thoughts.

@davidhurnphoto @magnumphotos @martinparrfdn @simoncroberts #flowers

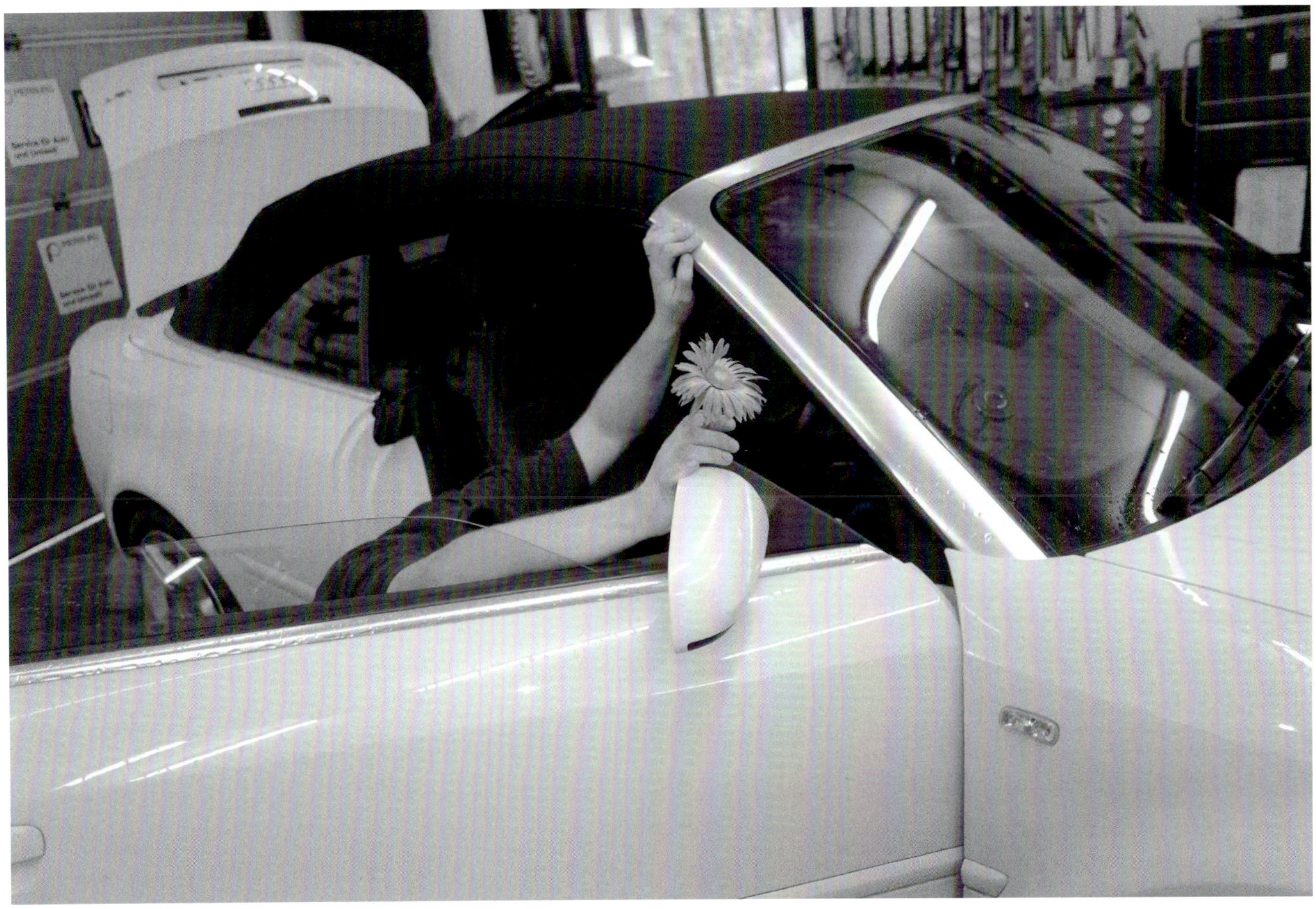

20 SEPTEMBER 2018 / TINTERN GARAGE, VALETING CAR (FLOWERS 4). *TINTERN, WALES 2012*

A few days ago I listened to Simon Roberts talk at the Martin Parr Foundation. It was a superb hour and a half. I pondered that when I was becoming a photographer, how constructive it would have been for me to have heard it.

Simon informed us he went to university reading Human Geography. His early photography was as a local newspaper photographer, graduating later to magazines. We learned that he did not feel fulfilled so developed a more considered approach – basically a development of his knowledge of Human Geography. We absorbed his tenaciousness – first self assignment a year in Russia, most later projects done over periods of years, all meticulously researched. In an hour and a half any student could have gained all the pointers for becoming a major photographer. No myths just facts from someone who has actually done it.

On reflection I mused that Martin Parr, Susan Meiselas, Paul Trevor, Markéta Luskačová, Chris Killip, Sirkka-Liisa Konttinen, Bieker Depoorter, Michael Christopher Brown, Niall McDiarmid, among others, had all passed on the same 'doer' information at the MPF. Siân Davey, Sir Don McCullin, will be doing the same soon.

I could conceive a photographic course in the future consisting of simply going to all these and future lectures. Over two years – enough initiation for anyone – you would hear the reality of at least 40 practitioners. Including travel/food/books it might cost £3500 per person. I would be interested in the result.

@davidhurnphoto @magnumphotos @martinparrfdn @simoncroberts #flowers #tintern #wales

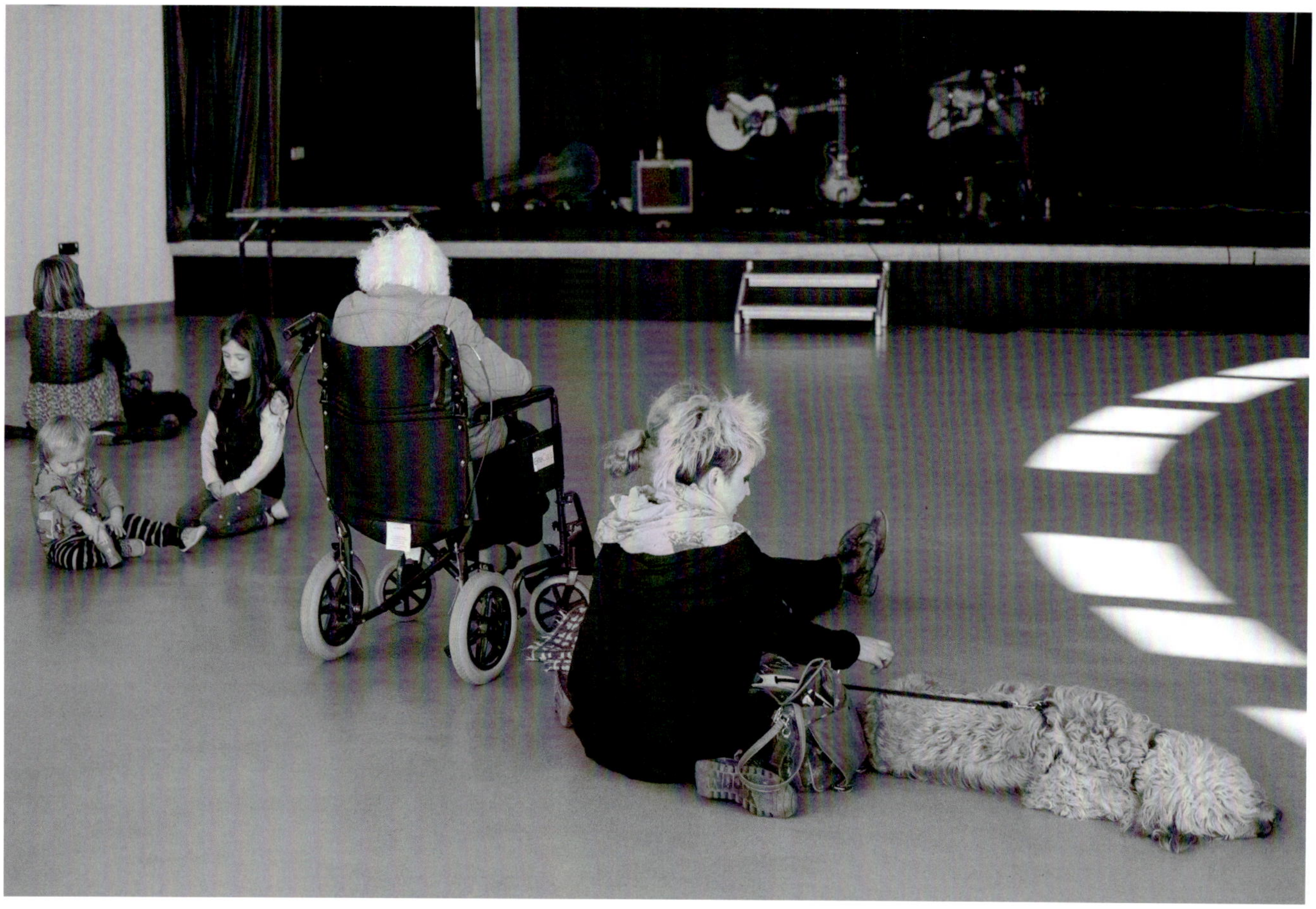

14 OCTOBER 2018 / FREE CONCERT ON ABERYSTWYTH PROMENADE. *WALES 2018*

Now home, I have been reminiscing about the recent EYE Festival.

I am puzzled by how few young came to the weekend. It was a chance for any aspiring photographer to hear true professionals from various photography mediums telling you their secrets. If you are a documentary photographer then there were three of major standing on show – so much real information was to be had.

Why do people not turn up? Why do course heads not insist their students attend? Why do they not come themselves? Is it too far for the next generation to get to Aberystwyth? Kate Holt, one of the speakers, managed to get there from Africa. Her flight was badly held up, she must have been exhausted, but still she managed to arrive for a late afternoon session instead of the morning one that she was scheduled for. She gave an enlightened talk, and explained exactly why I do not want to do what she does – I do not have that ability to care, I do not have her bravery – however, if I did want to be her she opened her heart to show how it might happen. All speakers spoke with the same passion and knowledge, I challenge any course in the country to give that much information in their total three years. We can all learn from every other genre. I repeat, if I were starting again, if necessary I would have walked to Aberystwyth to hear and meet them.

Just heard the 90-year-old composer Thea Musgrave on *Desert Island Discs*. What an inspiration – she talks about trying not to be be distracted from her continuing composing.

@davidhurnphoto @magnumphotos @niallmcdiarmid @danilobalducci @josesarmentomatos @kasiawozniak @bennettpix @kateholtphoto #theamusgrave #helenmarshallartist #eyefestival #aberystwyth #wales #desertislanddiscs #documentary

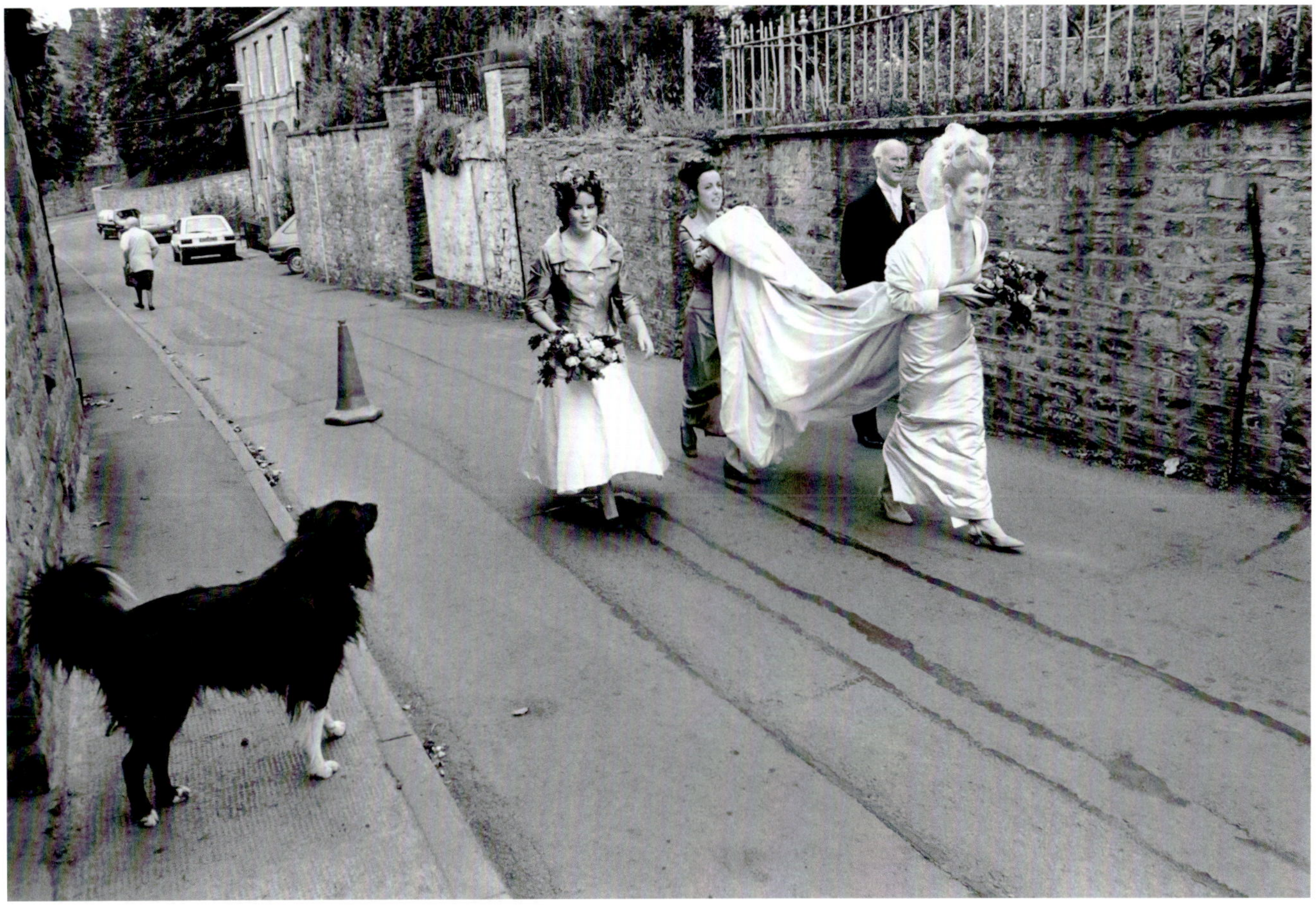

24 OCTOBER 2018 / LATE FOR THE WEDDING. *BRECON, WALES 1996*

Boy, do animals help in pictures. 'Used' well, they can add immediate humour, pathos, focal point, constructive ambiguity. They always seem relaxed. I think I will show some animal pictures.

I am fascinated by the seeming universal interest in food. I am quite structured in my eating habits, I have seven different breakfasts a week. Now I live by myself I need structure so that I am not distracted.

Earlier heard Sir Don McCullin speak at Martin's place. Not only one of the greatest of photographers but also one of the best of human beings.

@davidhurnphoto @magnumphotos @don.mccullin @martinparrfdn #brecon #wales

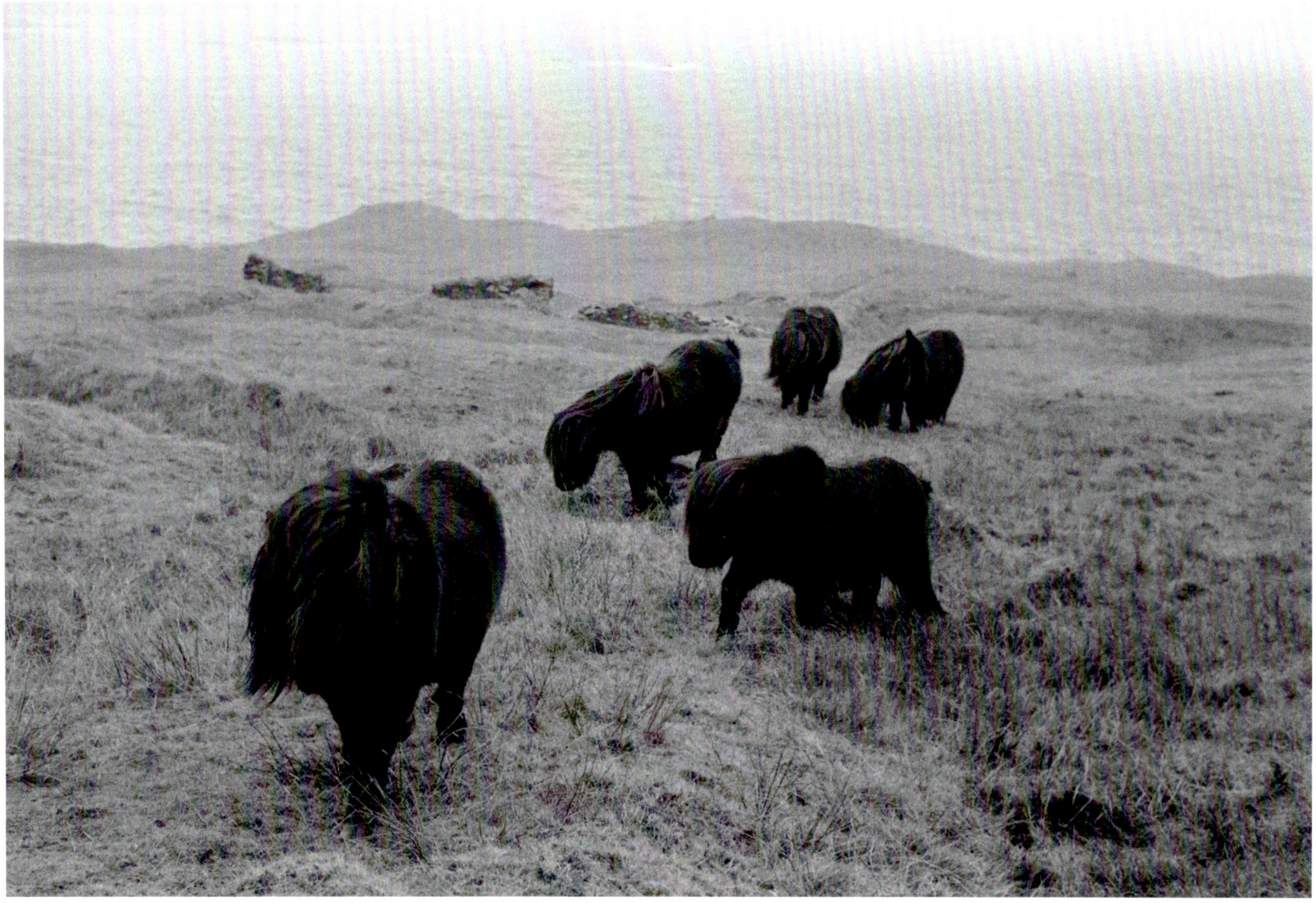

12 NOVEMBER 2018 / SHETLAND PONIES ON SHETLAND. *SCOTLAND 1967*

Still contemplating where it would be sensible to go for ten days.

In 1967 I spent an enjoyable few days at the 'Up Helly Aa' festival on Shetland. I suspect that modern health and safety rules would make it more restrictive than I can stomach.

I thought about doing a few more pictures in North Wales but the thought of being caught in a hotel there with the rain pouring outside does also not appeal.

I have never seen the Art Deco area of Miami but this seems over expensive.

Venice at Carnival has appeal but is very cold. Jan Morris's wonderful book about Venice is not complimentary about the city in the winter.

Separately, I have been reading some strange academic interpretations of the writing of Roland Barthes. However, the following I found for myself, and I think is significant.

'The photograph is authentication itself. The photograph is laborious only when it fakes. Photography never lies: or rather, it can lie as to the meaning of the thing, being by nature tendentious. Its force is nonetheless superior to everything the human mind can or can have conceived to assure us of reality. Every photograph is a certificate of presence'. – Roland Barthes.

@davidhurnphoto @magnumphotos #rolandbarthes #scotland #shetland

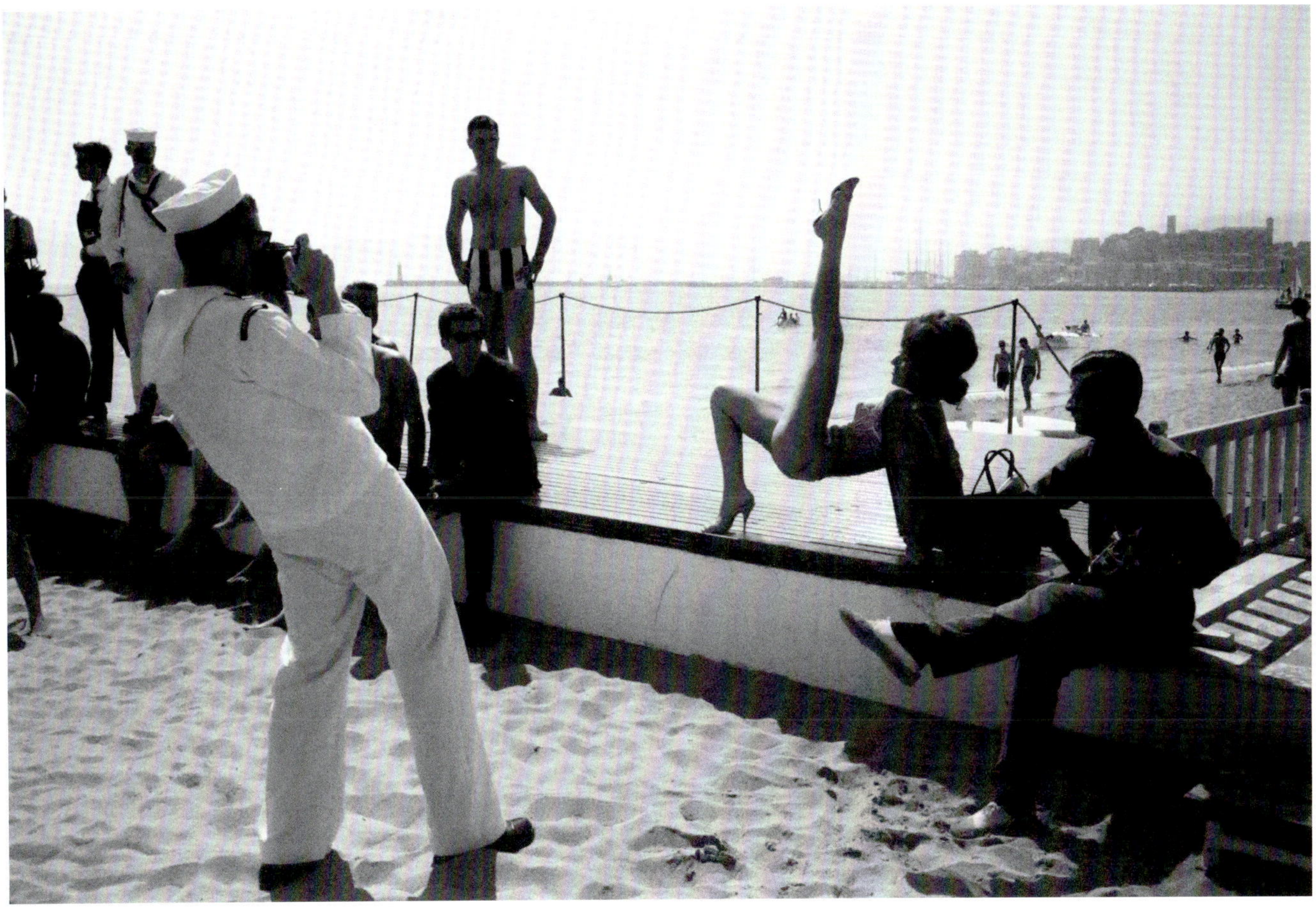

28 NOVEMBER 2018 / CANNES FILM FESTIVAL. *CANNES, FRANCE 1964*

Progress on my next year Mediterranean trip: I have decided to tell myself I am fit enough for it and have started to set it up. I start with Venice for Carnival, I soon discovered that I am booking late and have had to pay an arm and a leg for a room – only rather posh available, so at least I will be comfortable. I then go by train from Venice to Viareggio and come home via Pisa. By then I will know how tired I feel and what is my future. Later I will go to the Cannes Film Festival – I suspect security will be tighter than when I last went there in the early '60s, I will have to get passes.

I am continuing my photography around Wales – it's surprising how many people come up and say hello, I enjoy it, often an excuse to stop and have yet another coffee.

I am on my second Sjöwall and Wahlöö book, *The Man Who Went Up in Smoke*, full of sharp observations – these two writers would have been good photographers.

I am re-reading Gwyneth Lewis, a particular favourite. I love, and smile, at the opening line of *A Hospital Odyssey*, 'I'll kill you if you die on me now.'

@davidhurnphoto @magnumphotos #rolandbarthes #fujifilm #gwynethlewis #cannesfilmfestival

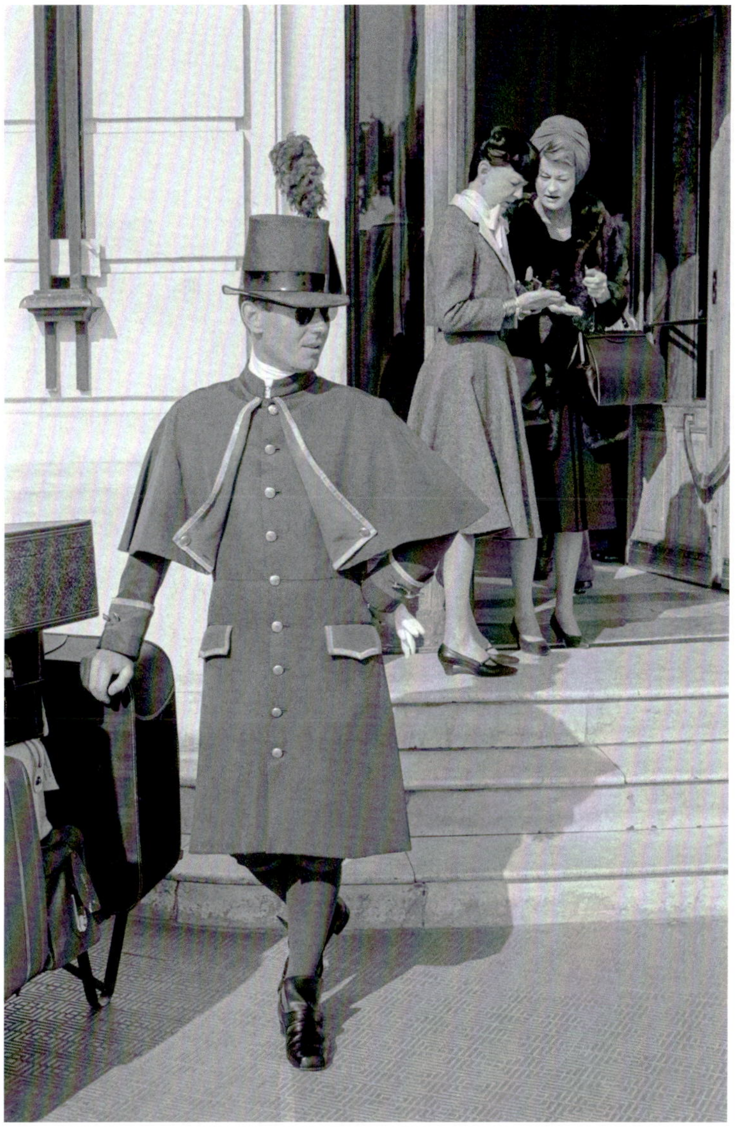

22 DECEMBER 2018 / DOORMAN, LE NEGRESCO HOTEL. *NICE, FRANCE 1964*

I am sorry that I have seemed to disappear. My computer was badly hacked and I was in a potential mess. Luckily, I have friends who know what to do and in the end I did not lose anything but pride. The rule is don't do anything that experts tell you not to do, however persuasive con persons are. It has taken me a couple of weeks to get all passwords etc changed but the worse thing is one's loss of confidence – how long does it take to get that back?

Good is that my Mediterranean trip is coming together. I have arranged Venice, Cannes and St Tropez. The rest will fall in place, it's a bit like doing a jigsaw puzzle.

I have known the photographer Paul Reas for nearly 40 years. For me he has always been one of the best – most interesting. A few days ago he gave me a copy of his new book, *Fables of Faubus*. It has not diminished my opinion of him or his work. It is an essential buy for anyone starting a collection of 'the books to have'.

@davidhurnphoto @magnumphotos @paul.reas #fujifilm

THE ONLY POSSIBLE BASIS FOR A SOUND MORALITY
IS MUTUAL TOLERANCE AND RESPECT: TOLERANCE OF ONE ANOTHER'S CUSTOMS
AND OPINIONS; RESPECT FOR ONE ANOTHER'S RIGHTS AND FEELINGS;
AWARENESS OF ONE ANOTHER'S NEEDS.

/ *A.J. Ayer*

2019

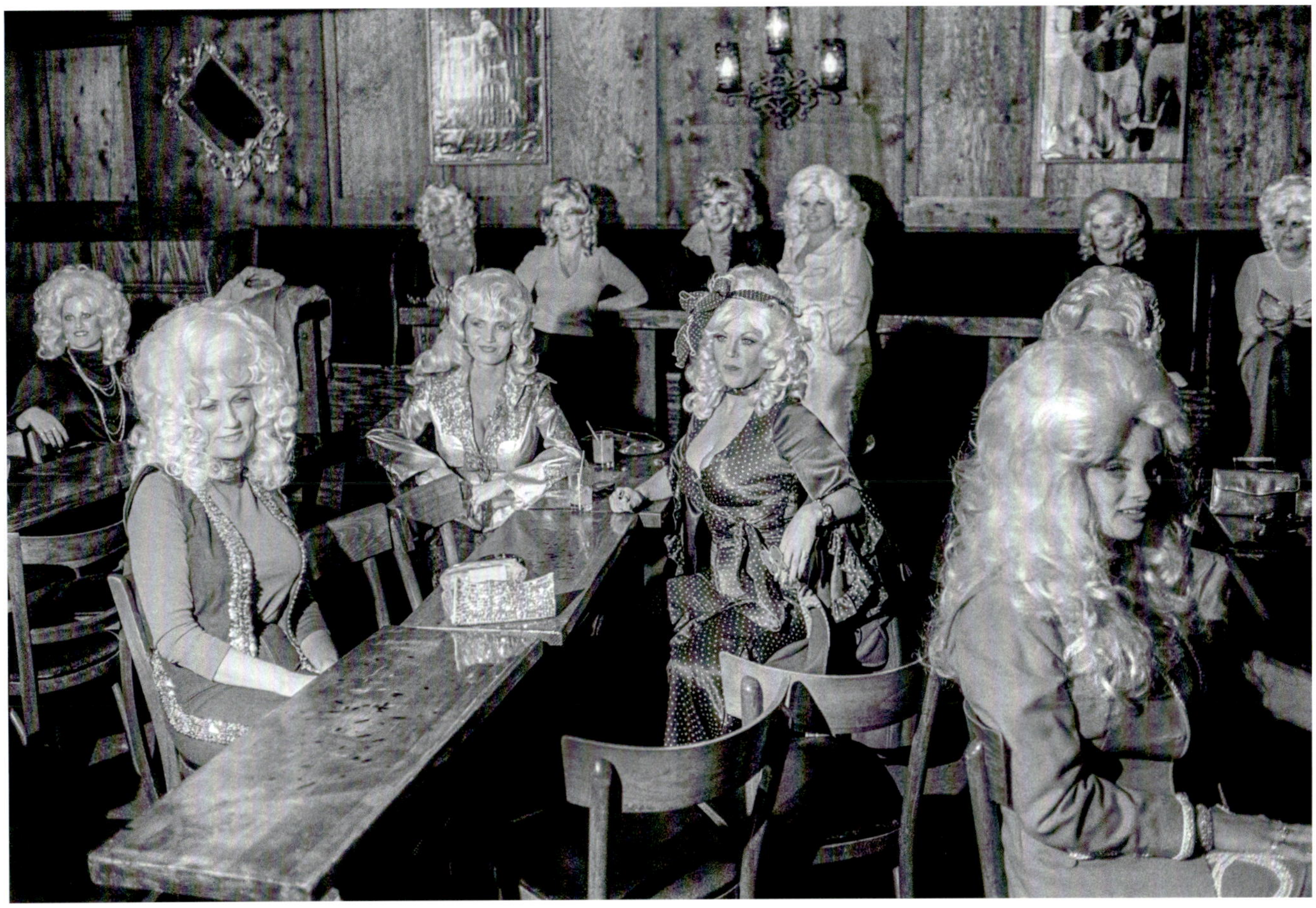

19 JANUARY 2019 / DOLLY PARTON LOOK-ALIKE CONTEST. *ARIZONA, USA 1979*

I am lucky enough to have an exhibition of my Arizona pictures in the splendid Etherton Gallery in Tucson starting 5 February. I am sharing the space with Bill Owens who produced the influential book *Suburbia* in 1973. I met Bill in 1986 when we were both invited to work on a book, *Ireland: A Week in the Life of a Nation*. My memory was that he was mainly interested in brewing. Also working on the book was Tony O'Shea whom I recently had the pleasure of seeing again, this time at the MPF – so many people turn up there.

A reminder that in the National Museum in Cardiff next week, Thursday 24, from morning till evening, there are a group of young women photographers – in my eyes now nearly everyone is young – talking. I suspect it will be a significant day.

For no apparent reason I had a dream involving George Rodger: great photographer and such a decent man. Thinking of him and his end of war pictures, I was reminded what Susan Sontag wrote:

'One's first encounter with the photographic inventory of ultimate horror is a kind of revelation. For me, it was photographs of Bergen-Belsen. Nothing I have seen – in photographs or in real life – ever cut me as sharply, deeply, instantaneously. Indeed, it seems plausible to me to divide my life into two parts, before I saw those photographs and after.' – Susan Sontag.

@davidhurnphoto @magnumphotos @martinparrfdn @ethertongallery @museumwales #fujifilm #nationalmuseumcardiff #susansontag #georgerodger #tonyoshea

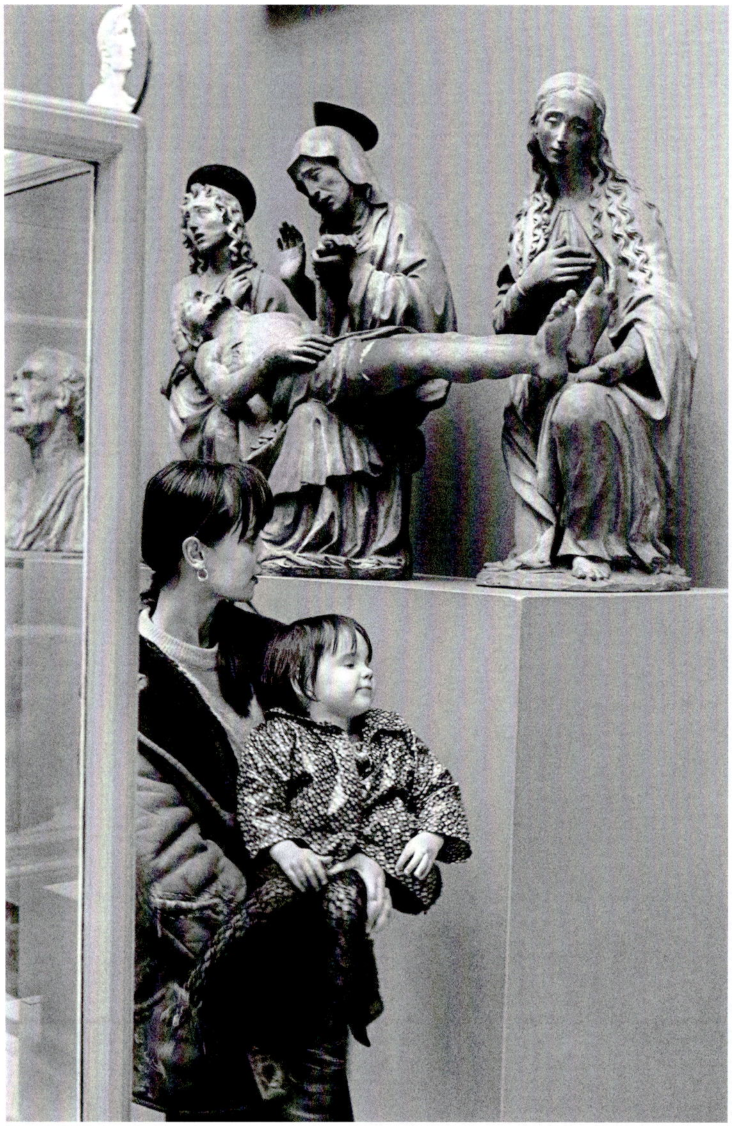

26 JANUARY 2019 / MOTHER AND DAUGHTER. *LONDON, ENGLAND 1967*

My wife at the time, Alita (we split in 1970), with my daughter Siân, now over 50, in the British museum passing by the beautiful sculpture, *Giovanni Della Robbia*. Alita has just died, but the good memories are not forgotten.

On a more upbeat note I have just spent two days in Cardiff at the *Women in Focus: Documentary and Citizenship* conference. It was extremely positive. I especially enjoyed Poulomi Basu, Lua Ribeira, Clémentine Schneidermann, Emma Lewis, Joanne Coates and Marcia Michael. All were full of the passion that I sometimes feel is lacking in many young photographers. It was very uplifting. One continues to learn. I hope the occasion is repeated next year.

@davidhurnphoto @magnumphotos @museumwales @poulomi07 @lua_ribeira @joannecoates_ @clementine.schneidermann @marciamichael_artist @_emmalewis__ #fujifilm #nationalmuseumcardiff #emmalewis

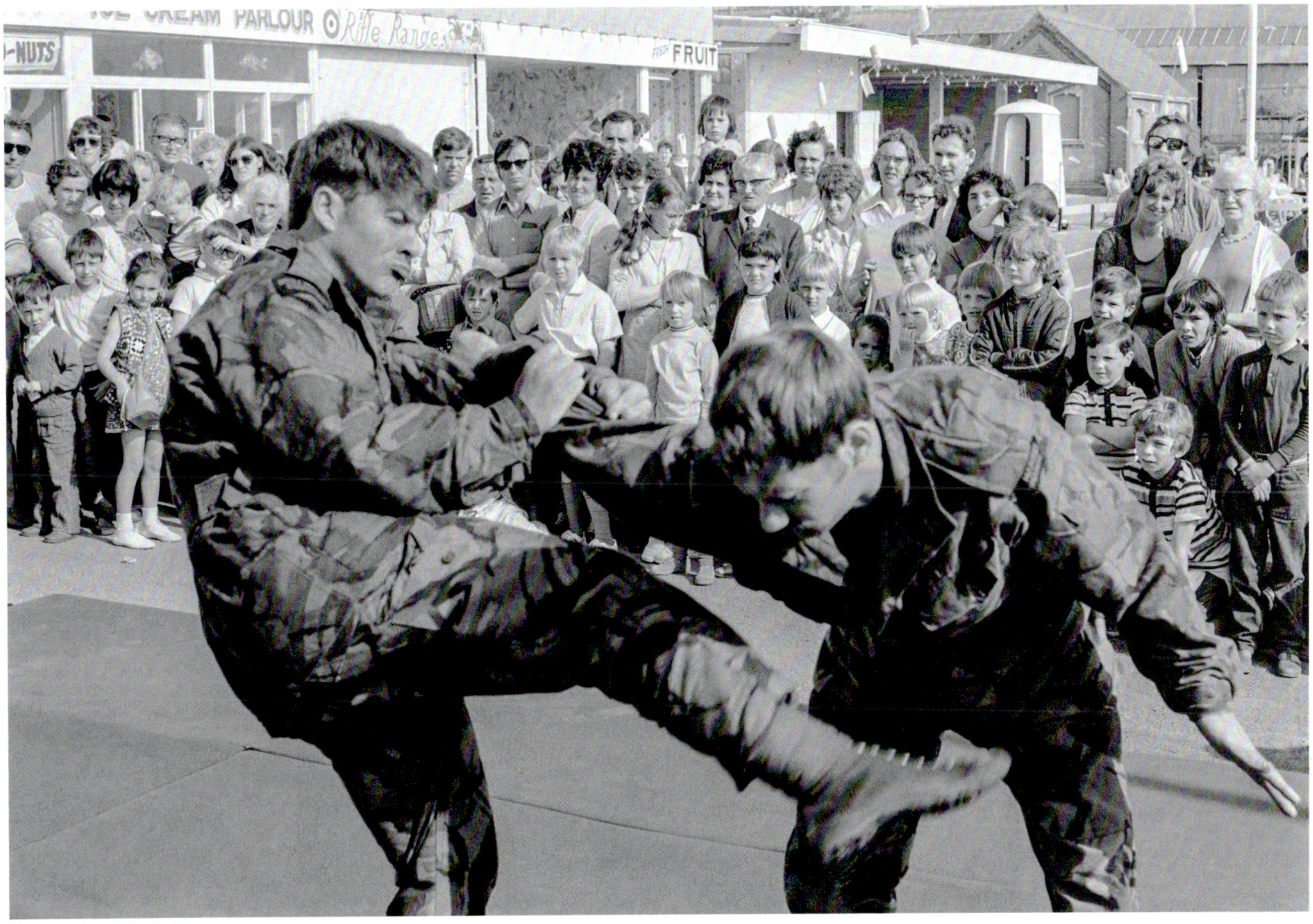

5 FEBRUARY 2019 / ON SHOOTING TRIP WITH DON McCULLIN. *RHYL, WALES 1972*

Last night I attended the private opening of the Don McCullin show at Tate Britain. As always, he does not let photography down. In an age where 'Artist' is a buzzword in certain genres, his pictures evoke words like empathy, beauty, poetry, social welfare, all of which I prefer.

It's a huge show and needs time to get around. I am sure it will have enormous audiences, I am sure many young might gain a greater understanding/sympathy of our messy world.

As an aside, during the initial speech Don was described as an artist. A voice from the side, Don, loudly proclaimed, 'I'm a photographer!'.

@davidhurnphoto @magnumphotos @don.mccullin #fujifilm #tatebritain

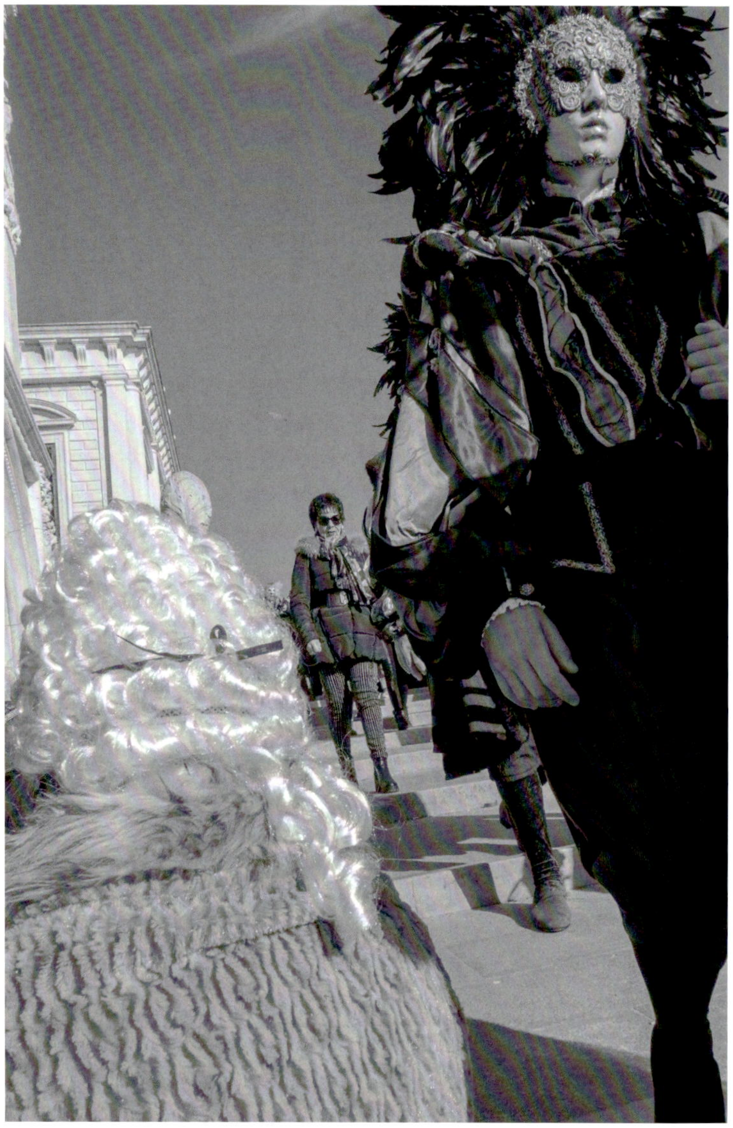

24 FEBRUARY 2019 / *VENICE, ITALY 2019*

My Mediterranean trip has started. Carnival is happening in Venice. In theory this sort of event should be easy to photograph. In practice I always find it difficult. I think the problem is because one feels so secure one does not fully concentrate – always a disaster. The trick is to try to isolate simple happenings and attempt to get these happenings slightly out of context. Personally I try to find a spot that instinctively seems right and wait to see what happens, flipping from place to place never works.

@davidhurnphoto @magnumphotos #fujifilm #mediterranean #venice

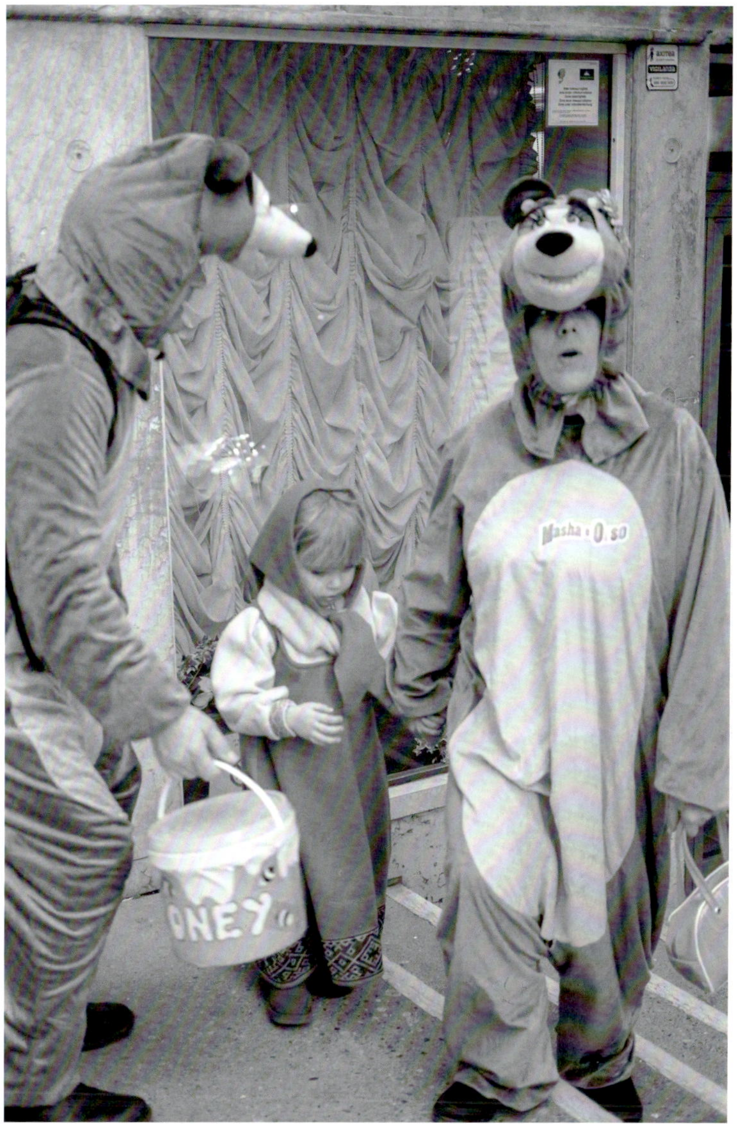

25 FEBRUARY 2019 / *VENICE, ITALY 2019*

So many people. All of us seemingly photographing the same wonderfully costumed people – in the main posing with members of the public. It's difficult to find wood for the trees – more clichés. I keep telling myself that this is really an exercise to see how I stand up after two weeks of exertion, at the moment not too well, I feel exhausted already.

I was asked what equipment I use. I have two Fuji X-Pro2. One fitted with the equivalent of a 50mm lens and one with the equivalent of a 28mm lens. I used the same set up with two Leica cameras for 50 years but changed to Fuji when digital arrived. For this trip I have bought a tiny flash that fits on the top of the camera – simply to deal with movement when attending 'Balls'. I have no idea how to use it, I presume it takes care of itself.

@davidhurnphoto @magnumphotos #fujifilm #mediterranean #venice

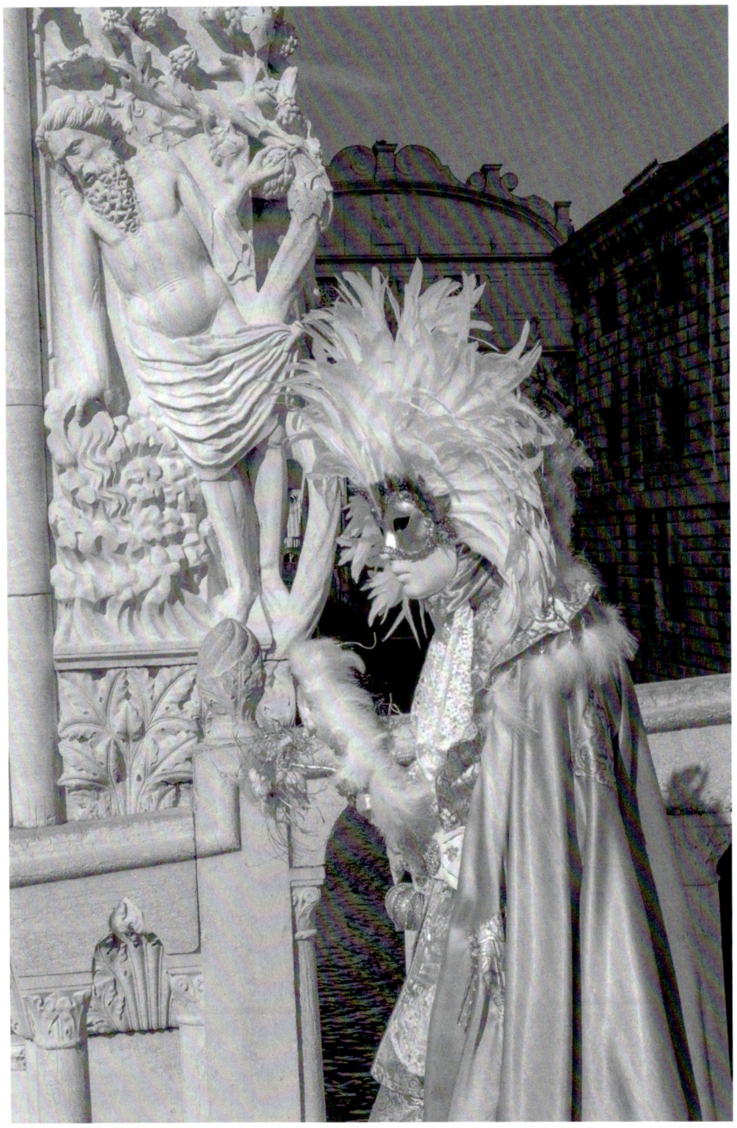

25 FEBRUARY 2019 / BRIDGE OF SIGHS. *VENICE, ITALY 2019*

If in doubt go back to what was a success before. The view from the Bridge of Sighs was the last view of Venice that convicts saw before their imprisonment. Myth, as you can't see from the window because of bars and the days of inquisitions and summary executions were over by the time the bridge was built. But in any case it's a frightening thought. I photographed there in 1964. So, go back to the same place and wait to see what happens – the lady turned up and passed by after half an hour.

By the way the magnificent sculpture is of drunken Noah. I have no idea who by but don't really care as it's very poignant whoever did it.

@davidhurnphoto @magnumphotos #fujifilm #mediterranean #venice

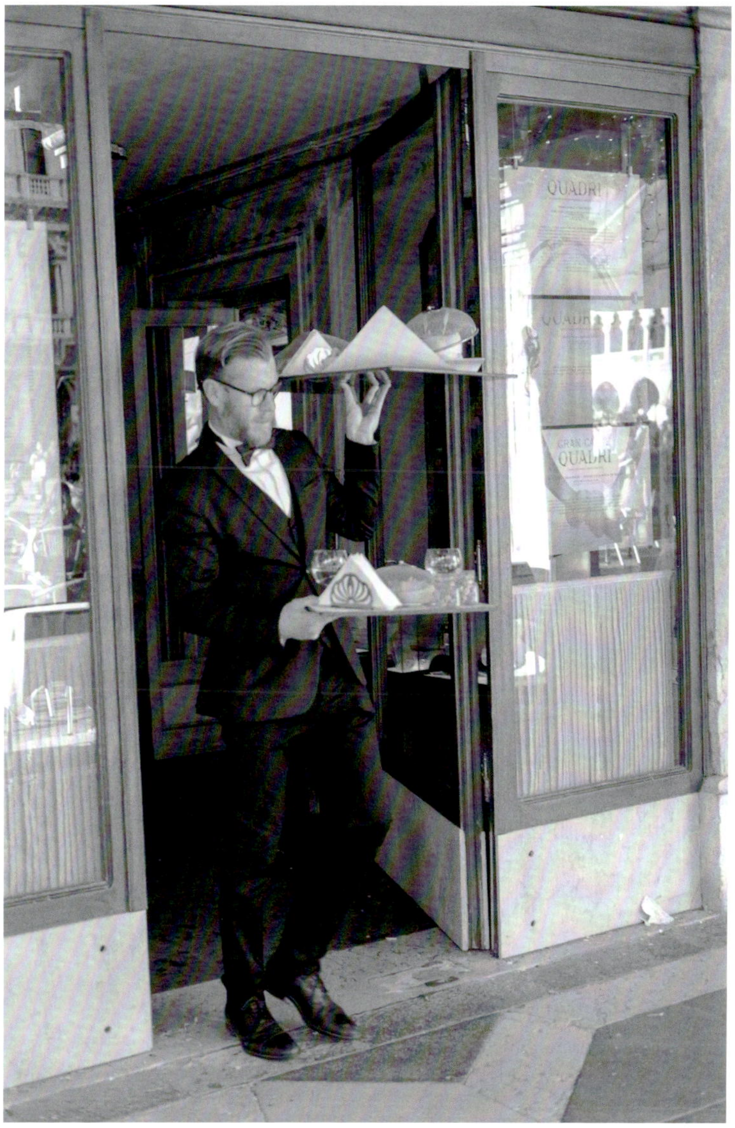

28 FEBRUARY 2019 / SAN MARCO WAITER. *VENICE, ITALY 2019*

Modern technology can keep one frighteningly on one's toes. I download into a program called Lightroom, it insists on telling me information that is slightly embarrassing. It seems I have pressed my camera buttons 1,408 times so far. I kid myself I don't shoot in a haphazard way so each press must have been for a reason. Why? Again Lightroom tells me I have so far only marked up 34 pictures and most of these are basically potential archive pictures. So far I have just eight pictures I might still like in ten years' time. What was I doing the 1,366 other times? Photography is difficult. Boy, does it need concentration.

@davidhurnphoto @magnumphotos #fujifilm #mediterranean #venice

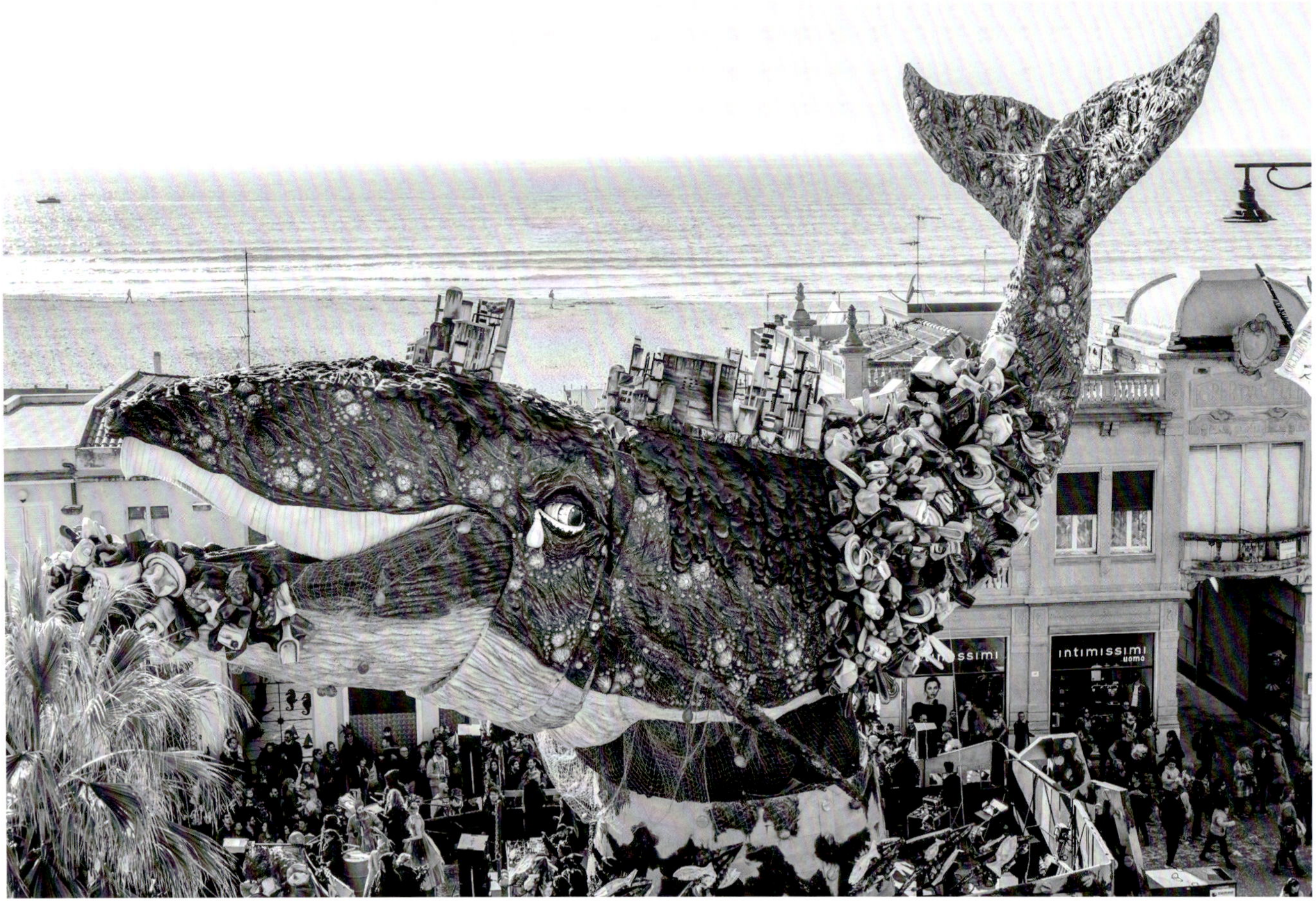

6 MARCH 2019 / *VIAREGGIO, ITALY 2019*

I am posting a picture that is virtually all content, but I think important. Viareggio is a town I really like, it's very family orientated. It hosts the biggest Carnival in Europe – some 200,000 people turn out to see art/craft at its very best, 5-story-high *papier-mâché* sculptures move in a circle up and down the seafront road. It's a wonder of people organisation, no rules, everyone wanders wherever they like, no police – and above all, I did not see a single drunk person. All were having fun, children mesmerised. I found it's far too crowded to isolate personal happenings but I did see the most moving monument against destruction of the living planet I have ever seen. An 80-foot high whale strangled by plastic. I wish I knew who designed/made it – sculptor of the decade?

@davidhurnphoto @magnumphotos #fujifilm #mediterranean #viareggio #whale #conservation #plastics

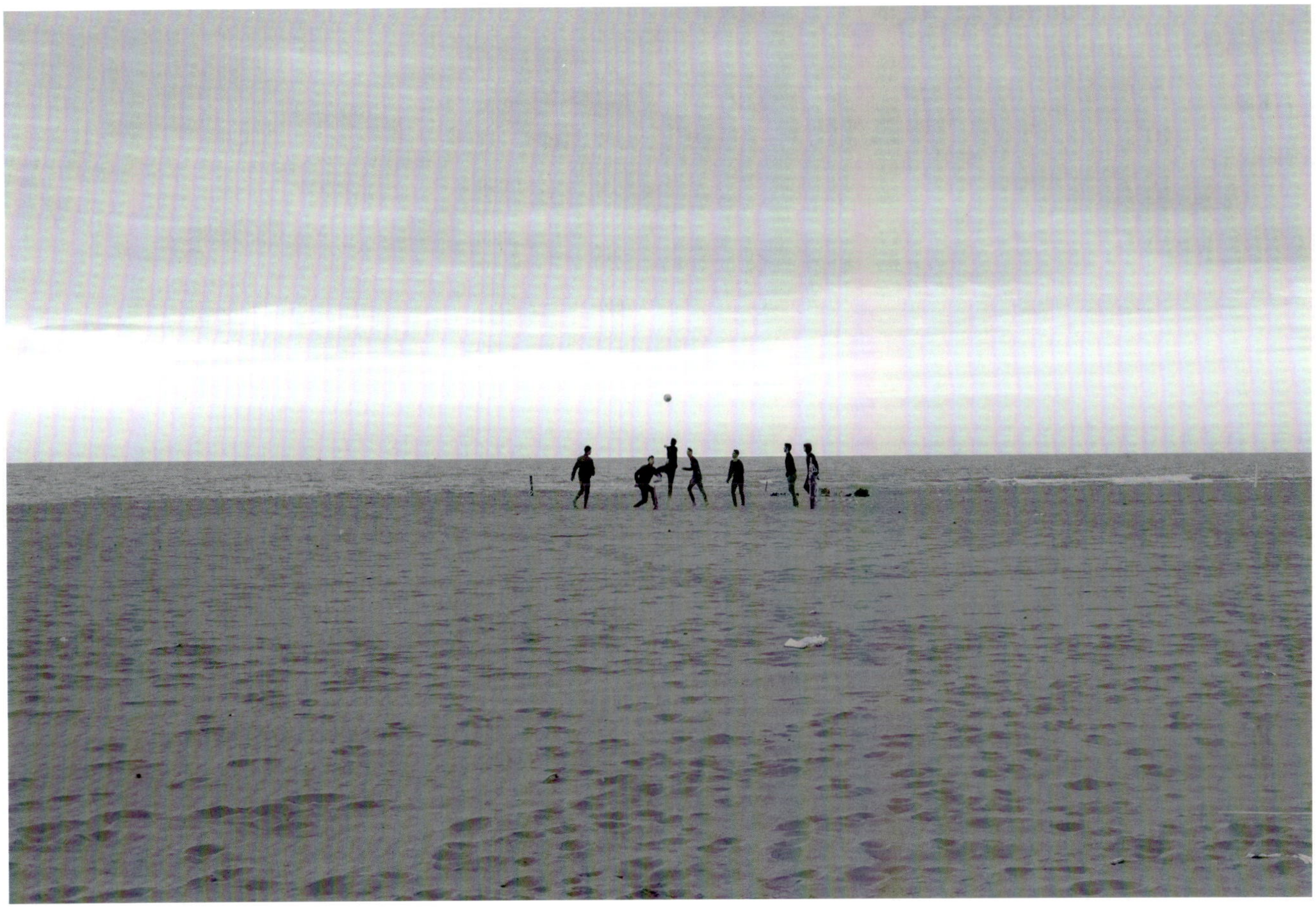

10 MARCH 2019 / *VIAREGGIO, ITALY 2019*

The very last picture I took before coming home to Tintern.

The wonderful beach is very sparse in winter. I wanted to get that feeling of space plus get a feeling of locals. The space is dealt with by – how far should I stand off? The locals by who is on the beach at the time. In the case of local Italian football something is always happening – then it is a matter of continuous shooting 'til you feel that you are seeing something visually pertinent. Be brave.

May I thank all of you who passed on information about the whale, it's extremely useful for me.

At home I need a few days rest, the trip was very taxing: two weeks on the trot is too much for my age. Next stages will be shorter.

@davidhurnphoto @magnumphotos #fujifilm #mediterranean #viareggio #beach #football

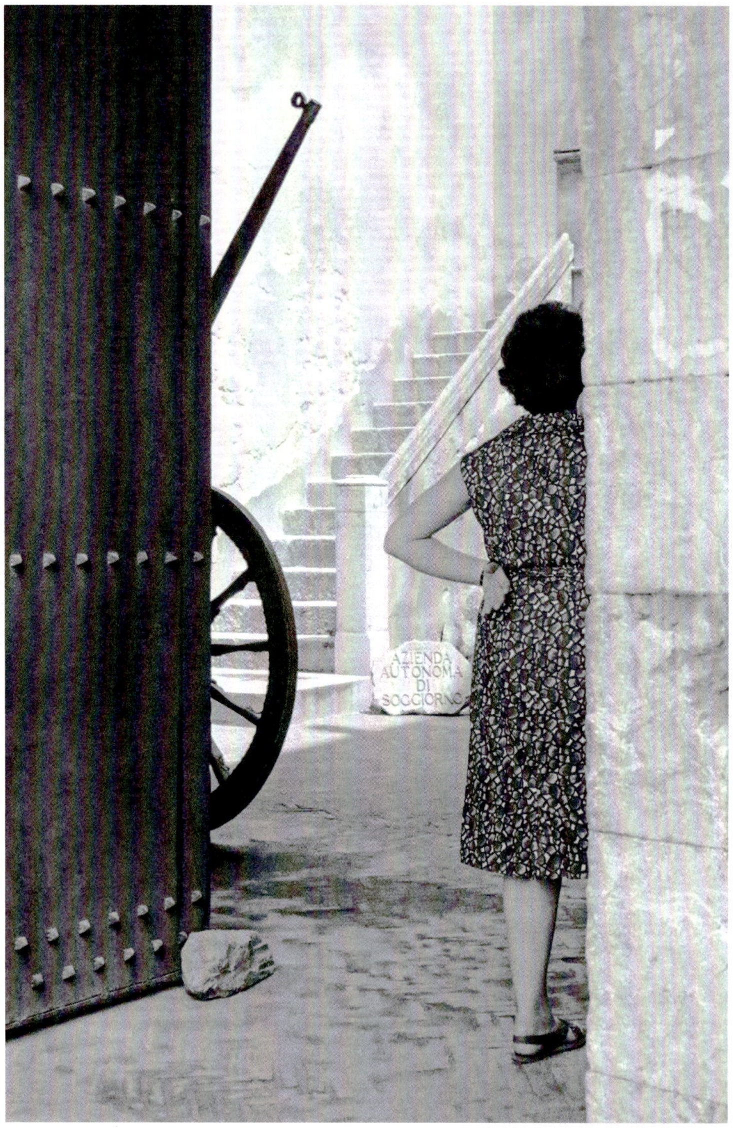

15 MARCH 2019 / TAORMINA. *SICILY, ITALY 1964*

Now I have realised that my re-trip around the Mediterranean is possible, it is time to start planning other individual sorties.

I have decided that my most productive blocks would be one day travel, three/four days shooting, and one day return.

I will try out this strategy at the beginning of April – give myself some good weather. First base, Catania/Taormina.

At home I notice that interesting photographer Clémentine Schneidermann is having an exhibition opening at the Martin Parr Foundation on 26 of this month, she is also giving a talk on 7 May – well worth a visit.

@davidhurnphoto @magnumphotos @clementine.schneidermann #fujifilm #mediterranean #taormina

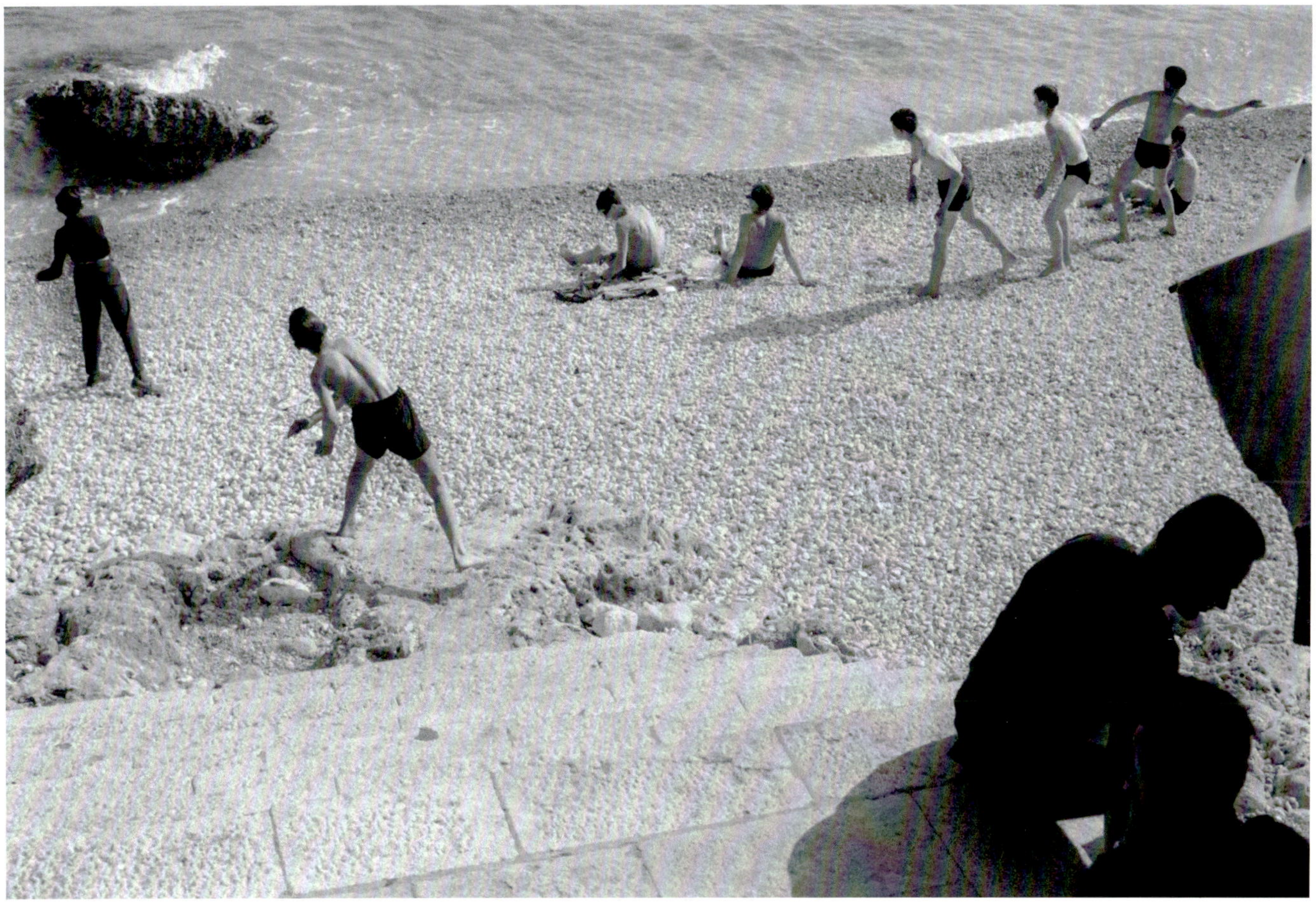

18 MARCH 2019 / STONE SKIPPING. *DUBROVNIK 1964*

One of the elements I love about being a photographer is that I see how many activities in this world are universal. Stone skipping, for example. As I have said so often, I enjoy the 'exotic of the mundane' and the fun in trying to capture that 'mundane' into a seen living picture.

I enjoyed the old city of Dubrovnik when I visited in 1964. Not sure why, as there is little there except atmosphere, limestone streets and Baroque buildings. Anyway, the city will be one of my 20 places to re-visit. I notice that there is a half-marathon around the city walls in April – just enough of a titillation to attract me. Before I cavort off anywhere, I prefer to have at least one focus that I might be able to extract a picture from.

To put this project into perspective, I have just come off the phone from my 'brother' Josef Koudelka who tells me he is in the final year of his 26-year project on 'archaeological ruins'.

@davidhurnphoto @magnumphotos @josef_koudelka #fujifilm #mediterranean #dubrovnik

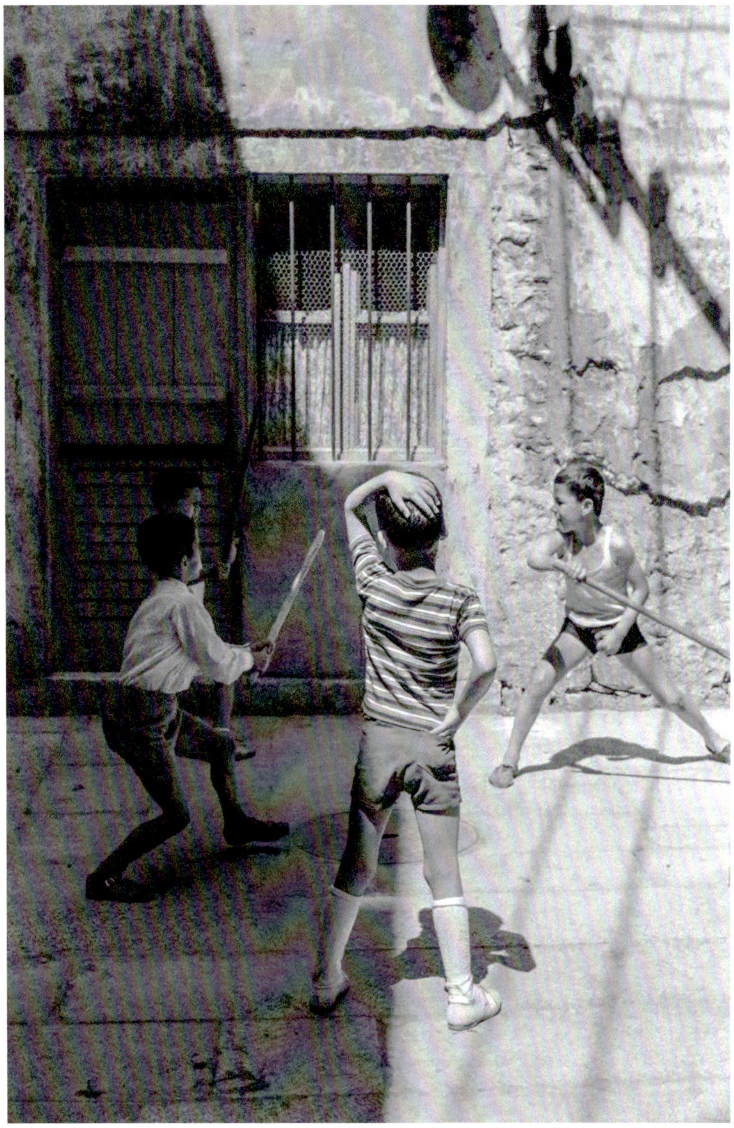

21 MARCH 2019 / YOUTH GAMES. *DUBROVNIK 1964*

(Nothing changes). I have settled on 16-20 April for my trip to Dubrovnik. I have a hotel booked near the gate to the ancient walls so that I don't have to walk too far at the start of my day. I might decide to do a *Game of Thrones* tour but at the moment I can only find tours that take about three hours, I would become one of the slain – of course, I could do the tour in Northern Ireland but somehow that does not seem so exotic.

I was asked yesterday what book would I recommend to enthuse the young about photography. I had no hesitation: *Looking at Photographs* by John Szarkowski. He shows and writes about 100 pictures selected from the collection of the Museum of Modern Art, New York. A very broad selection.

I enjoy the simplicity of his writing.

From the first description, a picture of a daguerreotype:

'When Daguerre announced his great invention to the public in the summer of 1839, he explained how it worked but not really what it was for. The process was obviously a miracle of the age of science, and like any miracle it was self-justifying. Painters said it would be a great aid to art, and physicists said it would be a great aid to science, but the important thing, on which everyone agreed, was that it was astonishing'

Later, on looking at a daguerrotype, he suggests:

'The image, though infinitely detailed and subtle, is elusive. The picture should be looked at with its case not fully opened, preferably in private and by lamplight, as one would approach a secret.'

@davidhurnphoto @magnumphotos #fujifilm #mediterranean #dubrovnik #johnszarkowski

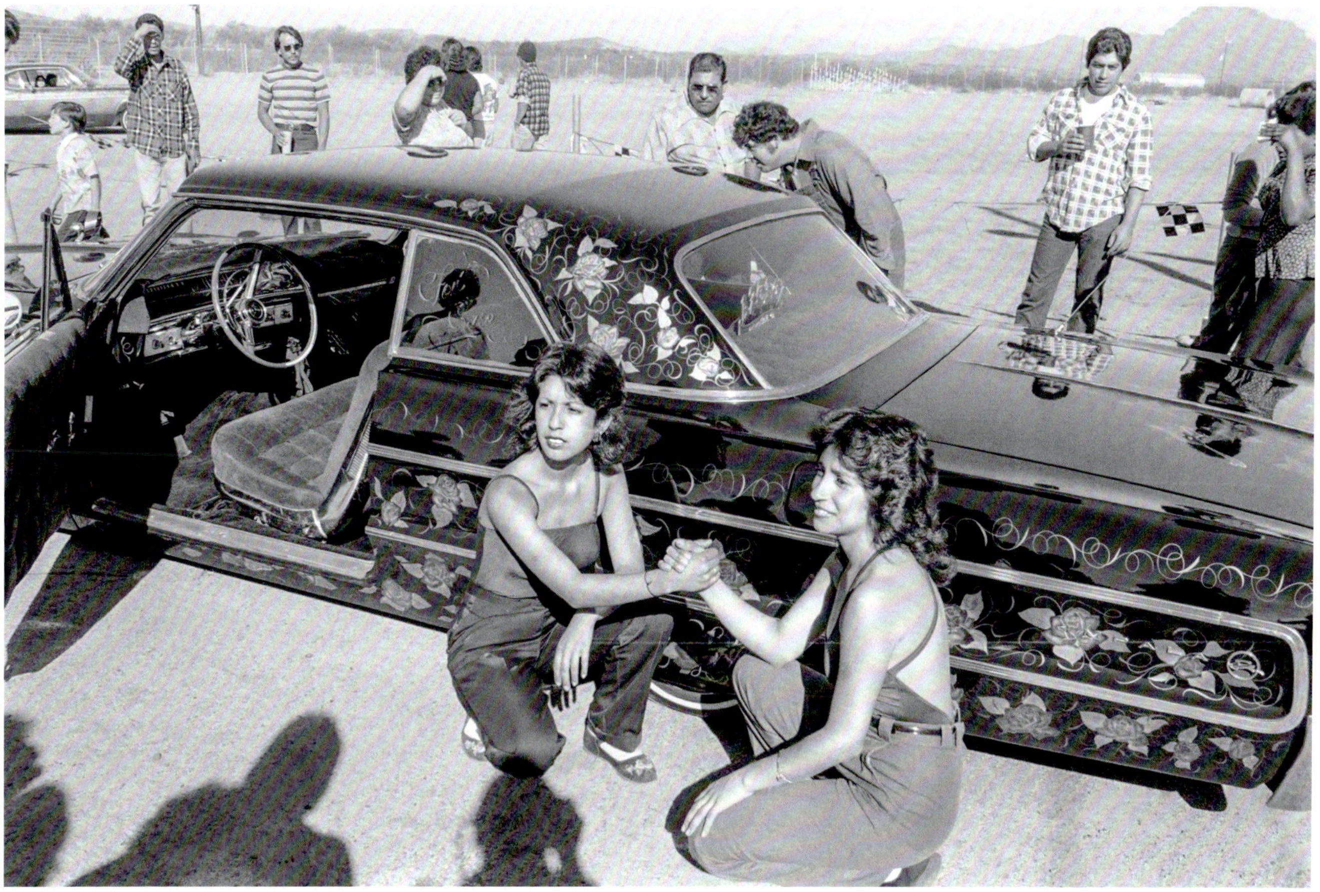

25 MARCH 2019 / LOW-RIDERS MEETING. *ARIZONA, USA 1979*

The Mexican/American border has always been an issue in the USA. When I was in Arizona I was particularly interested in cultural aspects of the 'Chicanos'. At that time it was a name for a chosen identity of some Mexican Americans in the United States. A word used by them to express pride in a shared cultural, ethnic and community identity. However, as is now the practice, with the pollution of language, the word is more and more used negatively by conservative members of the community.

Magnum has a good history of producing photographic essays along this border. They are about to embark on a group visual investigation. I have reluctantly decided that my Welsh Landscape, my Tintern Village, and my Mediterranean trip is all I can manage for this year so sadly will not be involved.

I suggest you look at the Alex Webb pictures as an example of producing an informative visual essay.

@davidhurnphoto @magnumphotos @webb_norriswebb #fujifilm #chicano #arizona

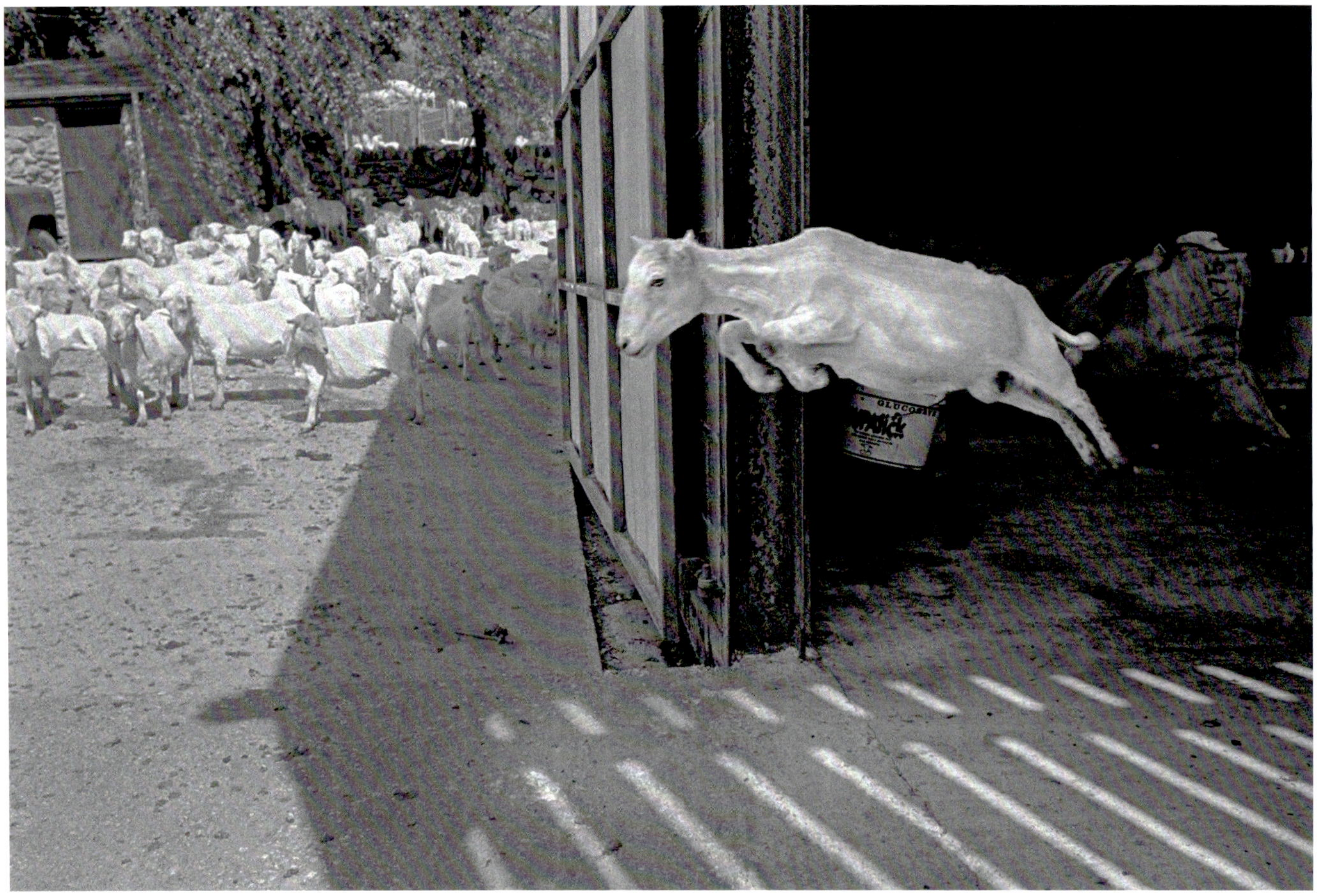

29 MARCH 2019 / SHEEP SHEARING. *SNOWDONIA, WALES 1997*

What a mess. I had felt I ought to try to do something on Brexit. I found it impossible as I couldn't find two people who seemed to have gleaned the same factual information. Virtually every farmer I talked to seemed to have a different source of 'facts' – this paper or that, this politician or that, this person in the know or that. Yet Welsh farmers are going to be greatly affected by whatever happens.

Before the Gutenberg press, the problem was lack of information, and now, due to the rise of social media, there is too much information – the former must have led to mental starvation but the latter leads to mental obesity. Once we hoped accuracy was sacrosanct, now the majority seem not to care.

Luckily, my photography life is simple:

'The subject matter is not that collection of solid, static objects extended in space but the life that is lived in the scene that it composes; and so reality is not that external scene but the life that is lived in it. Reality is things as they are.' – Wallace Stevens

@davidhurnphoto @magnumphotos #fujifilm #brexit #farming #wallacestevens #snowdonia #wales

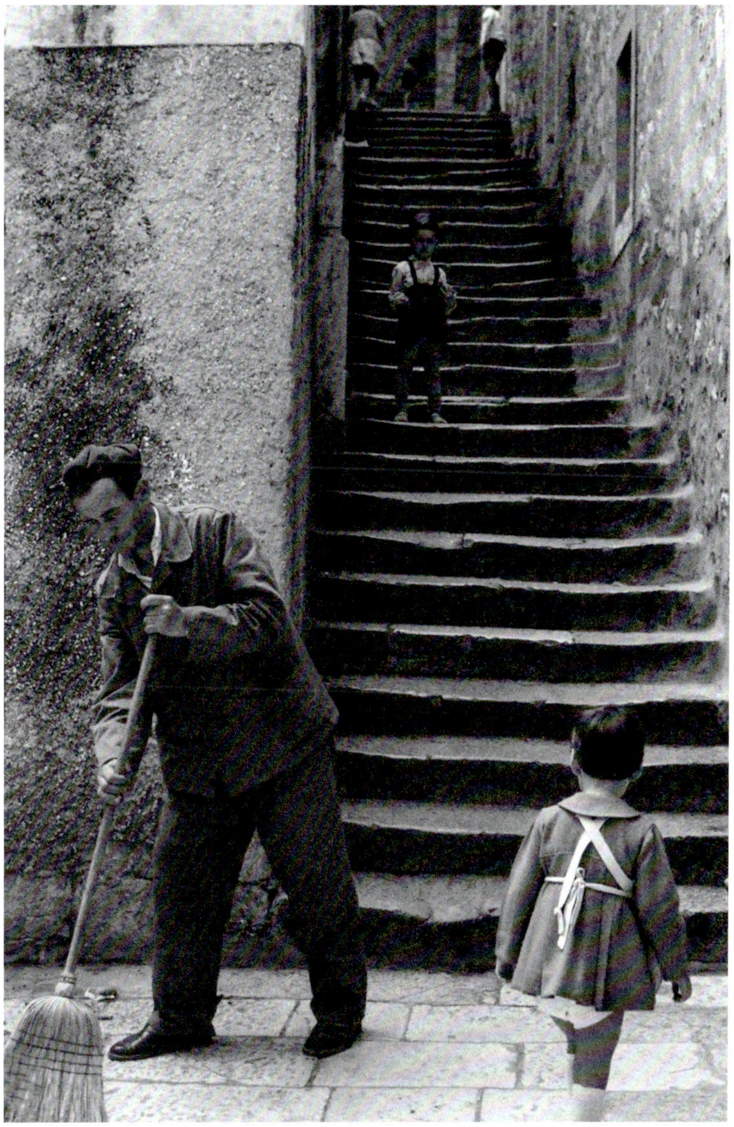

14 APRIL 2019 / CLEANING. *DUBROVNIK, CROATIA 1964*

I am off to Dubrovnik on Tuesday. The third of what I expect to be 20 trips to the coast of the Mediterranean. I went to this beautiful – perhaps most perfectly preserved – medieval city in the world in 1964. I wonder how much it has changed? Actually, it doesn't really matter that much to me as I am simply a recorder of that that is in front of me, whatever that that is, is OK. I am not a great believer that photography must 'progress', I love the 'wonder' of the world and I know tomorrow will be different from today and that's enough progress for me.

@davidhurnphoto @magnumphotos #dubrovnik #medieval

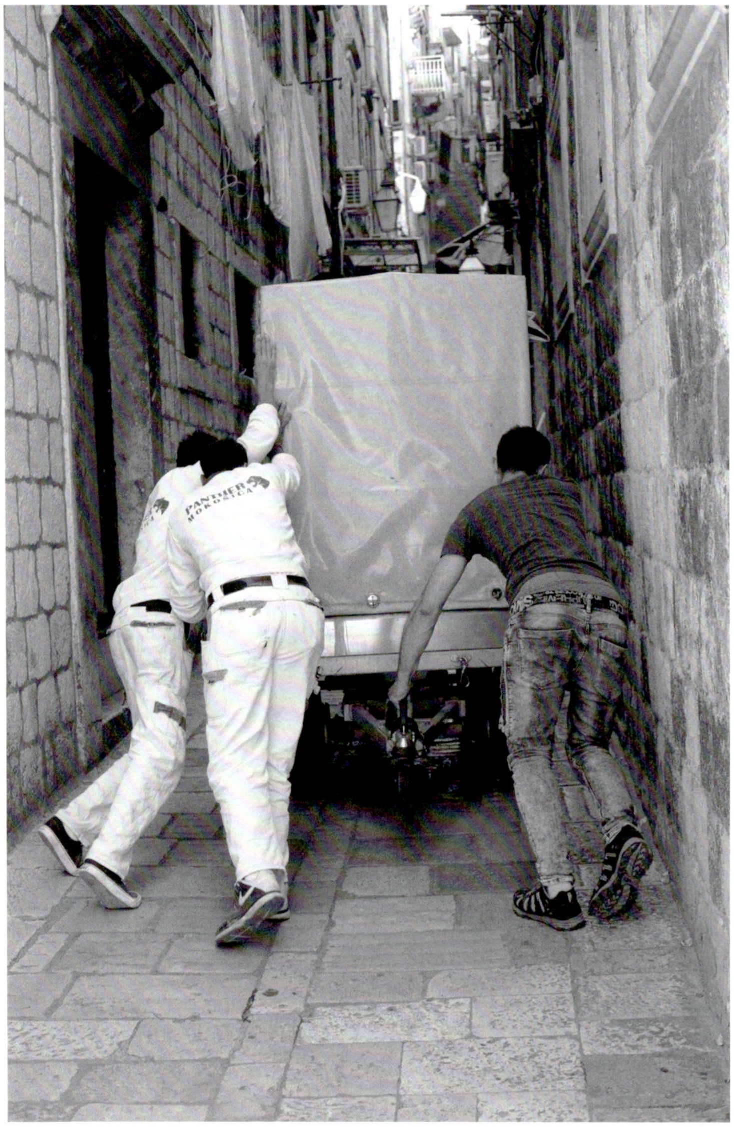

20 APRIL 2019 / EARLY MORNING. *DUBROVNIK, CROATIA 2019*

This trip has been a near disaster. After one and a half days' shooting I went down with dizzy spells and sickness. It totally laid me up and my main concern became whether I would be able to make it to the plane home.

I am beginning to realise that all the world's well-known towns or cities are now total tourist spots. All you can normally shoot is a potential advert for some iPhone camera or other. Boy, what a change from 1964.

Experience tells me that if you get up at 6am there is a potential for getting a few surprises.

@davidhurnphoto @magnumphotos #dubrovnik #medieval

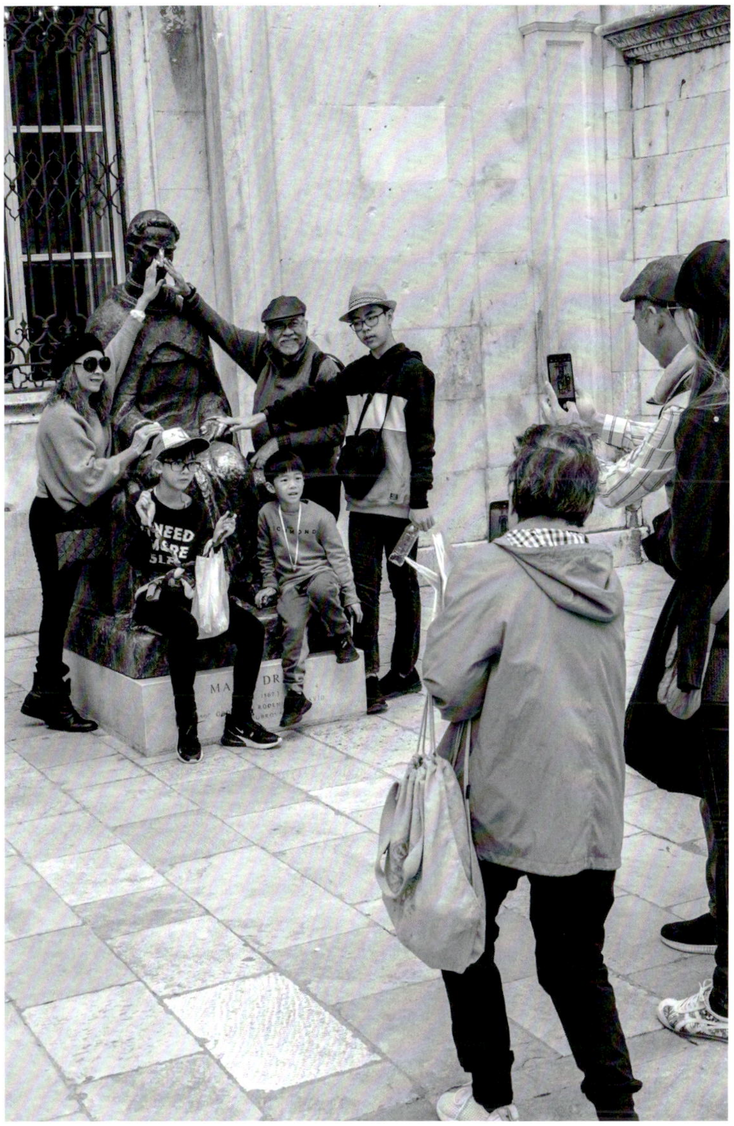

22 APRIL 2019 / NEED MORE SLEEP. *DUBROVNIK, CROATIA 2019*

Thank you for the many emails etc. I have always suffered from Ménière's disease. It's extremely unpleasant but I know how to deal with it. The problem is how much you gamble with it as you get older.

I did get home OK and it will all clear in a few days, so time to think.

I got a few more pictures than I at first thought so I will post a few quickly whilst I gather my thoughts i.e. what next.

Looking back on my 1964 pictures I realised that I don't have a single picture taken then with tourists in. I guess photography deals well with the passage of time. Be accurate, however upsetting and vulgar the trends seem.

@davidhurnphoto @magnumphotos #dubrovnik #medieval #tourist

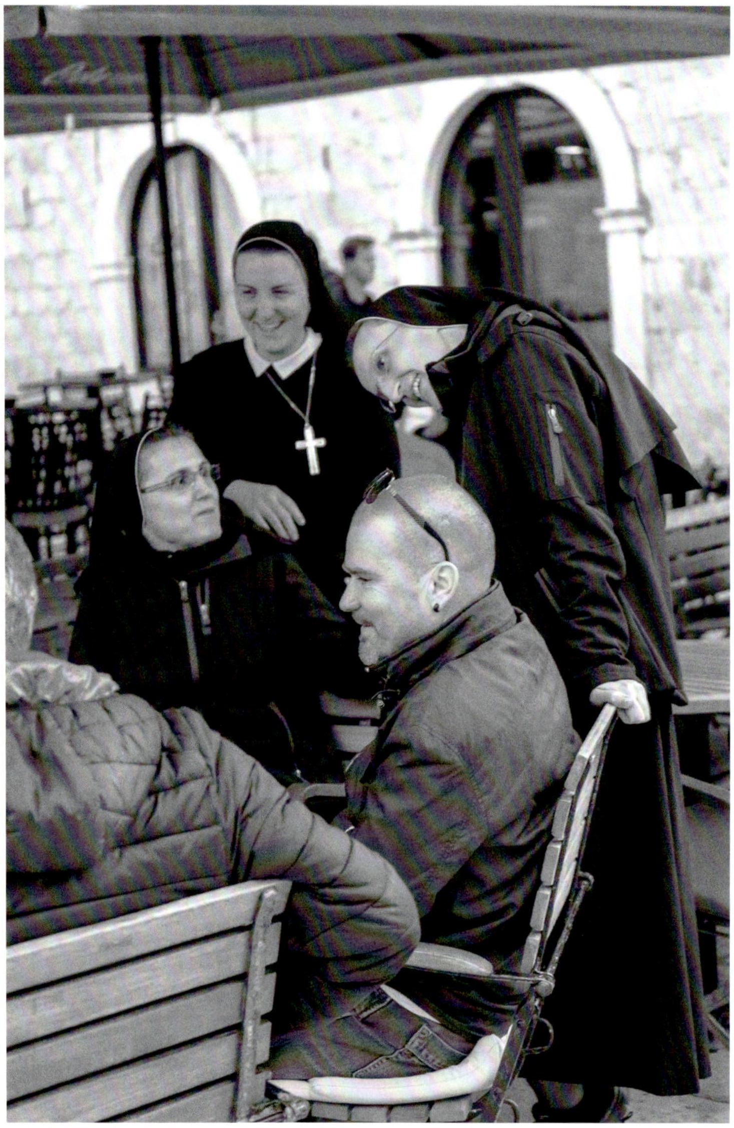

24 APRIL 2019 / COFFEE TIME. *DUBROVNIK, CROATIA 2019*

Well, my giddiness is receding slowly. The good is that I have had time to look at pictures, listen to music and read.

Have you seen the Instagrams of Matt Black? What a wonderful, caring photographer.

Reading has been mainly Ed McBain *87th Precinct* novels, they are so descriptive of place and there are so many of them. I have over 50. My memory is now so bad that by the time I get to have read them all I can start again.

At home I have an exceptional sound set up. Enjoy virtually anything classical, dependent on mood. But I love most music. Particular favourites are Paul Robeson, Chet Baker, Tim Hardin, Billie Holiday, Joni Mitchell, Barb Jungr, Stacey Kent, oh so many more. I suspect these are partly because I have seen a few of them live and in some cases have photographed them. Photography brings back memories of Chicago and Paris jazz cellars – and youth.

I am always slightly saddened/puzzled when so many ask 'what camera do you use'? Buying a camera that someone else has will not help. If you take enough pictures you will soon sort out what type of camera is most suitable for the way 'you' shoot. Since the invention of photography all cameras are basically the same, a box with a hole in its front and some method of letting more or less light through that hole. The viewfinder is the important part – it's your entrance to seeing. With most cameras you look down the lens and see an image on a ground glass screen. With others you look as though looking through a window. The Leica has dominated the second group. When I was using film I used the same Leicas for 50 years of my life. Since going digital I still use cameras with the window type viewfinder. I suspect my present camera will see me out. Most of the time I simply set it on automatic. I wish it had less buttons.

@davidhurnphoto @magnumphotos @mattblack_blackmatt @barbjungr @staceykent #dubrovnik #medieval #tourist #nun #edmcbain #johnszarkowski

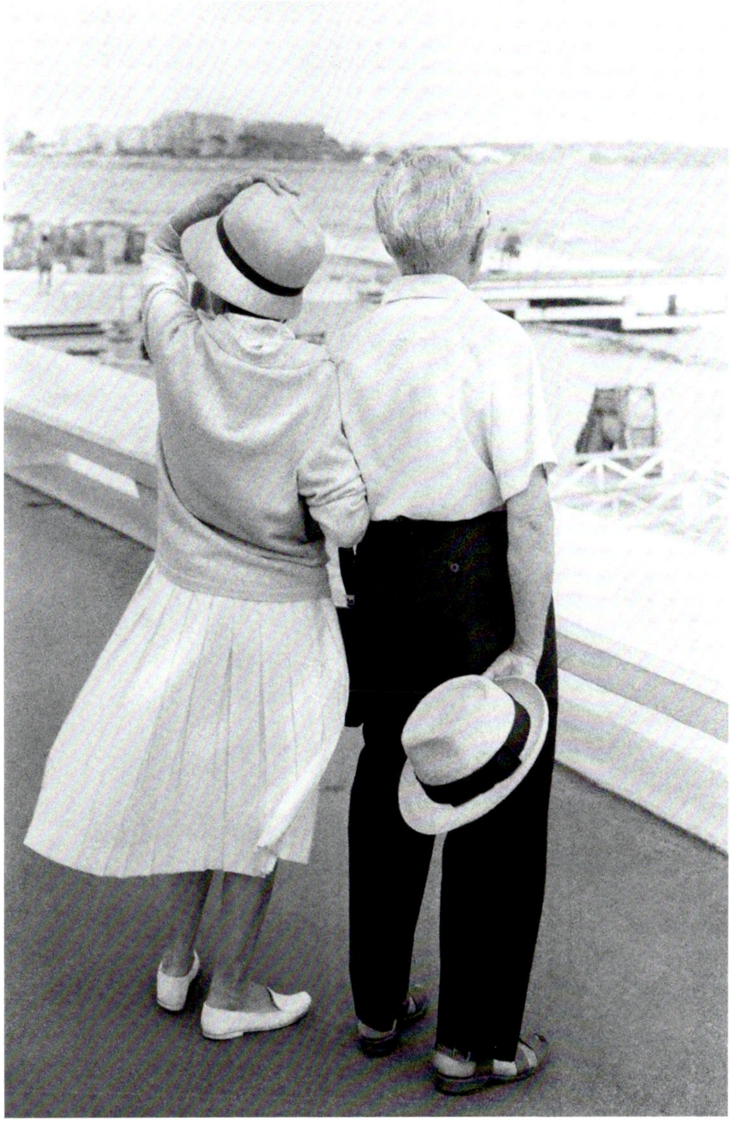

30 APRIL 2019 / CANNES. *CANNES, FRANCE 1964*

It has taken me longer than I would have hoped to recuperate. In fact, so long that I have decided to not take the gamble, and I have cancelled the Cannes trip. I hope to restart the Mediterranean project later in the year when I have taken more advice.

In the meantime I will concentrate on Welsh landscape. Hopefully the end piece in the jigsaw of my trying to understand what is meant by 'Welsh Culture'. I have about 20 more pictures to obtain – I can hardly believe it but I have now visited over 500 locations, a nightmare editing job, then the problem of what to do with it all?

Good thought: 'Life is really simple, but we insist on making it complicated.'
– Confucius

@davidhurnphoto @magnumphotos #confucius #cannes

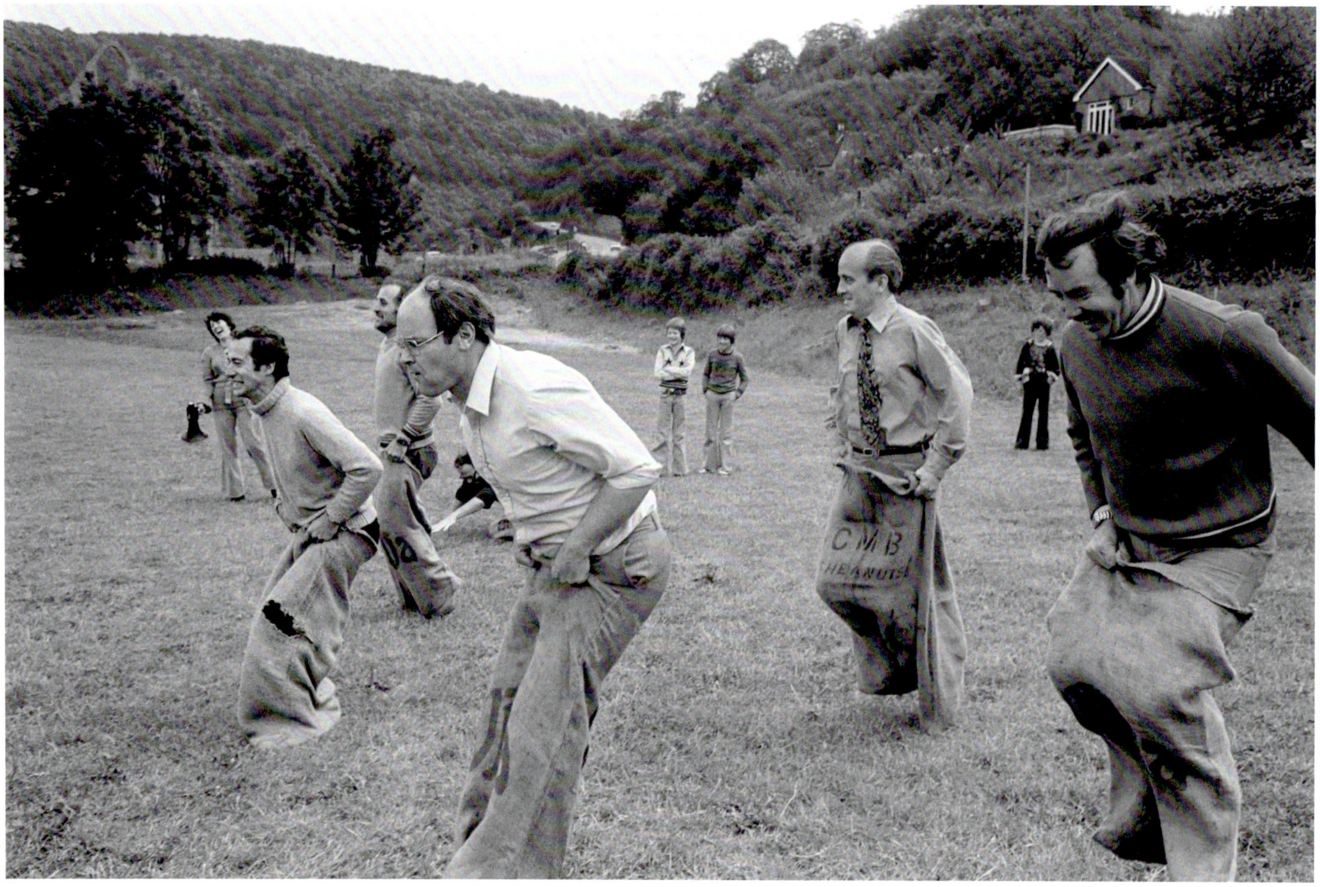

3 MAY 2019 / SACK RACE. *TINTERN, WALES 1977*

I love emails. Writing them allows me the time to think and perhaps be a little more precise, plus I also have something to keep for reference. To one person, particularly bright and precious to me, I have sent 1,228 emails since 2004 – a sort of Dear Diary.

I have just received an email from a dear friend and photographer I greatly admire, Chris Chapman. In 1975 he moved to Dartmoor, since when he has relentlessly documented aspects of Dartmoor life. He wrote me:

'I'm keeping busy and at the moment putting together an illustrated talk on my village, looking at photographs from the '70s and '80s. Quite extraordinary to see how much has changed. There are men sweeping the roads (you never see that now!), butcher, baker and grocery deliveries (so few of the elderly owned a car back then) and farming practice that has been replaced by one man and a machine.'

Photography deals so well with the then and now. I have always made it a rule for myself in Wales that if I hear something is closing/disappearing, I go photograph it on the simple assumption that no-one can do it later.

I got a real shock when I started my Mediterranean project, I saw the extreme change in places since 1964.

'Memory demands an image'. – Bertrand Russell

@davidhurnphoto @magnumphotos #chrischapman #bertrandrussell

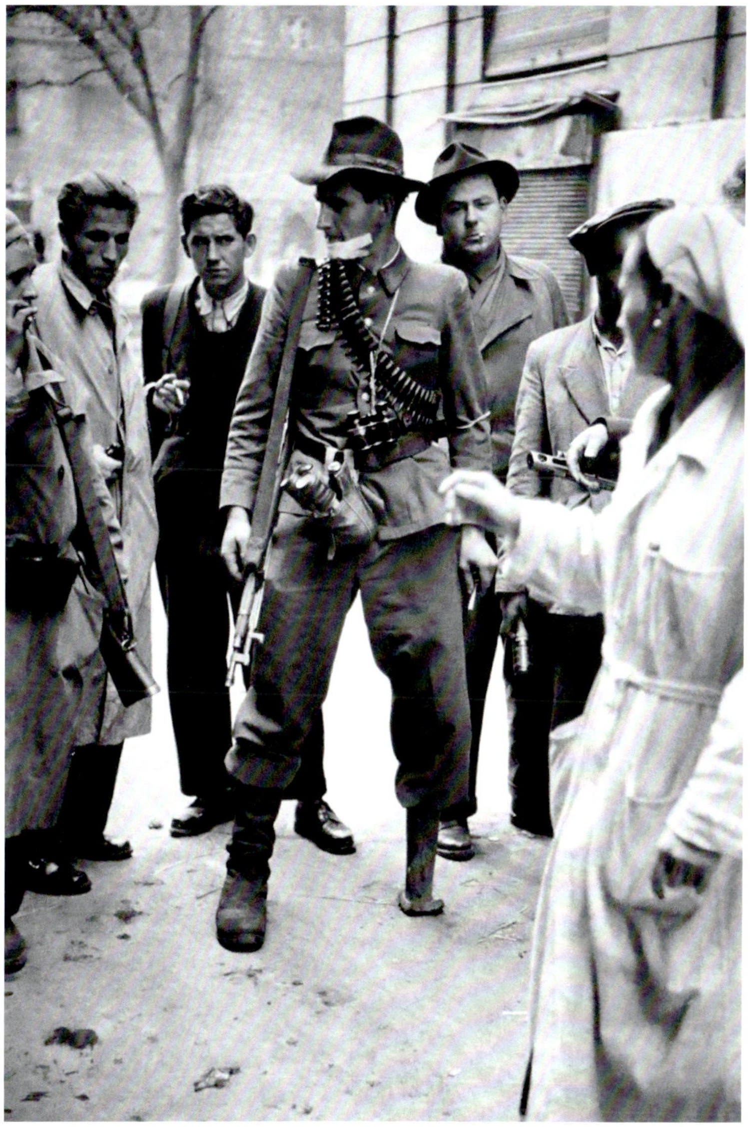

11 MAY 2019 / FREEDOM FIGHTER. *BUDAPEST, HUNGARY 1956*

I have just received my latest book, *La Storia le Immagini David Hurn*. A soft back, very elegant publication, by Italian publishers Hachette. Italy has some wonderful designers.

I see many self-published books. I wonder why so many photographers seem to think they are designers? Many photographers have spent three years in some form of photographic education and forget that designers spend the same amount of time on their courses. I would encourage young photographers to seek out designers and writers they enjoy, to maybe work with. I think results would be better.

My book is the editor's choice of pictures out of my 63 years of work so far. I normally let an editor I respect have a comparatively free hand. I enjoy seeing what others enjoy. I think I suggested one change in this book.

The first picture in the book is me with lots of hair looking very hip. To think I once was 24.

The second is from my first big gamble and adventure, the Hungarian uprising. What a gift, a peg-legged Freedom Fighter.

@davidhurnphoto @magnumphotos @hachettebooks

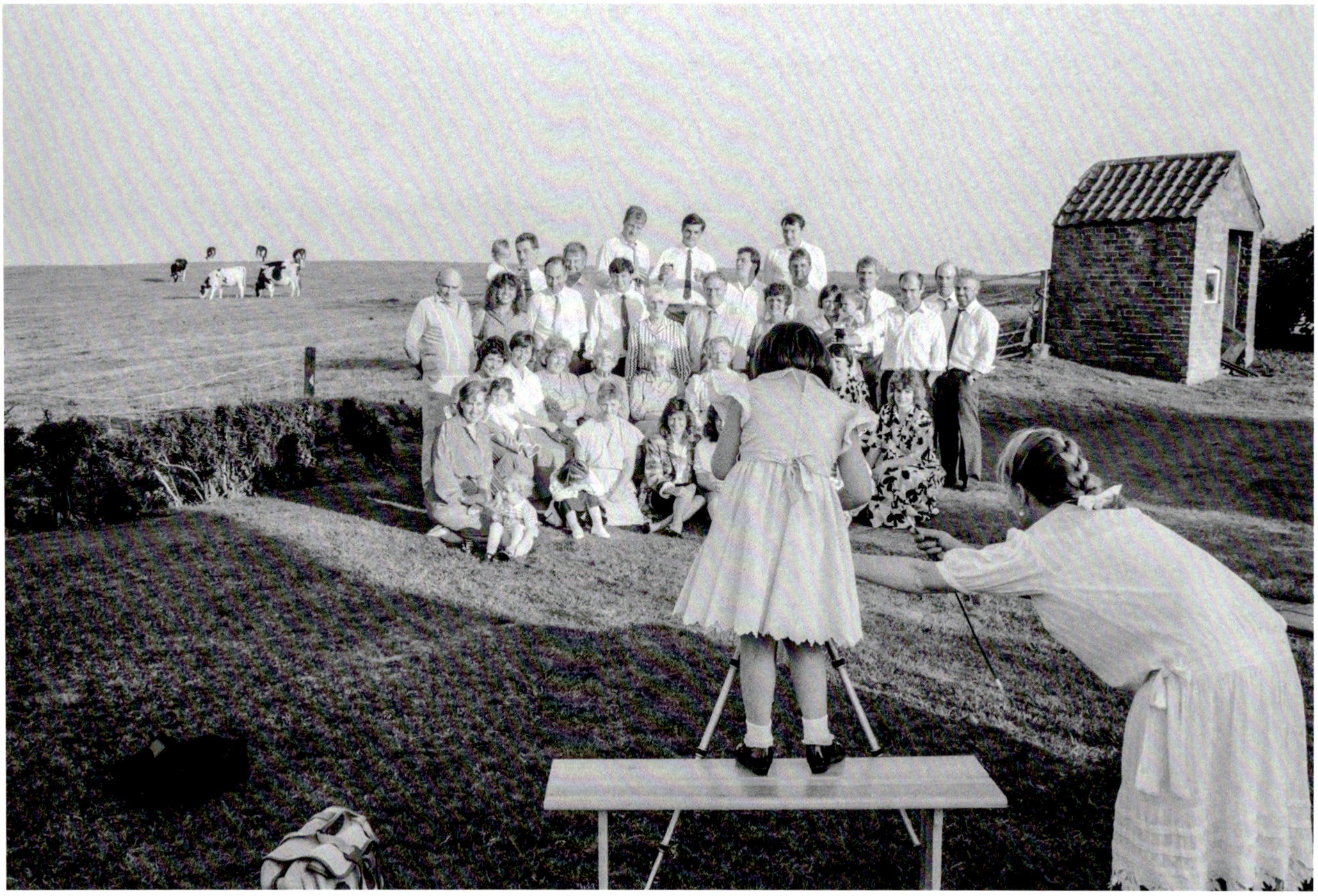

19 MAY 2019 / FAMILY PORTRAIT. *CASTLETON, WALES 1987*

A large farming family pose as one of the junior members take their photograph under the guidance of the photographer Sue Packer. This family get together at least once a year for a party (in this case for a Christening).

I have just returned home after one of my numerous trips around Wales – I have now photographed over 500 locations during my landscape project. During this last travel I came upon a lovely – small in number – wedding in a tiny village. I watched the local photographer at work. What responsibility. One hears that if there is a fire in a house, the first possession grabbed is the family and wedding albums. Surely this must mean something to those that discuss photographic theories. I have actually heard that within fire departments, if they can't find family or wedding pictures, they think of arson. I am not sure how true this is but it's a good start for thought. I suspect sometimes we get a bit too pompous about the importance of our particular genre.

@davidhurnphoto @magnumphotos #family

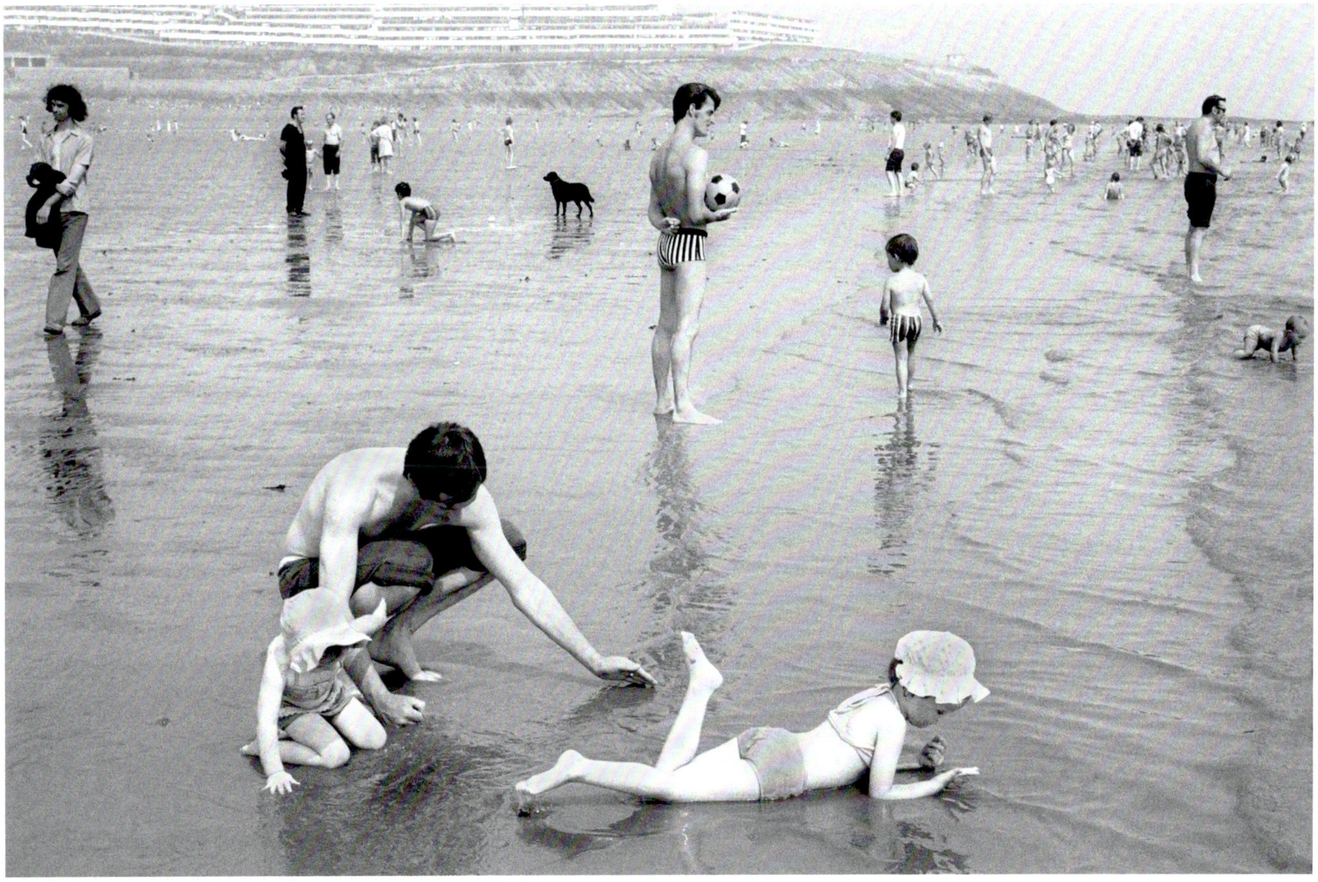

23 MAY 2019 / MINERS' HOLIDAY. *BARRY ISLAND, WALES 1973*

I have been reading a book called *Inside Photography*. Basically, it is ten interviews by David Brittain with magazine editors, published by Dewi Lewis. He is one of the true goodies involved in photography – he really has lasted the test of time.

David Brittain has been active in photography from at least the early '90s as a critic, lecturer, and one time editor of *Creative Camera* (1991-2001). He is a perceptive and articulate interviewer and has chosen editors of ten photographic magazines – sadly only one still functioning.

His choice is governed by: 'manifestations of the aspirations, fantasies and prejudices of readers, such magazines are part of the sociology of photography'. I think I can understand that.

In the past I have frequently looked at, or read, about half of the magazines. About a further 25 percent I have perused without much interest or understanding. About the final 25 percent I had not heard of. However, setting aside my particular prejudices, all interviews have one thing in common. They clearly show the passion and drive of the individual editors in question. The interviews are inspirational and tell us that with tenacity and commitment anything is possible, even though, sadly, it will probably finally fail.

I found it a very uplifting book.

@davidhurnphoto @magnumphotos @dewi_lewis_publishing #davidbrittain

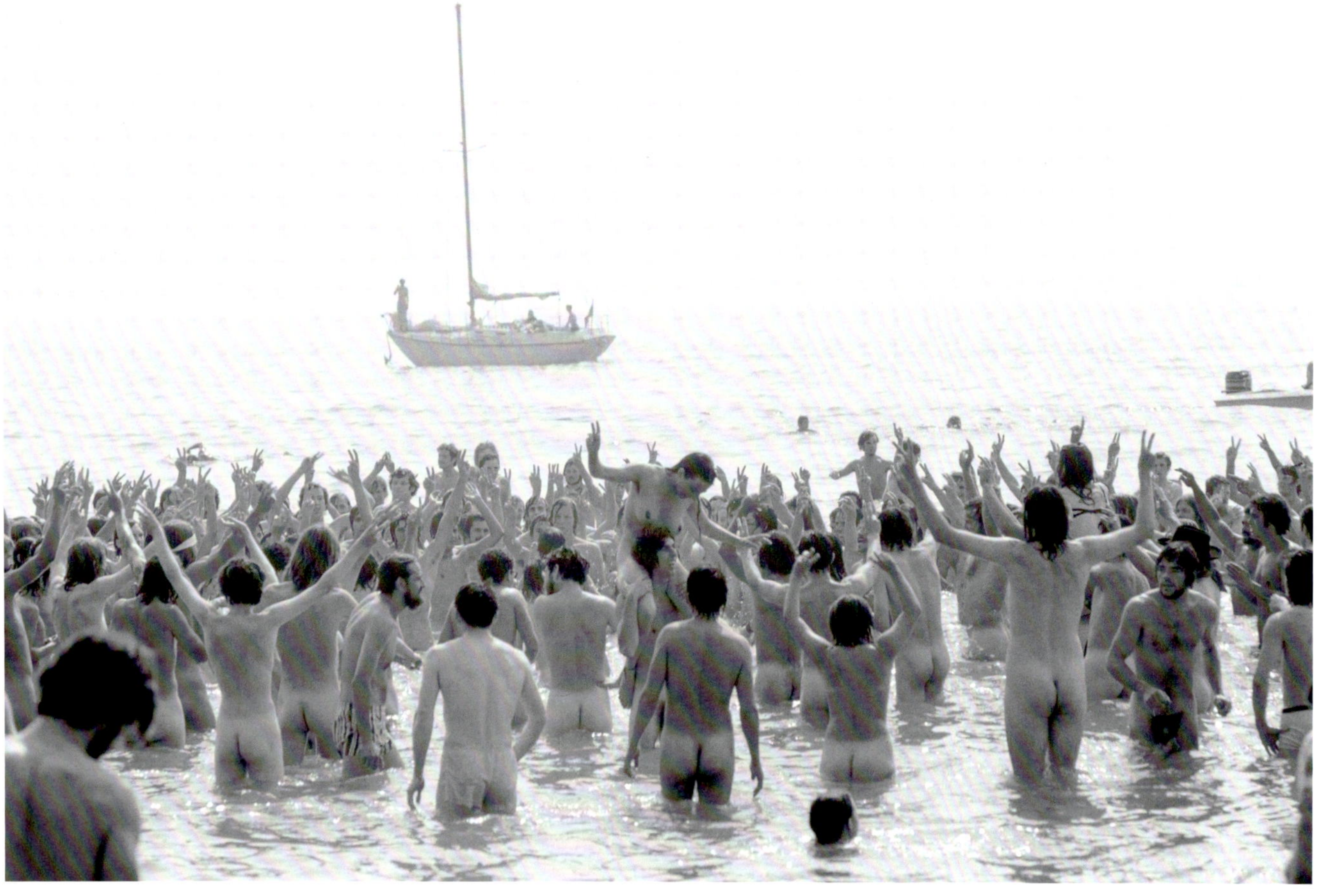

27 MAY 2019 / ISLE OF WIGHT. *ENGLAND 1969*

I have received an email from a friend, Brian Carroll of Ffoton, who had just discovered Gerry Badger's book, *The Pleasures of Good Photography* – in my opinion an essential book.

I think Gerry is one of the very best writers on photography. He has great knowledge, a point of view and writes in a language that I find pleasant to read.

In the introduction to the book Gerry writes: 'I still fundamentally believe – despite what many might say to the contrary in the furtherance of their careers – that most photographers make photographs not to illustrate theories but to make pictures.'

We all like quotes that support our personal point of view and, of course, I am no exception – other quotes by writers on photography I particularly like:

'In practice a photographer does not concern himself with philosophical issues while working; he makes photographs, working with subject matter that he thinks will make the pictures'. – John Szarkowski.

'Photographers, like kids, should be seen and not heard'. – Bill Jay.

'Philosophy can forsake too easily the details of experience . . . many writers and painters have demonstrated that thinking long about what art is or ought to be ruins the power to write or paint.' – Robert Adams

'I wanted to show the things that had to be corrected: I wanted to show the things that had to be appreciated'. – Lewis Hine.

'The photograph is authentication itself. The photograph is laborious only when it fakes. Photography never lies: or rather, it can lie as to the meaning of the thing, being by nature tendentious. Its force is nonetheless superior to everything the human mind can or can have conceived to assure us of reality. Every photograph is a certificate of presence'. – Roland Barthes

@davidhurnphoto @magnumphotos @ffotonwales @jazzyfingers #briancarroll #gerrybadger #robertadams #lewishine #billjay #johnszarkowski #rolandbarthes

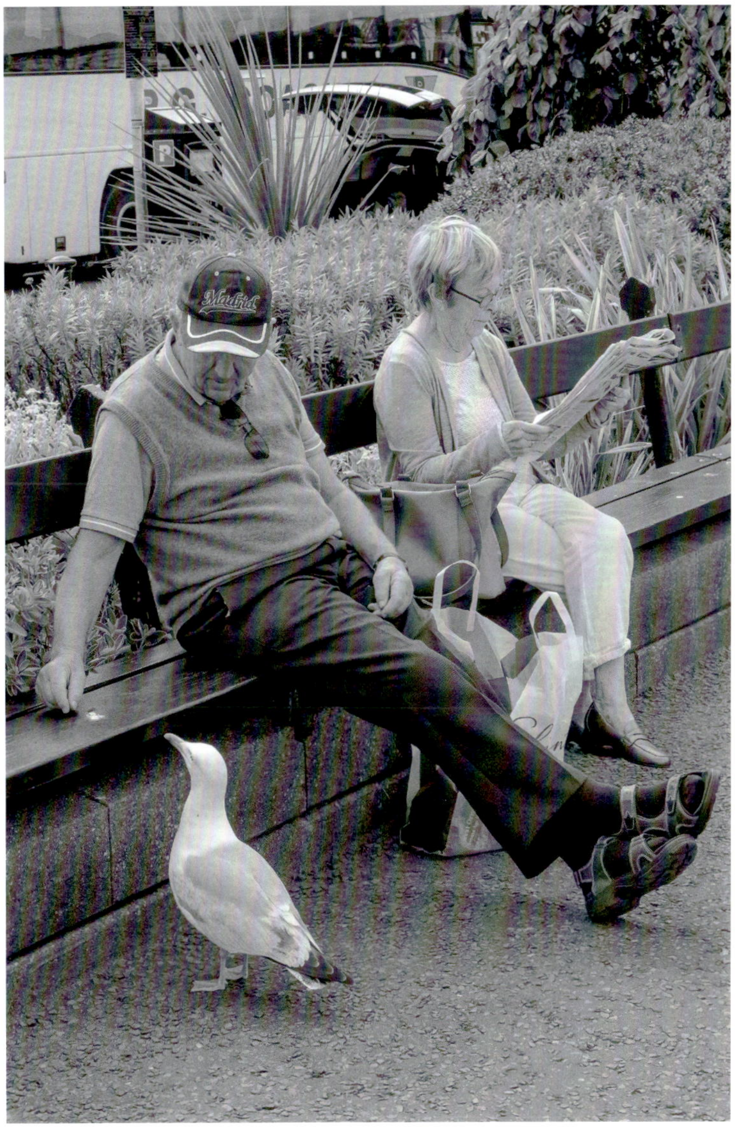

3 JULY 2019 / HOLIDAY IN LLANDUDNO. *WALES 2019*

I am sorry I have been so long not posting. I am totally bereft of any knowledge of IT and my method of dealing with the pictures went haywire.

Last weekend I was in Llandudno on my way to photograph an angle of Conway Castle that Francis Bedford had photographed in about, 1860? In what I could call spare time, I look at everyday life. I sometimes feel, 'I have seen that before'. But does it matter? Today is not yesterday and tomorrow is a totally new experience. The beauty of photography is that we are always recording something fresh if it is something we observe and think 'human'. I often remember T.S.Eliot:

'Each venture is a new beginning . . . what there is to conquer . . .
has already been discovered
Once or twice, or several times, by men whom one cannot hope
To emulate – but there is no competition –
There is only the fight to recover what has been lost
And found and lost again and again.'

@davidhurnphoto @magnumphotos

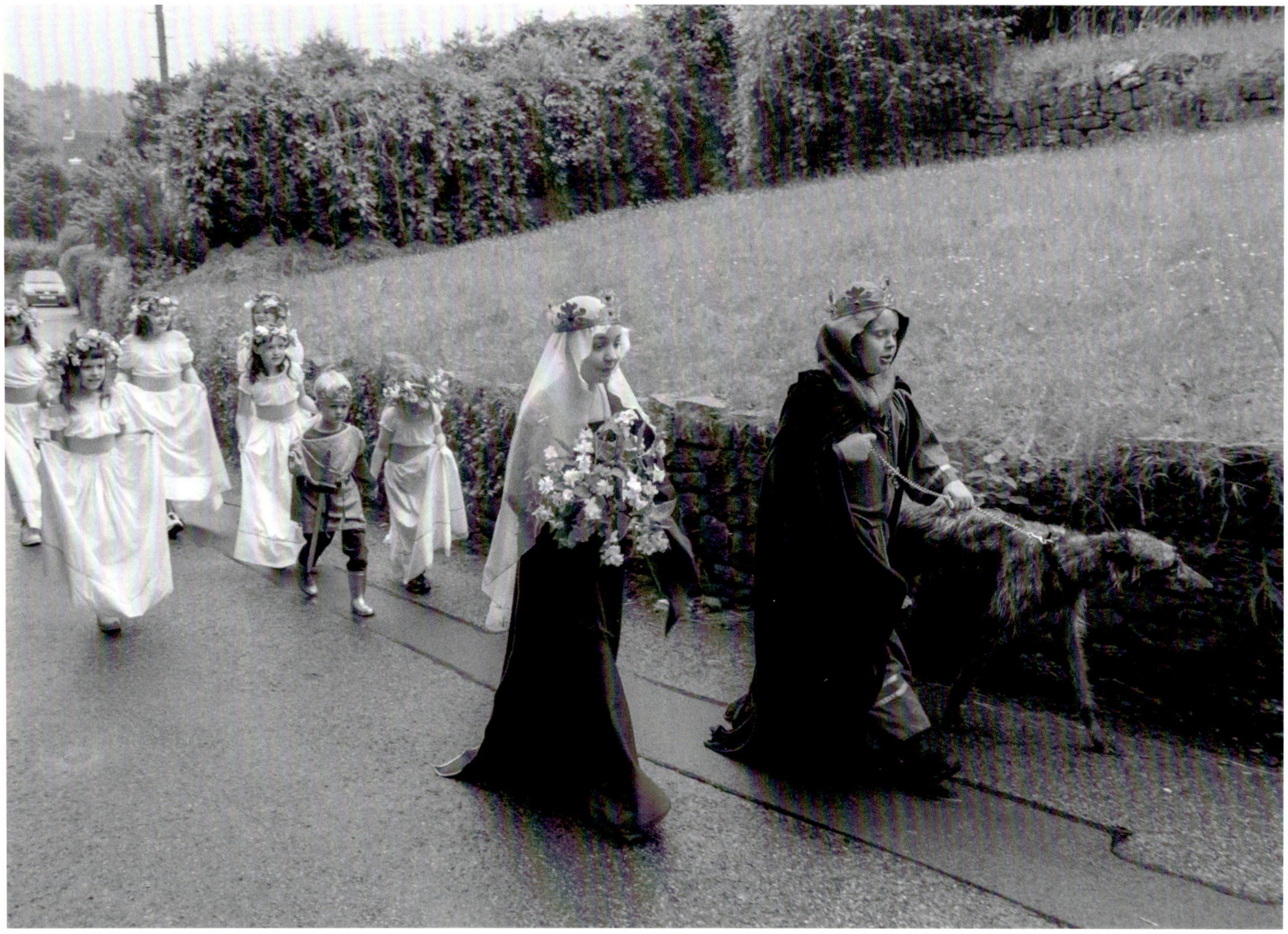

8 JULY 2019 / TINTERN CARNIVAL. *TINTERN, WALES 2002*

My village is jumping with activities during the summer. The fete was difficult because of road closures but the public are resourceful and the day was well attended. For children it's a time of make-believe.

'The subject matter . . . is not that collection of solid, static objects extended in space but the life that is lived in the scene that it composes; and so reality is not that external scene but the life that is lived in it. Reality is things as they are.'
– Wallace Stevens

@davidhurnphoto @magnumphotos #tintern #wales #wallacestevens

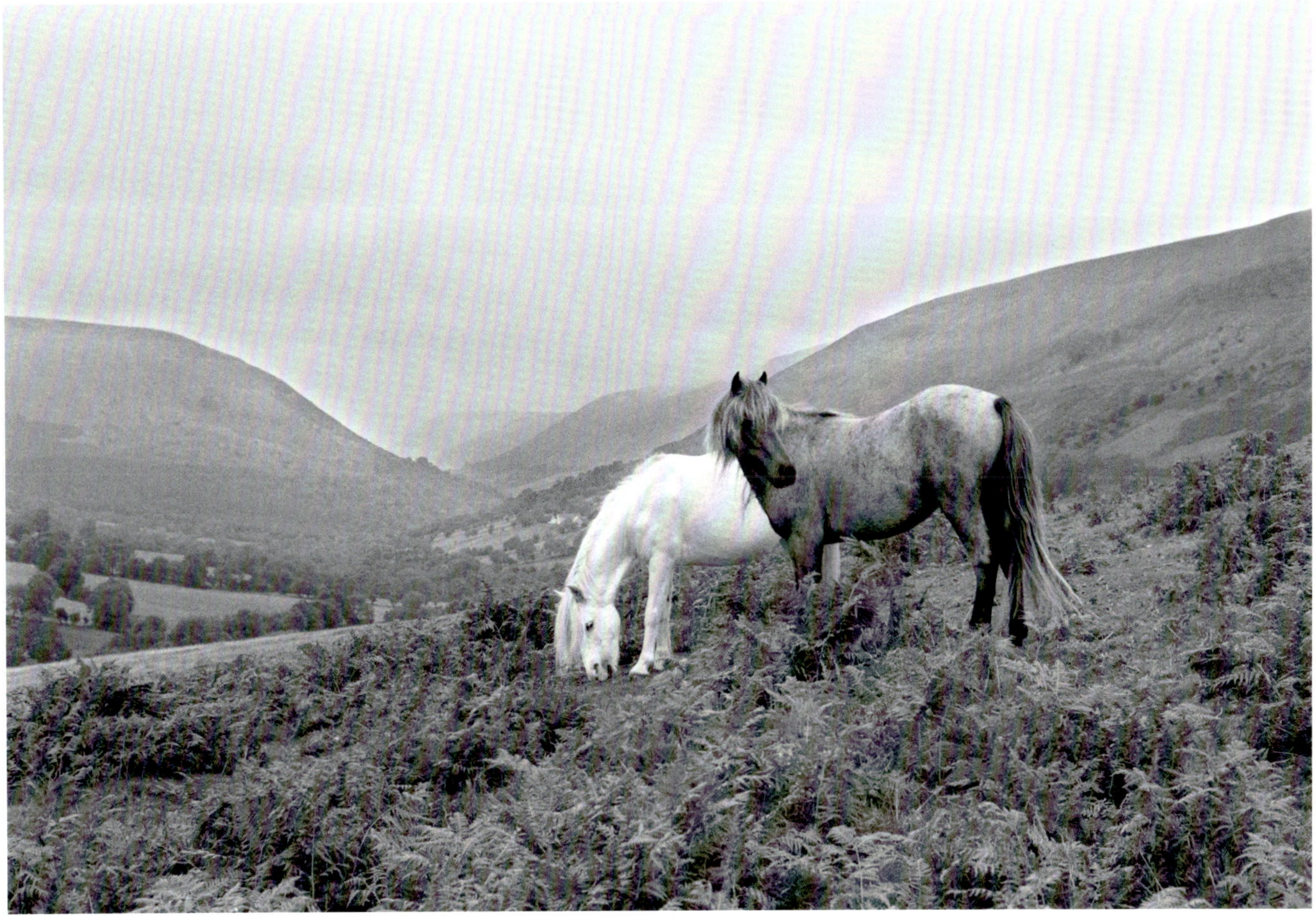

11 JULY 2019 / WILD PONIES, BLACK MOUNTAINS. *WALES 1987*

I was browsing eBay when I came upon *Planet* No 65 Oct/Nov 1987. It was an issue of the *Welsh Internationalist* in which I had two pictures, they both went with an article by Raymond Williams who was writing about 'People of the Black Mountains'; sadly, I believe it was one of the last articles he wrote before he died.

Raymond Williams and Stuart Hall were major influences on how I thought about the meaning of 'culture', a fixation of mine through many a year. I sometimes find writers writings difficult to comprehend but luckily in conversation they are always clear. The convention in conversation, and I hope photography, is to tell the truth in a language the listener can understand, otherwise no communication has any meaning.

@davidhurnphoto @magnumphotos #raymondwilliams #stuarthall #wales

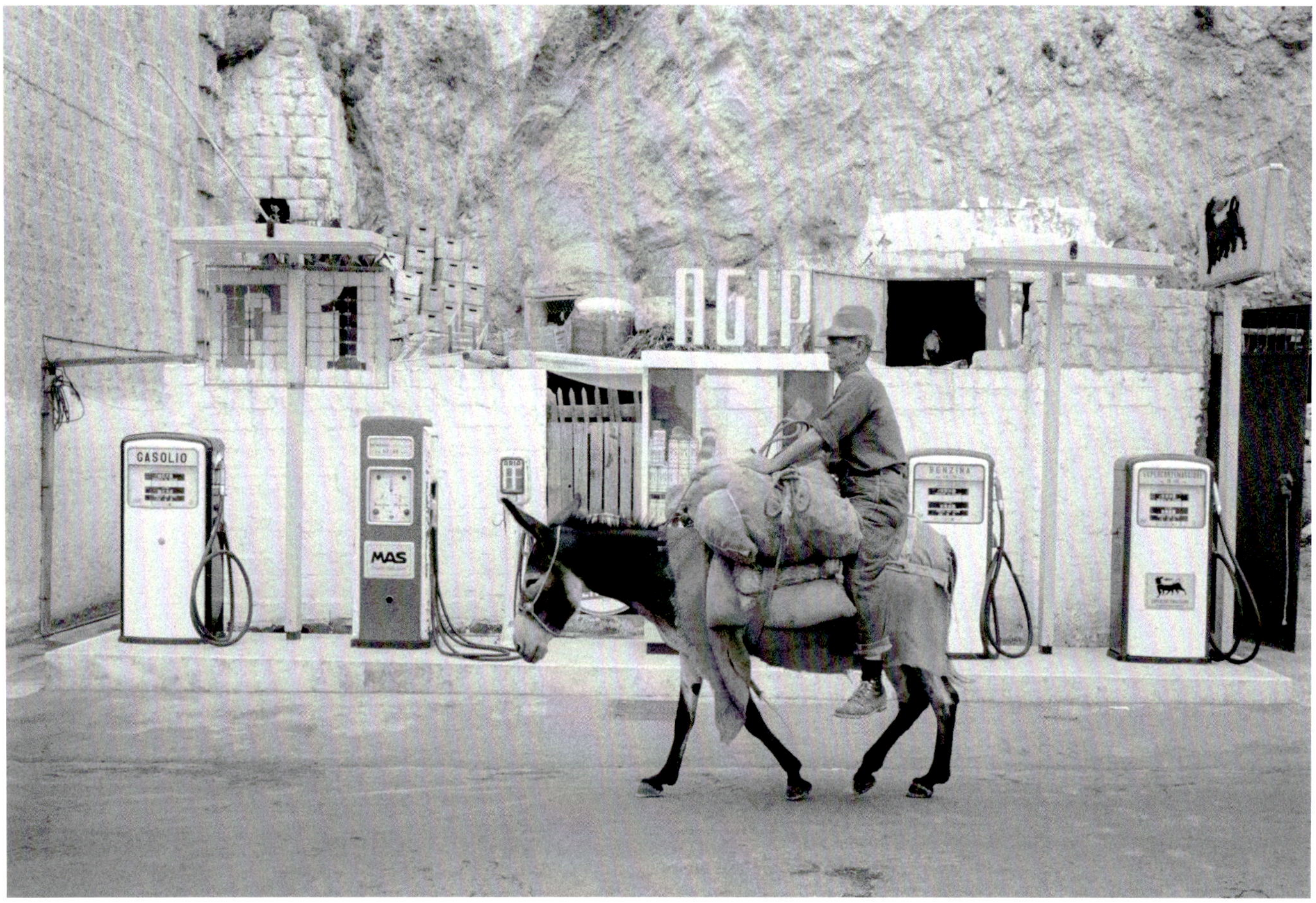

14 JULY 2019 / POLLUTION PROTEST. *PONZA, ITALY 1964*

It's no secret that I am not a fan of academic writings as a help for potential photographers to take better pictures. By academic I really mean the kind of writing that has become exceedingly odd: full of fine distinctions, full of seldom used words and opaque language. For me, the most constructive writing for photographers is not necessarily directly about photography. I suspect all the arts have an enormous amount in common thus, for me, Geoff Dyer, primarily a novelist, writes wonderfully about photography. Read Robert Adams, free of academic jargon, a fine photographer and one-time teacher of English at Colorado College, and Gerry Badger, once an architect. I have often championed Philip Pullman's *Daemon Voices* and John Carey, *What Good are the Arts*, both full of pointers.

I have just found *The Penguin Book of Art Writing*, 573 pages of enlightening writing – the opening essay is photographer Brassaï describing photographing Pierre Bonnard – but only being allowed to photograph from behind. Wonderful.

@davidhurnphoto @magnumphotos #gerrybadger #robertadams #johncarey #philippullman

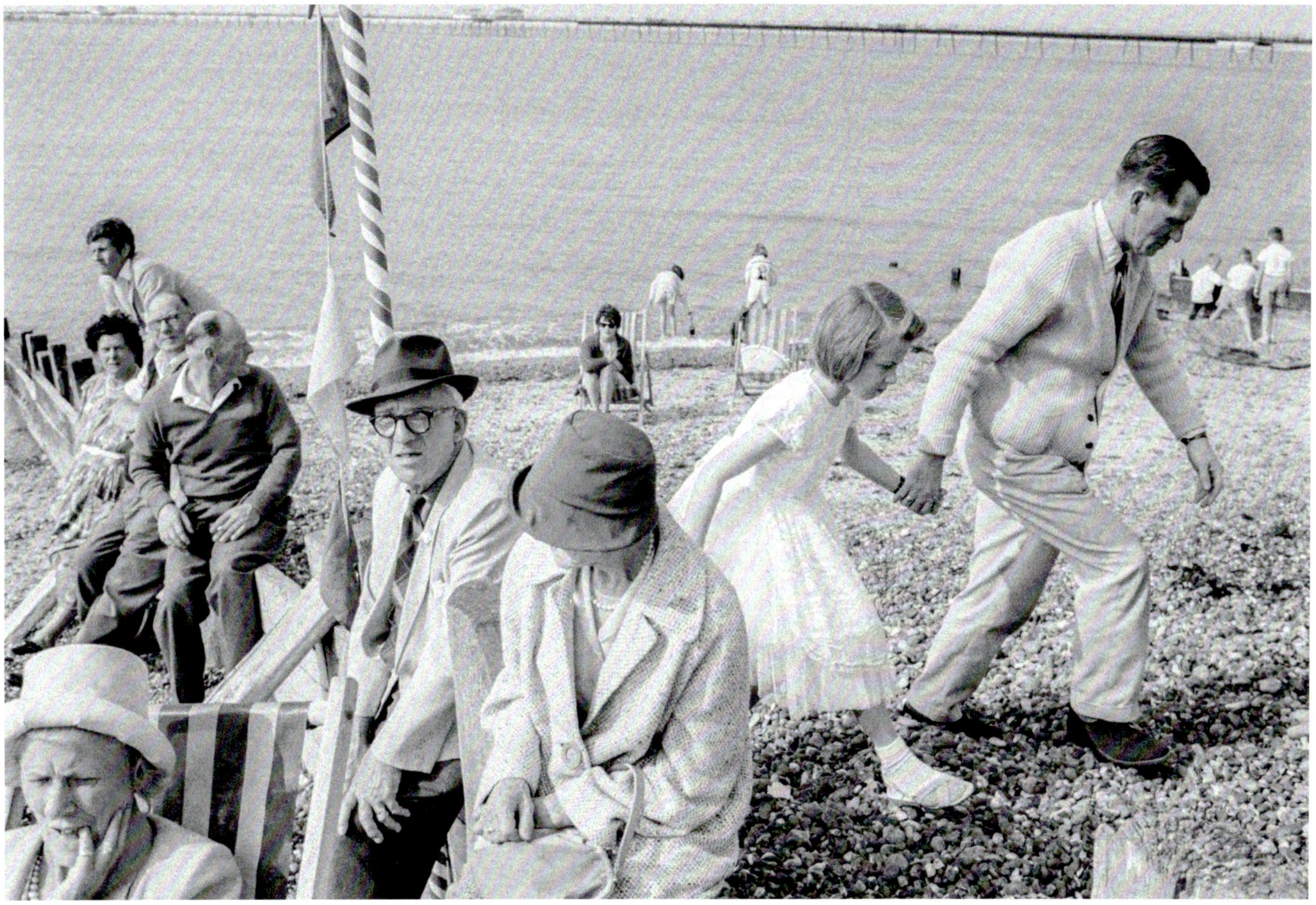

28 JULY 2019 / HEATWAVE. *HERNE BAY, ENGLAND 1960*

I was reading Bill Jay on the joy of getting new books in the '60s. Very few were published so most of us bought every one that came out. We treasured *Observations*, Richard Avedon; *The Americans*, Robert Frank; *Moments Preserved*, Irving Penn; *A Way of Seeing*, Helen Levitt; *Shadow of Light*, Bill Brandt; *Sunset Strip*, Ed Ruscha. I could go on. Every book is still being browsed over 50 years later.

Nowadays, there seems a vogue to publish one's own book. This seems to me a good or bad thing depending on motive. If its purpose is to show friends and boost one's ego then why not, but self-publishing can give you problems. Embryo photographers sometimes study on courses for three years but seem to forget that designers also study for the same amount of time, I presume writers the same. My advice is to sort out at least one designer and one writer you really like and work with them, not by oneself.

The trouble with books is that people who understand them immediately understand when the book is weak, but that weak book is going to be around for a long time, if it's ISBN-numbered, then forever. More and more people are going to be seeing a bad book. It diminishes your reputation and you can't unpublish it.

My advice is, make your book when you feel it has the merit to still be interesting in 50 years' time. If you have doubts, wait.

@davidhurnphoto @magnumphotos #hernebay

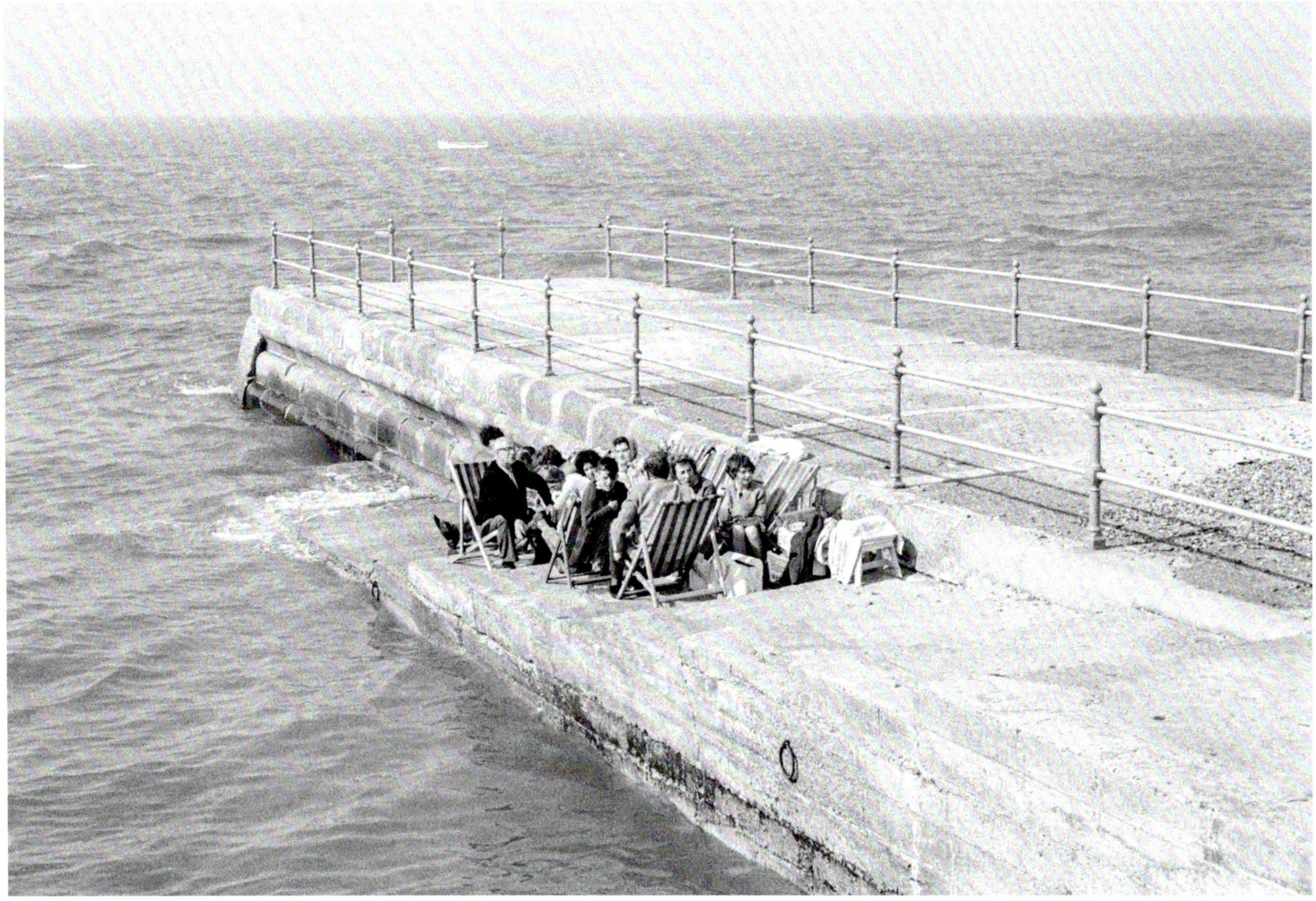

2 AUGUST 2019 / KEEPING IN COMFORT ZONE. *HERNE BAY, ENGLAND 1963*

I am frequently asked, how can I get myself a steady income, maybe small, but hopefully expanding?

My advice, look at your pictures, then invent yourself as the fantasy editor of any type of publication you can think of and ask the question of yourself: 'would I wish to publish this picture?'. If the answer is yes, then put the picture in a stock agency archive. I often hear 'they don't pay much' – well, they pay more than if the picture is not in the archive. I know more than a few photographers who make the major part of their income out of one archive or another. When you become very successful you can always transfer the pictures elsewhere. All archives have rules and for these to work you need to shoot a lot of pictures and caption them accurately – I suspect the lack of financial success of many is caused mainly because of not shooting enough images. If you shoot interesting and appropriate pictures there is a market somewhere.

I have heard that the Photojournalism course in Cardiff makes all students, on enrolling, immediately join a stock agency. Sounds sensible to me.

@davidhurnphoto @magnumphotos #hernebay

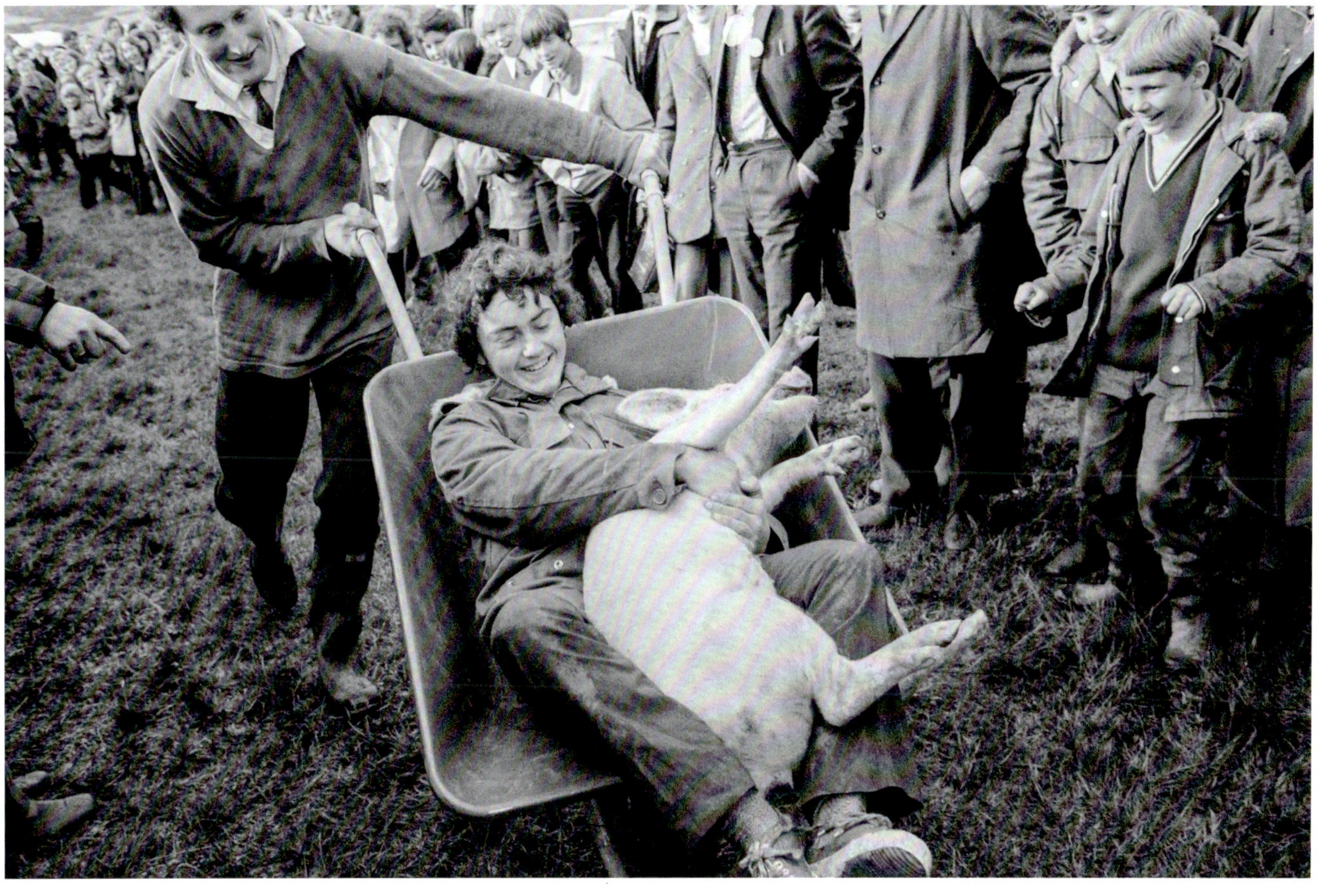

10 AUGUST 2019 / YOUNG FARMERS, *BRECON, WALES 1973*

Are cameras becoming too good? 'Crazy sharp' as Kertész once told me, and that was 40 years ago.

I work out what I actually need by thinking backwards. I have a 24-inch printer, i.e. I can produce a 24x36 inch print, so that becomes my norm largest print size. A majority of my 'living' pictures were shot on film – 50 years shooting on film, 15 years digital. I need prints from film period to match prints I now shoot. At the moment they more or less do so, if I have an exhibition I hope I am not worrying about obvious differences in appearance. However, every so often, I have no idea why, I get a file that produces prints so sharp, so smooth, that they become a problem. I certainly do not need more pixels in the future. And why so many potential adjustments built into the latest cameras? I was brought up in the age of Leica, Rolleiflex, Hasselblad etc, boxes with a hole in their front. Make the hole larger or smaller, let the light in for longer or shorter. I am sure most of the other stuff is better done outside the camera in far more sophisticated software.

@davidhurnphoto @magnumphotos #brecon #wales

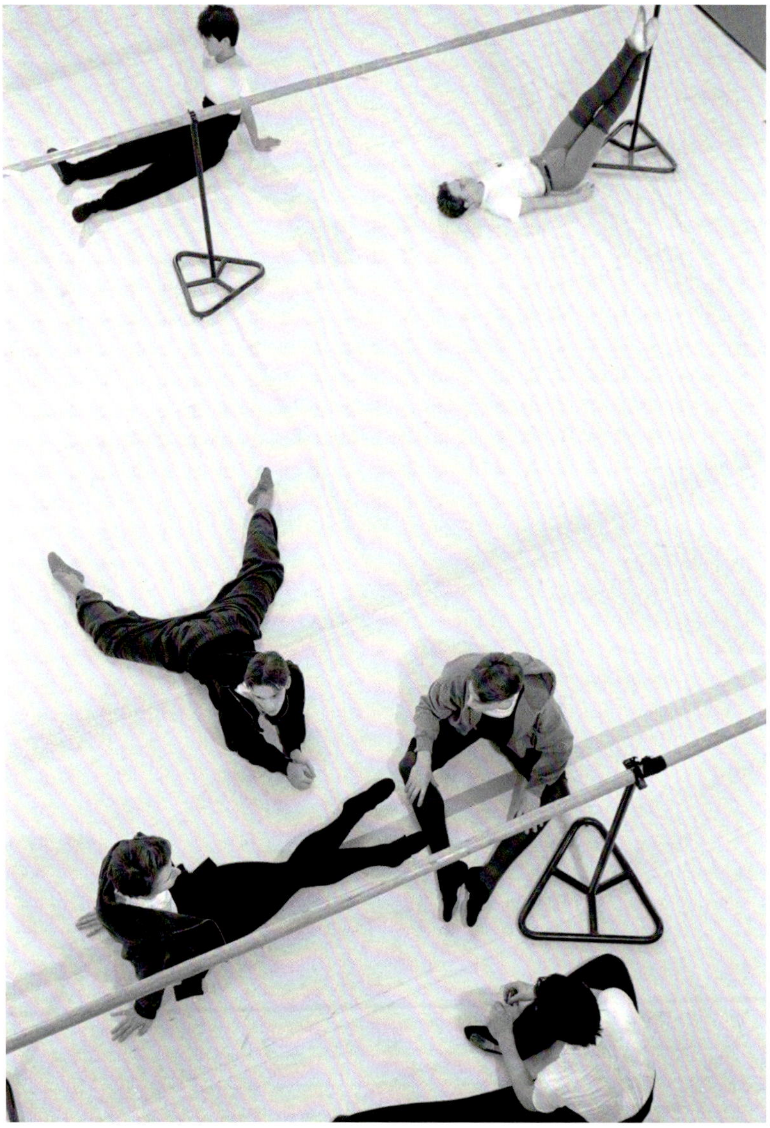

27 AUGUST 2019 / BALLET SCHOOL. *LUCERNE, SWITZERLAND 1991*

Recently I was corralled by a group of students who recognised me on one of my trips. We had coffee. Surprising to me, major questioning was about new travel needs. One of them had the book I had done with Bill Jay, *On Being a Photographer*, so I used the chapter on 'other essentials' as a reference as to what might have changed since 1995.

Nowadays I am older and weaker. Sight not so good. Hearing dodgy. I always travel with only carry-on baggage so the first requisite is a bag as near to the latest regulation maximum size as possible. My first essential is now a spare pair of spectacles – I have never had to use them but I am paranoid about not being able to see. I carry the smallest light computer, primarily to break up the evening loneliness by downloading the day's shoot and captioning the same evening. I seem to have a mass of chargers, cables etc, however, collecting advice, somehow I seem to be managing to make all this more efficient. All might seem heavier than previous but I no longer have to carry a radio, an organiser address book and up to 200 rolls of film, so I feel I have a bonus.

I always travel in a suit, a suit with pockets for passport, wallet, and iPhone – I wrote 20 years ago: 'it is better to be slightly overdressed than scruffy'. I have a pair of jeans in my case and a shirt and tie. Everything is machine washable – not that I machine wash on a trip but I do sponge down often. Pants, vests, socks now can all be washed overnight. I seem to have a lot of pills but they don't take up much room. My main indulgence is an extremely expensive raincoat, very light and long, down to my calves, I hate having trousers wet.

For me, very important, is a paperback book – I find it unrewarding to read off a screen.

And, of course, most important of all, 'good shoes'.

@davidhurnphoto @magnumphotos #switzerland

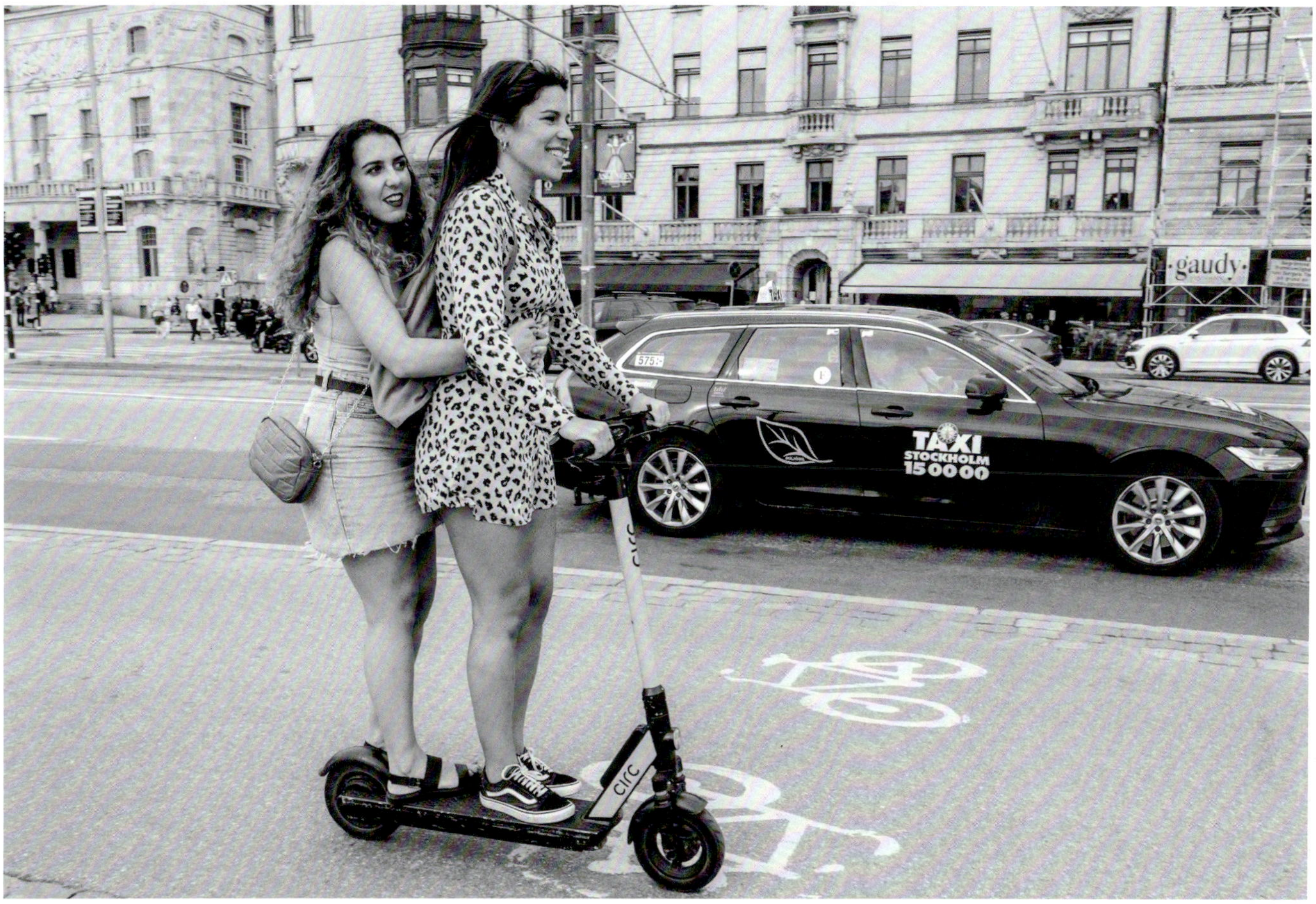

2 SEPTEMBER 2019 / STOCKHOLM TRANSPORT. *SWEDEN 2019*

I am not one who likes superlatives. I even hesitate at the dangers of the word 'good', certainly of the words, 'the best'. But I will break a habit. I timed my visit to Stockholm to catch the last days of Anders Petersen's photographic exhibition at the Liljevalchs Konsthall, he is given the whole gallery, or rather the whole eight galleries. It is a relentless show, picture after picture I envied his having taken. For me, it would be impossible to envisage a more invigorating set of pictures.

Stockholm is one of the world's more civilised cities, I would happily drift from island to island by the frequent boats, the most enjoyable of all forms of transport.

I also saw Castro's crocodiles – look them up, a lovely story.

@davidhurnphoto @magnumphotos #stockholm #castroscrocodiles #anderspetersen

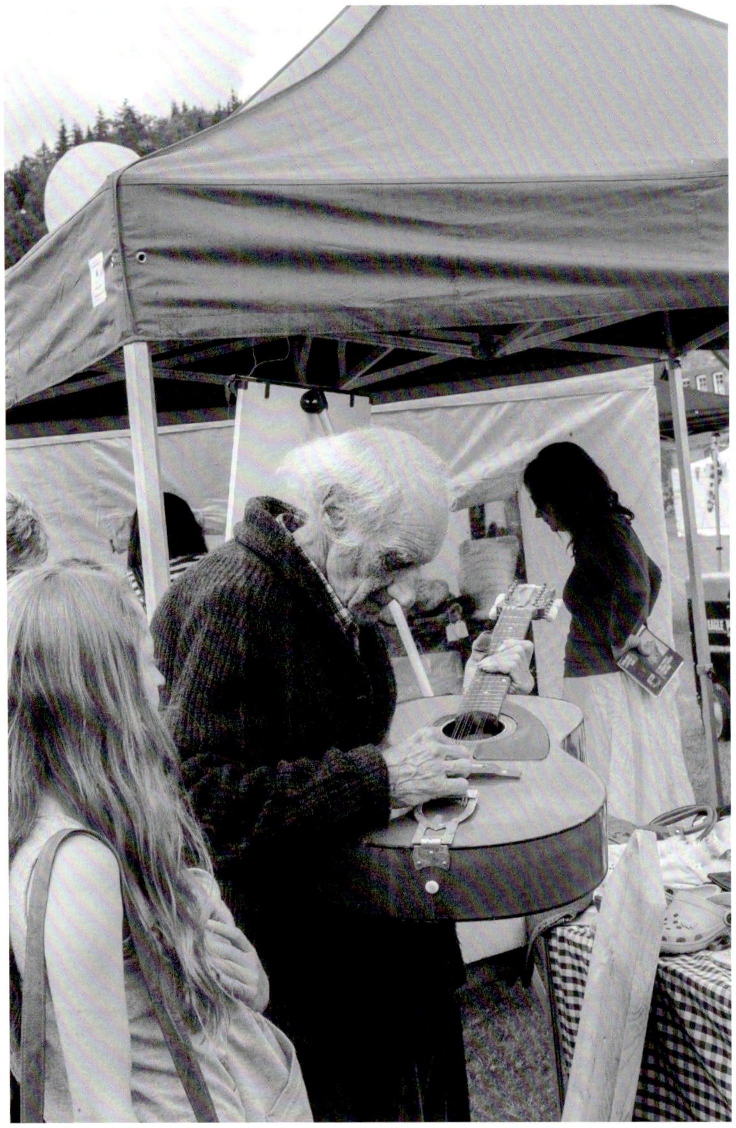

29 SEPTEMBER 2019 / MUSIC MEMORY. *TINTERN, WALES 2014*

I have just re-seen a photograph I took at a local 'bring and buy' sale where clearly love and memory are taking place.

What a photograph does was previously only done by reflection.

Before the camera we just had memory, now the photograph becomes a powerful nudge to memory.

No painting, sculpture or music has the connection to its subject that a photograph has. The photograph is not only an interpretation but a trace, like a footprint in the snow.

Perhaps one definition of a good photograph is that it evokes poignant memories.

@davidhurnphoto @magnumphotos #tintern #wales

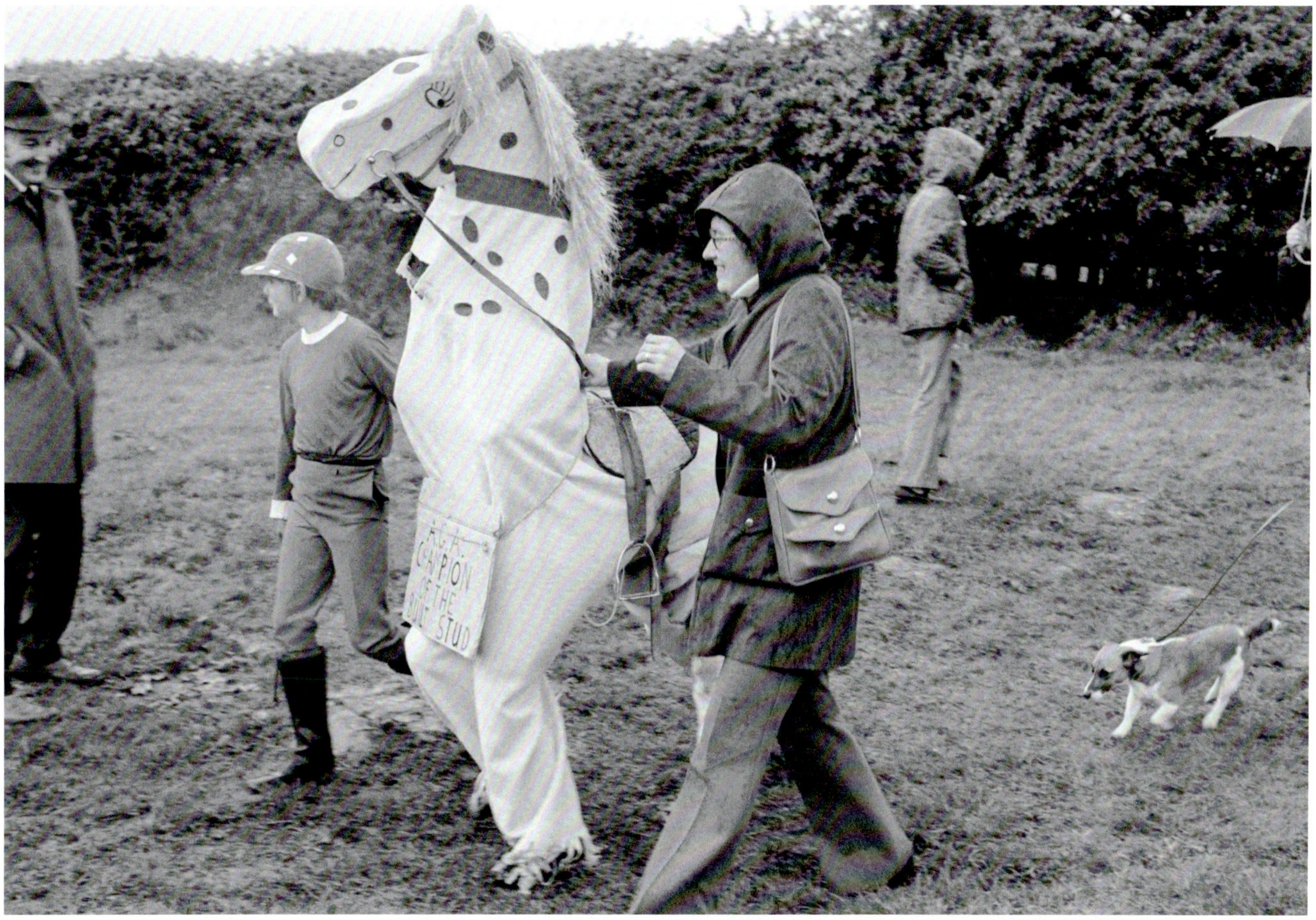

5 OCTOBER 2019 / CHAMPION 1973. *BRECON, WALES 1973*

A few days ago I was enjoying *Thinking 3D*, an exhibition including many Leonardo da Vinci drawings and books. It was in the Bodleian Library, Oxford, home of over 12 million items, including the Magna Carta, Gutenberg Bible, first folio Shakespeare, Fox Talbot's *Pencil of Nature* – a major place.

Three yards away, in the same hall, was another exhibition in a slightly larger space. It was an exhibition of photographs from an archive acquired – in my opinion with great foresight – by the Bodleian. The acquisition will raise the stature of photography in this country immensely.

The archive, and the pictures on show, were by the documentarist Daniel Meadows, the most modest of men, a man with a total lack of ego. His brief chat to the very full audience was all about others and directed to his subject matter, mostly people, a surprising number of whom were at the opening. They had flown in from Russia, New Zealand, and, of course, travelled from many parts of the UK. It was photography, and the use of photography at its very best.

As one of the subjects, I believe 'Neville', photographed in 1972, said: 'Wow, I'm with the Magna Carta'.

@davidhurnphoto @magnumphotos @danielmeadowsphoto #bodleianlibrary

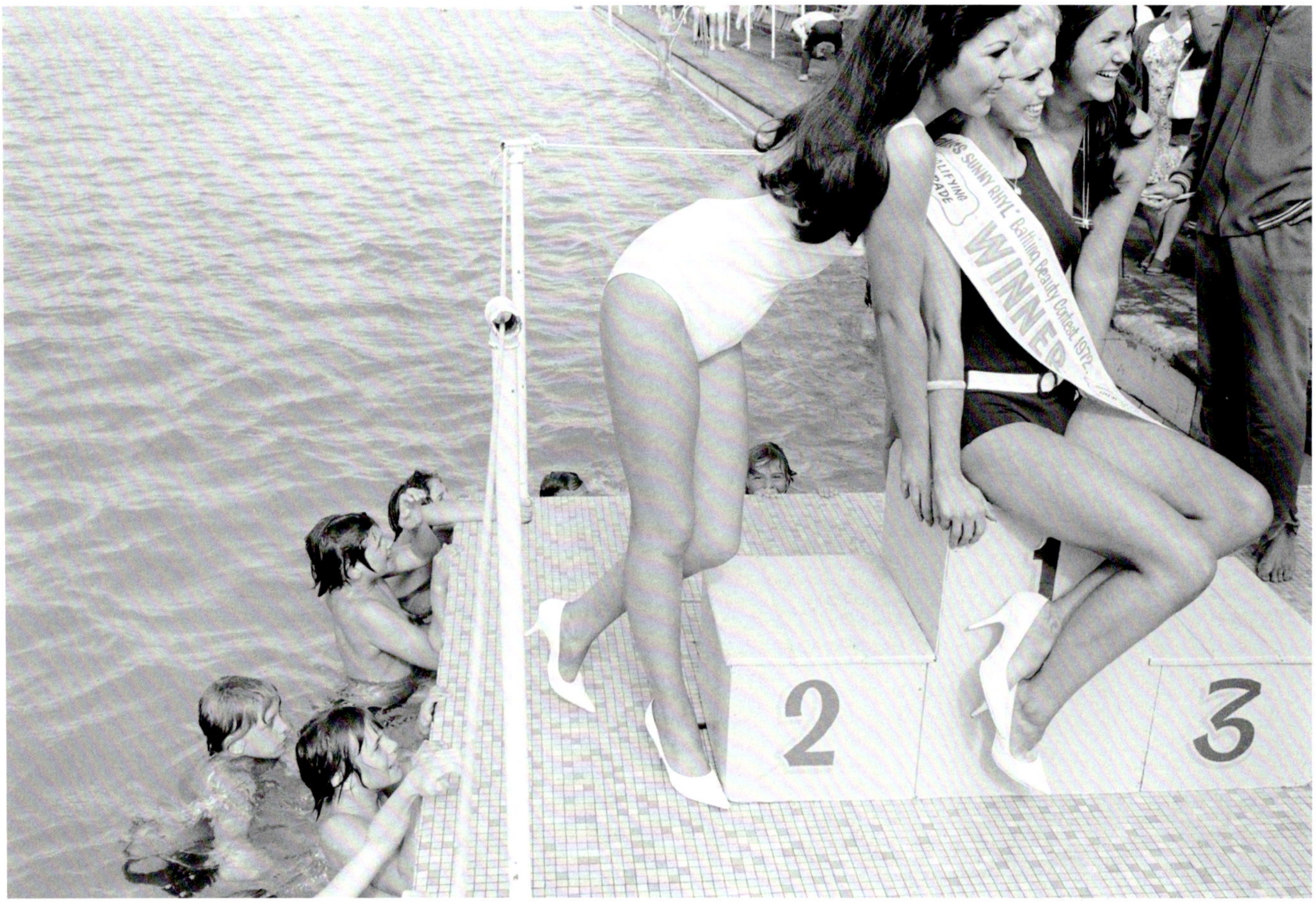

14 OCTOBER 2019 / MISS SUNNY RHYL. *RHYL, WALES 1972*

Sadly, I missed the first morning of the Northern Eye Festival. I had actually arrived in Colwyn Bay a few days early to hopefully shoot some pictures but was struck by a reoccurring illness and spent two and a half days in my hotel bed.

What do I look for in a festival?

Basically three essentials: a sense of community of similar interests; quality lectures broad in scope; exhibitions.

Maybe surprisingly, exhibitions are bottom of my list. Books are now of such high print quality that I don't gain much from seeing the originals, and with books I have the pleasure of time to browse, think, and re-look. Of course, exhibitions are important for many – particularly the exhibitors – it's just that if I have to miss out on something then it will be the exhibitions.

I tend to live in a bit of a bubble so I really enjoy the lectures as they allow me to make genuine assessment of persons I have often not heard of. For me the broader the scope, the better. Irritation is good for one. Often individual lecturers surprise me and I find gems of information I can steal from.

Most of all I love the ease of getting together. In Colwyn Bay it seemed particularly easy. Most met in the same cafe for breakfast. On the first night at least 40 had a meal together in the local Indian restaurant. It was easy to mix, easy to talk.

John Bulmer, that wonderful and extremely experienced photographer, was so very generous with his time and seemed to be continually in conversation with one person or another.

Wonderful.

@davidhurnphoto @magnumphotos @johnfbulmer #northerneyefestival

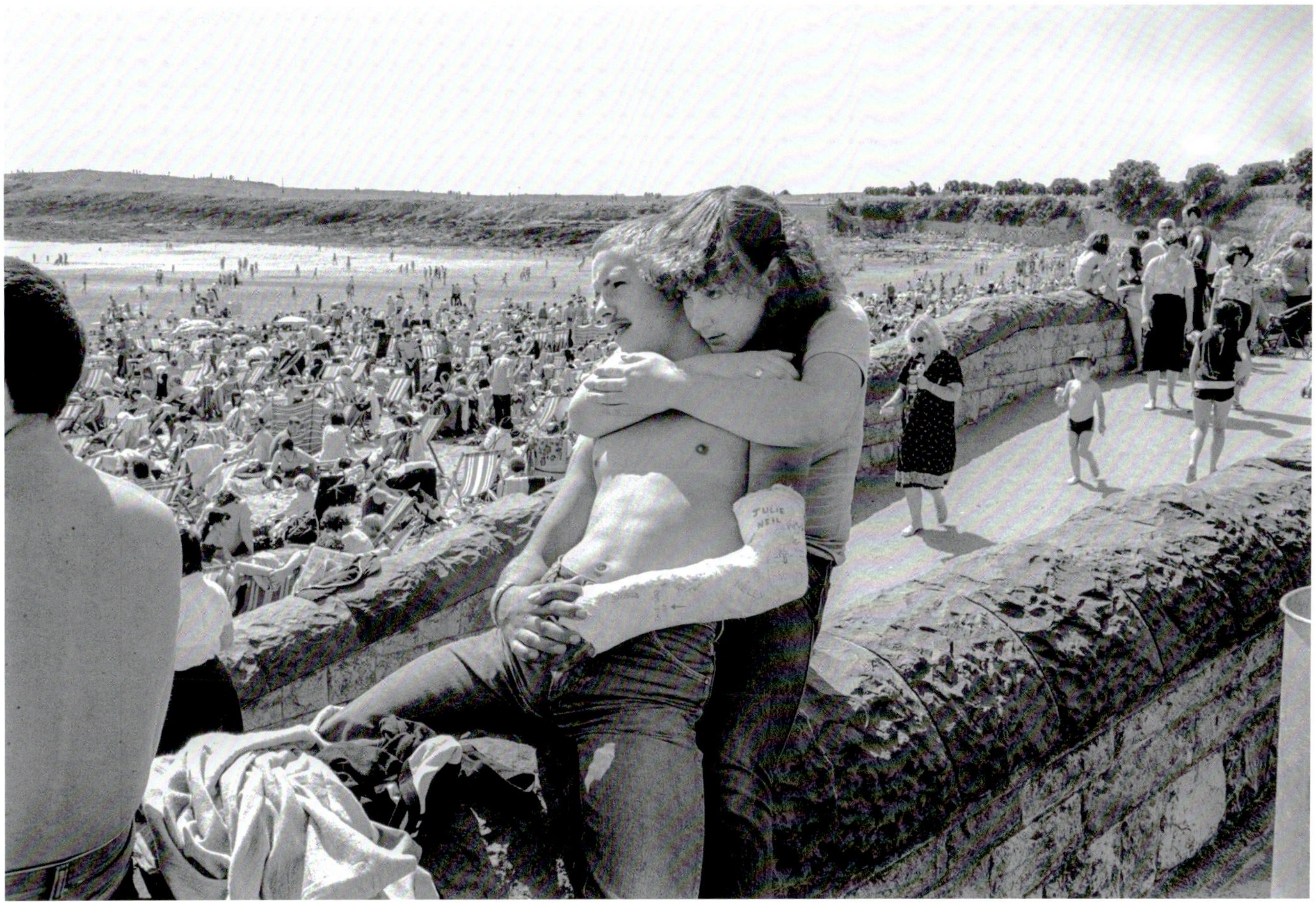

17 OCTOBER 2019 / *BARRY ISLAND, WALES 1981*

Last night at the MPF was an enjoyable party launch for another book/exhibition of Tony Ray-Jones pictures. The party was very well attended. The book was excellent as are all of Rudi Thoemmes' books. The exhibition had some surprises. I had only ever seen small Tony prints, here most of the prints were printed comparatively large – it worked well.

Tony sadly died at a very early age, 32. We can only speculate how interesting a photographer he might have remained.

He joined in the great British tradition of photographing the 'seaside', an obvious tradition being as we are an island. In a way, the photography tradition started with John Dillwyn Llewelyn whose first picture was in 1840, his family lived by the sea and he mainly photographed his family. My favourite group of pictures are by Paul Martin, photographed in 1892 and now published as a small book/catalogue, *A Yarmouth Holiday,* with an informative text by Mark Haworth-Booth. A collection of photographs by Francis Frith, *Victorian Seaside*, visits 68 seaside resorts.

British customs are particularly British, there are a mass of books doing your research for you, a good starting point. Two compelling visual books are by Sir Benjamin Stone, a member of Parliament, *Festivals, Ceremonies and Customs*, customs photographed primarily as participant groups, and a more modern selection is by Homer Sykes in his *Once a Year: Some Traditional British Customs*, a book that should be in everyone's library.

@davidhurnphoto @magnumphotos @martinparrfdn @homer.sykes @markhaworthbooth @rudi_thoemmes_rare_books #northerneyefestival #tonyrayjones #homersykes #francisfrith #paulmartin

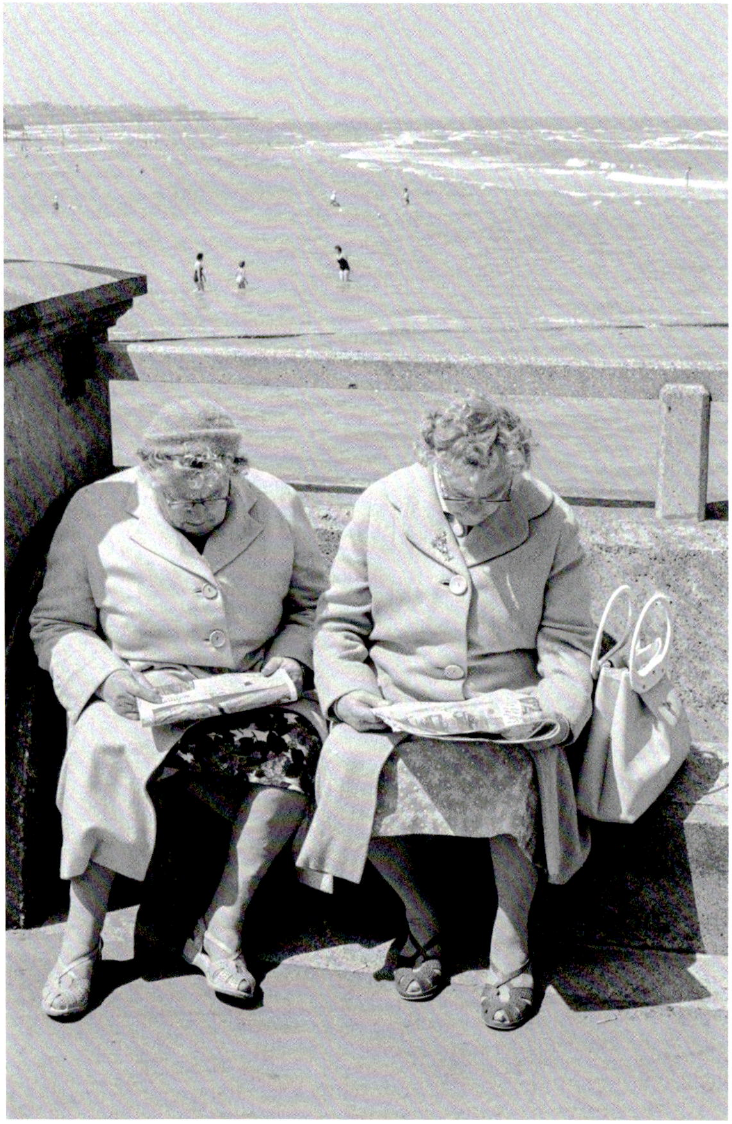

20 OCTOBER 2019 / *HERNE BAY, ENGLAND 1963*

I enjoy arguing with myself. It allows for controversial thoughts, clarifying muddled thoughts, and the ability to change one's mind. Knowledge of facts change thus opinions change.

I have just returned from the Photobook Festival in Bristol. My abiding memory is of amazing print quality.

If a major purpose of seeing an exhibition is to see print quality – are exhibitions really necessary anymore?

Letting this thought sink in, I will expand in my next post.

@davidhurnphoto @magnumphotos #hernebay #photobookfestival

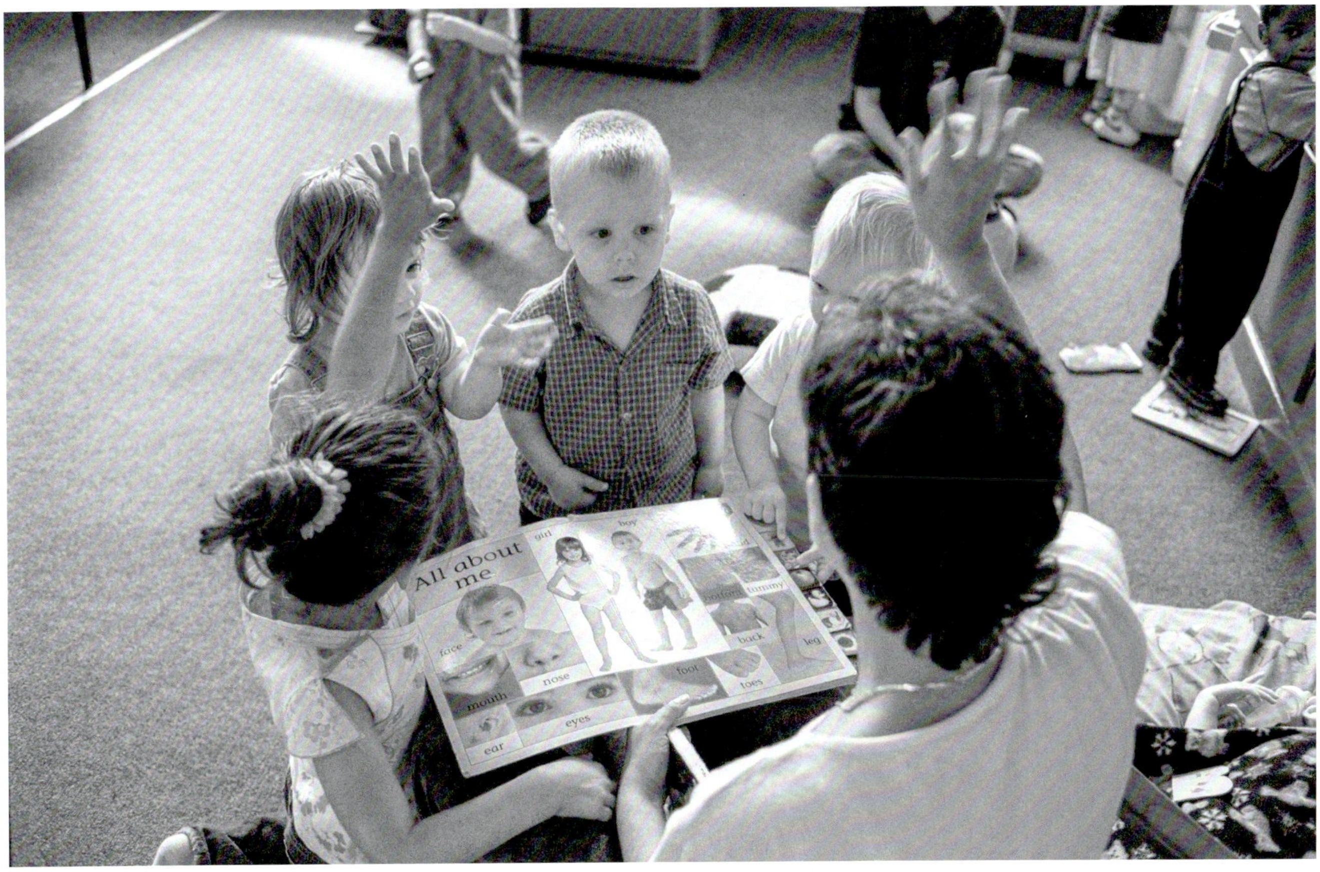

22 OCTOBER 2019 / ALL ABOUT ME. *CARDIFF, WALES 2003*

In the previous post I was, of course, not suggesting that exhibitions are totally irrelevant. They have many purposes, not the least that they give the photographer concerned some feeling of achievement. Large scale prints are becoming a norm and sometimes justified, I have read convincing explanations by both Thomas Struth and Andreas Gursky as to why they print very large. However, I can't but feel that so many large exhibition prints are large either because the photographer has few pictures or that they think somehow uninteresting pictures become interesting if they are printed large.

I think it is the memorability of individual prints that concerns me.

In the last month I have seen two massive exhibitions, each photographer I would count as a friend, and each, in my opinion, are as interesting a photographer as you can possibly get. Each exhibition was a credit to photography and undoubtedly in their own way help raise the status of photography largely because of their location, however, my overwhelming memory in both cases was 'being bombarded', the exhibitions became events, I remember few individual pictures. My enjoyment, and I expect it will be continuing enjoyment, is from the accompanying books from the exhibitions. I must have scrutinised each of these already at least 20 times. They are both on the table next to my favourite chair. I am sure in the future they will disintegrate through too much browsing. I suspect I will not re-visit either exhibition.

@davidhurnphoto @magnumphotos

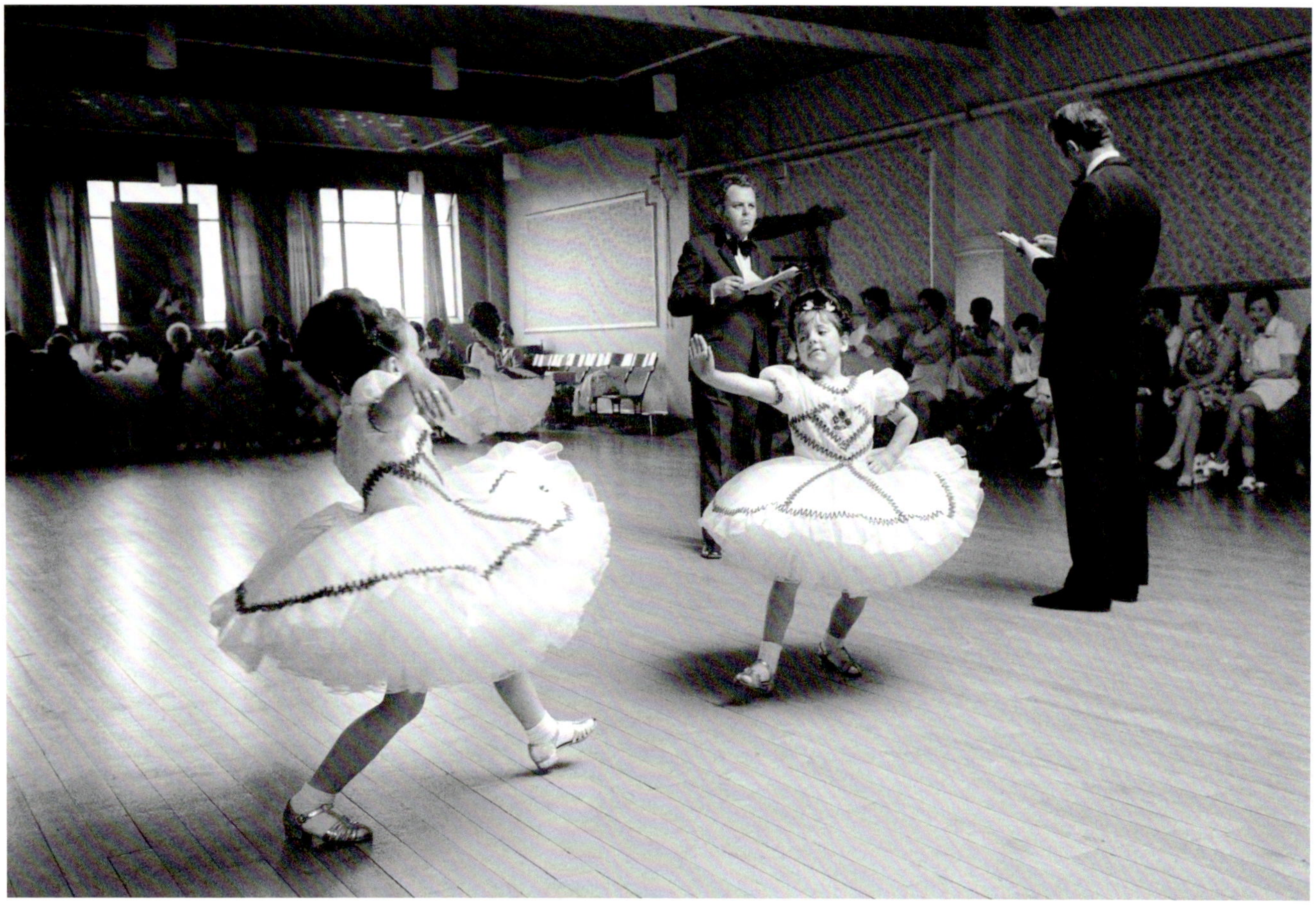

12 NOVEMBER 2019 / JUNIOR BALLROOM DANCING. *BARGOED, WALES 1973*

I apologise for not having posted for some time but I have been very tied up with a show starting on 21 November at the Workers Gallery in Ynyshir.

I enjoy working with smaller community galleries as long as there is a 'reason' for having the show in their area.

Me showing me is no longer a good reason.

However, I have shot so many pictures in Wales over the last 50 years that if I call a show '25 mile radius' I can always find 40 pictures I like shot within that area, the show thus becomes a community show relevant to visitors to the gallery. From this base one can expand more into the community – in my case shooting more up-to-date pictures of happenings taking place now, and with luck hanging fresh pictures during the run of the exhibition – one can involve the young in many ways, plus encouraging them to realise that photography is not some rarified activity out of their reach but simply a job that many of them could do and enjoy.

Showing in the gallery at the same time will be a tapestry made by ladies from the town based on a picture of a tree that I took that they liked – plus I am doing a day's portrait shoot to help raise money for the gallery, maybe 20 people, presumably mainly people from the area, all getting a signed print.

The opening will be 'tea and cakes' on 8 December, thrown in will be a discussion between myself, Dan Wood and Paul Cabuts, and virtually no speeches.

@davidhurnphoto @magnumphotos @danwoodphoto @paulcabuts #workersgallery #communityphotography #wales

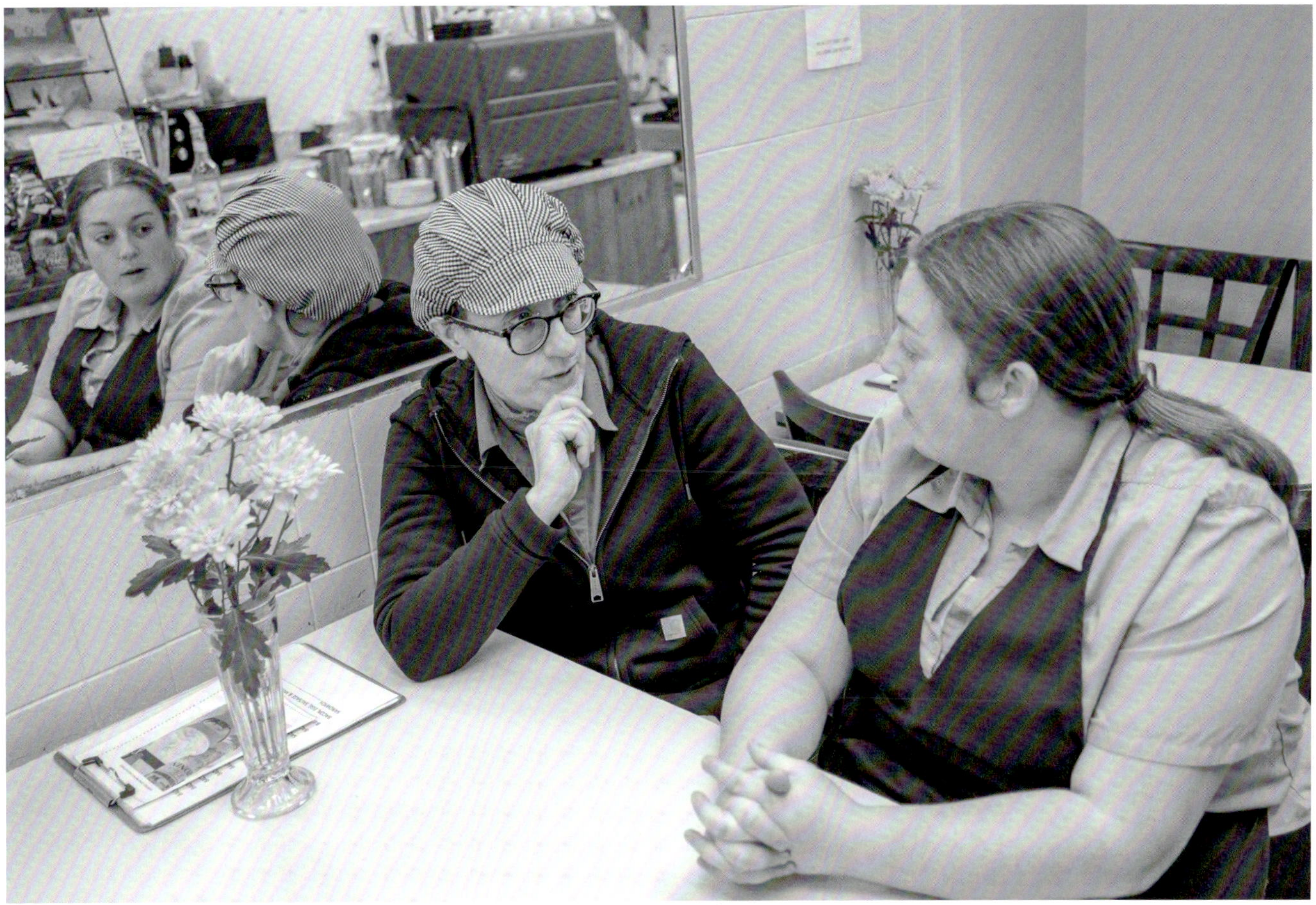

16 NOVEMBER 2019 / MARISA AND HANAH. *BARGOED, WALES 2019*

One of the delights of having curiosity is the way one thing often leads to another. I posted a picture of Junior Ballroom Dancing in Bargoed. I had a like from Marisa at the 'Rossi' cafe in Bargoed with information about where the picture had been taken – plus an invite to have tea. I was in Ynyshir at the Workers Gallery sorting final arrangements for the show there. Bargoed is just the other side of the mountain so I decided to make a visit. A lovely cafe – really excellent fresh food and real coffee, Marisa and Hanah, who were in charge, seemed to know everyone who came in. I had splendid scrambled eggs on toast. I took a quick portrait. Being a photographer is such a privilege.

@davidhurnphoto @magnumphotos #workersgallery #communityphotography #rossicafe #marisa #hanah #wales

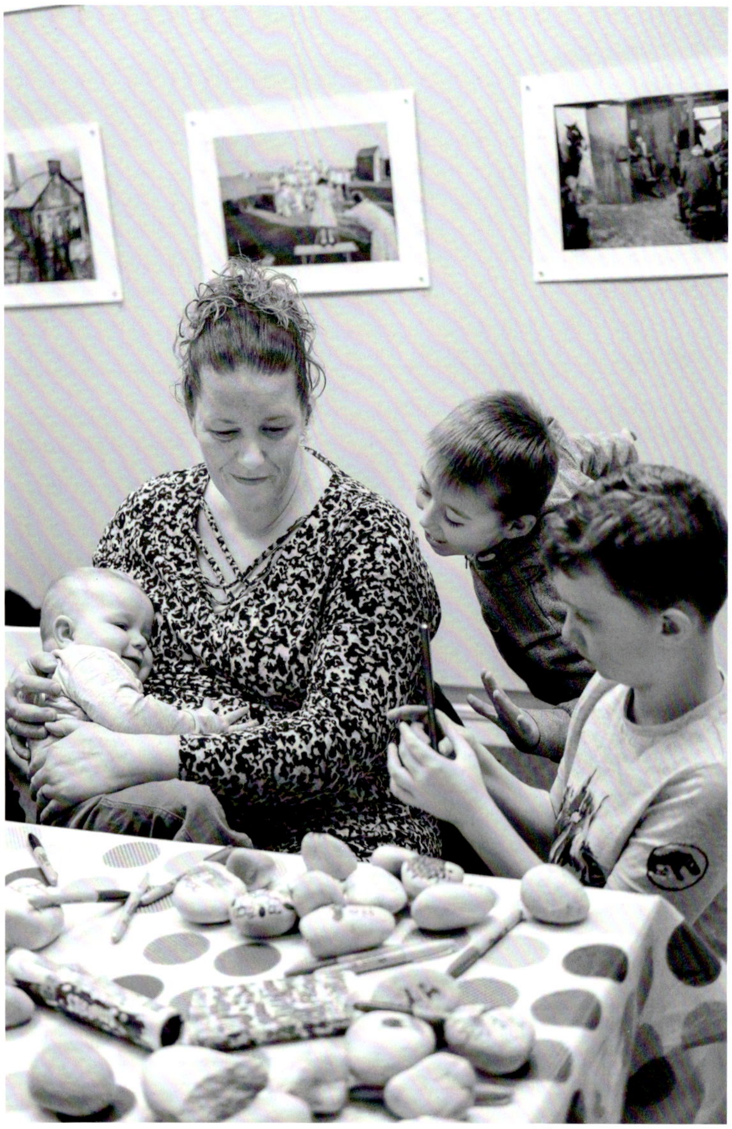

26 NOVEMBER 2019 / BUDDING PHOTOGRAPHERS. *YNYSHIR, WALES 2019*

One of the delights of having curiosity is the way one thing often leads to another. I am having a delightful time during the duration of my show at the Workers Gallery in Ynyshir. The gallery really is community based – my pictures are all taken within 25 miles of the gallery, but were mainly taken many moons ago – the pictures become the base for many other activities. We didn't really have an official opening, people just seem to continually turn up. A quilt is being sewn by one group based on a picture I took of a Yew tree, there is a day when the local school will all be taking pictures based on the idea of documenting, another group are writing on stones with comments, I will be spending a day taking portraits of locals. It's all so much fun and I enjoy the openness of everyone concerned. I am sure even more activities will emerge.

In conversation with the young and their parents, I keep emphasising that photography is a job and open to anyone, it should not be thought of as a rarified activity above anyone and it's much more fun than stacking shelves.

@davidhurnphoto @magnumphotos #workersgallery #communityphotography #wales

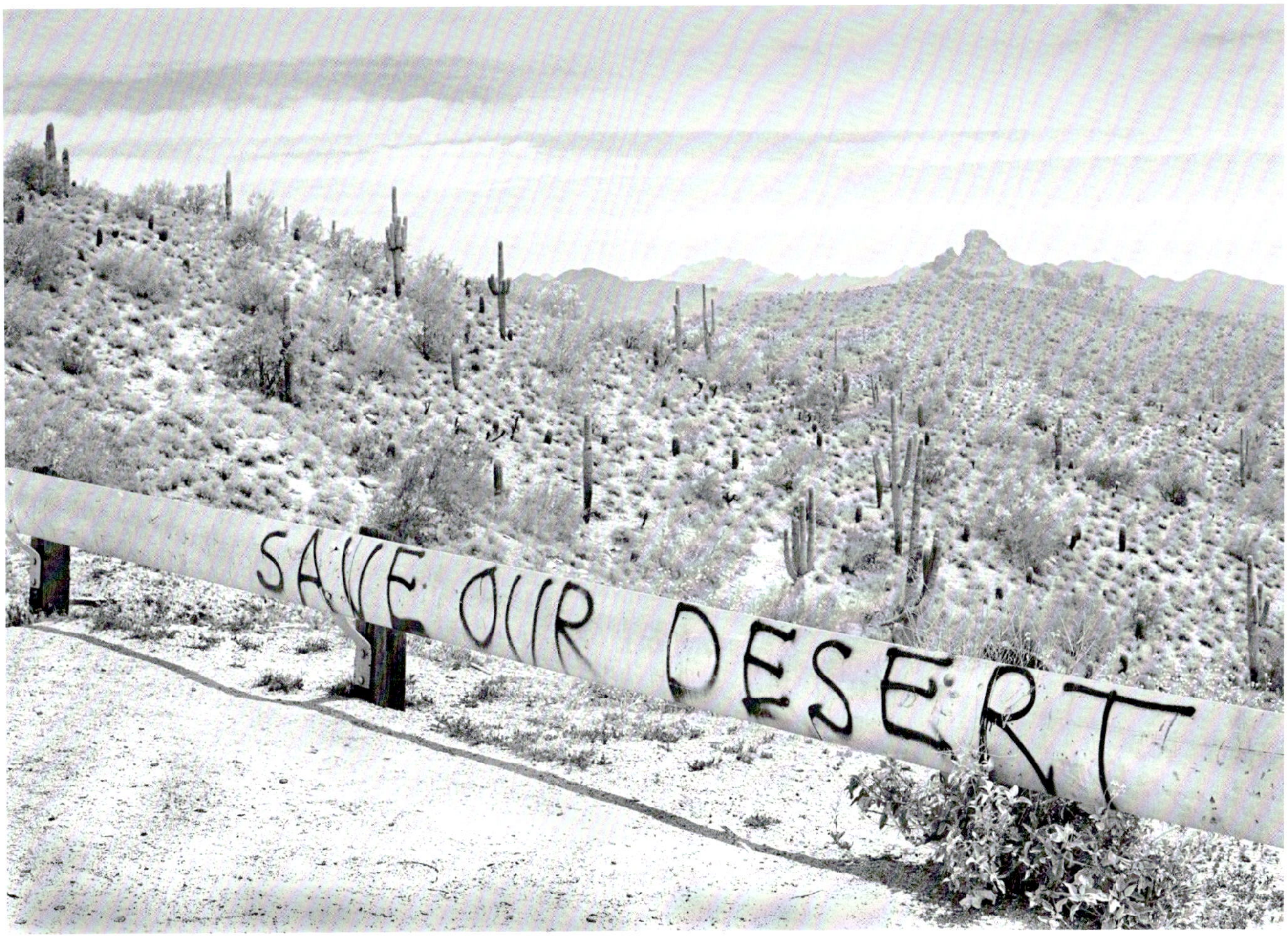

19 DECEMBER 2019 / MANY AMERICANS DO CARE. ***ARIZONA, USA 1980***

I don't claim to have the knowledge of a scientist or a politician but I feel despondent that the longest United Nations climate talks on record have ended in Madrid with what is called a compromise deal.

After two extra days and nights of negotiations, delegates finally agreed a deal that they say will, in theory, now see new improved carbon cutting plans on the table by the time of the Glasgow conference next year.

However, it seems that 'to address science' was opposed by a range of countries including the US, Brazil, India and China. While four of the major blocs in the world have so much tied up in coal and oil, I despair.

What this has to do with photography I don't know but I feel I have to get it of my chest. A feeble protest.

@davidhurnphoto @magnumphotos #arizona #pollution #climate

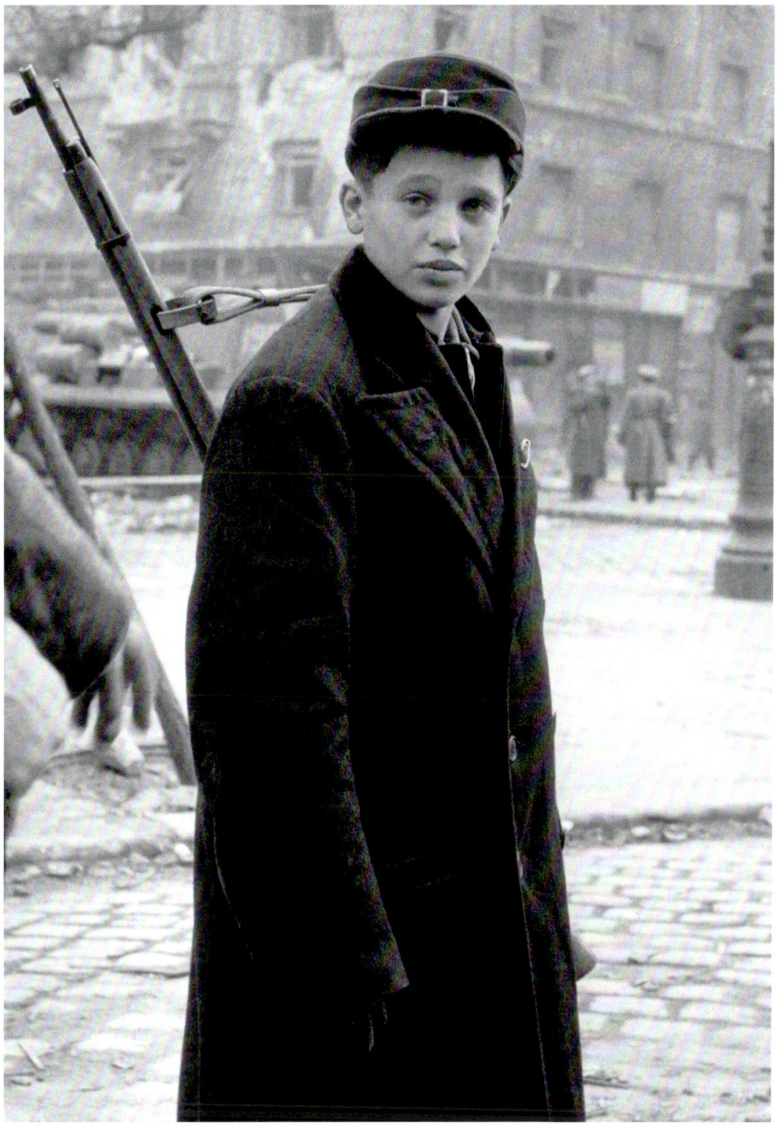

30 DECEMBER 2019 / CHILD OF REVOLUTION. *BUDAPEST, HUNGARY 1956*

I am reading an excellent novel by Henning Mankell, *Sidetracked*. In it he thinks about a deceased former colleague, 'He realised that he had difficulty remembering what Rhyberrg looked like. He's dying away inside of me, he thought. Soon even my memories of him will be gone'. As photographers we have an advantage, we have the perfect aid to memory, the photograph.

Every time I see the picture above it brings back the horror/sadness I felt at seeing for the first time a child with a loaded rifle. It was during the Hungarian Revolution. I was in Budapest. I was just 22, I guess he was ten years younger. I have forgotten non photographed peripheries to this picture, but not this boy.

My advice is to photograph everyone who has some significance for you. In the past I have photographed family, pets, lovers, and now I photograph friends. I photograph interviewers, filmmakers, and many photographers – I have 350 pictures of photographers but wish I had realised their significance earlier, I could have had more.

If you get an informative picture, what luck. If simply a snap, it still has memory merit.

@davidhurnphoto @magnumphotos #budapest #henningmankell

THE PHOTOGRAPH IS AUTHENTICATION ITSELF.
THE PHOTOGRAPH IS LABORIOUS ONLY WHEN IT FAKES.

/ *Roland Barthes*

2020

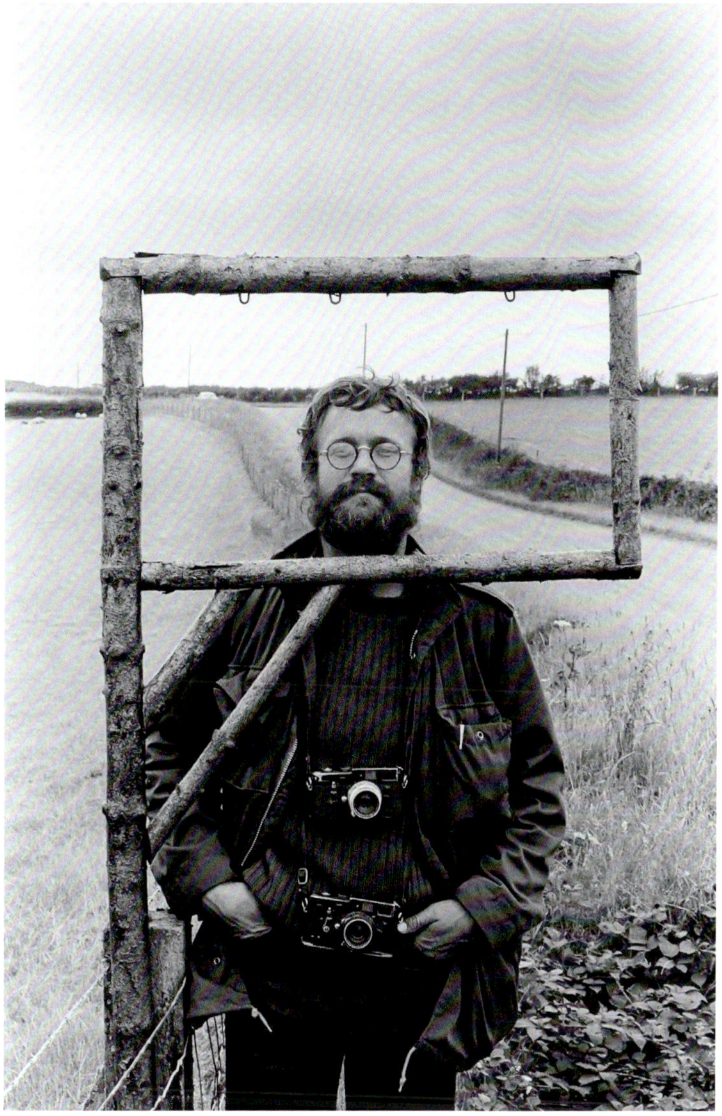

1 JANUARY 2020 / ROAD TRIP. JOSEF KOUDELKA. *TALGARTH, WALES 1977*

My New Year started out wonderfully as usual. I had a long phone call with my beloved 'brother', Josef Koudelka, who phoned me from Prague – we always phone each other first thing, first day, to make sure we are still around. His enthusiasm and energy have always affected me since I first met him in 1970. Every time I have contact with him I feel I want to rush out and take pictures. He has a large show opening in Paris in April, so that is my first entry in my diary.

I reminisce on the other male love of my life, Bill Jay. It's puzzling to think that we finished our constant conversations over ten years ago when he died in Costa Rica. During this month I will re-read his many articles and indulge his wisdom and humanity.

What more can you ask than friends who enrich your life.

@davidhurnphoto @magnumphotos @josef_koudelka #billjay

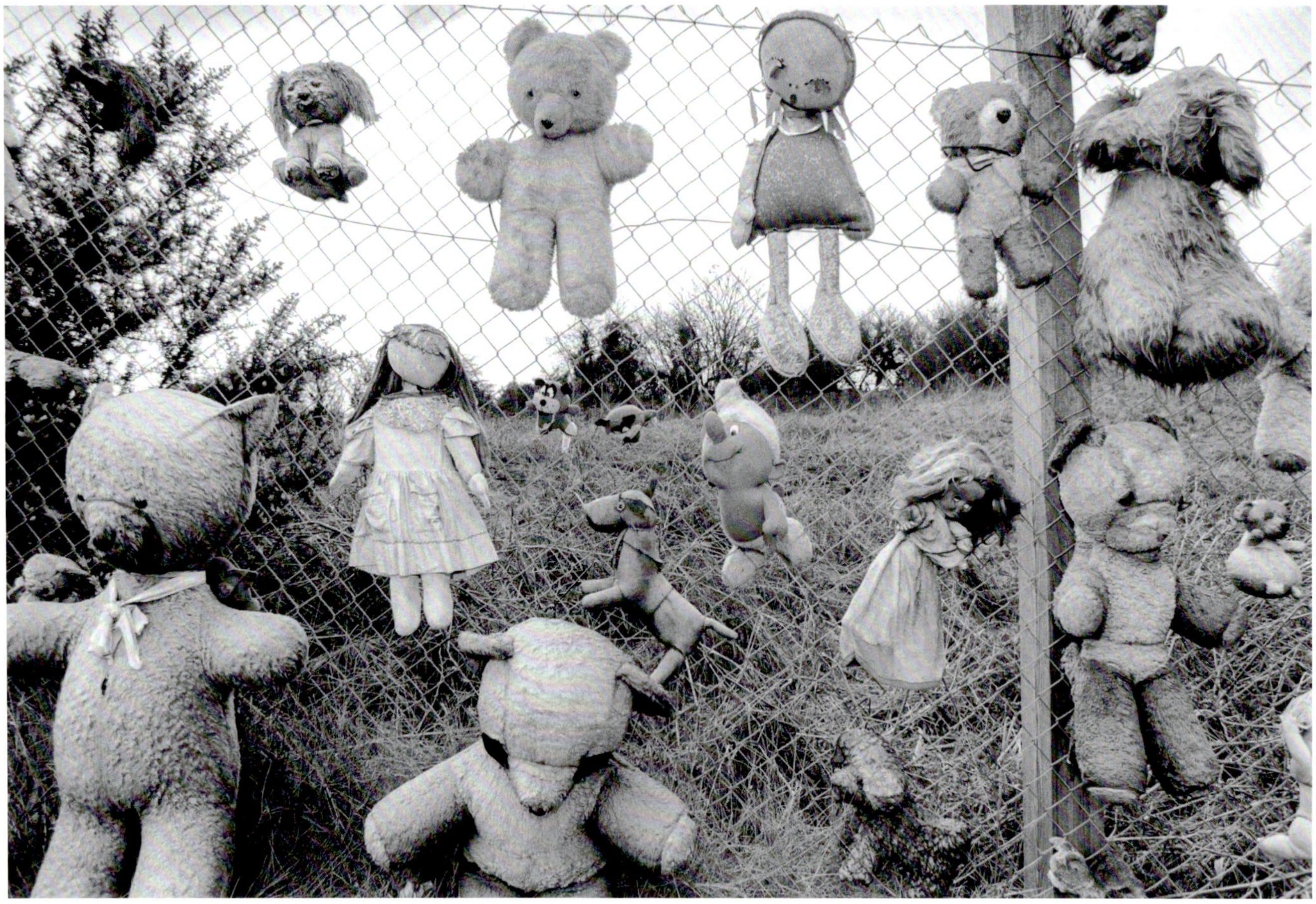

5 JANUARY 2020 / RUBBISH TIP. *PENPARC, WALES 1999*

I was recently asked why I read so many mystery novels.

An interesting question.

The simplest reason must be that a paperback is easily carried in my camera bag, I like holding/reading a paper book, and mystery is easy to read, put down, and start again.

I could argue that they produce a sort of research.

Henning Mankell, Peter Robinson, Ed McBain, and Simenon, I suppose at the moment my most read writers have in common a wonderful sense of place. I feel when I go to Sweden, Yorkshire, USA, I already have a sense/smell/feeling of what the landscape will be like. They all write well, in the case of Simenon, no less than William Faulkner wrote, 'I love reading Simenon. He makes me think of Chekhov'.

Read in sequence they all give a strong sense of cultural changes.

Henning Mankell was a left-wing social critic and activist. In his books and plays he constantly highlighted social inequality issues and injustices in Sweden and abroad. When you read his books in sequence you get a clear idea what has gone wrong with Swedish society.

They all seem to have love affairs that sadly ape many of my own.

Above all, crime novels do have a similar structure to photography. Solving mysteries means looking for the culprit, the discovery of sense, significance amid distractions, and irrelevant details of life.

Finding and taking a photograph is the end product of searching for the significant among distractions and making order out of chaos.

Maybe that's invented bullshit but it's the best I can do at this moment.

@davidhurnphoto @magnumphotos #henningmankell #peterrobinson #edmcbain #simenon #williamfaulkner #chekhov

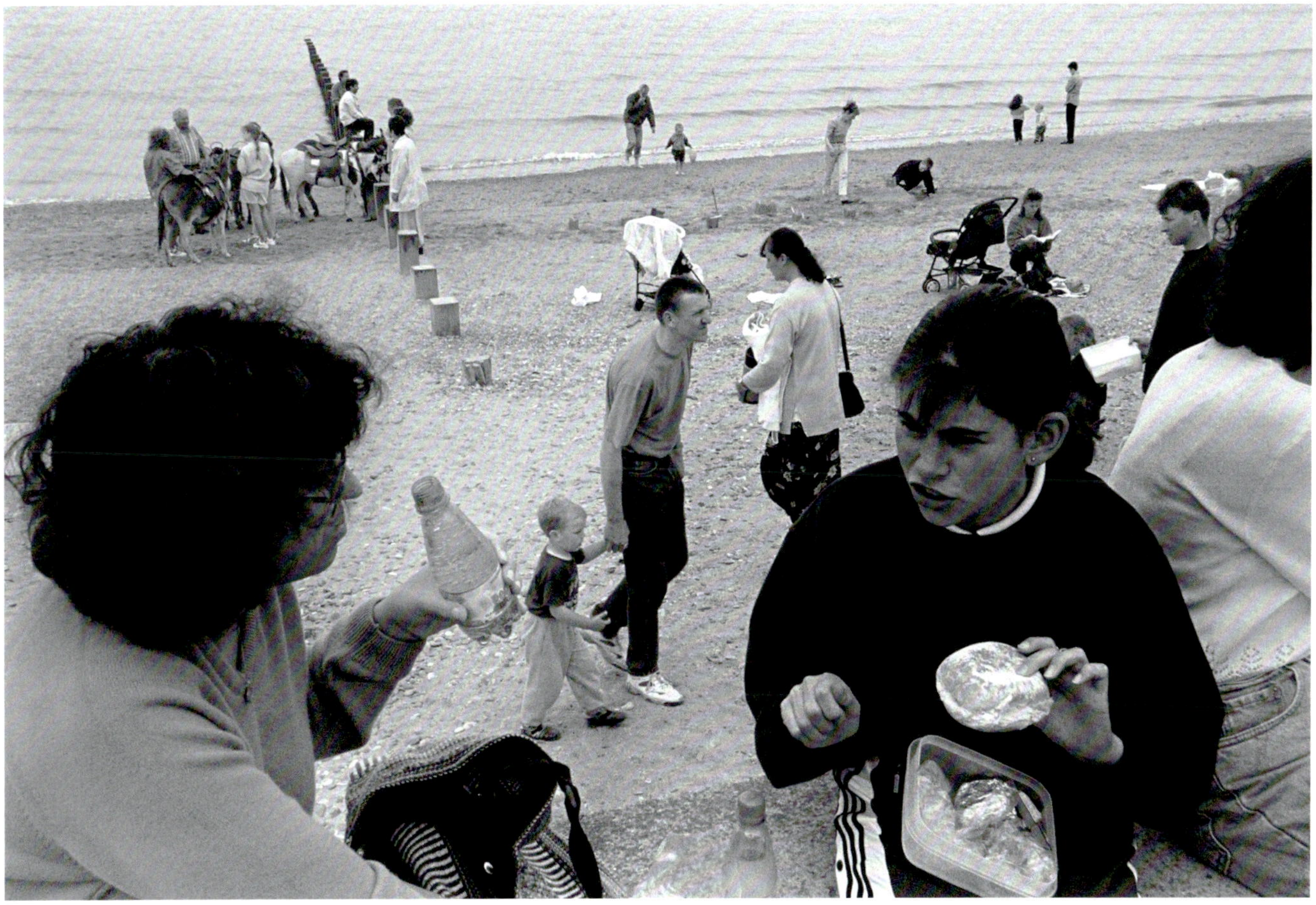

9 JANUARY 2020 / NEW YEAR'S RESOLUTIONS. *RHYL, WALES 1997*

I am quite good on fitness – when I am home I go to the gym three times a week. Of course, all could be done at home – the stairs are a wonderful base for so many exercises – but I find it very hard to get enthusiasm. Once in the gym somehow I feel I must fulfil my half an hour.

More problematic is diet. In weight terms I guess I am OK – I feel better seven pounds lighter than I normally am – don't have difficulty with my own choices of food, in fact cook quite well for myself – mainly using a steamer which deals with practically everything, I have a list of what recipes I can do – even thought of landing Instagram with my personal cookbook.

My difficulty is with visitors. I have a lot. Most are welcome, particularly if they phone/email first, however, too many bring gifts. Booze is fine, I don't drink any alcohol but that doesn't matter as others do. It's the habit of wanting to fatten me up that is a problem – too many bring cake, biscuits or chocolate, all generous but disastrous for me. I am fine if sugar is not in the cottage – weak if it is.

I think photographers are better if they are overall in good shape. I have often stated that shoes are the most important piece of equipment in the photographer's locker. My type of photographer must walk. Sadly as one gets older it becomes more and more difficult – I even find myself picking locations by how flat they are.

At the moment I am two pounds lighter than I was on 1 January.

@davidhurnphoto @magnumphotos #recipes

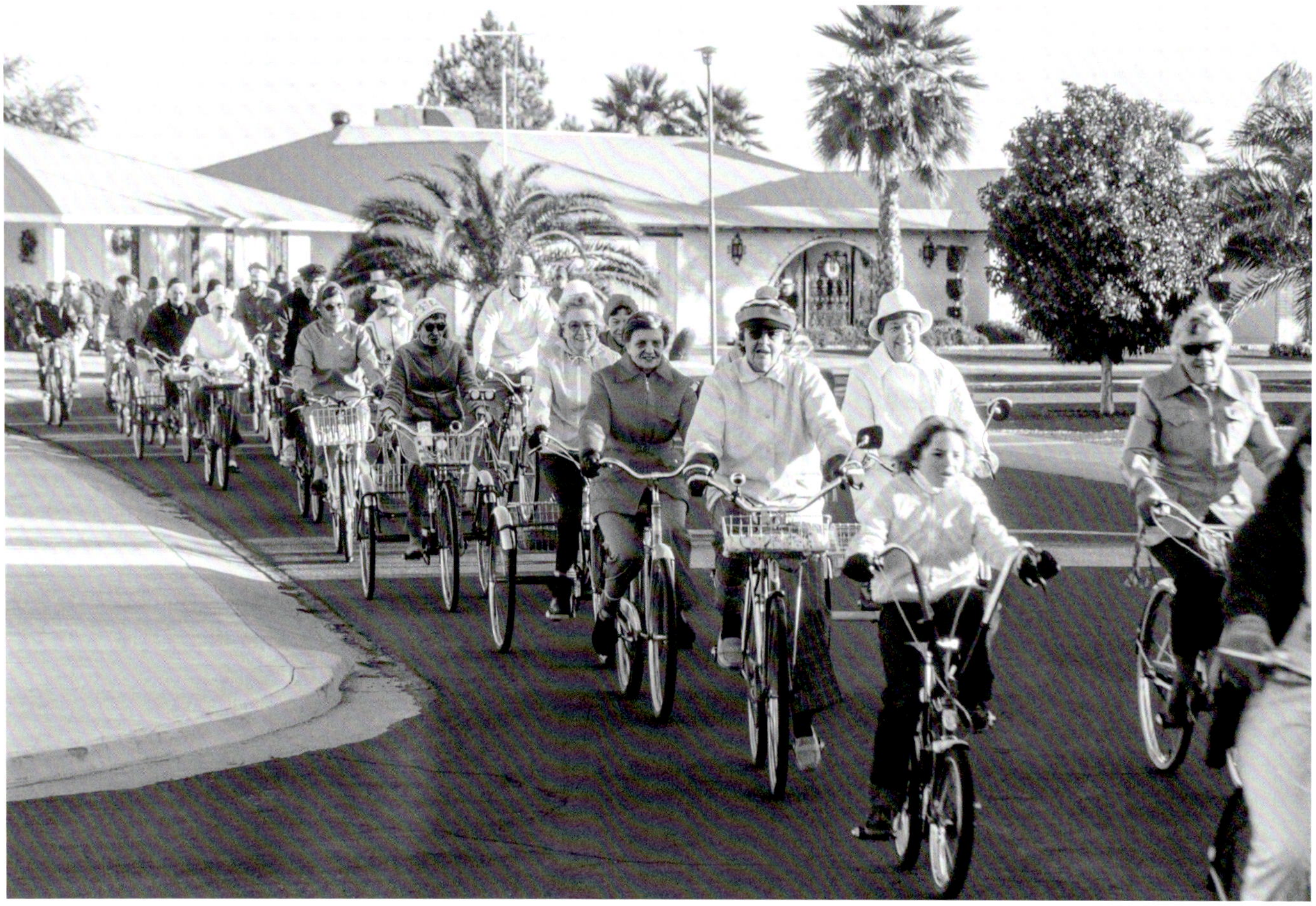

14 JANUARY 2020 / CYCLING. *SUN CITY, ARIZONA, USA 1980*

How I look at a photograph really applies only to me. You will read a photograph differently. So logically one should argue, take no advice, follow one's own instincts, own reason, own conclusions. Do not let others tell you how to look.

If you do all the above then I feel it lets me point, put forward, a few ideas to ponder on.

Maybe looking at lots of others pictures, with a discerning eye, is a good start. Find a few people whose photographic opinions seem to have some authenticity about them and filter what you like. By and large those that are admired by their peers probably have something to offer.

After all is said and done, more is said than done.

@davidhurnphoto @magnumphotos #cycling #environment #arizona

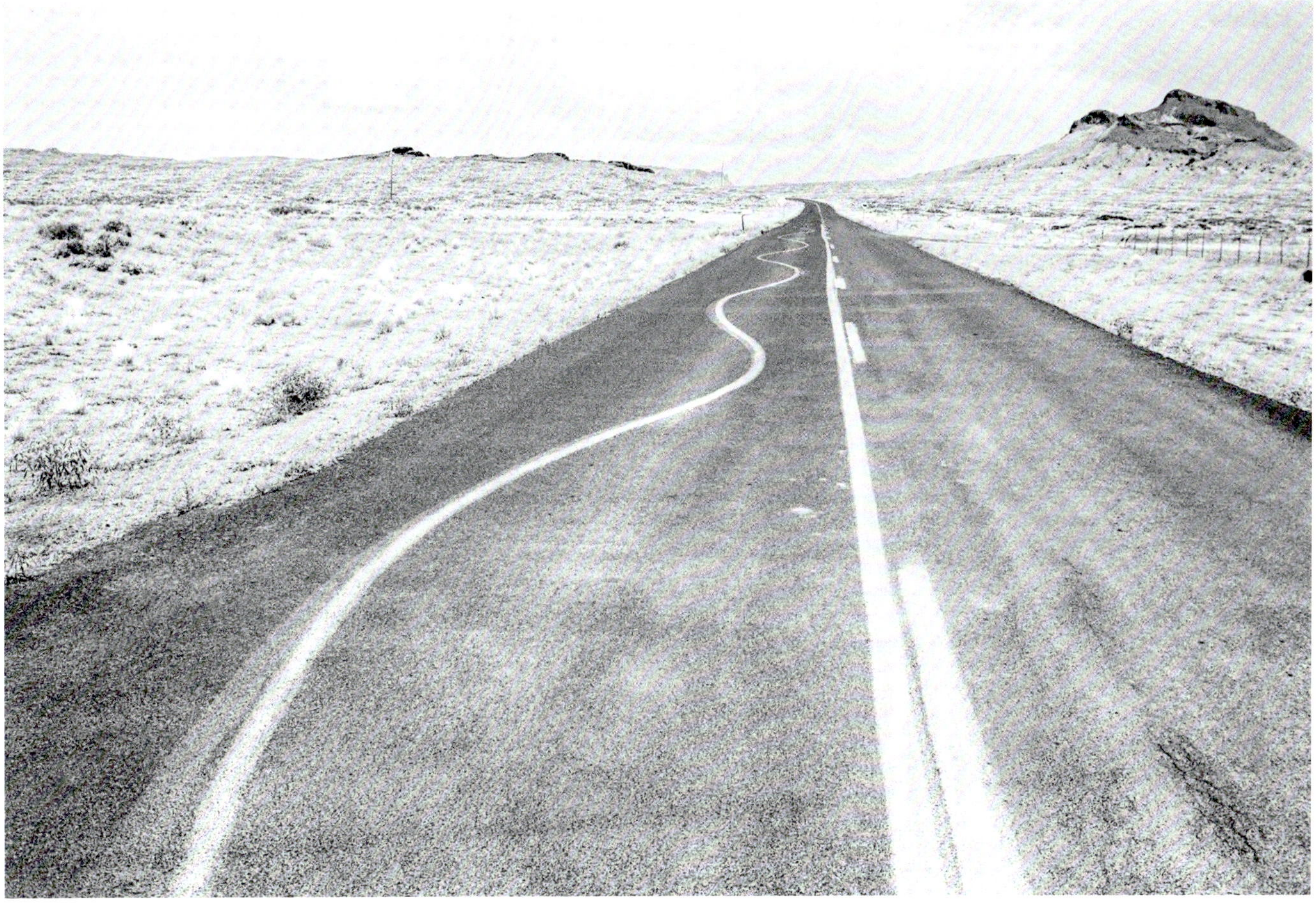

20 JANUARY 2020 / PAINTED DESERT. *ARIZONA, USA 1980*

I do enjoy pictures that set up a mental/visual puzzle.

At a time when so many people seem to think it is irrelevant whether what we hear or see is true or false, I am only interested in the true. What I see without falsifying manipulation. Doctoring simply makes bad pictures worse.

@davidhurnphoto @magnumphotos #painteddesert #arizona #visualpun

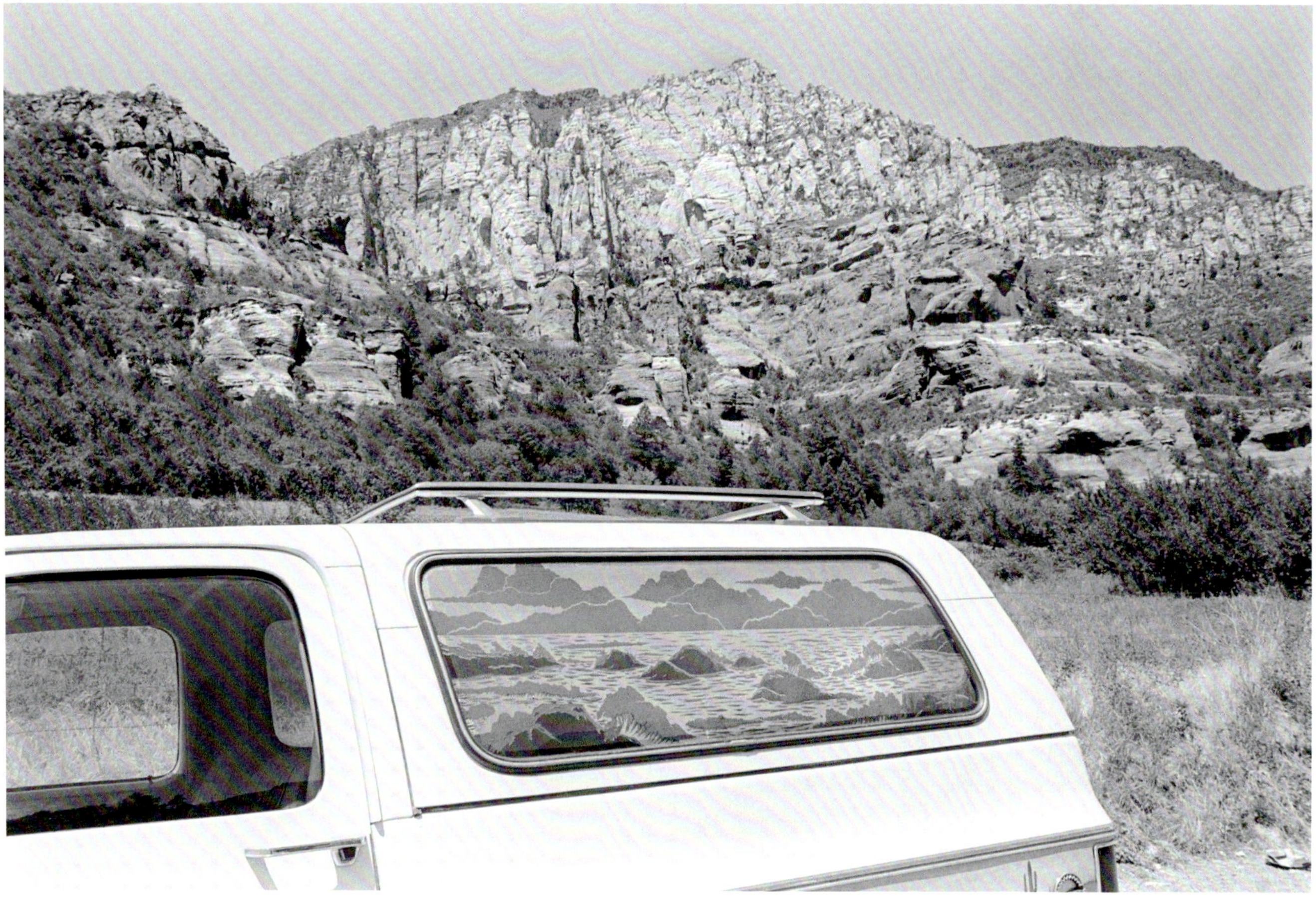

3 FEBRUARY 2020 / HEATWAVE. *ARIZONA, USA 1980*

Yet again I must apologise for my technical inadequacies, I am getting better but I seem to have been cut off towards the end of my previous post.

This is what was removed:

Amak Mahmoodian talked about her latest book *Zanjir*, which I will certainly try to see. The major part of her talk was about photographs taken by a very early Persian photographer, whose name I missed, I found these extremely interesting. She spoke with passion. From a lecture I want passion, entertainment, vulnerability. I felt Amak Mahmoodian had all three so I enjoyed and was informed by her slot.

I frequently get a question along the lines of 'how do I know if I should be a photographer?'. I refer to the conversation between the painter Renoir and a friend who asked him, 'how do I know if I should be a musician?'. Renoir's answer: 'how do you know if you want to piss?' Of course, this is really speculating about a rarified kind of painter/musician/photographer/writer. The likelihood of one becoming a Bresson, Koudelka, Weegee is remote but one can only do so if initially you have ambition. If you take this route you have to accept certain knowns. You have to have greater curiosity than others, work harder than others, be more tenacious than others, sadly, in a way, be more selfish than others. Above all, expect it is a full-time job.

But there are many genres of photography, perhaps not so taxing but also enjoyable, and in many cases perhaps even more worthwhile.

It always seems to me that potentially more 'good' is done in medical photography than in any other genre. Radiography is know as a very rewarding job and saves lives, X-ray crystallography had a major impact on the discovery of DNA.

If there is a fire in a house, it seems the first thing grabbed to save is the wedding album – that must mean something.

Perhaps the most looked at magazines are fashion.

From the start of photography audiences have demanded portraits.

People have wanted to sell you something by means of advertising.

So many choices.

Some even try to sell off gallery walls to merchant bankers.

@davidhurnphoto @magnumphotos @amak_mahmoodian

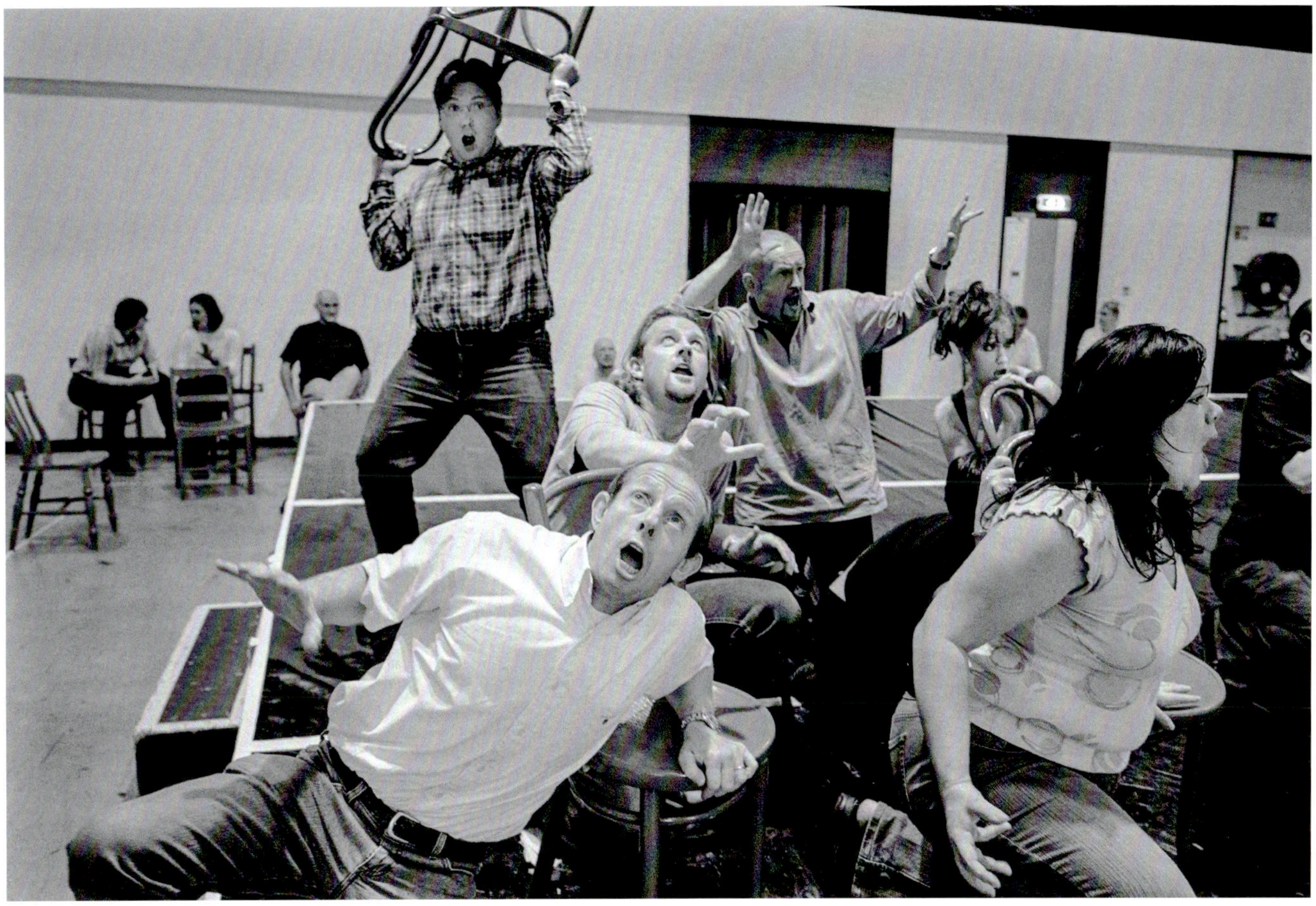

6 FEBRUARY 2020 / VIOLENCE. *CARDIFF, WALES 2004*

I am continually reading, in the introductions and publicity for many book and exhibitions, words like, 'in depth', 'significant', 'political', 'important'. I am often puzzled because they do not collate with my meaning of the words, particularly when I look at the work they are showing.

I have just been to talks given by Rhiannon Adam and Jon Tonks, at the Martin Parr Foundation.

Rhiannon Adam talked about travelling to the remote island community of Pitcairn in the South Pacific. Pitcairn measures just two miles by one mile and is home to just 42 British subjects, descendants from the Mutiny on the Bounty. A decade ago, the island's romantic image was tarnished by a string of high profile sexual abuse trials, as a result islanders are particularly reticent about accepting outsiders. Her trip duration was dictated by the quarterly supply vessel, there would be no way off for three arduous months. What clearly came forth through her talk was what a dedicated researcher she is.

Jon Tonks' work focuses on 'telling stories about people's lives shaped by history and geography'. He primarily talked about working on his book *Empire*, a journey across the South Atlantic exploring life on four remote islands, British Overseas Territories, intertwined through history as relics of the once British Empire. Ascension Island, Tristan da Cunha, the Falkland Islands and St Helena. He has photographed the people, landscapes and pockets of history embedded within each place. He spent up to a month at a time in each territory, travelling 60,000 miles around the Atlantic via 'military outposts, low-lit airstrips and long voyages aboard cargo ships, fishing vessels and the last working Royal Mail ship'. Now both these photographers fulfil my idea of working 'in depth'. In the case of Jon, also abstractly political. In the case of Rhiannon, blatantly political.

@davidhurnphoto @magnumphotos @martinparrfdn @rhiannon_adam @jon_tonks

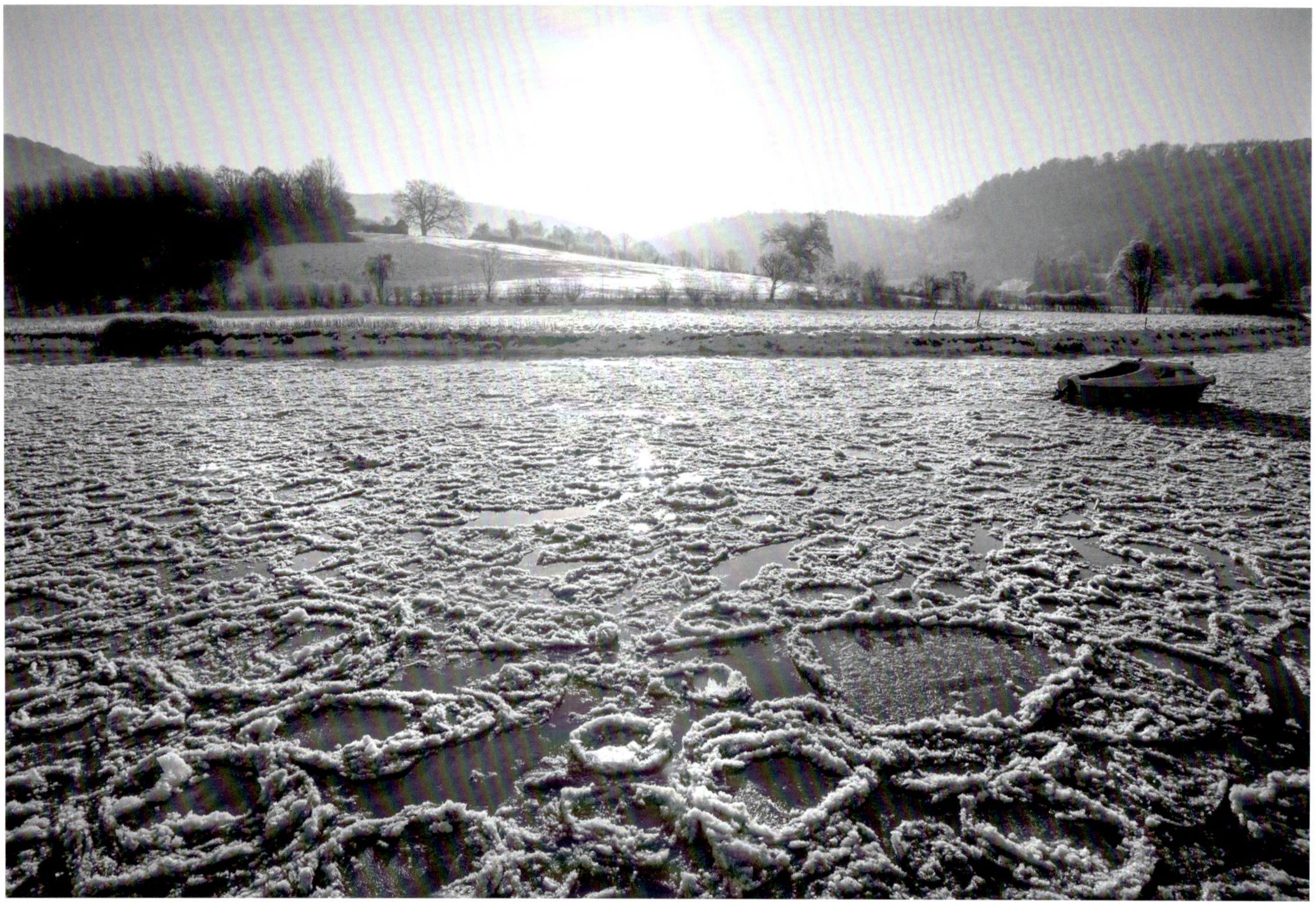

20 FEBRUARY 2020 / ICE FROM MY FRONT DOOR. *TINTERN, WALES 2010*

It seems to me one of the positives in the UK is the BBC. One of my favourite programmes is *The Life Scientific*, Radio 4. I am in awe of most of the people interviewed.

I urge you all to listen to the interview with Professor Myles Allen, conducted on 18 February. It was the clearest explanation of what we can and cannot predict and what we can and cannot do on climate change. Clarity and explanation.

Just listening to this series of programmes would set up a lifetime of ideas for projects for young photographers.

@davidhurnphoto @magnumphotos #mylesallen #lifescientific #bbc #tintern #wales

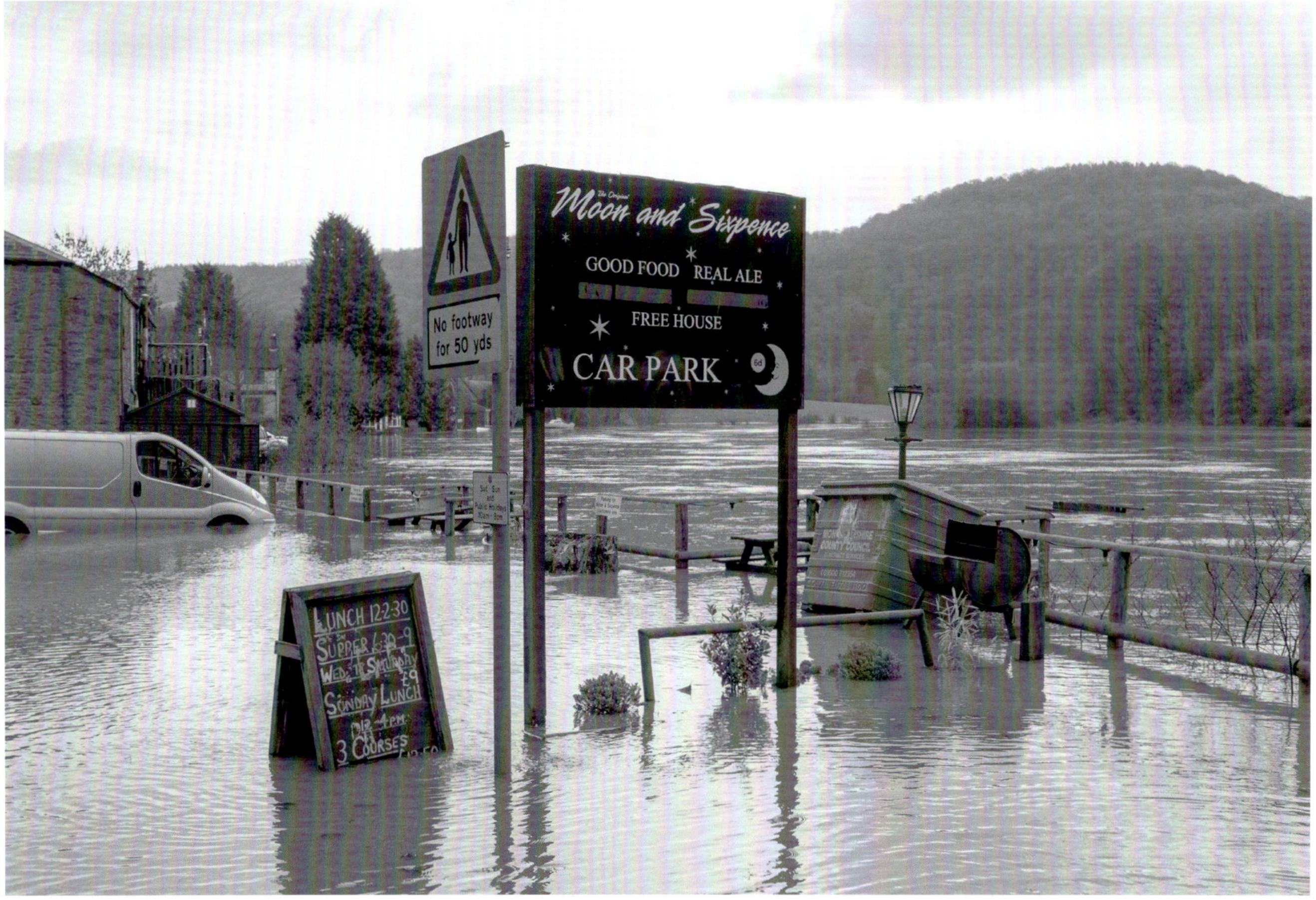

26 FEBRUARY 2020 / FLOODING. ***TINTERN, WALES 2014***

I think the flooding not only the most important visual story of today in the UK, but it will be in the future.

The realisation that I am physically not able to photograph this in any meaningful way is very distressing for me.

I had the same feeling with the pivotal fall of the Berlin Wall, I was teaching at the time and could not get away. The lack of being able to photograph there was a major reason for my resigning my head of department post.

What do I do now?

I suspect I will try to redo my 1963/4 trip around the Mediterranean, I started this last year and I enjoyed the sun.

Landscape is a possibility so finishing a long project on the landscape of Wales must be completed. I suppose I could do more of this but I would have to find a new initiative, but how do you not look like a mini version of John Davies, Mark Power?

Maybe a return to my early portraiture, spending time with people that have in some way enriched our lives, and photographing them in a natural way. Maybe scientists. I am already doing – or rather continuing to do – this with photographers I meet. I have about 300 specimens shot already.

@davidhurnphoto @magnumphotos @marktpower #tintern #wales

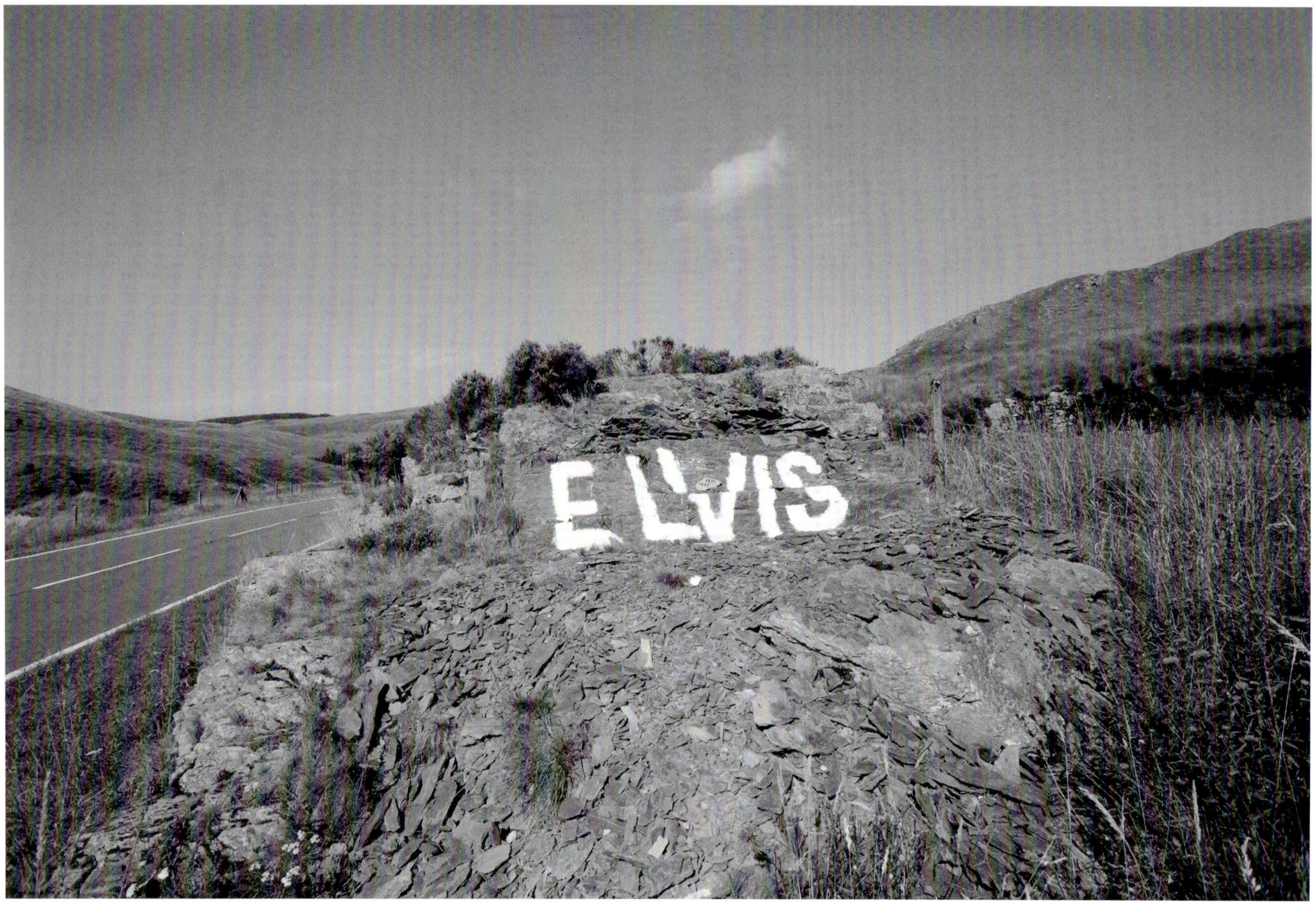

5 MARCH 2020 / NEAR ABERYSTWYTH. *WALES 2011*

At the start of the week I was in London for a UK meeting of local Magnum Photographers.

Hanging in the Magnum gallery – yes, all can come in and see – is a small exhibition of just 13 pictures, I presume culled from many more, by Mark Power.

I hope I don't offend when I suggest that Mark's authorship seems an amalgam of what, in my early days, would have been called architectural photography, and very pure documentary. Deceptively simple.

We all hear academics referring to Barthes, Foucault, and I am sure now others in fashion I have not heard of. Sometimes the more down to earth Raymond Williams or John Berger is mentioned, often misquoted, of a different genre, Steinbeck or my favourite Pullman essays. Anyway, it's as though the rest of us don't read or research.

I know that this is not true. The photographers I most enjoy have also read so much stuff but I think they feel that ultimately it's the 'picture' that must stand by itself – a picture backed up by thought.

Looking at the 13 was a feeling of connection each picture to each other, I am sure this feeling would be emphasised on seeing more of the series, but above all they are intelligent, clear, simple, beautifully executed 'pictures'. You sense authorship.

For the more amateur inclined, you can wallow in the exemplary craft.

For others, you can admire superb geometry.

For me, not only the above, but superb choice of place/time and connection between the pictures.

One extraordinary picture, looking down into a canyon, would not be out of place next to a painting by the elder Bruegel.

@davidhurnphoto @magnumphotos @marktpower #wales

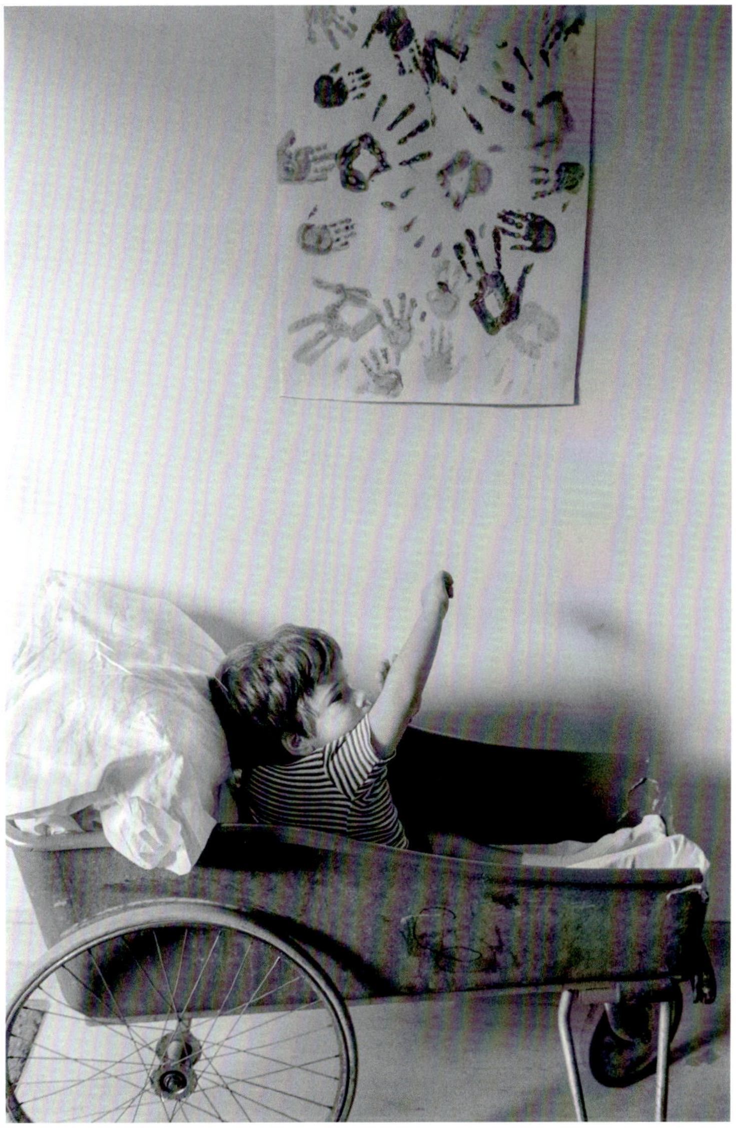

13 MARCH 2020 / HOSPITAL. *LONDON, ENGLAND 1969*

I spent a moving evening at the MPF. The content was based around people more unfortunate than must of us.

The evening started with four songs by a choir comprising people in recovery from problematic drug or alcohol use, as well as advocates of recovery. They were the Bristol recovery choir, Raising Voices. I was amazed by their standard, to my ears they were really excellent. I spoke to some of the singers – 'our choir is a place for people to come together, make friends and be uplifted by the power of song'. Well, it seems to work and I encourage anyone with problems in the Bristol area to contact them, perhaps they can help.

The second half of the evening was conducted by Julian Germain. The photographer showed a number of photography projects which are conceived and executed as collaborations with groups such as favela communities and street children in Brazil, they produce the imagery themselves.

The kids were given cameras and told to do as they liked. As with all kids with cameras the results are always excellent – we as viewers are not used to seeing technical deficiencies – this has a visual appeal – thus often support for Diana cameras. The pictures are full of life and action, there is no doubt in that children gain enormously when they gain some visibility importance, I am sure that gives an enormous lift to the kids, the project is unanswerably worthwhile – but the next question is, can they sustain this? Is there any way one can help them to become professionals and therefore a possibility of a new life?

Attendance was overflowing, there was even a student group from Madrid and one from Belfast. That's what I love to see.

@davidhurnphoto @magnumphotos @martinparrfdn @juliangermain #bristolrecoverrychoir #raisingvoices

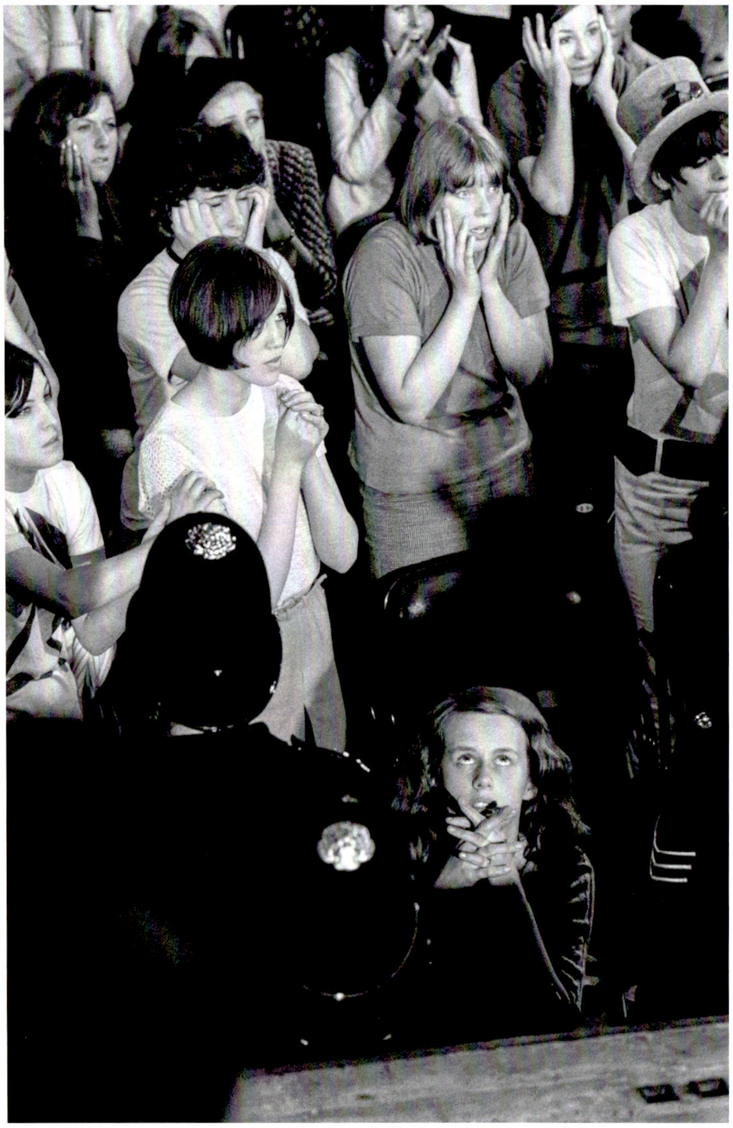

16 MARCH 2020 / AUDIENCE. BEATLES CONCERT. *BIRMINGHAM, ENGLAND 1966*

Well, I guess none of us knows what is happening. I will miss going to lectures/talks/conferences. I tend to go to as many as possible as I want to keep in touch, particularly with the young. I feel it irresponsible to criticise if you haven't tried to understand many points of view.

I guess I have self isolated, easy for me as I live in Prospect Cottage fortress. We have a wonderful health set up in the village – the NHS as it should be – and I am inundated by kind neighbours happy to supply food etc. My luck is that I have 51,408 pictures in my database. They need serious culling, re-captioning, and editing to best and to simply commercial. At last I can spend time doing it. Probably means bad computer back but a quick spin on cycle machine every hour usually deals with that.

I suspect my diet will be largely fruit and porridge. Luckily I have never smoked so my lungs are in exceptionally good shape. I intend to be fine.

I will do a daily walk and presumably do a set of 'landscape' of the village – I will pound the boundary. I have a very detailed map.

Should people knock on my door I have set up a table with a large gap between chairs either side plus lots of smelly soaps.

@davidhurnphoto @magnumphotos

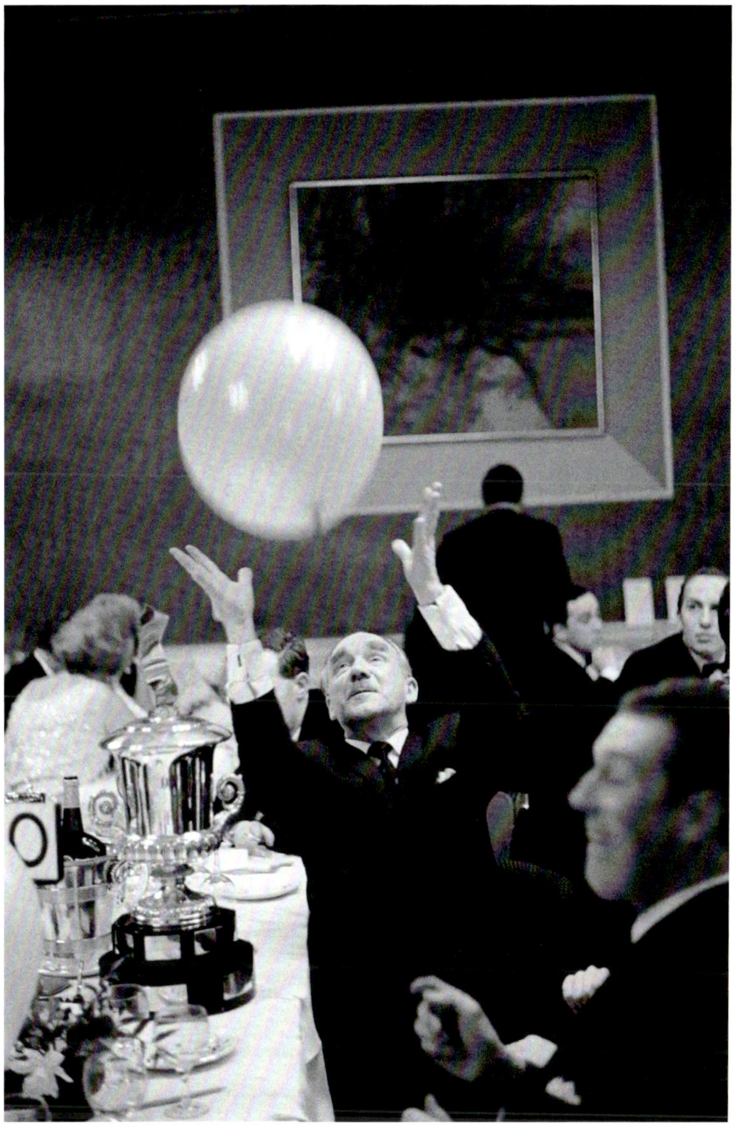

20 MARCH 2020 / HAPPINESS. ***EDINBURGH, SCOTLAND 1967***

Did you know, 20 March is the International Day of Happiness?

Surprisingly, I feel upbeat. So far I have managed to re-edit/caption/larger scan 273 key pictures taken from the past two years.

Arrived is a very accurate, up the bum medical thermometer. This, of course, doesn't tell you if you have or have not the virus, but it is a good indicator of something wrong if there is something wrong – I personally find it very reassuring.

I have bought the first six Elizabeth George books and am about to re-read *What Good are the Arts?* by John Carey. Plus Richard Holmes, *The Age of Wonder*. What a wonderful biographer.

I wish I had a dog to take for walks – perhaps I should buy a toy one and have it at the end of a stiff stick so that from afar it looks real.

Boy oh boy, are the villagers kind – so many offers of help not only from those I know but those I don't as well.

I suspect it's not the end of the world – let's hope the next phase is more sensible and less selfish.

@davidhurnphoto @magnumphotos #johncarey #richardholmes #elizabethgeorge

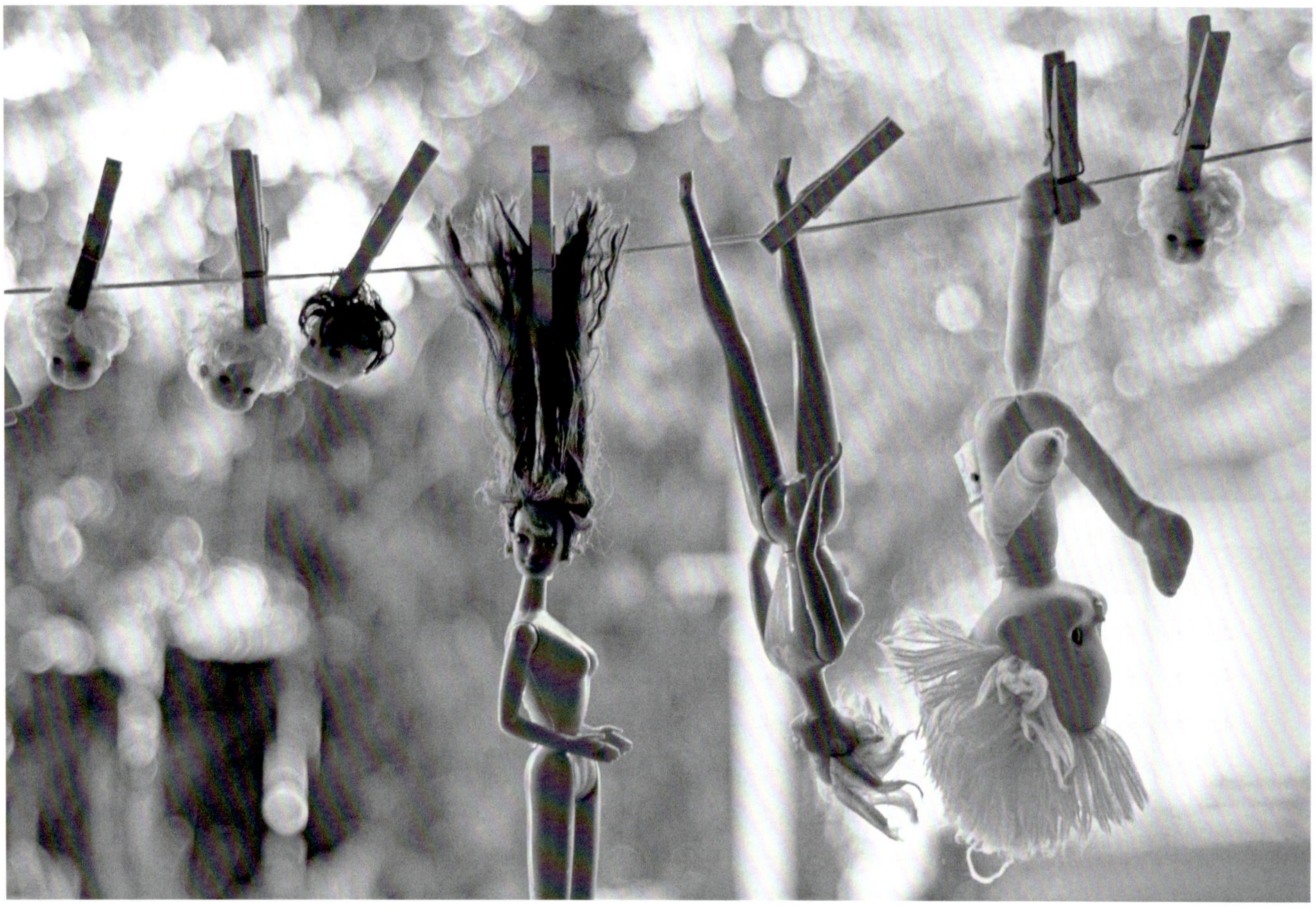

25 MARCH 2020 / DISINFECT. *ARIZONA, USA 1992*

Do remember, not the least important reason for inventing photography was to have a quick, accurate method of recording/collecting facts. I feel simple documenting is still one of photography's most important functions. I think it helps future history and certainly, for me, past memory.

It might not be your natural style but you can do worse than simply record your surrounds as they are now, be it stuff on the TV, what you are eating, reading, drinking etc. It's a kind of jigsaw puzzle game. I am sure you/I will not produce any pictures that will stand alone and pass the test of time but they will jog your/my memories in the future. Photography has many uses.

In the meantime Glenn Gould is producing Bach, *Goldberg Variations*, in the background. Now that certainly makes me want to wake up tomorrow.

@davidhurnphoto @magnumphotos #bach #glenngould

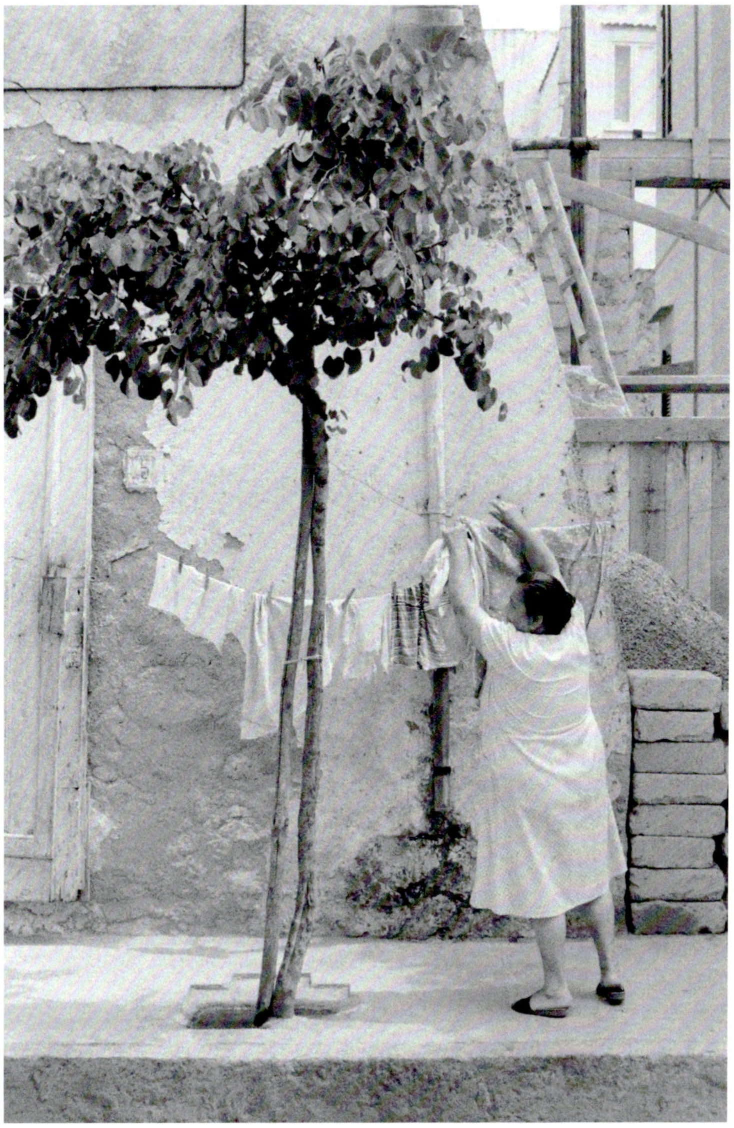

28 MARCH 2020 / D'ISCHIA GARDEN. *ITALY 1964*

We are at a time when, as *The Economist* tells us, 'A virus a ten-thousandth of a millimetre in diameter has transformed Western democracies . . .'. I am scrabbling for something that looks at the more positive side of life. My cottage is called 'Prospect Cottage'. I have always been aware of the more famous 'Prospect Cottage', home of that brave Gay Rights' activist , production designer, and film-maker, Derek Jarman.

In fact that Prospect Cottage is mainly know for its stark garden – as he wrote, 'Prospect Cottage, its timbers black with pitch, stands on the shingle at Dungeness . . . Prospect faces the rising sun across a road sparkling silver with sea mist. One small clump of dark green broom breaks through the flat ochre shingle . . . There are no walls or fences. My garden's boundaries are the horizon.' I actually met Derek when he was production designer on Ken Russell's *The Devils*.

Derek Jarman is, of course, now dead, and it appears the Cottage is 'at risk of being sold privately, having its contents dispersed, and its artistic legacy lost'. It appears that money needs to be realised by the 31 March to help save it and a little bit of beauty, for the future.

Photographer Peter Marlow lived close by. There is a rare opportunity to acquire a Peter Marlow photograph, *Overalls drying in Derek Jarman's Garden*, and provide vital support for the campaign. @artfund @magnumphotos

You can make this happen. Find out more at www.artfund.org/donate/art-happens/prospect-cottage

@davidhurnphoto @magnumphotos @artfund #derekjarman #petermarlow #prospectcottage

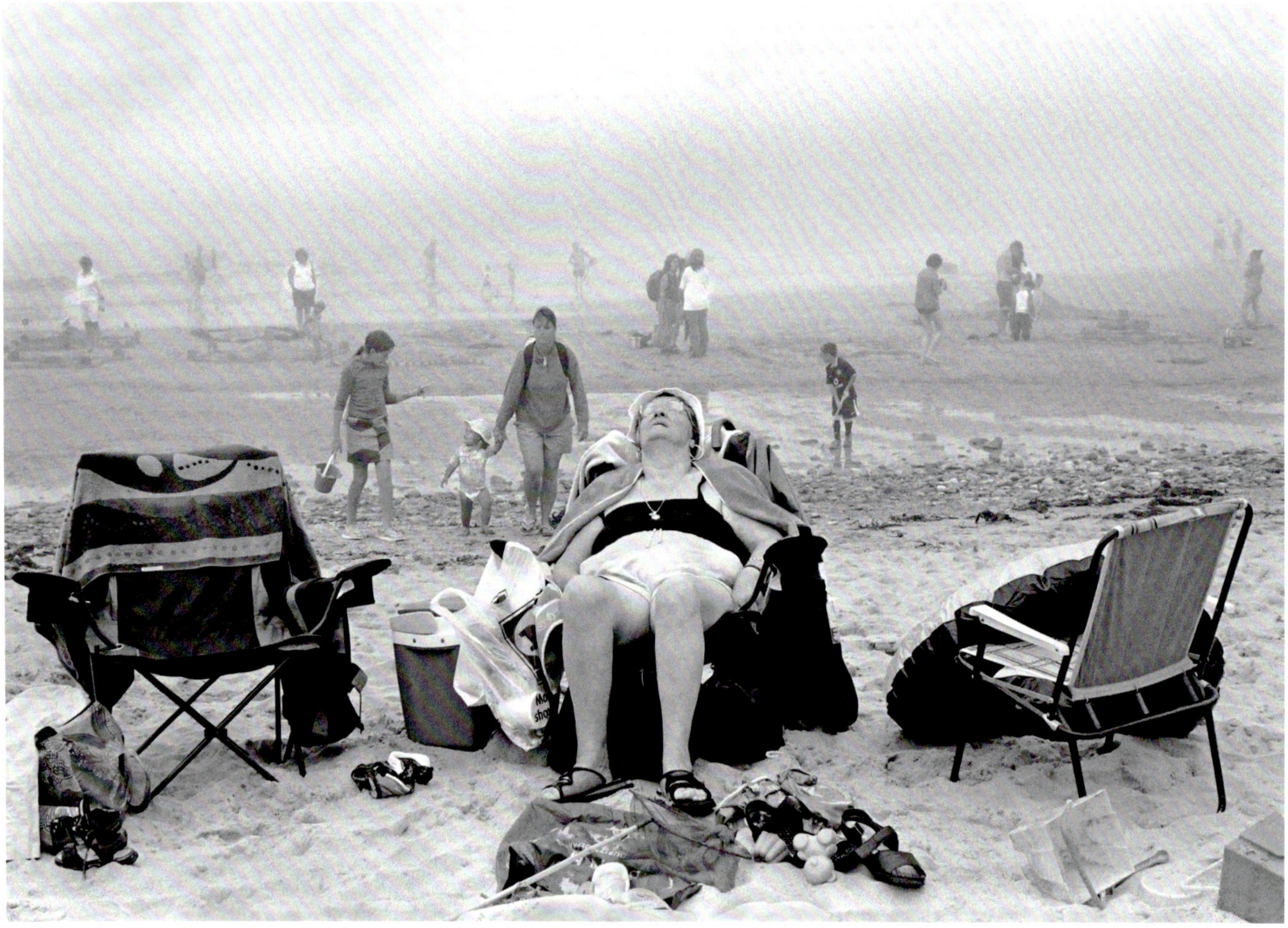

I APRIL 2020 / BEACH BATTLEFIELD. *PORTH OER (WHISTLING SANDS), WALES 2004*

April Fools Day. The world is feeling like a science fiction battlefield. *The Day of the Triffids*, *War of the Worlds*, *Blade Runner*, take your pick, I feel in the middle of the lot – everything is getting more and more surreal. Nothing seems real, I keep feeling I must surely soon wake up.

Scientists of stature are giving us something to believe in and have the honesty to change their minds if circumstances change. But politicians still flounder and bluster and the opposition still can't help but slide in their bickering remark.

Surely in the future there will be no excuse to not finance the NHS to the extent it can operate in the way we all hope for. We really do need more than enough doctors, more than enough nurses, more than enough beds, one can go on and on, but it's necessary.

How dare the BBC ever be threatened. Friends from abroad tell me the World Service is their first port of call. Friends with children tell me education, exercise, help programmes are springing up from seemingly nowhere.

Does any of this have anything to do with photography? Well, in a lateral way I think it does. The photography I love is that that is trying to enhance life, and transfer accurate, honest, information.

P.S. I have just heard that the money needed to save the Derek Jarman house/garden has been raised. I hope we helped in even a mini, mini, mini way, or if it was only by keeping the conversation going.

@davidhurnphoto @magnumphotos #coronavirus #selfisolation #derekjarman #wales

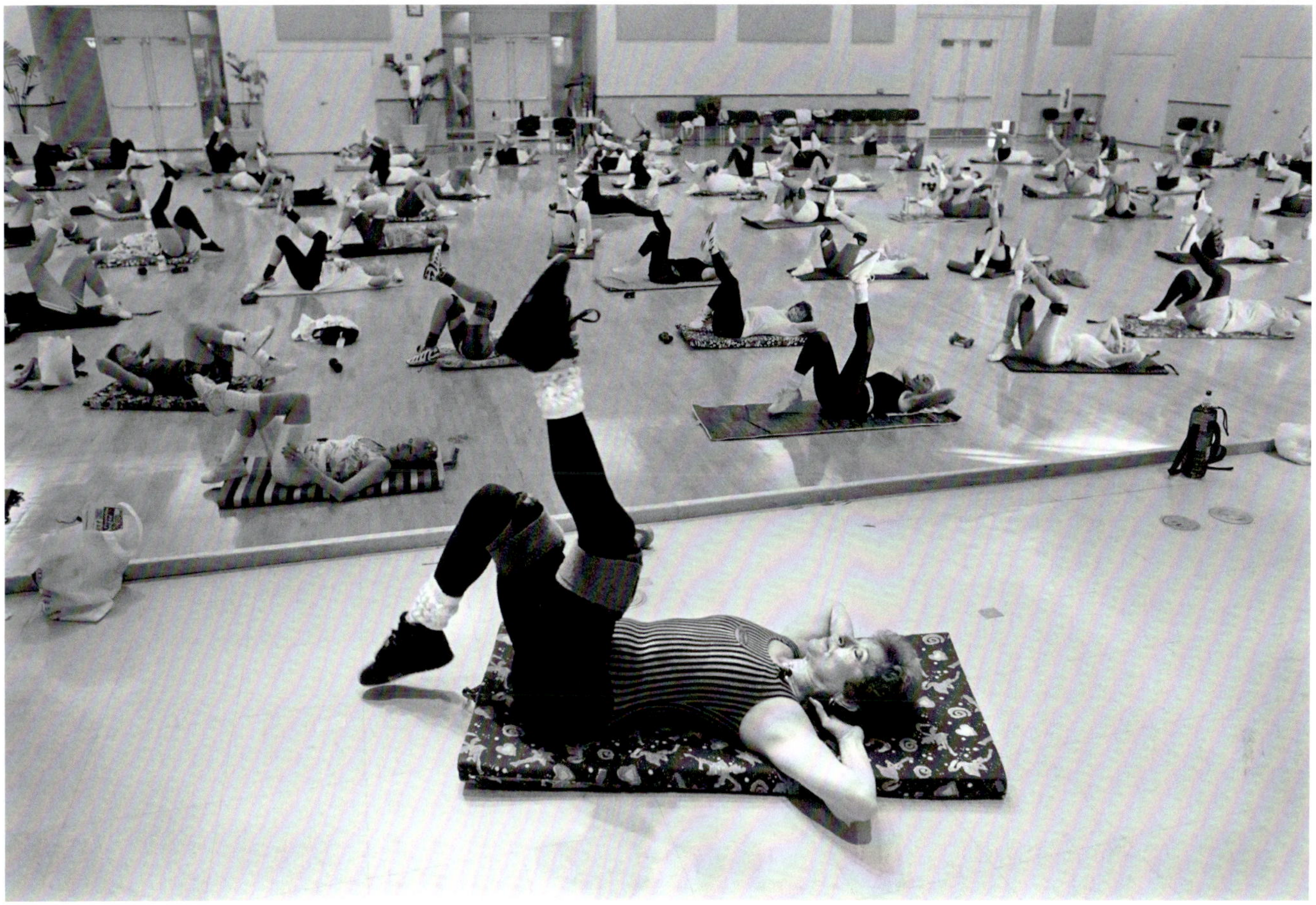

5 APRIL 2020 / JAZZ AEROBICS. *ARIZONA, USA 1997*

I normally try to go to the gym three times a week. Most photography I enjoy needs me to be active, and at my age I have to do forceful exercise to be fit. The gym's advantage is that once there you feel embarrassed if you don't do, in my case, my half an hour. At home it's much more difficult to get the discipline. Having a daily walk is fine but it doesn't raise the heart rate – it's more pleasure than effort. Lucky I have a cottage with stairs, stairs are a good exercise platform. I don't have the strength to do press-ups from the floor, but on the stairs I can do them at 45 degrees. I try 60 a day in two sessions. Step-ups are easy on the stairs, sitting on a firm chair and standing up become squats, sit-ups are good from lying down. I think I am OK, the discipline was difficult at the start but is better now.

To my surprise, I have enjoyed photographing my cottage. I gave myself an assignment as though being employed by an upmarket estate agent. I have tried to sell my cottage to myself. I have shot in colour and have enjoyed the precision and technical problems occurred. I enjoy solving problems. Boy, how much easier it is with digital, I don't know how I would have coped in the days of film and lighting. Anyway, I am aiming for a 25 picture set.

Just noticed a long line of walkers passing through the village, most almost hand in hand, looks like a fashion show – all new boots and sticks etc. Do they not realise they just could be jeopardising someone's life?

@davidhurnphoto @magnumphotos #coronavirus #selfisolation #exercise #arizona

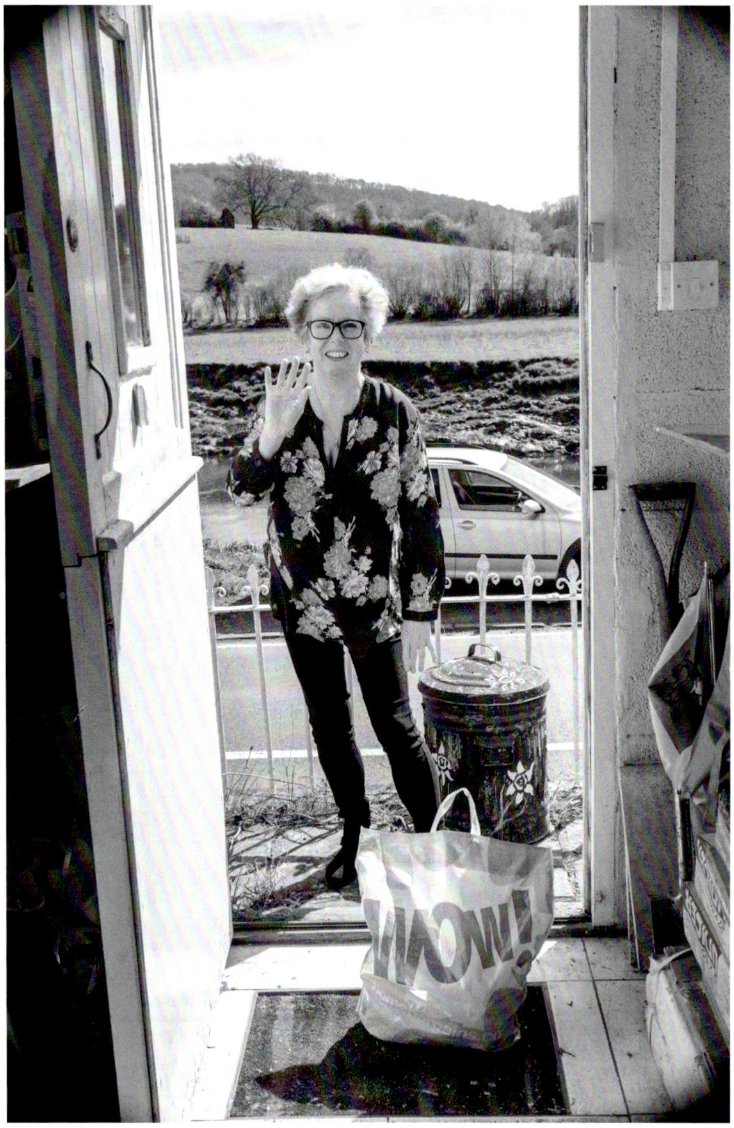

13 APRIL 2020 / TINTERN ANGEL. *TINTERN, WALES 2020*

Food seems to arrive miraculously at my front door. Neighbours can be just wonderful.

I have given myself the assignment of becoming an estate agent photographer photographing my own abode, the village, and what happens around me. It, of course, has commercial implications as if I conk it there will be a good set of images to help sell the cottage. Although not in any way my style, I am learning, and think I could now survive in a new genre, it's a matter of solving problems. So far I have 35 'in focus' pictures.

Whilst being isolated, a few things have happened that I can comment on.

A photographer, David Wilson, sent me a set of pictures he has been working on since the start of 2019. They are pictures of his village, Llangwm in Wales. As you know, I am a great advocate of documenting local community. Access makes life easier – as a freelance access is always a problem. Plus you meet more local people and become even more part of the community. All should be doing it. The problem is, what to do with the pictures once taken? Hopefully there is a local archive – but I suspect sadly no market – so one does it as a labour of love. Anyway, David's pictures are worth looking at.

Paul Cabuts, one who writes much better than most, has a new book coming out soon, essays – essential buying.

Plus *Offline Journal* gets better and better. 'No 6' is now available to pre-order. Everyone should subscribe – in fact it's my new question when I meet any new photographer: 'are you a subscriber to *Offline Journal*?'. The first essay in an essential book, *The Faber Book of Reportage* – basically writings from 430 BC 'til 1986, 701 pages, 296 essays – is by Thucydides, 430 BC, he wrote about plague in Athens. Within the essay he wrote, 'it attacked the extremities, the privates and fingers and toes, many escaped with the loss of these, though some lost their eyes as well'. Maybe we don't necessarily have it so bad.

Please all keep safe.

@davidhurnphoto @magnumphotos @offlinejournal @d_wilson_photo @paulcabuts #coronavirus #selfisolation

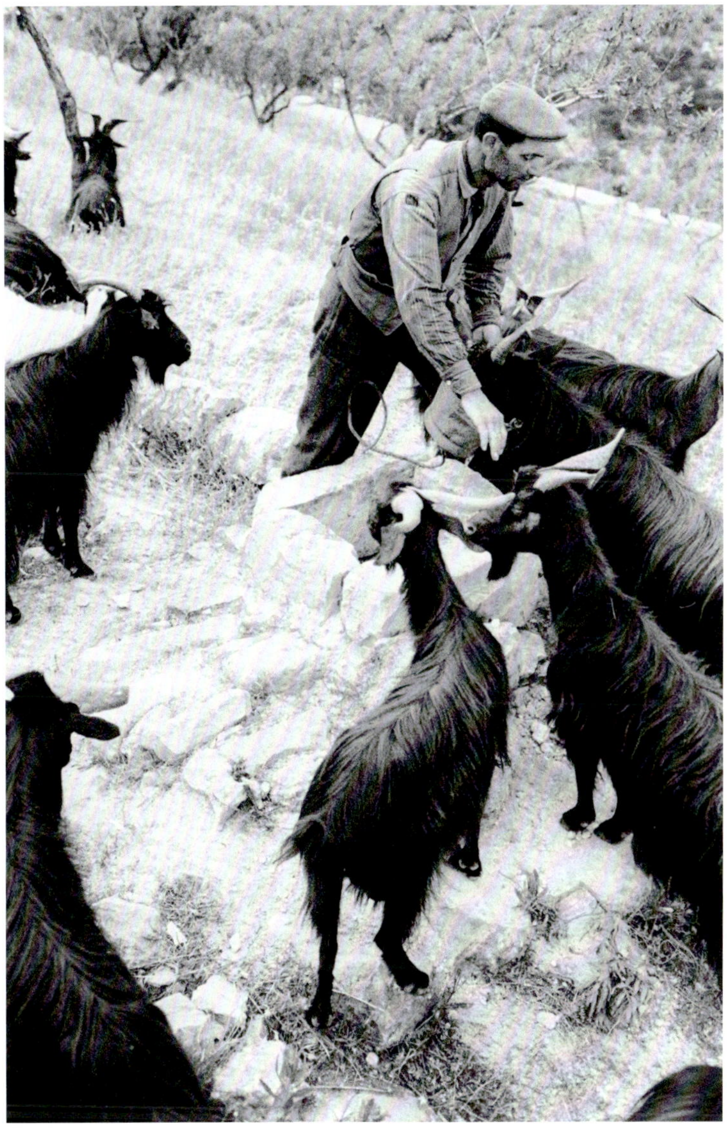

21 APRIL 2020 / GOAT HERDER. *BARI, ITALY 1964*

I have just heard dispiriting news. A major scientist says it is conceivable that: 'All persons over 70 years of age might have to self-isolate for a year or until an anti-Covid-19 vaccination is found'. If I cannot travel for a year I suspect that a part of my photographic life changes and has probably ended.

Could I finish my landscape project in a year's time? Could I face up to 16 towns around the Mediterranean in a year's time? It's all to do with energy, as one gets older it seems to react in an ever decreasing, clawing way. I suspect I will put on weight as I am not sure that I have the self-discipline to fully exercise from home.

The good is that I become my own paid assistant and if I learn a few new skills my archives can be put into good order.

The reality is that I suspect I would say to hell with it – as long as I can't give it to others, let's just get on with it.

In the meantime I will keep photographing as the estate agent me. I need it complete, then it has some merit in, say, the Tintern archive. Understanding what you are trying to do, who else is interested, where it can be seen is all part of the exercise, as far as I am concerned. I have never been a box of prints under the bed person.

@davidhurnphoto @magnumphotos #coronavirus #selfisolation

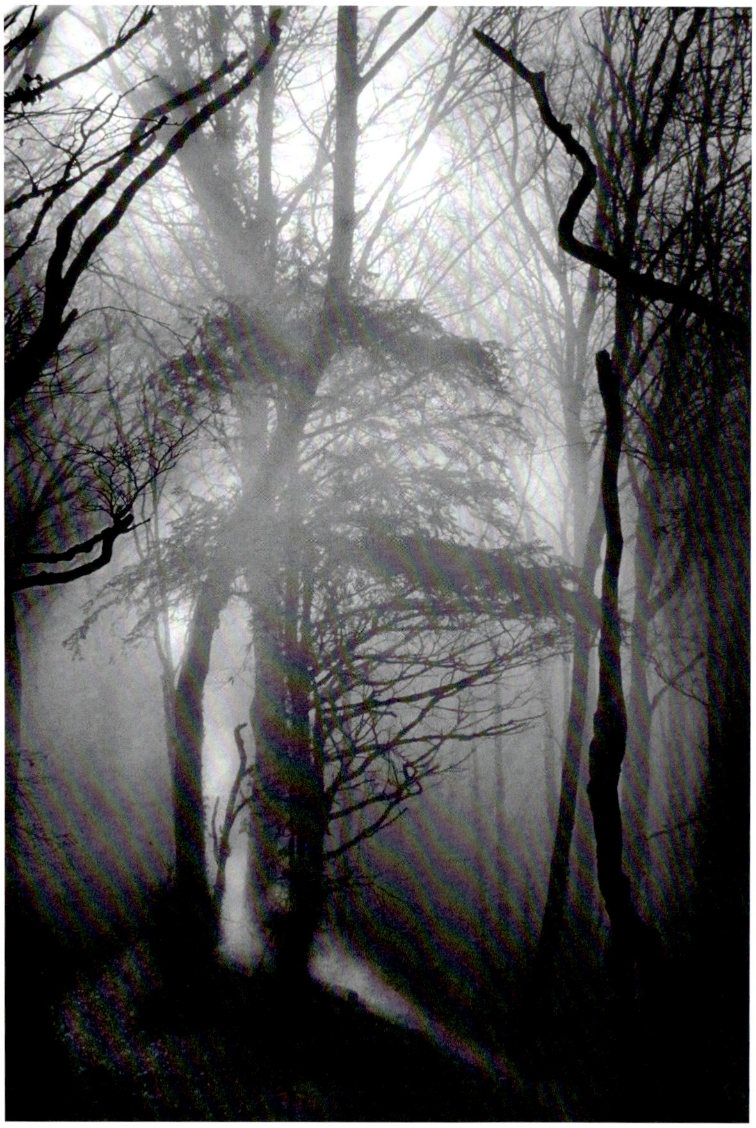

3 MAY 2020 / AT THE BOTTOM OF MY GARDEN. *TINTERN, WALES 1976*

I am in a complete muddle. I had presumed that the isolation would give me lots of time to catch up on archiving, re-organising, sorting CDs – of which I have 600 – how did I get so many and so many I have not heard for 30 years?

I started with a burst but have now found that I am simply doing stuff slower – same stuff but takes longer. I seem to have lost trace of time thus no Instagram for longer than I would have thought.

I am not seeing exhibitions, not seeing new books, not meeting photographers for chats – I always enjoyed those and they always sparked ideas.

In other words, I am wading through porridge.

I am about to photograph spring flowers in the garden – the woods at the bottom of the garden were photographed some years ago.

Well that's a lot of nonsense but at least I am trying.

@davidhurnphoto @magnumphotos #coronavirus #selfisolation #garden

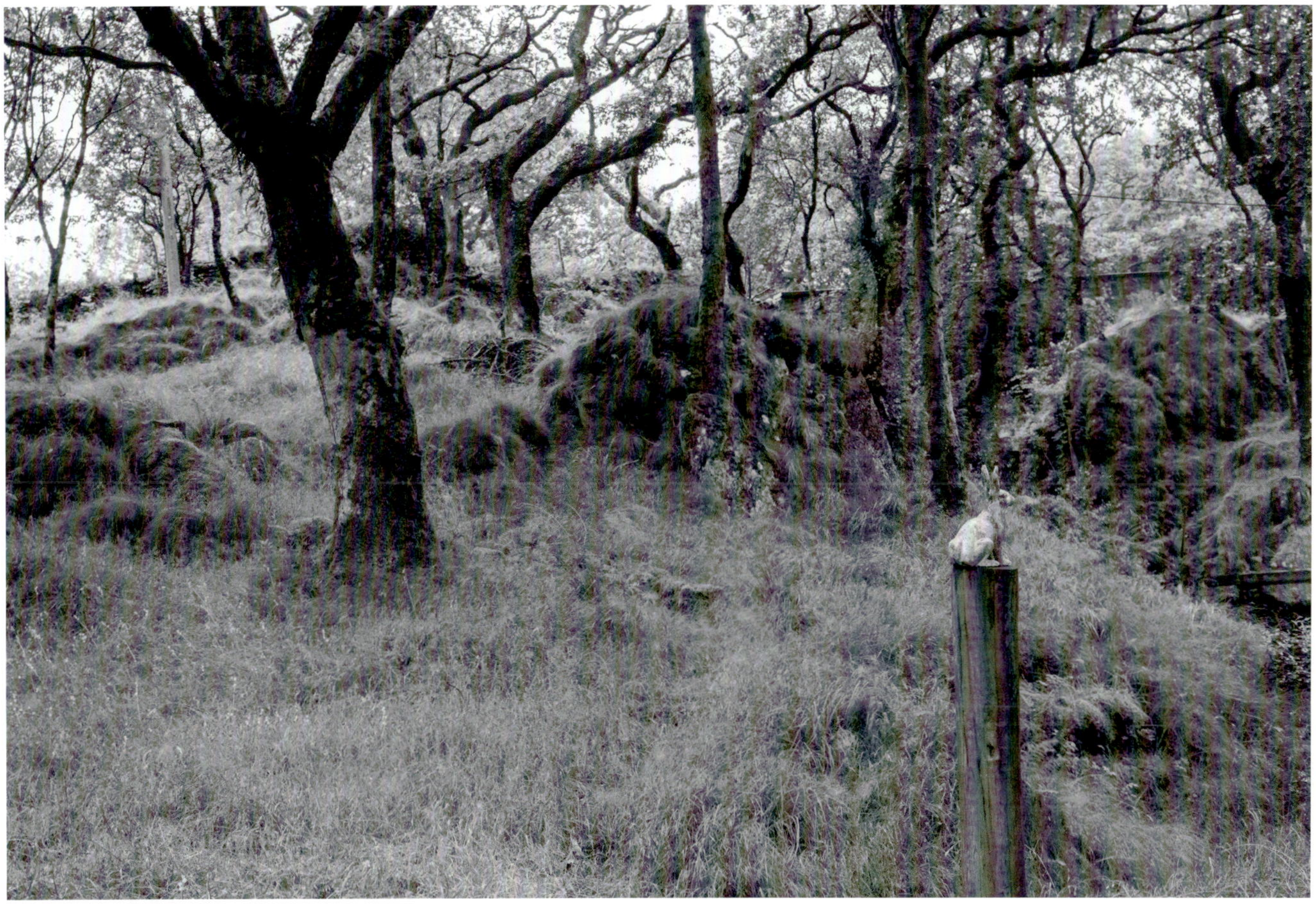

7 MAY 2020 / LIKE ALICE IN WONDERLAND. *GORDDINAN, WALES 1976*

I guess we are all hypocrites in some way. I don't really like awards, I think they are dangerous inflaters of egos, yet I have just received, and accepted, perhaps the most prestigious one, the Lucie Award for Documentary Photography. Previous recipients are impressive, among others, Mary Ellen Mark, Bruce Davidson, Larry Clark, Tod Papageorge, Danny Lyon, Eugene Richards, Martin Parr, but most pleasing to me, my 'brother' Josef Koudelka, who received it in 2008.

It means I don't feel anymore that I have to clean his shoes each morning when I stay with him in Paris.

I suspect the reality is, we all rely on the shoulders of those who went before us.

@davidhurnphoto @magnumphotos @brucedavidsonphoto @todpapageorge @larryclarkofficial @maryellenmarkfoundation @eugenerichardsphotography @josef_koudelka #lucieaward #dannylyon

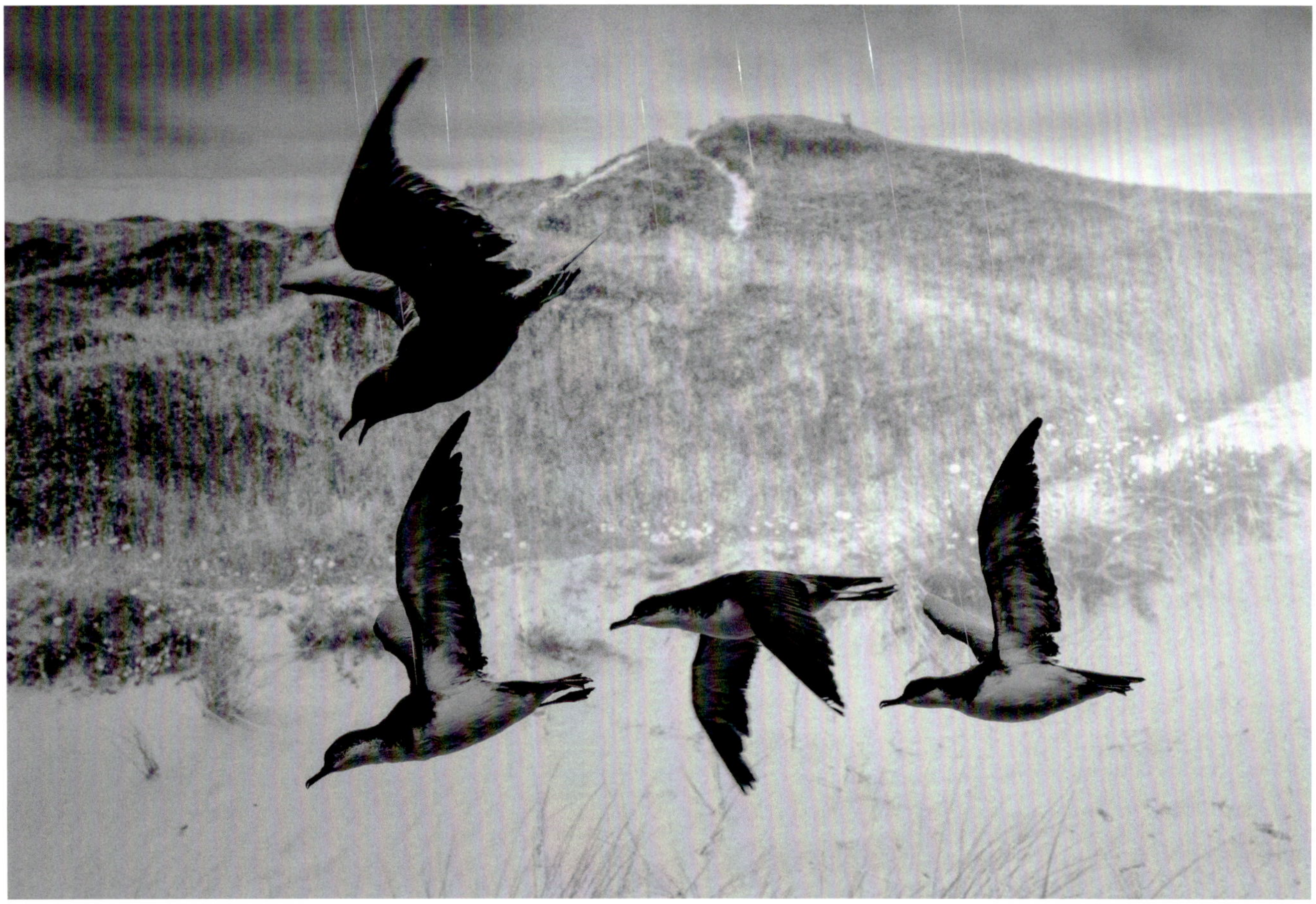

12 MAY 2020 / MUSEUM TABLEAU SHOWING WIRES. *CARDIFF, WALES 2006*

First, thank you so much for the kind words and happy emails. They really are greatly appreciated.

I have had subscriptions to two magazines for as long as I can remember, *Nature* and *The Economist*, both quite expensive, but I have never been a smoker so I have saved money. *Nature* claims, I think correctly, that it is 'a specialised organ for communicating science to scientists and the masses'. Its editor once wrote (very Orwell), we write in plain language, 'not the language of people who hide their meaning because of insecurity'. The magazine is authoritative and peer-reviewed.

It's sometimes difficult to define the truth, but we all know when we lie or are 'economical with the truth'. *Nature*, I feel, gives me some link to accuracy in a particular area.

Within photography's genres I must admit that I am most drawn towards pictures which are as the camera 'saw' them. I particularly enjoy some where the results are bordering on the ambiguous. I have less interest in the stage directed and no interest in the text swamped, or Photoshop exaggerated pictures. Elliott Erwitt once wrote, 'Photoshop makes bad photographs worse'. In the present environment, I personally think 'knowledgable misdirection' is dodgy.

@davidhurnphoto @magnumphotos #nature #economist #orwell

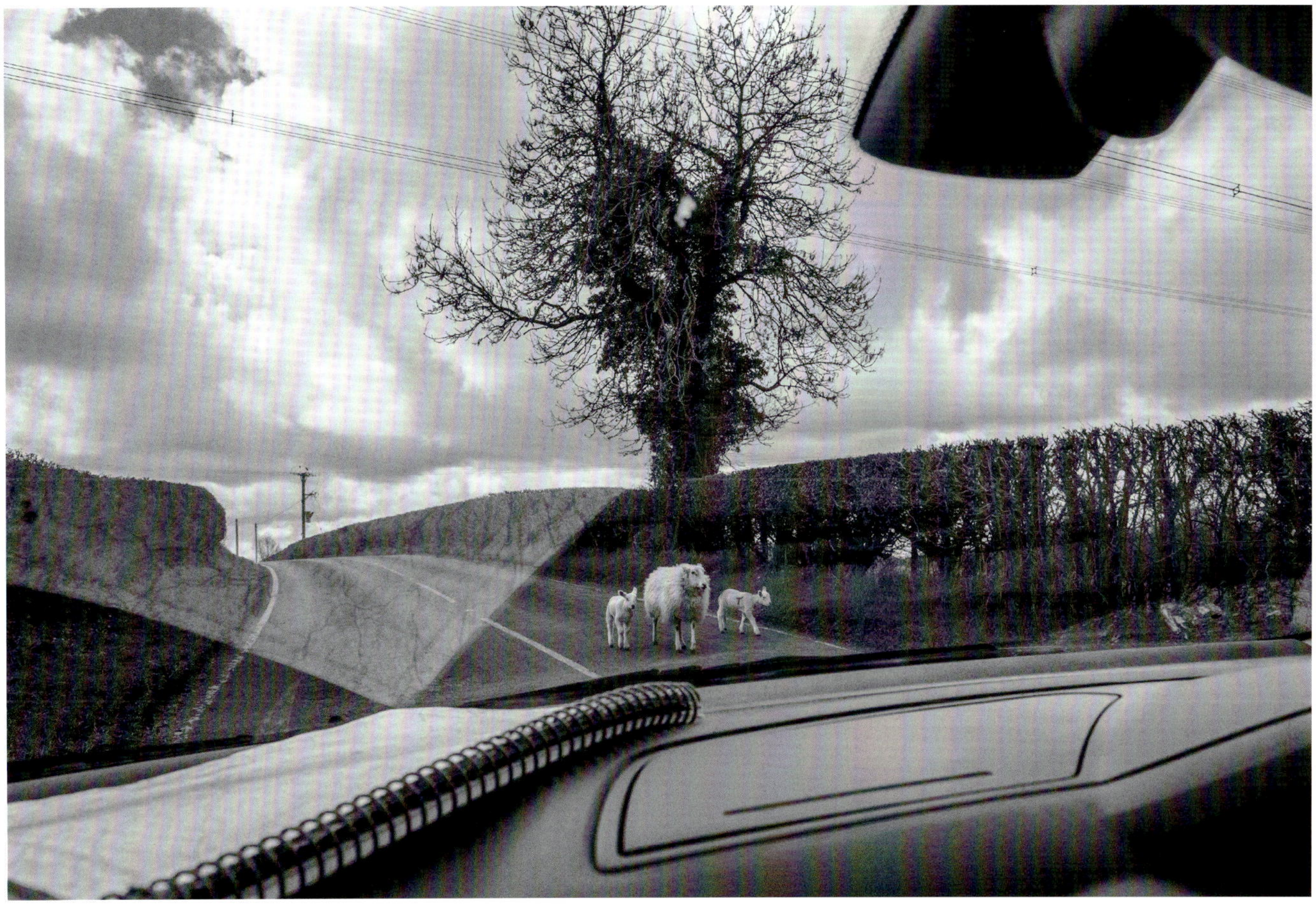

22 MAY 2020 / CAR WINDOW. *NORTH WALES 2016*

All my life I have had difficulty in reading, or rather concentrating when reading. After becoming a photographer I have deliberately gone out of my way to photograph writers, as knowing them I have found it easier to read all that they have written, for example I befriended: Romain Gary, Irwin Shaw, Jan Morris, Owen Sheers, and found it easy to read all their books.

I think I am just learning another tactic. I have been listening to *Book of the Week* on Radio 4. *The See-Through House*: I would never have read this book but being read to, I realise the book is a delight. It's by Shelley Klein and about her family home. Simple but lovely.

I am not sure what this has to do with photography but I sense for me it meets somewhere. I guess it's about solutions.

When I come out of first stages of lockdown, I suspect I will drive, or better still be driven, around Wales. Wales because it's where I live. I will take pictures out of the window or within close proximity to the car. If you decide to do this please be careful. If self driving make sure you are stationary.

My memory of my most disappointing miss was when a special lady from the BBC was driving me in rural Wales down a narrow lane, we had to stop as the local farmers were moving a large flock of sheep which were rampaging all over the road and up the hedge banks, pursued by three sheep dogs in full flight. It was potential perfect, very me – I had locked my cameras in the boot. Never again.

My publisher has asked me to include 'Head over to @reelartpress to pick up the *Arizona* book with free shipping, a few left.' I hate hustling, he is bending my arm.

@davidhurnphoto @magnumphotos @reelartpress @shelleyklein @owen_sheers

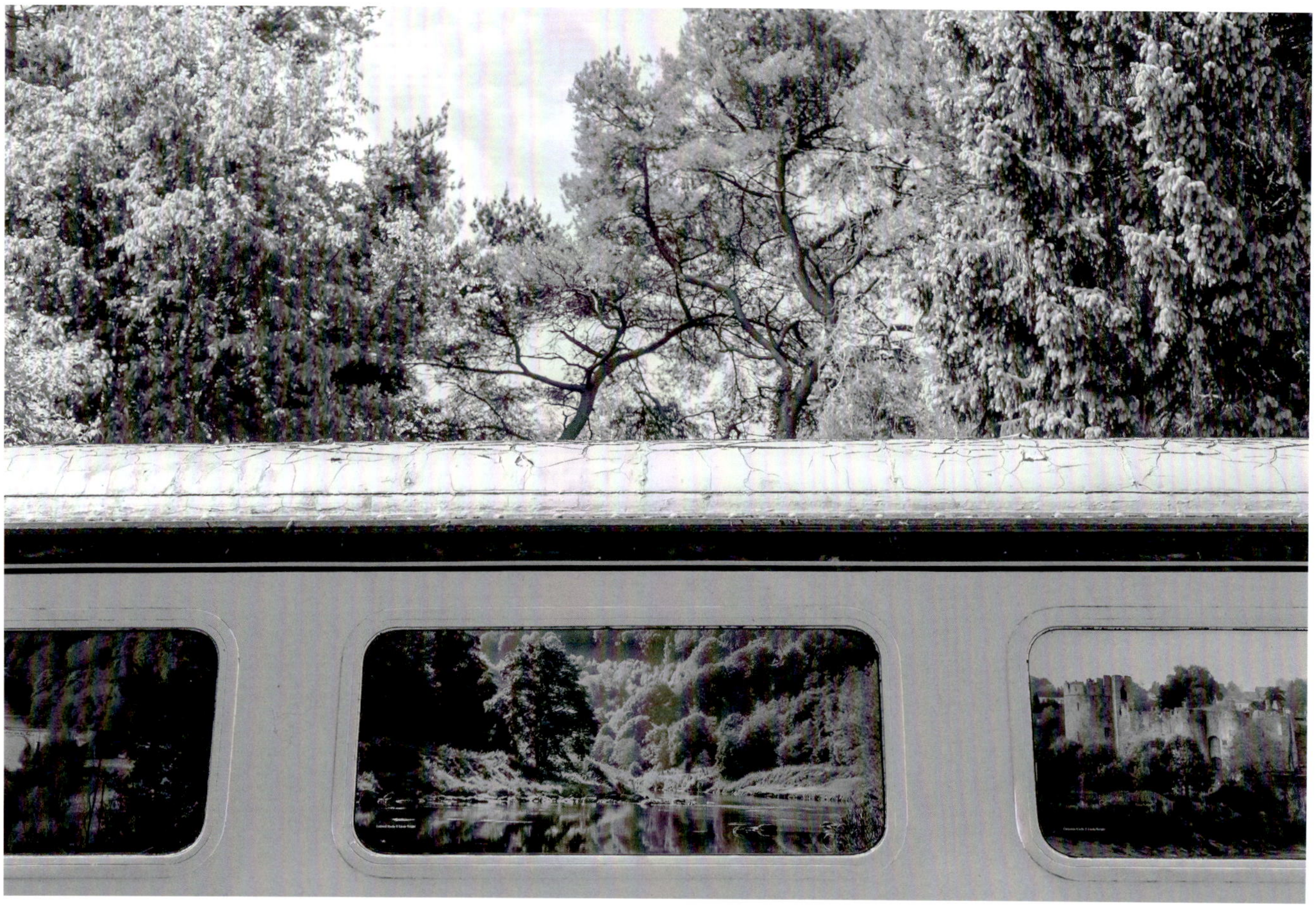

28 MAY 2020 / ONCE A STATION. *NORTH WALES 2016*

To me, Coronavirus seems to provoke one of two reactions. For so many, just settle down and do the paperwork. For a few, it's the sparking of innovation.

Last night I participated in an uplifting hour, listening enthralled, on Zoom.

Martin Parr was weeding out information from Stuart Franklin about his remarkable series of pictures from the hospital where his wife is a doctor. Stuart first showed pictures for half an hour and then answered a barrage of intelligent questions for another half hour.

One soon realised that there is no substitute for genuine experience and professionalism. No posturing, no exaggeration, just accurately observed moving facts. You sensed this was real.

I have seen other very worthwhile pictures from within hospitals in the UK, but they all seemed to lack a little something. The photographers had access, obviously had sincerity but sincerity is not enough. The photographer must understand how to produce a cohesive whole. Like any other profession, true quality comes from frequent hard work.

I think about 70 people paid a minimal fee to tune in. I believe this to be the first of a series. If you wish to advance yourself as a photographer, get signed up for the whole series.

@davidhurnphoto @magnumphotos @martinparrfdn @stuartafranklin

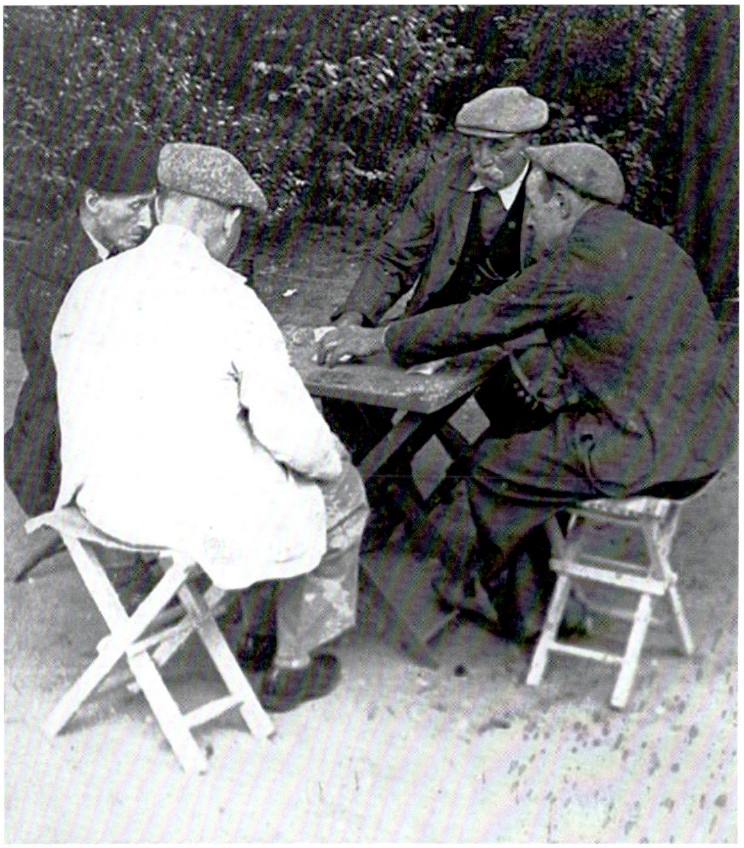

2 JUNE 2020 / 1954 CARDS. *BELGIUM 1954*

Locked down, I am delving into my archive in the hope that it will spark thoughts.

I found this picture – I might have posted it when I first started on Instagram – it's the first picture I ever remember taking. It's taken in Belgium, I only remember this because I was still at Sandhurst and was in Belgium with the army athletics team.

I have this strangely coloured print, no negative, no caption. Luckily now there is scanning.

I had not then learned how imperative archiving negatives, captioning and numbering are. If I help you in just one way, it's to make sure you always quickly note this information – you will thank me in 30 years' time.

I like the picture, it's accurate and honestly seen. If I had stood six inches further to the left one would see the man with the beret more clearly – but I have learned.

@davidhurnphoto @magnumphotos

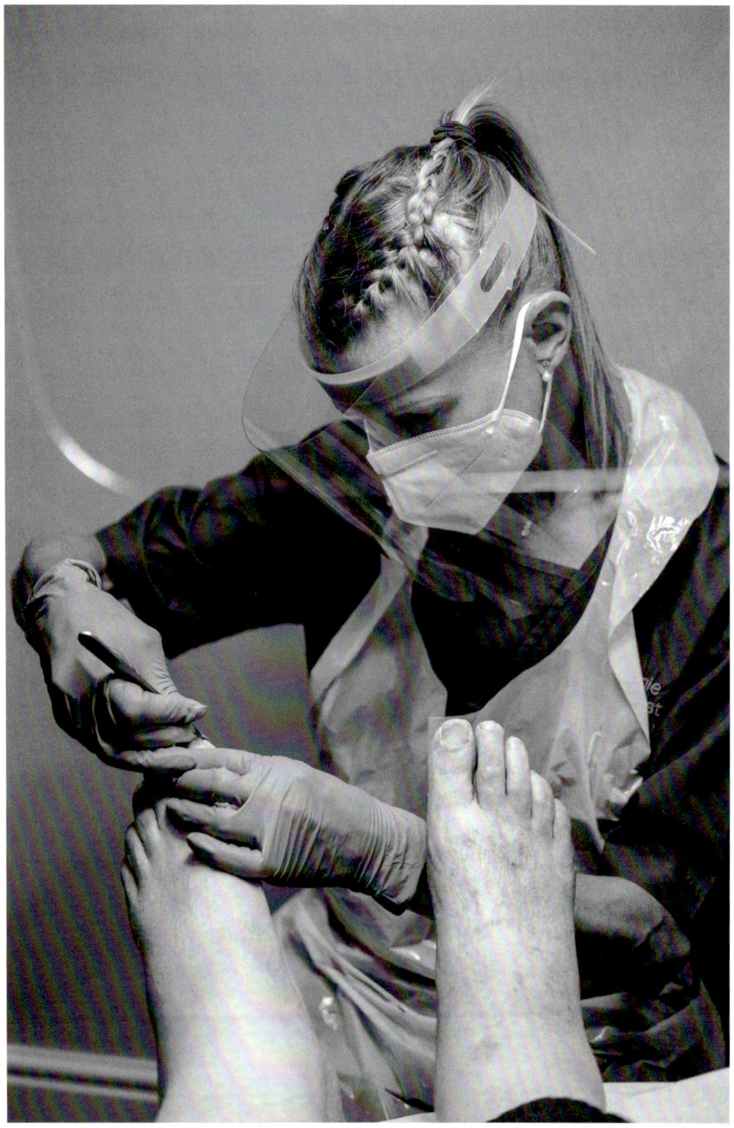

5 JUNE 2020 / MY FEET – YESTERDAY. *CHEPSTOW, WALES 2020*

Yesterday was excitement day. I could drive for more than five miles which meant for the first time in three months I could get into the local town, Chepstow. Three months of toe nail growth is difficult for someone who has trouble putting on their socks. What is bizarre is that podiatrists were open. I dashed to Hallux and now feel I can pleasantly walk again. At last I have a person picture.

Way back in the '60s, Bill Jay and I had many a spat with the Royal Photographic Society. How they have changed. The new premises in Bristol are magnificent, the 'power management' seem much more enlightened, they have a beautiful gallery – have shown some excellent exhibitions – have a beautiful lecture theatre, expanding reference/education rooms. Their *Journal* has just arrived, it's getting better and better with every issue, in fact I would go so far in suggesting I find it now the most interesting photo magazine in the country, mainly because it's not as incestuous as most. The last issue includes an obituary to Sue Davies, who was the founding director of the Photographers' Gallery in 1971. Boy, did she put on some worthwhile shows of photographers we still remember. An article showing pictures by one of the photographers who had access to a Covid-19 hospital, Jonny Weeks. Marc Aspland sports photographer for *The Times*. Heather Angel, a well-respected wildlife photographer. Exceptional photographs by Lewis Carroll, primarily of Alice Liddell. Deeply moving pictures by Moises Saman, and a new series by Mandy Barker. That's an eclectic high-quality mix.

Photographers stretching themselves to their limits in any genre are always interesting. I sometimes don't wish to do what they do, but I enjoy the looking.

@davidhurnphoto @magnumphotos @royalphotographicsociety @mikeyp1839 @marc.aspland @heatherangelphotography @moisessaman @mandybarkerphotography #halluxpodiatry #jonnyweeks

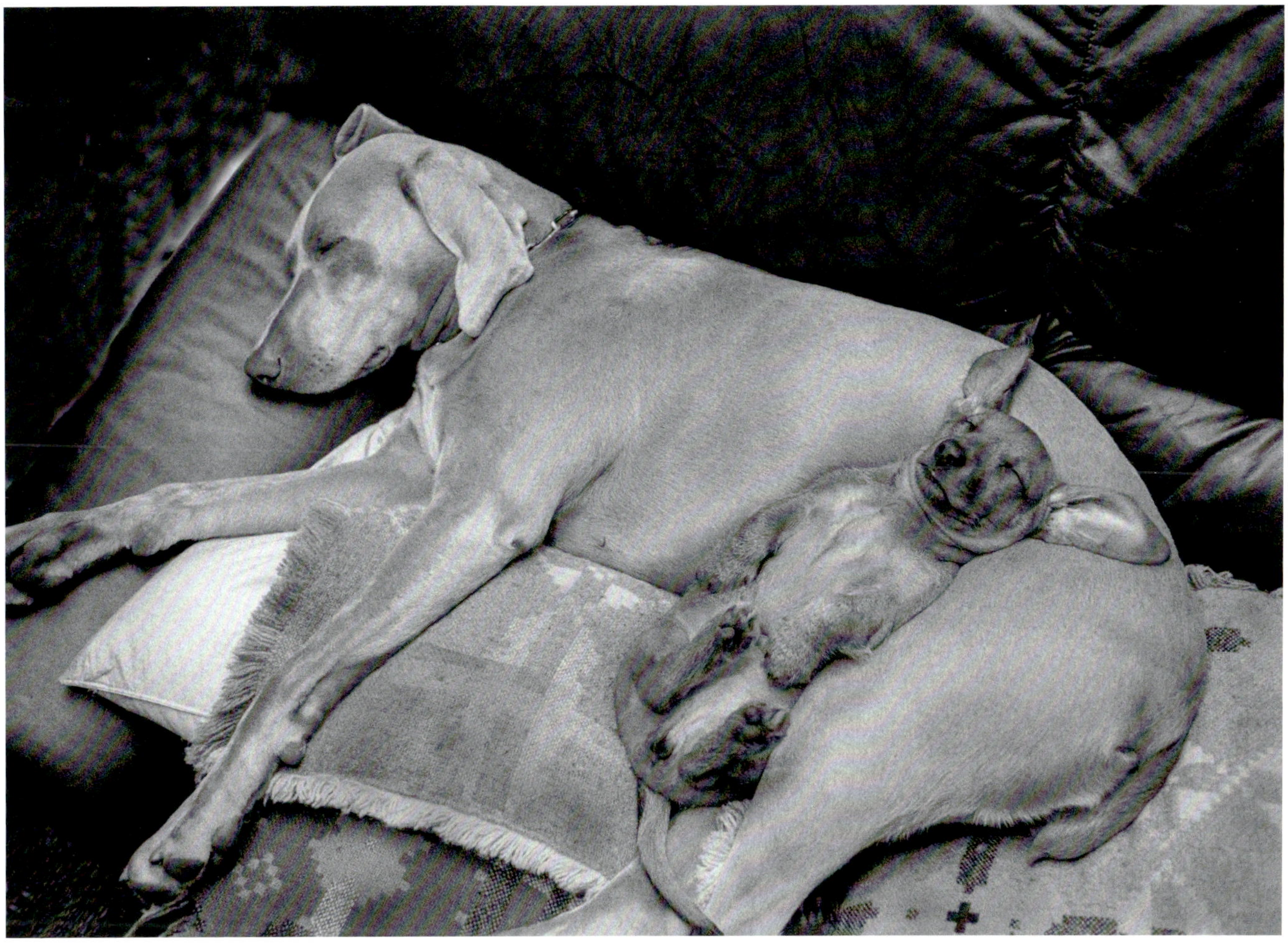

13 JUNE 2020 / PEEWEE & HANNAH. *TINTERN, WALES 1987*

I feel I have dealt well with the shutdown, after all I am surrounded by nearly 50 years of personally selected toys. An hour on this, an hour on that, the day soon passes. What I miss is something that moves, something that tried to put its tongue in my mouth – when will that happen again – I, of course, mean my dogs. Sadly, the last two are both long gone to a hole in the garden. I have always loved dogs. I have been, maybe still am, attracted to getting a new one. Advantages: real loving companionship; disadvantage: the acceptance that I was not going to travel again except within the UK.

I have a shelf of very favourite books, resting there is *The Dog in Photography: 1839-Today*, published by TASCHEN, I think, pictures collected/edited by Raymond Merritt. It's a dense book, over 650 pages. I can't think of a book that could possibly give one more joy.

Talking of joy, Jacques-Henri Lartigue is represented by seven pictures, Henri Cartier-Bresson by three, Elliott Erwitt by four, Ralph Gibson surprisingly by six, Frank Hurley of Antarctic fame by five, William Wegman by eight, but for me a not good selection. There are nude lady with dog, daguerreotypes, always slightly dubious, and nude lady with dog, albumen, also dubious. I think for me of most interest is a picture captioned 'unknown photographer' showing a large crowd, I suspect about 250 people, from the '30s, of which over 30 are holding a dog, usually a terrier, above their heads. I have no idea where it is or why. I would love to know?

For me this is photography at its best.

@davidhurnphoto @magnumphotos @taschen @elliotterwitt @williamwegman @ralphgibson_photography #raymondmerritt #jacqueshenrilartigue #henricartierbresson #frankhurley

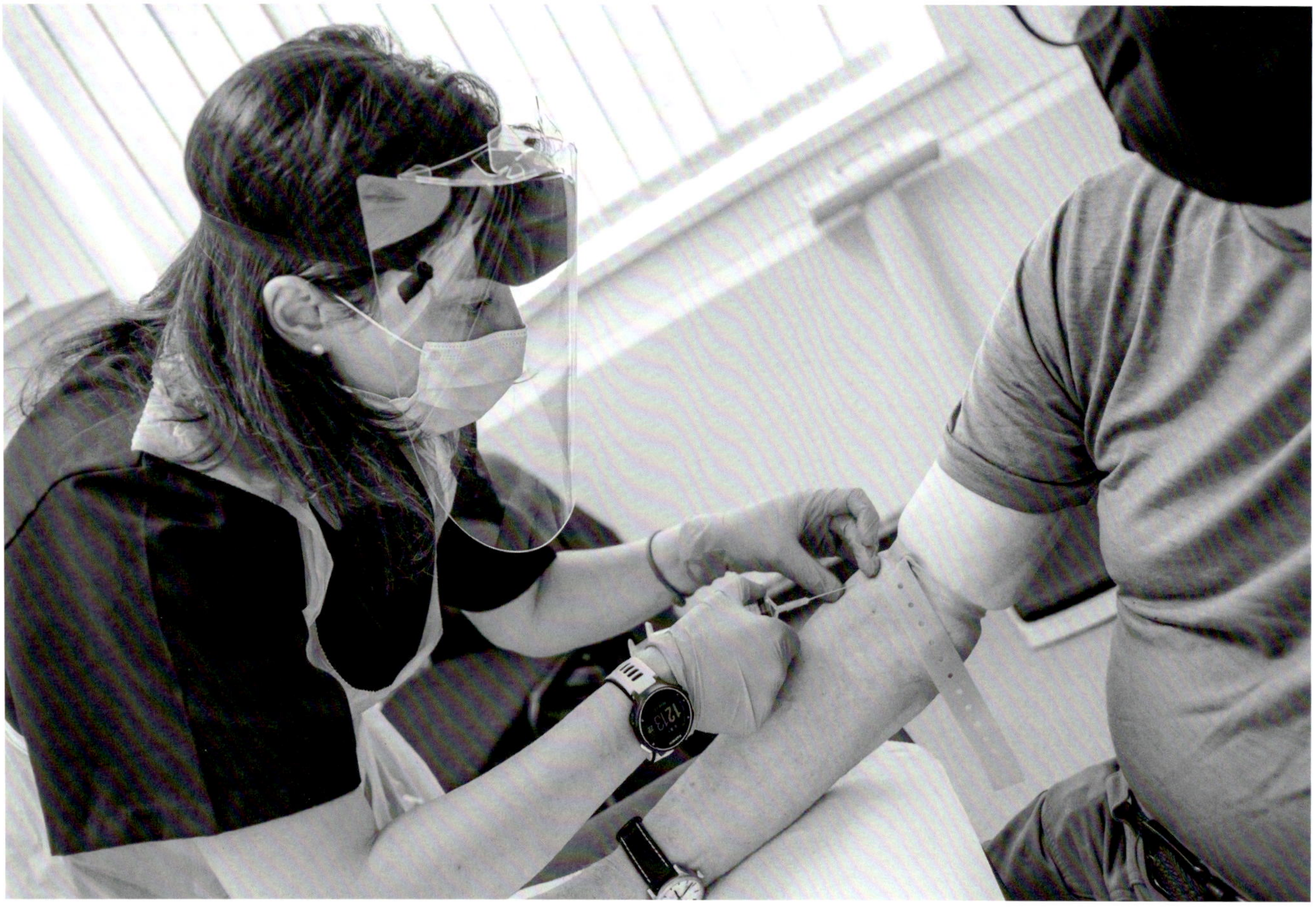

17 JUNE 2020 / COUNTRY DOCTOR, *TINTERN, WALES 2020*

Sometimes in life luck is on your side. I 'found ' Tintern, a wonderful place to live, but the surgery was already there and it has developed. Wye Dean Practice is as the NHS should be at its best, wonder team of doctors, nurses, healthcare and other staff. They have always made me feel I am in good hands and safe in their knowledge and care.

I am a coward, but had to have a blood test. Kate is best for that, I have never passed out. It seems the trick is, don't be dehydrated.

She let me take pictures of me being done. Maybe I shouldn't have been surprised but the concentration in trying to shoot a picture, unseeing, left handed, one handed, was such that I had no time for hysterics.

How I would love to be able to re-do Eugene Smith's wonderful essay, *Country Doctor*, well worth looking up.

I think so much of the attitude and strength of the photographers I find most interesting is bound up in concentration.

I remember my first meeting with Sergio Larrain, we were both in Trafalgar Square shooting pigeons – I remember him saying, 'I knew you were serious, you looked so concentrated'.

@davidhurnphoto @magnumphotos #wyedeanpractice #katestafford #sergiolarrain

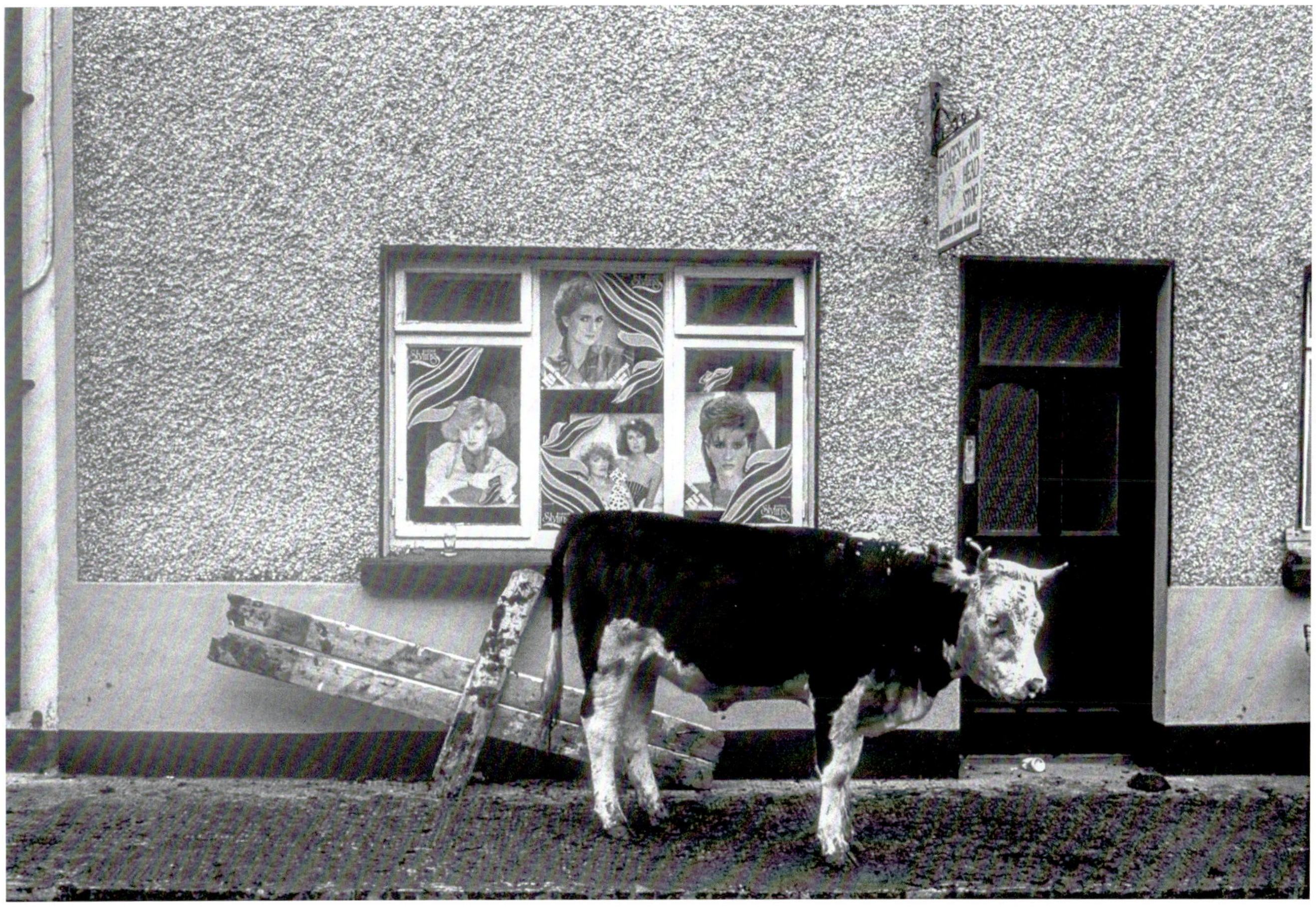

20 JUNE 2020 / HAIRDRESSING OPEN. ***KILLARNEY, IRELAND 1984***

Ha, ha – well I have found out that people don't like pictures of needles.

I have just heard that Ireland is letting you get your hair done/cut. Maybe Wales soon. I was beginning to look like a '60s hippy of the particularly lazy type. I bought, online, electric hair clippers, put on a number two and did a self shearing – looks OK at the front and I can't see the back so who cares.

I have had many very enjoyable trips to Ireland, two for *GEO* magazine. Once to cover David Lean, 'film director's country', this included photographing the intelligent, lovely, Julie Christie. Second was a project on 'Puck Fair' a strange event: every year a group of people go up into the mountains and catch a wild goat, the goat is brought back to the town and the 'Queen of Puck', traditionally a young schoolgirl from one of the local primary schools, crowns the goat 'King Puck'. The next few days are a photographer's delight, cliché after cliché, but then sometimes clichés are actually true.

A fun holiday, and after, you can judge your pictures against the many who have been there before.

@davidhurnphoto @magnumphotos #puckfair #juliechristie

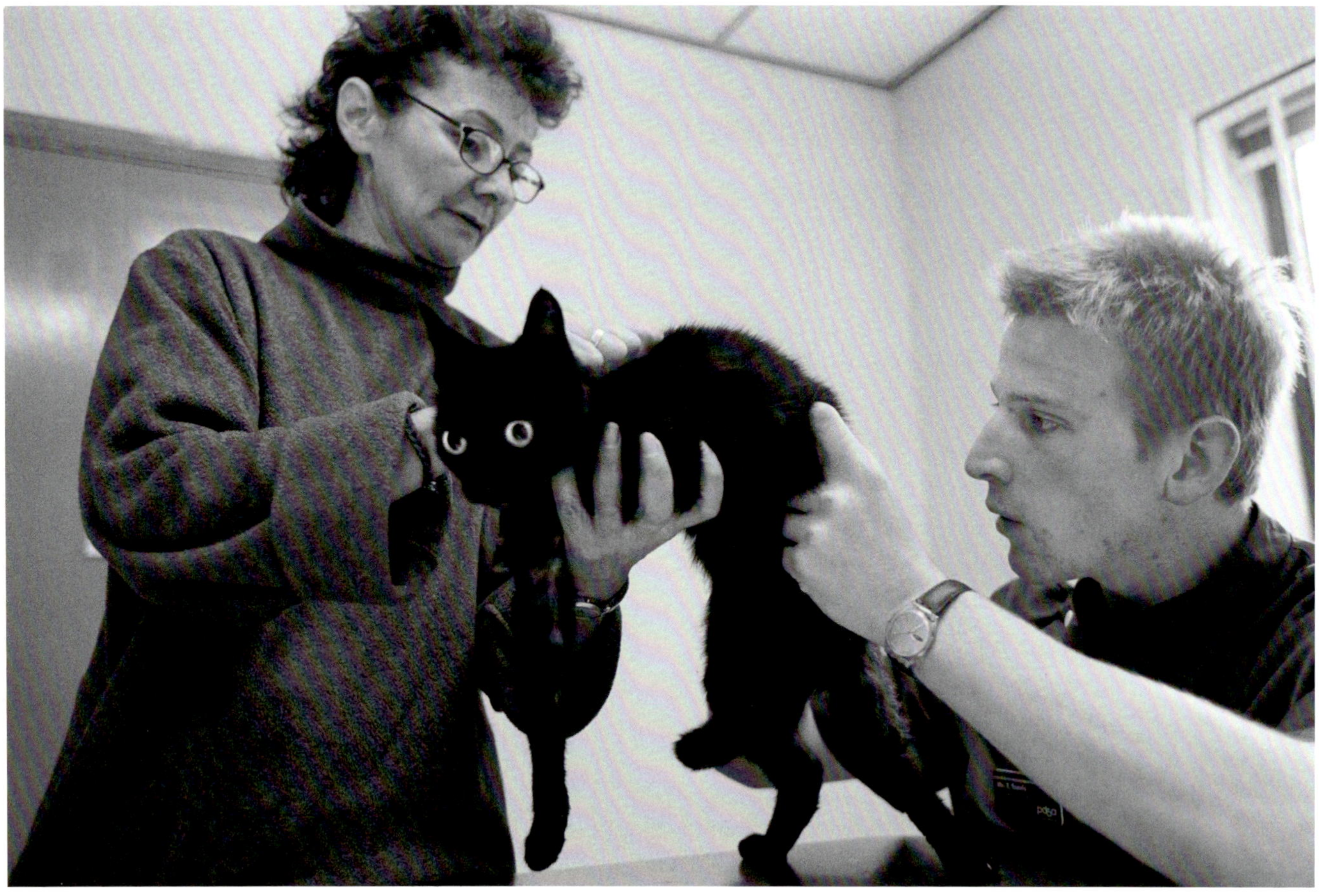

2 JULY 2020 / A NEW LOOK. *CARDIFF, WALES 2003*

A long time since posting, mainly due to Magnum business – we had our annual board meeting and it seemed to stretch out over time. I was suspicious of Zoom but it worked remarkably well, it or similar platforms will certainly have a major effect on business in the future. At one time we had 97 participants on the screen – two screens of 40 something, that one could switch between. Organisation depends on having a very good/firm chairman, we did. In many ways it was very democratic, for the first time the introverted seemed to get an equal say, however, in my opinion, it can foster a 'herd instinct' and some ideas seemed in danger of gaining momentum in an unthinking way.

We took in five new nominees, sadly experience tells us that probably two will not make the final cut.

Magnum has set up a new site to create discussion on what is happening to individuals during the close down: Magnum Flow. I think it is worth looking at. magnumphotos.com/flow

We have a new CEO, Caitlin Hughes, and a new Photographers' President, Olivia Arthur, both frighteningly bright.

@davidhurnphoto @magnumphotos #caitlinhughes @oliviarthur

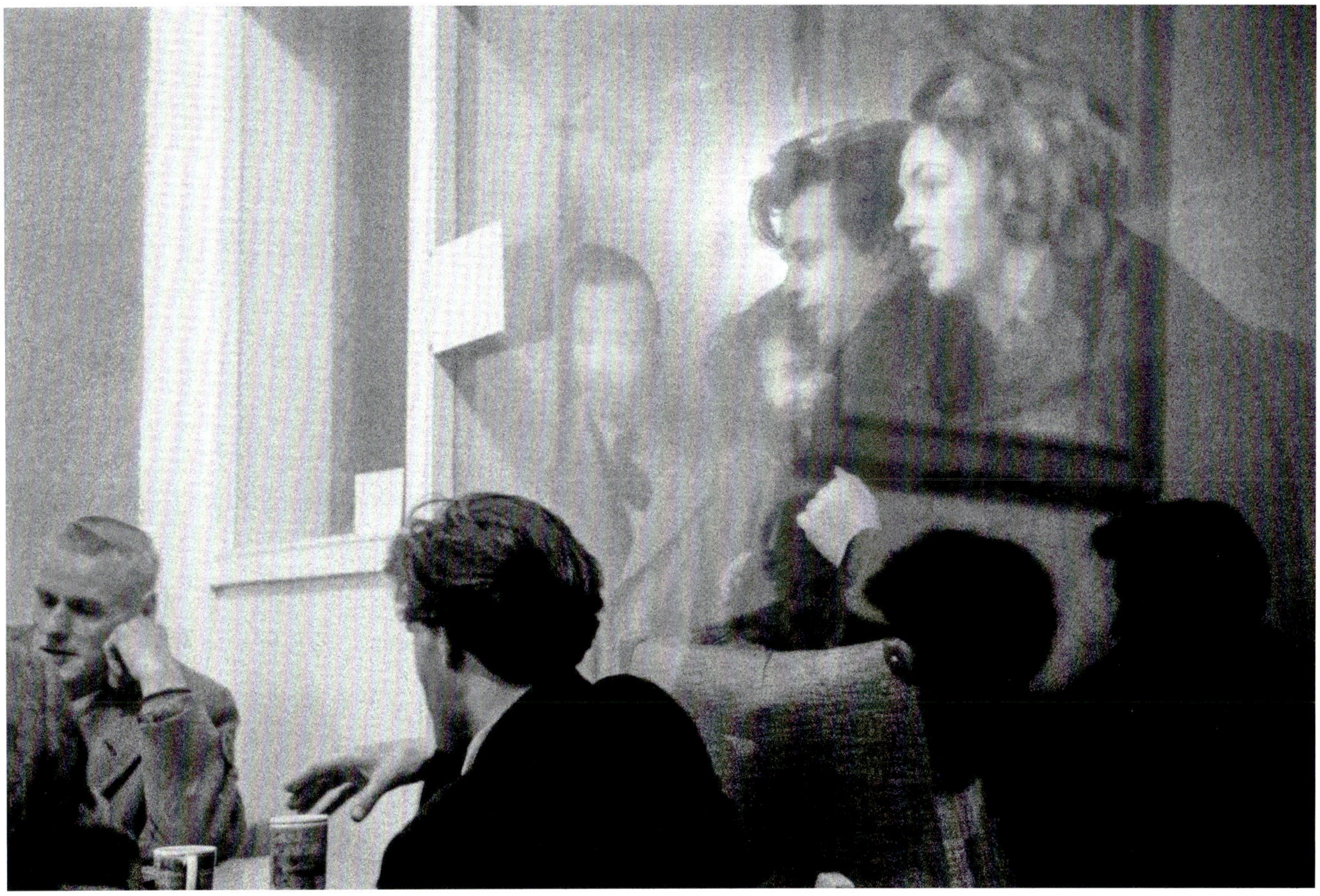

10 JULY 2020 / PARTISAN COFFEE HOUSE. *LONDON, ENGLAND 1958*

I am losing track of what is open or not open. I think under some circumstances, cafes are open on Monday.

Will there ever be another coffee house like the Partisan? Set up in 1958 by the radical historian Raphael Samuel, with the help of Stuart Hall and the Marxist academic Eric Hobsbawm. Home of radical talk, where subversive thinking was encouraged and a cup of trademark mediocre coffee came with a complementary side-order of socialist discourse – it is said that Special Branch officers used to come in and play chess so that they could listen in to the conversations.

It was here that the CND's 'Committee of 100' was named and the first Aldermaston marches were arranged.

I remember seeing or photographing Doris Lessing, Ken Russell, Arnold Wesker, Colin Wilson, Quentin Crisp, John Hurt, Barbara Steele, Raymond Williams, John Antrobus, among many others who later became well known by 'doing stuff'.

It was in places like this that I honed my photography and interest in the world.

@davidhurnphoto @magnumphotos #partisancoffeehouse

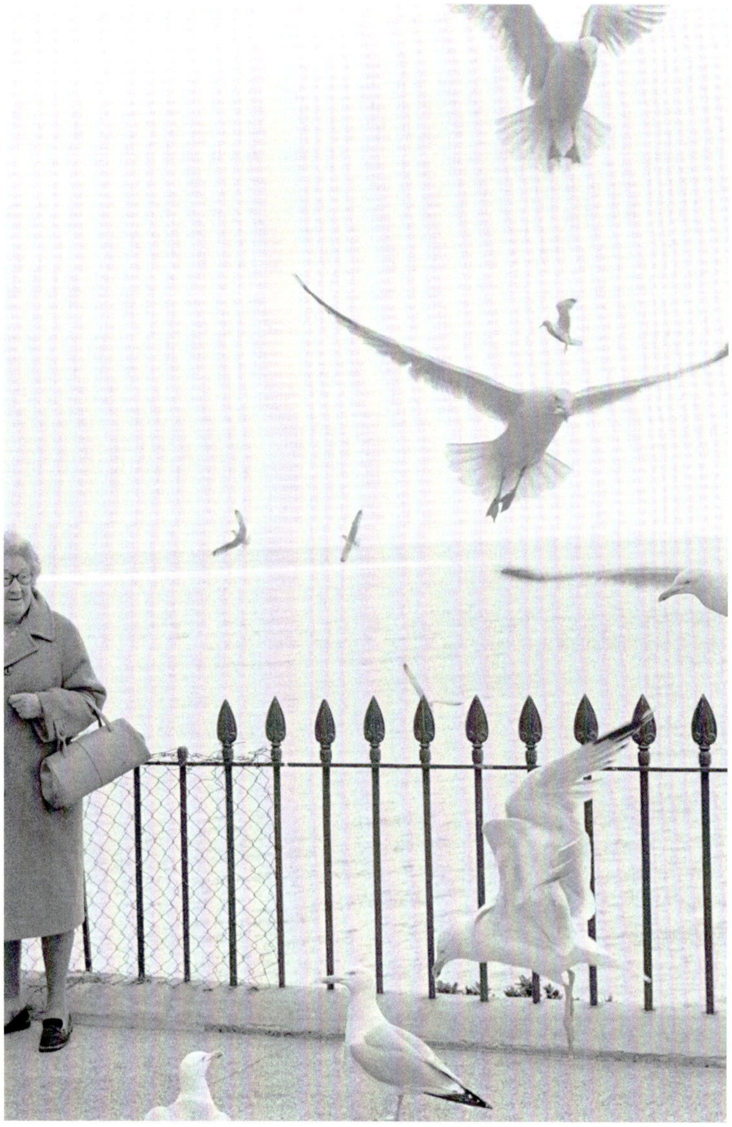

16 JULY 2020 / TENBY SEAGULLS. *TENBY, WALES 1974*

A dear friend of mine has just died.

The great photographer Paul Fusco.

His photo essay 'RFK Funeral Train' is, in my opinion, as great a use of photography as ever achieved.

He was a wonderful person. Totally thoughtful of others.

He was a photographer who symbolised Magnum at its very best, always interested in what was happening in the world and wishing to document it in as human and accurate a way as is possible within all the shortcomings of being a human being.

He had no ego.

@davidhurnphoto @magnumphotos @paulfuscoestate

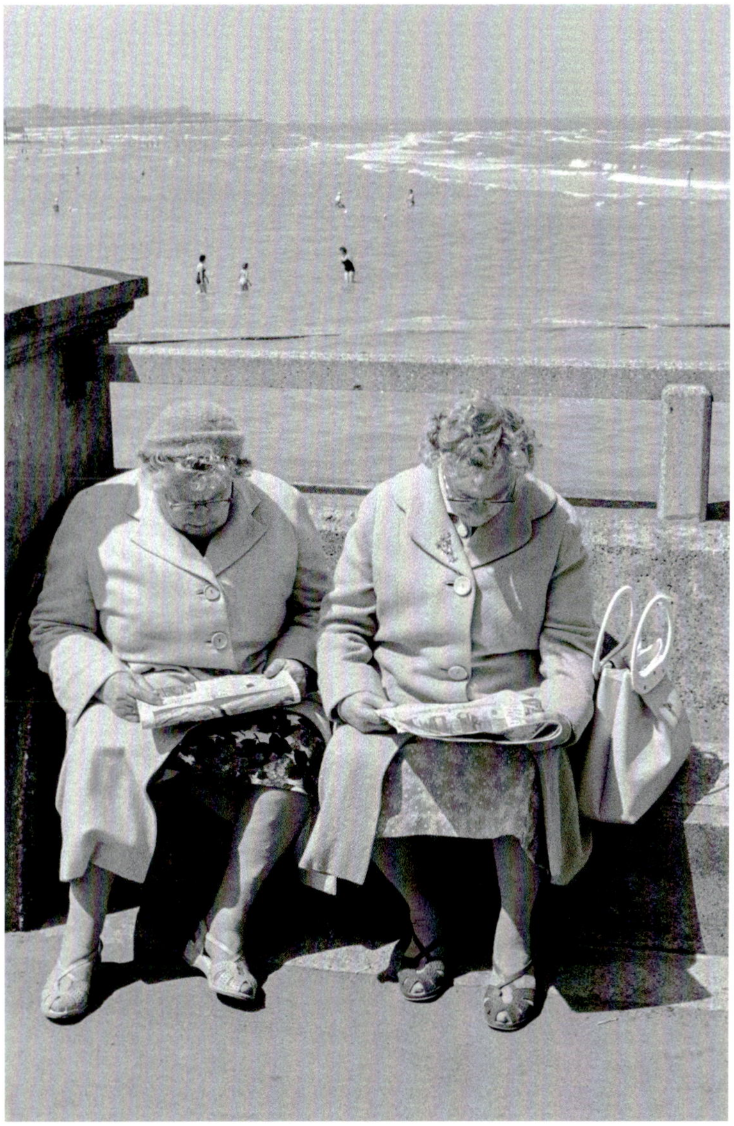

3 AUGUST 2020 / *HERNE BAY, ENGLAND 1963*

I was looking at a picture by Kertész, the great Hungarian photographer, it was in his book, *Sixty Years of Photography*, and was captioned 'Broken Bench', September 15, 1962, New York. We seem to see a park bench with a broken back, to the left of the picture is a figure of a man in a dark coat hands behind his back with head cut off, in the background two small female figures. The picture gives a feeling of menace. How? Why?

One of the unsolved mysteries/joys of photography is how a group of items/facts in a photograph can seemingly produce a different reaction than the obvious when one simply analyses the component parts. It's as though we seem to have two kinds of visual process; one is factual, simple record, and second the ability to combine separate elements and invent thoughts and personal explanation.

I remember I once had two dogs, 'Poo' and 'Peewee' their names. 'Poo', a German Shepherd, when seeing animals on the TV would growl. 'Peewee', a Weimaraner, didn't react at all except with puzzlement at Poo's reaction. Which was the more intelligent? Poo, who recognises animals on TV, or Peewee, who pays no heed? I guess it's simply a matter of seeing the world in different ways, coming to different conclusions though seemingly having the same facts.

Ultimately, the really intelligent are willing to debate their viewpoints, putting aside prior prejudices, so they can build on the best that we all have to offer.

@davidhurnphoto @magnumphotos @andre_kertesz_estate #hernebay

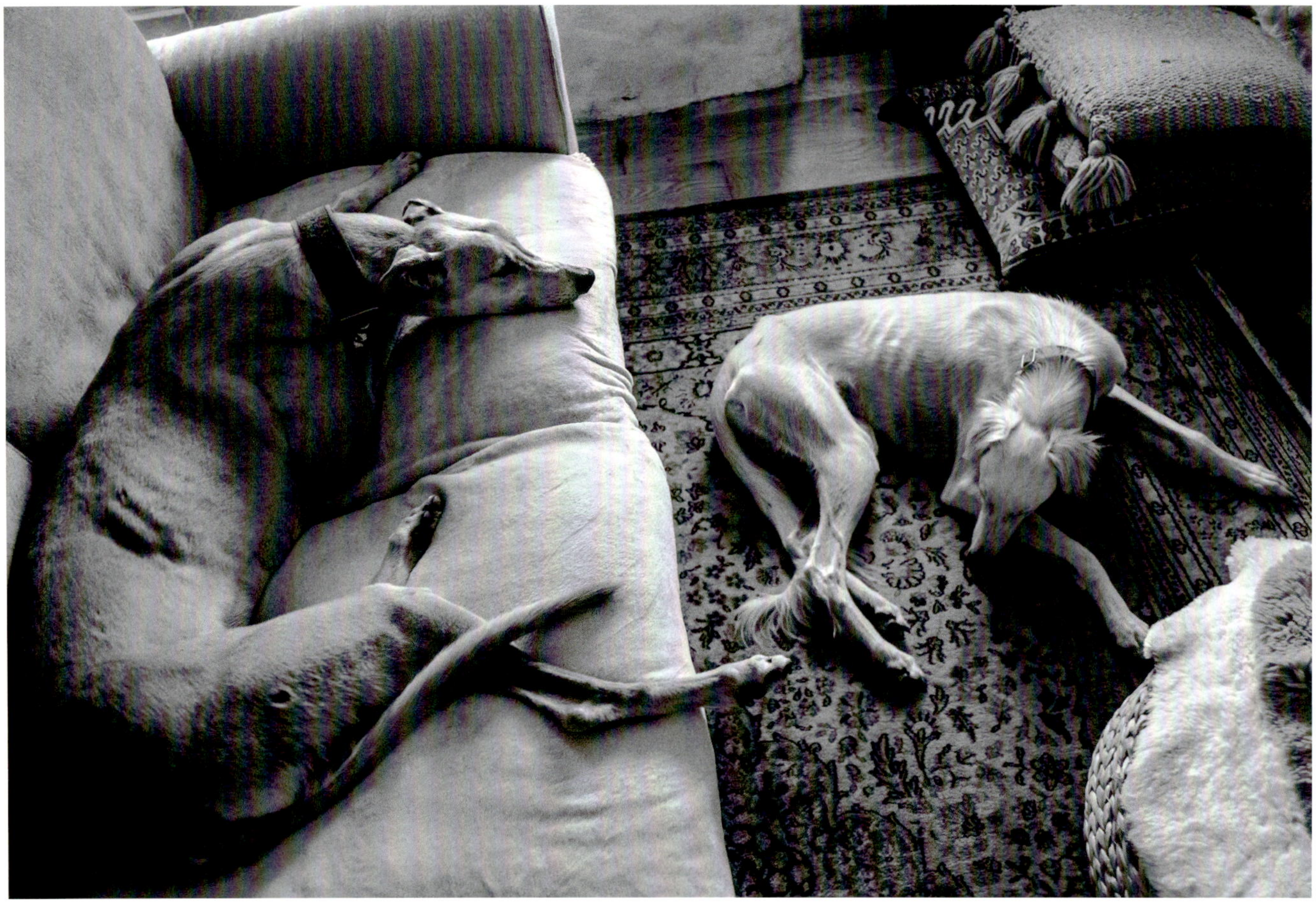

20 AUGUST 2020 / ELEGANCE. *WALES 2020*

I enjoy elegance. I decided to test my semi coming out of lockdown with a drive to see the special lady a couple of hours away. To say she likes dogs is a gross understatement. She has three – all from refuge greyhoundrescuewales.co.uk – why would anyone ever buy a dog? – a Greyhound, a Whippet and a Saluki.

So much of what I enjoy most in photographs is content being projected by elegant design.

I don't set up pictures so for me it takes a lot of patience and a lot of misses. But when it works, boy does it bring back memories, and that's worthwhile.

@davidhurnphoto @magnumphotos #greyhound #whippet #saluki #dog

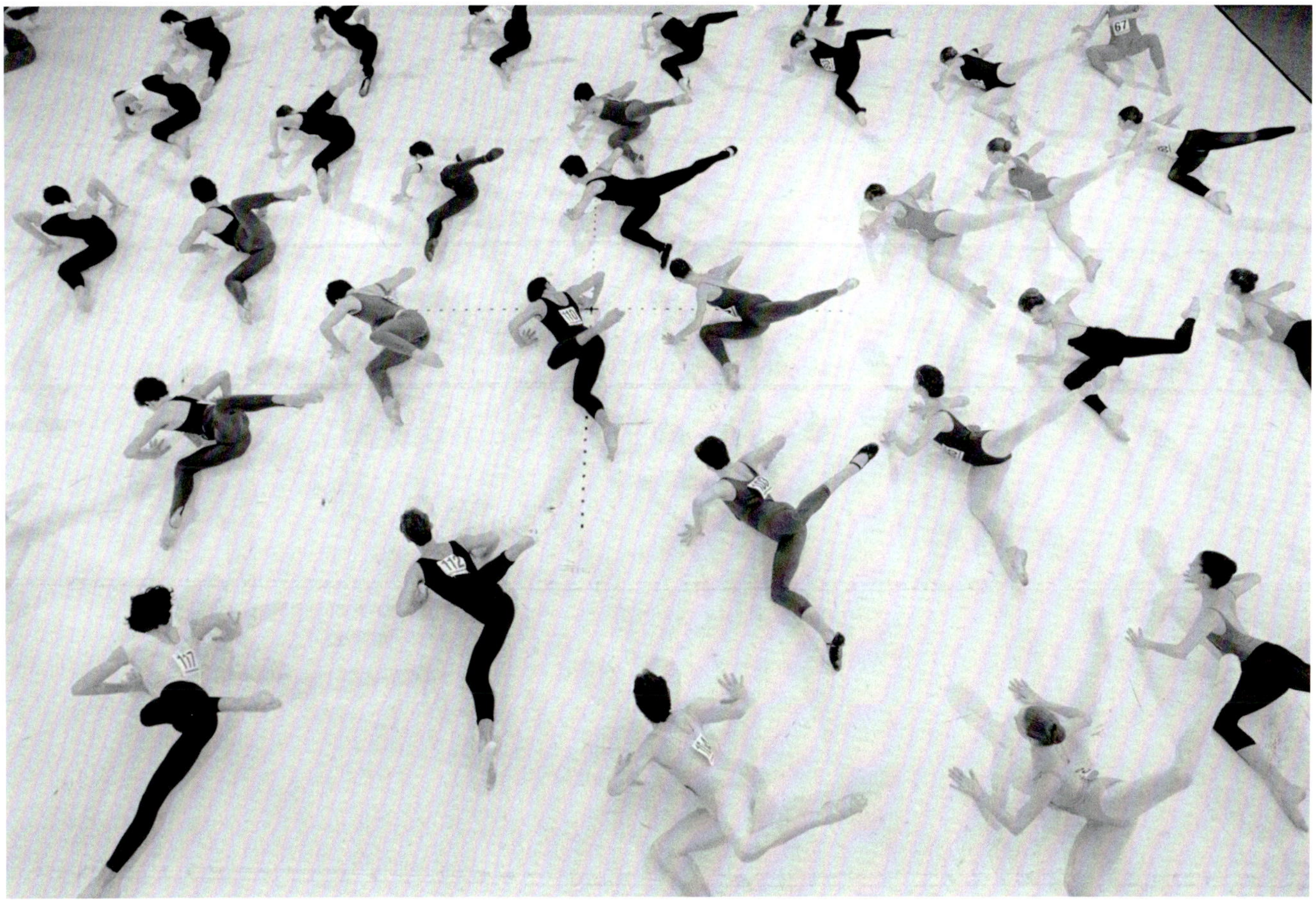

29 AUGUST 2020 / PRIX DE LAUSANNE. *LUCERNE, SWITZERLAND 1991*

On my last post was an observation of visual relationship between greyhounds and elegance. It brought back good memories of being at the *Prix de Lausanne*, an international competition for young dancers seeking a professional career in classical ballet.

I hope budding professional photographers have the same work ethic. I remembered the extraordinary tenacity, dedication, sheer hard work that dancers have to put in. I guess it's my mantra – it's the same for anything done really well.

I have just obtained a book, *The Valleys* photographed by Anthony Stokes. I am puzzled that I have not seen it before. It was first published in 2007, publishers, serenbooks.com. It seems to me to cover all the criteria I have laid out above. Tenacity; the pictures were taken over a five-year period. Dedication; the subject matter is clear and obviously dear to the photographer's heart. Plus the photographer has a wonderful, personal, consistent, eye. I highly recommend the book. Much to be learned from it.

@davidhurnphoto @magnumphotos @serenbooks #anthonystokes

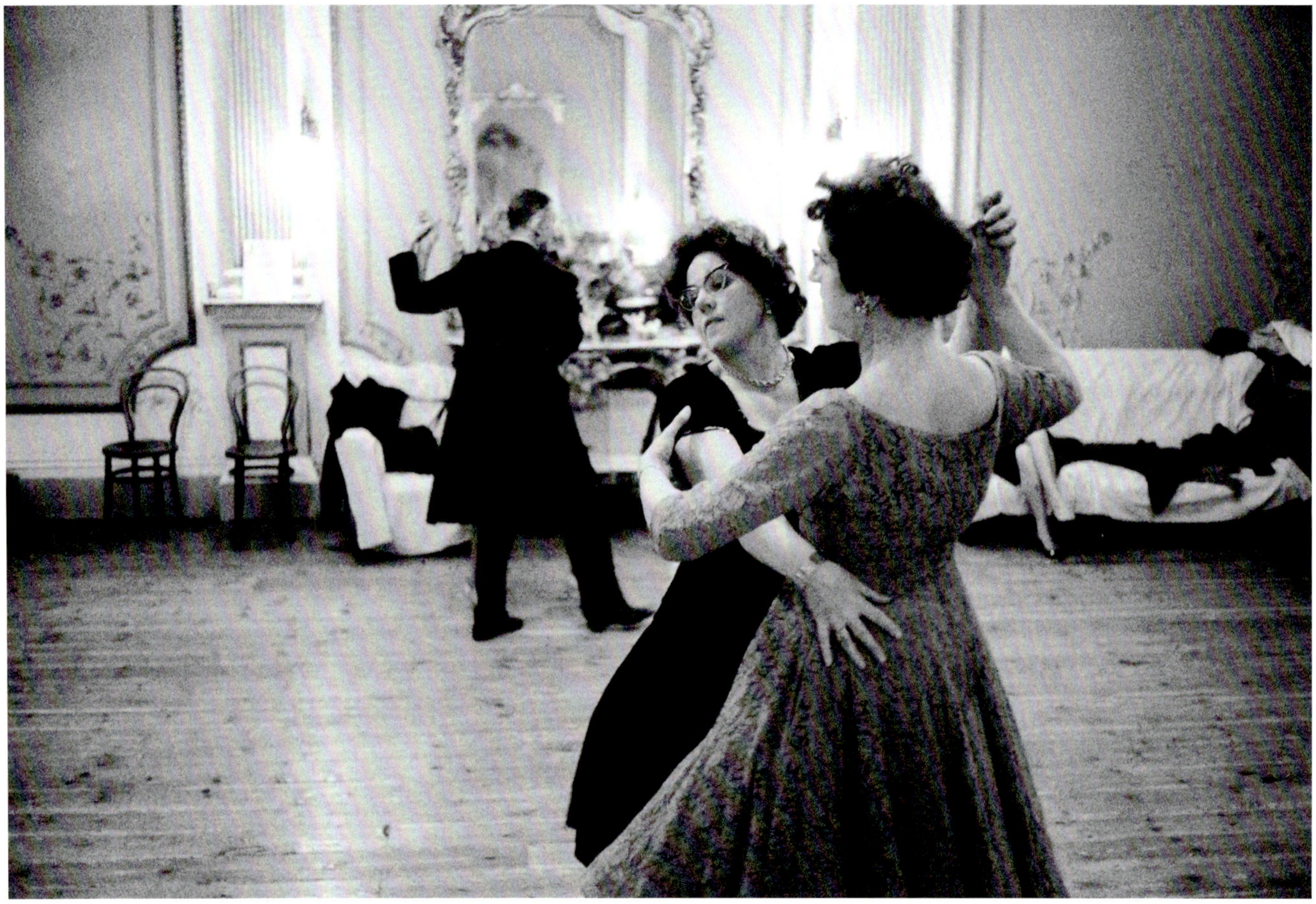

8 SEPTEMBER 2020 / EARL'S COURT HOTEL. *LONDON, ENGLAND 1960*

I have recently heard that *Strictly Come Dancing* is allowing same sex dancers. Now I have never seen *Strictly* but I understand it is very popular. It is licensed to over 42 territories – in USA called *Dancing with the Stars*.

During my passage as a photographer I have frequently covered activities that although I have no real interest in participating in, by the sheer numbers of other people being interested in them, they become of interest to me. Ballroom dancing was one such. I did a reasonable, thorough essay in the '60s. I was amazed by the engagement of the people engrossed. The amount of practice, the making of costumes, the sheer skill, the personal contact. I learned to understand the pull. I remember photographing one aspect in a hired hotel room in Earl's Court London for a dancing club. Many of the couples dancing together were women, to my recollection never men. I enjoyed the joy they seemed to be achieving, there is something about being attached to another human that is very loving. I applaud the TV programme.

Slowly we seem to be moving forward on many fronts. It just needs open discussion, decency and respect.

@davidhurnphoto @magnumphotos #strictly #ballroomdancing

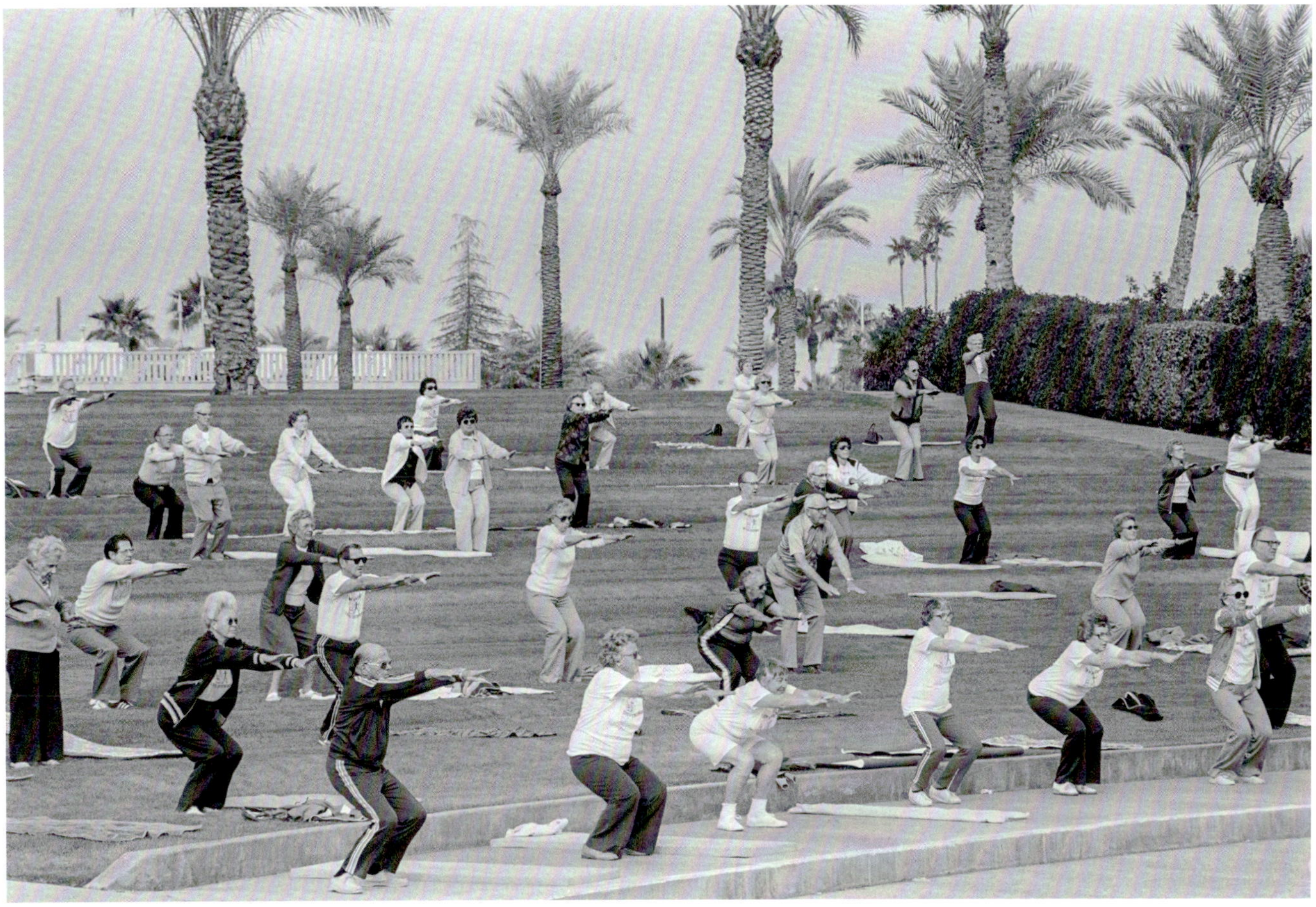

16 SEPTEMBER 2020 / UNREAD ARIZONA 5.30AM. *ARIZONA, USA 1980*

Now only six in a group.

Doesn't really affect me as I only really enjoy small numbers in any case.

Am back at the gym – it's amazingly efficient, plenty of spare space and I feel very safe. I have a sort of nostalgia for Arizona days when 5.30am, most mornings – it's very hot midday there – there were exercises classes together, many members of which then were my age now.

I enjoyed photographing in USA, I sensed less hang-ups there than here, more understanding as to what one was trying to do. More respect for photography. My dear friend Bill Jay and I had a splendid idea of buying a large RV mobile home – we had a nostalgia for an Airstream. The idea was to wander USA for a couple of years, reading local newspapers as we went, picking up mundane stories that had international interest. He writing, me photographing. We felt we could easily make a living. Sadly, Bill went down ill and our enterprise never got off the drawing board.

@davidhurnphoto @magnumphotos #airstream #arizona #billjay

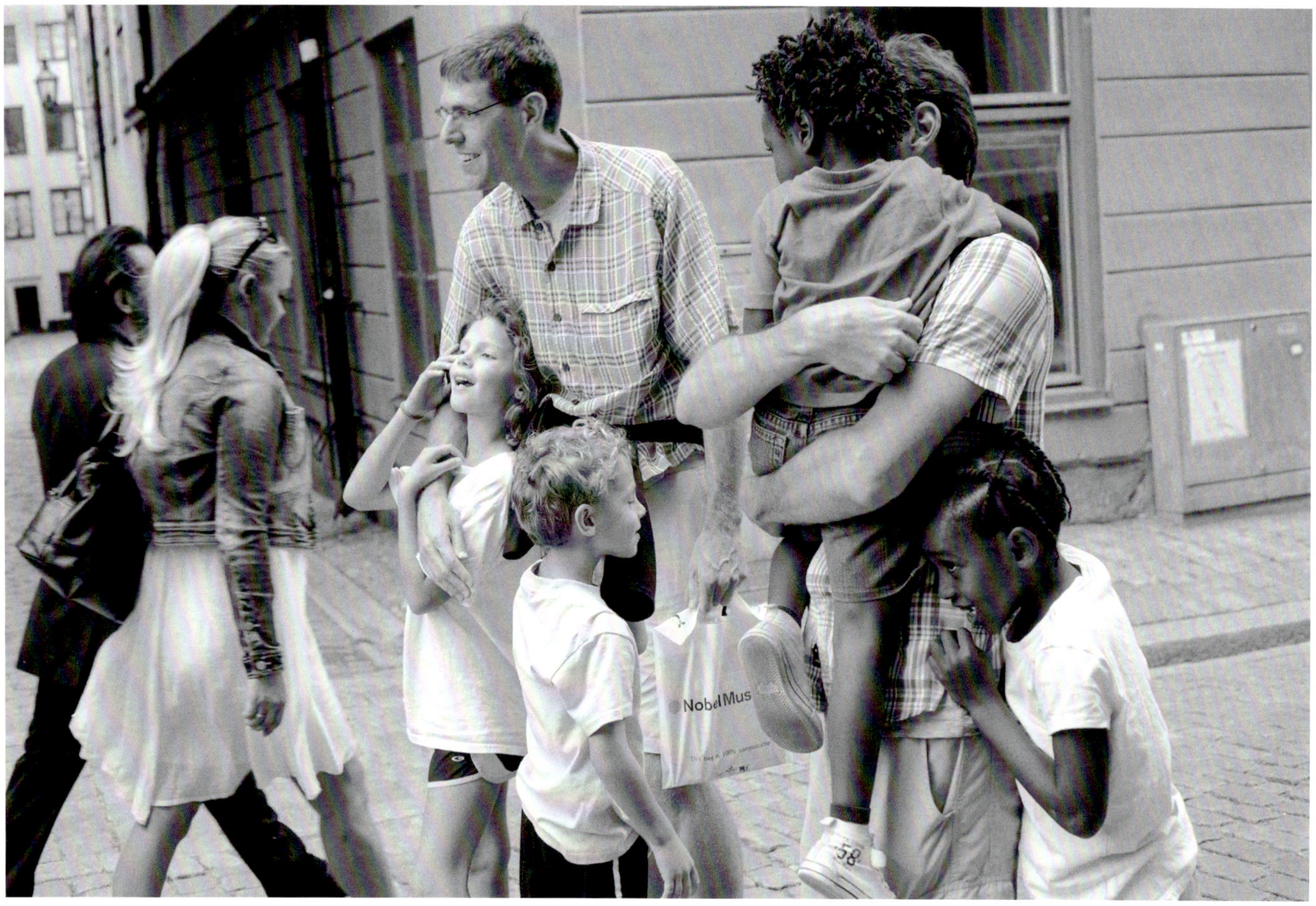

5 OCTOBER 2020 / THE LAW OF SIX. *STOCKHOLM, SWEDEN 2011*

I yet again admit a bias: I am closely linked to the Martin Parr Foundation. Just last week I watched a Zoom projection of an extraordinary interview of Don McCullin by Jonathan Dimbleby. One soon understood that even in interviewing, talent will out. Jonathan teased out of Don a memorable conversation. As I have said before, students should really think about becoming members of the Foundation, in an age of online learning you are going to get much more from the series of lectures from here than from anywhere else.

I am in depressive mood, I get like it when I can't get out to shoot pictures. I remember once back in the late '60s an actress friend of mine saying that we were maybe the last generation that were going to die – it was the start of the age of body parts replacements. The slow slide of us all becoming robots without knowing it. I think it could still happen but not yet. Now the extreme thought is are we the last humans to live? The truth is that the rest of the world will not care.

If so, we had all better get stuck in and do something worthwhile.

I do think that, ultimately, the camera will be our eye and we will take pictures by blinking, the results being beamed back to our computers to be stored.

@davidhurnphoto @magnumphotos @don.mccullin @martinparrfdn #jonathandimbleby

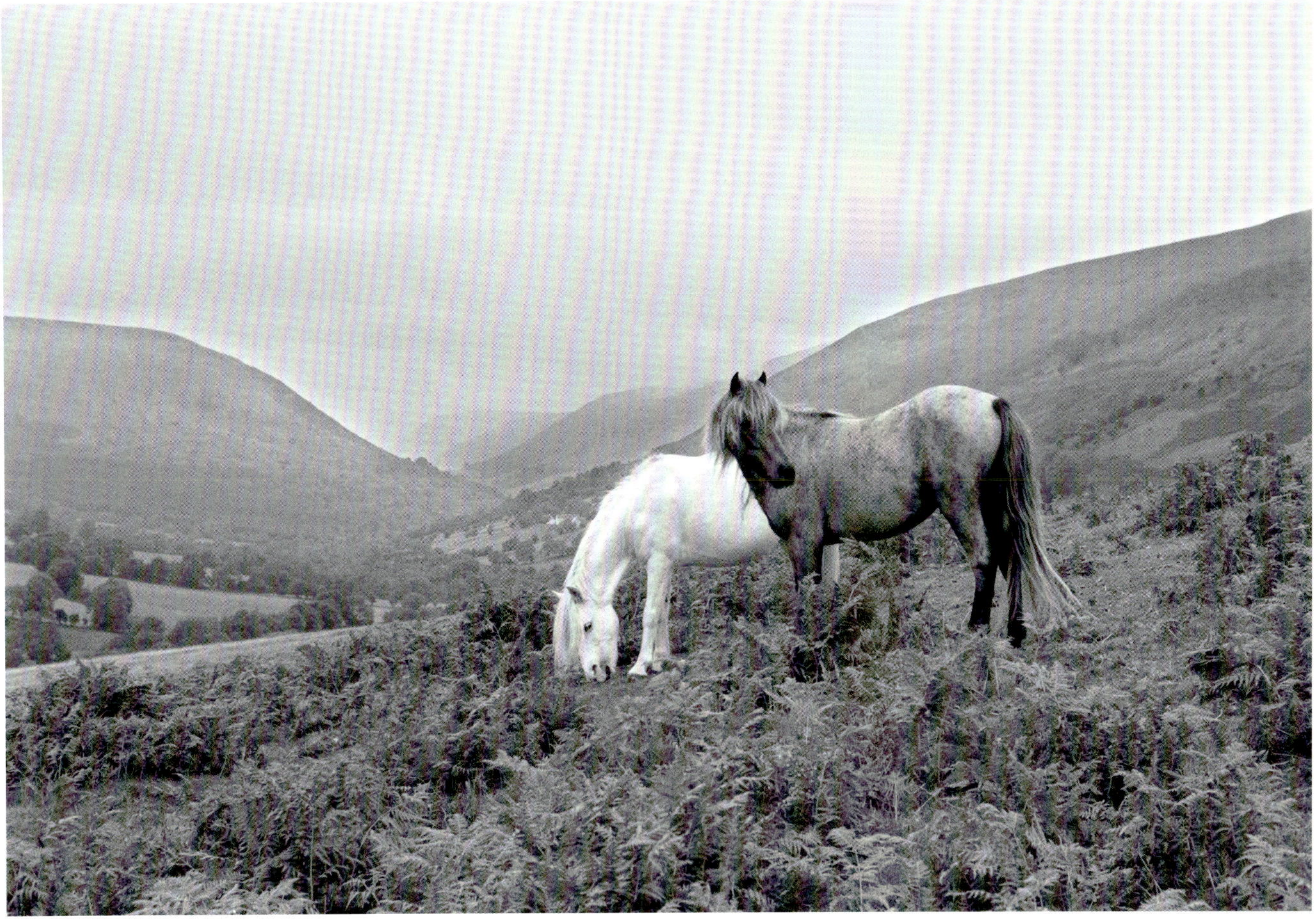

14 OCTOBER 2020 / BLACK MOUNTAIN PONIES. ***BRECON, WALES 1987***

Sadly, I have just heard that Chris Killip died yesterday – it was not unexpected. Chris was undoubtedly one of the UK's greatest photographers – in fact, undoubtedly one of the world's greatest photographers.

His book, *In Flagrante*, is as good a photographic book as has ever been published.

He was a founder/advisor for the original Side Gallery in Newcastle, an organisation that has had very positive vibes in British photography ever since.

He was Professor of Visual and Environmental Studies – whatever that means – at Harvard University from 1991 to 2017.

He was a friend and always a pleasure to be with. I am sure he will remain a positive influence on discerning students throughout the future.

@davidhurnphoto @magnumphotos #chriskillip

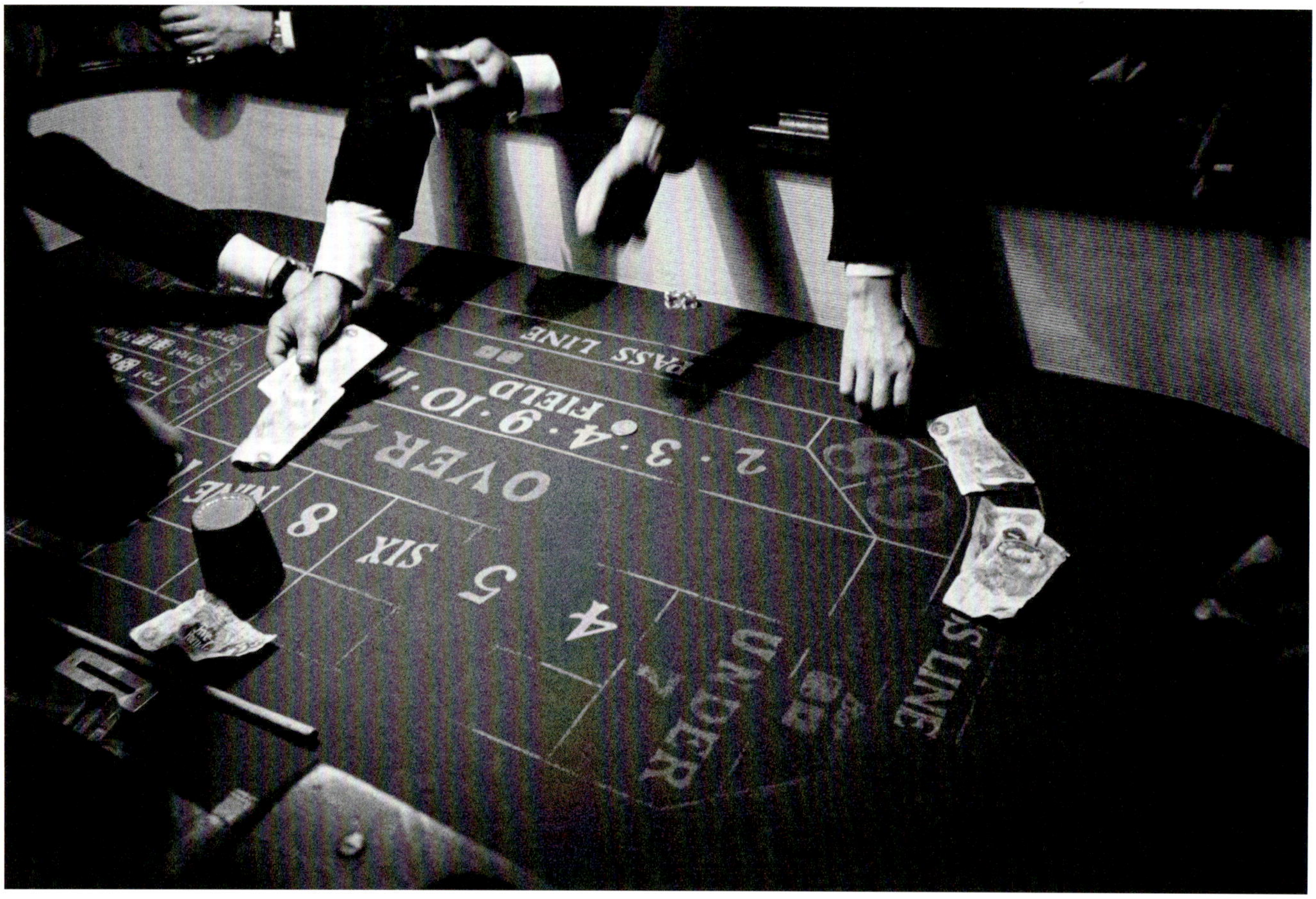

26 OCTOBER 2020 / GAMBLING, SOHO. ***LONDON, ENGLAND 1966***

Well, a first for me – I have had my previous picture taken down by Instagram, for 'nudity reasons'. I am slightly puzzled by present day conventions – but who wishes to consciously offend? Offend who I do not know. Certainly not the lady in the photograph who I later knew well and was actually a nurse – inadequately paid.

I repeat previous text, Craig deserves acknowledgement.

I have just ordered and received some books from 'Cafe Royal Books'. I have often suggested that one could make the argument that these books form the most important archive of photography by Brits around. Craig Atkinson has been pouring his heart into his enterprise for 15 years, it seems impossible, but there have been 700 publications.

During the lockdown I have been making fantasy layouts of – so far – six new possible books to submit to Craig and I hope that he agrees to at least a couple. It's a way of getting large 30-picture essays into print, wonderful as there are no longer magazines able to do the same.

However, of course, you have to actually shoot the pictures.

@davidhurnphoto @magnumphotos @craigatkinson @caferoyalbooks

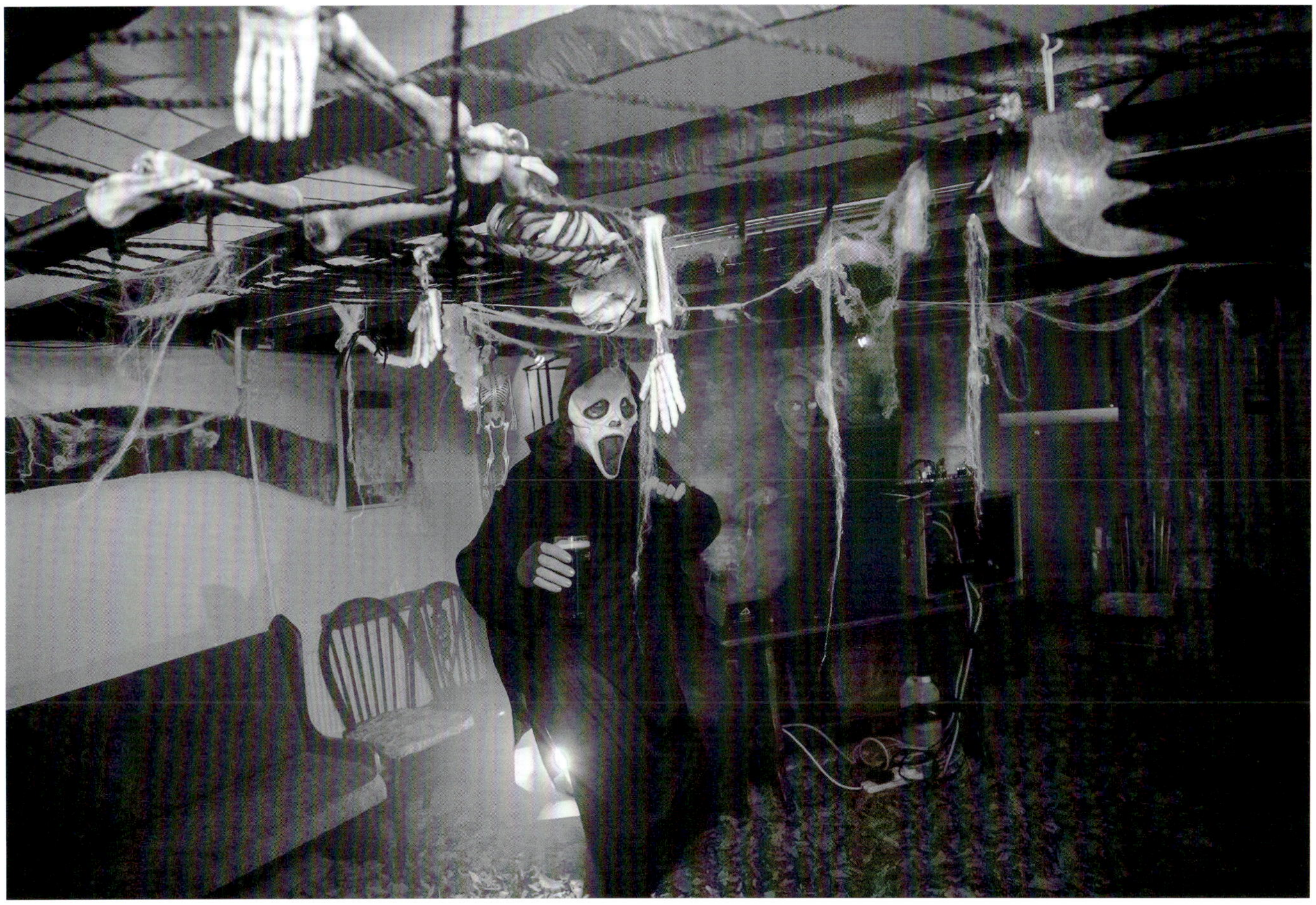

31 OCTOBER 2020 / COVID-19 HALLOWEEN. *TINTERN, WALES 2007*

One of the advantages of living in a village is that one knows what is going on. Access is always a problem for photographers – how do you get it? Perhaps the most useful ploy is getting to know people in some sort of authority who have some clout. Having contact with magazines can be useful but if you live in a country where few journals have much influence, you have to venture more worldwide. Writing polite letters can occasionally work but seldom with people/organisations that are guarded. In other words, photography is not just about taking pictures. Networking can be learned, so learn.

Some time ago I suggested I was going to find a new way of finding subject matter to write about. I decided to see what happened if I collected others questions. To make things easier I talked to the local Doc Photo course at University of South Wales to which I had some contact. I have received a list of 30 very interesting questions. My problem is how to answer an intelligent question in 2,200 characters including spaces.

@davidhurnphoto @magnumphotos @docphotusw

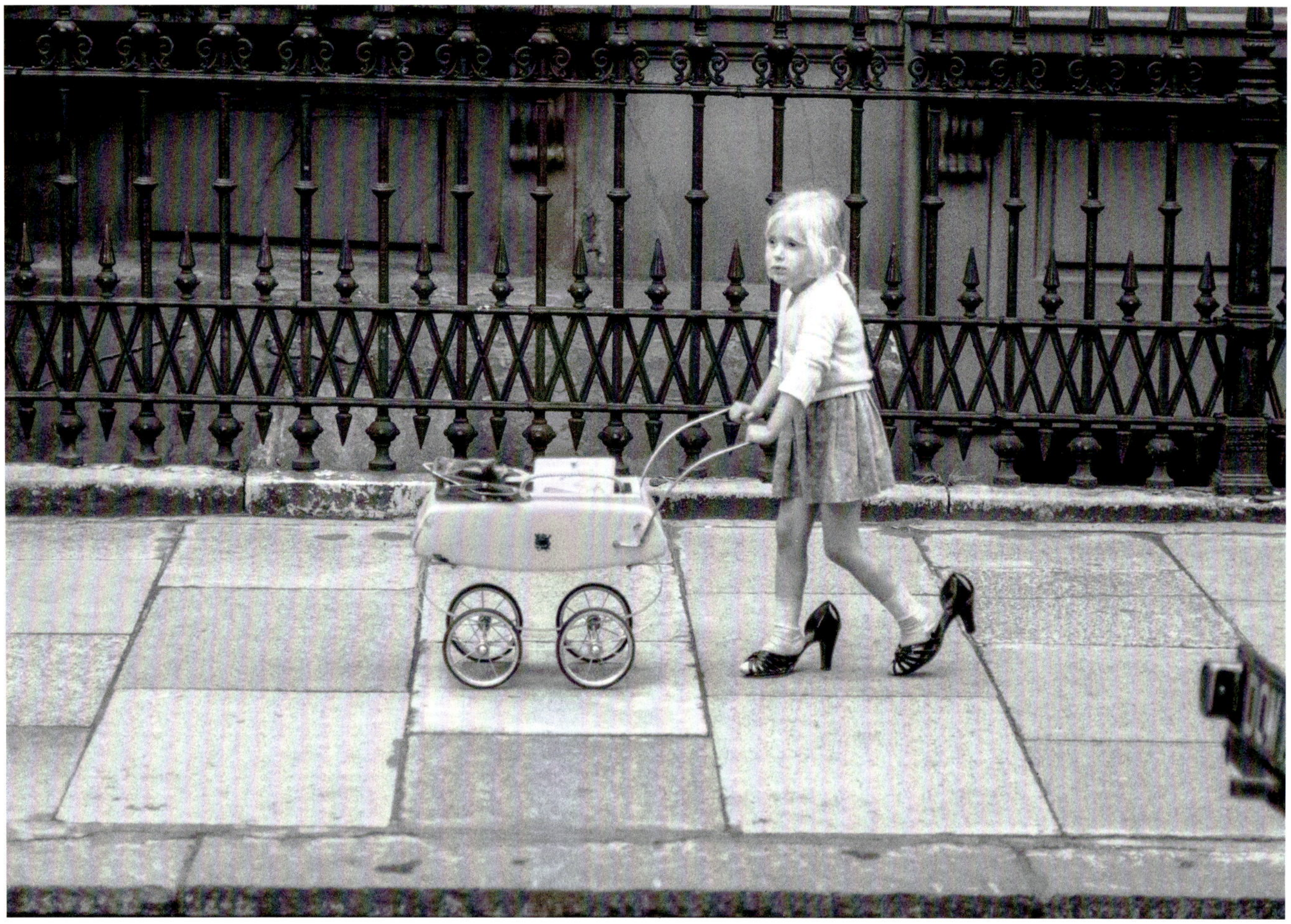

6 NOVEMBER 2020 / GOING FOR WALK, NOTTINGHILL GATE. *LONDON, ENGLAND 1958*

I am one of the very lucky ones. I am locked down in a pleasant cottage and I have plenty to do. I have been laying out fantasy books, 60 years of pictures, plenty to look through.

I am frustrated at not being able to wander shooting. At heart I am a *flâneur* – wander the streets with no particular destination, and no purpose other than to absorb surroundings, muse on whatever takes your fancy and end up somewhere interesting. I admire Charles Dickens and his miles a day walking London streets to absorb happenings that he can write about.

Previously I have tried photographing my personal surroundings, I think reasonably well, but on looking back I feel a bit of a fake – it's just not me. For the first time ever I actually thought of destroying the pictures – I haven't, we should live with our mistakes.

I look forward to Monday. In Wales I am let loose, I suspect I will head North. I need a picture in Conway. It depends where the tide is.

@davidhurnphoto @magnumphotos

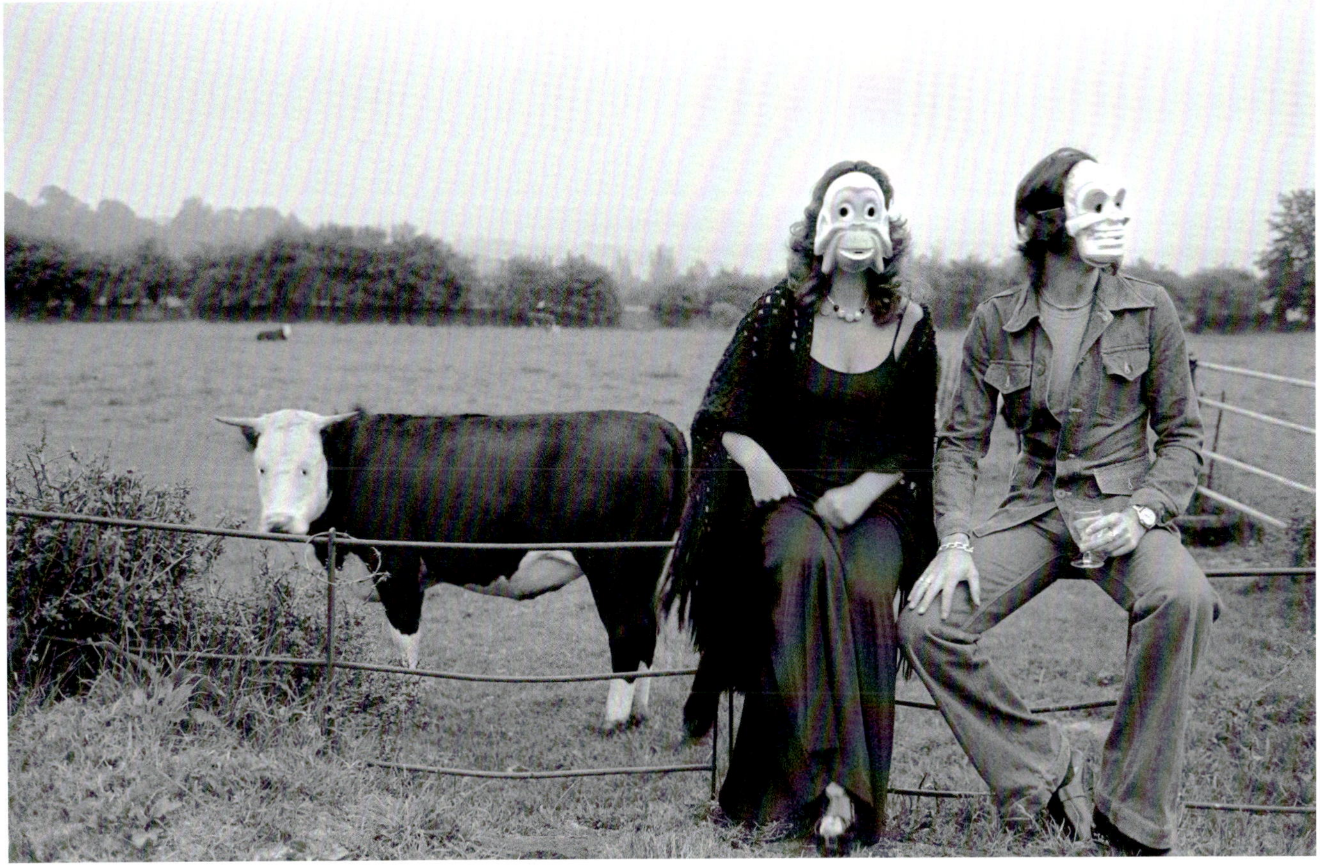

20 NOVEMBER 2020 / MASKED PARTY. *USK, WALES 1974*

A wonderful day yesterday. My friend Brian suggested a trip to Hay-on-Wye to see the Thru The Lens Gallery. The gallery was set up in 2019 by Andra Milsome and her co-curator, the excellent local photographer Billie Charity.

I had not seen it previously.

The gallery is small – I guess it can handle an exhibition of on average 20 prints. It's a beautiful space, clean and uncluttered by extraneous bric-a-brac. Above all, it has the essential ingredient, someone running it with experience and enormous enthusiasm.

The present show is by John Bulmer, someone whom one can safely call a great of British photography. The show is pictures of 'A Very English Village', a book accompanies the show – in fact, there are many books for sale including Billie Charity's latest, *A Strange New World*.

It is galleries like this that should be supported. Whoever gives money should be making sure that some of it goes in their direction.

@davidhurnphoto @magnumphotos @thruthelens_gallery @johnfbulmer @billie_charity

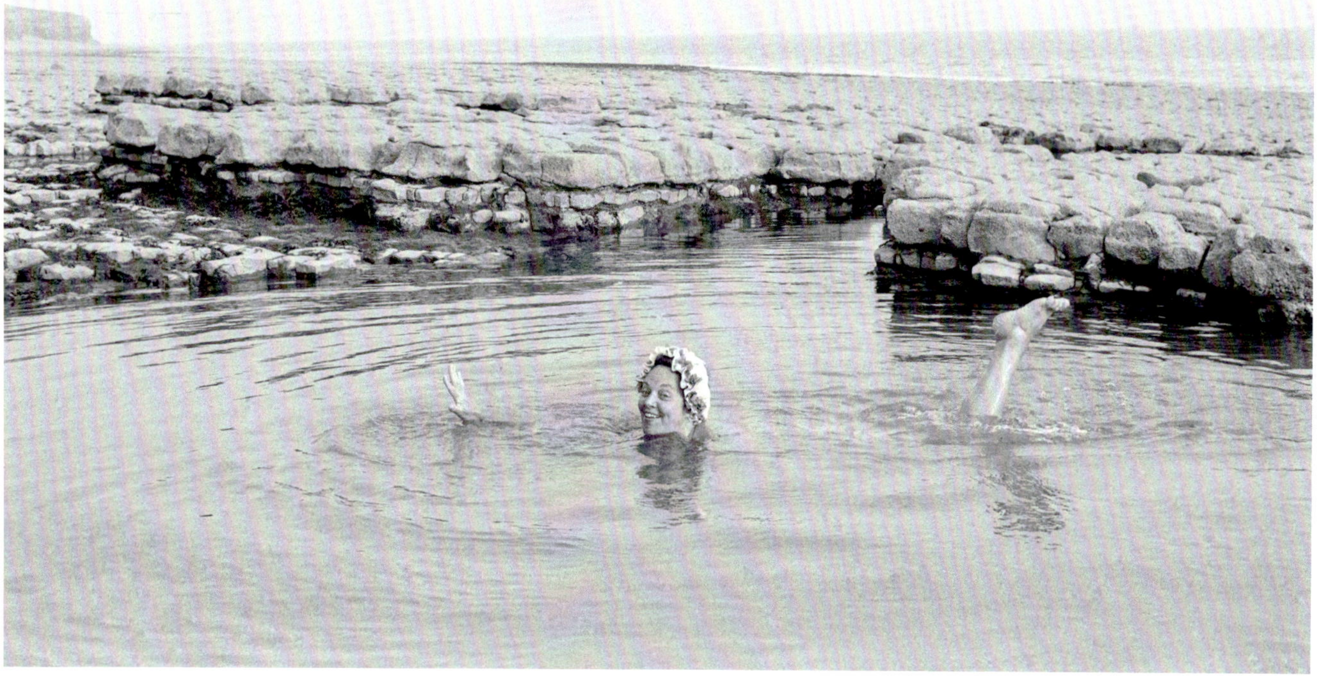

29 NOVEMBER 2020 / ROCK POOL LADY. *LLANTWIT MAJOR, WALES 1971*

I realised that it was the anniversary of the lovely lady in the rock pool above. I wished to do a print of the picture for myself but was puzzled that the 'scan' only allows a 9x6 inch print.

When I shot film I would always make 'contact prints' – do you all know what that was/is? – filed those all together and had a duplicate file of the negative with duplicate numbering.

Panic fell on me. I had the contact sheet but the negatives were missing.

I checked my outgoing delivery slips – I had not sent the negatives away.

A dream came finally to my rescue. I realised, to keep in step with previous practice, I had made a contact sheet from the equivalent of a digital roll of film, but of course, there are no negatives – my first digital pictures were buried way back in my computer.

I say all this simply to plead – make sure you do your filing well, you will thank me.

My scans now average 120MB. My first scans were just 6MB. Then 32MB, then 64MB, who knows what in the future? The 120MB seems fine for me as it correlates with the maximum print size I want from my printer, i.e. 24x36 inches. It does mean I am having to re-scan much from my past. The actual scanning is quite fast, the spotting – boy, how I now love digital – takes, on average, 42 minutes to spot to 66.67 percent size.

Then there is re-captioning. Simplest, people die. It seems rude not to state this in your caption. Sometimes we include awards. I was looking at a picture I took of Andrew Davies, writer, early in his career, it seems I have to add another award every year passing. I ask myself should I simply put only his name in my IPTC.

Of course, keeping up with new terminology in race, ethnicity, colonialism can be a nightmare. I have recently seen/received an authoritative document on the matter, it is 100 pages long.

What does all this mean? Simply, early on in your career, make sure you have a very accurate numbering, filing system. Make sure you caption well and simply (no opinions, only facts). Make sure you keep up to date – again, advice is keep it simple in the first place.

@davidhurnphoto @magnumphotos

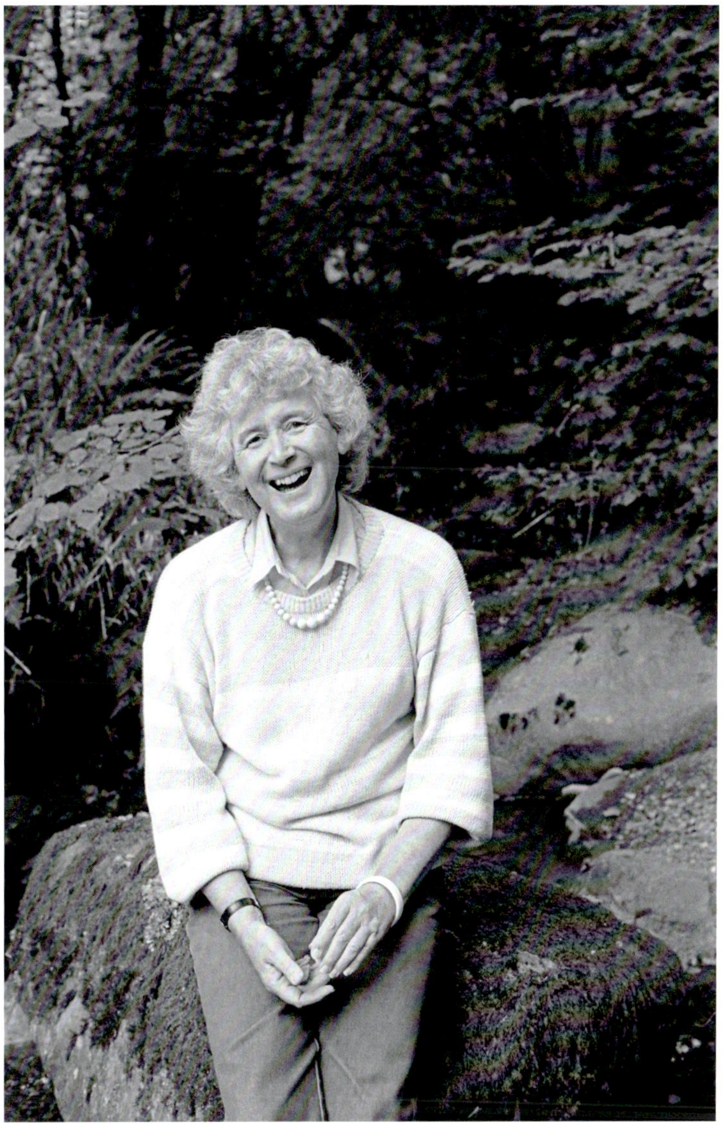

1 DECEMBER 2020 / JAN MORRIS. *LLANYSTUMDWY, WALES 1986*

Portraits don't seem to work for me on Instagram. I hope the smaller numbers of viewers that I expect are not seen as disappointment with her. She was, for me, a dear friend – her book, *The Matter of Wales*, was undoubtedly the platform for everything I have photographed in this country. She wrote in perfect and readable English. Her essay on the Zoo in Central Park New York for *Rolling Stone* magazine is as moving as I think writing can be.

She has just died and I will miss her.

@davidhurnphoto @magnumphotos #janmorris

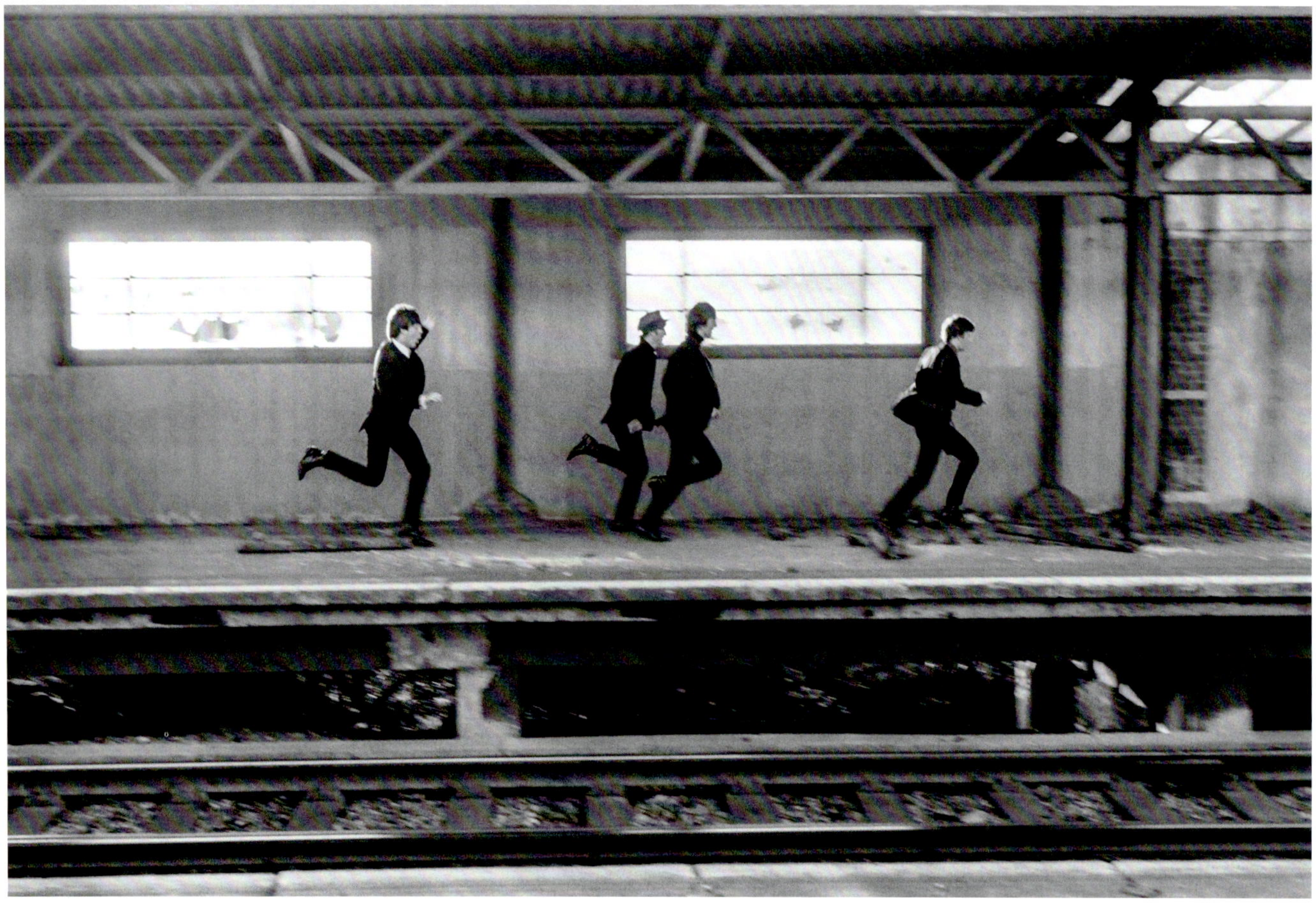

8 DECEMBER 2020 / RUSHING FOR VACCINATION. *LONDON, ENGLAND 1964*

For some time I have been worried that photography is on a fast track to self-destruct.

I have previously written that photography does one thing better than anything else:

'A major reason for the invention of photography was that it was needed. It was the time of scientific collecting and tabulating. A quick method of recording was needed. Need normally produces results, photography is by far the best method of making an accurate trace – the 'Thing itself'', as someone once said.

Either we look at the world directly and try to record what we see with as much integrity and intelligence as we humans can muster, or we can use our intelligence to direct visual happenings to illustrate a narrative. Neither is more important than the other. However, what is important is transparency. All of us should let the audience know exactly what we are trying to do. If we are observing we should not manipulate our pictures and we should state we don't. If we're a director then we should explain. A fashion photographer could say that the picture is a directed picture using models. The more conceptual artist photographer could say, 'this picture is constructed', my feeling is that it would actually enhance the process and engage the audience more. It removes the ambiguity or implication the pictures are from actual life.

These thoughts were resurrected during an inspiring Zoom talk by Fred Ritchin. He suggested that we, who called ourselves Documentary Photographers, should use a new term and call ourselves 'Non-fiction Photographers', this then implies a second section 'Fiction Photographers'. Neither term is demeaning, but both give clarity. Within IPTC one could have a symbol for one style and a second symbol for the other.

If we leave it as is I feel the general public is fast losing faith in the central point of photography – a trace – suddenly nothing is real, science becomes fake, all pictures are considered manufactured. I think we are really near this position – if it happens, photography no longer exists in any meaningful way.

@davidhurnphoto @magnumphotos #fredritchin #beatles #aharddaysnight

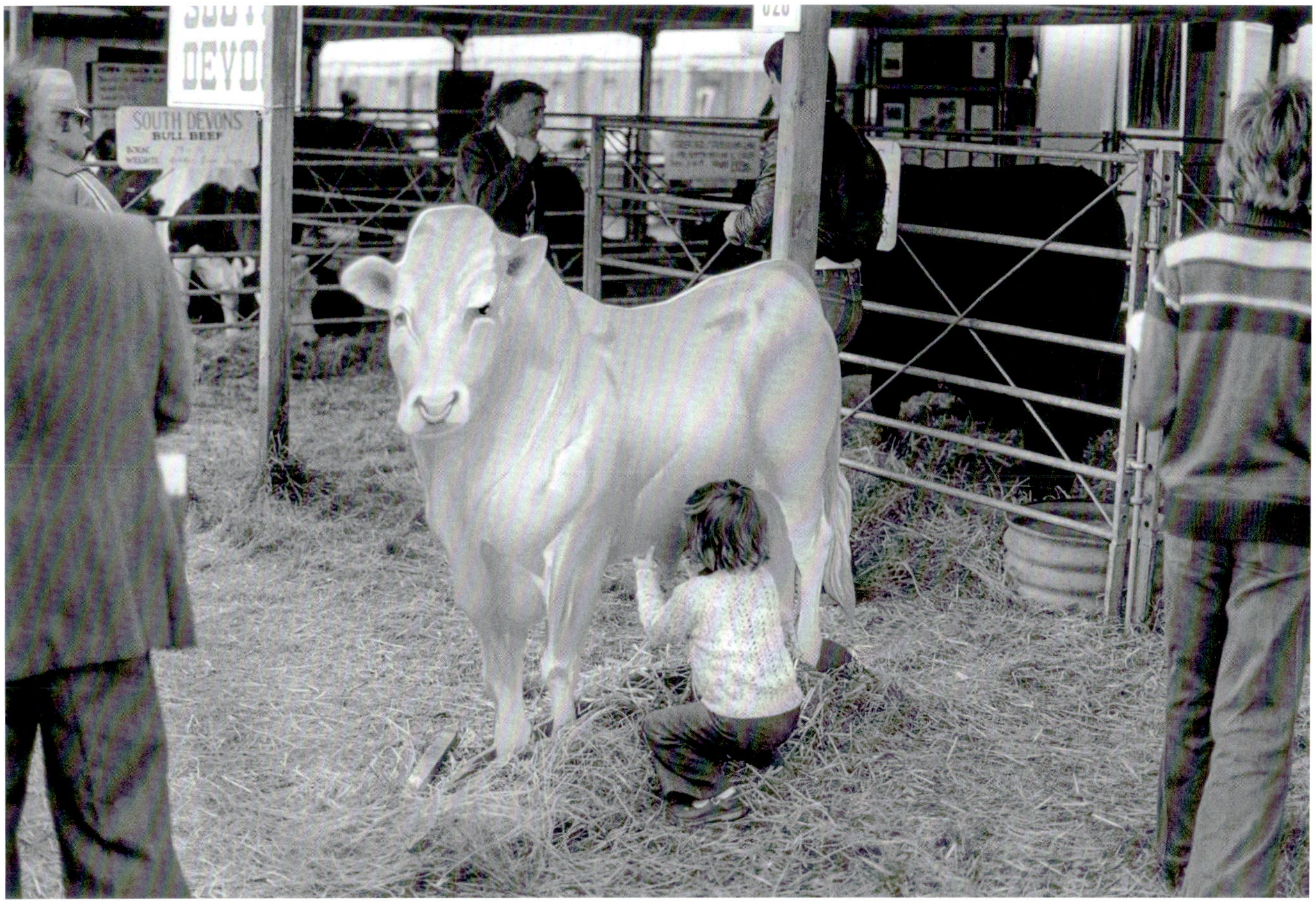

11 DECEMBER 2020 / IMAGINATIVE MILKING. ***BUILTH WELLS, WALES 1978***

I found the replies to my previous post interesting. But I was obviously not as clear as I had hoped. Basically I am saying that if the general public begins to presume that all photographs are constructed then we are in trouble. I am suggesting that if we followed literature and had fiction and non-fiction categories we would clarify a little to everyone's advantage – of course, I don't think it will happen.

What was even more surprising was that some thought I was making a plea for shooting on film and printing in dishes – you would have to drag me kicking and screaming to do that. Firstly, I never enjoyed smelly hands. But more seriously, digital gave me so many advantages.

For 40 years, to all intents and purposes, I have shot pictures using two Leica cameras, one with a 50mm and one with a 28mm lens. If possible using Ilford film – I found it less aggressive that Kodak. The maximum print size I printed was 20x36 inches. The second I could produce that size naturally by digital cameras I switched camera, i.e. 2007. For me, the important part of the camera is the viewfinder so I switched to a camera that had the most similar finder to the Leica. I have since had many exhibitions of prints made from both film and the digital mixed prints showing side by side. I have never had anyone comment on any difference in the print quality.

However, I have had a couple of negatives that I had mis-exposed, and now for the first time I was able to save.

Of course, if one prefers the aura of film and developer then that's wonderful for you, as I suspect is making cyanotypes, making albumens or even daguerreotypes, each to their own.

I don't shoot in any way different from before, basically, stand in the right place, press the button at the right time, it doesn't matter what camera you use. As for feeling one shoots more, and concentrates less, well that seems to me a definition of a poor photographer. I would suggest get disciplined.

The ethics of photography is what is important for me, I know when I lie, and I try to know the opposite.

@davidhurnphoto @magnumphotos

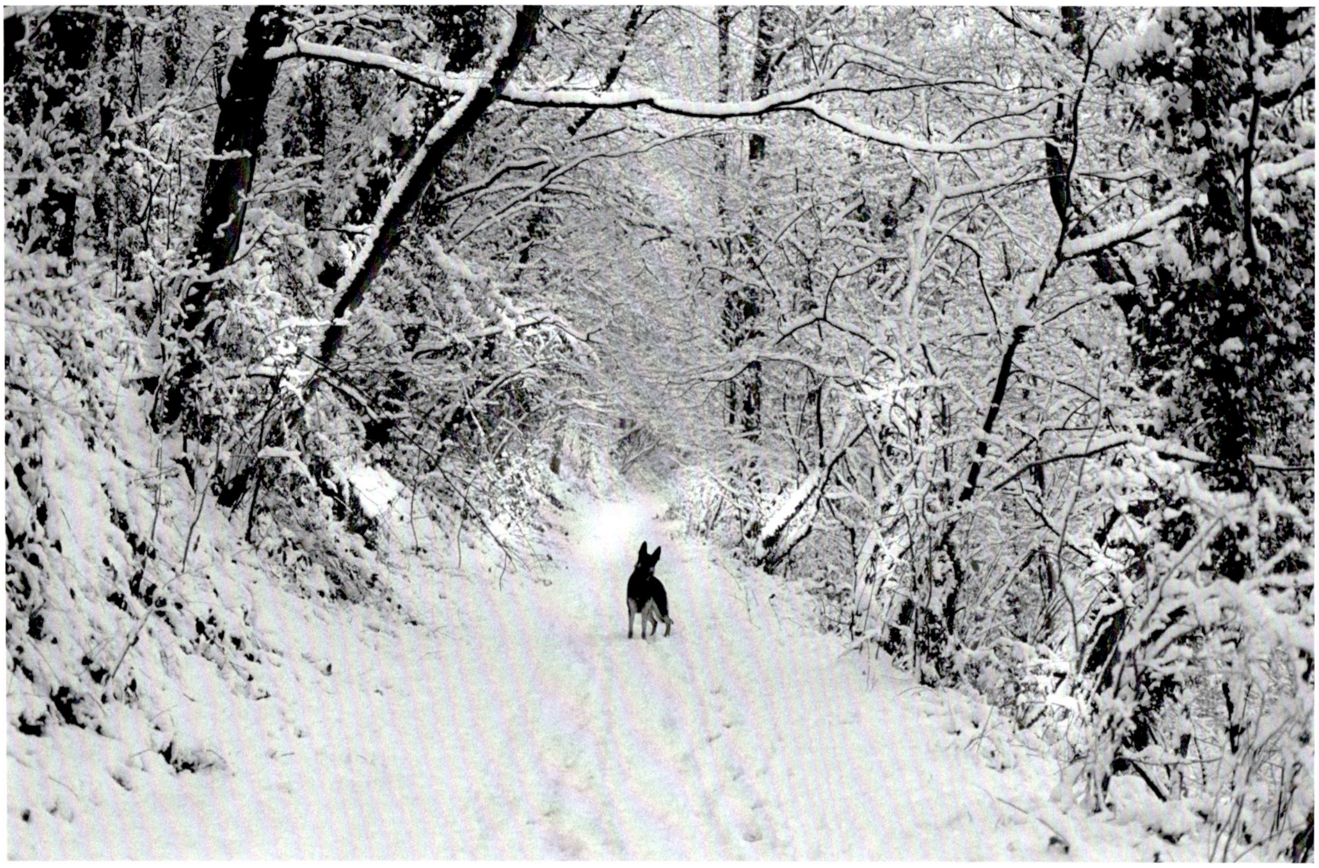

25 DECEMBER 2020 / BE SAFE THIS CHRISTMAS. *TINTERN, WALES 1979*

I am not a natural TV watcher. I much prefer radio, not only because I can do jobs on my archives whilst listening, but for me it seems to have more illuminating programmes and longer interviews.

Many friends whom I respect kept mentioning a Netflix production, *The Crown*. I started to watch, was quickly enthralled – it's superbly produced, acted, and directed. However, I was most interested in episodes that had content dealing with events I had also covered or, in a minor way, been part of.

Starting with the 1952 great fog/smog, the depiction was extraordinary and it rushed back memories. I had just finished school, I remember clearly it was impossible to see anything three feet in front of oneself.

I, of course, knew first hand of the pomposity of the various photographers represented, each was exactly as I remember them.

I remember Lord Altrincham's attack on the monarchy – his advice to cancel Queen Charlotte's Ball spurred me to do an essay later.

Above all, I found it almost impossible to watch the Aberfan section. Coverage of this obscenity was undoubtedly the two most affecting days of my life.

What I think I am trying to convey is that photography, whether moving or still, has an amazing ability to bring back memory. For me it is one of the main justifications for doing it. History.

However, the results need to come out of passion, ability and accuracy and I am not sure that *The Crown* is always accurate. Its problem, in a way, is that it's too convincing, even though it is honest and presented as fiction, its feeling of authenticity ingrains itself within us – or it certainly did for me. What is accurate? What audience grabbing?

I personally don't like the blurring of the lines without transparency.

@davidhurnphoto @magnumphotos #nonfictionphotography #thecrown #aberfan

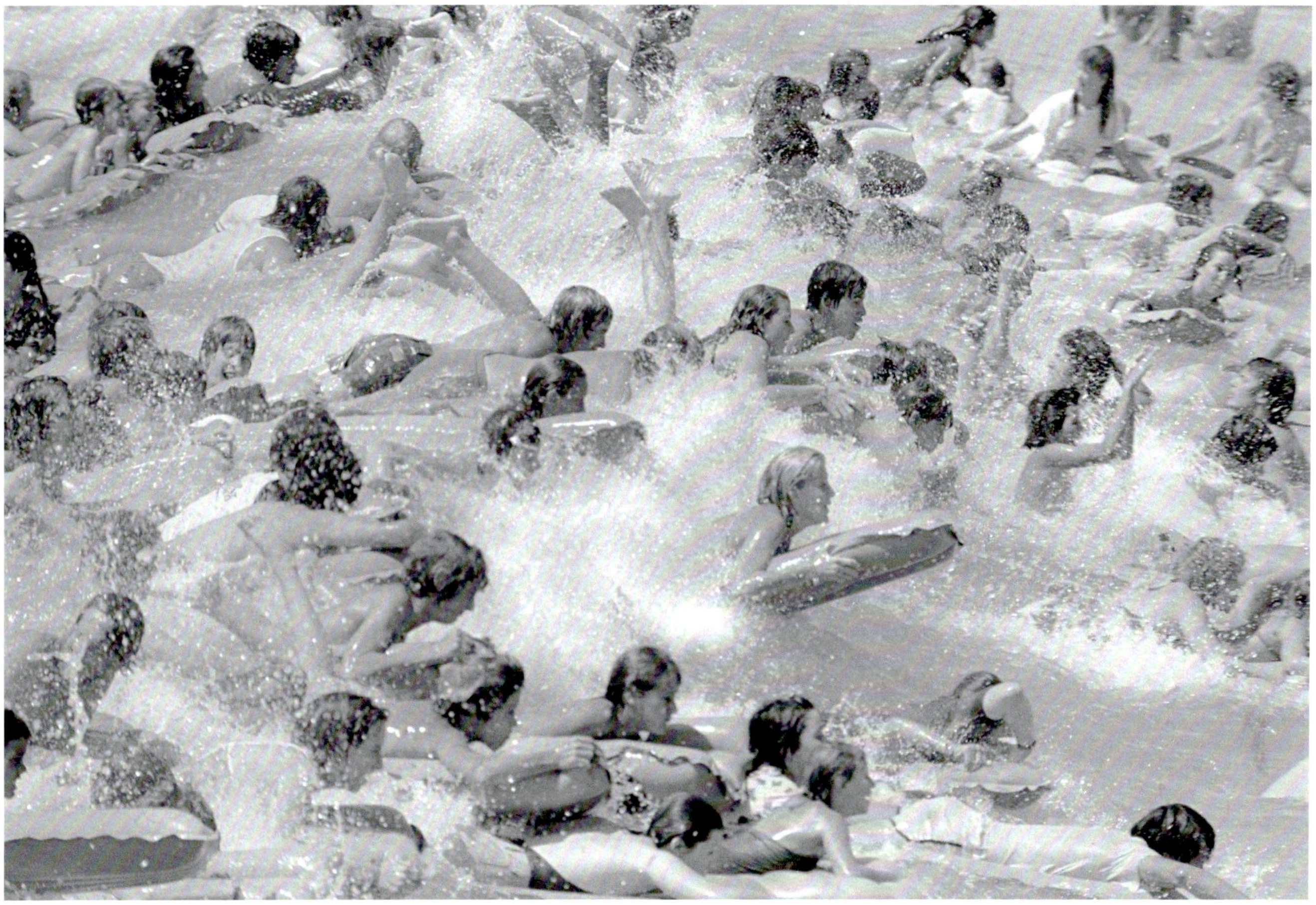

29 DECEMBER 2020 / INTO THE FUTURE. *ARIZONA, USA 1980*

In lockdown I have plenty to do. At the moment I am working on the 538 edit I have of photographs of photographers. To my surprise, no portrait before 1959 and even more of a disappointment no portrait of my dear friend and great photographer – in my opinion one of the greatest – Sergio Larrain.

Certainly at the beginning I found it difficult to photograph friends.

Please don't ape me. You will not regret it.

The working on past pictures is laborious. More than three quarters of the pictures were originally shot on film. At least I have scans of most, however, many of the original scans were scanned by original scanners and have very small files, these have all had to be re-scanned. Scanning from negatives means massive spotting, where does grot come from? I only spot at 66 percent but it takes a laborious age. All numbering has to be re-checked – in the future others will have to find pictures only by having these numbers for guidance. And finally I realise how feebly I have captioned. So often I must have thought, 'well, I will not forget who this is', so often I did. And,of course, there is the problem of change/advance of language for keywords – I have just noticed 'flight hostess' is now 'flight attendant' – I have only one and that caption and keyword is now changed.

I give the same advice as many times before: get numbering, captioning and scanning as complete as you can from the start. You will not regret it.

@davidhurnphoto @magnumphotos #nonfictionphotography #sergiolarrain

SOMETHING, LIKE NOTHING, HAPPENS ANYWHERE.
I AM ALWAYS TRYING TO 'PRESERVE' THINGS BY GETTING OTHER PEOPLE
TO READ WHAT I HAVE WRITTEN, AND FEEL WHAT I FELT.

/ *Philip Larkin*

2021

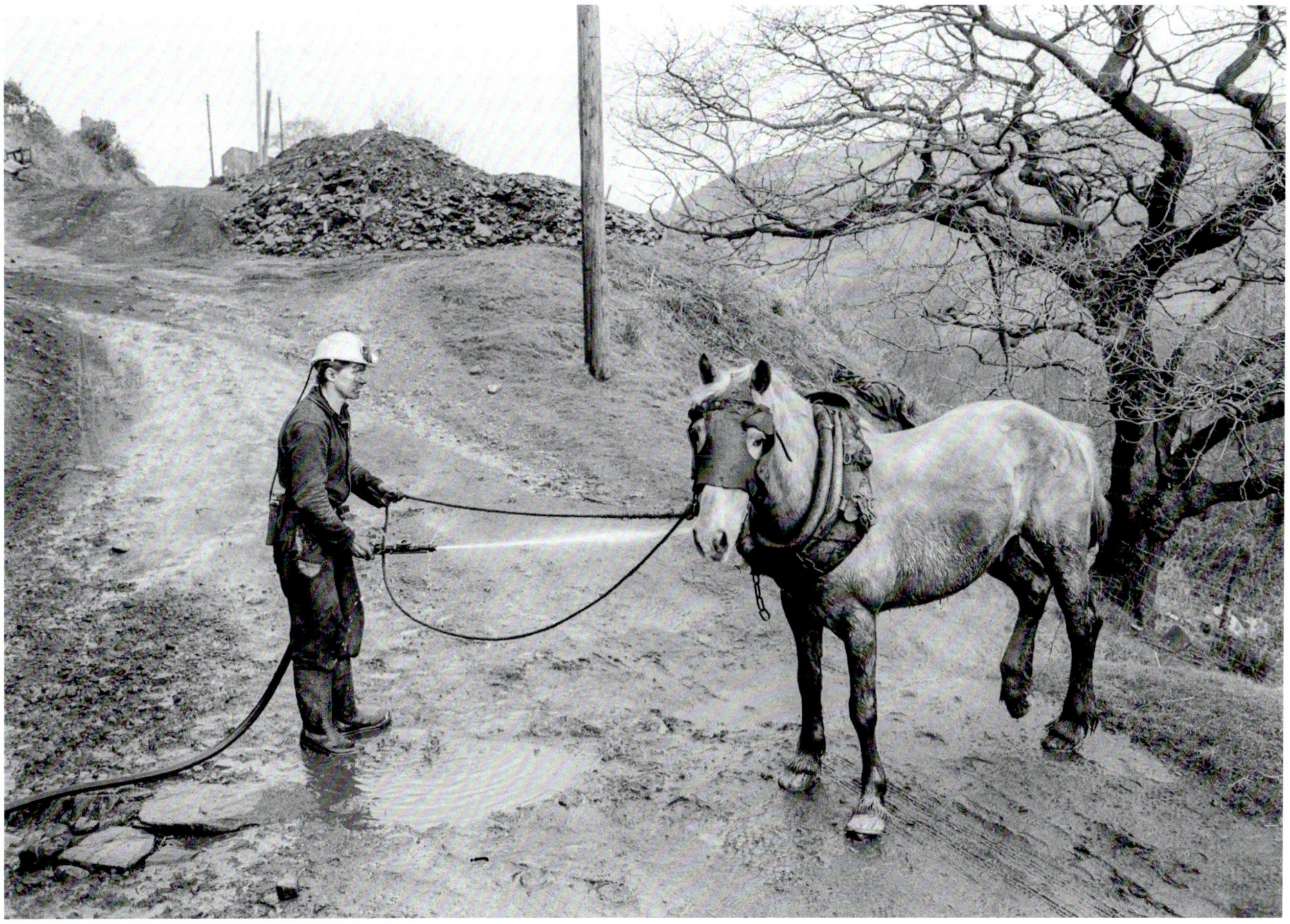

11 JANUARY 2021 / LAST PIT PONIES. *NEATH VALLEY, WALES 1993*

Even more so than usual, I have been struggling to find something of interest to say pertaining in some way to photography.

I have just received *The Journal* of The Royal Photographic Society, Jan/Feb. A journal that in the not too distant past I thought lightweight but, for me, now seems to be giving more interesting information than most other photography publications. In this issue is a four-page obituary for Chris Killip who sadly died on 13 October last year, he is called 'A quiet giant of British Photography', an apt heading. Also included in the journal is 'Legend Maker' an article about the late Richard Avedon, again aptly titled. However, I know a lot about both of these photographers who were friends.

For me, the most interesting article was about X-ray photography. It spanned 125 years' history. Now this is an article I might not have noticed elsewhere. Suddenly I was looking at pictures I found enthralling. At one time I tried to collect X-ray pictures – the most startling was featured in a newspaper and showed a suitcase going through an airport X-ray surveillance protocol. Clearly showing in the suitcase was the X-ray of a live dog. Wow, the naive cheek of some people.

I must say, nowadays I am even more drawn towards virtually any form of non-fiction photography. As I have said many times, simply looking at the world and recording as accurately and honestly as humans can has always been photography's strength. It seems to me that fiction photography, however intelligent, however well crafted, immediately loses the advantage photography has over other mediums of communication and expression.

@davidhurnphoto @magnumphotos @royalphotographicsociety @avedonfoundation #dogs #nonfictionphotography #chriskillip

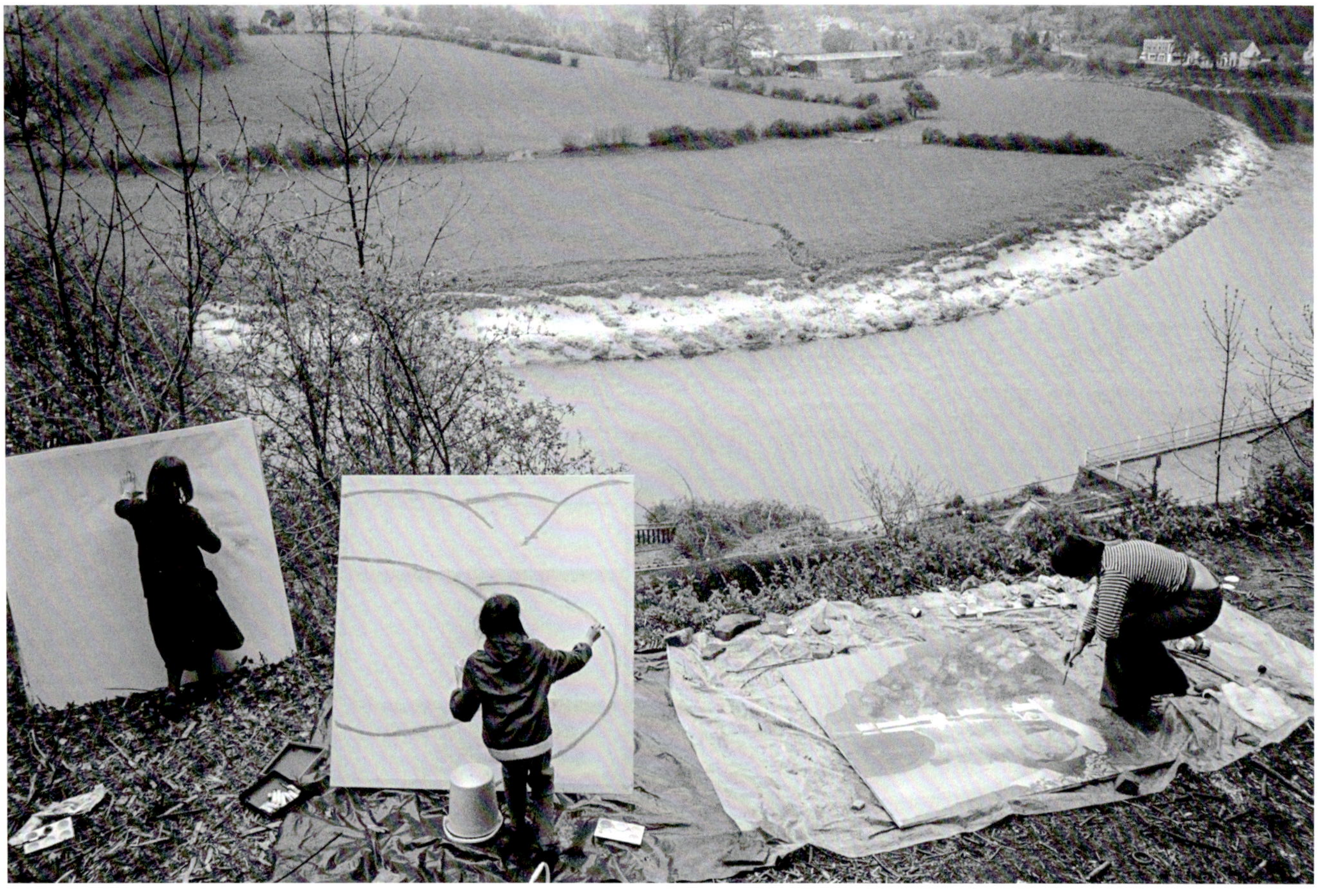

16 JANUARY 2021 / GARDEN ART CLASS. *TINTERN, WALES 1976*

It is the time of plant catalogues, and I like gardening. My large garden has now become a wild garden – this actually means that I have not touched it for three years – I now have a fantasy idea of strimming the whole and making it a meadow garden. At the moment, it is adored only by wildlife.

For me, by far the most seductive catalogue, and new to me, was from Sarah Raven. On the inside page is a smiling picture of, presumably, herself and at the moment I can do with a few smiles. However, what really attracted me was that for some reason the pictures of the flowers seemed 'better' than others – it made me question what I meant by that. I have no idea. Are the pictures shot in better light? Are they more accurate? I can't really tell, all I know is that I bought some stuff and am about to re-structure my small front space based purely on the catalogue.

I have always enjoyed garden pictures – I suspect interest coming from my first meeting with Bill Brandt who shot the landscape so mysteriously – later, my favourite photographer was Edwin Smith who shot distinctive vignettes of English gardens, landscapes and architecture. One of my all-time favourite books is his *The English Garden*, 172 photogravure plates and one colour plate, an odd design choice. I enjoy the black and white as it emphasises the structure of the plants and the design of the gardens, I sometimes feel aspects now often forgotten.

In my library I have a cookbook, photographs by Robert Freson, *The Taste of France*, I bought this purely for the photographs – again, why do I like these food pictures more than any others I have seen?

I insist there is something important floating in the word quality.

@davidhurnphoto @magnumphotos @sarahravenperchhill #nonfictionphotography #gardens #edwinsmith

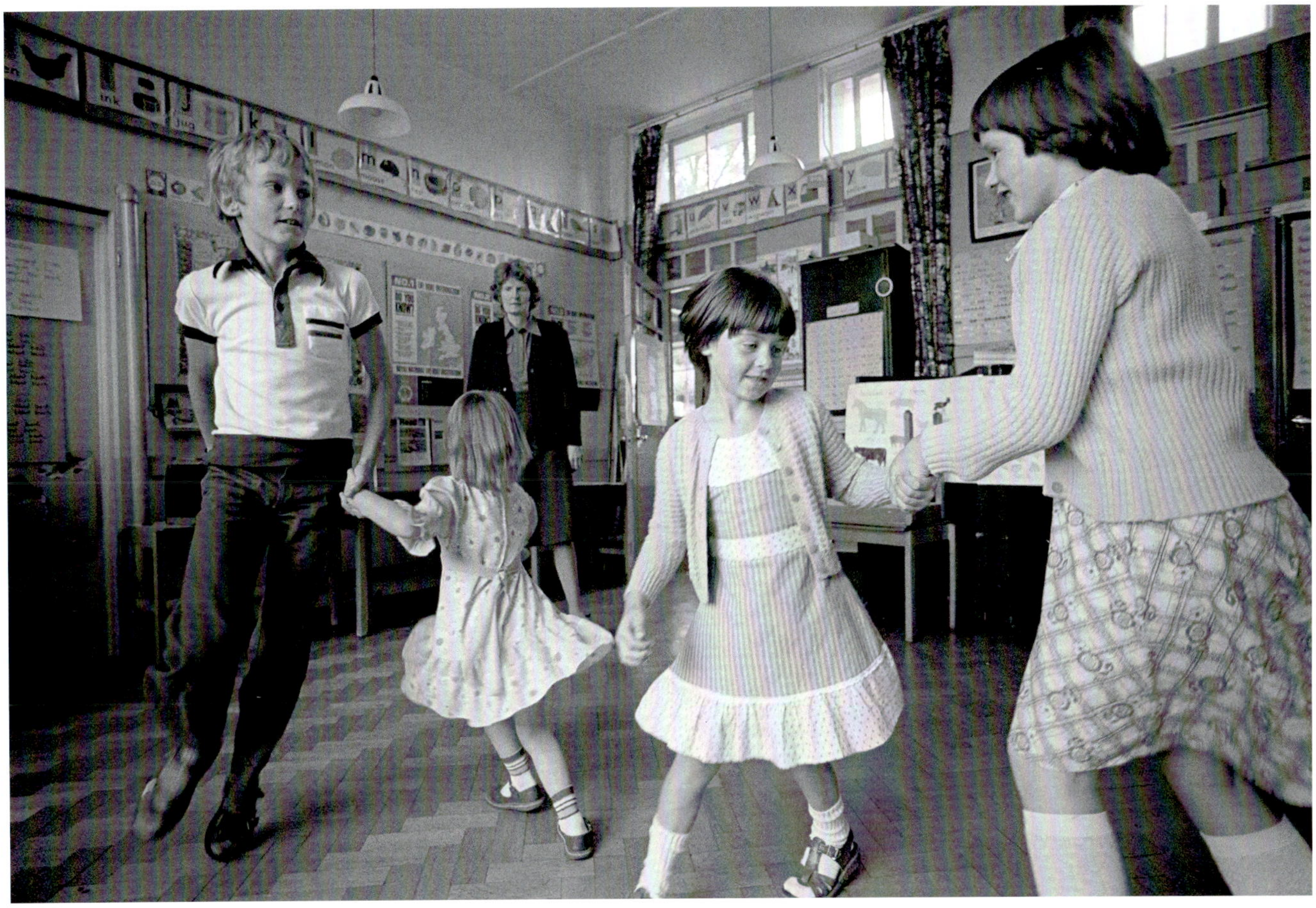

23 JANUARY 2021 / SMALLEST SCHOOL. *LLANEGLWYS, WALES 1997*

Half by chance, I got involved with a Zoom conversation between Brian Carroll and Mohamed Hassan. I like the consistency of Mohamed's photographs, both landscape and portraits – as an aside, he reminded me that he had introduced himself to me, some years ago, when I was shooting in North Wales and I suspect we had had a pleasant coffee together. These conversations, whether on Zoom or in person, usually end up with questions and advice, which I nowadays feel less and less able to give. I have never had ideas on equipment (not in this case mentioned or thought about) as I have used roughly the same cameras for 60-odd years and still don't understand the buttons on the back of my present boxes. But, equally, I no longer have ideas on clients – in fact, I would think I would be going to the young on advice where to go with my pictures – I do know that audience is important for me, the maximum the better, I have no truck for prints in a box under the bed.

Most of my advice is now on the practicalities of personal survival. I have had the same accountant since the early '60s, Seymour Gura, who was then in Fleet Street, his clients were mainly journalists, he knew all the ins and outs. I inherited his son and later grandson etc, all have all of my books and like photographs. I suspect I pay exactly the correct amount of tax, but not more than I should. Sadly, I have never had a lawyer who was a friend – a few barristers – but it's a basic lawyer who understands photography who would be useful. I befriend writers, designers, sociologists. In other words, I accept that once the pictures have been taken it needs a team to do something with them. Doing something with them means I don't die of malnutrition, which in turn means I can shoot next week.

@davidhurnphoto @magnumphotos @jazzyfingers @mohamed_hassan.photo #nonfictionphotography #briancarroll

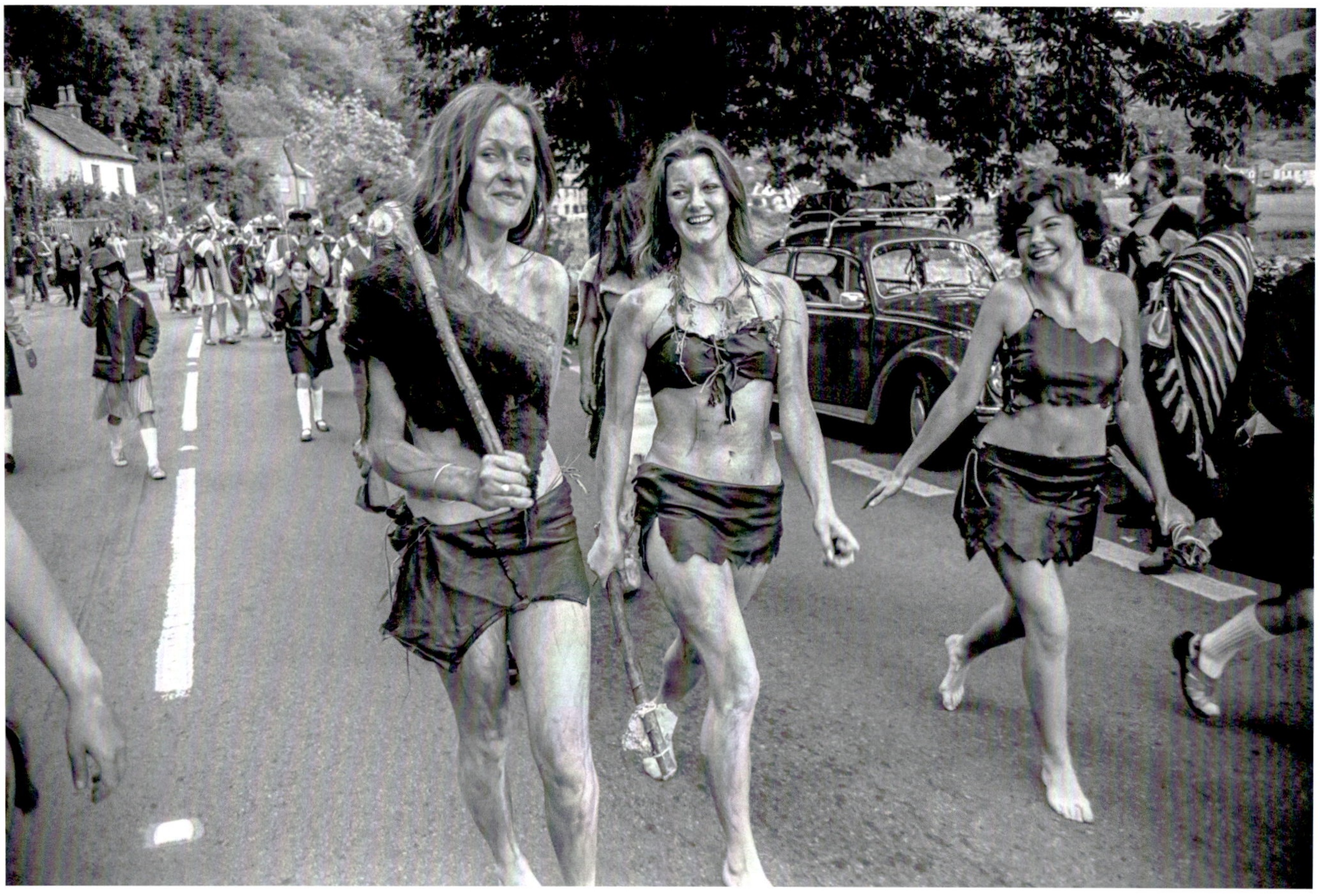

28 JANUARY 2021 / FETE PARADE. *TINTERN, WALES 1977*

I am sure I have mentioned it many times, but the quote: 'I wanted to show the things that had to be corrected: I wanted to show the things that had to be appreciated' by Lewis Wickes Hine was influential for me. I have always enjoyed living so I have leaned towards the 'appreciated'.

I was drawn to the above picture because I was in a gardening equipment shop and the friendly woman behind the counter surprised me by telling me I had once photographed her and the picture was on her wall: she is the laughing figure on the right of the picture, axe in hand. The central figure I still know and, of course, now I need to discover the one on the left.

I have photographed carnival over many years in my village – it is always a time of great joy, hair is let down, male and female flaunt themselves and happy memories made, I enjoy the recording. When will it happen again?

I am at an age where one ponders on 'time left' to function.

My life in photography has been keeping a photographic journal of life as it unfolds in front of me, as honest as I can be, or certainly as honest as I think I can be – rather blank at the moment. But I have a series of memories, I am not sure they add up to anything significant, but it doesn't really matter, the pictures are there and I can keep trying.

@davidhurnphoto @magnumphotos #nonfictionphotography

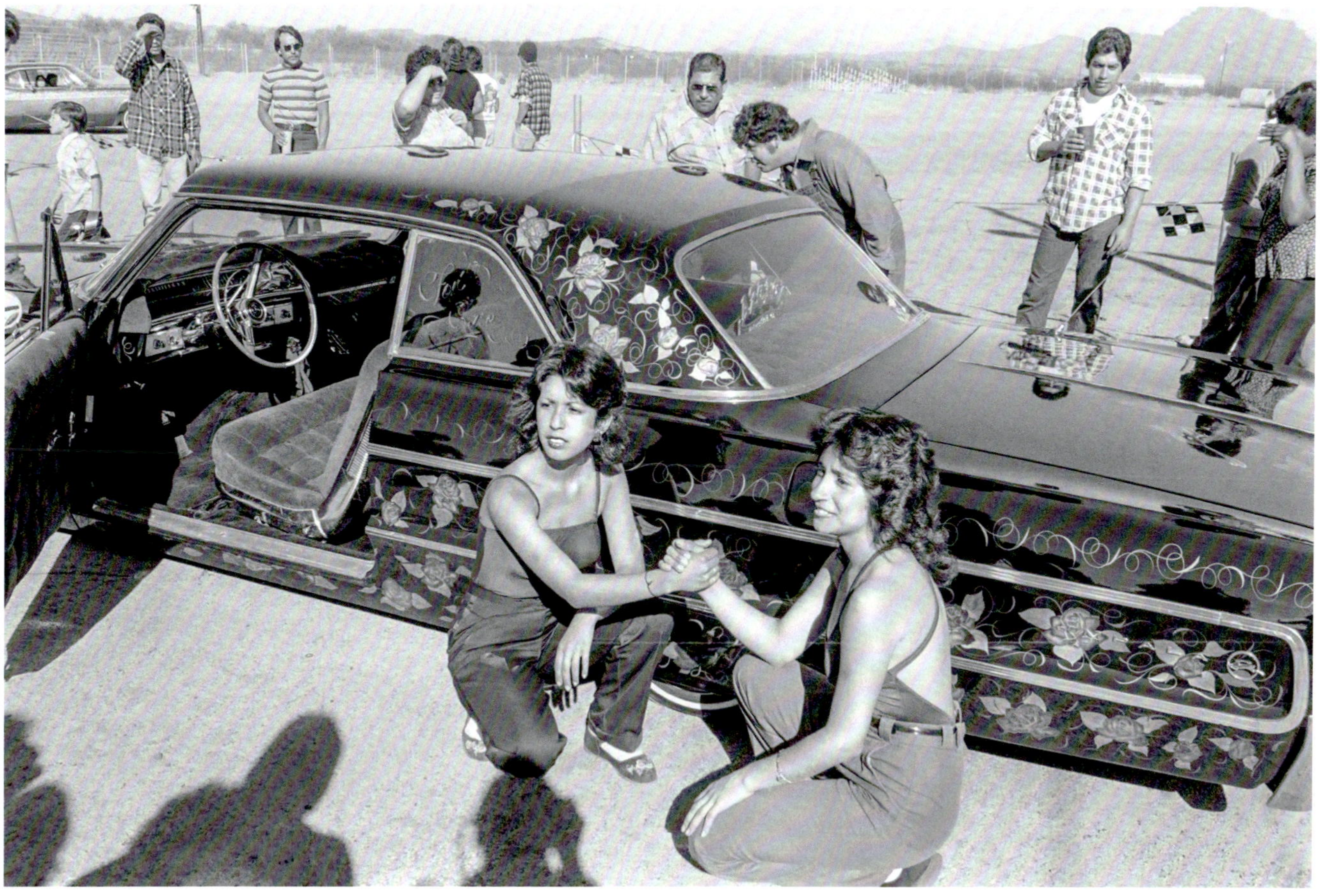

2 FEBRUARY 2021 / CUSTOM CAR. *ARIZONA, USA 1979*

I was randomly thinking of culture, and whether I should change my car. At the time of the photograph the friends in the picture were known by themselves as Chicano – then Chicano/a, now I suspect something else.

I have just received the latest *Nature* magazine and have read the lead article on epidemiology. It explains how 'Epidemiology itself is expanding, with the involvement of researchers from other fields, such as physics, mathematics, computer science and network science'.

I couldn't help thinking that as photographers we should benefit/grow from interest in many other fields.

Further on in the article it states, 'These challenges provide a chance to showcase science as it is happening in real time – something that only researchers normally see. The pandemic has helped people to understand that science, by its very nature, needs to be continually corrected and refined, its conclusions changing as the balance of evidence changes. This contrasts with the way many may have previously viewed science – as a body of knowledge that is fixed and unchanging. The change in how science is perceived might give the impression that scientists are changing their minds, but doing so when the facts change can only be a good thing'.

A difficult problem for photographers is keeping up to date with captions and keywords, meanings of words seem to be continually changing – a simple example is the problem I have with keeping track of people I have photographed who have died, and changing a reference to that fact. We as photographers continually make mistakes both culturally and verbally – by all means peer review and point out mistakes – but give us a chance to rectify.

Most of us realise as painters we are not going to be Rembrandt or Matisse, as composers not Bach or Beethoven, as photographers Koudelka or Weegee or Brandt, but we should keep trying. If we work hard, take lots of pictures, cull sensibly, we will each find our own level and that would be wonderful.

@davidhurnphoto @magnumphotos #nonfictionphotography #koudelka #brandt #weegee

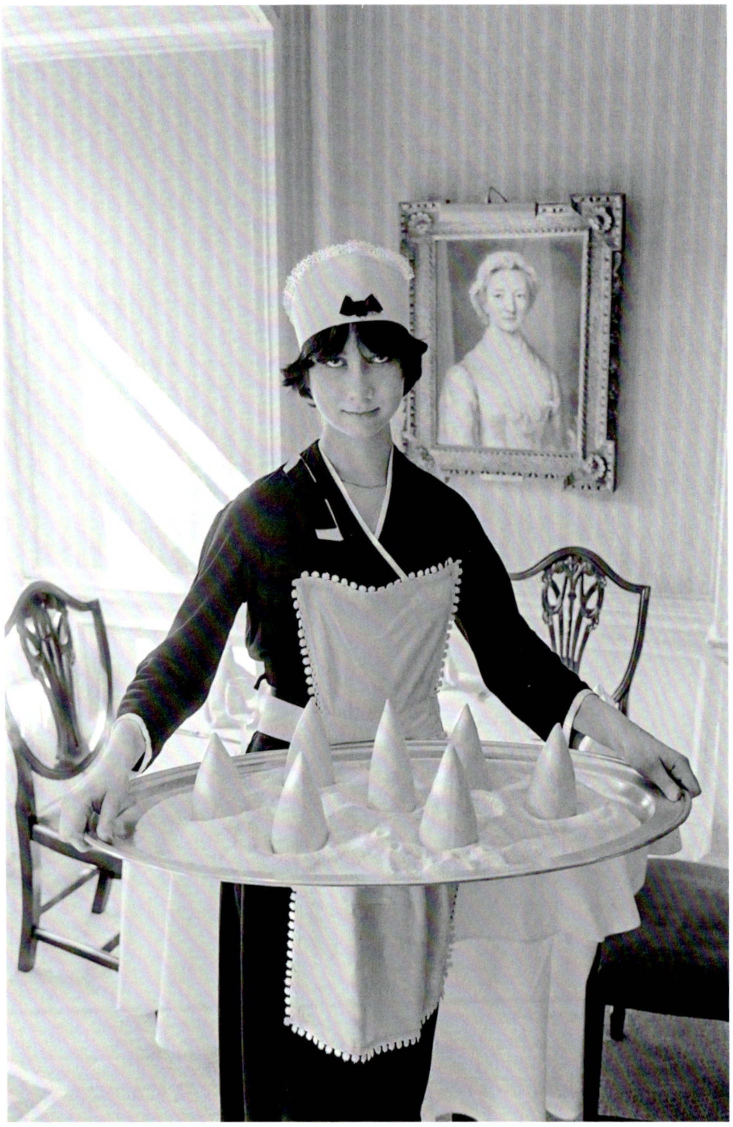

6 FEBRUARY 2021 / METAPHOR & ROMANCE. *BATH, ENGLAND 1981*

I have said many times before and expect I will again, you cannot learn from the angry photographer who has already failed.

Again, I have often suggested that if I were starting now I would spend a lot of time listening to, and digesting, those who are respected by their peers, whatever genre they were in.

All this is to introduce that I recently listened to a Zoom talk – with open questions – by the photographer Robbie Lawrence.

One hundred and eight-four persons tuned in, each paying a minimal fee – boy, money well spent.

I am continually amazed by the constructive nature of the Martin Parr Foundation – this lecture was put on by them. They obviously have the respect of the most ambitious of photographers as their series of lectures is a growing series of the world's best. There is a network of quality, the foundation obviously has trust.

The photographers I like best seem all to be generous, inquisitive, decent people. They seem constructive. Robbie was no exception. I have never enjoyed a talk more. Maybe the pictures were bordering on the romantic, which is not normally my choice, but he is a gentle, loving, honest man and this radiates in his pictures. The pictures, basically of a gardener and his garden, radiate many repeat shootings, hard work, perfect technical skills and, dare I say it, love.

He certainly is one of my goodies. I am sure we will meet up in the future and I look forward to it and will enjoy debate. Debate and openness is what the world should be fostering.

@davidhurnphoto @magnumphotos @robbiel1 #nonfictionphotography

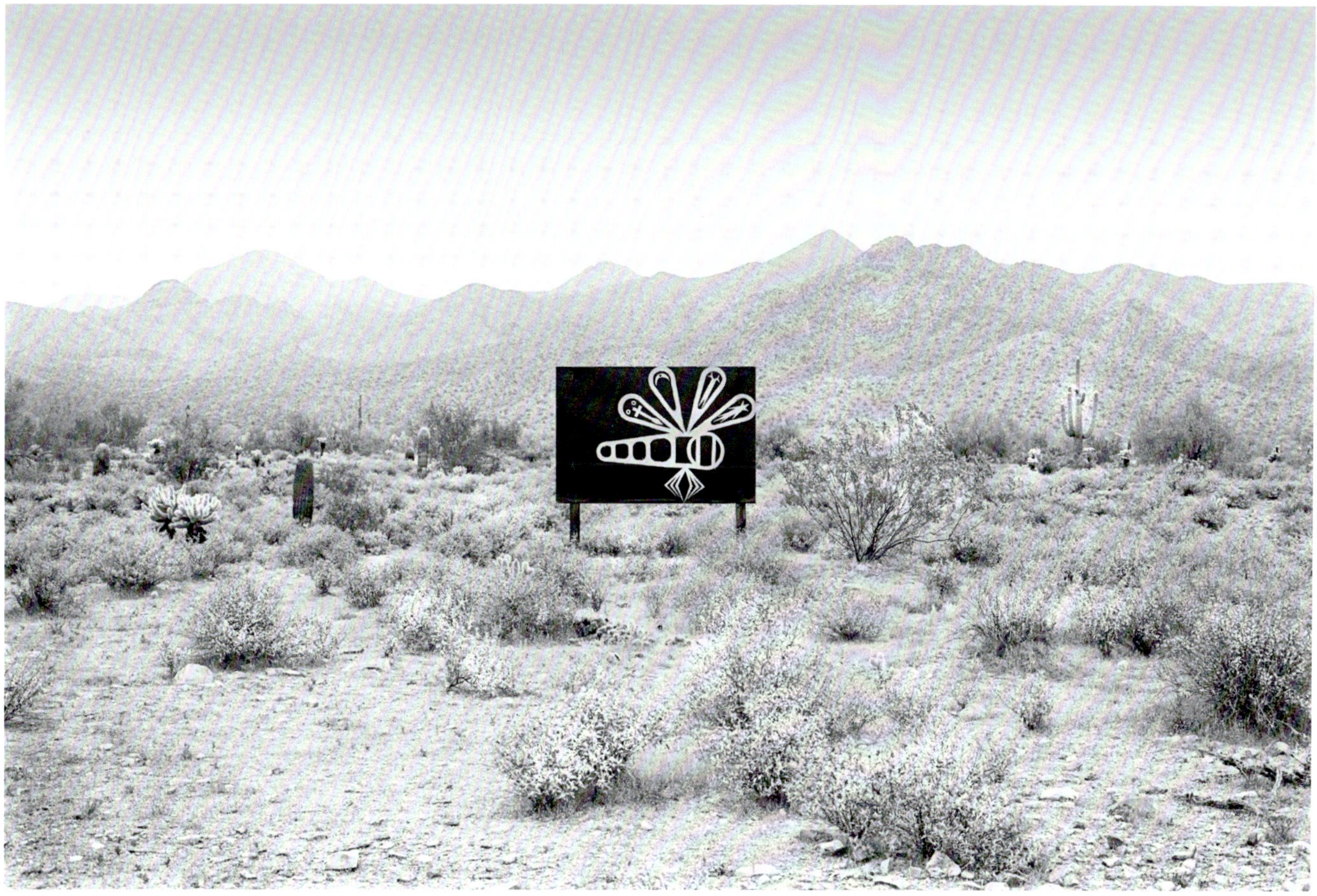

10 FEBRUARY 2021 / DESERT SIGN. *ARIZONA, USA 1980*

I enjoy simplicity and clarity. In USA they do both wonderfully when inviting you into their wilderness. Who doesn't totally understand the above sign?

It seems to me that non-fiction photography – a trace – should be trying for the same.

Can your viewer reasonably be asked to make an intelligent stab at what your photograph is inferring? If not, why not? Or can one be deliberately obscure for some rational reason? I must say I cannot get very interested in deliberate abstruseness, it certainly doesn't , as some seem to think, equate with quality.

Have faith in your own thoughts but clearly understand what those thoughts actually are visually, make them simple. Then, have the knowledge, skills and tenacity to follow those ideas to where they end up.

You have something to show, you think you get it right, you try to show it, wait for intelligent constructive criticism, if necessary amend or start again.

My favourite radio programme is *Life Scientific*. I love the commonality of the people involved, their passion, their tenacity, their openness to peer review, their delight at discussion. If I was young again I would be stealing these programmes for the basis of my research and start on a never-ending project of portraits of scientists. Boy, how interesting and valuable that would be.

@davidhurnphoto @magnumphotos #nonfictionphotography #lifescientific

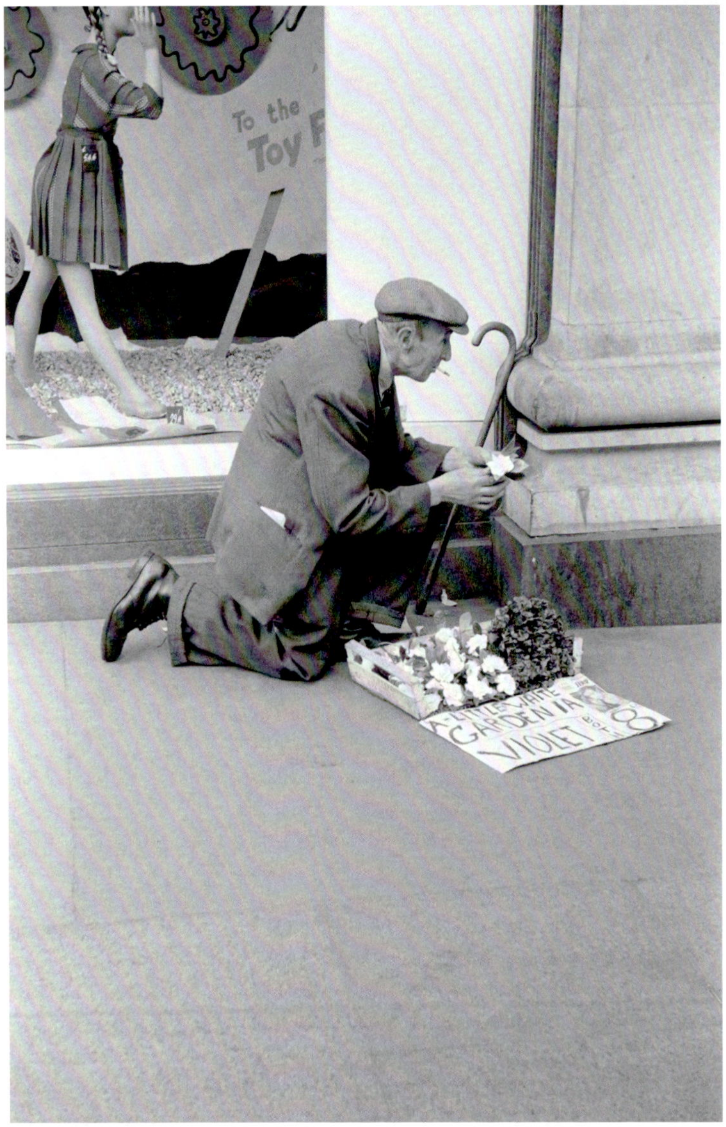

14 FEBRUARY 2021 / VIOLET SELLER. *LONDON, ENGLAND 1955*

It's Valentine's Day and for me the time to contemplate past and present loves and the nature of photography that brings you so close to some people and then forces you to abandon them.

I think I have had eight true loves in my life – five female and three male. If I followed the Greek six words for love then, of course, more.

Being a photographer is very difficult. If you are photographing people you are, almost by definition, very close to them. Then suddenly you are whisked away somewhere else and most times feelings quickly dissipate. I think it is the biggest downside to taking up this profession, a profession I love and could and would not change.

I am a natural hugger, kisser, smiler. What does the future offer? Will we ever have a time when we can feel relaxed kissing another on two cheeks – three times in some countries? Will I ever again look forward to rushing into the office and giving hugs all round? It was my shy way of demonstrating respect and friendship. I suspect if I now had to ask permission first, I would not bother.

I might have stated before that perhaps my all time favourite book is just 10x12 cms in size. Size is not everything. I take it with me whenever I go on a trip. It boasts 266 uplifting joyous pictures taken by, in my opinion, many of the world's greatest photographers. It is published by Abbeville Press and called *Hugs and Kisses*.

@davidhurnphoto @magnumphotos @abbevillepress #nonfictionphotography #hugsandkisses

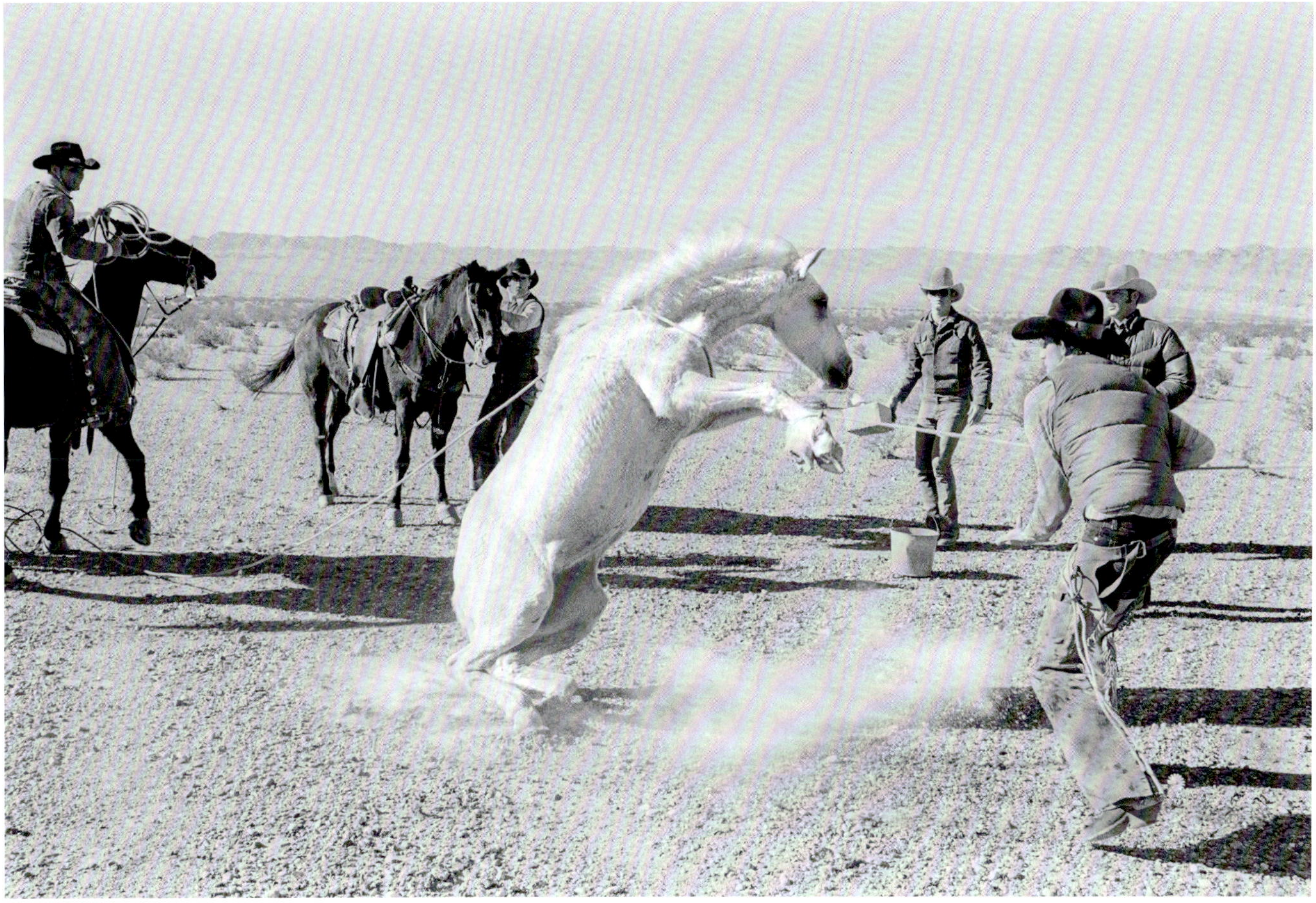

19 FEBRUARY 2021 / LAST WILD HORSE. *ARIZONA, USA 1980*

Sometimes it is difficult to read a picture without knowing the context. The above picture is in fact very positive.

It is from one of my favourite self assignments. I had read that the last 11 wild horses in Arizona were to be rounded up. The horses were being harmed, as they were getting onto the highways to get throwaway food, and were getting hit by trucks.

The Arizona desert is largely a rock desert with many hills and gullies. The wild horses know the terrain and are very fit, consequently difficult to corral. Local cowboys were given the task. It took two weeks.

I had a wonderful time turning into a make believe cowboy from a John Ford movie. One had to ride a horse, which luckily I had learnt to do in Spain – another story. One had to wear 'chaps' to protect from the vicious cactus. A large stetson type hat to deal with the sudden rain downpours. We all were woken before sunrise – the wild horses would gather together at that time – breakfast was usually steak and eggs. I just love being a photographer.

The horses were finally all caught, never more than one a day. I followed this beautiful white one, who ended up as the riding horse of a young girl on a large ranch.

@davidhurnphoto @magnumphotos #nonfictionphotography #horses

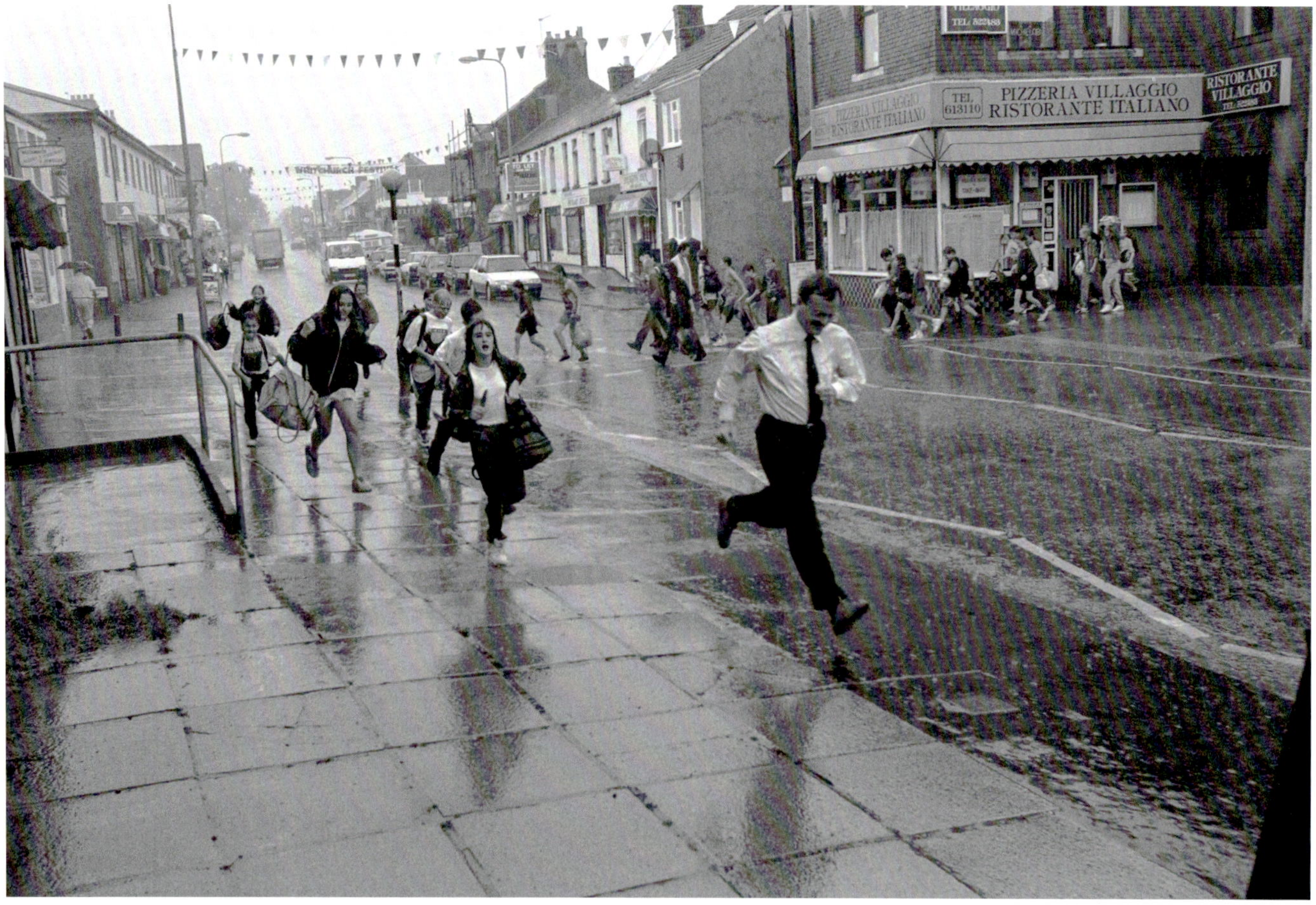

24 FEBRUARY 2021 / WEATHER GRAB. *CARDIFF, WALES 1995*

I have just been given an award: 'Exceptional Achievement in Photography Award' given by *Amateur Photography* magazine.

The magazine has had a distinguished continuous circulation since 1884.

I was, of course, delighted but puzzled.

As far as I know, I know no-one at the magazine. Who makes these decisions?

Although not a habitual reader, the magazine has often been of use to me throughout my career, particularly through their reviews of equipment, which I have always found extensive and accurate, and also because they seem to get excellent writers to do their interviews. The present edition of the magazine – I think dated 27 February – has an accurate but rather flattering essay on me by Amy Davies.

It's always nice to be liked and it has certainly been a lift during the shutdown. I thank them and all involved.

At this point it seems pertinent to also thank those that say nice/constructive things about my Instagram dabbles. Right at the beginning I said that in the main, I would not be making replies – hopefully not through laziness – but simply because thoughtful remarks need thoughtful replies and these are better discussed between friends and like-minded practitioners in your own vicinity. I wish to encourage more group activities and discussion.

Very occasionally I do reply but usually by personal email. I assure you that whenever you make a nice/constructive statement to anyone, it is appreciated.

@davidhurnphoto @magnumphotos #nonfictionphotography #amydavies #amateurphotographer

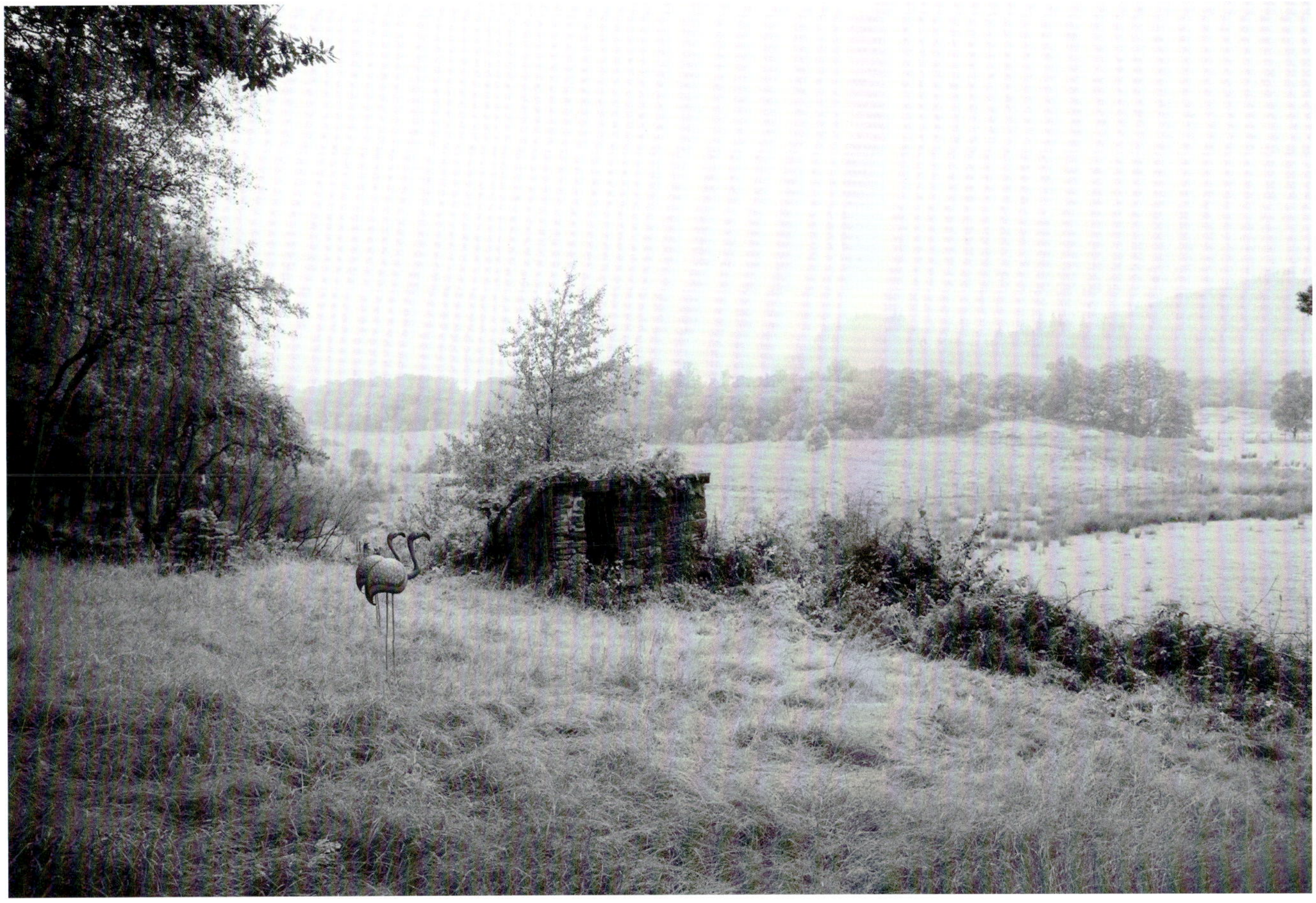

1 MARCH 2021 / INVASIVE GENUS. *GORDDINAN, WALES 2017*

I have watched two Zoom talks, one through MPF, one through Ffoton.

I enjoy Zoom more and more as everyone learns the mechanics and protocol, sadly I expect the trolls to invade soon.

The first talk was by that established, universally respected photographer, Susan Meiselas, brave, tenacious, whose heart is always involved with others. Most know of her work with the Prince Street Girls, Nicaragua, Carnival Strippers. All photo essays of the highest quality.

Perhaps less is known about her collaborative work and it was this she talked about in the Zoom – I had to take a portrait of a distinguished Kurd in Cardiff, when I said I was from Magnum he hugged me and said 'you must know Susan'. She is the hero of the Kurds because of her book, published in 1997, *Kurdistan*. Susan is an extraordinary researcher, organiser, collector of talent – she set up the Magnum Foundation, which in my opinion has done more for young photographers around the world than any other organisation.

She talked about her latest two books: one, *Tar Beach*, a collaboration, Susan organising/collecting a series of pictures taken on the roofs of the area of New York, called Little Italy; two, *Eyes Open: 23 Photography Ideas for Curious Kids*.

I won't elaborate more – just go buy them – they will make you feel better, part of that outside world.

The second was Euan Ross, talking about his large collection, primarily of landscape books.

I try to be in the background of as many Zoom calls as I can where I suspect there will be young participants. I know what I think about my contemporaries and how they/we work, but we are all yesterday and by and large should shut up. I want to get a feel of what is the future.

At the moment I am wary of the seeming emphasis on self-publishing of books and what seems to me the fetishising of books as an object. If I compare with the written word – at the moment I am re-reading *A Tale of Two Cities* in the Penguin edition, clear text, no frills.

I enjoyed listening to Euan, he seems a most forward thinking person and I suspect his website, circa35mm.com, is very worthwhile visiting.

@davidhurnphoto @magnumphotos @circa35mm @ffotonwales @susanmeiselas #nonfictionphotography

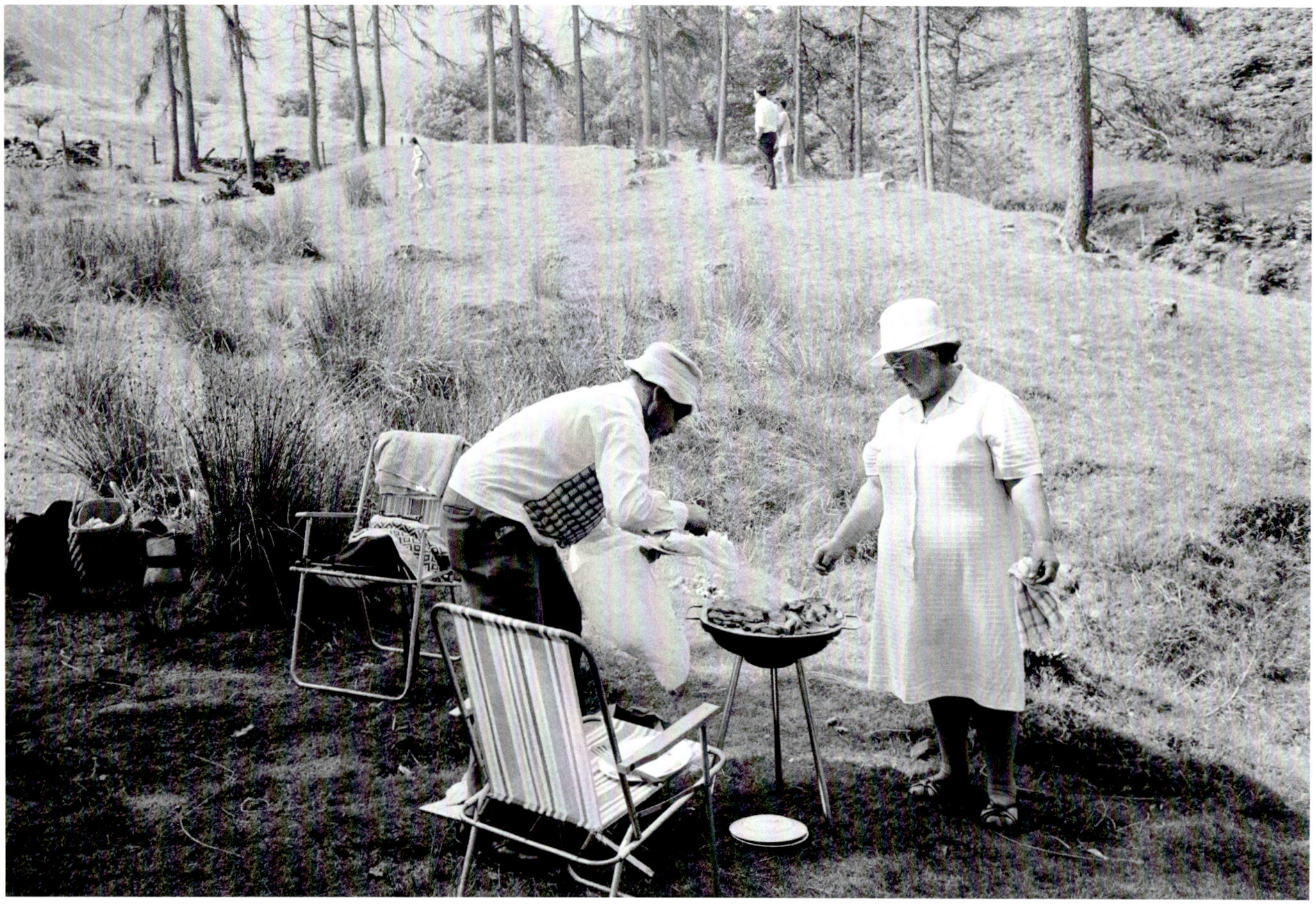

5 MARCH 2021 / BARBECUE SHINDIG. ***BRECON BEACONS, WALES 1973***

I am so looking forward to the end of my lockdown and to have the ability to venture into the Beacons and 'rave' again.

Whilst at home I have tried – among other subjects – to photograph flowers and produce. Difficult, as Blossfeldt, Weston, Mapplethorpe, and a favourite, Charles Jones, hover above me.

I think one good way to initially learn is to have heroes that you try to emulate, if they were good enough, you won't, because they are they. However, if you try and try and try and take lots and lots of pictures I suspect you will gradually discard the hero and gradually find your own voice – that is, if you are good enough, and have the stamina.

Sadly, time is not on my side so I flunked.

I will return to my landscape, 'Man's influence on the Landscape'. So far I have photographed just over 500 locations (I have been doing it for five years), my notes suggest that I have 15 more spots that need visiting. I need to get them finished this year whilst I can still stand up.

My first trip will be Conway, view of castle based on a photograph by Francis Bedford also in Conway, one of the two Elizabethan houses in the town. Maesgeirchen, the first housing estate in Wales. Barmouth, first area of land donated to the National Trust. Fairbourne, a village being abandoned to the sea because of climate change.

In theory, in total a two-day trip, but knowing my new slowness, perhaps three or four days. At least I have a plan and that gives me forward hope.

@davidhurnphoto @magnumphotos #nonfictionphotography #blossfeldt #edwardweston #robertmapplethorpe #charlesjones

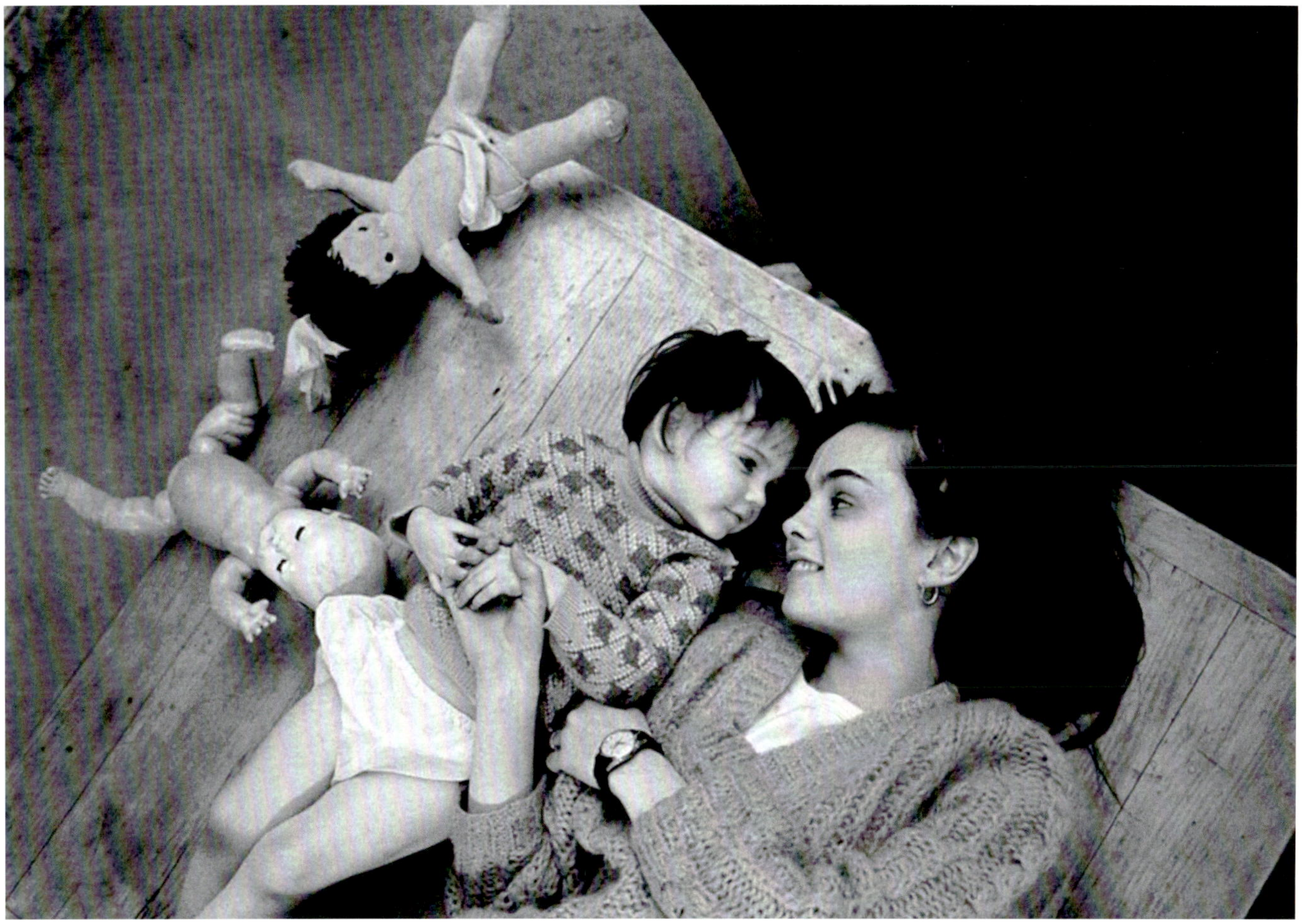

9 MARCH 2021 / MOTHER AND CHILD. *LONDON, ENGLAND 1965*

I love contact sheets – although I see there are all sorts of advantages from digital and the ease of results ending up in a computer – I get endless pleasure in re-living my life through looking at pages of 1.5x1 inch pictures.

Whatever some others might analyse about pictures as memory, they work for me. I am at a stage in my life where failing memory is a growing worry. Re-looking at what I think are the most successful of my pictures, they bring back almost total recall of the incidents seen. Unsuccessful pictures don't, it's almost as though the bigger the memory gain equates with the success, for me at least, of the picture.

When seeing a situation in front of me, instinctively I analyse and search for the moment that encapsulates the event, I guess thus its memory.

After what was for me – most of the time – one of the happiest times of my life, the picture above, wife and child, totally recalls the moment, the place, the happiness. It becomes a very precious picture.

I think one of the biggest mistakes I have made is the one that most of us make, I did not live in the moment enough. I think one should try to live life to the fullest while you can and collect memories like fools collect money, because in the end, that's all you have – hopefully, happy memories – maybe sad memories, together they make life.

Moral: take more pictures of everything.

@davidhurnphoto @magnumphotos #nonfictionphotography #motherdaughter #love

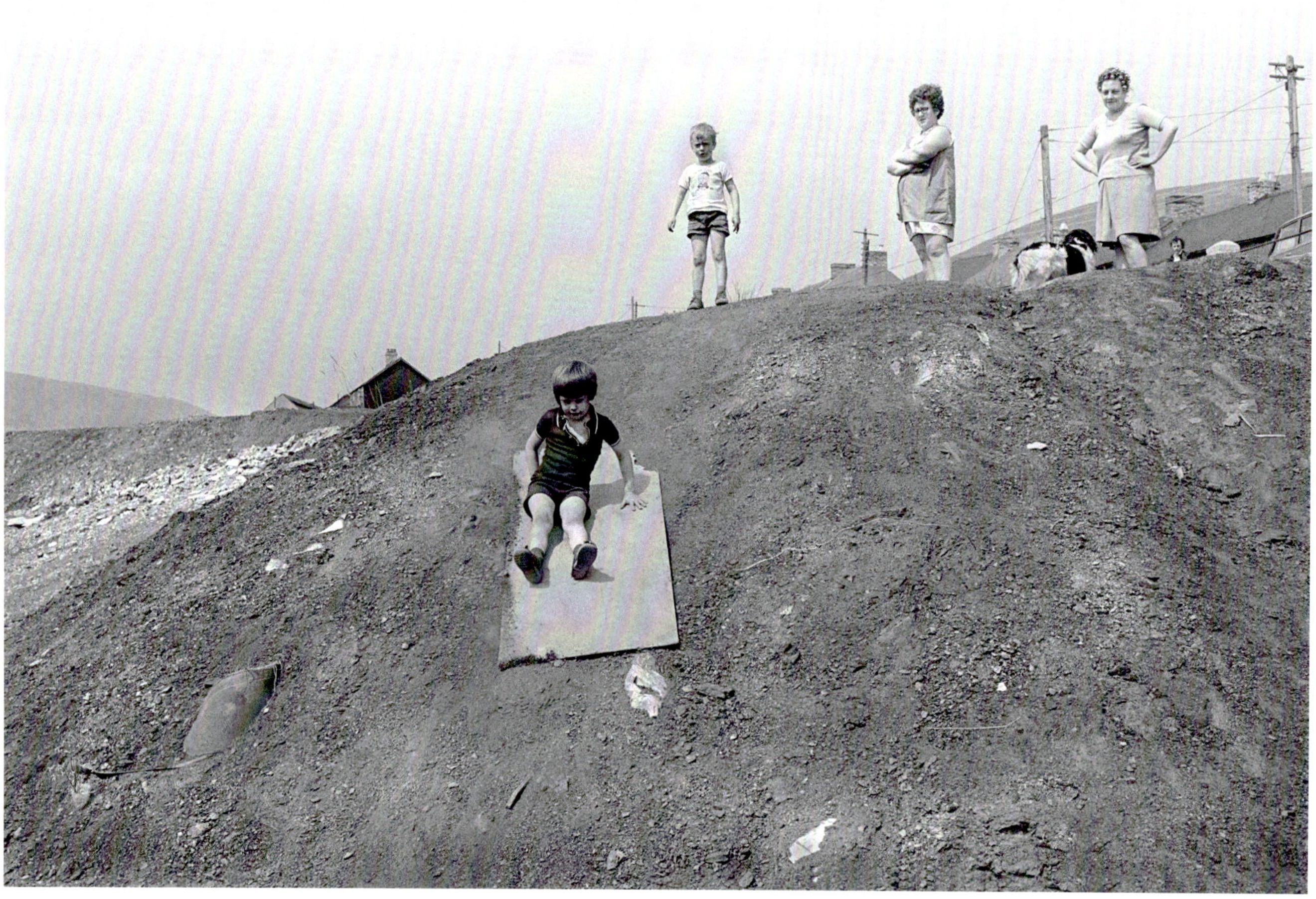

15 MARCH 2021 / SPACING AND BUBBLE. *ABERTILLERY, WALES 1977*

I think, for me, a problem I have with lockdown is that I think too much, maybe invent problems, and too many solutions. I am having difficulty in finding relevant stuff to write about so have decided to stagger my posts a little, i.e. post every Tuesday, an arbitrary day but why not.

My stay-at-home diary is fast filling up. I am finding Zooms very fruitful. I have tuned in to – is that the right terminology? – Harvard, Arizona, ICP, etc, always to hear very established people sound forth, I learn a lot and find plenty to absorb/steal.

The Format Festival is launching in Derby – formatfestival.com – this week. Brian Griffin talks on Zoom 27 March. I have my ticket. I always enjoy Brian, extremely innovative and passionate about photography, he can be very funny, he is at the top of his tree.

MPF has just published its latest programme. Trent Parke; Joel Meyerowitz; Peter van Agtmael; Tariq Zaidi is new to me so that is always exciting, pictures exploring self-expression through fashion, style and art on the streets of Congo.

Essential for every woman photographer; Fiona Rogers, extremely intelligent, progressive, smart, founder of Firecracker; if every woman photographer doesn't tune in to this, and after contact her, they would be mad. She is talking to Margaret Mitchell, a photographer I have never met. Of course, if you are male join in as well.

It's an extraordinary line-up, I expect to commandeer lots of stuff for future Instagrams. If I were a budding photographer, in fact now as an experienced photographer, I would/will sign up for every one – you would/will learn.

I will continue to promote when I find events of quality – it's simply that I think it's such a constructive and inexpensive way to pick up true information and progress.

I am afraid I am a bit of an elitist. You will always learn a little from those you admit are better than oneself.

@davidhurnphoto @magnumphotos @martinparrfdn @chillioctopus @pvanagtmael @joel_meyerowitz @tariqzaidiphoto @firecracker_foto @margaret.mitchell #nonfictionphotography #format

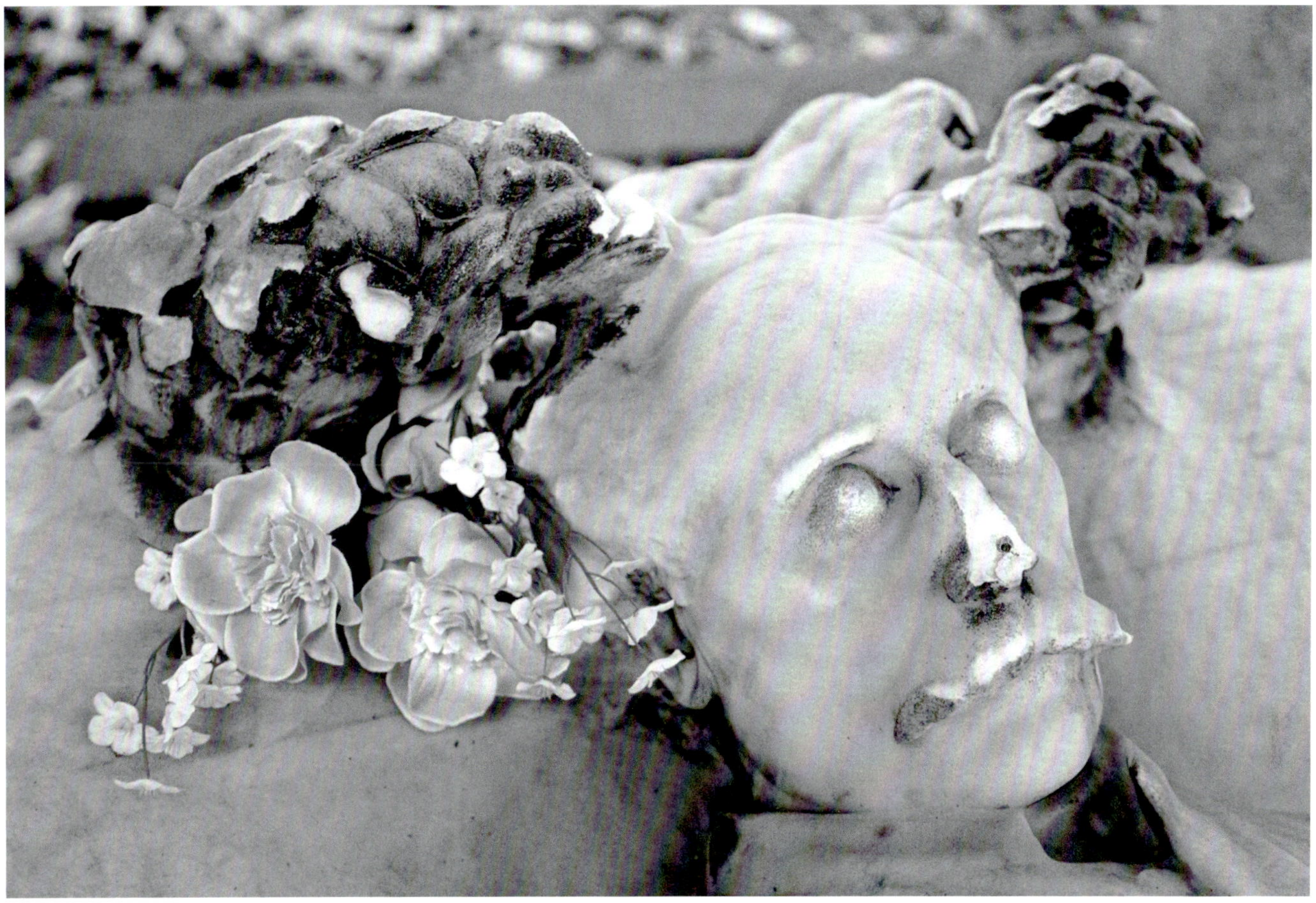

5 APRIL 2021 / ALEXANDRE DUMAS. ***PARIS, FRANCE 2001***

To carry on my theme of seeing pictures from different sources, I have just received a book, *Buckingham Palace: A Royal Garden*. A quick check on Google shows that there are 37 magazines concerning gardening. A good market. There has been a distinguished history of pictures and photographers specialising in this area. I have books by Edwin Smith, I love a book of vegetables by Charles Jones, and, of course, I hope you all know the pictures of Bill Brandt. Earlier period, one can see Karl Blossfeldt whose book, *Art Forms in Nature*, actually became an international best-seller. I am sure there are many worth visiting pre this time – a quick perusal shows many female photographers – worth a research project in itself? Flowers seem more difficult, there is a strong history of flower painting, interesting flower photography is more sparse. A good book is *Flora Photographica*. Recent photographers that seem to have made it work include John Blakemore whose picture series on tulips are refined, and Robert Mapplethorpe and Edward Weston, both of whose work seem to have sexual overtones.

I am sure the *Royal Gardens* book will have an enormous sales potential, the subject matter has international appeal, a good start. Luckily it's a fine book, in no way pretentious, but way above the normal brochure, with at least two pictures that I will attempt to swap. One picture I particularly like views the central island like a tropical rainforest. The whole shows an enormous amount of early morning wake-ups, great tenacity, a real sense of form. I suspect the photographer John Campbell will instantly be top of the garden tree.

My picture of flowers are part of the grave of the writer Alexandre Dumas in the Cimetière de Montmarte in Paris.

@davidhurnphoto @magnumphotos #buckinghampalace #johncampbell #edwinsmith #charlesjones #billbrandt #alexandredumas

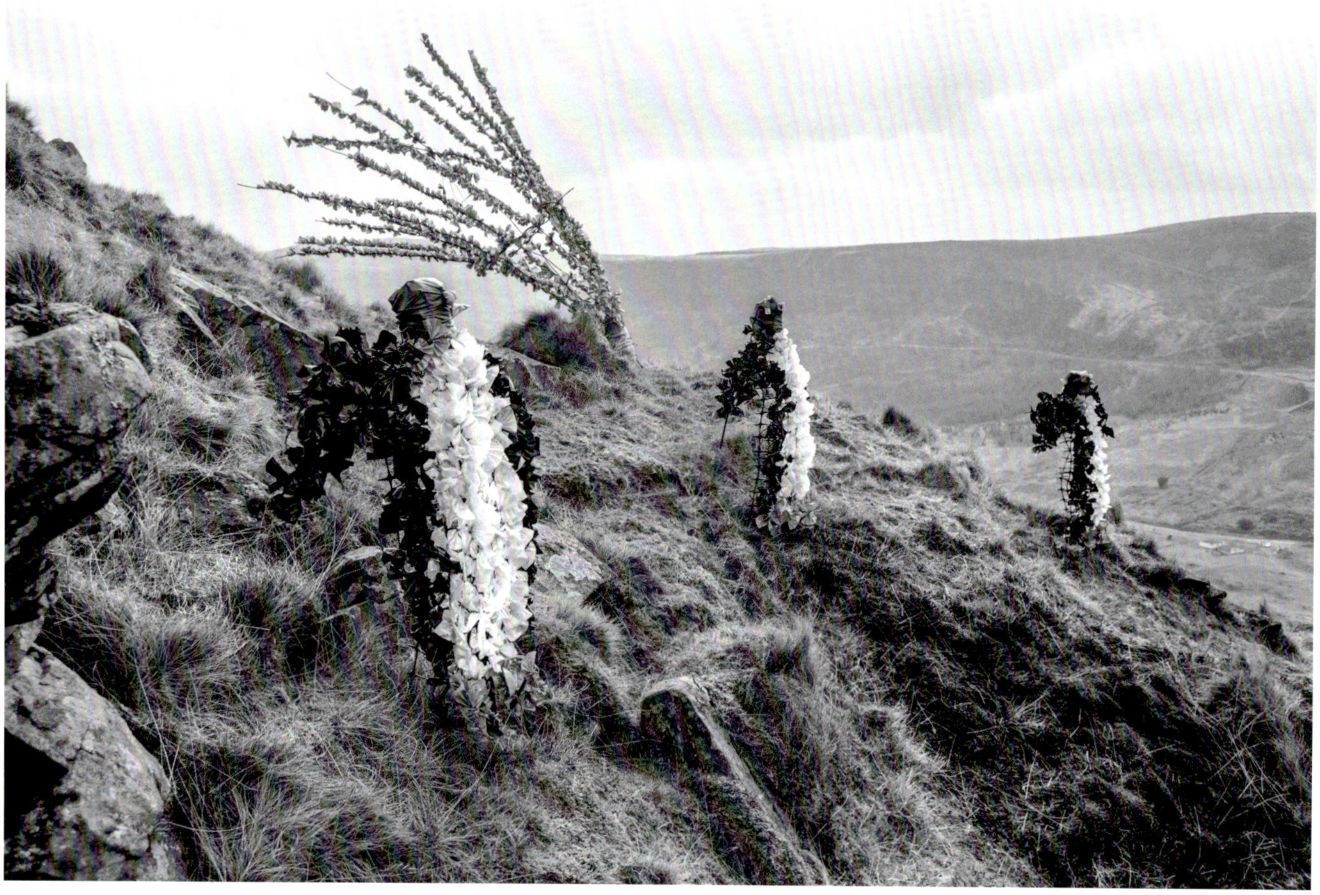

7 APRIL 2021 / WELSH PENGUINS. *TREHERBERT, WALES 1993*

My picture is taken on the road separating the Rhondda and Cynon Valleys in Wales. It is of plastic and wire sculptures made by a local 'watchman', George Cole, who was employed to deal with falling rocks off the hillside and ranging sheep on the road – in his spare time he adorned the hillside with wonderfully inspired sculptures. In 1993 I tried to get the Arts Council to acquire the complete set – I presume it wasn't high enough art for them. At least I have a set of pictures.

Another inspirer who I photographed for my book, *Living in Wales*, was Mark Bourne, he was a retired caravan owner who lived in Corris. He would do a yearly Italian trip with his beloved wife, photograph classical buildings and then make six feet high models of them, in concrete, in his garden – they were magical. I have heard that he has since died, but it seems the cottage and garden has been acquired by a local artist whom one hopes is keeping the sculptures in good order – I will explore when I am in the North. Any information would be helpful.

A photographic record of sculpture is, of course, historically useful and in a way that is enough, however, some have tried to do more, I am not sure that works. I have a book, *The Kiss of Apollo*, which I quite like but it is not totally satisfactory, I am not sure why. Perhaps it is simply that sculpture is essentially three dimensional and in a way asks to be touched.

Sets of sculptures are a different thing as each seem to gain from their togetherness. I thought Lee Friedlander's *The American Monument* a very worthwhile and thought-provoking enterprise, it was said to be influenced by Walker Evans – was he influenced by Hoppe's *Forty London Statues and Public Monuments*? and he by 'In 1851 five artists, utilising the recently-introduced waxed paper negative process, were sent to four regions of France to record relevant ancient and medieval structures'? The nature of influence is interesting.

@davidhurnphoto @magnumphotos @leefriedlanderarchive #georgecole #markbourne #nonfictionphotography #walkerevans #hoppe #sculpture

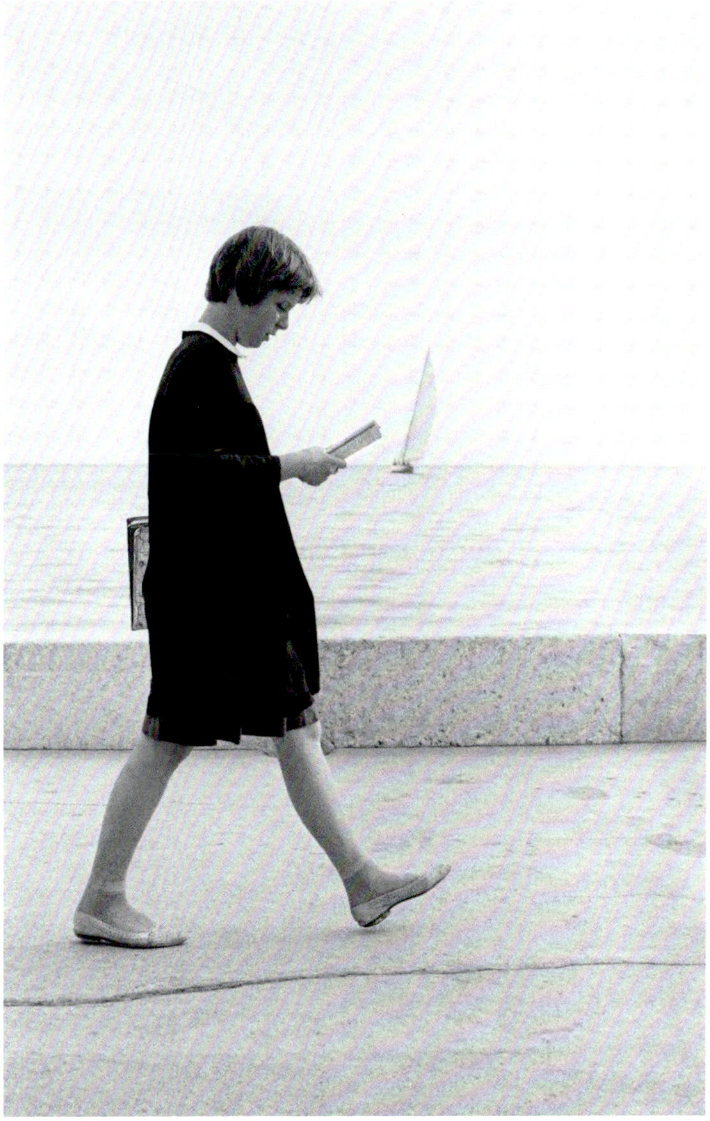

27 APRIL 2021 / STROLLING. *DUBROVNIK, CROATIA 1964*

Links are intriguing.

I have just been watching a TV programme about the painter Manet – I have often suggested that if one buys a dozen Manet postcards, studies them thoroughly, you will learn everything to know about form/composition – at least of the type of pictures I most enjoy trying to take.

I did not know that Manet was a close friend of Baudelaire – if anyone has had an influence on me picture-wise from what they wrote, it would be Baudelaire (1821-1867) writing on the *flâneur*. He refers to 'somebody who observes the city or their surroundings, and experiences not only an actual physical stroll but also a way of philosophical thinking and a way of seeing/feeling things. Walking for walking's sake and not in a hurry to just get from one place to another, but to just experience/wandering in the urban cityscape, hidden corners and nooks, observing the immediate'. Elsewhere, 'His passion and his profession are to become one flesh with the crowd, an immense joy to set up house in the heart of the multitude, amid the ebb and flow of movement, to be away from home and yet to feel oneself everywhere at home; to see the world, to be at the centre of the world, and yet to remain hidden from the world'.

Manet and Baudelaire often walked together through Paris.

In the UK, Charles Dickens was a supreme example, 'Dickens clocked up a huge number of miles on foot. He is estimated to have walked at least 12 miles per day'. – Peter Ackroyd.

Dickens' descriptions can easily be seen as photographs, read, *A Tale of Two Cities*, chapter 5, The Wine Shop. It reads like a shooting script.

Previous to Baudelaire, Edgar Allen Poe wrote a short story in 1840, *The Man of the Crowd*, 'The unnamed narrator sits in an unnamed coffee shop in London. He was fascinated by the crowd outside the window – he takes time to categorise the different types of people he sees.'

One can learn so much about being a better photographer from other sources than photography.

@davidhurnphoto @magnumphotos #baudelaire #manet #flaneur #charlesdickens #edgarallenpoe

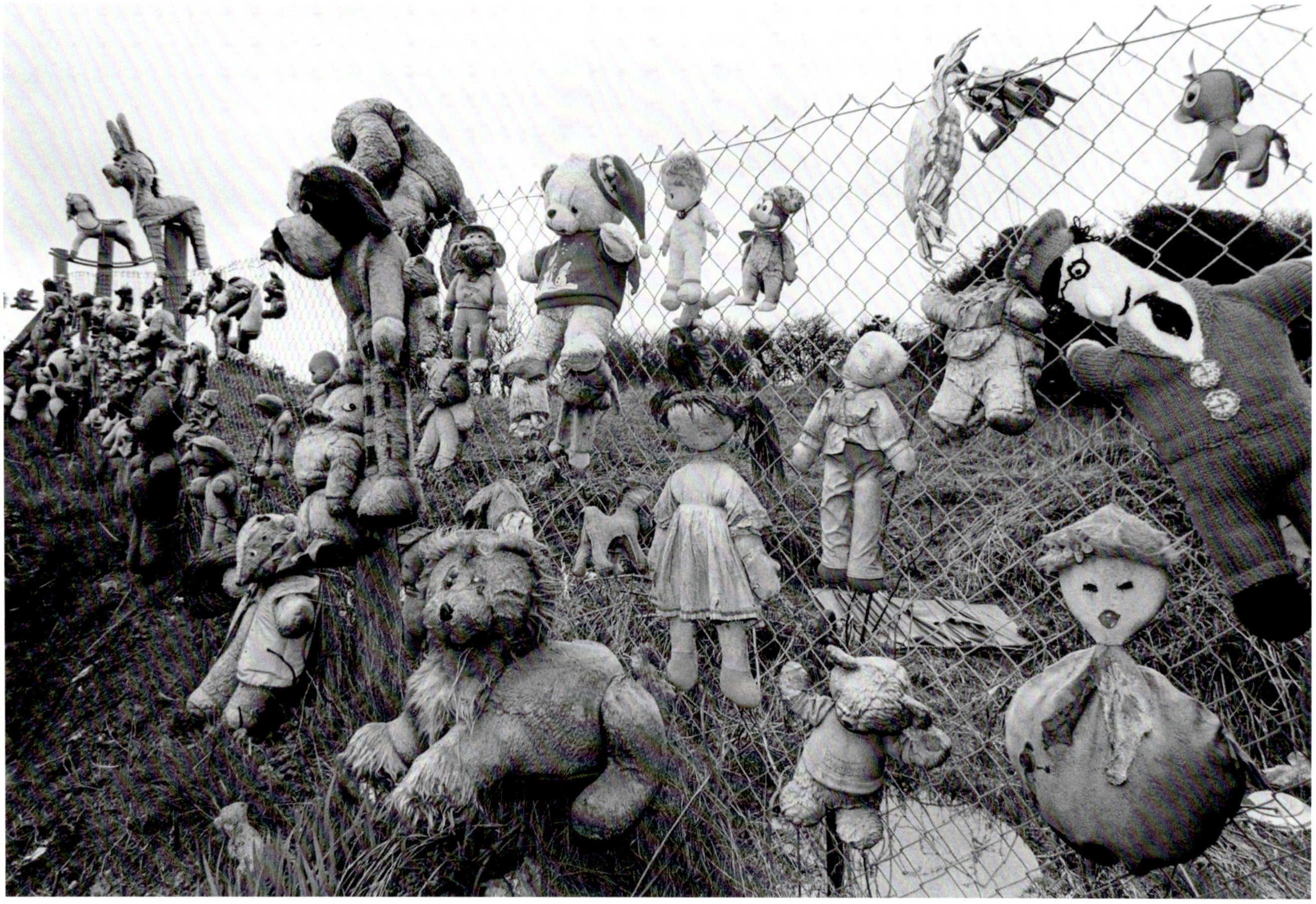

4 MAY 2021 / DISCARDED LOVES. *PENPARC, WALES 1999*

During my perusing of past pictures I have noticed how many I have of things and advents that no longer exist. Of course, this is not a coincidence as whenever I read of, or have heard that something was likely to fold/disappear, I would try to photograph it, perhaps on the simple assumption that what in the future is no longer there cannot then be photographed. I knew that with my hat on of photography being my way of making a living, these pictures at some time were likely to be worth at least the price of a meal. Yet as I was photographing something of my choice, something that I was interested in, it was a win-win situation.

In an age of social media and academic theoretical writing, this sort of seeing, thinking, trying for self-honesty genre of photography can be under attack.

But I am glad Jacob Riis and Lewis Hine photographed for social change. I am glad George Rodger documented arriving to enter the concentration camp at Bergen-Belsen in 1945. His photographs of the survivors and piles of corpses were published in *Life* and *Time* magazines and were highly influential in showing the reality of the death camps. I am glad Robert Frank produced The Americans, I am glad Donna Ferrato photographs the way she does. I am glad Josef Koudelka photographed the Gypsies and Sergio Larrain photographed London. I am glad Elliott Erwitt loves dogs.

There is, of course, no doubt that in the past and, I expect, unfortunately in the near future, photography has/will be dominated by white males, often very colonialist, photographers. But let's not too often look for the negative. My experience is that I have known so many photographers and people in the photography industry who worked their butts off, in often extreme conditions, because they really cared and in some minor way wished to help – plus they often had more knowledge than most.

We must all be open to advancement and change, but we should not be suppressed by anonymous bigotry.

I have hope for the future.

@davidhurnphoto @magnumphotos @josef_koudelka @elliotterwitt @donnaferrato #georgerodger #nonfictionphotography

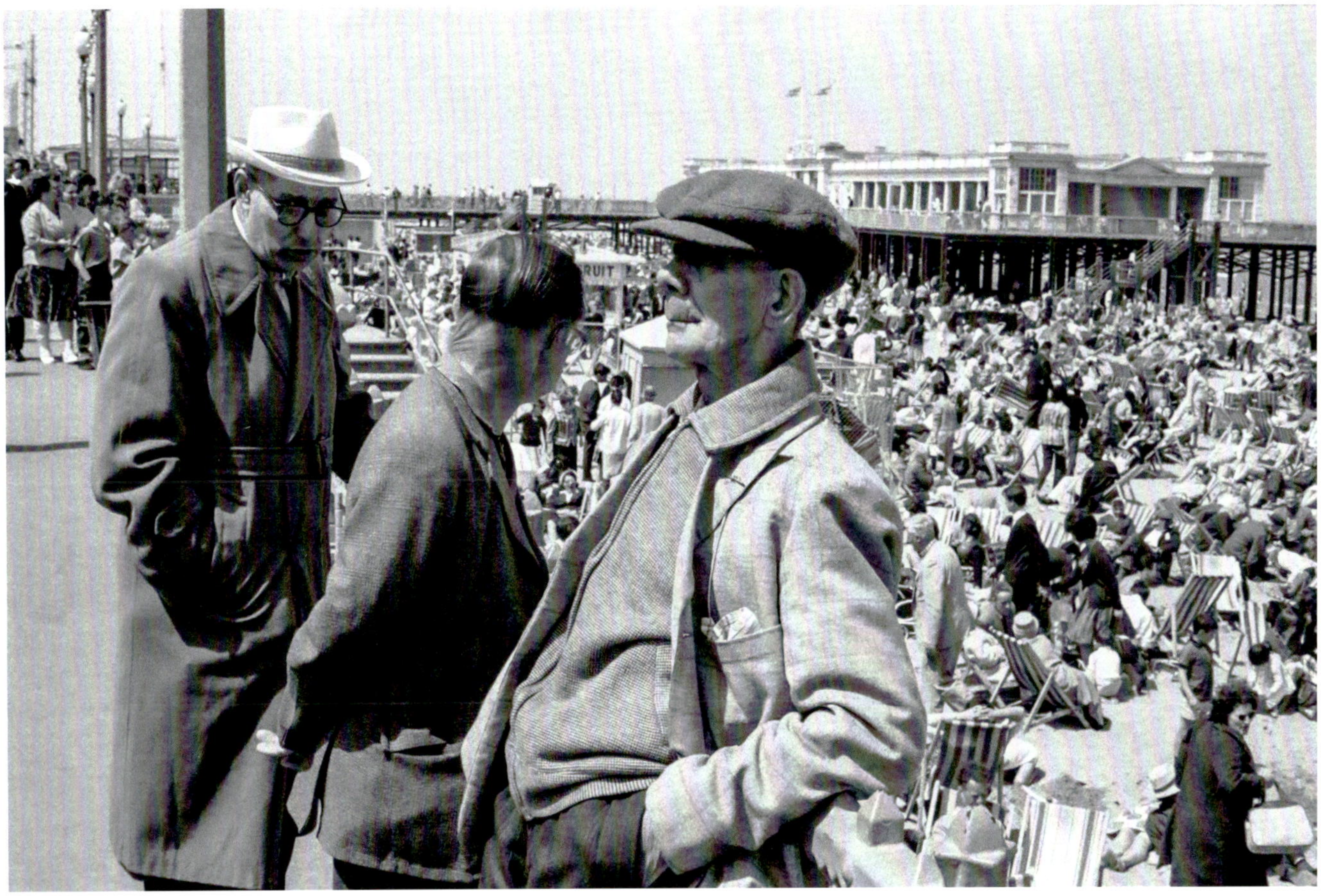

11 MAY 2021 / NOT IN LOCKDOWN. *HERNE BAY, ENGLAND 1963*

A writer who has always had influence on me is/was John Szarkowski, from 1962–1991 director of photography at New York's Museum of Modern Art. Among quotes of his in my quote collection he says, 'photography's central sense of purpose and aesthetic: the precise and lucid description of significant fact'– it's not difficult to completely concur.

However, I would suggest that this 'description of significant fact' is more precisely projected by some than by others.

I have heard it suggested that more pictures are taken in a present hour than in the total history of photography before the iPhone. I would suggest that most do not deal with 'significant fact' – that is not to denigrate the pleasure many get out of the simple selfie, undoubtedly fun and good for well being, however, so many of these pictures lose any potential long term historical/sociological value because they are not accurately captioned by the simple who, why, what, where, when.

I have suffered badly from inaccurate or absent captioning of my own pictures. For some reason I was prone to 'putting it off', it never worked, I ultimately always forgot details, and then sometimes guessed/invented them. Photography should be about accuracy and honesty. On honesty – we are all humans and prone to mistakes but we should try.

An example from my past is the picture above. I have it captioned as being in Margate 1963. However, on recently trying to confirm, I can't locate the pier.

Can anyone help me and confirm for me the location?

@davidhurnphoto @magnumphotos #nonfictionphotography #margate #hernebay

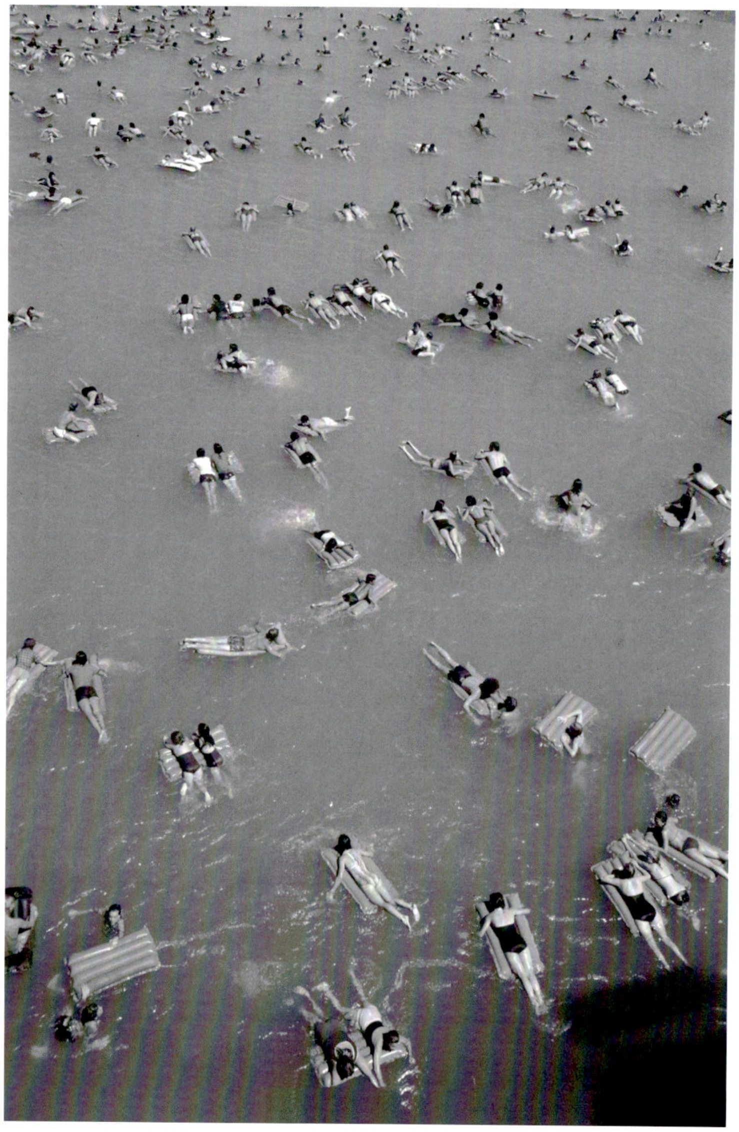

17 MAY 2021 / SOCIAL DISTANCING. *ARIZONA, USA 1980*

Ever since I can remember I have loved going out for breakfast. The idea of a walk, food being brought to me, and being able to read an essay, has always had great appeal. I feel perfectly relaxed. A good start.

When I was teaching, but during holidays, I went virtually every day to the Little Chef in Redbrook. It opened very early, was by the river, and was the perfect location to start a walk with my dogs – three of them. Soon students, mainly from other colleges, heard of my ritual and would turn up at 7am. Many an enjoyable constructive conversation emerged.

I have posh memories of the terrace of the Negresco in Nice, paid for by someone else, opulence at its most seductively obscene. Even more expensive, Hôtel du Cap-Eden-Roc, Antibes.

The funniest was perhaps in Cardiff. The morning after the opening of the wonderful new photography gallery in the National Museum of Wales – Sir Don McCullin had done the opening and other friends had turned up – we met for breakfast the next day. Myself, Don, John Bulmer, Ian Berry and, I think, Patrick Ward. Was it an intellectual conversation about photography? No, it was completely discussing our deafness, our bad eyesight, our inability to get up once sitting down, our continual aches and pains – it was so refreshing.

All this to say, I was the first for breakfast at the opening at our local Hare and Hound, a walk along the river bank, a delightful food room with Thames Green walls, marble tables and leather-backed chairs. I had a 'full English', it could not have been better. Between sips of coffee, a leisurely re-read of John Berger's *The Suit and the Photograph*. I had found total bliss again.

@davidhurnphoto @magnumphotos @don.mccullin @ianberrymagnum @johnfbulmer @patrickwardphotography @museumwales #nonfictionphotography #nationalmuseumwalescardiff

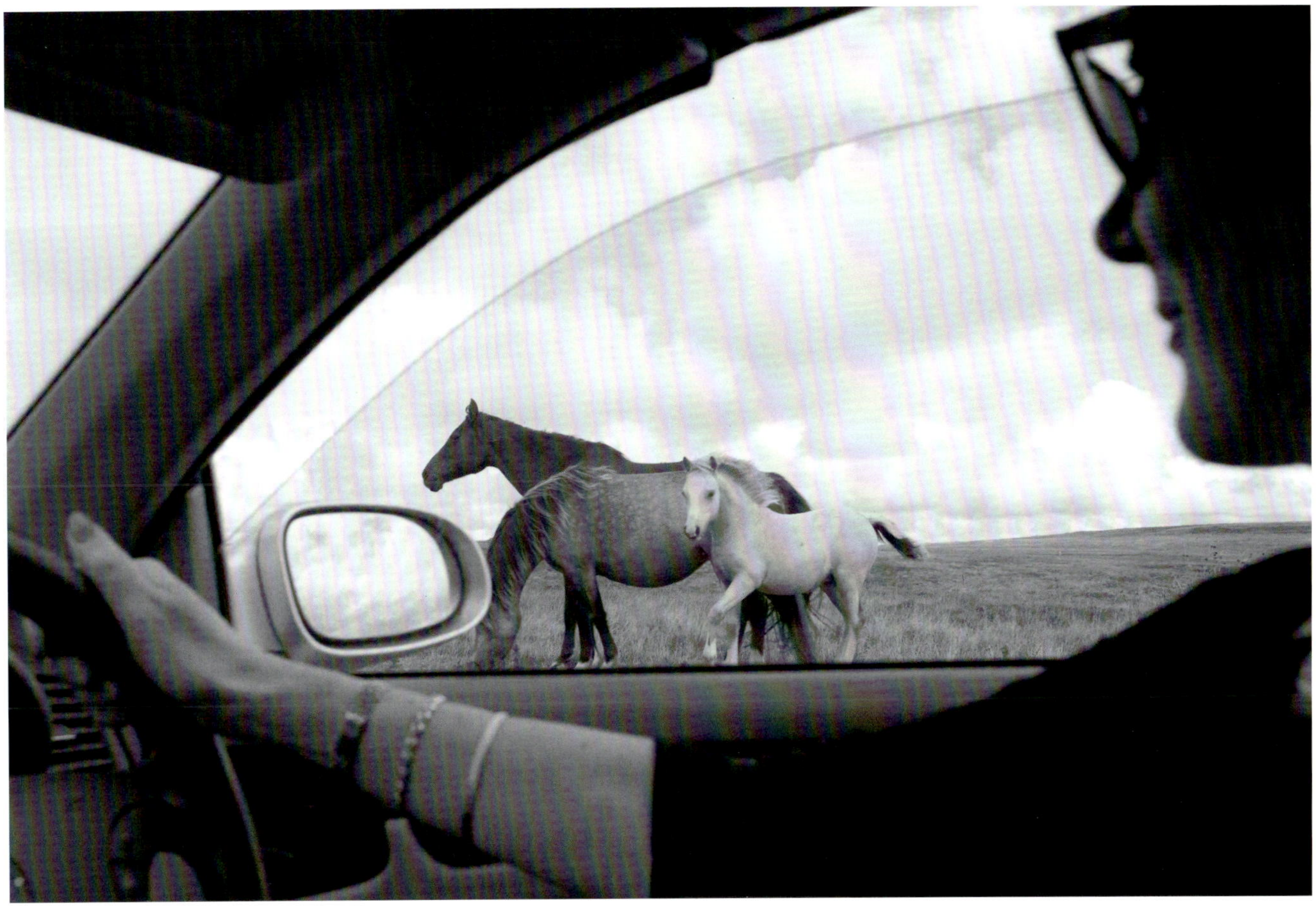

24 MAY 2021 / ON THE ROAD AGAIN. *WALES 2014*

How wonderful to get the location of my previous post but one – Marine Terrace, Margate – confirmed by so many, plus even the possibility of added captions. Thanks.

Many of my early pictures were shot on film. To get one into my database I have to scan it, 15 mins, and even though it might be a reasonably clean negative it takes over one hour to spot. I am thinking, 'I wish I had been able to shoot digitally.'

I now shoot everything digitally and make pigment prints.

Why? Answers, but not in any particular order:

For most, an obvious reason could be cost. When I went to involve myself in the Hungarian Uprising, 1956 – I was just 22 – I had with me a new second-hand 35mm camera with 50mm lens, and 20 rolls of film. I was not trying to save weight, I simply could not afford more. Film and its processing has always been expensive. Now a card hardly costs anything so you never have to worry about film costs.

Film speed was: colour, either 25 or 64; black & white, 400 – could be pushed to 800. Now I can easily shoot at 3200. It makes a difference and expands possibilities.

If you study Wilhelm Imaging Research you will see that pigment prints on the right papers, I use Canson Platine, have a far greater archival expectancy in sunlight than silver or CP prints.

But by far the most important asset for me is what I might call 'continuity of contact print'. From when I could afford it, I have always worked with two cameras, one fitted with a 50mm lens and the other with a 28mm lens. I shoot about 90 percent on the 50mm and ten percent on the 28mm. When I was shooting on film it meant that the 28mm contact sheet was never in sequence, in fact it only appeared every ten contact sheets – a nightmare to edit. I now download into Lightroom by date and whatever camera I use the pictures are shown on my computer in sequence. I would shoot digital for this asset alone.

If I now have any reservations it's that pictures seem 'too' sharp. I am tempted to soften them. I keep telling the manufacturers of the cameras I use: 'I don't need more pixels, I need less buttons and a better viewfinder'.

@davidhurnphoto @magnumphotos

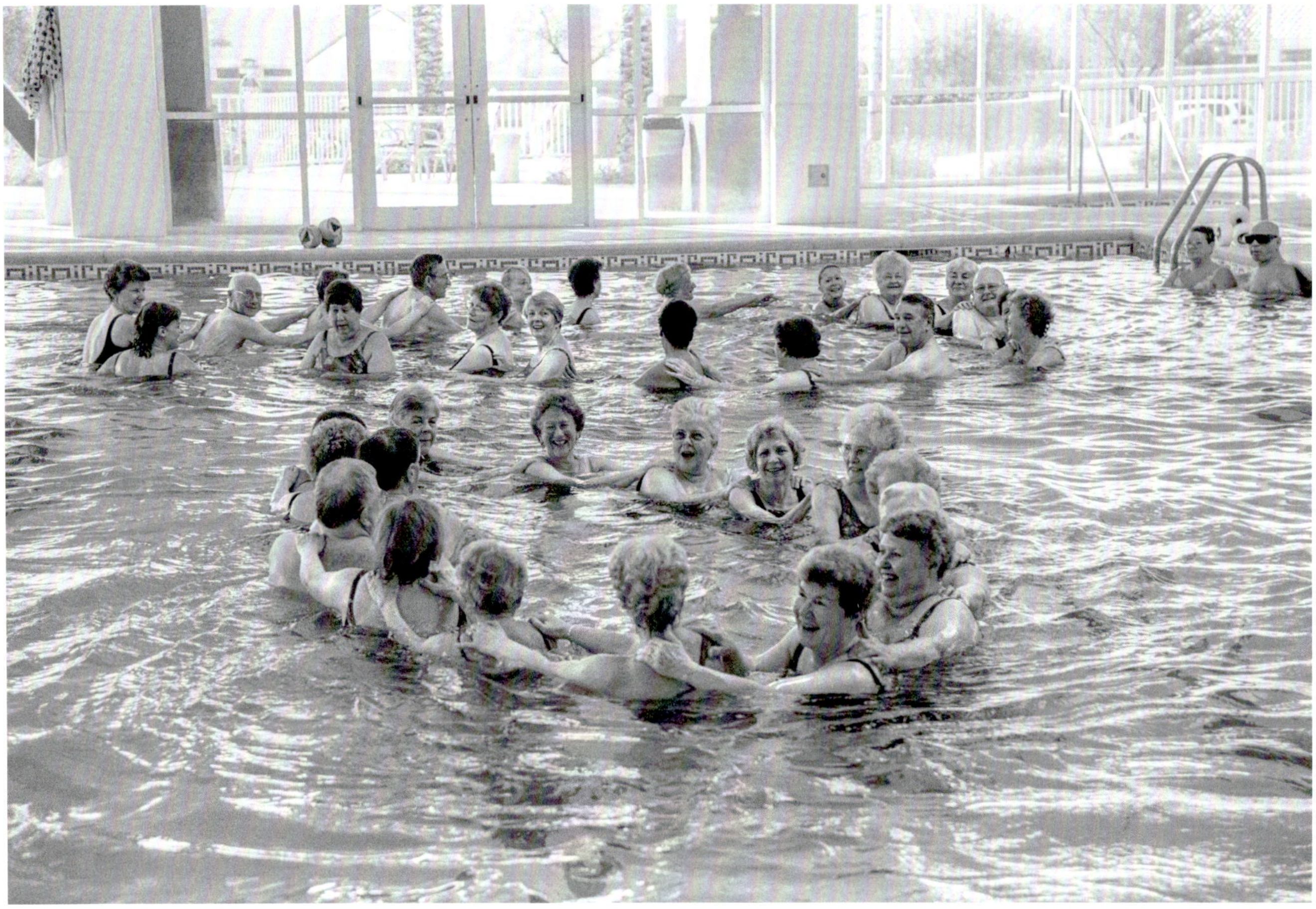

31 MAY 2021 / MEMORY OF FITNESS. *ARIZONA, USA 2002*

John Berger suggested that, 'A photograph fixes the appearance of an event. Before the invention of the camera nothing could do this except the faculty of memory'.

At last I can get back into the gym, keeping fit is an essential part of my photography repertoire. I have pleasant memories of photographing exercise in other countries. I always enjoy that all participating seem to enjoy it.

I love looking at pictures. I suppose I make mental choices, he/she is interesting, he/she needs watching. But can I explain what is great photography or a great photographer?

Speculating, I think, for me, the category could be linked to the number of pictures I can remember by an individual that are ingrained in my mind. If I can *instantly* remember over 12 pictures by someone, I think that maybe that's what makes them slot into my greatness: Julia Margaret Cameron, Weegee, Bresson, Thurston Hopkins, Davidson, Koudelka, Larrain, Avedon, Levitt, Lange, Parr, Doc Edgerton (I must admit I only remembered seven pictures), Arbus, Griffiths. All easily fill the criteria.

Maybe if I recall four pictures they become, for me, a good photographer.

If one then they are worth following.

I am not enamoured by those who ape someone else, or latch on to the latest 'trend'. By definition, at best, it means you can only be second best. The only way to improve is shoot lots and lots of pictures, keep discarding those that don't seem right, then shoot more, self criticism is all important. If you have exceptional talent it will slowly come through.

Of course, this *great* is great simply for me and maybe only for me. However, it gives me a base to argue from.

@davidhurnphoto @magnumphotos @brucedavidsonphoto @diane_arbus @philipjonesgriffiths @avedonfoundation @josef_koudelka #nonfictionphotography #weegee #cartierbresson #sergiolarrain #helenlevitt #martinparr #dorothealange #docedgerton #juliamargaretcameron #thurstonhopkins

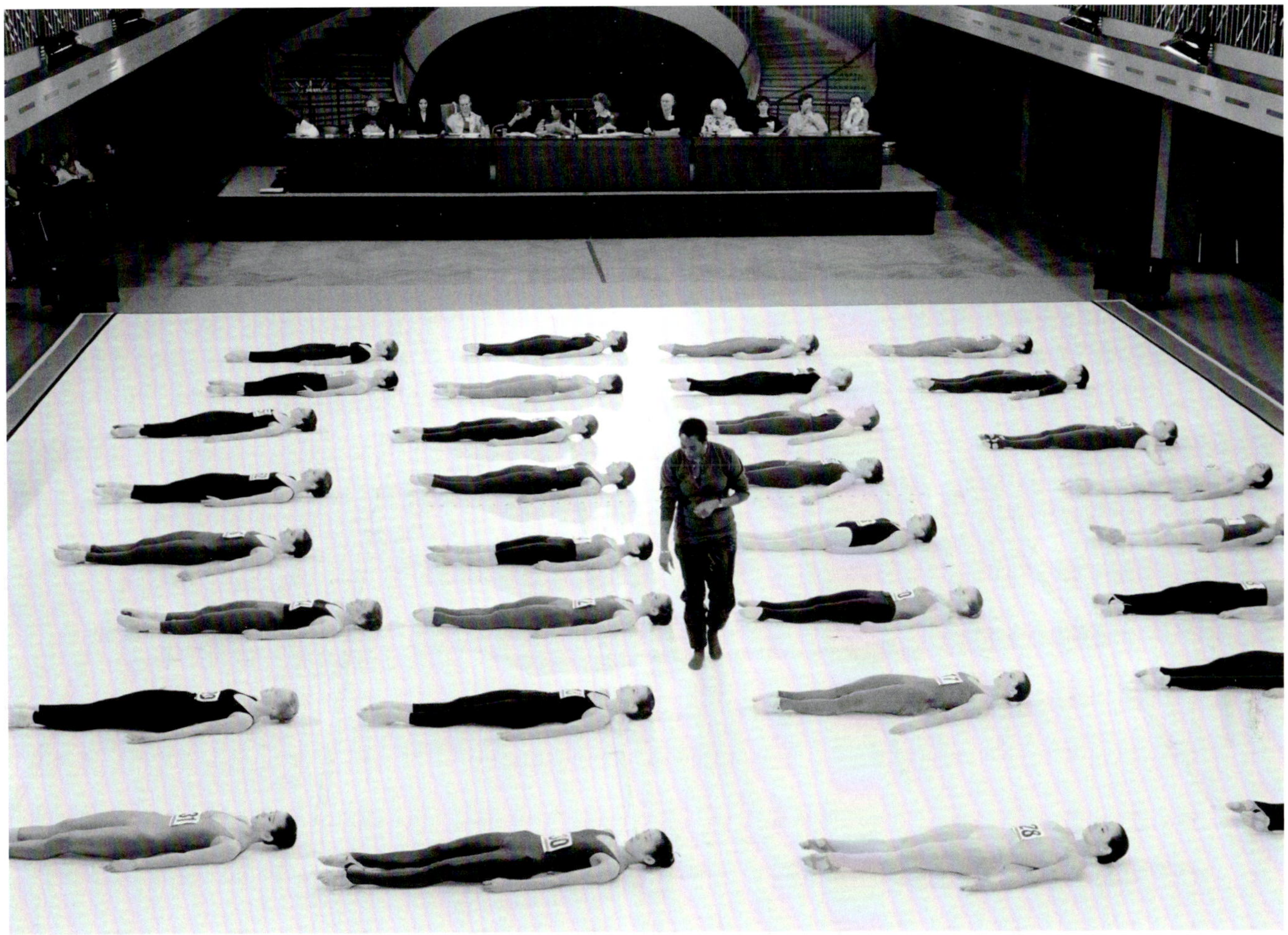

14 JUNE 2021 / LYING. *LUCERNE, SWITZERLAND 1991*

The above is a picture I hope sets up a myriad of speculations, not answers. Photography is not good at answers – I doubt that many serious photographers think it is. Unlike other visual images, photographs are not an interpretation of a subject but a trace, the equivalent of a footprint in the snow or a death mask. The photograph fixes the appearance of an event, it is a finger pointing at possibilities not answers, the best photographs ask more questions.

What photography reproduces has occurred only once. I hope to choose subjects which in their ordinariness are ordinarily representative. The photograph does not invent, it is authentication, it says, at a fixed time, in a fixed space, this happened. That's why it is useful in history and memory: 'the photograph is laborious only when it fakes.' – Roland Barthes.

A fact: there seem 32 figures lying on a floor, I thought the moment worth recording. I am not saying why, I suspect I didn't actually know why, instinct from experience? All viewers who find the picture interesting will have their own interpretation, that's the joy of photographs, you have a mixture of facts/traces, put together they set up infinite possibilities of interpretation.

May I do a self promotion. That wonderful publisher caferoyalbooks.com have published my essay on the 'Isle of Wight Festival 1969'. I am not sure of its cost but it's inexpensive and I hope worth it.

@davidhurnphoto @magnumphotos @caferoyalbooks #nonfictionphotography #rolandbarthes

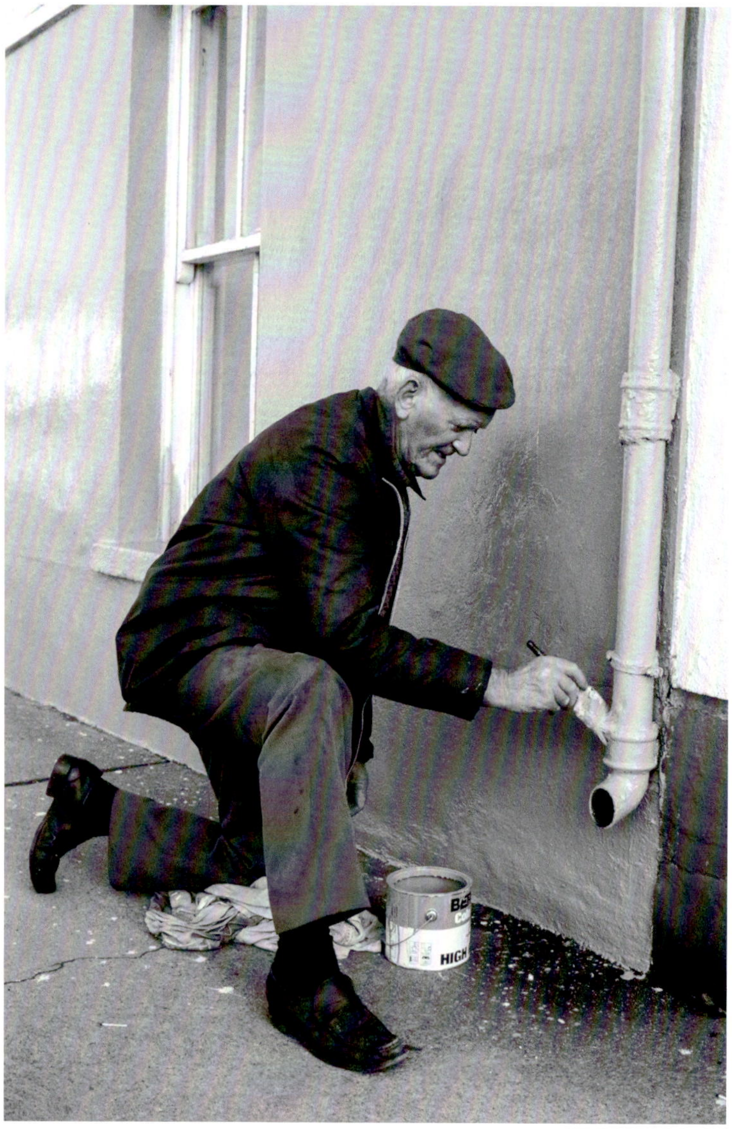

14 JUNE 2021 / IRELAND. MAN AT WORK. *KILLARNEY, IRELAND 1984*

I happened to be browsing in the magazine section of Waitrose in Monmouth whilst a friend shopped. I must say I was surprised to discover that they didn't have any magazine in any way dealing with photography. There were three on sewing, a worthwhile occupation, three on psychology, etc, etc, but not a mention of my obsession.

Maybe we photographers all get a bit pompous about our choice of activity and fantasise its interest to the rest of the world.

On getting home, I looked up the Sky Arts Awards; Literature, Theatre, Visual Art, Film, Opera, Classical Music, Pop Music, Dance, Comedy, TV Drama – no mention of Photography as a category on its own. I looked through the Visual Arts awards over previous years, no-one mentioned who was even vaguely to do with being a photographer.

I then looked up 'UK Arts Competitions 2021'. Listed were over 100 possible awards one can apply for. Many actually specifically listed 'no photography'.

One competition was mentioned from my own country, Wales, the 'Waterfront Gallery, Milford Haven', states – Wales Contemporary / Cymru Gyfoes now in its second year is an international open competition developed by the Waterfront Gallery in association with the Welsh Government. Wales Contemporary celebrates all aspects of the country by inviting artists to submit work that is 'Inspired by Wales', i.e. by its ancient history, its art history, its heritage, its landscape (rural, urban or political) and its contemporary culture. For this second iteration both 2 and 3 dimensional work will be admissible.

Medium: 2 or 3 dimensional artwork in any medium apart from photography or film. (2D max length: 140cm, 3D max length: 50cm)

All sad. However, I think I am right in saying Picasso never called himself a prize-winning painter.

@davidhurnphoto @magnumphotos @waterfront_gallery #nonfictionphotography

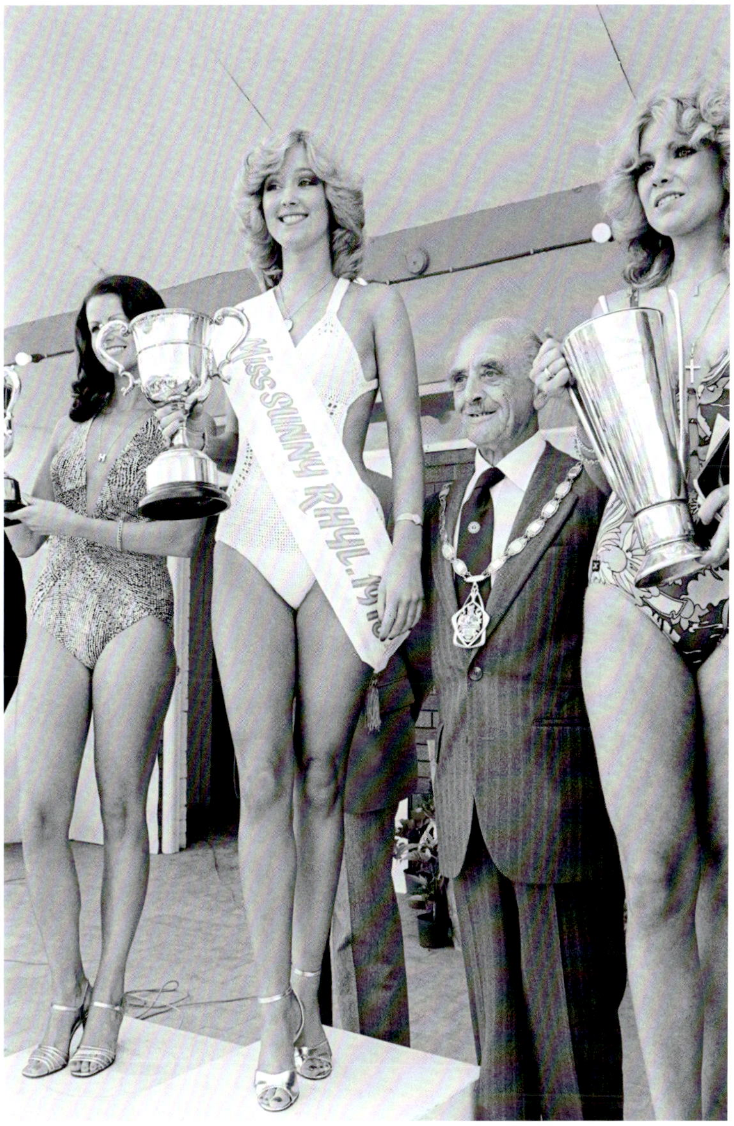

16 JUNE 2021 / AWARD. *RHYL, WALES 1978*

I have known Martin Parr for many years, in fact from the time of his final year photography show at the Arnolfini in Bristol, early '70s. I think I am right in saying I probably bought the first print he ever sold – I think for £6.

I know of no-one in photography who has poured more of himself back into photography – he is outrageously generous with his time, so rare. My guess is that it would be impossible to count up the number of students who have become better photographers because of his advice – always accurate, always constructive, never possessive. When I ran the course in Newport, the visiting lecturers most looked forward to were always Martin Parr and Josef Koudelka – enough said.

I have often preached that every student in the country should be a member of the Martin Parr Foundation. Listening to all their interviews/talks would be an education in itself – to say nothing about meeting with so many other working photographers, editors and gallery owners. There is no substitute for meeting those who have actually done it.

Martin has now been awarded the CBE. Maybe awards are worthwhile, after all, if they are given for the merit that this one has been given for.

@davidhurnphoto @magnumphotos @martinparrfdn #nonfictionphotography

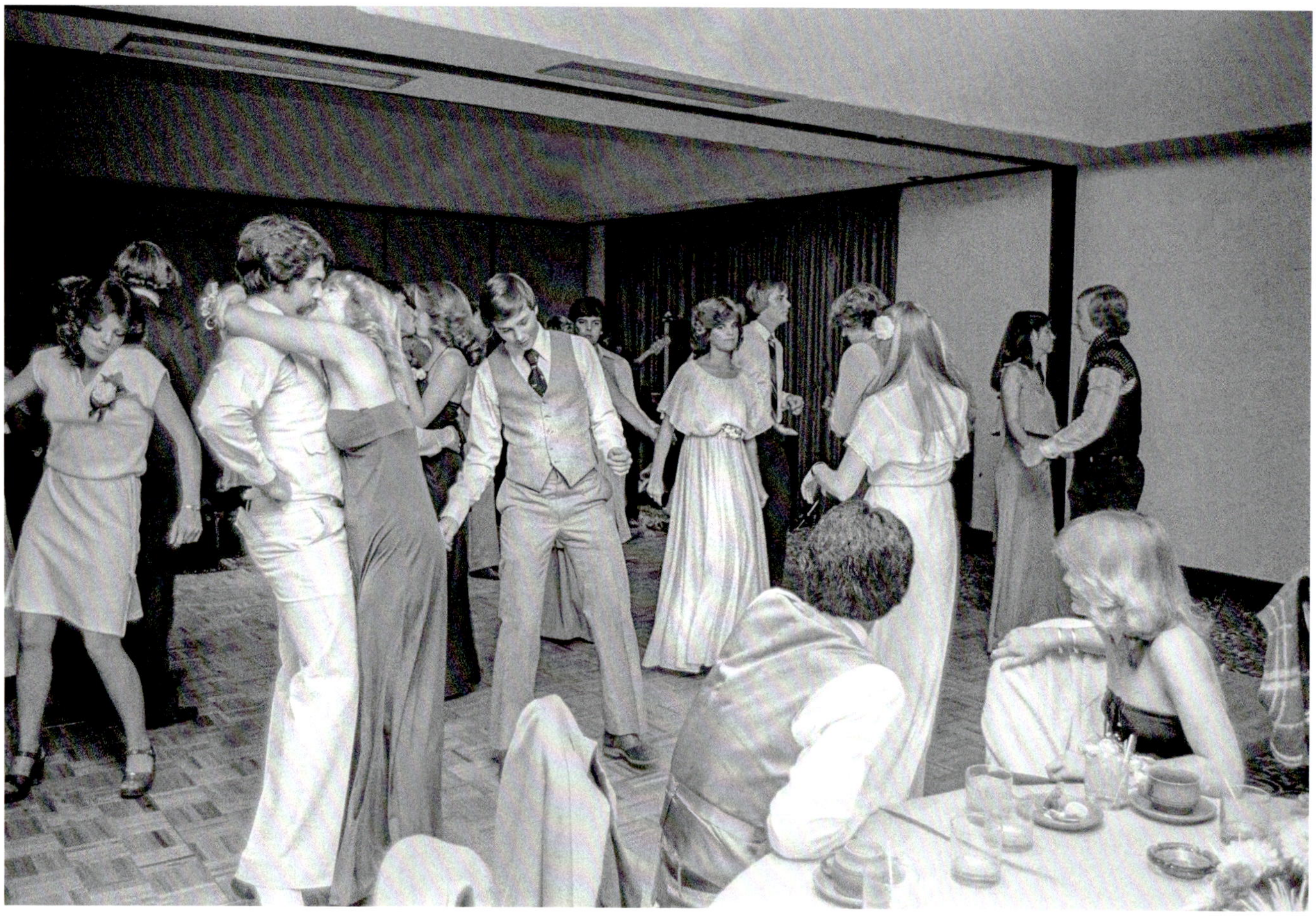

22 JUNE 2021 / TOGETHER AGAIN. *ARIZONA, USA 1979*

Late last week I enjoyed a gallery opening, at the Thru The Lens Gallery in Hay-on-Wye. I do relish these smaller galleries, they seem open to taking risks. They are usually run by persons with great enthusiasm, passion, and knowledge of their community, in this case, Andra Milsome and the photographer Billie Charity. I so hope they get the support they deserve, and survive. At the moment I sense that the cash available from various obvious sources is not ending up in the most productive places.

The exhibition was the first gallery exhibition of Veronika Lavey. She suggests, 'I am a self-portrait artist. I photograph myself taking on the persona of an autobiographical or a theatrical character.' The pictures are beguiling and extremely well-crafted. Together with her show is a book/catalogue of her pictures and poetry, unpretentious.

Billie was, of course, also there, and on sale is her book *Colour*, the title is self-explanatory.

Visiting the gallery was Glenn Dene, who is an Operating Department Practitioner – thus access – at Nevill Hall Hospital, he is also a photographer. Around the world we see many who are professionals in hospitals, are also photographers. The dedication of staff dealing with Covid-19 within hospitals is well documented. I tended to want to hug anyone moving – I suspect not sensible. I suddenly realised the dangers of mass gatherings – contact is very seductive.

Sadly, the pizza van in the square had run out of dough – a sign of an adventurous entrepreneur doing very well.

@davidhurnphoto @magnumphotos @veronikalavey @billie_charity @thruthelens_gallery #nonfictionphotography #glenndene

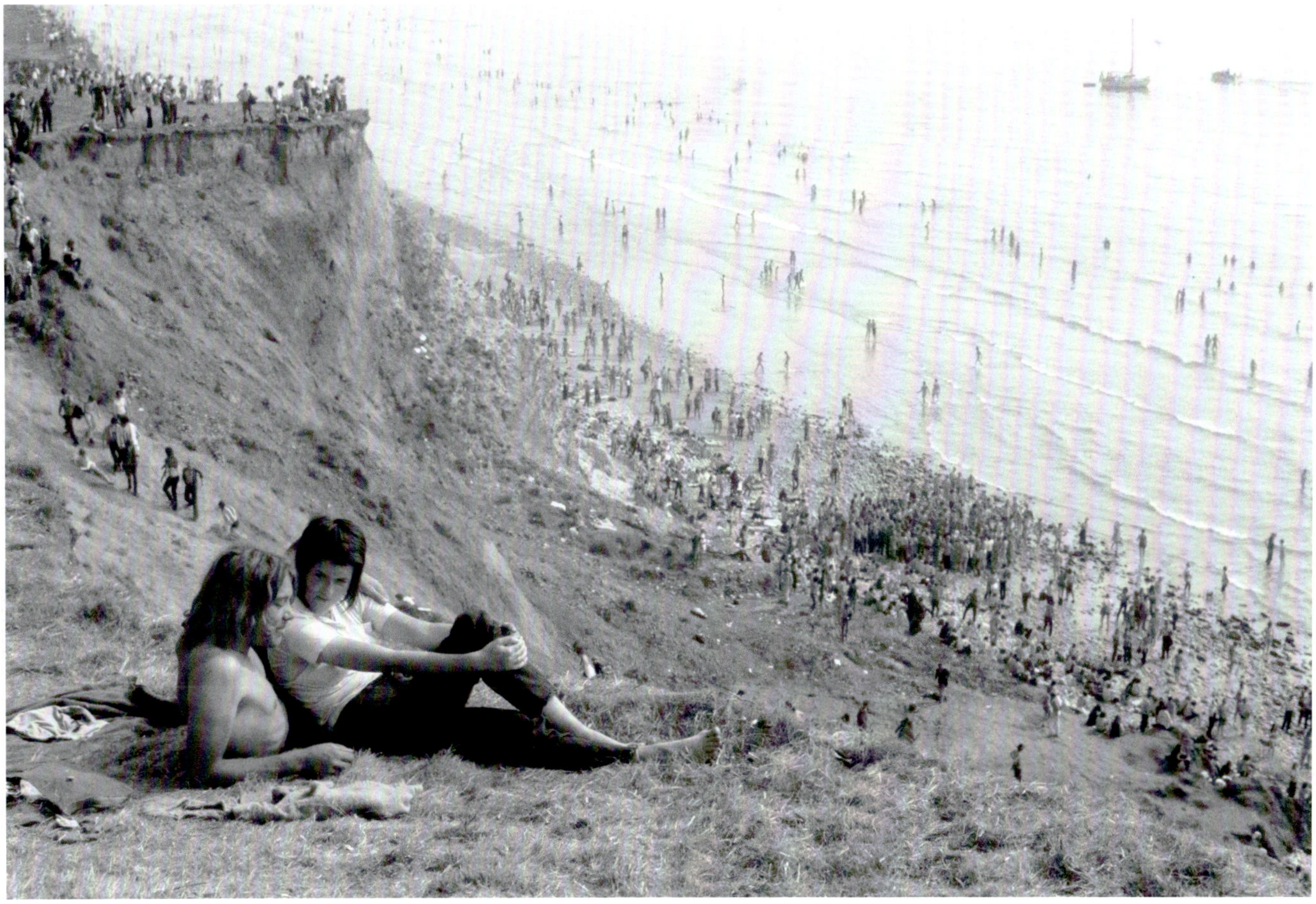

29 JUNE 2021 / FESTIVAL. ***ISLE OF WIGHT, ENGLAND 1969***

Cafe Royal Books have recently published my coverage of the 1969 Isle of Wight Festival. It was politely pointed out by Ray Foulk, who with his brother Ron were organisers of the1968-1970 festivals, that the 1969 title was incorrect and should have been 1969/1970. As he suggested, accuracy in captioning is all important since 'others will copy what is published'.

He is, of course, absolutely right, captions are not just for Christmas, they last as long as the pictures are shown and they are read by sociologists, historians, journalists, beside the general public. They must be as honest, accurate and as transparent as we humans can produce. It is invaluable when others, with superior knowledge, point out mistakes – hopefully in a polite manner.

For people of my age and persuasion we have a particular problem. Our initial market was primarily magazines. In my case I would distribute to up to 15 countries. This meant making 15 sets of prints to be sent by post, or in the case of colour, 15 sets of dupes. Pictures would be circulating all over the place and end up re-captioned in many different languages. Captions might be changed by mistake. Photography was not that rarified practice as many treat it today, as soon as you dispatched one 'story' you were doing the next. One didn't really have the time or ability to keep total control of anything.

Two things happened to change dealing with a potential market:

1. Prints became valuable as an object in themselves, often editioned, it was/is imperative to keep control.

2. The coming of digital meant that you can attach 'IPTC' information directly to a picture so the caption should always remain the same.

The fundamentals are the same. To have future validity/use pictures are always helped by attaching a simple, where, when, who and maybe why.

@davidhurnphoto @magnumphotos #nonfictionphotography #rayfoulk #isleofwightfestival

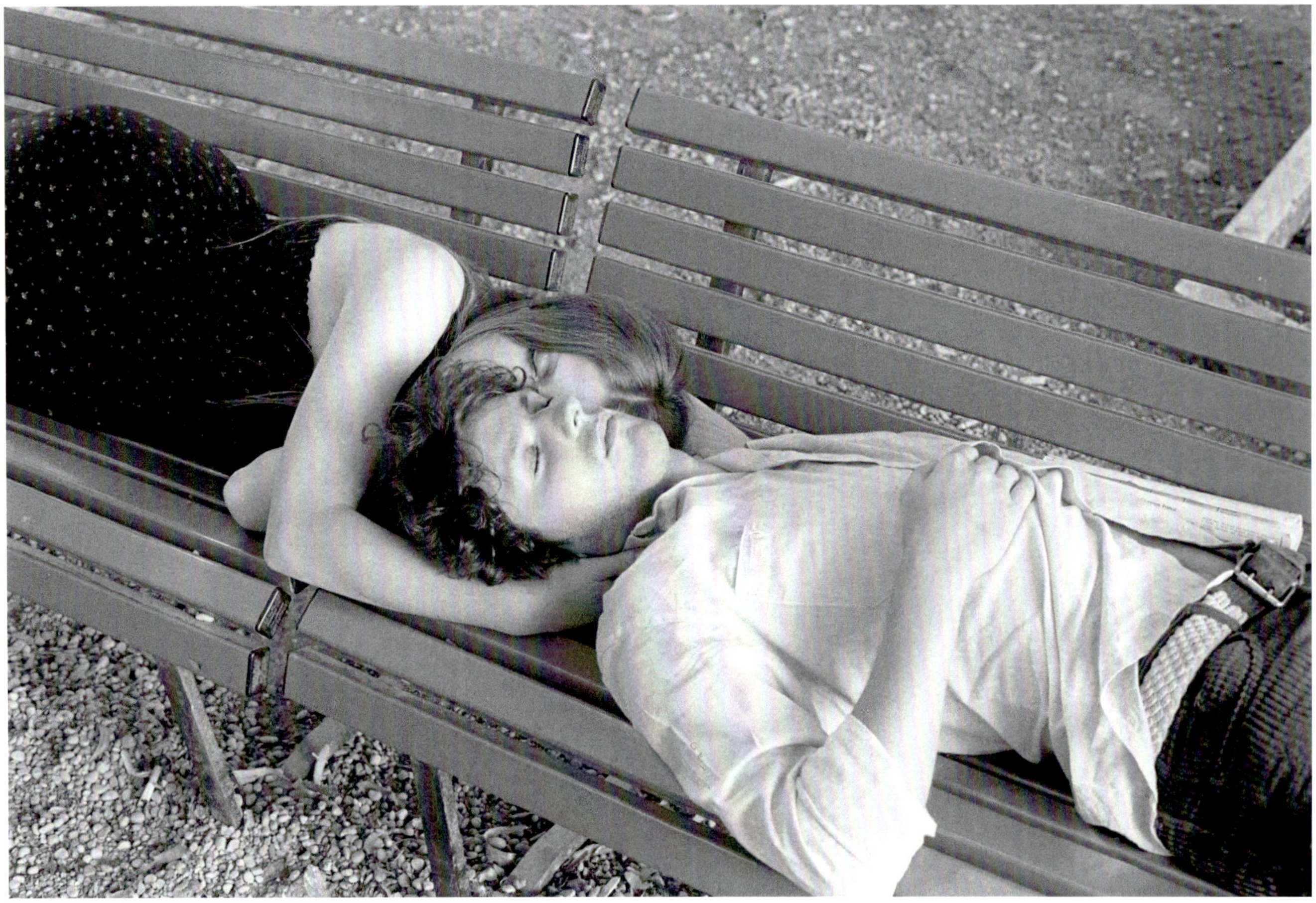

7 JULY 2021 / DREAMS OF FUTURE. *VENICE, ITALY 1999*

I have been watching a series of 'free' – i.e. no cost – Zoom lectures titled *Beyond Magnum*: an in-depth talks programme created to address and explore some of the challenges facing the photographic industry today. (*Beyond Magnum* YouTube Channel.)

Of course, I can be accused of bias but most people with photographic knowledge would agree that the series, in chapters addressing Archives, Representation and the Future of Photography, had highly thought of speakers who shared ideas and engaged in debate across a range of issues. Each section was led by respected figures from the world of photography who, in turn, invited an array of other speakers doing critical work, ranging from practitioners to academics, to subjects of photographs.

I would suggest that any lecturer not advising their students to watch all are either ill-informed or totally narcissistic.

For me, the most interesting speaker was Fred Ritchin – nowadays, I think, the most informed thinker on the future of photography.

I am personally most interested in photography that confirms existence.

A few quotations by, I think, respected people:

Bernard Kouchner, the co-founder of Médecins Sans Frontières and Médecins du Monde: 'Without photography, massacres would not exist'.

Roland Barthes: 'The photograph is authentication itself. The photograph is laborious only when it fakes. . . . Its force is nonetheless superior to everything the human mind can or can have conceived to assure us of reality. Every photograph is a certificate of presence'.

John Berger: 'A photograph is not only an image (as a painting is an image), an interpretation of the real, it is also a trace, something directly stencilled off the real, like a footprint or a death mask'.

The 2,200 character limit to Instagram means I must put in a brake. I will re-engage on 19 June, subject, 'Post Truth Age'.

(Square Print Sale is in between)

@davidhurnphoto @magnumphotos #nonfictionphotography

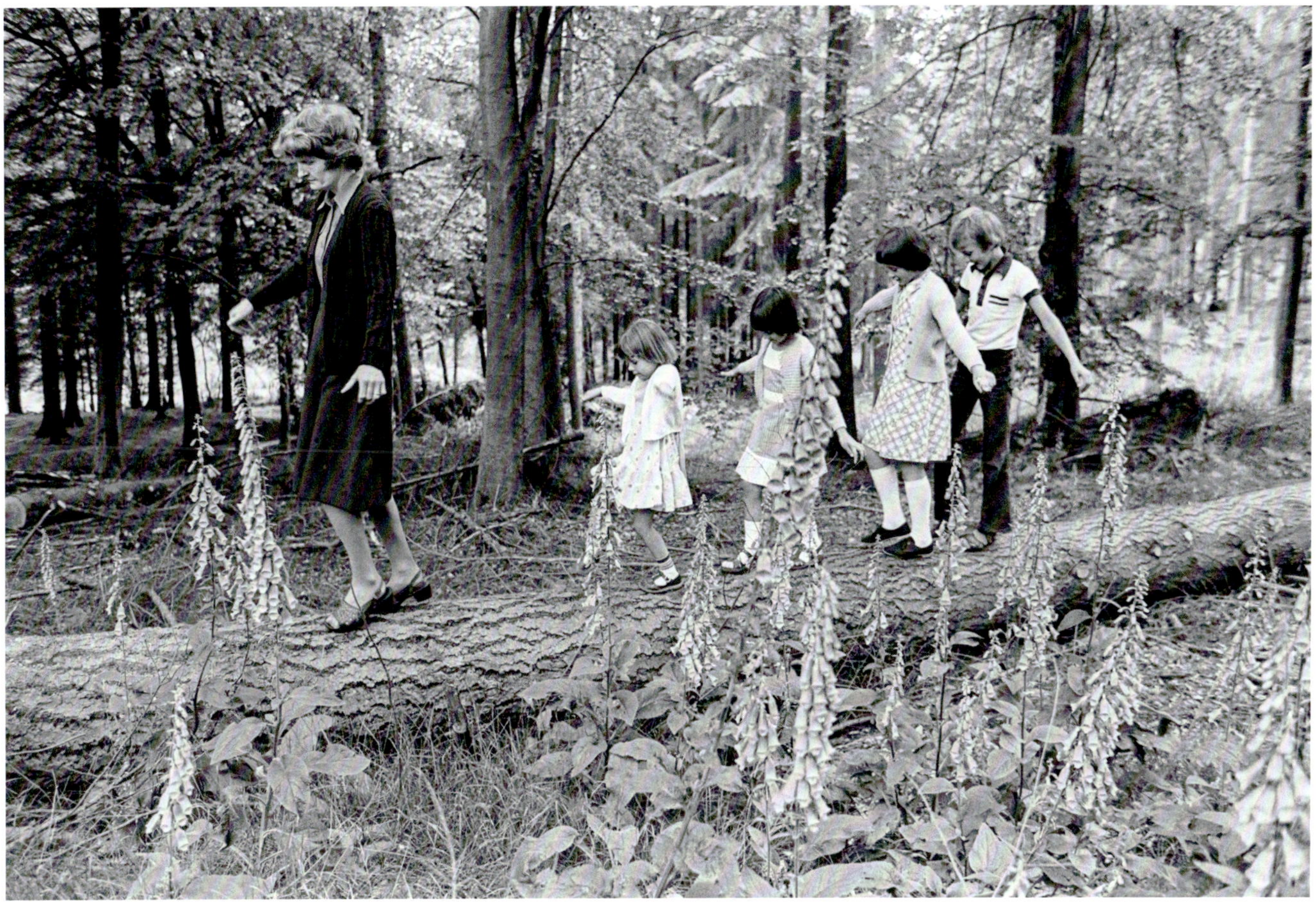

19 JULY 2021 / SMALLEST SCHOOL. *LLANEGLWYS, WALES 1978*

Post Truth Age:

I have always functioned in an age of eye witness. I made my living through publication. Journalism (the keeping of a photo journal) was considered honourable. Writing was happy to loosely fall into categories of fiction and non-fiction, so why not photography? I was always insistent I enjoyed primarily being in the non-fiction area of photography, of course, I strayed into the fiction area – for financial reasons – but I hoped that the context made the distinction obvious. Fashion was obvious, portraits more problematic. I thought all genres of photography to have potentially equal value, one has preferences, not silly competitions – I often said, if you must have a hierarchy then medical is the most important.

Up until the '70s there were very few photo galleries, 'art' was not really in the equation. But there became a diminution of current affairs publication. Then, together with 'art', academic theory, deconstruction and writing, gradually the new methods of making a living moved more and more to non-fiction. The selling of a product continued but the conceptualising of an idea and the illustrating of such vastly increased.

My feeling is there is about to be an even greater 'paradigm shift'.

I was given two introductions: one, a series of videos shown me by an architect friend – they showed a series of apartment, office, environments, all of which were superbly artificially visually constructed, I was totally convinced they were 'real', they are not fact, not really fakes either, but facsimiles of possibilities in the future.

The second, a website called 'This person does not exist'. At the moment this consists of two and a half million portraits of people, all free, *all* synthetically produced, artificial imagery – not a real person in sight – catalogues include male/colour of hair/with beards/colour of skin/shades of skin etc. Female obviously similar. I repeat, *not* a single image from reality.

Can you imagine the future when the general public think no picture relates to reality? My guess, within ten years?

Starting again, I suspect I would pursue my school time ambition of being a vet.

@davidhurnphoto @magnumphotos #nonfictionphotography

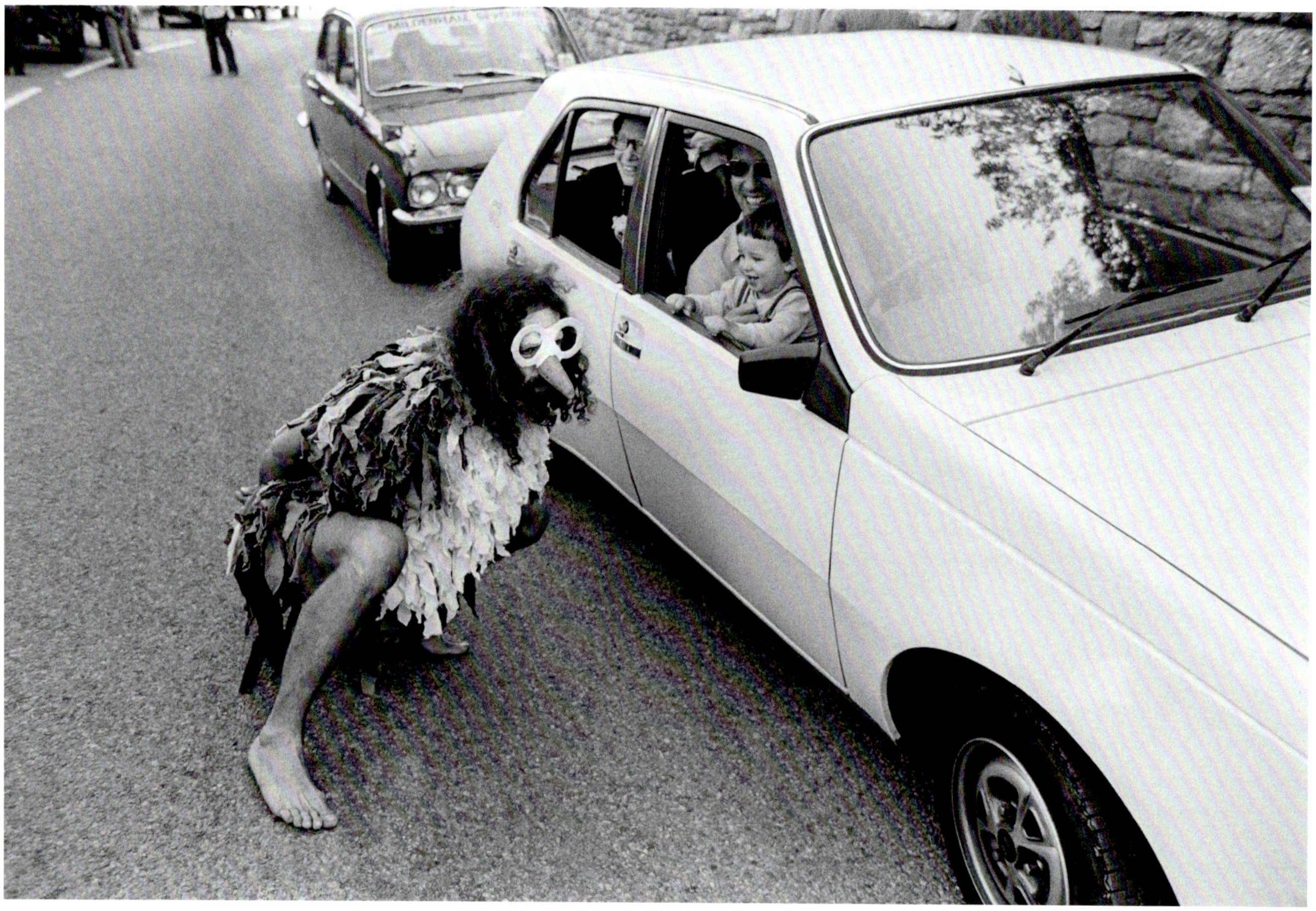

29 JULY 2021 / VILLAGE ARTS. *TINTERN, WALES 1979*

I have been mesmerized on the TV by the Olympics. The power of that is real. It is so uplifting to see so many young from so many countries giving their all. Some have more ingrained talent than others but all put in the absolute maximum of effort in the training and dedication to get to where they are. They all seem to conduct themselves with laudable dignity even in extreme disappointment. Is there something we can learn from this as photographers?

My biggest disappointment of the week was watching the South Bank Sky Arts Awards for 2021. For two hours three minutes I watched 'The only awards show in the world celebrating every genre of the arts', suggests Melvyn Bragg. All wonderfully grand, best clothes, plus the Household Cavalry with four trumpeters on tap to welcome in the winners. Categories for Theatre; Visual Art; Drama; award for the design of the physical awards themselves (in my opinion a wonderful, sensible design); Literature; Film; Pop; Dance; Opera; Classical Music; a new category for Innovation during the Pandemic, both institutional and individual; plus an award for Breakthrough for a Young Artist – the best of the same ten options above. 'The Arts are in good hands in the future' we are told . . . I waited and waited for any mention of photography – nothing.

I am not in any way criticising any of the above, each area had persons of enormous talent and each absolutely deserved their individual gong.

But is this really what we feel about photography in this country? Could you imagine this happening in USA or France or, in fact, anywhere in Europe, or probably large amounts of Asia?

I just don't know what is wrong. I would love people to explain to me.

@davidhurnphoto @magnumphotos #nonfictionphotography #skyartsawards #melvynbragg

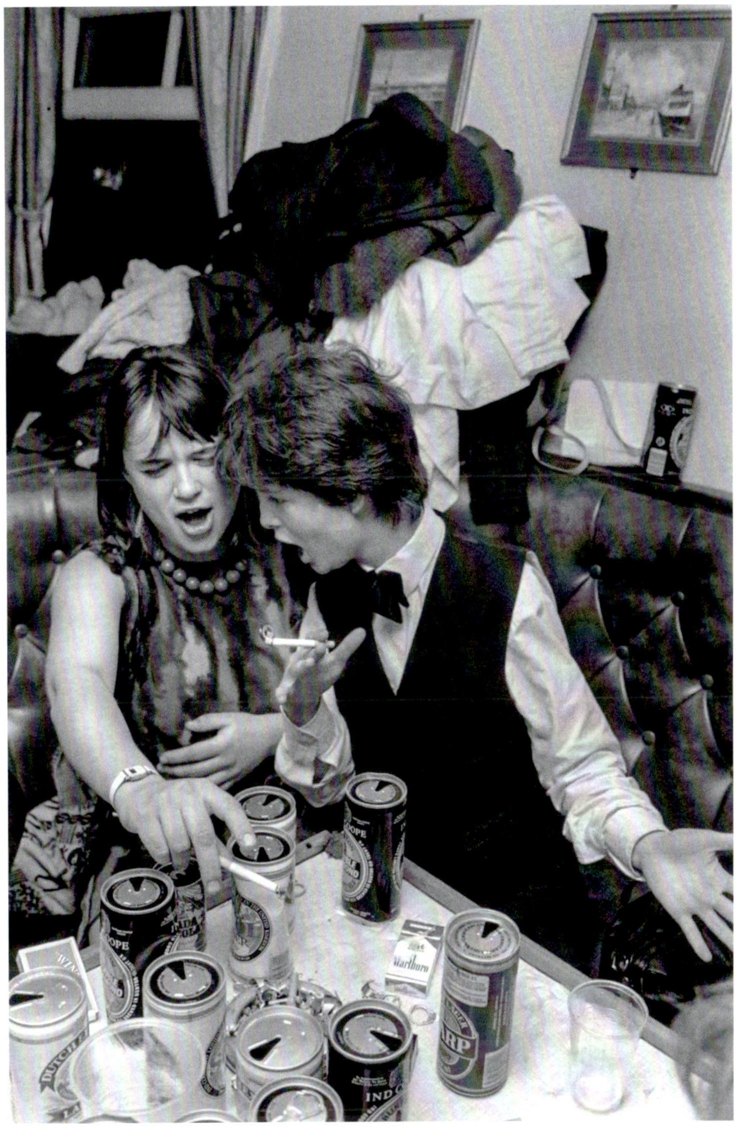

29 AUGUST 2021 / DOC PHOT PARTY. *NEWPORT, WALES 1985*

I was browsing the Instagram of that very fine photographer, Thomas Hoepker. In his text he quotes the New York painter, Chuck Close:

'Inspiration is for amateurs. The rest of us just show up and get to work. If you wait around for the clouds to part and a bolt of lightning to strike you in the brain, you are not going to make an awful lot of work. All the best ideas come out of the process; they come out of the work itself.'

It seems to me that this is the message from so many I admire in so many different fields – certainly, for me, it is true that if I need to be operated on I want it to be by someone that performs every day, not someone that performs an operation every other weekend.

I have always thought that teaching/learning has a few simple basic rules. You have someone who really wants to learn and you have someone who has real experience to pass on – mix them and you have a chance. I always felt that students learned most from 'hero' visiting lecturers, as varied as possible. When I was teaching it was simple, someone came to stay with me, I conned them into coming into college and we worked out details later as to how they could receive some money. Boy, how have things changed.

I have been talking to a trusted friend who suggests that now, in at least some universities, if they want to invite guest lecturers they have to physically meet them and see and make copies of both their passport and proof of right to work (National Insurance number) before they are allowed on campus. I wouldn't have had a course. Boy, do I sympathise.

I think one of the most significant/productive purchases I have ever made were glasses set up to focus at just my eye distance from my computer screen. I suspect I spend on average at least a couple of hours a day editing and spotting. You don't even have to worry about having fancy frames.

@davidhurnphoto @magnumphotos #nonfictionphotography #thomashoepker

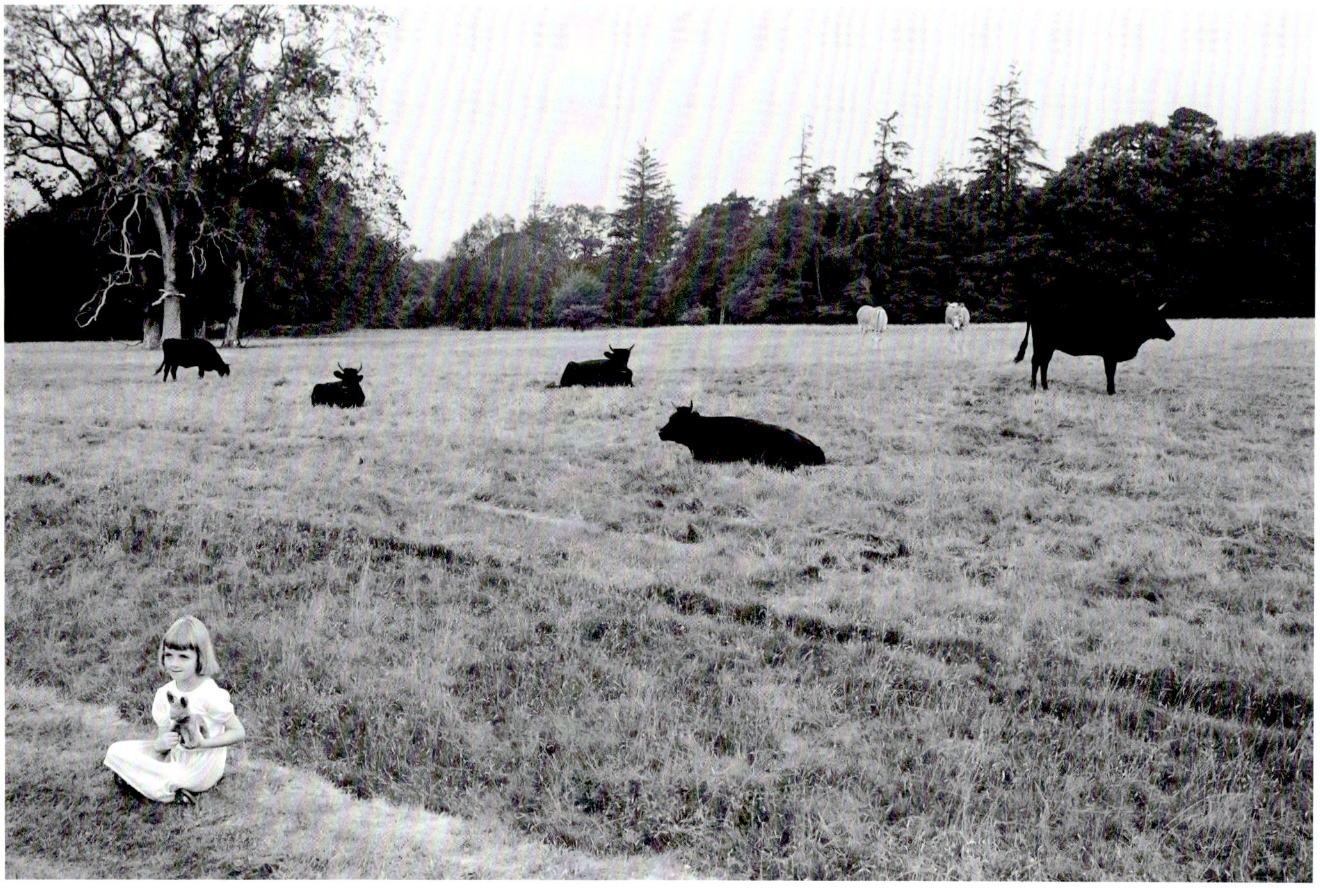

9 SEPTEMBER 2021 / MEMORIES. *KILLARNEY, IRELAND 1984*

I overslept last night, surely a good sign. I was staying in the Angel Hotel in Abergavenny, my vote for my most perfect hotel – amazingly polite, helpful staff. I had been involved in 'Conversations at the Chapel' with Alastair Laurence, a modest interviewer who makes chat easy. Talking about me by me is, of course, simple as I know all the facts, what's as important is the ambience of the place chat is taking place, in this case a chapel, 'something' is on one's side. Audiences continually surprise me – I was emotionally stymied, there, smiling at me, was perhaps the most important person in my life, Mr Richard Blackett, looking exactly as he had 20 years ago when he had undoubtedly saved my life – he was, now retired, a cancer surgeon. Also Rita and Jack Tait, Jack had once re-adapted a Rolleiflex camera of mine so that I could actually critically focus with it, it helped me produce another book. Also numerous photographers I had previously come in contact with – it was very uplifting. I held back a gulp and a tear.

All this through being a photographer. I have had a blissful life. Blissful because it's always been a struggle and that can be fun. I am slowly bowing out, I am puzzled by the future that I don't seem to understand. Now, more and more, I just wish to be an observer.

@davidhurnphoto @magnumphotos #nonfictionphotography #alastairlaurence #richardblackett #jacktait

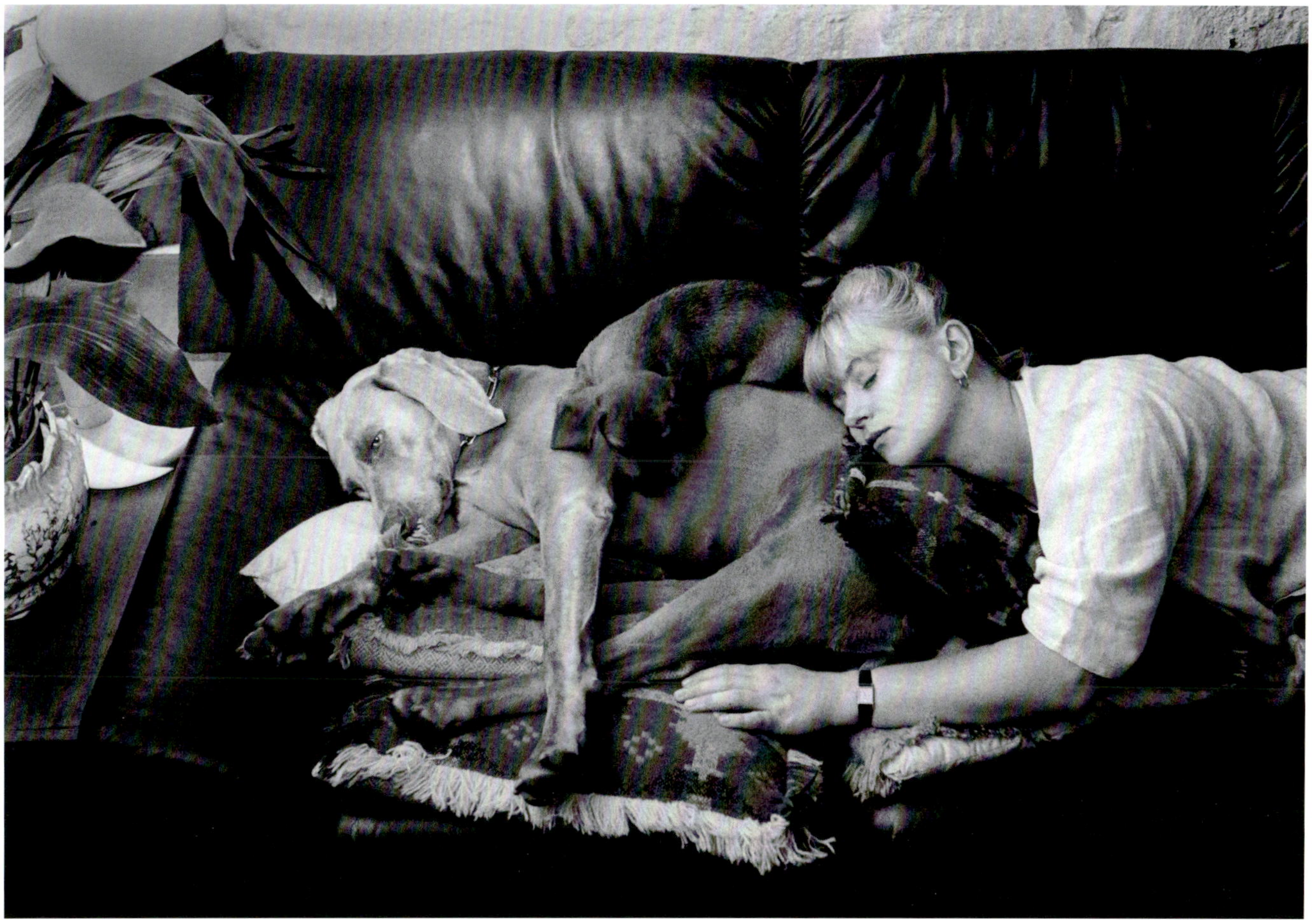

21 SEPTEMBER 2021 / ULTIMATE BLISS: REAL. *TINTERN, WALES 1987*

Interesting. There were precisely no comments about my last post. I guess that is a comment in itself.

Please read – absolutely essential – *The Book of Veles: How Jonas Bendiksen Hoodwinked the Photography Industry* – on the present magnumphotos.com site, but I don't know for how long.

It brilliantly puts into real context what I was struggling to suggest in my post of 19 July. I think the future is worrying if you hope that photography should be about observation and facts.

I repeat, everyone who pertains to have an interest in photography must read and digest this. I will be testing if I ever meet you.

@davidhurnphoto @magnumphotos @jonasbendiksen #nonfictionphotography

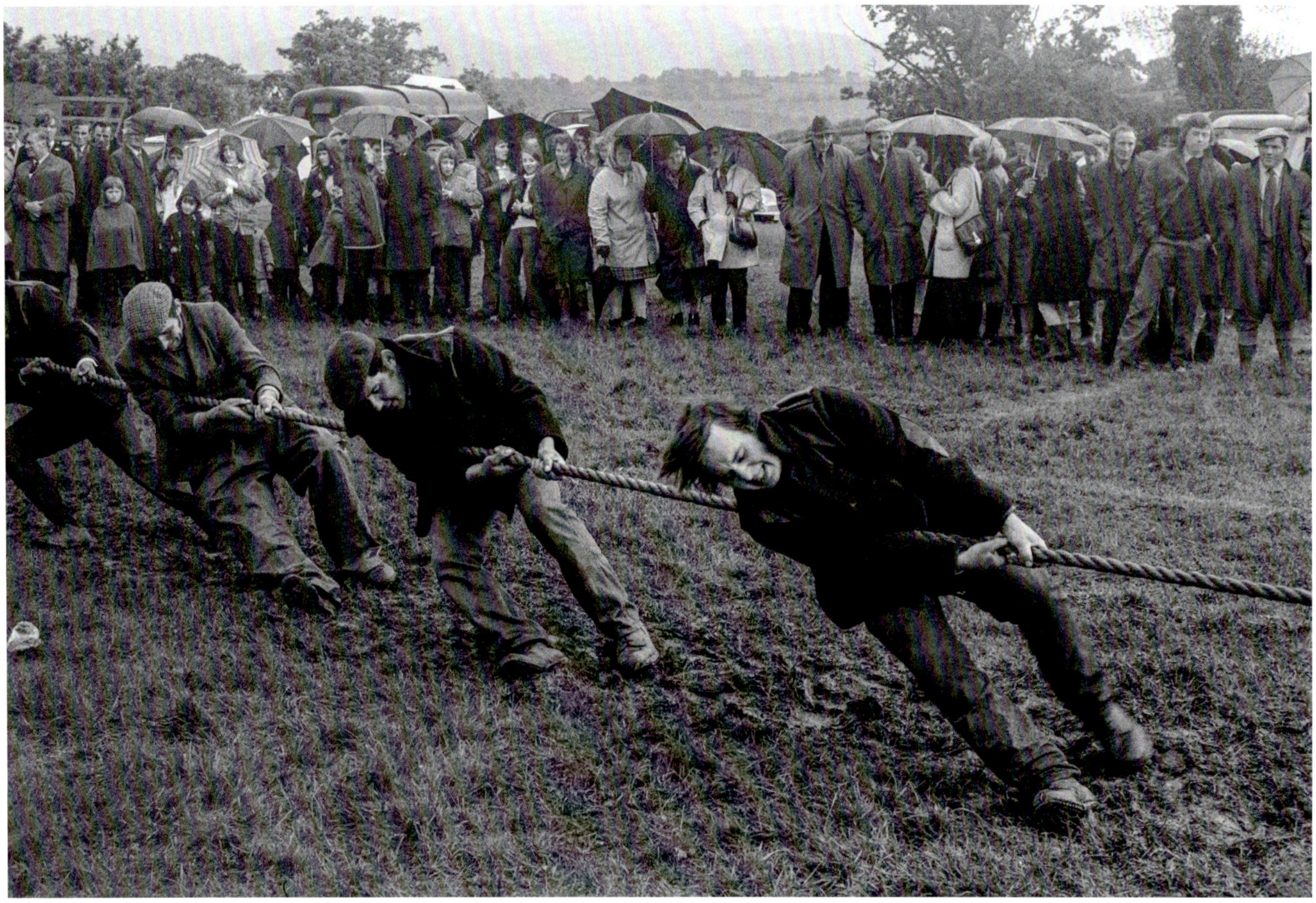

14 OCTOBER 2021 / EFFORT. *BRECON, WALES 1973*

A reader queried my use of the word steal.

I use it as the *Oxford Dictionary* suggestion, 'an idea taken from another work'. In my mind 'inspiration'.

I steal from many sources and often in very lateral ways.

I look at Rembrandt's self portraits and marvel at the 'honesty' of the pictures.

Bach shows 'work rate' and 'tenacity.' I remember Daniel Barenboim – I asked him what makes a concert pianist – he replied, 'you play the piano a lot'.

I think I was absorbing from when I was about 15, I had postcards by Manet, Seurat, Bruegel, on my wall. On reflection, I think what they had in common was a powerful sense of form/design/geometry, whatever you wish to call it – at that age I had never taken a photograph and certainly no way fostered the idea of professional photography.

The other night I saw a wonderful documentary about Simon and Garfunkel, it showed they fostered a fantastic attention to detail, never being satisfied, building little by little.

Orwell: 'I write because there is some fact I want to draw attention to'.

I presume none of us think we are as good as we hope we will be. How do we get better?

Well, as I have said many times before, the one thing most persons I admire have in common is that they work their butts off. If you are not doing that then that's a good place to start. If you have an idea make sure you know more about your subject than anyone else and make sure it's visual.

Importantly, don't be too proud to listen, look, learn from others – one's heroes.

Not being quite good enough is the norm for most of us. It should not be a worry.

@davidhurnphoto @magnumphotos #nonfictionphotography

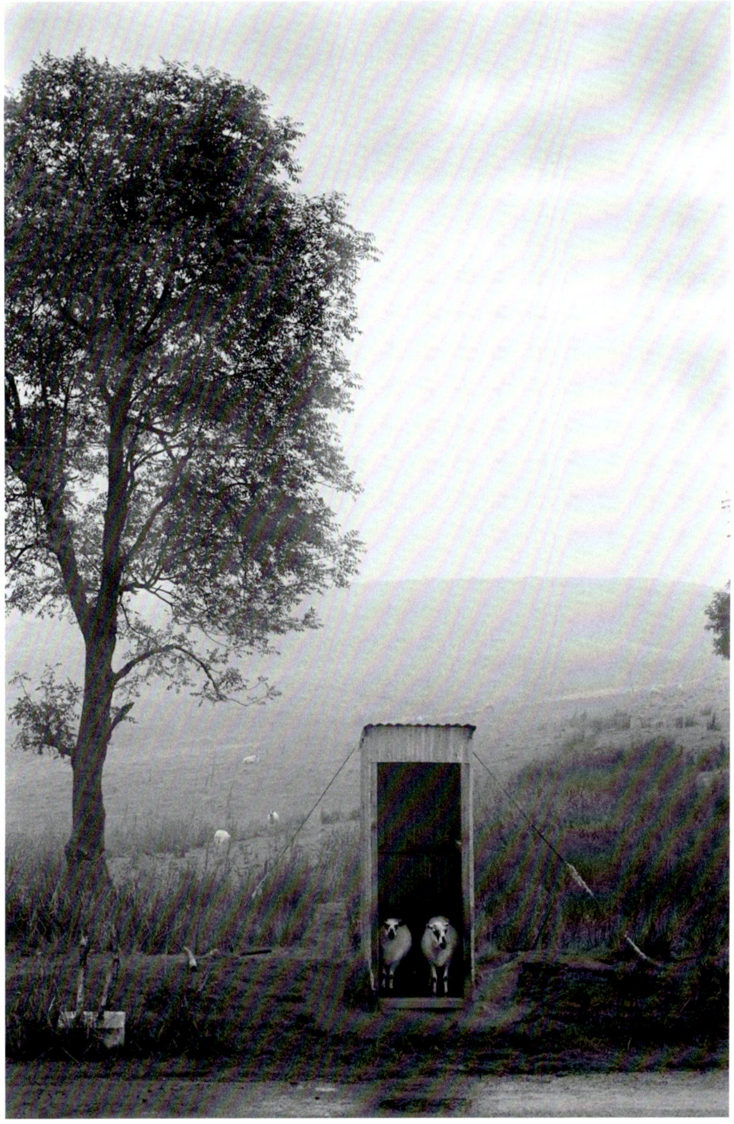

25 OCTOBER 2021 / ON GUARD. *MYNYDD EPYNT, WALES 1973*

I visited Bristol to see the book fair and at the same time had the opportunity to hear 11 lectures, all by lecturers worth learning from. If anything the whole was too dense. Every talk had a packed audience. How come Bristol seems to always get these events right?

I will not name the speakers – too many – but as I hinted above – the only problem was fitting in listening with time to look at the book stalls.

I am conflicted by the amount of books now being produced.

There was a time when I started when, perhaps, a new book came out every other week. My photographer friends and I each bought every one, the genre variety was broad yet standards so high that though battered through looking, they are still on my library shelf and looked at.

I now hear of so many book titles that I am sure if I had them in my front room they would only get one viewing.

I like looking at pictures very simply shown.

I hate folded pages, tissue or fancy papers, books that you feel the designer seems more important than the photographer, text that tells you how to look at the photographs.

On the other hand, publishing any book is an achievement, good for one's morale and ego.

As a portfolio, one should remember that if your pictures look like everyone else, it is not very useful.

I just warn, remember once you have published, it is there somewhere forever.

@davidhurnphoto @magnumphotos #nonfictionphotography

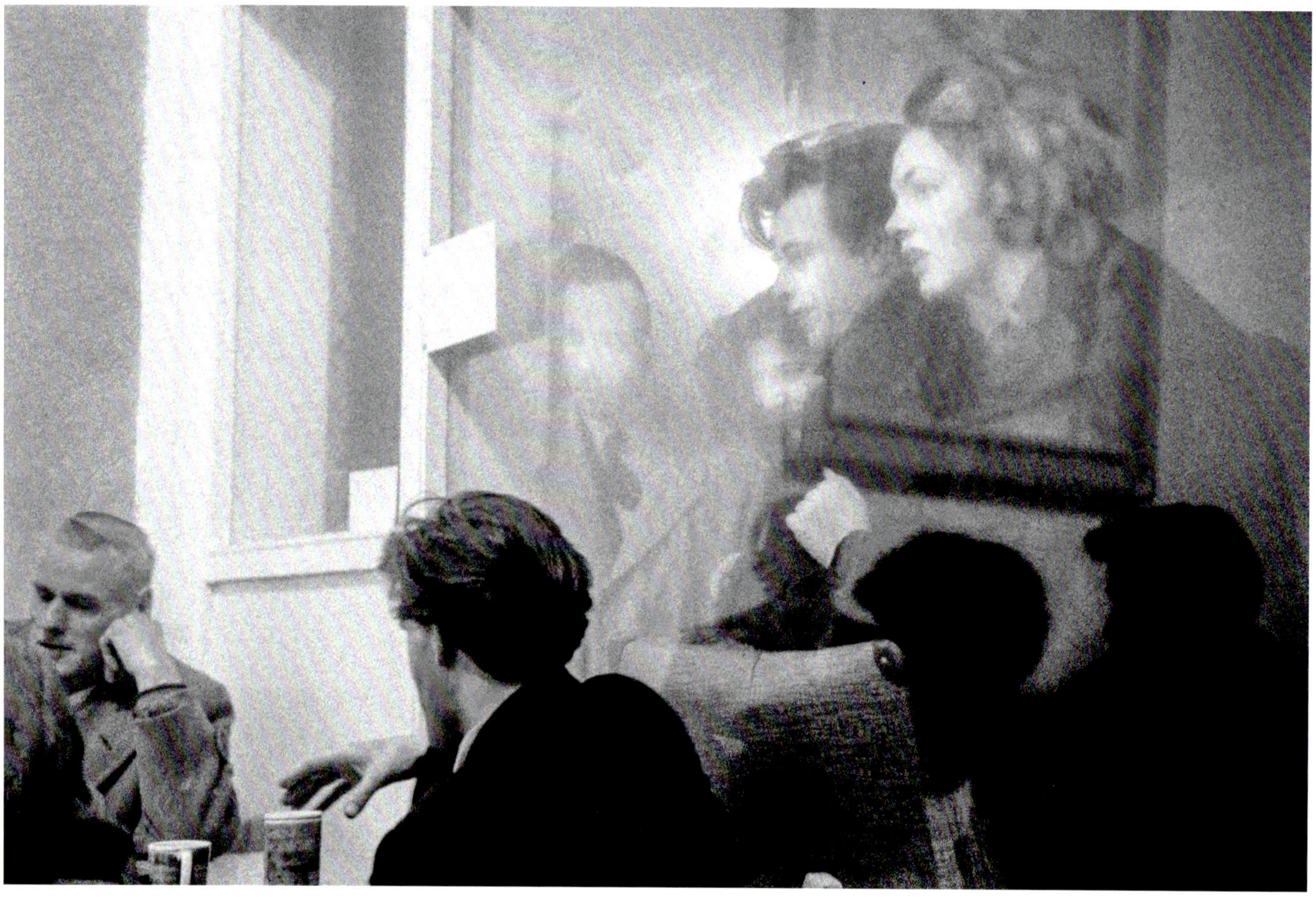

30 OCTOBER 2021 / COFFEE #1. *LONDON, ENGLAND 1957*

A few days ago I met up with friends in a coffee house in Monmouth. Conversation/ discussion, what a delight. I am always suspicious of those not willing to talk. Daniel Meadows recommended a book, David Mayne showed *newport-land* – well worth looking at.

On perusing at home, I discovered coffee houses first opened in London in 1652, they came from Turkey. The idea was largely economic, they served as informal office space.

In Charles Dickens' *Nicholas Nickleby*, Mr. Squeers, the schoolmaster, makes the coffee house a meeting place to pick up new scholars and to interview parents who wish to send their children to his lonely boarding school on the bleak moors of Yorkshire. Even though his novels are obviously fiction, it is interesting to see them as 'slice of life' pieces, showing us where people went and what they did. Apparently business and banking transactions took place in them; Freemasons had their Lodge meetings in them. They even gained a reputation for being meeting places for religious or political dissidents, and hence at one point were 'under suspicion as being centres of intrigue and treasonable talk'.

But later it is also suggested they also functioned as social venues, that many artists and writers began to congregate and hold meetings in them.

The British called their coffee houses 'penny universities.' That was the price for the coffee. A nobleman who visited London in 1728 described them as one of the great pleasures of the city. How it is 'a Sort of Rule with the English, to go once a day at least' to coffee houses 'where they talk of business and news, read the papers, and often look at one another'.

They quickly became England's premiere egalitarian meeting places, where all patrons were considered to be more or less equal. The forum through which the notions of freedom of speech and the public sphere emerged. A place where the honesty, reliability, and prudence of one's fellow patrons were safe.

All this to say 'bring back the era of the coffee house meetings'. Photographers discussing over liquid and a bun seems good to me.

@davidhurnphoto @magnumphotos @danielmeadowsphoto @projectymahere

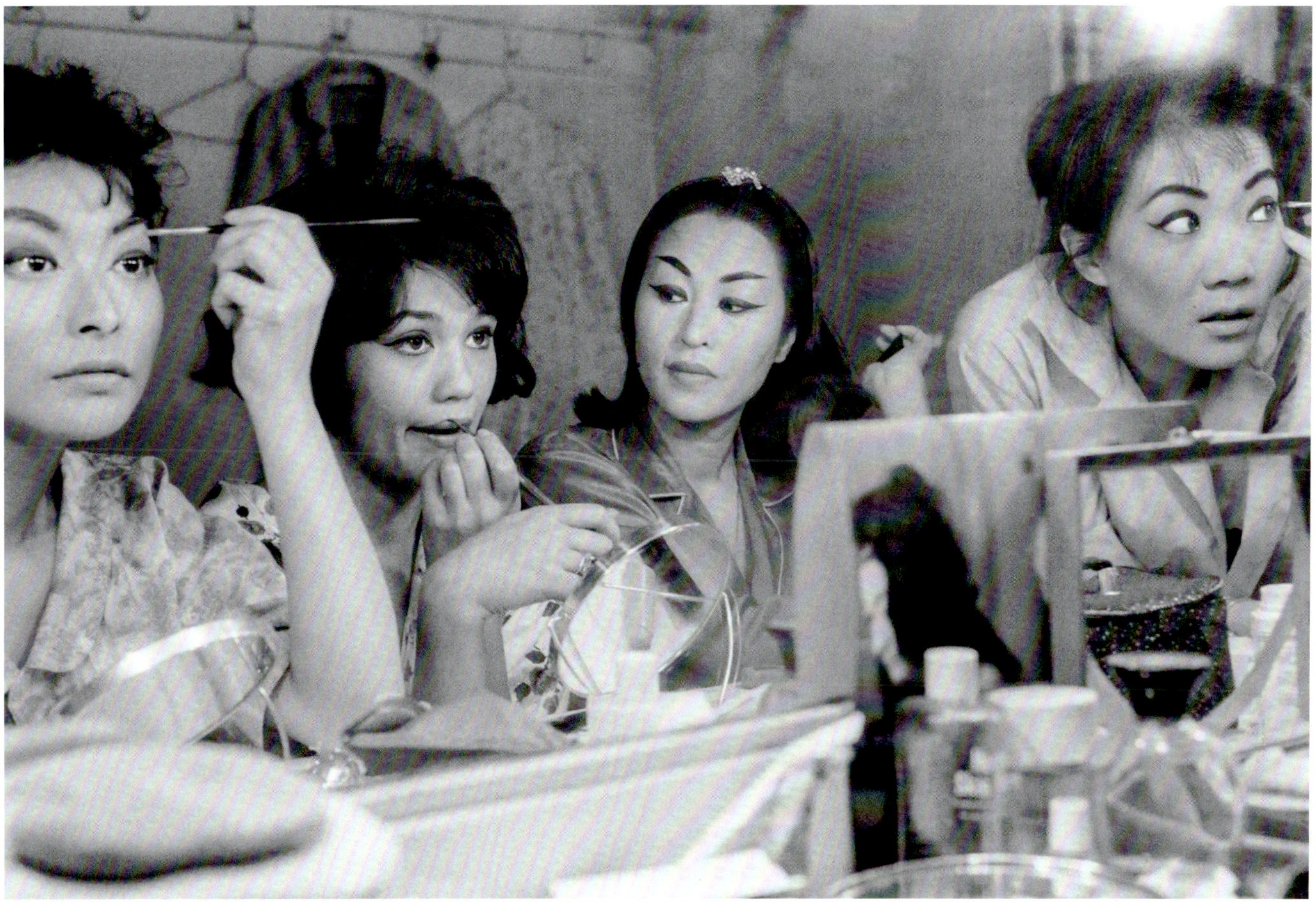

4 NOVEMBER 2021 / CLOSE FRIENDS. *LONDON, ENGLAND 1961*

The more I decide to relax from most things photographic the more my mind seems to enjoy contemplating fantasy.

I was reading about the Paris cafes – OK, perhaps they were mainly drinking bars – but I envied the idea of lively companionship. I love the idea that 'doers' tend to congregate. That in Les Deux Magots could have been found Jean-Paul Sartre discussing with Simone de Beauvoir, somewhere/sometime could have been found Hemingway, Camus and Picasso – the cafe now gives a major literary award every year. In La Rotonde could be found Braque, Modigliani, Soutine, Diego Rivera. Magnum's first space was in a flat above a Paris cafe where many assignments and stories were talked about and thrashed out. There, one might have bumped into Bresson, Capa, Seymour, Arnold, Erwitt, Morath.

When I started, I learned largely by photographing in Soho coffee bars; The Partisan, Nucleus, Macabre, The Two Eyes, not only how to shoot pictures, but I also learned networking (not a word then), met Ken Russell, Colin Wilson, John Antrobus, Michael Foot, Stuart Hall, Raymond Williams, Spike Milligan, they were all people I showed my pictures to and who all generously gave constructive comments. Many stayed friends. The Fleet Street wine bars were frequented by Bert Hardy, Thurston Hopkins, Grace Robertson, etc and the young McCullin, Griffiths, Bulmer, Berry, and editors, Rand, Jacobson, etc, it was very constructive.

If I lived in a major town/city I would love somewhere central where I could go with the likely outcome of meeting someone interesting, someone to learn from, i.e. a really good cafe with maybe some pictures on the walls and certainly some books for whiling away time whilst waiting. Its main function would be as a meeting and talking place. Of course, in my fantasy world there might be an adjacent room which one could call a gallery to show groups of pictures. Small/medium gallery space these days can be very flexible, it does not need to be constant.

@davidhurnphoto @magnumphotos

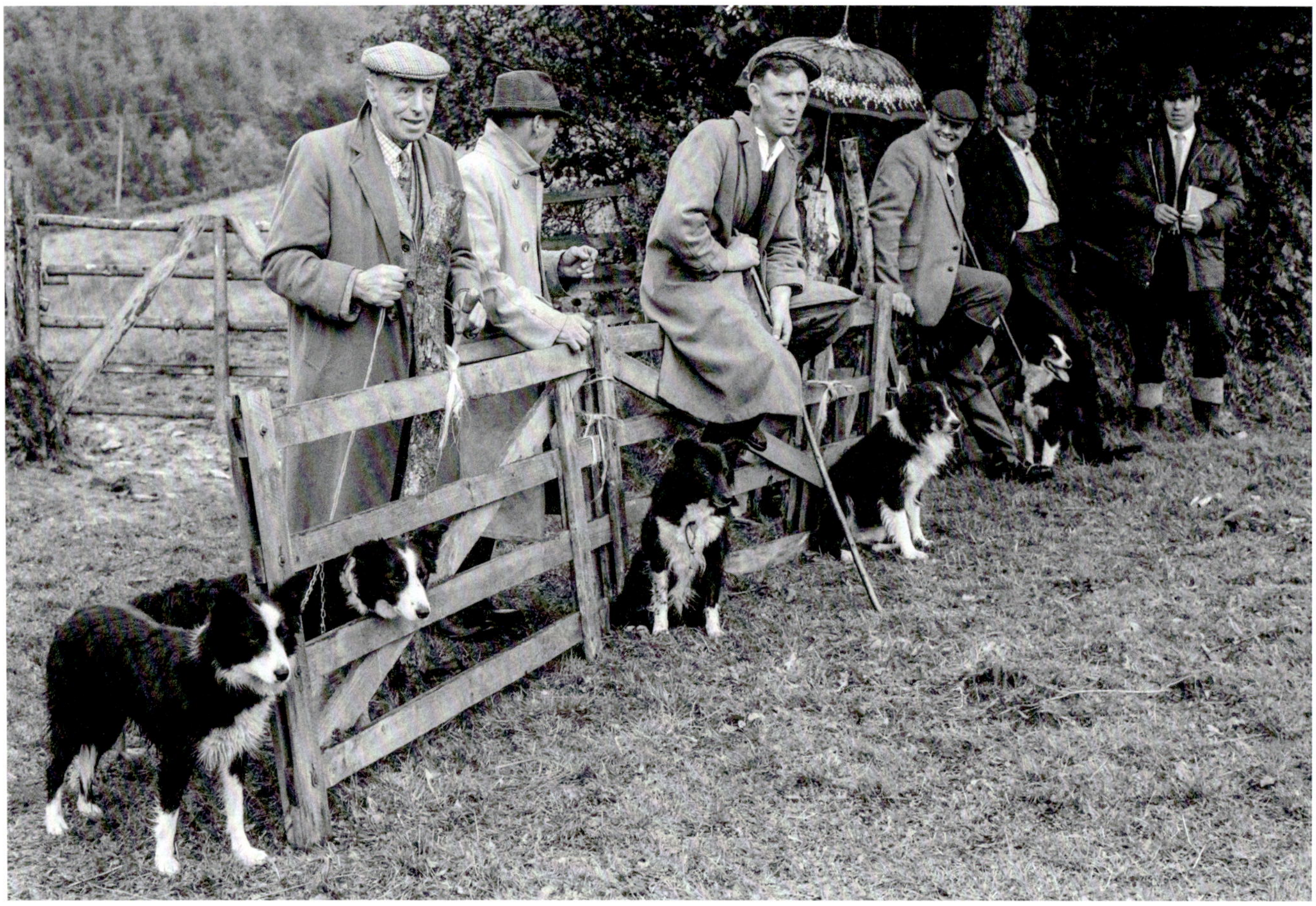

15 NOVEMBER 2021 / REAL WALES. *GWERNOGLE, WALES 1971*

I was pondering why I do or do not buy books.

Of course, I know what I like and dislike. However, it's not always simply pictures that persuade me.

MoMA recently launched a yearly celebration of the photobook. They list their ten favourite photobooks of 2021; I have, of course, not seen them.

I do know I am put off by some of the descriptions: 'The thrill of this book lies in the invitation to manipulate the uncoated paper into new photo-sculptural configurations that the concertina fold encourages,' certainly not attractive for me.

Nor, 'some images are cut by the external edge and continue on the following double page. Even more interesting: the volume, which was Japanese bound, has other images hidden in the folds of the pages, as if there were a book within the book'.

I have recently come upon four books that have interested me.

The first, *The Book of Veles* by Jonas Bendiksen, is in many ways, for me, one of the most important photobooks ever produced. Jonas asks, 'I started to ask myself the question – how long will it take before we start seeing "documentary photojournalism" that has no other basis in reality than the photographer's fantasy and a powerful computer graphics card? Will we be able to tell the difference?'

The book looks like a very thorough documentary book, in fact all the actual content is deliberately fake. A problem is that many who analyse photography were taken in – they didn't like being hoodwinked. Jonas was amused by fellow Magnum friends; 'In my experience my colleagues here are normally really sharp and see through a lot of bullshit. The fact that none of my colleagues caught me red-handed was a good measure for me that I was headed in the right direction. Or wrong direction, depending on how you view it all'.

My question is, when the general looking public think everything wonderful is fake, what does this mean?

Well, I have run out of space – I will write thoughts on other recent books in next post if I haven't completely given up on the world.

@davidhurnphoto @magnumphotos @jonasbendiksen #nonfictionphotography

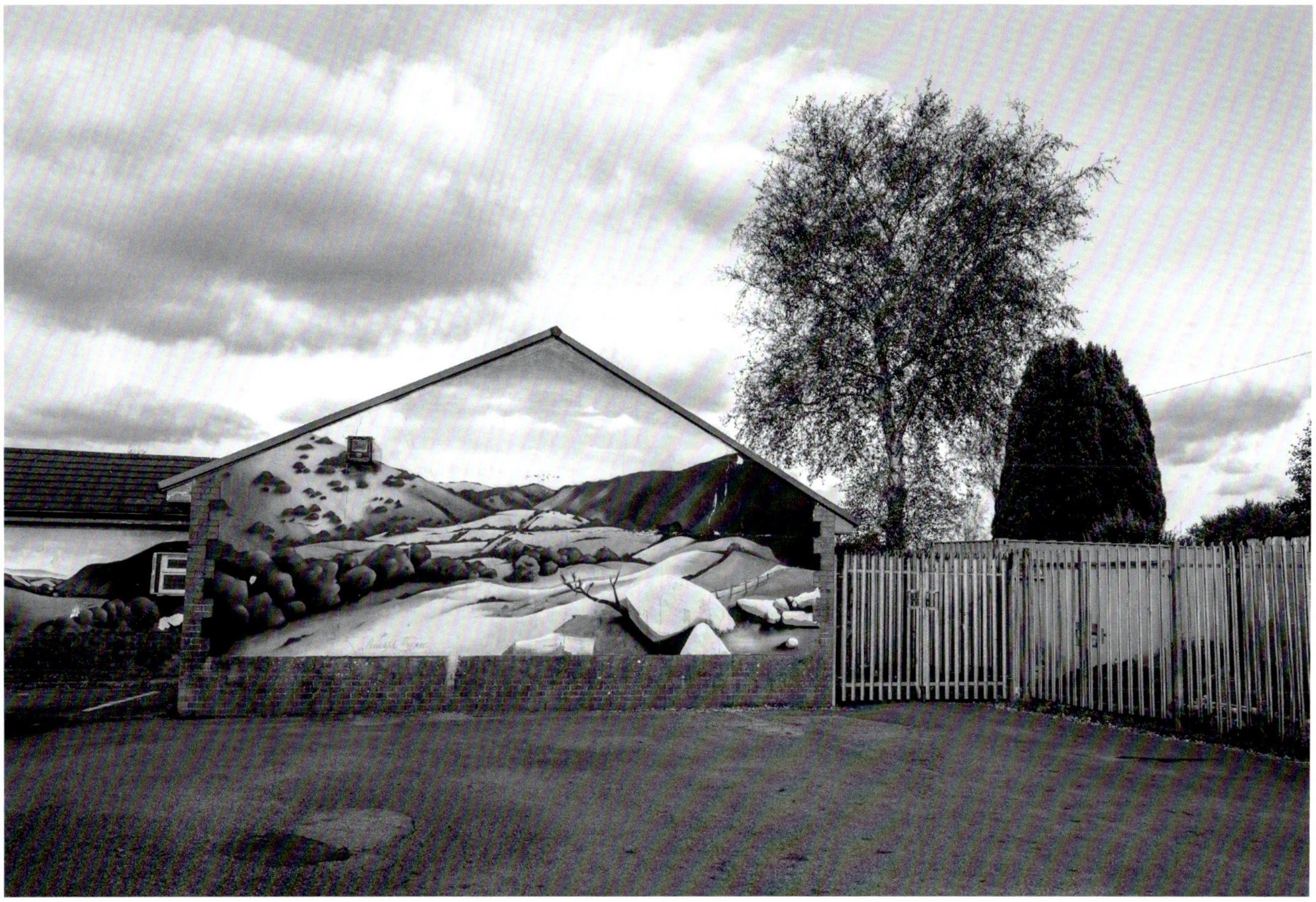

18 NOVEMBER 2021 / NON-FICTION GABLE. *BLACKWOOD, WALES 2015*

The second of my books slots into my 'too good' section. Books that I would not really want to own for fear I dropped a cup of coffee over them.

I like books that I wish to see the pictures so often that finally the book drops to pieces and I have to buy another copy.

The book is by Gilles Peress – may I make it very clear that if I were to make a list of my ten favourite photographers, Gilles would be there.

Gilles has a new book, *Whatever You Say, Say Nothing*, pictures from Northern Ireland conflict, published by Steidl.

I remember seeing an Ansel Adams exhibition for the first time. I was totally thrown by what I suppose one would call the print quality. However, on leaving the exhibition I realised I didn't remember any individual picture. They were each a haze of perfect black and white.

Gilles has two volumes of pictures and one of text, including a glossary of terms. They come in a 14.4x10 inches handsome tote bag. We are informed, Tritone 2 four colour process, 2 greys on black, 42 light grey – 92 dark grey – 198 black, printing on Italian GardaPat Kiara paper. Forgive me if I got some of this slightly wrong, but you get the gist. There is a section I glazed over, explaining finding a perfect black. But the pages/photographs themselves are as perfect prints.

Volume I, 504 b/w pictures and 8 colour.

Volume II, 444 b/w and 23 colour.

Cost, about £300. Actually I feel inexpensive – people pay thousands for a single separate print.

Anyway, one gets a sense of the book-maker's perfect book.

Every picture is outstanding. I am mesmerised by perfect picture after perfect picture and all just from Northern Ireland.

It is, undoubtedly, what should be my most perfect book, but I am never enthralled by knowledge of paper and ink and I keep thinking of my coffee.

I do not know what rumours abound but I am basically fine. I have dizzy spells, which at the moment confine me close to home but I have plenty to do and welcome passing visitors.

@davidhurnphoto @magnumphotos @gillesperess @steidlverlag #nonfictionphotography

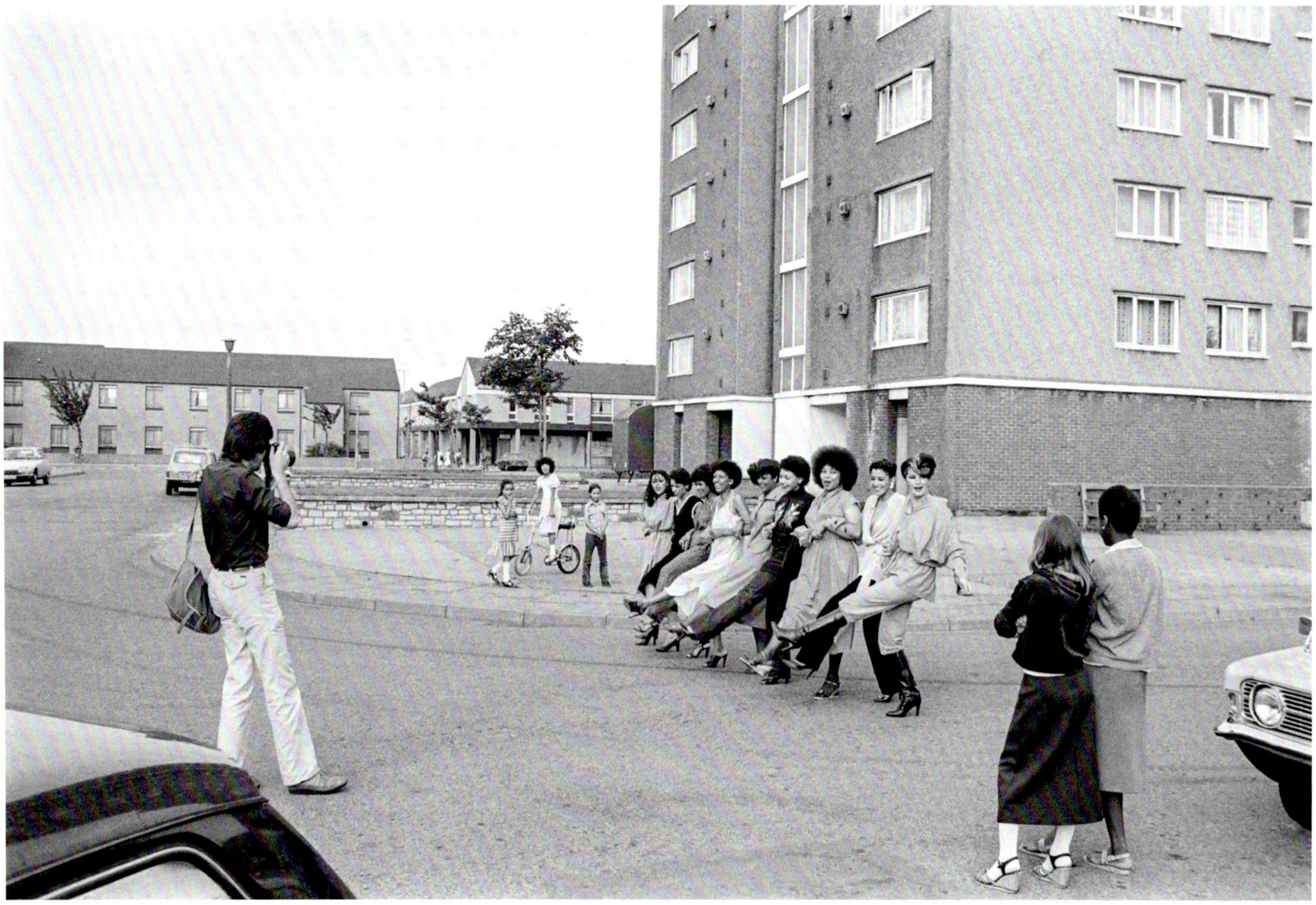

22 NOVEMBER 2021 / FASHION. *CARDIFF, WALES 1979*

I am still pondering what I want from a new photographic book. I suspect not only pictures of interest but also that the book invites discussion afterwards – this seems to imply a good print run and good distribution.

Next in my book list is Matt Black's *American Geography* published by Thames and Hudson – so thankfully its print run is probably large. Price £35, so I hope most can afford it.

You can have a pre-browse as he has an exhibition at the Magnum Gallery in Gee Street London. I think on until 17 December.

Matt Black is from California's Central Valley, a rural, agricultural area in the heart of the state. He started photography working at his hometown newspaper. In 2013, he began photographing isolated communities. In 2015, Black expanded the project to encompass the United States and completed his first cross-country trip, a three-and-a-half-month journey visiting dozens of communities across 28 states. Since then, he has completed four additional trips, travelling over 100,000 miles and making work across 46 states.

What had begun as a story of individual, isolated communities grew into a portrait of an increasingly divided and unequal America, created during a time of rising disparity and disunion.

The opening pages are a graphic representation that clearly outlines the distances and places covered. The effort involved.

For me, it enhances the question, what do photographers mean when in so many book introductions they claim 'an in-depth study' – 'deep investigation' – 'thoroughly researched' – 'explores the relationship' – 'widely published' – 'internationally known' – 'collected' – 'ongoing project' – 'a study of'?

As dear Greta might say – blah, blah, blah.

At the moment Matt is, for me, probably the most illuminating photographer working today. So, of course, I wallow in the pictures.

@davidhurnphoto @magnumphotos @mattblack_blackmatt @thamesandhudson #nonfictionphotography

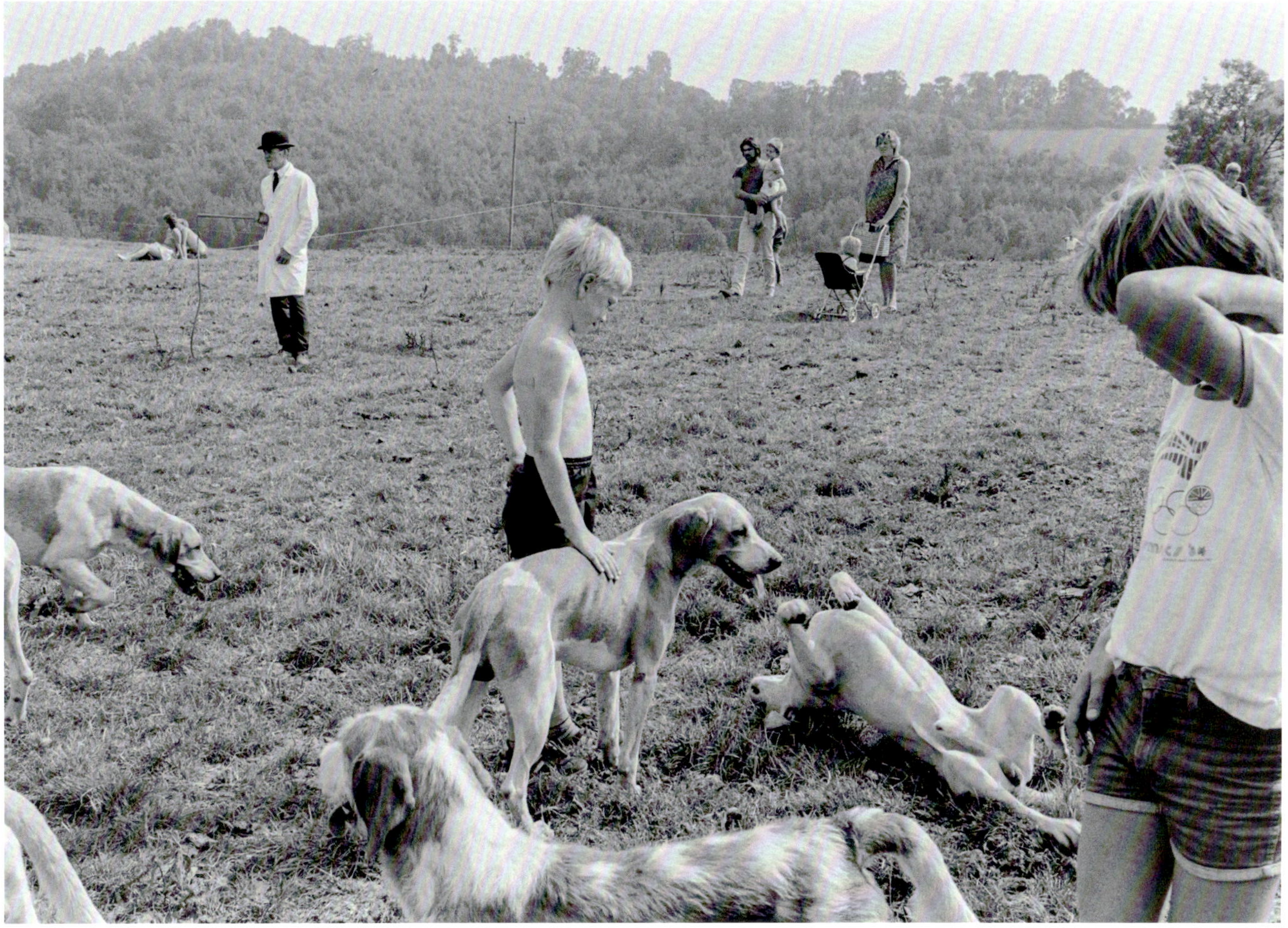

25 NOVEMBER 2021 / DOGS. *MONMOUTHSHIRE, WALES 1984*

To add to my list of banal phrases, I have just been told, 'Story Teller'.

My desert island book would be *Hugs and Kisses*, published by Abbeville Press. Author, Mimi Coucher – who, we are informed, normally writes about food, fashion, life and love, including sex and love quizzes for *Cosmopolitan*. She writes a splendid introduction essay. The book is small, 4.5x4 inches, has 270 pictures and costs about £4.

I give it as presents to people I like a lot. I think it might now be out of print. It might be difficult to get as I tend to buy every copy I can find in very good condition. I cannot think of any more pleasurable visual experience than viewing – as the title says – a mass of hugs and kisses.

I now see so many books that seem totally interchangeable so that if you took the 'artist's' name off the cover I doubt you could tell much from which. I guess I like discernible authorship.

I am still puzzled by a chance meeting I recently had with some young photographers in a local cafe. During conversation they informed me 'there is no such thing as quality – we are all equal'. Now I have no reason other than to believe they sincerely believe this. But I was saddened.

I think part of the joy I have had throughout my life is in searching continually to be a 'little better' – whatever that might mean for any of us – pushing myself and, as I have said before, 'stealing' little bits from others to help me do so.

I know I am never going to be a Bresson, Koudelka, Lange, Evans, but they show me what was/is possible and I can have fun trying to understand how to claw myself up the ladder.

I remember once listening to Jimi Hendrix at, I think, the Troubadour. I am sure he was more accomplished than most pub guitarists. Of course, I am not decrying the pub musician, they are helping a fulfilling and enjoyable evening – but for me, he was different.

I think Kazuo Ishiguro writes better than most. Aretha Franklin sings better. Judi Dench acts better. I just want to make an attempt.

@davidhurnphoto @magnumphotos @abbevillepress #nonfictionphotography #mimicoucher

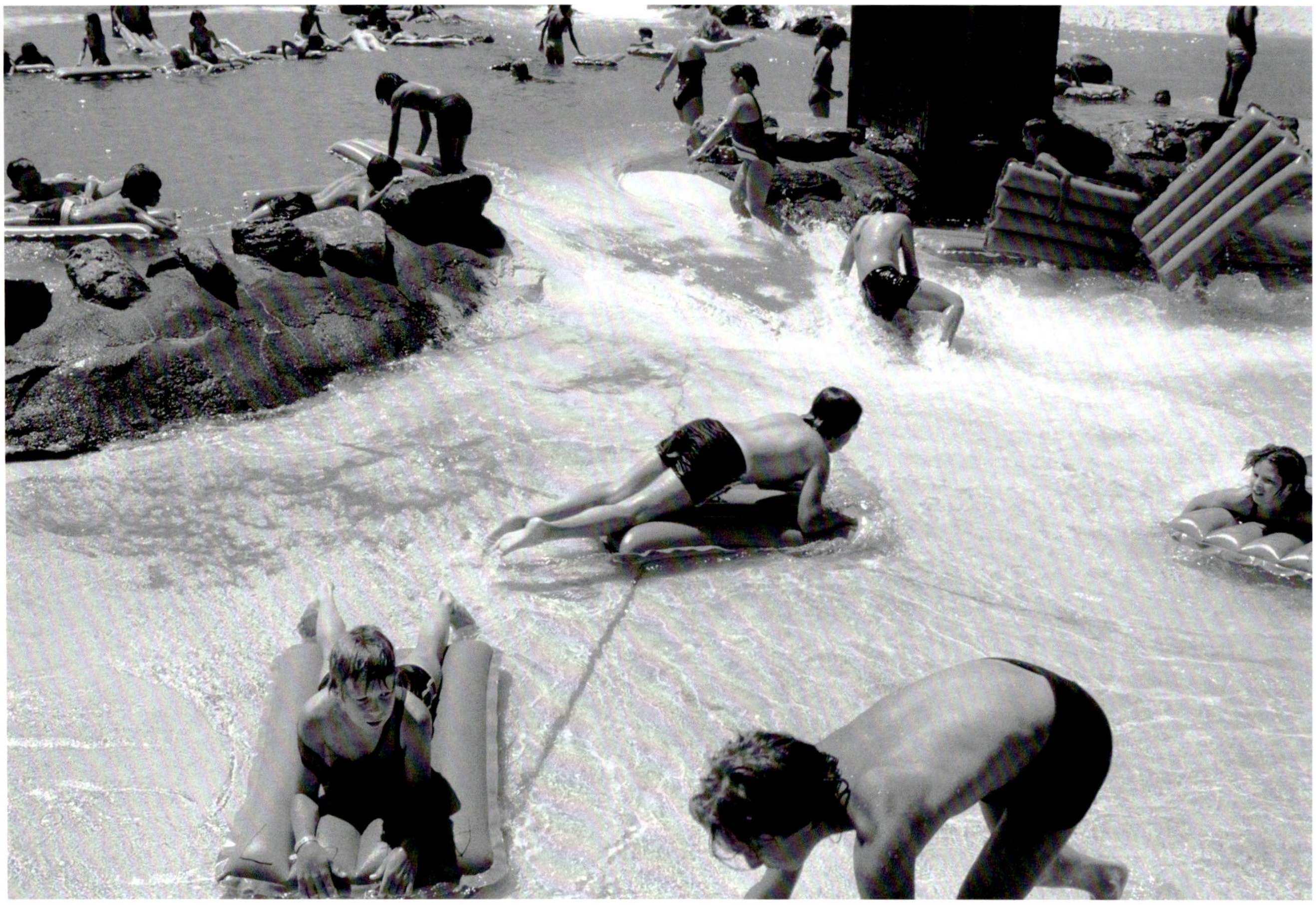

2 DECEMBER 2021 / THANKS FOR MEMORY: IT'S GETTING COLD. *ARIZONA, USA 1980*

It is difficult enjoying being a recluse yet wanting to invade everyone else's privacy. Even more puzzling – I enjoy having visitors.

When I returned to my home, Wales, in 1970, I felt happy. I bought a cottage in Tintern – an inspired choice.

In theory I would continue working as before but would now spend one third of my time doing a lifelong project on Wales – 'What is my Culture?'

Of course, I did work in Tintern, but it surprises me how blind we can be about that close to home.

The village has an extremely progressive mind in my friend Andrew, who has lots to do with making a truly excellent film society. But more important for me, in setting up a first class website. I said I was going to start a lifelong project – he gave me a slot.

I do believe there is merit in a singular voice looking at a village over an extended period of time. If done honestly, with a point of view and with accuracy, I am sure one's pictures will end up in a museum or village history society, or such like, sometime.

I am saying this because anyone can do it in their own area. It just needs tenacity, a willingness to find a small slot for the rest of one's life. I encourage others to start.

Please look at Andrew's and my efforts – tinternvillage.co.uk – go to 'David Hurn's photographic project'. Lots of pictures.

I hope it encourages others. There will be difficulties but difficulties should not stop you, they are there to be solved.

The family album will no longer exist – something needs to replace it.

@davidhurnphoto @magnumphotos #nonfictionphotography #andrewreid #tintern

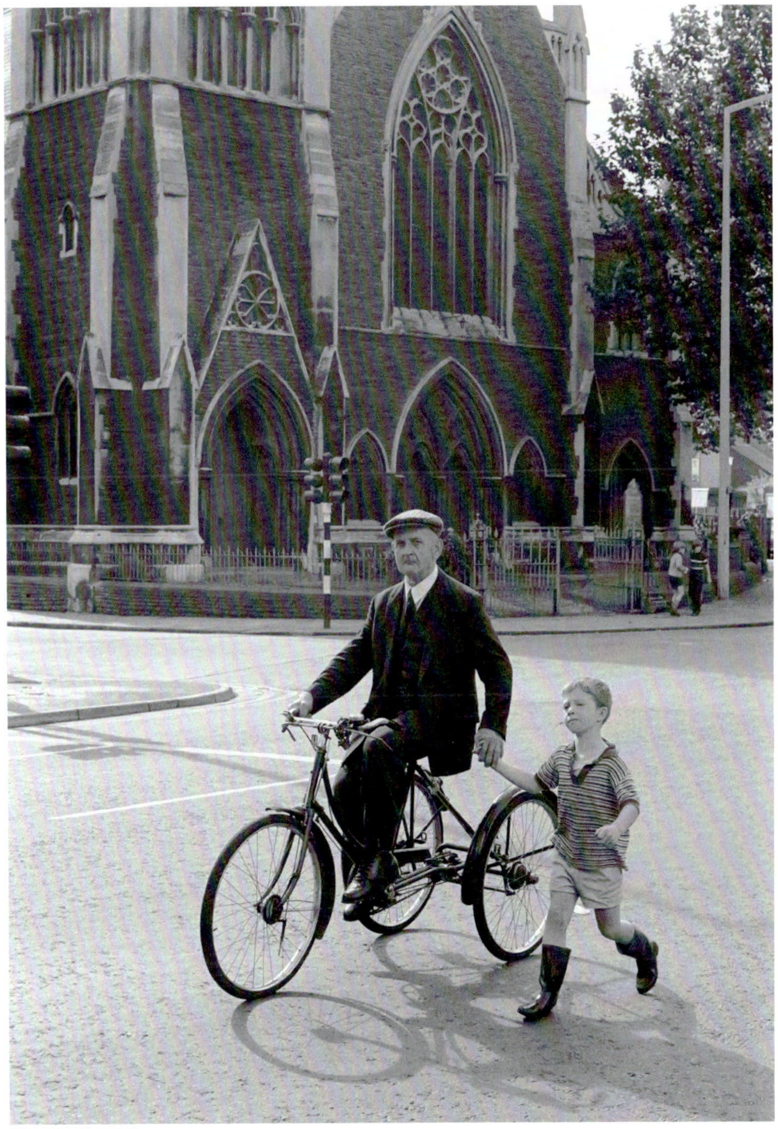

6 DECEMBER 2021 / RELATIONSHIPS. *CARDIFF, WALES 1973*

I am totally flummoxed by the result of my last post. I thought it was a sensible suggestion how to do something of social use in the community and possibly ultimately historically wider. It was a way of meeting people and gaining their trust – especially children, now difficult to photograph. A way of learning and perfecting how to put together a set of pictures, and in my case also gaining some rudiments of knowledge of IT and the internet.

There was just *one* smattering of interest. The least I have ever had from a post. Are we so disinterested in our fellow human beings other than our immediate family?

This might now be culturally true and, of course, all I can do is gape from afar and feel it's not an attitude for me.

I have absolutely no religious feelings/aspiration but I must admit many highly intelligent persons for many hundreds of years have disagreed with my views. I admit to being in a minority, so be it. I am puzzled by Love, there seems no logic there either but luckily it happens. How can some transmit music so blissfully – better than I would think humanly possible?

This was triggered by the Torchlight Carol Service held in Tintern Abbey. There is something – dare I say spiritual about this location, even more so at night. I am moved by people singing together.

I enjoyed photographing as part of *my* Tintern project. My gift to the community. I have eased back into shooting, nervously, but practice, I hope, will make perfect. Well, maybe not quite.

@davidhurnphoto @magnumphotos #nonfictionphotography #tinternabbey
www.tinternvillage.co.uk

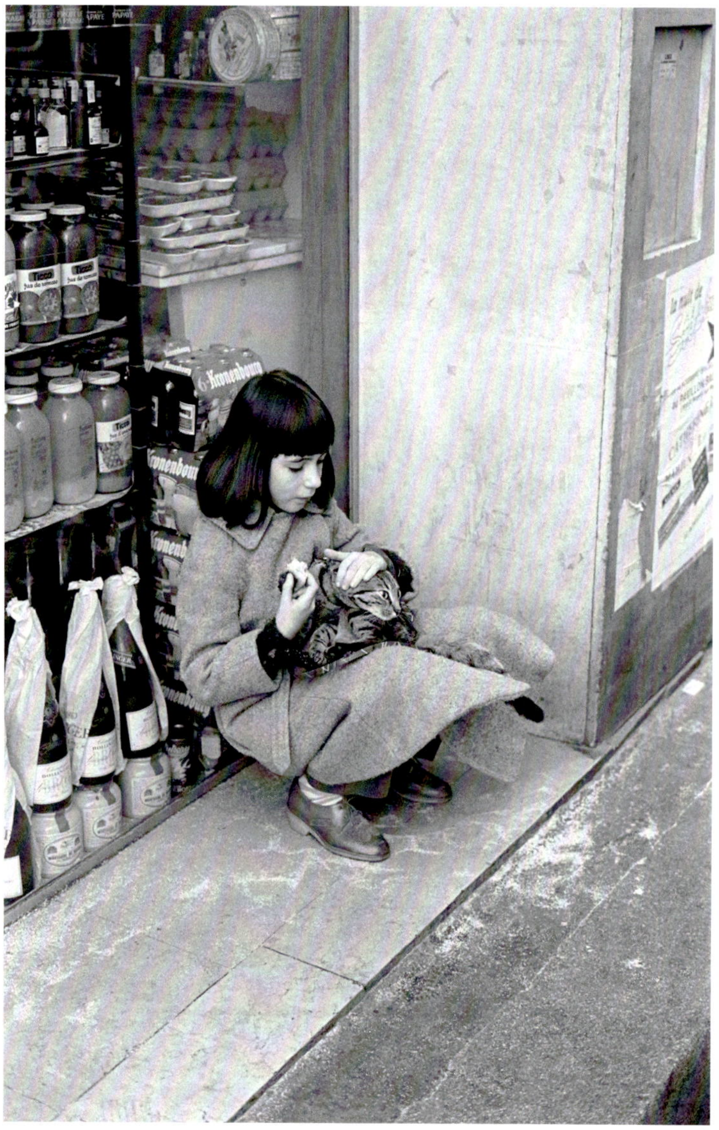

16 DECEMBER 2021 / PARIS LOVE. *PARIS, FRANCE 1980*

Another three trips cancelled. Sweden, Paris, London. I have to ruminate at home.

I have become very nostalgic and have been browsing through seldom looked at family albums. Boy, are memories jogged. The three most important pictures in my life lend nothing to art galleries, strong geometry, impeccable technique or latest trends. They are all to do with content and emotion.

First is a picture of my dead mother lying on the floor of her Cardiff home. I sadly discovered her when I visited to take her for a walk in the park. The essential was that she had a smile on her face. I felt I wanted to remember that smile – it meant to me that she had not died in pain. An observation later endorsed by our family doctor.

Second is a picture of a smiling father, waving to me as I left him after a visit to him in his Newport nursing home. He had died before I had arrived back home to Tintern, but a happy picture.

Third is a picture taken up my backside – a colonoscopy, a picture of a cancer. No discussion in the radiologist's mind about 'what is truth', or 'space'. Just accuracy. An accuracy which allows a brilliant surgeon to cut in the correct place and save my life.

Photography has many genres. I would maintain none more hierarchical than the next. I just feel we should always have a purpose and how 'good' we are is judged by how near that purpose we manage.

I also like a picture of my two dogs snuggled up together, asleep on my couch. It radiates love and contentment.

@davidhurnphoto @magnumphotos #nonfictionphotography

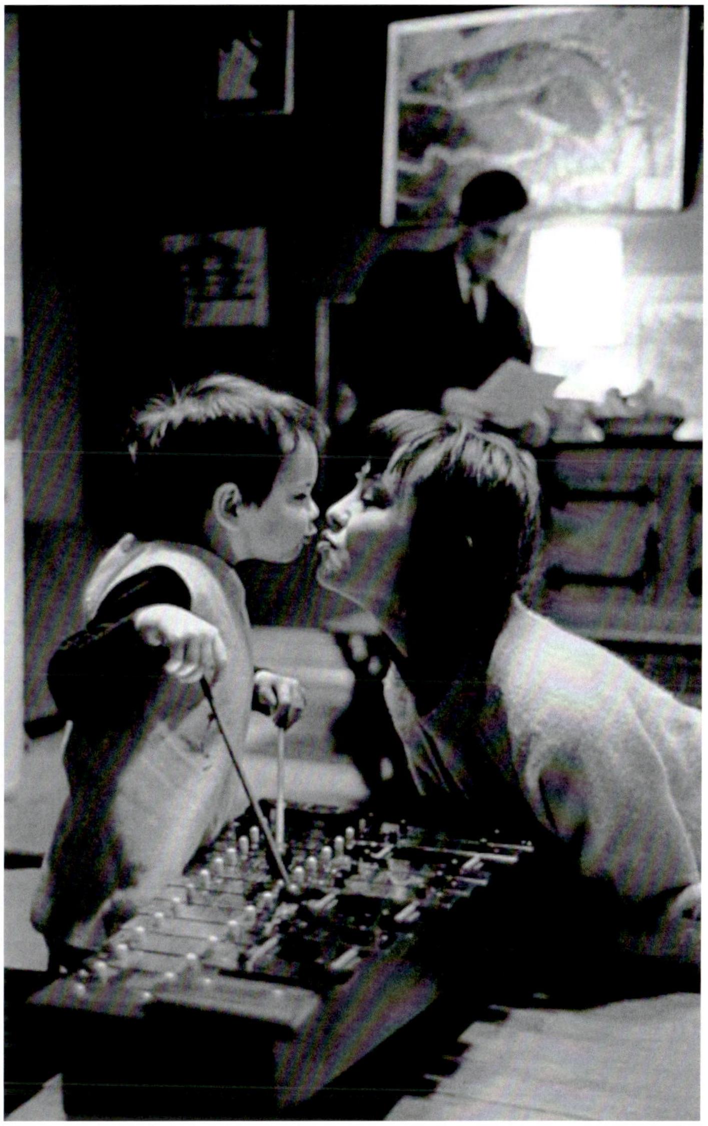

21 DECEMBER 2021 / TRUE LOVE. *LONDON, ENGLAND 1967*

I don't think I have ever killed anyone. I would be sickened if I did so this late in life. I have no faith in the words of politicians whom en-masse seem incapable of ever answering a simple question with what most of us would call a simple answer. Surely each should be honest, intelligent people? In theory they represent us.

I do have faith in scientists, most of whom have put in more than ten years studying in minutiae their particular branch of knowledge. What I like about scientists is they admit the nature of what they do is not always exact and therefore their decisions could be fallible – but they are open and peer reviewed – I would prefer to follow them than 'I have a friend who's friend knows someone who . . .' etc.

I am happy to wear a mask, have my jabs – even though I hate needles – be careful where I go, if that means I will not kill someone else.

The irony is that it now means that it is the few friends I continue to meet who are the vulnerable ones.

It also means that the little photography I was doing is put on hold yet again.

Christmas wish: that all put their address on cards or envelopes. I have four Johns, three Susans, I have no idea who is who.

@davidhurnphoto @magnumphotos #nonfictionphotography

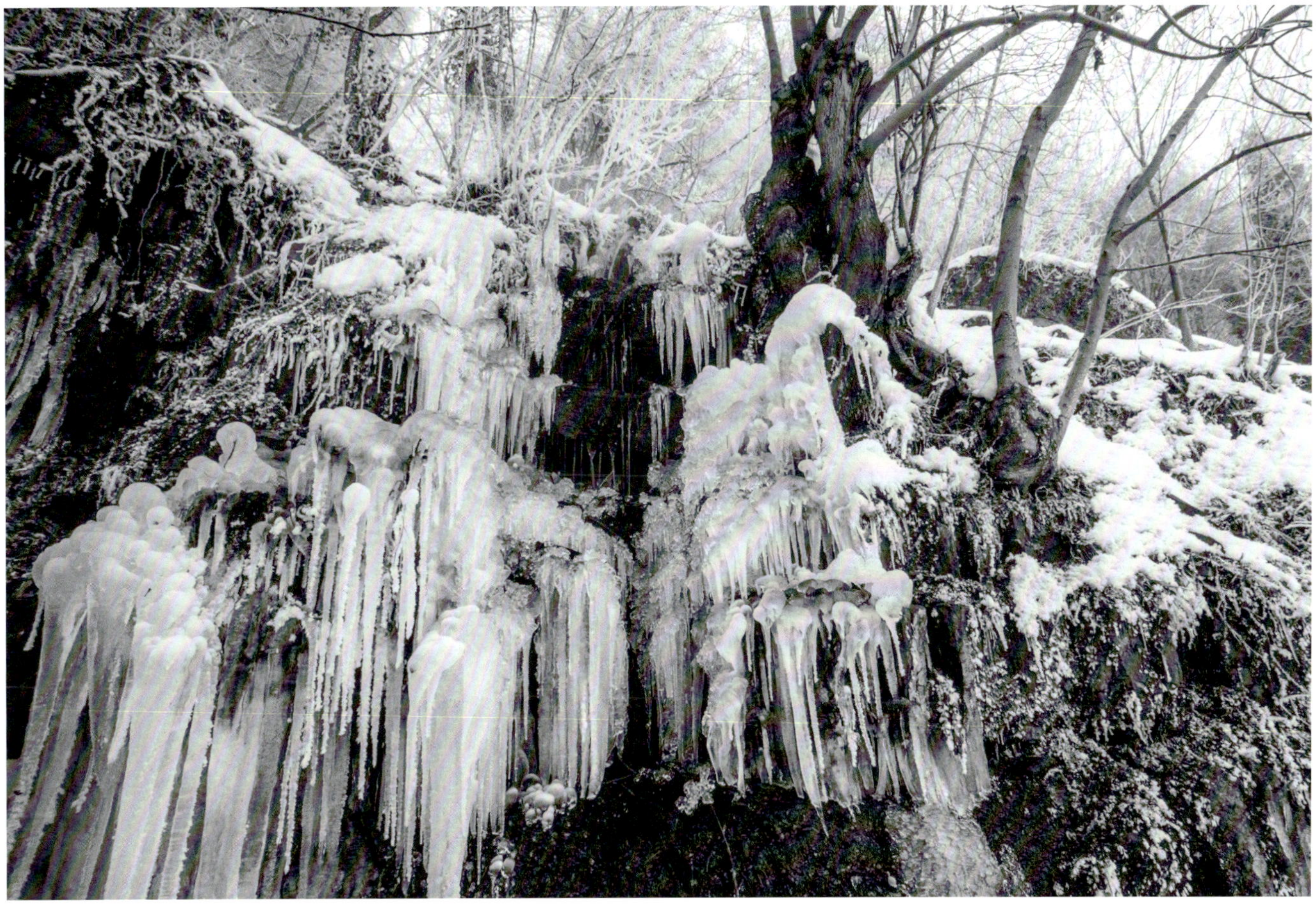

26 DECEMBER 2021 / PROSPECT COTTAGE, COLDER IN '79. *TINTERN, WALES 1979*

Normally I spend Christmas Day with long time friends who are neighbours. I have to trek at least 50 yards to get there. They always have a large happy family group. A mum and dad, three children, five of their children, plus brothers and others. I have nothing similar in my life and I find it joyous and uplifting and enviable – I also enjoy photographing exaggerated eating, pulling crackers, and the chaos of unwrapping presents.

We/I have decided that I would be entering a risky environment this year.

Luckily, I have other friends, a couple, who also live in the village, they are comparatively isolated and they invited me. People can be very kind. We had a wonderful meal. Of course, I had my cameras.

I am hoping for a very icy holiday period. There is very little for me to photograph close at hand apart from landscape and I never feel at ease in that genre – icy views make formalism easier and I feel a little more comfortable there, however, I do feel I am cheating a bit.

I like special Christmas cards. Photographers have the enormous advantage in that they can send something very personal and something someone else can cherish and wish to keep – I am puzzled that more don't do this.

I have just received a card from Jem Southam, in my opinion among the very best of the landscape photographers. I recently had a very enjoyable lunch with him, we swapped opinions on some favourites – Mark Klett, alive today in Arizona, and that wonderful group of 19th century American photographers, A. Gardner, W. H. Jackson, T. H. O'Sullivan, C. E. Watkins, E. J. Muybridge, A.J. Russell, etc – some of whom worked with Mathew Brady – 'Brady's Photographic Corps' – as war photographers during the American Civil War, and switched to landscape when the war ended and they were out of work.

The best photographers simply work tenaciously to a simple, clear brief – but often self-imposed.

May the world stay in focus for you.

@davidhurnphoto @magnumphotos @jemsoutham #nonfictionphotography

IF I COULD TELL THE STORY IN WORDS,
I WOULDN'T NEED TO LUG AROUND A CAMERA.

/ *Lewis Hine*

2022

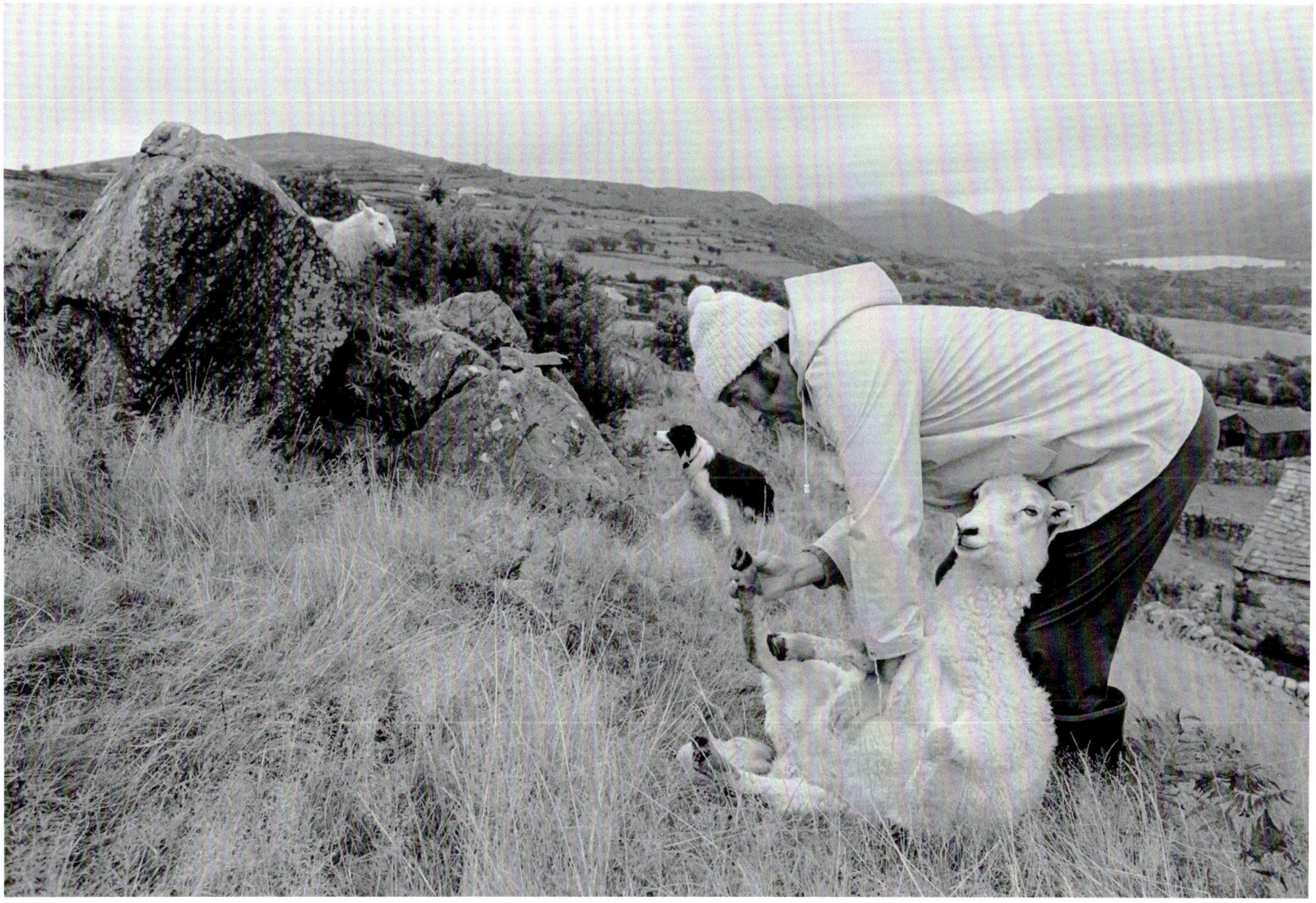

2 JANUARY 2022 / FEELING THE FUTURE. *NANT GWYNANT WALES 1983*

I heard a charming German phrase – *Guten Rutsch*. It translates as 'A good slide into the New Year'. I therefore wish *guten rutsch* for all of us.

For me 'sliding into the New Year' asks who am I with on New Year's Eve?

I spent it here, in Prospect Cottage, with a favourite writer and friend. I can't remember when I first met Bella Bathurst. I had probably been asked to photograph her, but sadly, on archive investigation, I most certainly didn't get a worthwhile picture.

I suspect that had I not known her personally I would never have read any of her books.

Why should I be interested in – an account of the construction of Scottish lighthouses by the ancestors of Robert Louis Stevenson – a history of shipwrecking and maritime skulduggery around the coast of Britain – the losing of one's hearing and the regaining 15 years later – an anthology of writing about cycling and bikes?

If I hadn't started reading, boy would I have been missing out on gems. She is mesmerising, so accurate, the language so right – 'I went with a group of friends on a cheap last-minute skiing holiday in the early nineties. So cheap, it turned out, that the resort had forgotten to include any snow.' Or 'Everything those old acid casualties from the sixties said is true: there really is no hallucinogen more effective than smashing a hole through your own skull.' Both from the book *Sounds*.

Anyway, my advice is treat yourself and start reading everything she has written.

Does this have anything to do with photography? Of course it does. It shows that if you have a passion for something, have the technical abilities to transfer what you are feeling, are accurate with your research, have tenacity – i.e. the ability to start and finish – one can achieve anything in whatever medium you work in, whatever your interests are.

@davidhurnphoto @magnumphotos #nonfictionphotography #bellabathurst

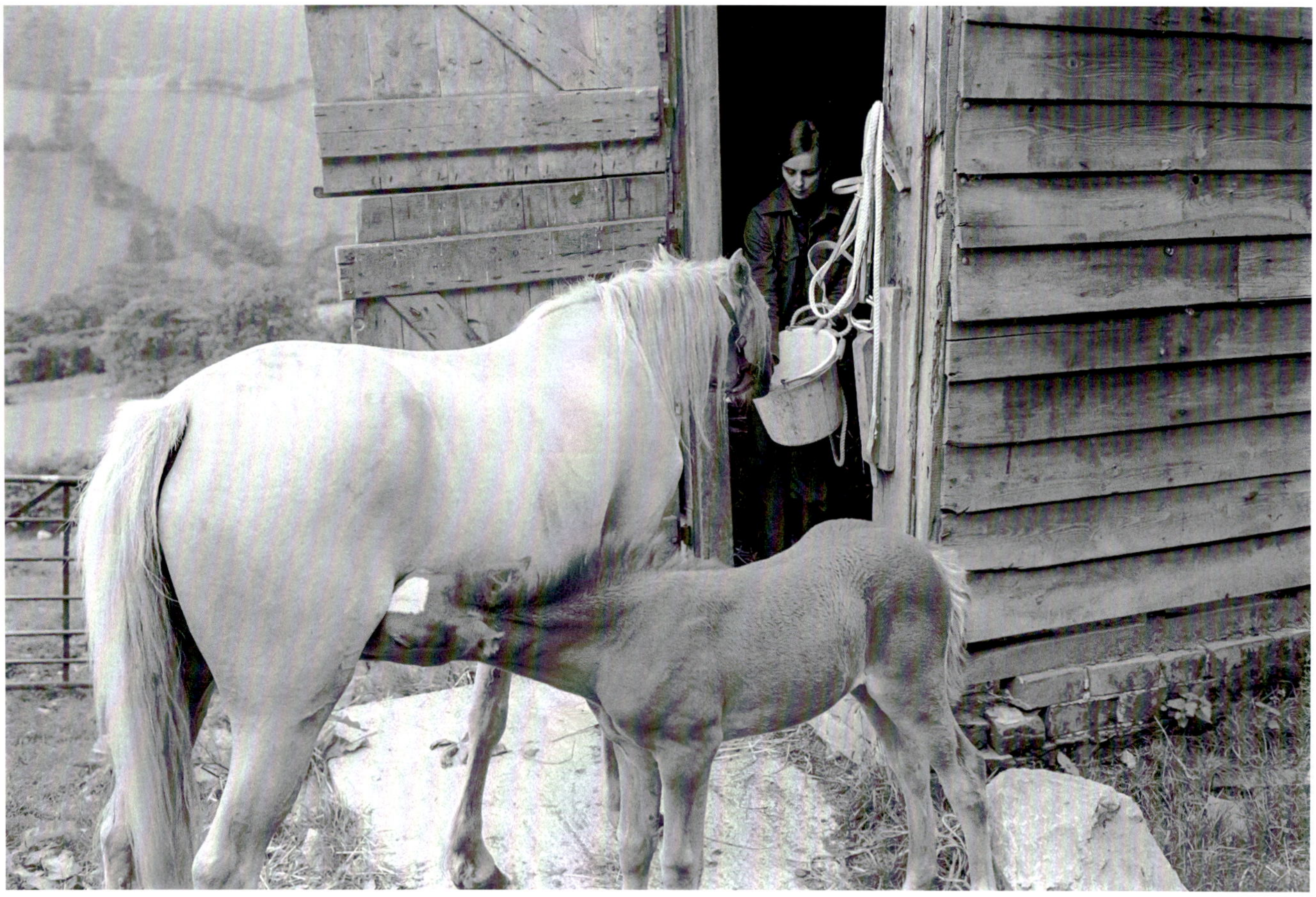

10 JANUARY 2022 / LUNCH TIME. ***DUTLAS, WALES 1975***

I have a gut feeling that I will be able to start photographing seriously again soon. I guess I should stop and ask, why? Is it to continue to make a living or to say something? I suppose a mixture of both.

Although I am fine driving it does tire me so that I can't really shoot till the following day. Luckily, I am getting offers of friends willing to come on trips, and apart from accommodation nuances, I feel positive.

My biggest problem is actually self-confidence. Over the past two years I seem to have absorbed so much information as to how I have to shoot pictures by people who don't actually shoot pictures, that I think it will take time to have a mental clear out.

Theory is fine, and for many I expect enjoyable – even gets them jobs – for those that indulge. But in my observations it doesn't produce photographers, i.e. makers of significant pictures.

We live in a visual world. The integrity of the photographer and the quality of their images are vital to the recorded history of our time.

I am still influenced by Lewis W. Hine:

'There were two things I have wanted to do. I wanted to show the things that had to be corrected. I wanted to show the things that needed to be appreciated'.

I rely primarily on instinct, whatever that means, or what romantically could be called 'a mixture of head and heart'. One searches for the significance and meaning of a situation, a situation that, hopefully, will still have interest many years in the future.

I try to listen, to observe, to make sense of. I come to decisions – that I am often willing to change. I hope for companionship, even love, in other words, to be a decent normal human being. Everything after will take care of itself.

@davidhurnphoto @magnumphotos #nonfictionphotography #lewishine

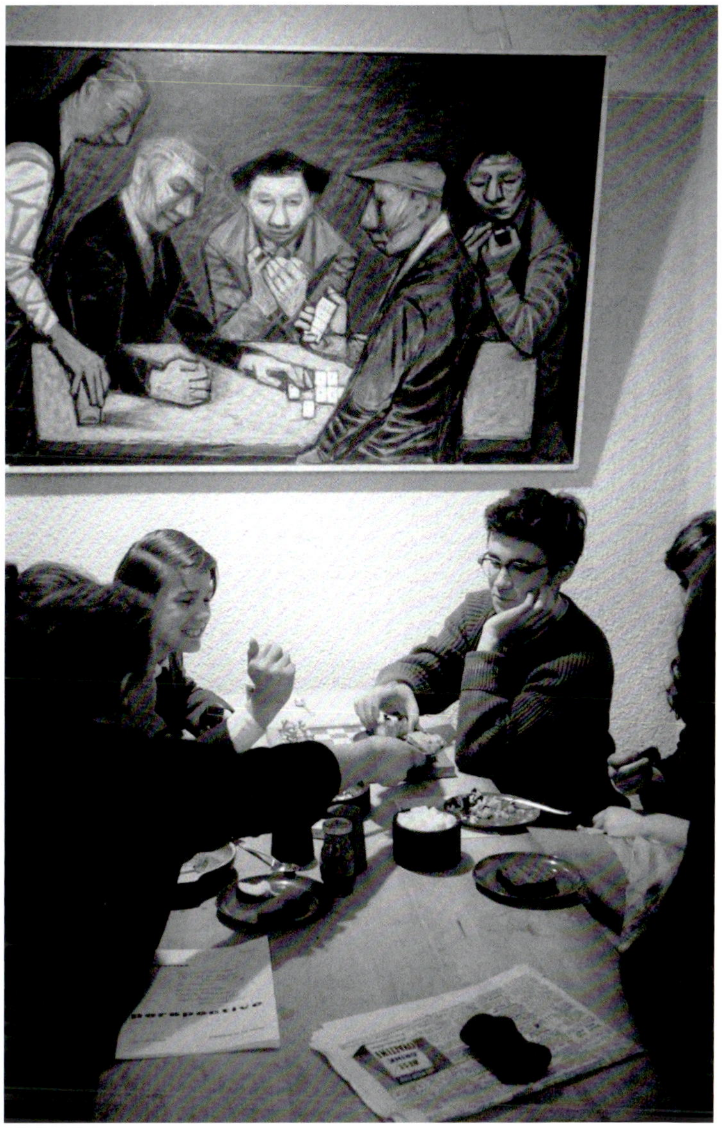

17 JANUARY 2022 / COFFEE BAR. *LONDON, ENGLAND 1957*

How did I start?

Seeing a photograph that made me cry and realising a photograph could create emotion and/or counteract propaganda.

My only time to learn was evenings. I simply went to my haunts, coffee bars, and pointed my camera at anything that interested me. I did it relentlessly, evening after evening.

I processed film in a lightproof metal canister, two films at a time. I only made contact prints. If I needed to give someone a print it was a 9x6inch made in a commercial lab – I think Grove Hardy. Does this ring a bell with anyone?

I worked with a Kodak Retina 11 camera. It is a bellows camera that you, of course, had to guess focus and manually set aperture and shutter speed.

Coffee bars were good training grounds – lots happening but taxing conditions.

I soon discovered there were two types of patrons, Doers and Talkers. Each tended to group together with their own.

I would show my pictures to any/everyone. People preferred pictures to be in focus and correctly exposed so one quickly learnt how to do that. Once technical matters were dealt with one could get on with learning how to observe and react. The self brief was point the box with a hole in the front at something that interested you and hope – it wasn't rocket science.

I saw photography as my way of making a living thus next stage was getting published. This largely meant slogging around and showing my pictures to whoever would look.

I learned how to put together a picture story from editors telling me I had messed up. Learning needed to be fast.

I knew Magnum's agent in London, John Hillelson. I spent hour after hour looking at the contact sheets of other photographers. One can read in a contact sheet the similarities of ways of working between photographers. That was the basis of the Documentary course I much later set up in Newport.

Advice: Link up to an agency. Agencies help you think about what the world thinks is interesting. Find an archive to sell your individual pictures – pictures might not command large fees but under the bed produces nothing. A few small cheques let you continue to function.

@davidhurnphoto @magnumphotos

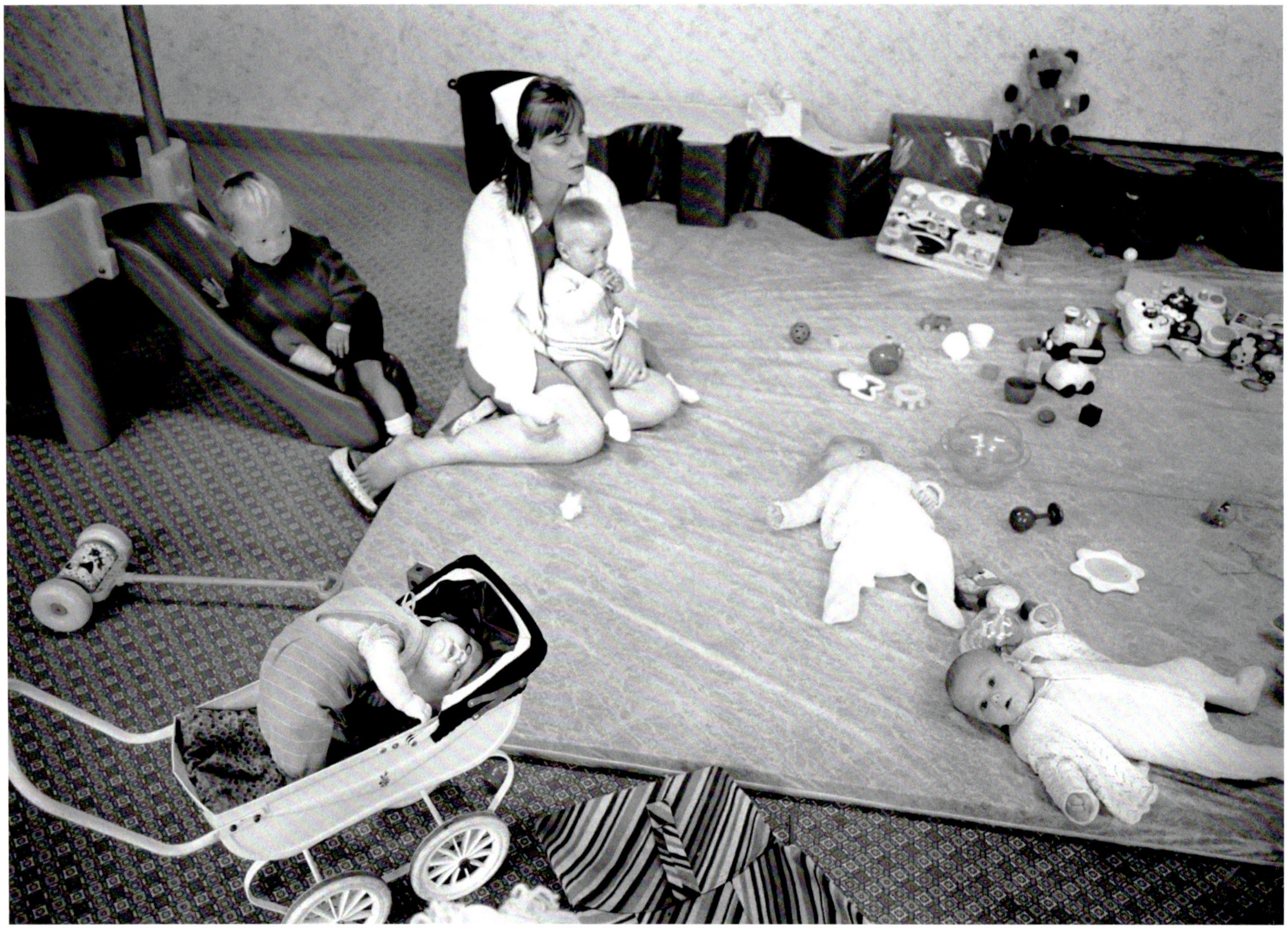

24 JANUARY 2022 / CHILDMINDING. *PWLLHELI, WALES 1986*

Photographs seem to be everywhere now. You could argue that photography has never been more popular?

Has the omnipresence of photography devalued it?

'It is the democratic art, i.e. technical skill is practically eliminated – the more foolproof cameras become with focusing and exposure the better – and artistic quality depends only on choice of subject'. – W.H. Auden

Ah, the choice of subject. Agreement, that is what it's all about. Do you have unique interests? Are others interested in your interests? They have to be if you wish to be professional.

My guess is that the photography profession has always been, and will always be, like a rather tall ladder which has a finite number of rungs on it, and to be a success you have to fight onto the bottom, then try to climb. There are, of course, many genres of photography, many different ladders. If you feel that the 'mass' is your competition, and you feel they have as much right on your particular ladder as you, then you will not make it anyway.

Luckily, there will always continue to be a Bach, a Bacon, a Gormley, a McCartney, a Hambling, a Zephaniah, a Koudelka. One can strive to reach them. One might not get there but a few rungs down is pretty good.

Of course, you can simply praise your circle on Twitter or Facebook or whatever, in which case I advise training to be a plumber, always needed, and well paid.

@davidhurnphoto @magnumphotos #nonfictionphotography #auden #francisbacon #paulmccartney #maggihambling #benjaminzephaniah #antonygormley #koudelka

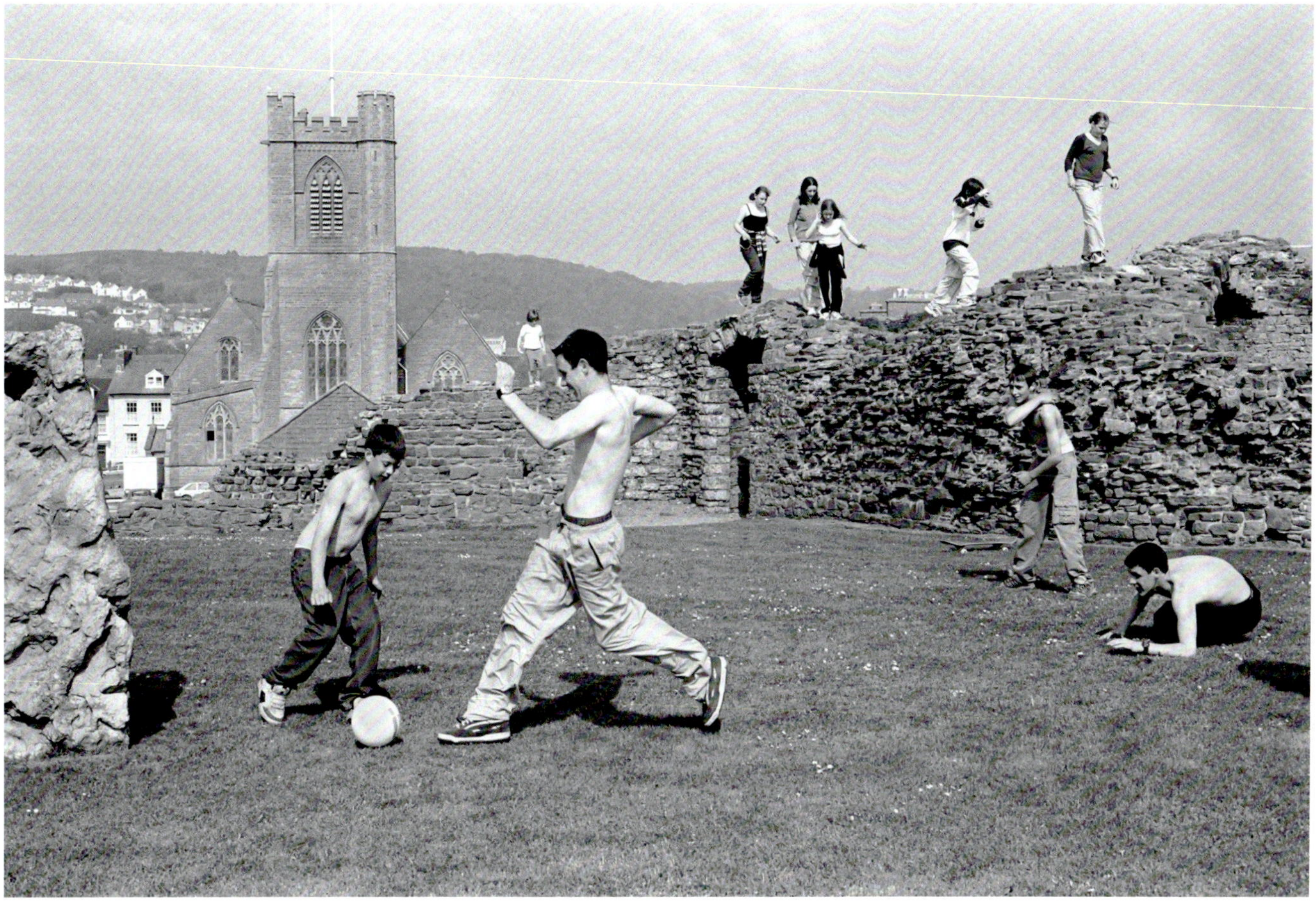

7 FEBRUARY 2022 / HAVE FUN. *ABERYSTWYTH, WALES 2000*

It's strange where thought can come from. I have been walled up at home trying to get through a series of dizzy spells. I listen to a lot of music, mainly BBC classical. I was intrigued to hear that part of the influence for Beethoven's *Tempest* sonatas, Op.21, was to write to test out the limits of latest technology.

I began to think about technical advances in photography.

The dry plate, the Leica, digital photography and the iPhone, etc.

From when I first started looking at magazines, I remember a picture of an owl in flight by Eric Hosking. He started as a photographer in 1929 photographing mainly birds. Birds were mainly photographed at the nest because the camera needed to be pre-focussed to where the subject was expected to be. The light sensitivity of the film was very low, about ISO 10. His pictures were very popular, his *Birds of the Day*, published in 1944, sold more than 50,000 copies. He gave many lectures, often 100 in a year to audiences of up to 3,000. Boy, have we gone backwards. He kept up with innovation as needed, he was the first person to use electronic flash to record birds in flight.

Miriam Rothschild wrote of him, 'Eric Hosking brought birds into all our lives. He opened our eyes to the beauty of their world, their grace and fascination. He probably achieved more for avian conservation than any other naturalist of our day.'

One of my favourite all time pictures – the picture to hang longest on my wall – is by Dr Harold Edgerton, a professor of electrical engineering at MIT. He obtained a patent for the stroboscope – a high-powered repeatable flash device, in 1949.

If you could stop time, here is what you might see: a bullet being shot through an apple, an amazing picture that made me see the essence of what photography is about. It showed me that a bullet shot through an apple caused visually the same explosion when it entered the apple as when it passed out. I am still amazed every time I see it.

Doc Edgerton's philosophy, 'Work hard. Tell everyone everything you know. Close a deal with a handshake. Have fun!'

@davidhurnphoto @magnumphotos

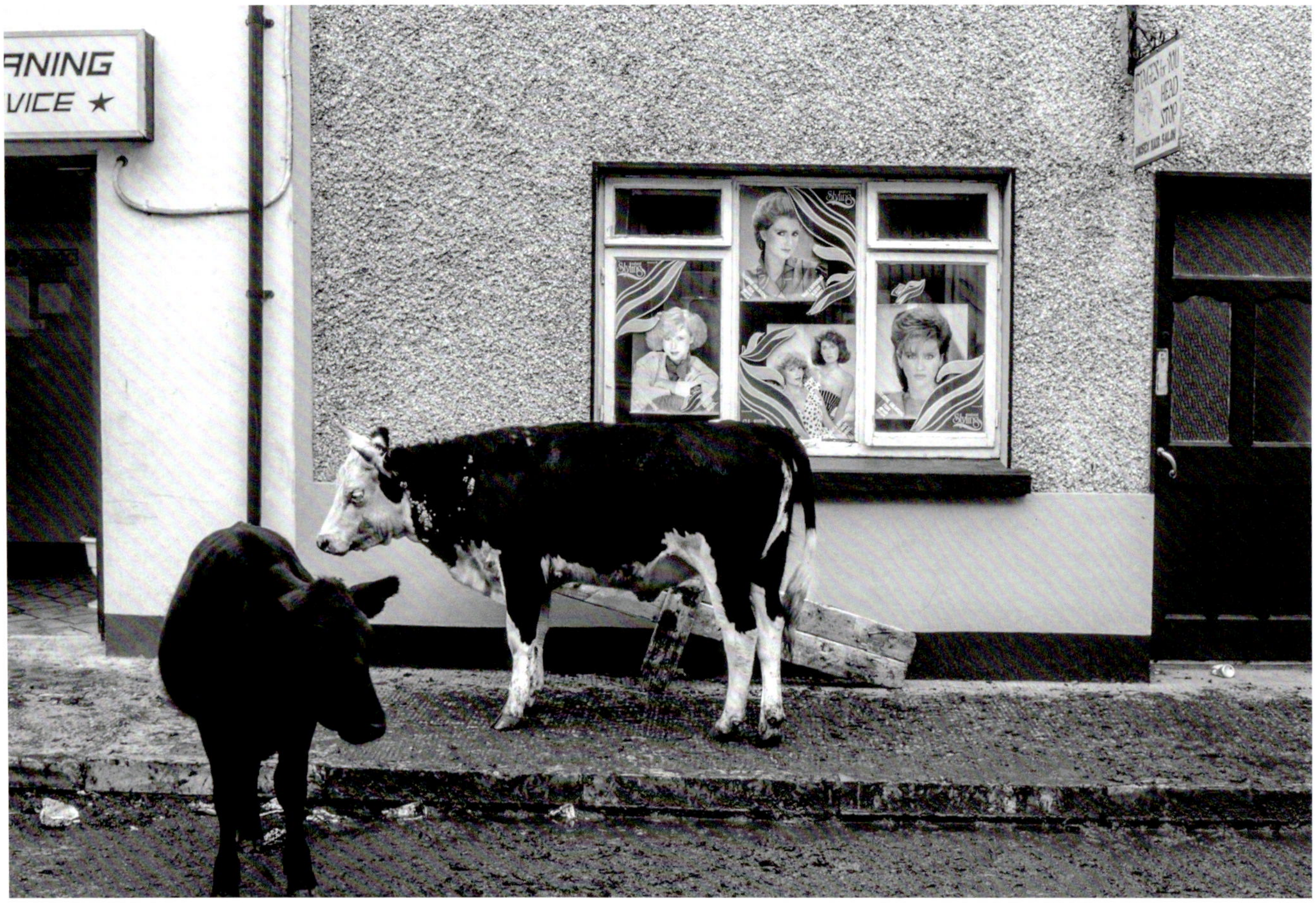

14 FEBRUARY 2022 / KILLARNEY HAIRDRESSER. *IRELAND 1984*

At last I have had my haircut. I was beginning to look like many photographers' subject matter when they visit Kentucky for the first time.

I hope I am not judgemental. I try not to be critical of other persons' pictures, it's the reason I do not do portfolio reviews or ever act as a judge – well, maybe at the local carnival fete.

I am, however, intolerant of technical incompetence. I was recently looking forward to a worldwide Zoom talk – an interview with a photographer, who I think is one of the very best photographers still working, a person of knowledge and passion, well worth listening to and learning from. The sound was totally inadequate, I could hardly understand a word said. There can be no excuses. Sound is difficult but professionals, I presume the set up was run by professionals, should know what to do – basically connect up the correct equipment into the correct slots. I was so disappointed.

However, sometimes I am puzzled by, what seems to me, over indulgence in 'quality' for quality's sake. I remember coming out from seeing my first Ansel Adams exhibition, and realising I didn't remember a single picture – only the 'quality' of the prints. Very black blacks, very white whites but the whole not really looking real. Maybe real is not for everyone – it is for me.

I continually hear young photographers complain about monetary problems but in their next breath paying what I would call fortunes on frames. I can't remember ever going to an exhibition and feeling I should examine the frames.

Maybe I am very lax – I tend to shoot on auto, download into Lightroom and then press the auto button there. However, my special screen is very accurate and checked at least twice a week, my printer very high-end, and the paper the best and rather expensive.

Not infrequently, I get told, 'lovely prints'.

I then worry the pictures aren't interesting enough.

@davidhurnphoto @magnumphotos #nonfictionphotography #anseladams

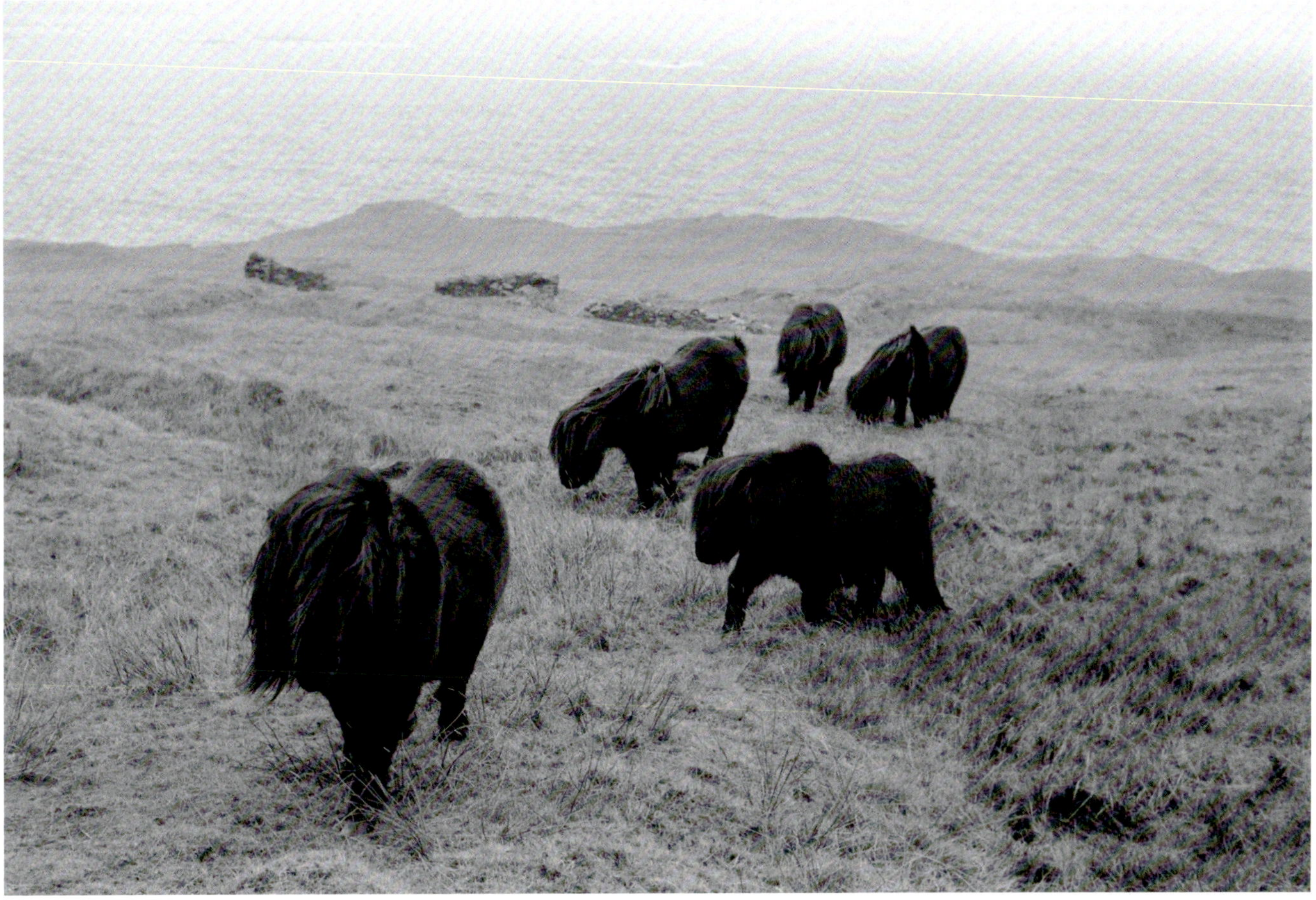

21 FEBRUARY 2022 / SHETLAND. *SCOTLAND 1967*

'Now the years are rolling by me. They are rocking evenly. I am older than I once was and younger than I'll be; that's not unusual. Nor is it strange. After changes upon changes, we are more or less the same'. – Paul Simon.

I now find small nudges often link me to memories. A recent reply, to a previous post, comments, 'I was wondering about lenses the other day. Some are so sharp the images almost look "too real" or "hyper real" if that's such a thing?'

I was invited to participate in an extremely well-organised photo event, 'A Day in the Life of London'. One hundred photographers were to photograph in London on Wednesday, 14 September, 1983. Among those asked to participate was one of my 'heroes', André Kertész, then aged 89. I cut my shooting participation in half so as to meet him, we had breakfast together and later we wandered around Hyde Park – by the way, I think his resulting picture was one of the most representative of self in the resulting book. We talked a lot, me mainly asking questions, and letting him ramble. Among other gems he suggested 'lenses are now "crazy sharp"', he wished he still had his original camera.

In a sense I agree. In recent talks with a Fuji technical member who was talking about 'more pixels' I remember offering, 'I don't want more. I have enough'.

I plan backwards. I live in a small cottage. The largest printer I can cope with will make a 24x36 inch print. How many pixels do I need to make this? – Well, certainly less than I have from my camera at the moment.

I love the actual prints of Cartier-Bresson, Robert Frank, Sergio Larrain, all have a sort of 'soft feel'. My favourite all time book is *London 1959*, photos by Sergio Larrain, published by Thames & Hudson. Very simple layout, beautiful printing, yet every picture looks veiled or out of focus. Perfect.

@davidhurnphoto @magnumphotos @thamesandhudson #nonfictionphotography #henricartierbresson #robertfrank #sergiolarrain

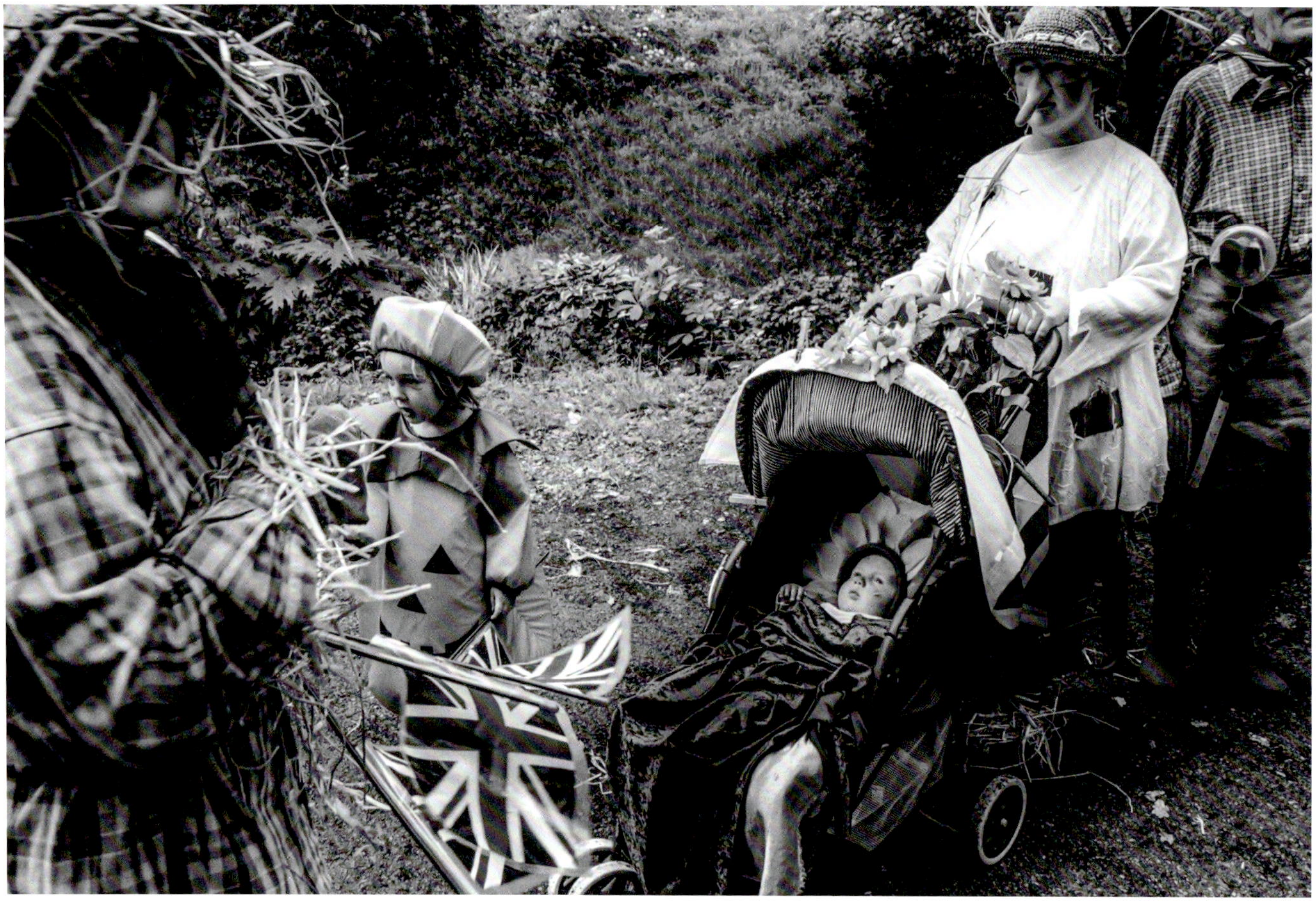

31 MARCH 2022 / FESTIVAL. *TINTERN, WALES 2002*

Finally I have sallied forth. London. All booked online, all seamless – how quickly conventions move on, much of my mind still clings to the past. Train nine minutes late, some things don't change.

A two years' break, my first visit is to the Magnum office to absorb changes. Mid-morning tea and scones have been laid on for me, a packed group sitting around a white table, doing business but awaiting me. I am flabbergasted – the world seems so young: I remember my father commenting that policemen seemed to be getting younger.

Only four I knew. I chatted to all one by one – a quick pic (by camera not by iPhone) to remember who was who – they were all so bright, so enthusiastic – I am in good loving hands, perhaps we are family again? I still have no idea what each does. They all have titles but language has also changed and I am not up to date: the word 'digital' is prominent, as is 'producer', 'co-ordinator', none of which clarifies much for me. Individual jobs seem to have been replaced by 'teams'. This seems progressive and positive. Am I worried? No. They breed trust. The future of Magnum is positive in their hands.

In the evening I go to an exhibition and gallery opening. James Hyman has a new space in Maddox Street. A strange layout on different floors with stairs and corridors very prominent – it feels intimate. I was impressed.

The opening exhibition is *Telling stories: Picture Post and its Legacy*. – Some of the key photographers of *Picture Post* magazine and a curated selection of some later British photographers of documentary tradition, including me – what's not to like? In person at the opening – meeting in the flesh is always the most important and enjoyable happening at openings – Anna Fox, Brian Griffin, Dafydd Jones, Charlie Phillips, Homer Sykes. Of course, many others are no longer with us, still they are lucky and live on with their pictures, a lucky bonus of our profession.

Beautiful pictures, all about something, refreshing, very well worth a visit.

@davidhurnphoto @magnumphotos @jameshymangallery @annafox61 @brian_griffin_photographer @dafyddjonesphotographer @charlierootsfoto @homer.sykes

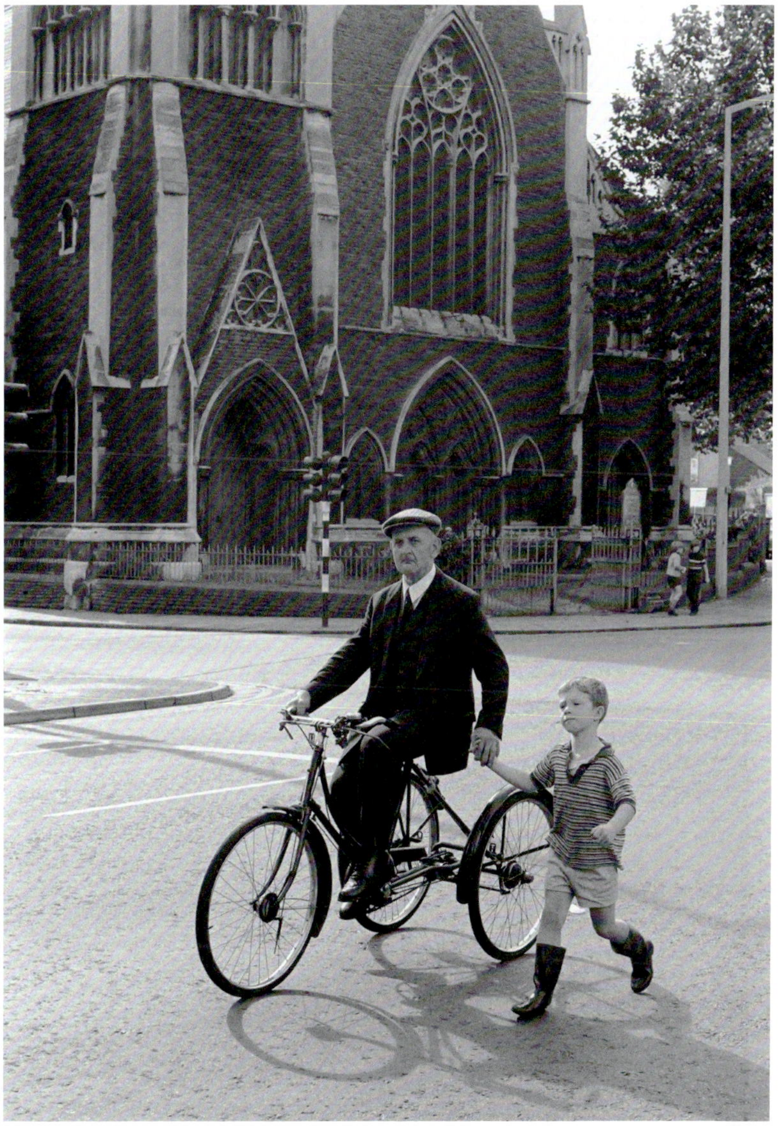

4 APRIL 2022 / SUNDAY STROLL. *CARDIFF, WALES 1973*

There is much value in networking. At the Hyman gallery opening I met Duncan Forbes, Head of Photography at the V&A and Fiona Rogers, the inaugural Parasol Women in Photography curator – or rather, I already knew Fiona from her innovative time at Magnum, so she introduced me to Duncan. Whatever, it was arranged to have a guided tour of the V&A photography section the next day.

Duncan has been overseeing photography development at the V&A, and now the second phase of the project will add a further four rooms, interactive features, and a reading room dedicated to photographic books. It seems the V&A are supporting photography big time. When the new gallery is finished it will be of international significance. You have the space, what do you put into it? How does one see a collection of 800,000 prints, a puzzle. Certainly not quickly. The two shows that are on at the moment are there for two years – yes, two years – I presume to do with building works.

Museums seem to have rules on light, the spaces are very dim, pictures are spotlighted, all too reverential for my taste. Luckily, what for me is the main exhibition, Maurice Broomfield, is in no way pompous. He was a working photographer dealing mainly with industry – he happened to be very good and his pictures will last the test of time. I enjoyed the broadness of the exhibition, on show besides some outstanding pictures were contacts, layouts, his cameras, it all added up to a complete experience. Why do some establishments think of archives as only pictures?

The other space was mainly newly acquired pictures, most of which were not to my taste. Still 50 percent is OK by me. I recommend going.

On the other side of the road is the Natural History Museum and on show *Wildlife Photographer of the Year*. I was amazed by the vision and nature knowledge in the 'Under Ten' section. Within the grown-ups I coveted a drone shot showing the difference in canopy of a forest and the growth in a crater in its centre. Such clear information. A great show for anyone over three years old.

@davidhurnphoto @magnumphotos @vamuseum @natural_history_museum @firecracker_foto #mauricebroomfield #duncanforbes

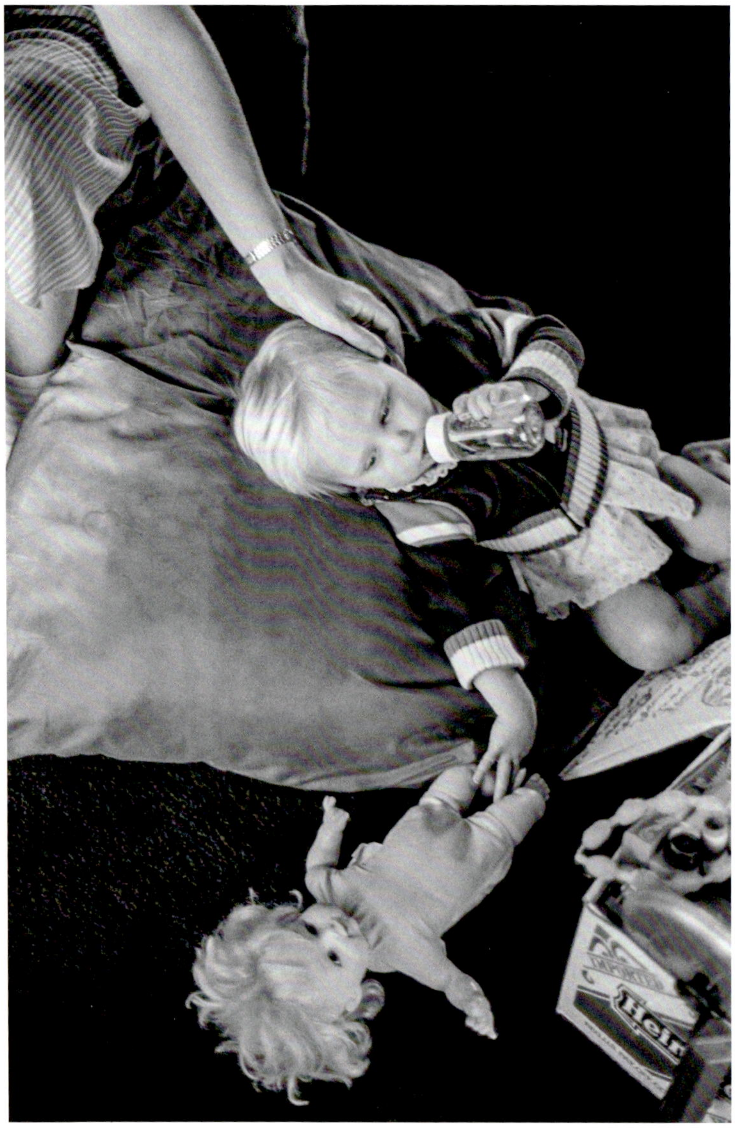

18 APRIL 2022 / TOUCHING. *CALIFORNIA, USA 1980*

It is worth repeating, 'Photographs bring back memories'.

I so remember that hand – the child must now be in their late 40s – does the doll still exist?

Last Thursday I attended the ultimate memory jogger, a celebration of 'zines' by Café Royal Books at the Martin Parr Foundation (MPF). It is magnificent.

Craig Atkinson founded Café Royal Books in 2005 and produces weekly publications focusing on post-war documentary photography linked to Britain and Ireland, in an accessible and affordable zine format. This show presents 300 zines (of the 550 so far produced), exhibited alongside 167 prints from work CRB has published.

During my lifetime in photography I have seen the work of many whose images I have enjoyed. Often these photographers seem to reach a plateau and then disappear, one suspects for very definable reasons. Most have not had the recognition they might have hoped. Craig has remedied this. With extraordinary research and dedication CRB seems to have been able to find these talents and has thus documented, for posterity, what was achieved. Intermingled is also the work of some who managed to survive the pace.

I would be happy to defend the proposition that CRB are the most important publishers for promoting photography of the UK. Every museum, arts organisation, government arts department, should have a complete set as a starting reference point.

Twenty yards away The Royal Photographic Society are hosting their *International Photography Exhibition*. Now in its 163rd edition. The selected photographs were chosen from a worldwide open call in which over 3,944 photographers from 114 countries entered. A total of 105 works are shown. I particularly liked the studio portraits of Alys Tomlinson, North London teenagers and Aneesa Dawoojee, sports people. I would be happy to have their lenses 'invade my space'.

@davidhurnphoto @magnumphotos @caferoyalbooks @craigatkinson @martinparrfdn @royalphotographicsociety @alystomlinson @aneesaimages

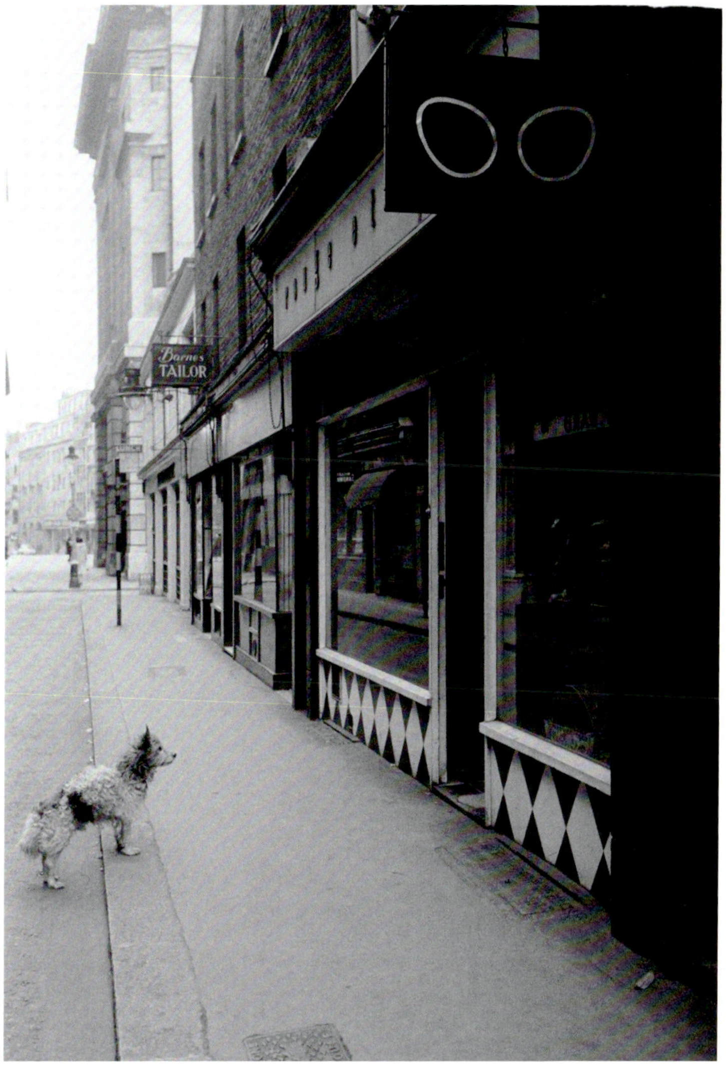

20 JUNE 2022 / WAITING. *LONDON, ENGLAND 1959*

I must be appearing very frail. On a recent trip to London I found that others continually offered to carry my case up and down stairs, and on the underground, someone always offered me their seat. I thank them all, it makes trips so much more enjoyable. People are kind.

Out of the blue I was in London for a rather surreal 'secret' assignment. I really enjoyed it.

I spent an extra day visiting an exhibition at the Barbican, I think it was called *New Art in Britain 1945-1965*. I am not sure as the cover of the accompanying brochure seemed designed to confuse. Mainly on show were paintings, some sculpture, far too few ceramics, and far too little photography.

I am not a great lover of most fussy, abstract paintings, especially when they are accompanied by text that is very subjective and actually puzzles even more.

I was deeply moved by two portraits, a portrait of Jean Cooke, by John Bratby – Jean was his wife – and a portrait of him by her. I found them together very emotional. Also a powerful self portrait by Jean Cooke, titled *Mad Self Portrait*, it tells so much. There was a lovely portrait by Lucian Freud, *Girl with Roses* (his first wife) – I covet this. A discovery was Sylvia Sleigh, a portrait of Lawrence Alloway, Sleigh's very young lover dressed as a bride, the cross dressing was very poignant.

For me the 'star' of the paintings was by Frank Auerbach, a portrait, *Head of Gerda Boehm*. Virtually all white thickly-layered paint, quite remarkable.

The curator obviously does not champion photography. Bert Hardy was hardly shown, two pictures and one cut contact sheet which seemed to have little relevance to the other pictures, surely more could had been made of this great photographer. I wondered why Grace Robertson was not included. Bill Brandt was represented by his nudes, all a bit precious for me – I think his nudes are seen so much better in his book. The revelation was Roger Mayne, I have always rated his pictures but I had seen very few. I feel the selection shown here showed him as a genuinely great photographer.

@davidhurnphoto @magnumphotos #barbican #jeancooke #sylviasleigh #frankauerbach #rogermayne

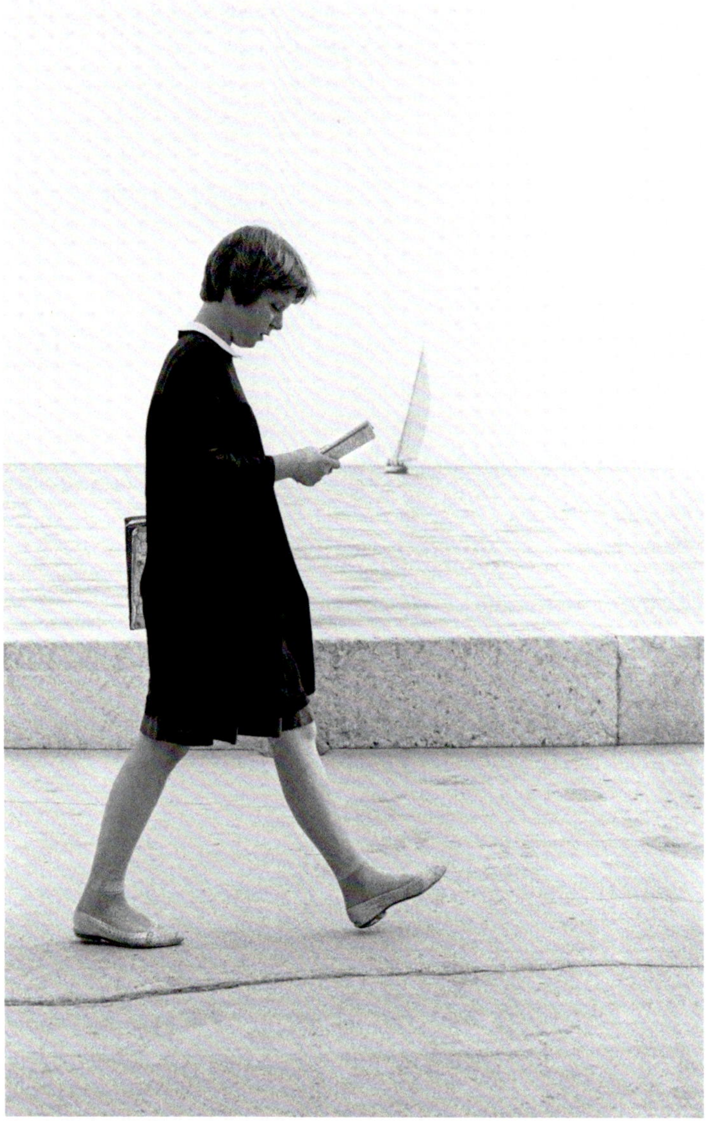

2 AUGUST 2022 / READING. *DUBROVNIK, CROATIA 1964*

Very recently, I was sitting under a tree reading, having a picnic, and contented.

I discovered: 'I will never be an old man. To me, old age is always 15 years older than I am'. – Francis Bacon.

In 2002, botanist David Bellamy signed a certificate giving the age of the Llangernyw Yew in Wales as 4000-5000 years old. Whether this is accurate I do not know, but he was a reputable scientist.

It makes me think. This tree was established long before the initial Roman invasion. It was giving shade slightly pre the pyramids. And I could sit there, for free, having my smoked salmon and cucumber sandwiches and bottled tap water, what a joy of being a photographer.

Taking its picture was easy. After all, there is no point to be proved, or if there was a point it is to do with humanity, its life, the richness of life – just be sensitive.

Please Leave No Litter.

I feel a set of pictures projects the photographer's personality. That is why there is no competition in our work – maybe in the marketplace. Competition does not exist because relaxed, talented people see things differently.

To help clarify my mind I need communication. I love being with people of progressive interests, whatever field they might practice in. I love to know I am not isolated. One keeps learning from each other – reading helps, looking at pictures helps, listening to music helps, listening to the radio helps.

I guess I will shoot more and more about man's effect in/on the landscape – if I get it wrong I can always go back. But I can progress slowly, finding my own pace.

@davidhurnphoto @magnumphotos #nonfictionphotography #davidbellamy #botany #llangernywyew

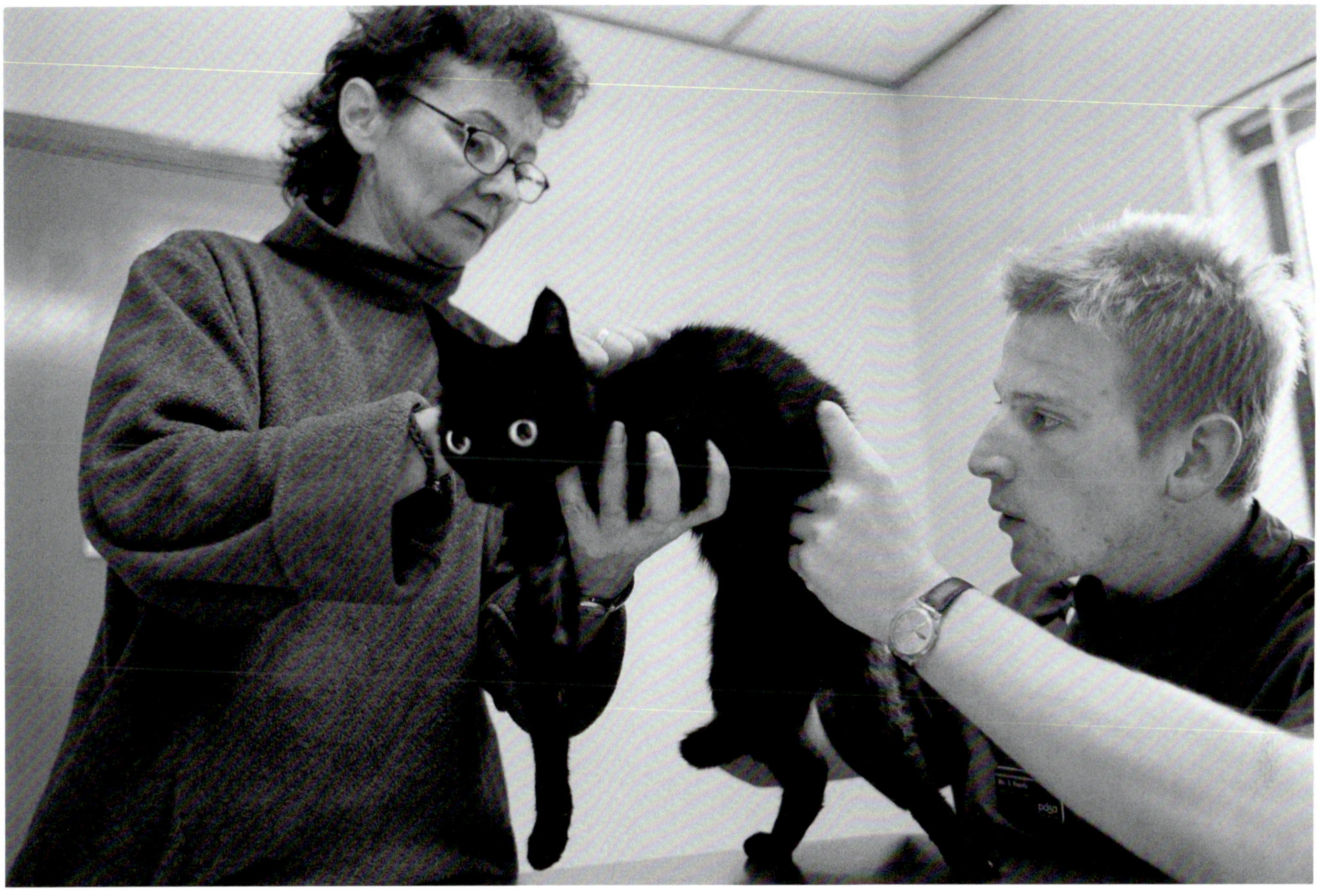

9 AUGUST 2022 / EXPRESSION. *CARDIFF, WALES 2003*

Photography is the only means of expression that fixes forever the precise yet changing moment. Photographers deal in sights that are continually vanishing and, of course, once they have vanished, there is no getting them back.

It's why photography is important, because at the same time that it's great fun simply getting all the components right, it is showing a statement about our world – even though one might not be totally aware as to what one is actually doing at the time.

It's the results that count, and the results are the finished prints; without the print there would be only memories of what might have occurred and memories are often myth.

Occasionally, we get a single image that seems to sum up what had happened. A trace of reality. I'm always hoping to get that one picture about which people will say, 'Ah, this is true. You plucked it right'.

I wish to pass on my visual 'non-fiction' thoughts/feelings. I always shoot as though telling a flowing story – my 'single pictures' come from inside a set. This 'set' approach has to have become instinctive, you must not miss any component part, afterwards is too late.

@davidhurnphoto @magnumphotos #nonfictionphotography

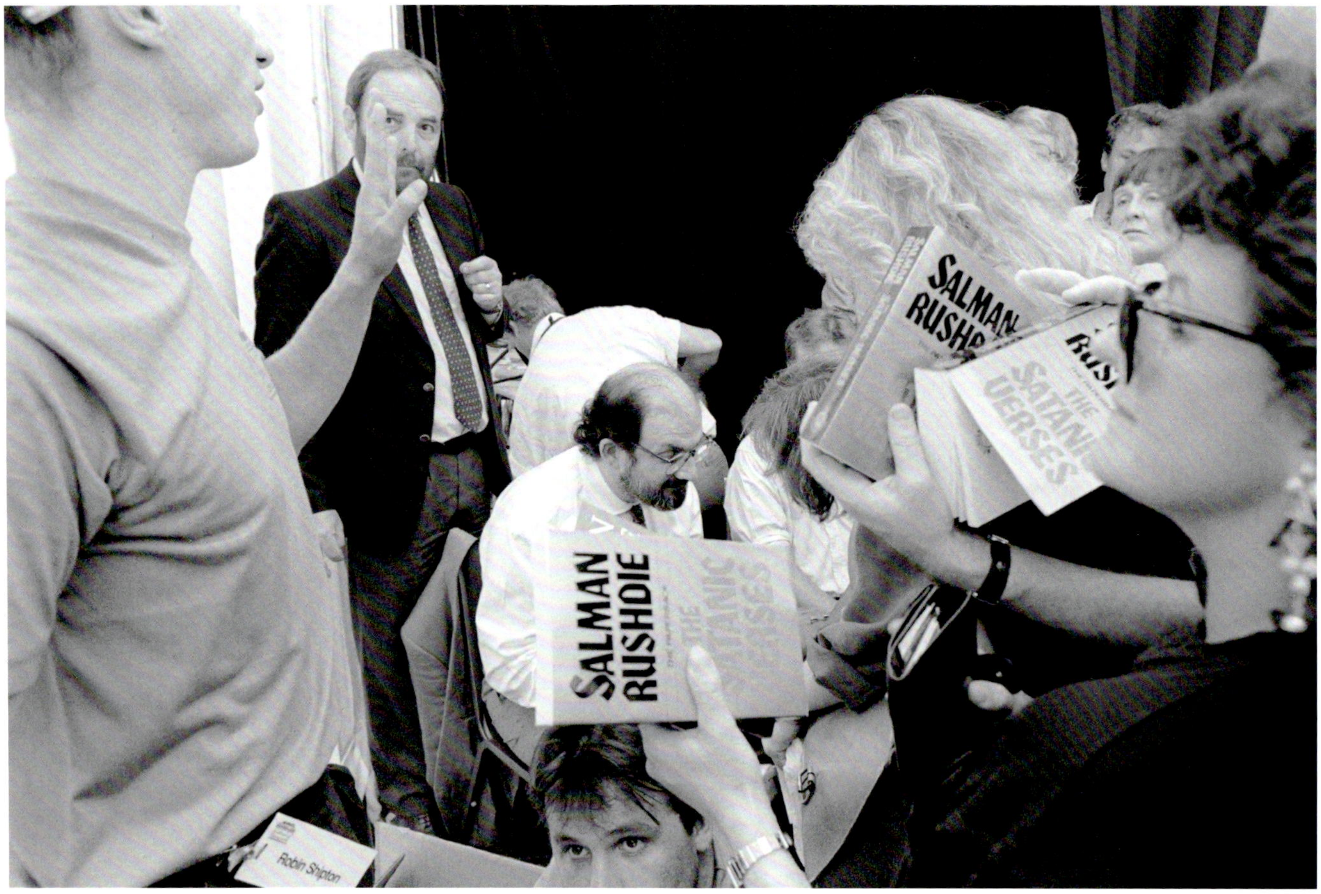

15 AUGUST 2022 / SALMAN RUSHDIE. *HAY-ON-WYE, WALES 1992*

I photographed Salman Rushdie almost by mistake. I was at the Hay Literary Festival in 1992, he was not supposed to be there – his novel, *The Satanic Verses*, had aroused worldwide controversy and promoted death threats. I knew little about him, I certainly had not read any of his writings, but his being there in front of me seemed very brave. Fans are frightening, killer fanatics even more so.

I travel little now but when I did I was always wary of countries that had pictures of their leaders plastered on too many walls. Of countries that waved too many flags – always the suppression of free speech. Am I wrong, but do I sense that there is, as yet tiny, a creeping malaise starting in this country?

I am not a 'believer' but I admire belief but not if it promotes the maiming or killing of someone else, however greatly they offend you or your God.

I hate the banning of books and freedom of speech seemingly creeping into universities.

I hate the hounding of persons on social media, seemingly to promote the hounder but with no willingness to debate.

I have heard of photography lecturers banning their students from talking to established photographers outside the university umbrella. Boy, how insecure can one be?

I disagree with a group of students who told me 'there is no such thing as quality, we are all equal'. Have not Bach, Bruegel, Bresson, Rodin, maybe Rushdie if I had read him – influenced my life? I think for the good. I disagree with the students but do believe it's their sincere point of view – what worries me is it totally stifles debate.

I suppose all the above is why I love photography that keeps to its core values. The destination of photography is to reveal what something or someone looked like, under a particular set of conditions, at a particular moment in time and to transmit the result to others. It must be accurate, it must be honest, it must be clear.

@davidhurnphoto @magnumphotos #nonfictionphotography #salmanrushdie

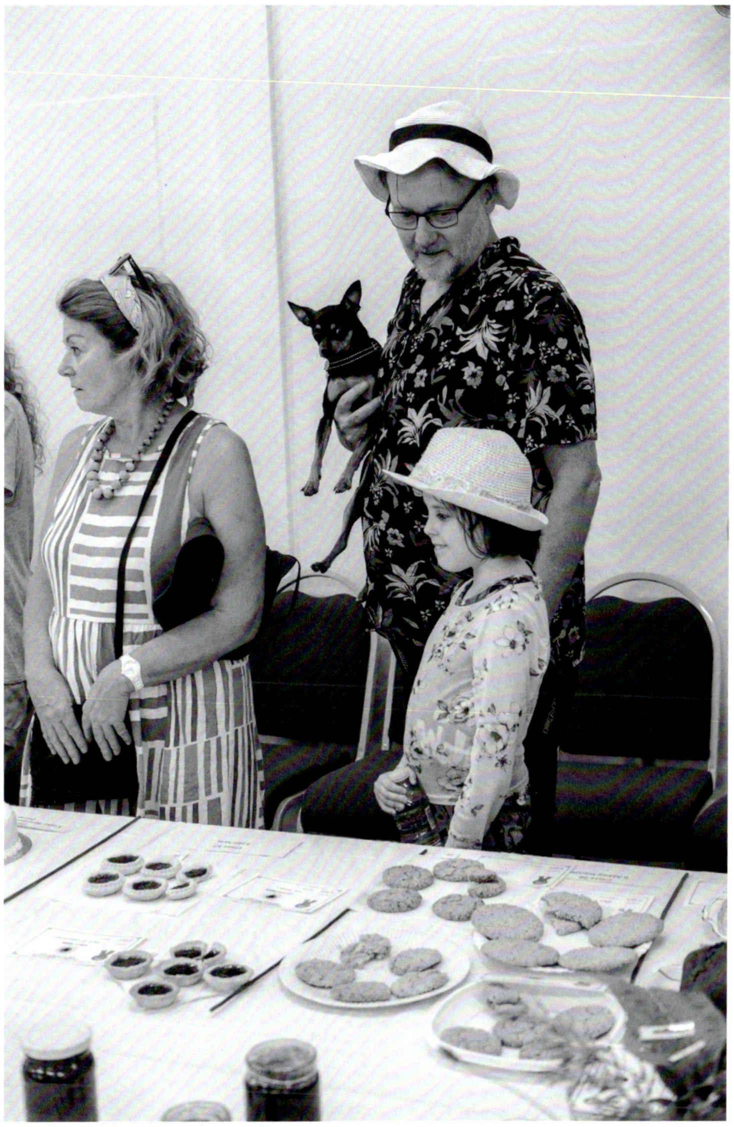

22 AUGUST 2022 / GARDEN CLUB PRODUCE SHOW. *TINTERN, WALES 2022*

You are not a photographer because you are interested in photography.

I think too many 'teachers', workshops, books etc, imply that how a picture is made, what techniques were employed, why it looks different and artistic, is more important than the subject matter. Yet I am sure the most interesting photographers are actually subject-selectors.

So what to photograph is the first decision. This curiosity should lead to intense examination, reading, talking, and many failed attempts over a long period of time.

Your curiosity, fascination and enthusiasm for this subject can be communicated to others through the pictures you take of it.

Taking my own advice I always carry a notebook, ballpoint and highlighter.

If I hear, see, absorb anything that takes my fancy I note it down. Don't worry if it does or doesn't relate to photography. Later, when you have time or the urge, you filter down.

Self questions:

Is it visual? You can eliminate anything touching philosophy or the abstract, thought is difficult to see.

Is it practical? If you can't afford it you can't do it.

Is it a subject about which I know enough? Be cautious of exploitation rather than exploration.

Is it of interest to others? From your crowded notebook, if you are lucky, you will be left with a couple of possibilities. You have shown yourself they all have equal interest to you and are possible to do, so – select the topic which others are more likely to have interest in viewing – some things are more interesting to look at than others.

Above all, make the idea 'simple'. No outline, either in the head or written, should take up more than a couple of lines of text.

One of my permanently ongoing projects is documenting my village. It ticks all the above boxes. The village website gives it voice.

@davidhurnphoto @magnumphotos #nonfictionphotography #gardening tinternvillage.co.uk

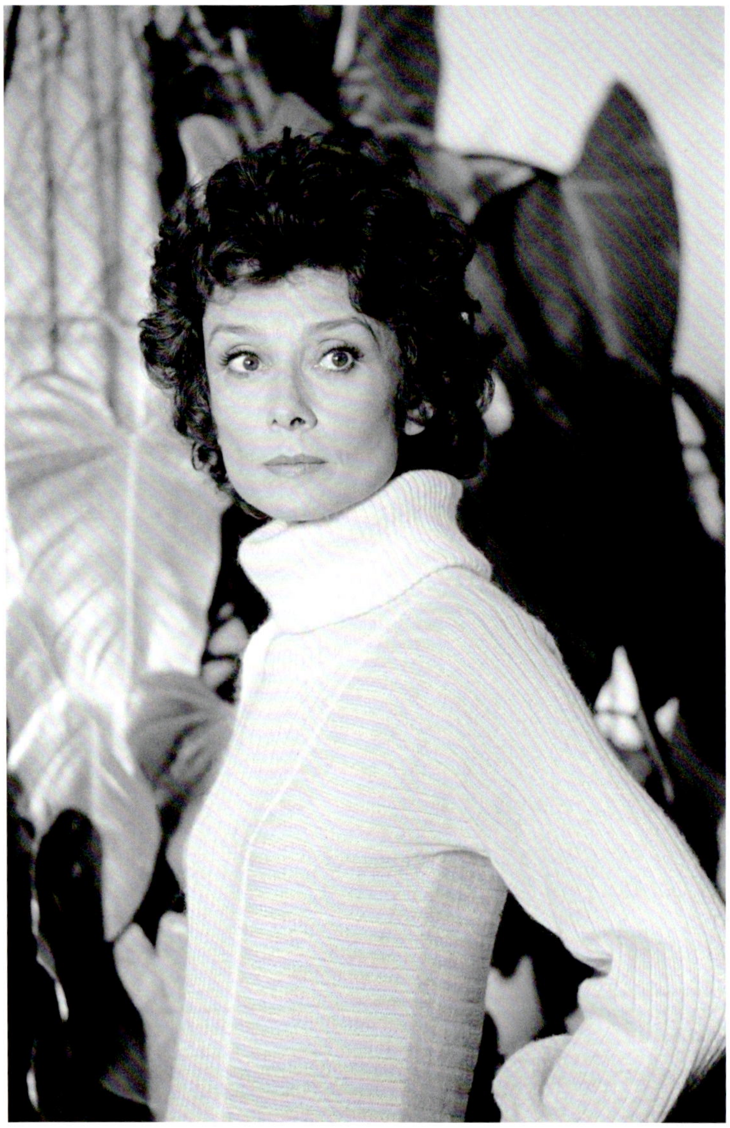

29 AUGUST 2022 / AUDREY HEPBURN. *SARDINIA, ITALY 1978*

Last night on TV, I re-saw the film *Roman Holiday*. It brought back memories.

In 1978 I was asked to go to, I think, Burghausen, to photograph Audrey Hepburn coming up to her 50th birthday.

I am sure the only time I was ever genuinely star struck was then at our first meeting. She was so polite, so beautiful, so elegant yet seemingly vulnerable, a powerful combination.

I don't smoke, my first confusion was when I heard/saw she increased her smoking habit to 60 cigarettes a day when filming.

When we knew each other better, she confided she was actually only paid $12,500 (1953) to do *Roman Holiday* – she also offered, oft quoted 'I was asked to act when I couldn't act. I was asked to sing "Funny Face" when I couldn't sing, I was asked to dance with Fred Astaire when I couldn't dance . . . I simply tried like mad to cope with it, basically, hard work'. By the way, she spoke five languages: English, French, Spanish,Italian and Dutch. Yet she was the most modest of persons.

So often 'hard work' comes into my posts.

Photographers depend so much upon the relations they establish with the people they are photographing, it is a strange relationship, a wrong word or attitude can ruin everything. When the subject is in any way uneasy, the personality goes away where the camera can't reach it.

When relationships work the photograph offers itself up. In a way, the photo takes you. The creative part of photography is very short. A painter can embellish, a writer can embellish, but we have to pick that moment, that essential moment, if it is there.

In 2002, at the United Nations Special Session on Children, UNICEF honoured Hepburn's legacy of humanitarian work by unveiling a statue, 'The Spirit of Audrey', at the New York headquarters.

Since Hepburn's death, her grave site in Tolochenaz, Vaud, Switzerland is one of the biggest tourist attractions throughout Europe. People from all over the world visit it, garnering hundreds of thousands of people year round.

@davidhurnphoto @magnumphotos #nonfictionphotography #audreyhepburn

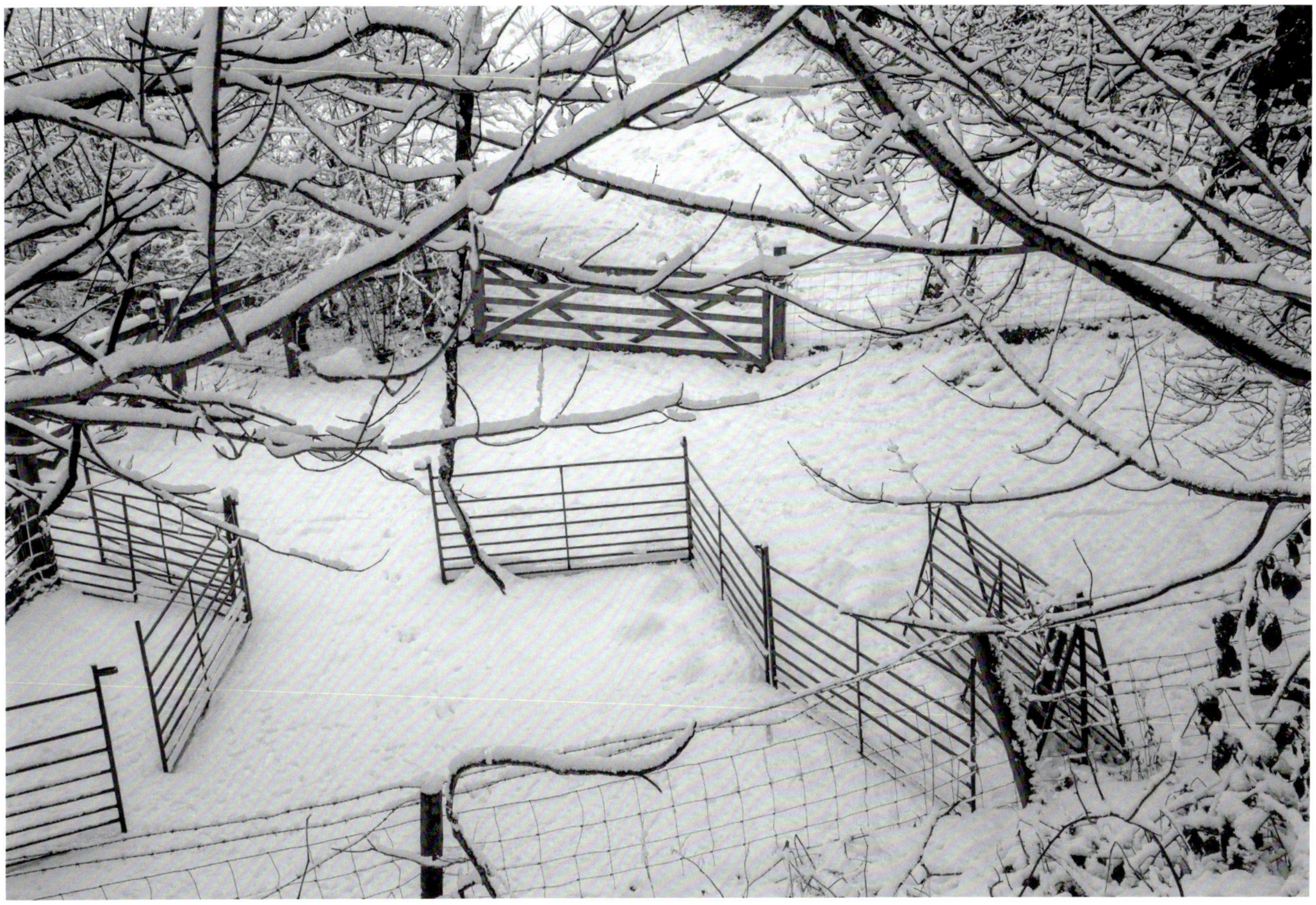

8 NOVEMBER 2022 / TINTERN LANDSCAPE. *TINTERN, WALES 2010*

Why do we have books? To enjoy pictures; to learn from pictures; for research; because they were given as a present by friends; for investment; for collecting like postage stamps; etc, etc?

I think I have books primarily for the enjoyment of looking at what others see, and for research. In both cases, books need to be used and not simply take up space.

When I started dabbling in photography very few books were published. We, who called ourselves photographers, bought every one.

The Decisive Moment, Henri Cartier-Bresson (1952); *Observations*, Richard Avedon; *The Americans*, Robert Frank; *Aaron Siskind Photographs* (all 1959); *Moments Preserved*, Irving Penn (1960); *Perspective of Nudes*, Bill Brandt (1961); *A Way of Seeing*, Helen Levitt (1965); *Every Building on the Sunset Strip*, Ed Ruscha; *Shadow of Light*, Bill Brandt (both 1966). The buying of a book was an event, it provoked dinners and discussion.

They are all still there on my 'Library One' shelf, all very well thumbed. Others were added, Arbus, Atget, Walker Evans, all on the shelves with the above.

My library has two other parts: Two and Three, 'Three' actually in another room; Two are those books that I think there is a possibility of viewing one day in the future, in practice very unlikely; 'Three' is those books I suspect I will never look at again; One sometimes gets relegated to Two, seldom the other way.

This explanation is because I am delighted to add two more books to One.

A Photographic Friendship, pictures by James Ravilious and Chris Chapman, edited by Mark Haworth-Booth, and *Four Winters*, pictures by Jem Southam.

I will expand on the two books in my next effort in about a week.

@davidhurnphoto @magnumphotos @avedonfoundation @markhayworthbooth @jemsoutham #nonfictionphotography #robertfrank #henricartierbresson #billbrandt #helenlevitt #jamesravilious #chrischapman

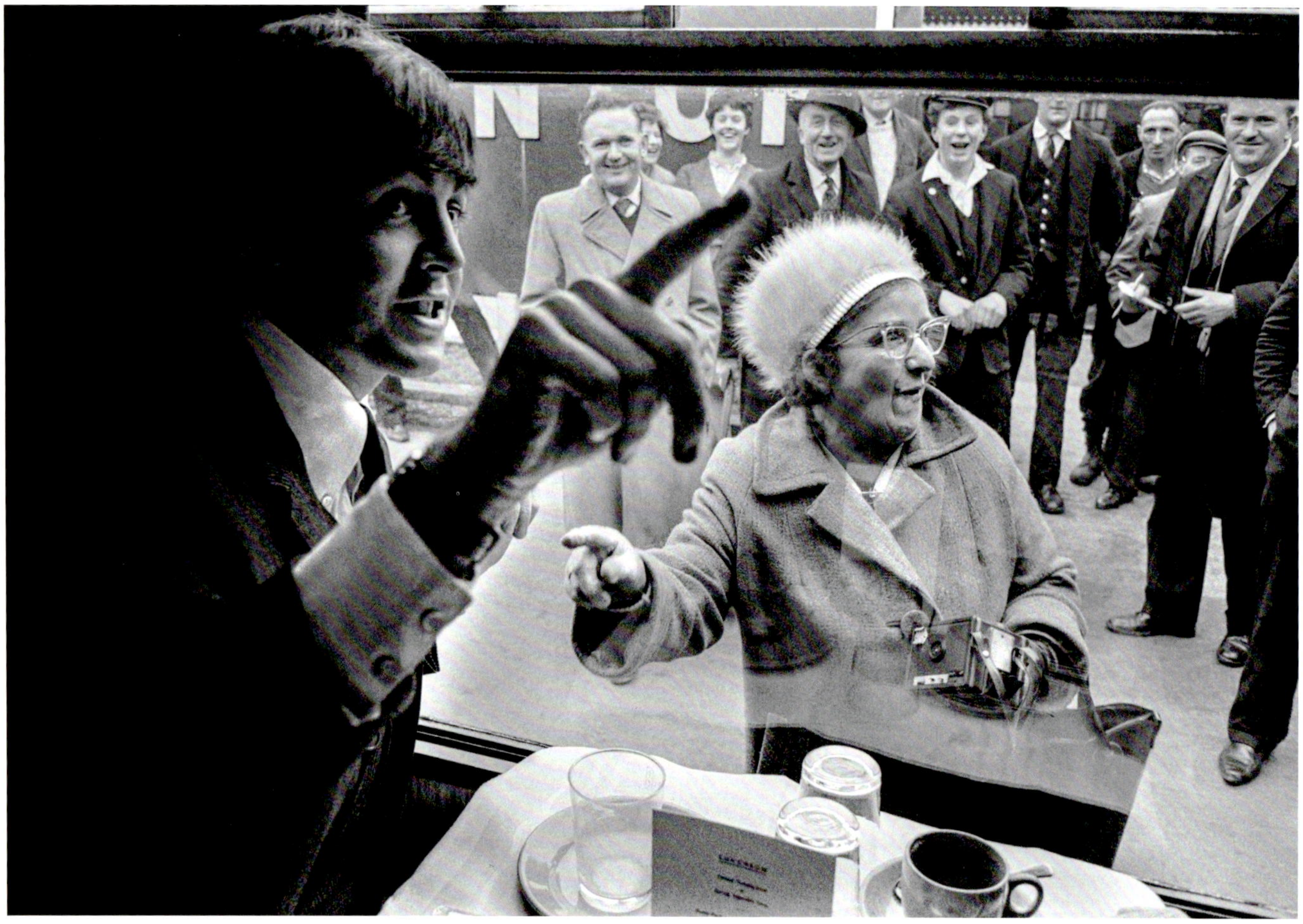

29 NOVEMBER 2022 / VISITOR. *ENGLAND, UK 1964*

I have often suggested that, besides a camera, the most important tool for the photographer is their shoes. Photographers walk a lot, I wish I could walk more. Although I don't think I am overweight, I would gain by losing ten pounds, it could be comparatively easy if it was not for the overwhelming kindness of many people, visitors continually bring me cake. I feel obliged to eat with them and that equates with another session at the gym. I just wish people would not bring me stuff – I don't drink alcohol, never have, but anyone looking at my kitchen shelves would think I was an alcoholic. On one shelf alone I have, Tobermory whisky single malt, Glenfiddich 12 Year Old single malt, William Grant whisky, Croft Late Bottled 2004 Vintage Port, Stock Slivovice – I suspect this was brought by Koudelka for his own use on frequent visits to the cottage, Mount Gay brandy, Mount Gay rum, all unopened and this is only one shelf of three. The latest gift phase seems to be plants, a real nightmare as they need perpetual care and that in a home where I am continually trying to get rid of stuff to own, or stuff to do.

Please don't get me wrong, I love getting visitors, however haphazard; that someone puts themselves out to ring my bell is lovely. Tintern is an attractive village for a visit and many know where I live. Most get a positive response, but if I am busy, after a cup of coffee, I will say so. I just wish that someone generously giving their time to say hello would know that's more than enough to give and is very appreciated.

I enjoy conversation, particularly if visitors wish to discuss ideas they wish to pursue – I am good at expanding ideas and enjoy the game – nowadays anything that stretches my thought process is good for me.

Please keep coming, but please don't bring anything other than yourself.

I did have one particularly dear friend that came down for the weekend complete with vacuum cleaner, mops, cloths and bottles, having decided she 'liked' cleaning.

@davidhurnphoto @magnumphotos #nonfictionphotography

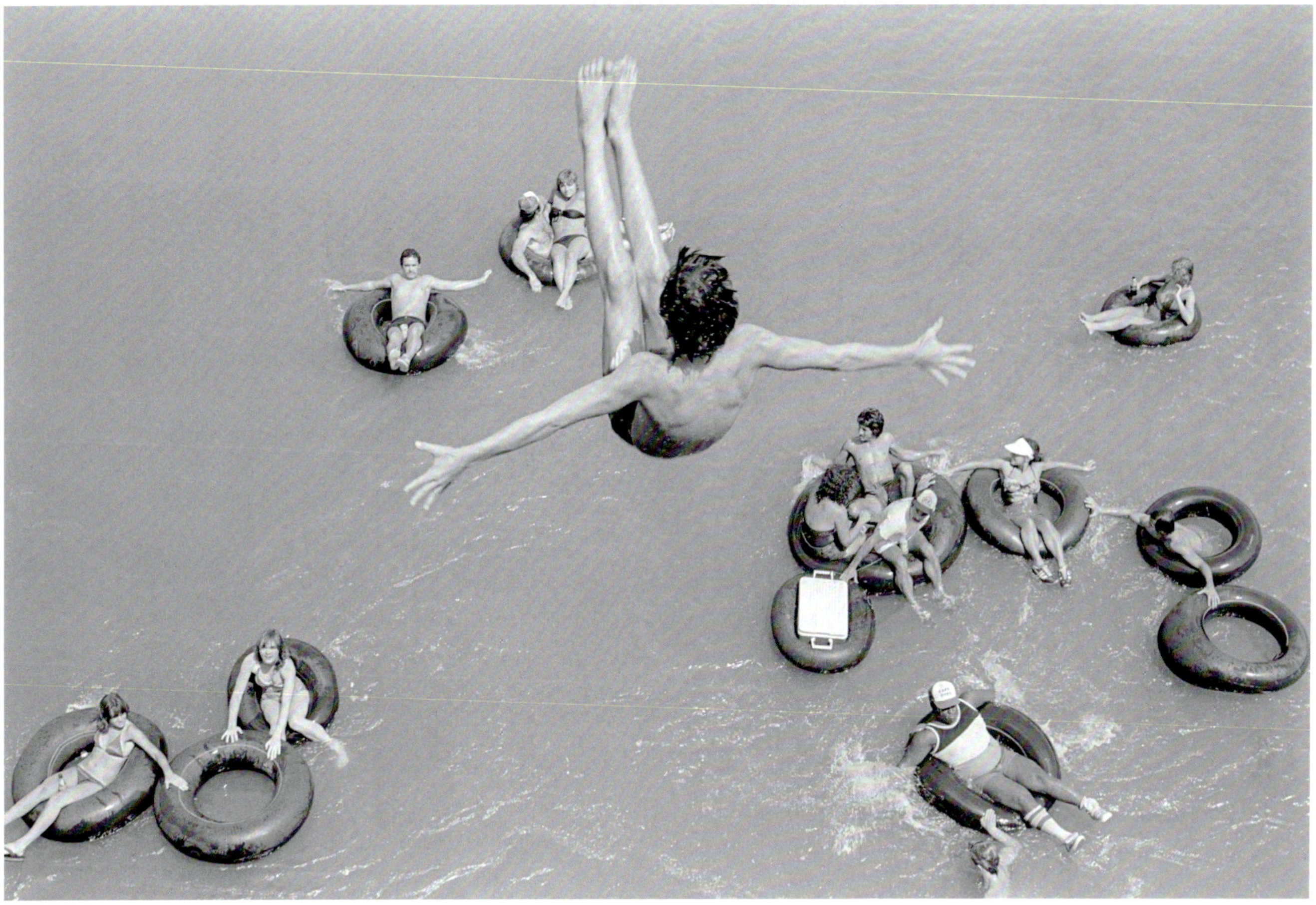

8 DECEMBER 2022 / FREEDOM. *ARIZONA, USA 1980*

I have had an enriching past week. First I heard the BBC Reith Lecture – first of four – the first lecture was by Chimamanda Ngozi Adichie, to my shame someone I did not know of, she is a Nigerian writer. She explored freedom of speech in what I think the most perfect lecture I have ever heard, clear and erudite and with deep passion. Please all look it up. Boy, is the BBC licence fee a gift.

I went up to London – by train, a painful experience, cancelled trains even though not a strike day. Usual excuses, signals or points – how can we in 2022 have signals and points that don't work? Anyway, in the end it was worth it. It was my 'groups' team Christmas party. It was wonderful, full of bright young people, I am in good hands. I chickened out when karaoke started – I did not wish to show everyone up!

I spent most of the day trying to mimic Sergio Larrain's pictures from the top of a bus – total disaster.

Then to the National Gallery, here to see the Lucian Freud exhibition. What an inspiring painter. I am fascinated by his consistent authorship even as he moves from early pencil and crayon to the final large pictures, mainly nudes, often plus animals – I loved these – among all a beautiful picture of buttercups.

Lucian Freud wrote, 'I go to the National Gallery rather like going to a doctor for help'. I think that is wonderful.

I guess I would go to the same place. So many great works to be inspired by that Constable's *The Hay Wain* is tucked away in a corner and could be easily missed.

Sadly, I have to admit that photography will never be of the stature to warrant a museum of its own. The best we can expect is a few – critic-chosen – works being reluctantly let into other museums.

@davidhurnphoto @magnumphotos #nonfictionphotography #chimamandangoziadichie #reithlecture #freedom

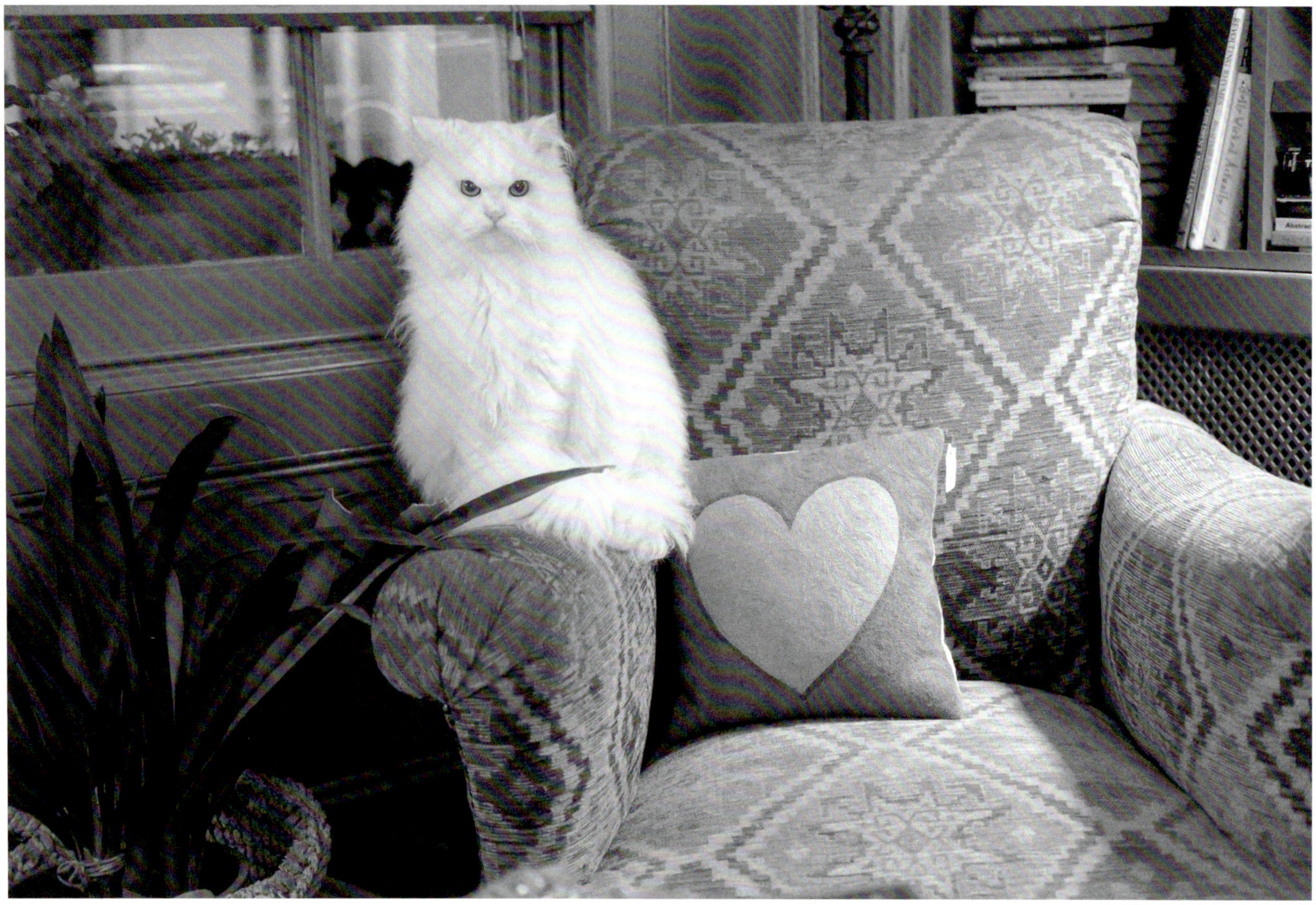

14 DECEMBER 2022 / WHITE CHRISTMAS. *ENGLAND, UK 2016*

The last post certainly had interesting responses – many places for me to check out – however, I am still to be convinced there will ever be a dedicated museum with dedicated space, showing permanent pictures from the history of photography on show.

Someone suggested, 'Maybe photo books are the museum of photography'. I see a lot of potential merit in this idea. Books of paintings are rarely totally satisfying – much of the attraction of painting is the paint surface and the use of paint. You can't see this on a flat page. Photography does not have this problem – I would argue that book printing can now be as good as an actual print – in some cases better – I have even argued that in some ways exhibitions are redundant except for personal gratification, or hopefully, for a mass, probably uninformed, audience. The problem with books is that there are too many of them. Most certainly will not stand the test of time. Museums of painting and sculpture tend to show only the best of the best and that's very enriching and informative to see and ponder.

I am afraid that I might be a bit elitist. I feel a possible definition of the best, in any field, is that it uplifts. The not so good tends to depress and stultify.

@davidhurnphoto @magnumphotos #nonfictionphotography

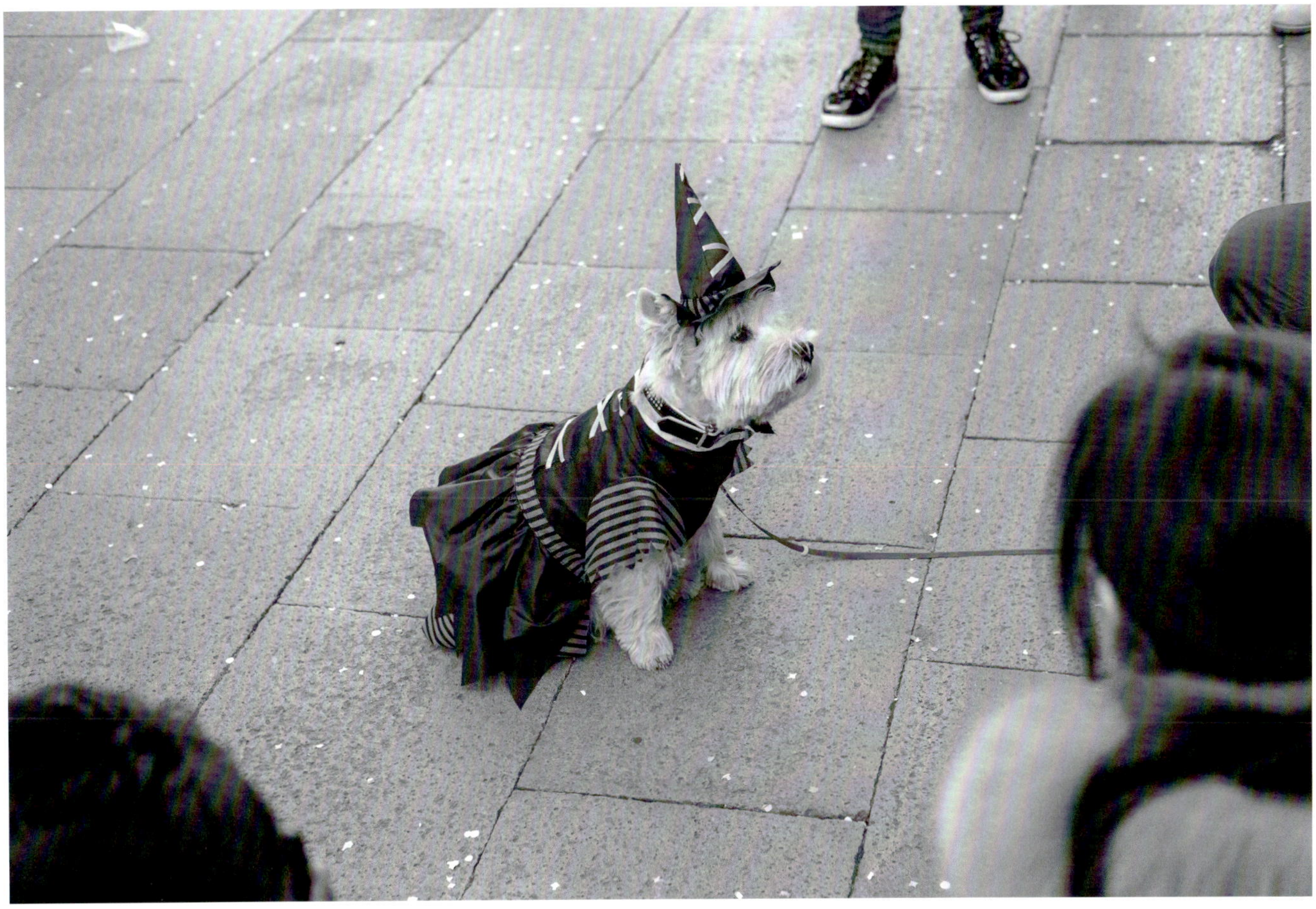

28 DECEMBER 2022 / CURIOSITY VENICE. *AVEBURY, ENGLAND 1993*

I see my scratchings primarily as pointing a finger. I hope not too many times in the wrong direction.

Do I contradict myself?

'Very well then I contradict myself.' – Walt Whitman.

I have just received the latest issue of the RPS *Journal* and am heartened by the opening section, 'Preview of 2023'. It seems some positive activities might be unfolding.

I read that the Imperial War Museum will have, opening in late 2023, a 1,000 square meters dedicated gallery space, housed there will be 11 million photographs – I presume that is a correct number? Let's hope photos get a good showing among art and film.

This spring, at the V&A, the largest permanent gallery dedicated to photography in the UK will be unveiled. Again, I presume that this is an extension to that already there.

In January, a new 8,000 square foot space dedicated to British photography from 1900 (what's happened to 1839-1900?), is opening in Jermyn Street, London.

Sad no mention of activity in the North – to think there was once a wonderful photography museum in Bradford, very progressive, quality exhibitions and commissions, with large audience numbers when the knowledgeable Colin Ford was in charge.

Two/three exhibitions I already look forward to: *A New Power: Photography in Britain, 1800-1850*, at the Bodleian Oxford. And Tom Wood retrospective at Liverpool's Walker Art Gallery. Already showing – and I will certainly go to see – is the exhibition of English (I wish he had done Welsh as well) cathedrals, all 42, photographed by the late Peter Marlow and shown inside St Paul's Cathedral. Only until 26 January.

I am still photographing but mainly in my village. A couple of hours at a time – I have the joy of a slot on the village website – I guess I continue to collect curiosities of human life just as natural history enthusiasts collect shells and fossils as they wander on beaches. But please capture things as they are rather than they 'should' be. Allow the world to be as it is.

@davidhurnphoto @magnumphotos @imperialwarmuseums @vamuseum @centre_for_british_photography #streetphotographyinternational #nonfictionphotography #petermarlow #stpaulscathedral

EACH VENTURE IS A NEW BEGINNING . . .
WHAT THERE IS TO CONQUER . . . HAS ALREADY BEEN DISCOVERED,
ONCE OR TWICE, OR SEVERAL TIMES,
BY MEN WHOM ONE CANNOT HOPE TO EMULATE
BUT THERE IS NO COMPETITION
THERE IS ONLY THE FIGHT TO RECOVER WHAT HAS BEEN LOST AND
FOUND AND LOST AGAIN AND AGAIN.

/ *T.S. Eliot*

2023

♥

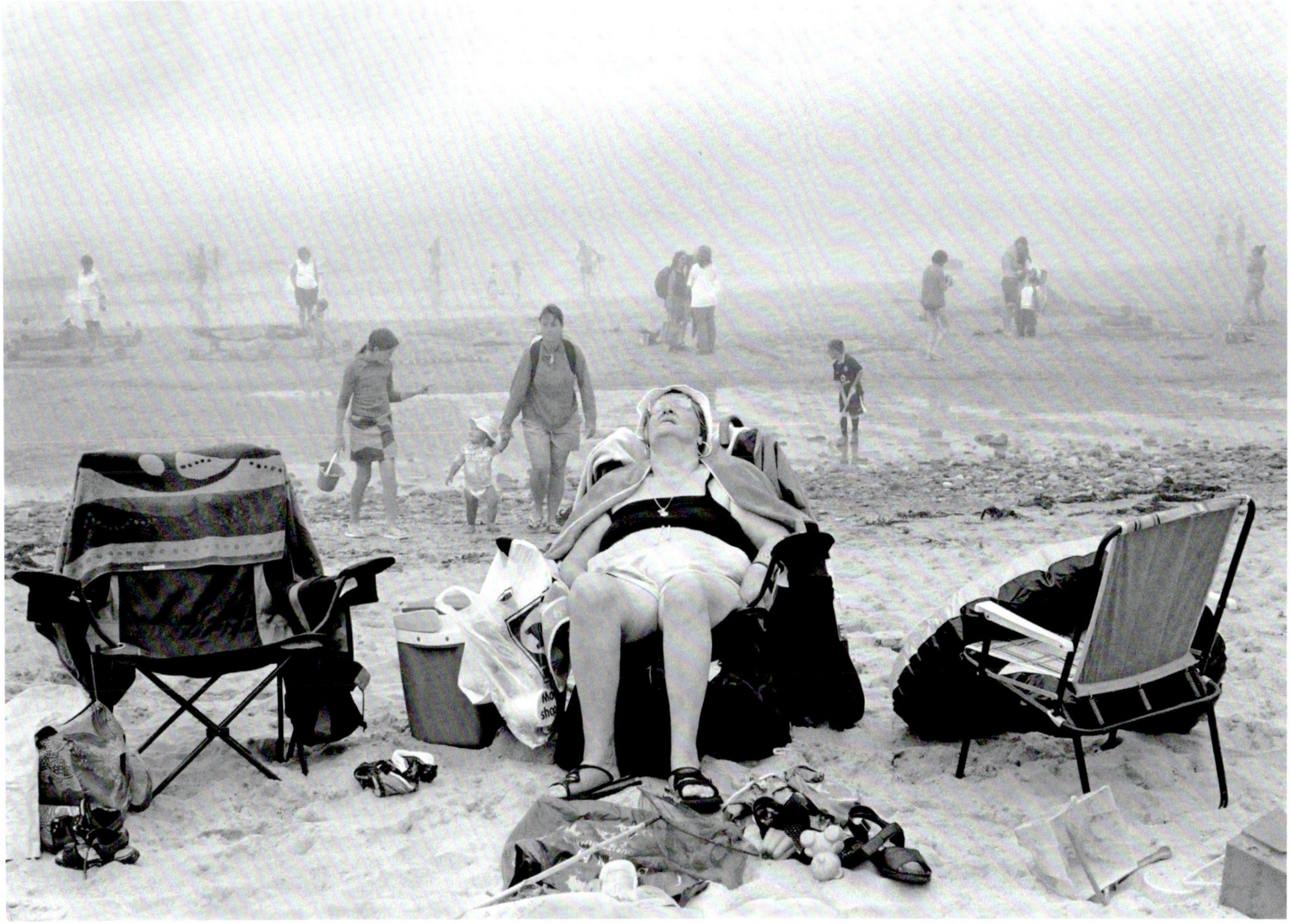

18 JANUARY 2023 / ENTHUSIASM. *ENGLAND, UK 2016*

I have been stuck to my bed, able to amble but not with enthusiasm. I am glued to my computer struggling to get my archives into a useable state. I am a believer in absorbing from heroes, from Rembrandt and Beethoven I feel humanity, from Shakespeare the ability to question, Bach and Turner sheer hard work, Orwell clarity and simplicity.

I have the radio permanently on. It's my constant source of ideas and stretching thought. The BBC is a treasure-trove, I suspect the best money I have ever spent.

High on my list is *Life Scientific*, interviews with the world's top scientists. I am enthralled by how they started, their tenacity and love of what they do. If I was starting again from scratch, I think I would attempt to document all interviewed – a wonderful group to meet – and one's research done for you. *More or Less*, *Start the Week*, *In our Time* and *This Cultural Life*. *From our Own Foreign Correspondent* is wonderful for variety of story told in a contained time. How we photographers can learn from them. The 'Reith Lectures' are always erudite. And I recently was mesmerised by Professor of Forensic Anthropology, Dame Sue Black, explaining to a lecture theatre full of transfixed children – they were being shown a full skeleton – how she could discover biological gender from the skulls, show the age, discover how death came about, etc. When I started there was virtually no TV, no iPhones or computers. I read at least four newspapers a day, I suspect my core information came from a subscription to *The Economist* – the starting point of daily conversations with my friends – it's the one magazine that I still subscribe to. I hardly travel abroad anymore, but it does make me feel slightly in touch with what, from one intelligent point of view, is going on.

When I started the course at Newport, we had a contract with the local newsagent to deliver the most significant papers plus many major magazines from USA, France, Germany, Brazil – I felt it important to show the UK was a small part of the potential publishing world.

All this to cover up that my mind is fuzzy at the moment and I have little to say.

@davidhurnphoto @magnumphotos

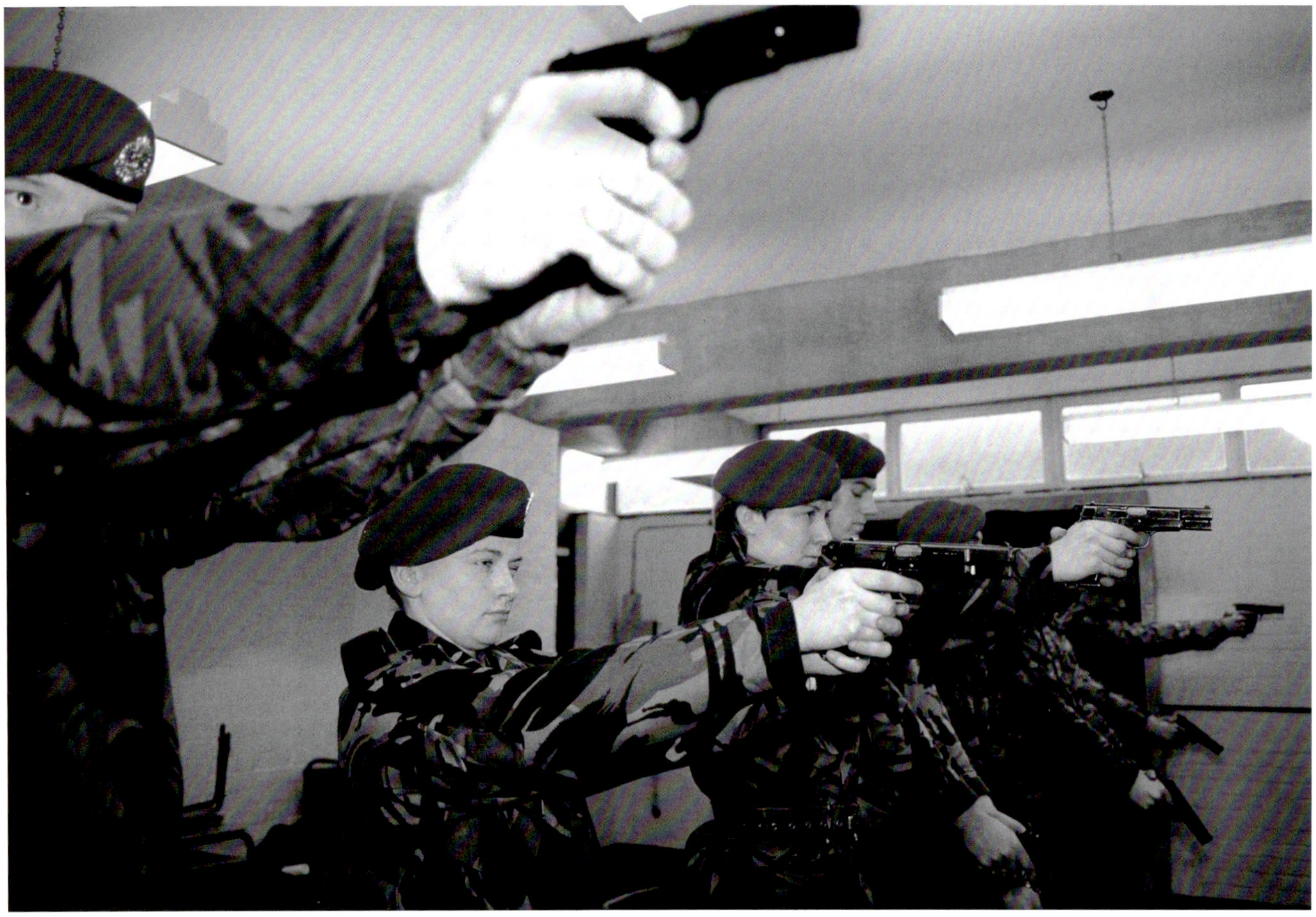

24 JANUARY 2023 / WOMEN MILITARY POLICE. *ENGLAND, UK 1987*

I read from a professional, i.e. someone who makes the major part of their living out of a camera, calling themselves an 'Artist'. I have never been comfortable with this title as I don't know what it means – maybe someone can enlighten me? It seems such a vague term and seems to be applied to virtually anything, I have heard, 'Artist Plumber'.

I wish to be called a photographer, but that in itself is not very precise, there are so many genres. I like the literary categories of fiction and non-fiction as a good starting point. I class myself in the non-fiction grouping. A start. When I set up the course in Newport I called it 'Documentary'. I felt most aspiring young photographers would have an idea what that meant – but it is not very accurate. The word 'documentary' was coined by Scottish filmmaker John Grierson in his review of Robert Flaherty's film *Moana* (1926), published in the *New York Sun* on 8 February 1926, this title refers to film, and very often re-staged film. Soviet film-maker Dziga Vertov's was tighter; to present 'life as it is' (that is, life filmed surreptitiously) and 'life caught unawares'. Early film (pre-1900) was dominated by the novelty of showing an event. They were single-shot moments captured on film: a train entering a station, or factory workers leaving work. These short films were called 'actuality' films. Maybe 'actuality photographer' would be good. I rather like 'reportage', from old French 'reporter', 'to tell, relate, bring back', but I suspect that the French connection is too much to stomach for some Brits. Photojournalist is another possibility, but academics seem to wish to disparage this activity – however, if it is the keeping of a journal, then I think it is rather fine. Most I like *flâneur* – according to Baudelaire, the *flâneur* moves through the labyrinthine streets and hidden spaces of the city, partaking of its attractions, but remaining somehow detached and apart from it. Perhaps it sounds too exotic.

In the end, when asked, I still say I am a photographer. When asked 'of what?' I just mumble.

@davidhurnphoto @magnumphotos #nonfictionphotography

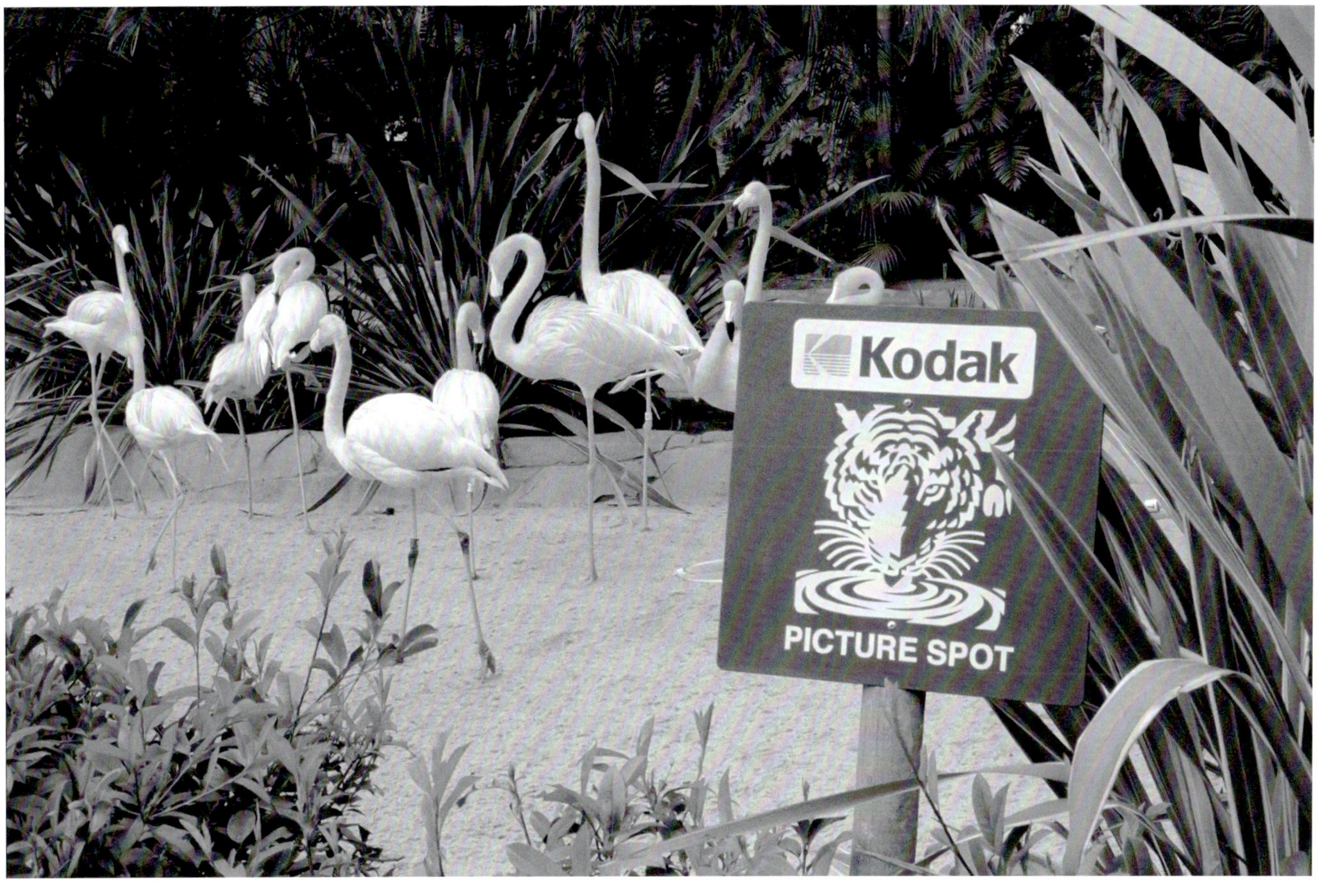

14 FEBRUARY 2023 / PICTURE SPOT. ***SAN DIEGO, USA 2001***

Floundering around at home I have been thinking about how one picks subject matter.

I have close friends gone to Ukraine, Turkey and I expect soon Syria. For them where to be is mainly obvious. I have such respect for those who often rush, with no assignment, on the hope that someone will cherish their efforts enough to buy. They have the will to show history, aspects of how the world is. Early on I went to the Hungarian Uprising, but my head didn't really enjoy the experience. Not for me.

I love *From our Own Correspondent* on BBC, they have fine describers covering a mass of different ideas, with such clear and passionate writing, many of which I would have loved to photograph. Sadly, no longer. It's now more a matter of 'how do I get to a place' and 'what could I do in a couple of hours' – that's my maximum physical possibility. And always, 'would anyone else be interested?' Luckily I have thought long term, so most of my income comes from archive, pictures taken over a 60-year span, and more recently print sales – I was then often called a journalist, now galleries want those pictures and I become, in their terminology, an *artist*.

Over the last ten years I have been dabbling with an essay on 'Human involvement in the landscape'. I have photographed in over 500 locations in Wales. My Mind-Node shows me I have about 12 more pictures to complete. I have just had the luck of a well-respected author saying he would love to write an essay to compliment the pictures. It means there is now a good chance of a book. Interesting for me as it would be in colour.

I am continuing the 'My Village' saga.

I love a little book by André Kertész called *On Reading* – his father owned a bookshop – throughout my active life I have always filtered out people reading – I might try to see if I can get a small edit of these. I don't think he would mind me pinching his idea.

I keep hinting at others to drive me around. Browsing contact sheets I see I have a dozen pictures 'Through a Car Window' – I think that is a good title so I suspect that might be a final project that will occupy me for a couple of years.

@davidhurnphoto @magnumphotos #andrekertesz

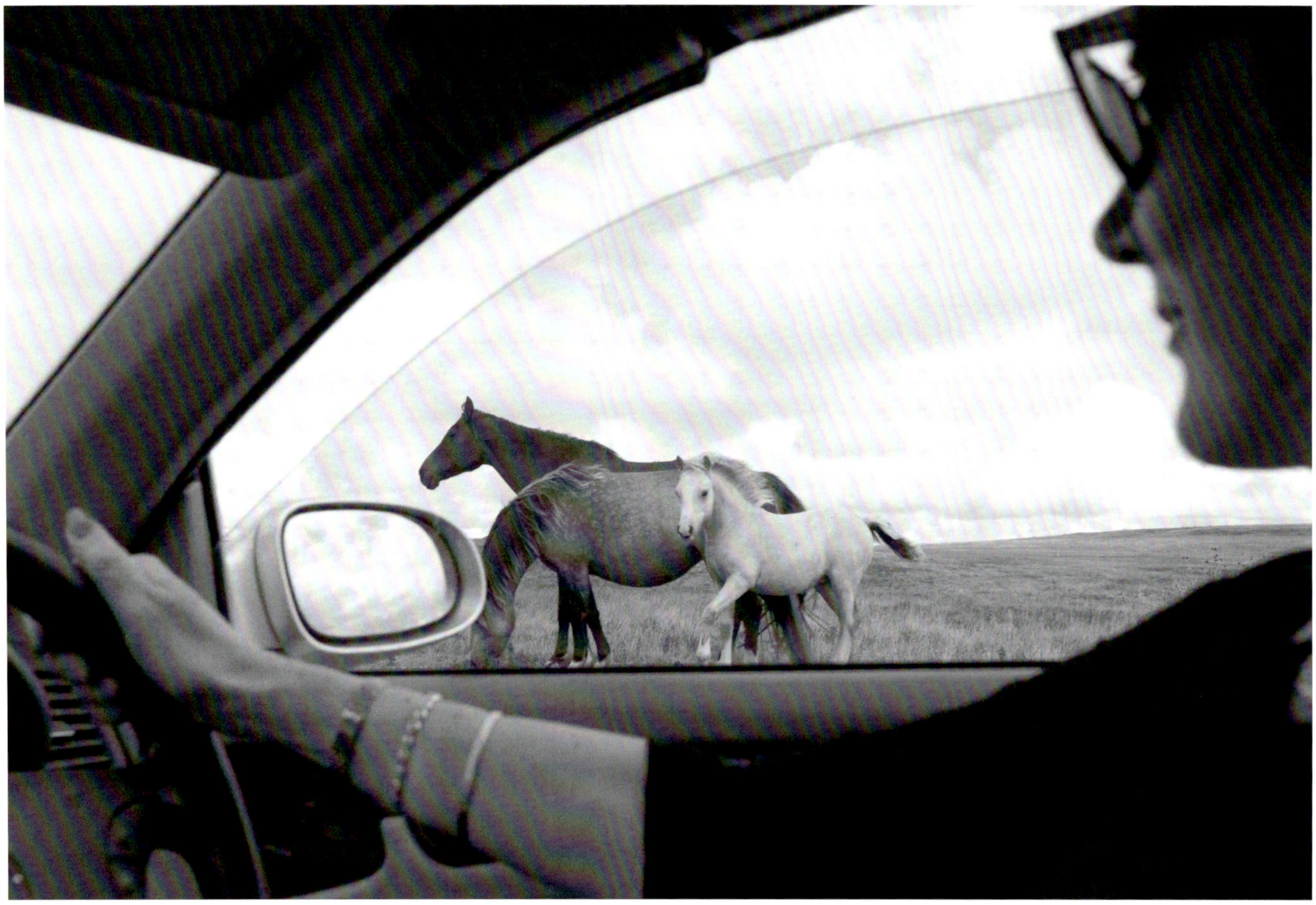

17 MARCH 2023 / WINDOW ON WORLD. *WALES 2014*

It's fun to be a photographer. Not a good photographer, or a bad photographer but simply a photographer. Everywhere I go I see a mass of people all enjoying photographing each other, they get enjoyment, delight and togetherness. However, I wish everyone, at what ever level, thought more about the aftermath. Once we kept family albums – most were informative. Those with captions are sociologically invaluable – sadly I suspect most of the positive of the iPhone is the instant gratification, wiped out by the next exposure – no-one writes information, who, why, what, where.

I often hear the mantra that everyone now has a camera and that there is so much competition. My feeling is that if you feel these efforts are competition to yourself you are not going to make it anyway. There are just so many places on the ladder, I suspect the same number now as there ever has been. Its markets that have changed, but markets have always been changing, it is part of one's profession to understand and adapt. Sadly, the explosion in markets is mainly in fiction so that rules me out. However, research is now so much easier than ever before. At random I looked up 'magazines in Poland':

'In terms of frequency, the Polish magazines are mostly weeklies and monthlies. Women's magazines are a significant part of the press market. Magazines targeting youth and university students also exist. Poland has a long tradition of architectural magazines. In 2001 there were 5,792 magazines – this number has increased since'.

There is then a list of all the magazines.

The world has many countries, I am sure in many the results would be similar.

I am convinced with individual contact and perseverance one can make a living.

@davidhurnphoto @magnumphotos #nonfictionphotography

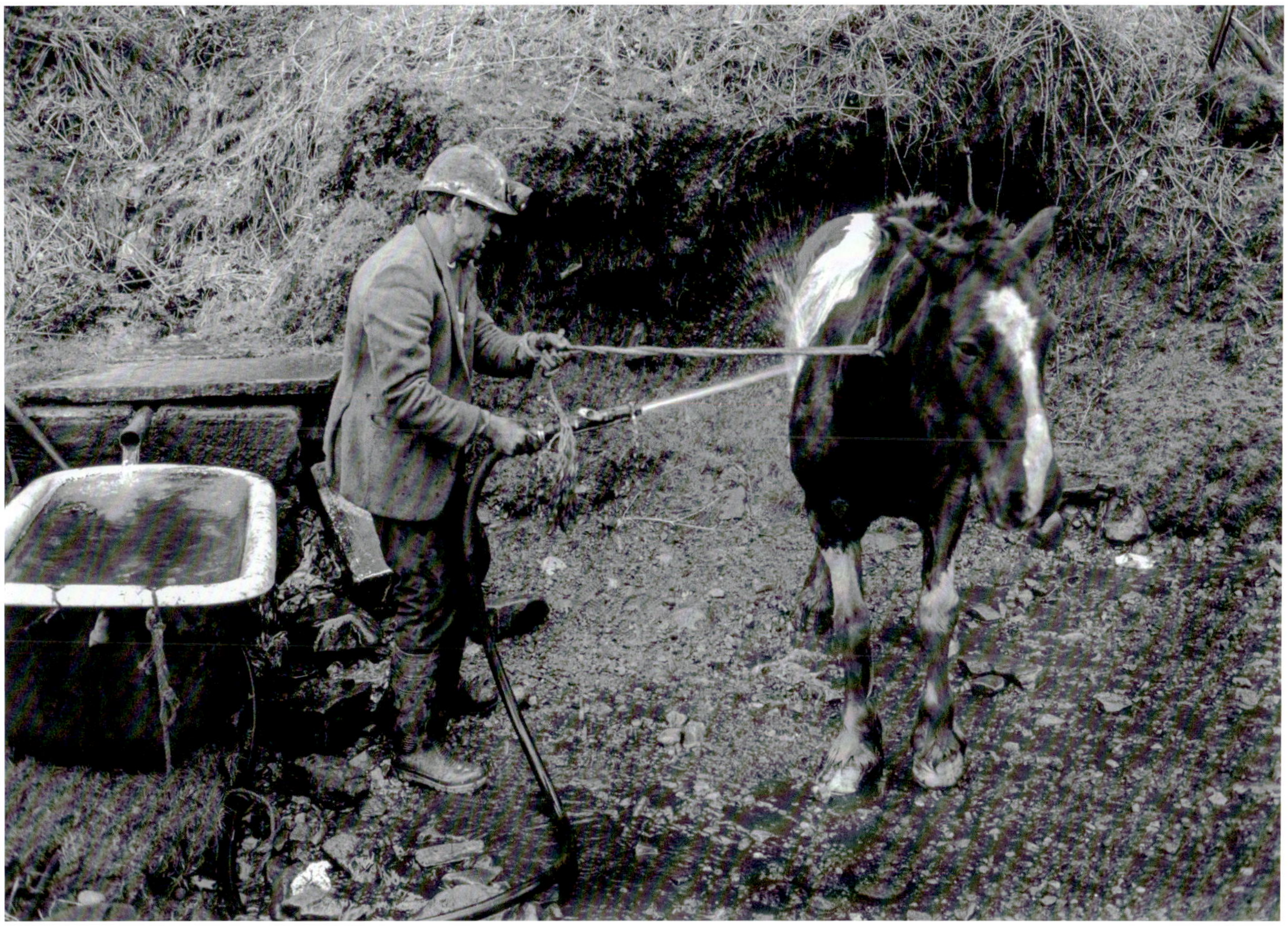

7 APRIL 2023 / WASH TIME. *NEATH VALLEY, WALES 1993*

I heard that on social media, pictures showed the Pope apparently wearing a very stylish white puffer jacket by Balenciaga. I am an atheist but I am very aware that there are at least 1.2 billion Catholics in the world, fervent believers, 27 percent of them in Europe, 277 million. That's a formidable believer block – I presume a large increase in puffer sales.

The problem is that the picture is a very convincing *fake*, a picture constructed by means of a readily available bit of software.

Is this a problem? I was taken in, too trusting, a bit like talking to someone, there are things that I feel ought to be exact, correct. My immediate reaction had been amusement. Of course, I was aware that many were being offended, but I am not particularly worried about offence, there is a long – I would argue healthy – history of offending people. Hogarth, who died in 1764, was one of the founders of visual satire, *Spitting Image* more recent. Offending seems to me one sure sign of civilisation. I am offended by the triviality of game shows on TV, so I simply don't watch them, I don't wish to ban them, and certainly don't wish to take up precious time being irate and organising petitions.

It appears that in March, images of former US president Donald Trump being arrested similarly went viral, again *fake*. I have no time for Trump but this foray directly into politics seems to me even more dangerous – technologies being pushed into our societies without oversight, regulation or standards.

I feel fact as opposed to fiction is important, particularly when the fiction is in the guise of fact.

Photography can help clarify our thought on democracy. Pictures help us see what happened when a mob attacked the United States Capitol Building in Washington. George Rodger photographed the mass deaths at Bergen-Belsen concentration camp at the end of the Second World War. A permanent reminder of the Holocaust.

Does it affect my love of my genre of photography? Well I think, yes. The second that a group of 1.2 billion people either think all pictures are 'fact' or surmise 'all pictures are fiction', what I think is very worthwhile is in trouble.

@davidhurnphoto @magnumphotos #nonfictionphotography

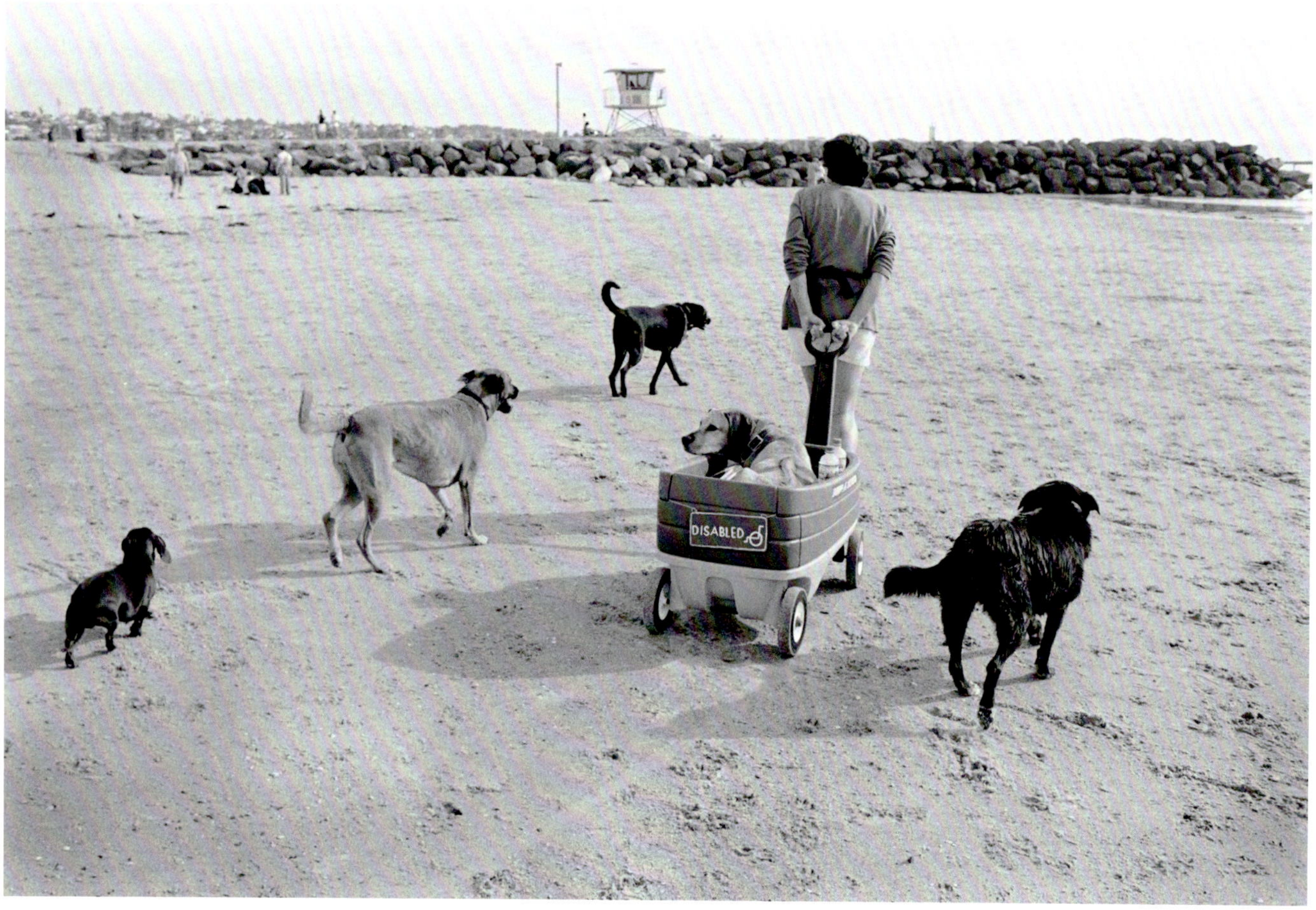

14 APRIL 2023 / DOG BEACH. *SAN DIEGO, USA 2002*

Occasionally, I hear people put forward the idea that we should only look at our own community. I don't understand this idea. Do they mean their own home, street, town, area, country or what?

I have a fear that photographing 'one's own' almost by definition ends up as propaganda.

Certainly, in my case, I make no pretence that I am ever doing anything more than looking and saying – I found this interesting, do you?' In my own country I do not sense the same vibes in Tintern as I do in Cardiff, or Pembroke, or the Isle of Anglesey, yet all are in the same country.

The classical conception of objectivity was the earliest scientific thought dealing with things and objects. We were objective when our own wishes and fears and hopes are excluded from the observations. Dealing with non-human objects is easy. For most, it does not matter which way an amoeba acts. Detachment gets more and more difficult as we go up the phyletic scale.

In most cases, humans find it practically impossible to be cool, calm, detached, uninvolved, non-interfering spectators. We should try.

Examine one's own prejudgments, know/accept, be aware of them in advance.

If we can understand ourselves and we then love or are fascinated by or are profoundly interested in something, we are less tempted to interfere, to control, to change, to improve. We do not wish it to be other than it is.

To the extent that it is possible for us to not interfere, be non-suggestive, non-improving, to that extent we achieve a particular kind of objectivity. A certain kind of truth.

But remember, be aware, that love produces a certain kind of blindness.

@davidhurnphoto @magnumphotos #nonfictionphotography #dogs

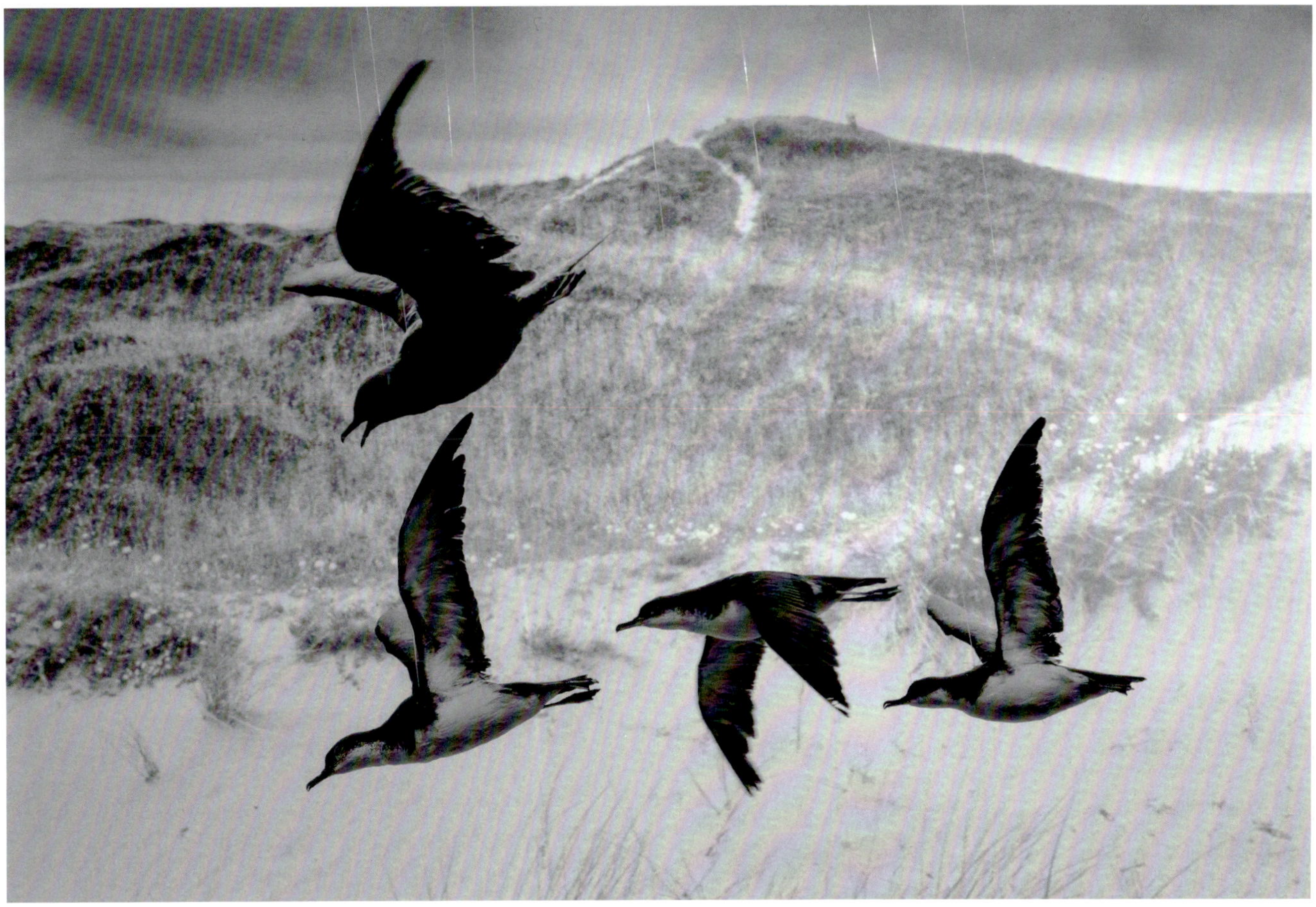

20 MAY 2023 / MUSEUM TABLEAU. *CARDIFF, WALES 1993*

The truth is not irrelevant.

I was recently overhearing a group being lectured by someone who should know better. They were being told why I (Hurn) shot in black and white. A mass of speculated philosophy. Fascinating but mumbo jumbo. The reality was almost certainly that when I started, the local chemist only stocked black and white film.

We are talking the buying of film in the mid '50s. Ilford HP3 film was, I think, 200 ASA. Colour was available – Ernst Haas shot his memorable colour essay for *Life* magazine on Kodachrome – 10 ASA, later to be upgraded to 25 ASA.

To learn how to control any medium takes time, after maybe a couple of years I think I understood black and white – why would I ever change and then have to absorb again from scratch?

This repetition of using a medium is the most useful teaching ploy. Gradually you discard – if you are sensible – that which doesn't work for you and gradually, by definition, end up with that which does. You very gradually shoot more which is really you. The process continues for ever if you leave yourself open and vulnerable. If somewhere you have extra ability it will come.

@davidhurnphoto @magnumphotos #nonfictionphotography #birds #museum

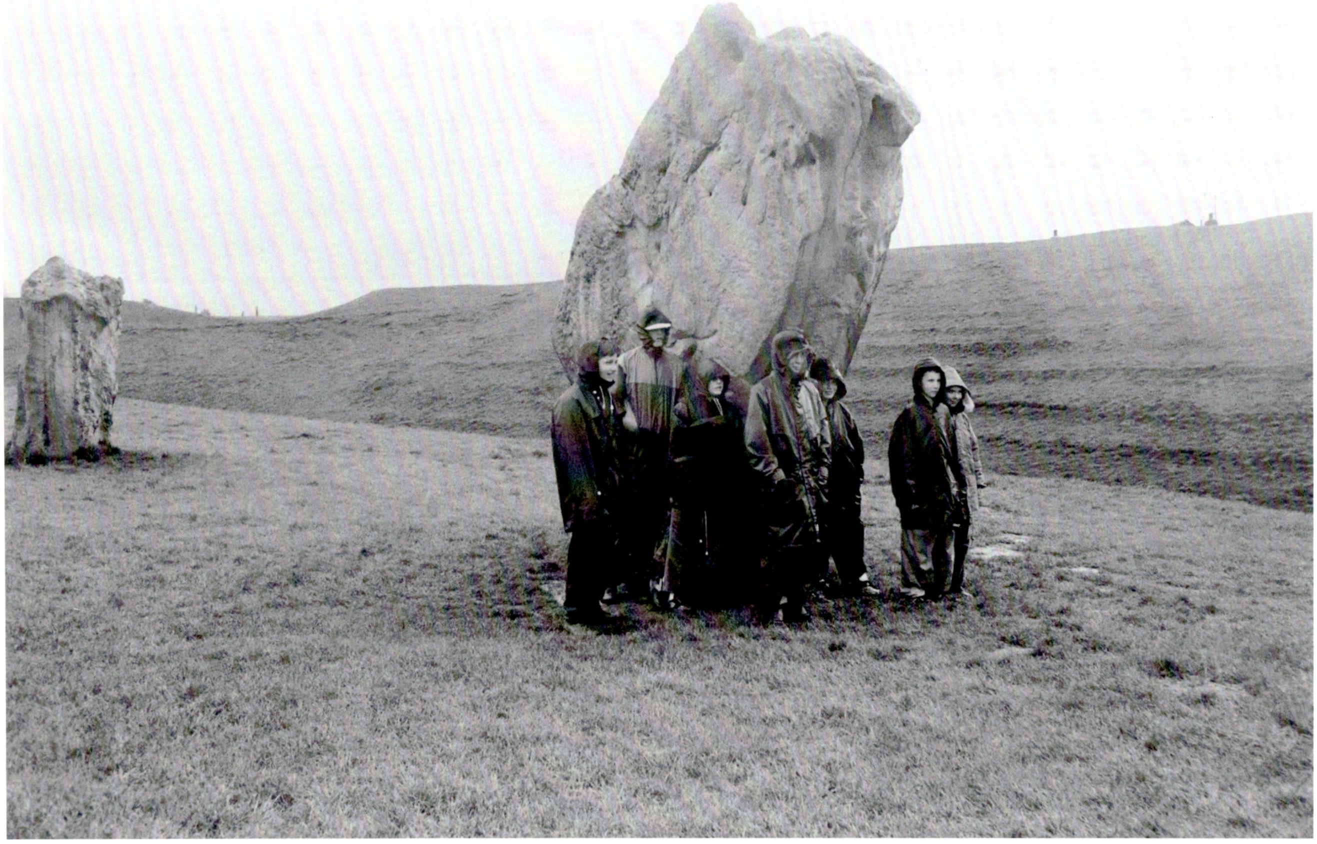

8 JUNE 2023 / FRIENDSHIP. *AVEBURY, ENGLAND 1993*

Next to good shoes, the most important asset a photographer can have is a knowledgeable honest friend. I have one and I hope he knows how much I actually rely on him.

I have been trying, photographically, for 60-plus years to work honestly and without bias. It's sacrosanct to me in my genre of journalism (the keeping of a journal). I promised myself if I ever had the luck to have a book done of the pictures I liked most, I would be very stringent in my needs.

RRB publisher offered me that choice and *David Hurn 1955-2022* is about to come out. I am not sure what gripes I take in from my above friend, I suspect few, but he keeps me thinking.

The team at RRB were wonderful and absorbed my insistences. Waiting for picture proofs is one of the tensions of one's life – they have just arrived and I am over the moon, what did I expect, well these were better.

I think the ability to have conversation and advice from those you trust as knowing what they are talking about – even if you disagree with everything they say – is totally invaluable.

What I sense is that too many people are too complicated, I suggest reading Orwell rather than some convoluted philosophic text full of words few of us use. I suggest any text alongside pictures should be short, tight, and accurate.

For me, a burden is now lifted. I now can get on with something else.

We photographers are lucky, we have something that lives after we are gone – but remember we are actually judged by time, not by our friends or enemies. It's only when we die that true appreciation good/bad comes out and then it is too late to matter for us as individuals. We never know.

@davidhurnphoto @magnumphotos @rrbphotobooks #nonfictionphotography #archaeology

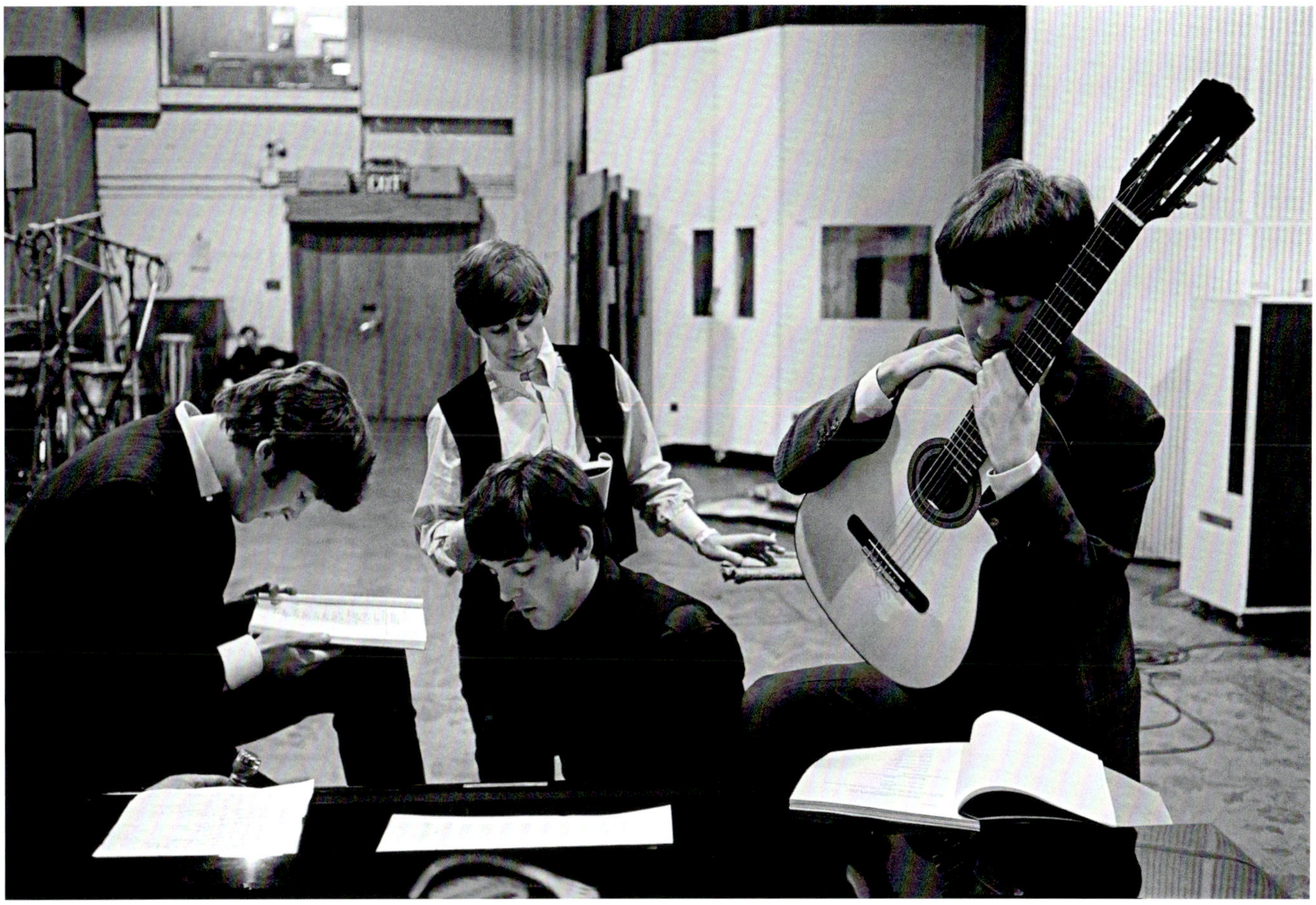

6 JULY 2023 / THE BEATLES. *LONDON, ENGLAND 1964*

The Beatles will release a new and final record this year. Extraordinary.

More good news:

My book of pictures *1955 to 2022* to be launched – with talk by me (mainly to do with what is luck?) – 13 July, Magnum office, London. To my relief there are very good reviews and hearty advance sales.

I am delighted that four photographers I greatly admire, Nanna Heitmann, Gregory Halpern, Rafał Milach and Lua Ribeira, finally made it as full members of Magnum – younger blood. From nominee to member is a tortuous four years. I think we have a very fair system but it is tough. It's difficult to cope with the dedication involved.

I have been struggling physically for four months – thus no Instagram recently – but am now on the mend again. The NHS may be taking a hammering in some quarters but luck is on my side and we have a superb surgery in Tintern and I thank them all for looking after me.

I have re-equipped with new batteries for my camera – with luck they will last longer. I do have everything set to the fastest responses I can get but that uses a lot of power – I work on the principle that I would prefer to carry a little extra weight in my pocket than miss a picture – nowadays pictures become rarer and rarer, I wonder why? Maybe imperceptible lack of concentration. Total concentration is so important – certainly for me.

@davidhurnphoto @magnumphotos @rrbphotobooks @nannaheitmann @gregoryhalpern @rafal.milach @lua_ribeira #nonfictionphotography

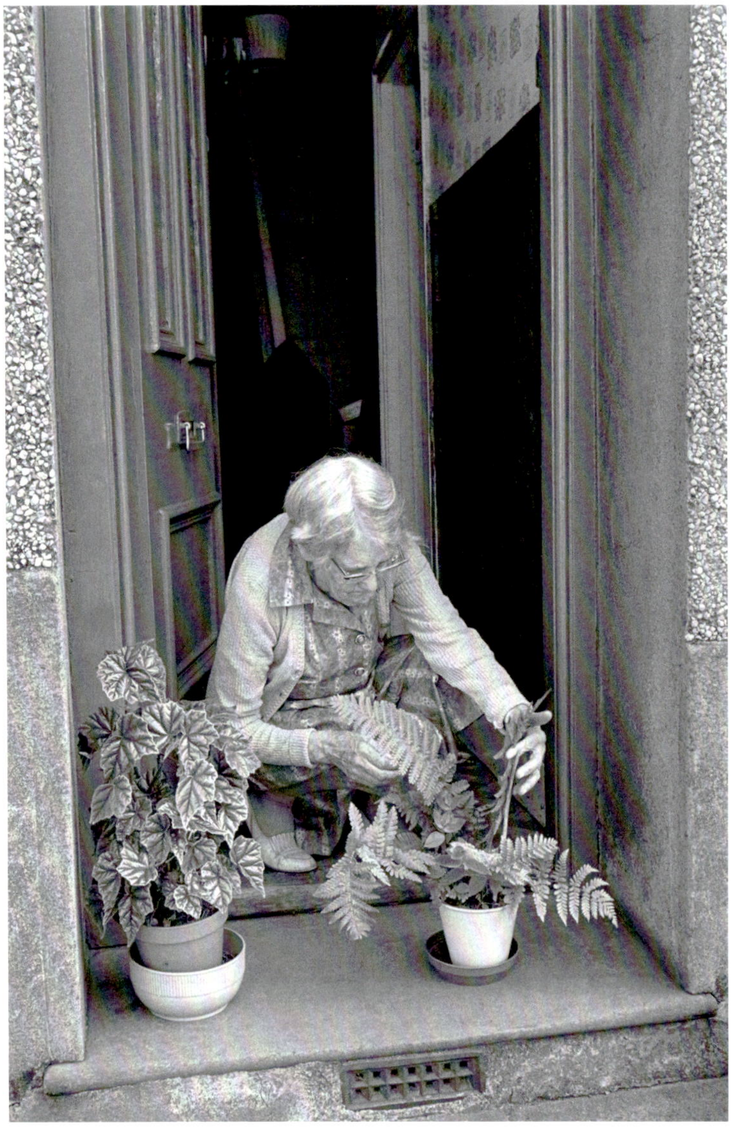

16 JULY 2023 / MEMORY. *PORTHMADOG, WALES 1976*

It's interesting how some obvious things can suddenly show importance in our lives.

I have finally accepted that I am on the mend and tested myself with a trip, ostensibly to go to the launch of my new book and to give a chat. A couple of years ago I had said no more talks, but since, I have just invented a new format not praising my own pictures but asking questions about luck.

Travelling to London I realised what a wonderful invention is the wheeled suitcase, plus I really found out how generous most people actually are; at no point did I have to carry my bag up any stairs and at no point did I not have a seat on the underground.

The talk was to a packed audience who I think found luck interesting – as for the book, it seems to be selling well. Reading on the train, I think the *New Statesman* probably now has the most interesting writing – if Orwell were alive I think he would have written for them. Back home, on TV, I found a repeat of the series *The Newsroom*, anything written by Aaron Sorkin is worth a watch. I had, of course, seen the series before, but luckily my memory is so appalling that it was like watching afresh.

It is that ability to reboot and get a memory jog that I so love about non-fiction photography. My only regret about the past is that I didn't shoot more. So many friends I have forgotten and certainly don't remember what they looked like, so many places are only a blur. A good motto is 'if in doubt, shoot', always take more than you think you need. You don't have to look at what you then don't find interesting, but that you do is a treasure.

@davidhurnphoto @magnumphotos

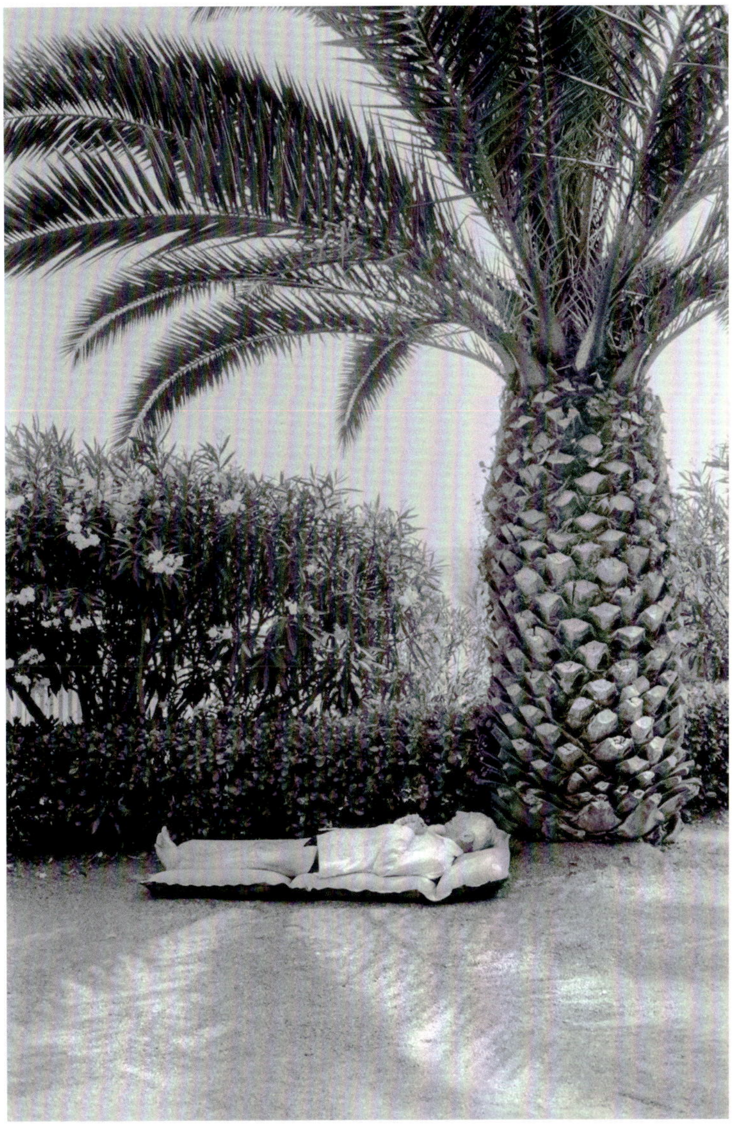

21 JULY 2023 / THINK. *MONTE CARLO, FRANCE 1964*

I suspect the producing of books is in jeopardy. Costs have jumped. Often photographers are asked to pick up some of these costs rarely to be recuperated by royalties. I suspect a greater variety of cheaper possibilities will have to be found to get to the audience. The established publisher has the advantage of being professional and has designers etc who really know what they are doing. Most self-publishers don't – at the moment it shows. Type, paper, printing, colours, binding really do matter – it's important that the end result is correct for the hoped-for audience, knowledge of this audience is important.

Café Royal Books have been successful because they have a policy and have kept to it. Consistency is attractive. I received a zine by a person who takes photos, I suspect he would not call himself a professional. It is basically a family album, the effort is commendable. The family album is important, apparently in case of fire it is the first item that owners grab. Some albums, if complete with good captions, have a future sociological value. This zine is not dissimilar in look to Café Royal but family albums need charm in abundance, it has something to do with love of pasting individual pictures – something to do with colour of paper, elaborateness of the container book. The future needs to ape this in the modern way, cheaply. I am sure it can be done. If you get a chance look out the original Lartigue family album.

I feel that zines could be made of what in the past would have been a major *Life* magazine or *Picture Post* essay. The problem is, that although minimal, text was always a part. I think it would need to be in conjunction with a very savvy journalist who was not worried about taking a minor role. Someone might try it but remember the audience, don't bore them with your subject matter. Jem Southam's publishers have now produced a little boxed set 6x4.5 of his pictures of Bristol, they are beautifully printed, I am sure they will have large sales in cafes etc around the water in Bristol.

I guess I am saying it is the time for experimentation but do it from knowledge, quality is always seeable.

@davidhurnphoto @magnumphotos

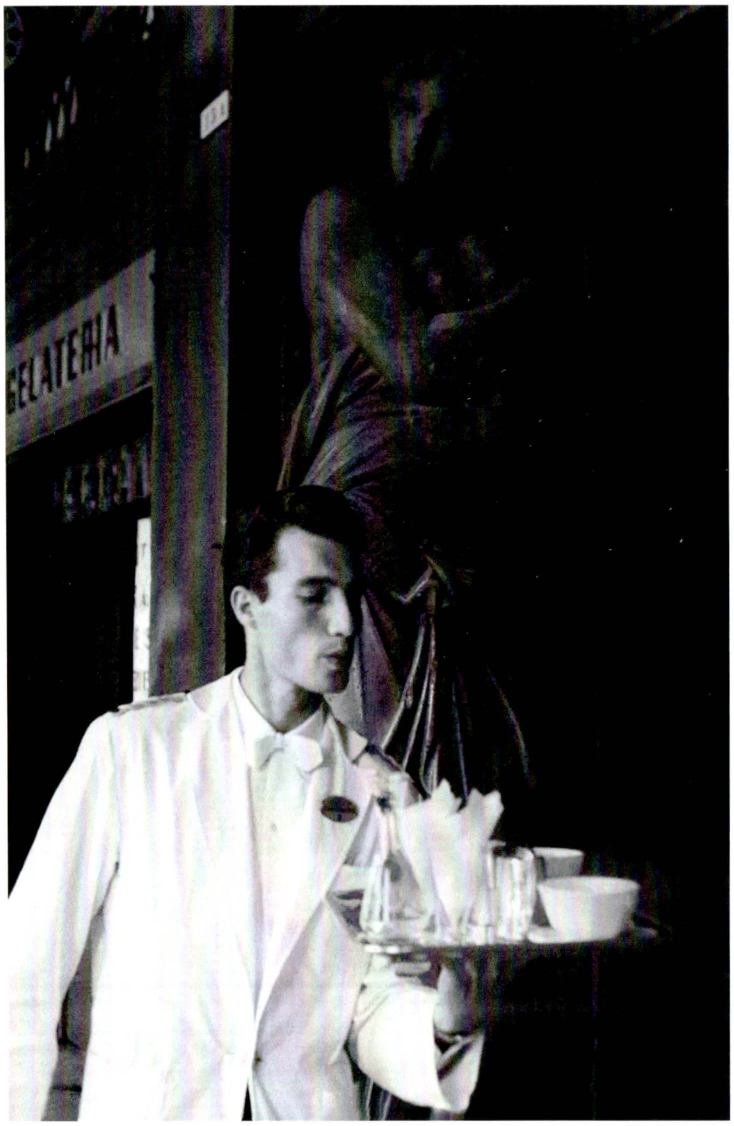

25 JULY 2023 / CAKE. *VENICE, ITALY 1964*

I am often asked how I would try to teach now. I still think the best method is the combination of genuine experience on the one hand, chatting to potential on the other. Biggest danger are teachers who think they are 'right' and stifle debate. I would still champion non-fiction photography as this is mainly what I am interested in.

Josef Koudelka's book, *Ikonar*, has just arrived – he certainly has genuine experience. It's a different book from Josef in that it is full of insights into his life and work methods – reading/absorbing would be a good start. Add Robert Frank's book *Looking In*, full of like information and full of contact sheets – the very best way of understanding how someone works. *Walker Evans at Work* shows hundreds of pictures, often variations of the same subject. *Magnum Contact Sheets* and *Magnum Stories*, titles that speak for themselves. *Master of the Photographic Essay*, Eugene Smith, shows the very broad edits of individual pictures in his main essays. This group gives a very good template for learning. I would add John Szarkowski's *Looking at Photographs* to get a feel of how one might interpret pictures other than just 'it's what I like', plus Bresson's *Interviews and Conversations*. Being vain, I would include *On Being a Photographer* by Bill Jay and myself. By the way, this is the template for the course that I devised in Newport. Bill Allard who has worked with *National Geographic* from 1964, wrote wonderfully about his work methods in *The Photographic Essay*.

Later, to feel more intimate contact with photographers, I would research for quality videos. Magnum produce many, I suspect NOOR and IPC also.

I would certainly include a simple introduction to the history of the medium – we need to know shoulders we all stand on – a tight summation is *The Invention of Photography: The First Fifty Years*.

I would try to find a beginner's book on book-keeping and accountancy, i.e. basic numbering, filing, budgeting, law – I might have to write this myself to keep it as simple as is needed.

That would be my basic ingredients – all I would now have to do is work out how to actually bake the cake.

@davidhurnphoto @magnumphotos

REMINISCING / DAVID HURN

Bill Jay wrote way back in the late '70s that with the starting of specialist photo galleries and photography education being embedded in the art departments of universities, the judgement of the merits of photographers would pass from the practicing photographers themselves to academics and students of academics and have a radical influence on photography as a whole.

I would argue that he was right, certainly in the field of documentary/reportage/journalism/*flâneurism* or whatever one wishes to call it. I prefer to simply say non-fiction photography.

I hope my Instagrams have been seen as simply me asking questions – I would love to cause debate, I doubt it will happen as debate needs real drive, passion, ideas, accuracy and a lack of narcissism.

Only the young can enforce the future.

LOVE YOU, BILL JAY

Art Direction and Design: Brian Carroll

Editor-in-Chief: Tony Nourmand
Managing Editor: Alison Elangasinghe
Editorial Assistant: Adam Reich
Pre-Press: HR Digital Solutions

First published 2024 by Reel Art Press, an imprint of Rare Art Press Ltd., London, UK

reelartpress.com

First Edition

10 9 8 7 6 5 4 3 2 1

ISBN: 978-1-909526-94-5